THE CAMBRIDGE

History of the Book in Britain

*

VOLUME VII

The Twentieth Century and Beyond

The Cambridge history of the book in Britain is an authoritative series which surveys the history of publishing, bookselling, authorship and reading in Britain. This seventh and final volume surveys the twentieth and twenty-first centuries from a range of perspectives in order to create a comprehensive guide, from growing professionalisation at the beginning of the twentieth century, to the impact of digital technologies at the end. Its multi-authored focus on the material book and its manufacture broadens to a study of the book's authorship and readership, and its production and dissemination via publishing and bookselling. It examines in detail key market sectors over the course of the period, and concludes with a series of essays concentrating on aspects of book history: the book in wartime; class, democracy and value; books and other media; intellectual property and copyright; and imperialism and post-imperialism.

ANDREW NASH is Reader in Book History and Deputy Director of the Institute of English Studies, University of London. In addition to books on Victorian and Scottish literature he has edited or co-edited *The culture of collected editions* (2003), *Literary cultures and the material book* (2007) and *New directions in the history of the novel* (2014).

CLAIRE SQUIRES is Director of the Stirling Centre for International Publishing and Communication at the University of Stirling. Her publications include *Marketing literature: the making of contemporary writing in Britain* (2007) and, with Padmini Ray Murray, *The digital publishing communications circuit* (2013).

I. R. WILLISON held several senior posts in the British Museum Library from 1955 until his retirement in 1987. As Senior Research Fellow in the Institute of English Studies he has played a leading part in the development of book history as a field in the English-speaking world. He edited volume 4 of the *New Cambridge bibliography of English literature* (Cambridge, 1972) and has authored numerous essays on bibliography, book history, and librarianship in Britain and in a global context. He was awarded a CBE for services to the History of the Book in 2005.

History of the Book in Britain

The history of the book offers a distinctive form of access to the ways in which human beings have sought to give meaning to their own and others' lives. Our knowledge of the past derives mainly from texts. Landscape, architecture, sculpture, painting and the decorative arts have their stories to tell and may themselves be construed as texts; but oral tradition, manuscripts, printed books, and those other forms of inscription and incision such as maps, music and graphic images, have a power to report even more directly on human experience and the events and thoughts which shaped it.

In principle, any history of the book should help to explain how these particular texts were created, why they took the form they did, their relations with other media, especially in the twentieth century, and what influence they had on the minds and actions of those who heard, read or viewed them. Its range, too – in time, place and the great diversity of the conditions of text production, including reception – challenges any attempt to define its limits and give an account adequate to its complexity. It addresses, whether by period, country, genre or technology, widely disparate fields of enquiry, each of which demands and attracts its own forms of scholarship.

The Cambridge history of the book in Britain, planned in seven volumes, seeks to represent much of that variety, and to encourage new work, based on knowledge of the creation, material production, dissemination and reception of texts. Inevitably its emphases will differ from volume to volume, partly because the definitions of Britain vary significantly over the centuries, partly because of the varieties of evidence extant for each period, and partly because of the present uneven state of knowledge. Tentative in so many ways as the project necessarily is, it offers the first comprehensive account of the book in Britain over one and a half millennia.

JOHN BARNARD . DAVID MCKITTERICK . I. R. WILLISON
General Editors

THE CAMBRIDGE
History of the Book in Britain

*

VOLUME VII
The Twentieth Century and Beyond

*

Edited by

ANDREW NASH
Institute of English Studies, University of London

CLAIRE SQUIRES
University of Stirling

I. R. WILLISON
Institute of English Studies, University of London

CAMBRIDGE
UNIVERSITY PRESS

CAMBRIDGE
UNIVERSITY PRESS

University Printing House, Cambridge CB2 8BS, United Kingdom

One Liberty Plaza, 20th Floor, New York, NY 10006, USA

477 Williamstown Road, Port Melbourne, VIC 3207, Australia

314-321, 3rd Floor, Plot 3, Splendor Forum, Jasola District Centre, New Delhi - 110025, India

79 Anson Road, #06-04/06, Singapore 079906

Cambridge University Press is part of the University of Cambridge.

It furthers the University's mission by disseminating knowledge in the pursuit of education, learning and research at the highest international levels of excellence.

www.cambridge.org
Information on this title: www.cambridge.org/9781009010474
DOI: 10.1017/9780511862489

First published 2019
First paperback edition 2021

A catalogue record for this publication is available from the British Library

ISBN 978-1-107-01060-4 Hardback
ISBN 978-1-009-01047-4 Paperback

Contents

Contents

Contents

Illustrations

Contributors

CHRIS ATTON is Professor of Media and Culture in the School of Arts and Creative Industries at Edinburgh Napier University. His books include *Alternative media* (2002), *An alternative internet* (2004), *Alternative journalism* (2008) and *The Routledge companion to alternative and community media* (2015). He is co-founder of the *Journal of Alternative and Community Media*. He has produced studies of fanzines and the media of new social movements, as well as the cultural value of avant-garde and other 'difficult' forms of popular music.

PETER J. BOWLER is Professor Emeritus of the History of Science at Queen's University Belfast. He is a Fellow of the British Academy, a Member of the Royal Irish Academy and a past President of the British Society for the History of Science. He has a PhD from the University of Toronto. Recent books include *Science for all* (2009), *Darwin deleted* (2013) and *A history of the future: prophets of progress from H. G. Wells to Isaac Asimov* (2017).

SARAH BROMAGE is Deputy Curator for the University of Stirling Art Collection and archivist for the Scottish Political Archive at the University. Sarah has held various roles within the heritage sector, and between 2001 and 2010 worked as a researcher for the Scottish Archive of Print and Publishing History Records (SAPPHIRE), investigating the working lives of those who worked in the print and papermaking industries in Scotland. She is currently involved in managing the newly established Pathfoot Press at the University of Stirling.

SEBASTIAN CARTER was a letterpress printer at the Rampant Lions Press in Cambridge, and is a writer on typographical design. His *Twentieth-century type designers* was published in 1987 and he wrote the type history section of *The history of the Monotype Corporation* (2014). In 2013 he received the individual Laureate Award from the American Printing History Association. He is European editor of *Parenthesis*, the journal of the Fine Press Book Association.

GAIL CHESTER has worked in the radical, feminist and small press book trade since 1973. She researches in twentieth- and twenty-first-century book history and is widely published in academic and general publications. With Eileen Cadman and Agnes Pivot she co-authored *Rolling our own: women as printers, publishers and distributors* (1981). Major articles in the field include 'The anthology as a medium for feminist debate in the UK' (*Women's Studies International Forum*, 2002) and 'Publishers' readers' in *The Oxford companion to the book* (2010).

CAROLINE DAVIS is Senior Lecturer in the School of Arts at Oxford Brookes University, where she teaches publishing studies and book history. Her research interests focus on literary publishing in Africa, and she is the author of *Creating postcolonial literature: African writers and British publishers* (2013) and co-editor of *The book in Africa: critical debates* (2015). Her recent articles have appeared in the *Journal of Southern African Studies*, the *Journal of Commonwealth Literature*, the *Journal of Postcolonial Writing* and *Book History*.

DAVID FINKELSTEIN was Head of the Centre for Open Learning at the University of Edinburgh. His research interests include media history, print culture and book history studies. Recent publications include the co-authored *An introduction to book history* (second edition, 2013), the co-edited *Edinburgh history of the book in Scotland*, vol. 4 (2007) and the edited essay collection *Print culture and the Blackwood tradition* (2006), which was awarded the Robert Colby Scholarly Book Prize for its advancement of the understanding of the nineteenth-century periodical press.

SARAH ANNE HUGHES is Principal Lecturer at Oxford Brookes University where she teaches on the masters programmes through the Oxford International Centre for Publishing Studies. Her doctorate (University of Leicester, 2011) addressed the central question of why museums and galleries publish. Prior to a career in academia, she worked in museums in the United States and at the National Museum in Botswana where she set up a publishing unit. She is currently working on a book on museum and gallery publishing.

PETER HUNT is Professor Emeritus of English at Cardiff University. He is the author of many landmark studies in the field of children's literature, including *An introduction to children's literature* (1994), *Understanding children's literature* (1999) and the four-volume *Children's literature: critical concepts in literary and cultural studies* (2006). He has also published novels and shorter books for young adults and children.

MICHAEL LEDGER-LOMAS is Lecturer in the History of Christianity in Britain at King's College London. He is the co-editor of *Cities of God: the Bible and archaeology in nineteenth-century Britain* (2013), *Dissent and the Bible in Britain, c.1650–1950* (2013) and *The Oxford history of Protestant dissenting traditions. 3. The nineteenth century* (2017). He is currently completing a religious biography of Queen Victoria.

KATE LONGWORTH is completing a doctoral thesis at Magdalen College, Oxford on twentieth-century poetic drama and its context in philosophy and social policy.

MICHAEL MABE is CEO of the International Association of Scientific, Technical and Medical Publishers, the global trade body for scholarly publishers large and small. He read chemistry and did research at Oxford on radiocarbon dating before joining Oxford University Press. He has worked in a series of editorial, management and communication roles with BSI, Pergamon Press and Elsevier over a career spanning thirty-seven years. He writes on publishing issues and is a Visiting Professor in Information Studies at University College London.

ALISTAIR MCCLEERY is Professor of Literature and Culture at Edinburgh Napier University where he directs the Scottish Centre for the Book. In addition to numerous books and articles on twentieth-century and contemporary literature and publishing, he is co-author of *An introduction to book history* (second edition, 2012), co-editor of *The book history reader* (second edition, 2006) and co-editor of the *Edinburgh history of the book in Scotland*, vol. 4 (2007).

RONAN MCDONALD holds the Gerry Higgins Chair in Irish Studies at the University of Melbourne. His books include *Tragedy and Irish literature* (2002), *The Cambridge introduction to Samuel Beckett* (2007) and *The death of the critic* (2008). Recent edited collections include *The values of literary studies: critical institutions, scholarly agendas* (2015) and *Flann O'Brien and modernism* (2014).

ANDREW NASH is Reader in Book History and Deputy Director of the Institute of English Studies, University of London. In addition to books on Victorian and Scottish literature he has edited or co-edited *The culture of collected editions* (2003), *Literary cultures and the material book* (2007) and *New directions in the history of the novel* (2014). He contributed essays to volume 6 of the *Cambridge history of the book in Britain* and volume 4 of the *Edinburgh history of the book in Scotland*. He is an editor of the *Review of English Studies*.

MARK NIXON is an independent historian based in Scotland with particular interests in popular political history, material culture and book history. Much of his work is collaborative in nature, with community groups and local history societies. He has curated or co-curated exhibitions on twentieth-century popular culture for more than twenty museums and galleries, including 'More than just the Beano' for the Auld Kirk Museum, Kirkintilloch, which has since toured.

LUCY PEARSON is Lecturer in Children's Literature at Newcastle University. Her research focusses on the development of British children's literature in the twentieth century. She is author of *The making of modern children's literature: British children's publishing in the 1960s and 1970s* (2013) and editor of *Jacqueline Wilson: a new casebook* (2015). She is currently working on a major new history of the Carnegie Medal.

SARAH PEDERSEN is Professor of Communication and Media at Robert Gordon University, Aberdeen. Her current research focusses on women's engagement with the media during the early twentieth century. Her book *The Scottish suffragettes and the press* was published by Palgrave Macmillan in 2017. She is currently working on a Heritage Lottery Funded edition of the correspondence of Caroline Phillips, Aberdeen journalist and suffragette.

SUSAN PICKFORD is Associate Professor of Translation Studies in the English department at the Université Paris-Sorbonne. Her main research interests are the sociology of the translation profession and the interface between translation studies and book history. She is a co-founding editor of the Society for the History of Authorship, Reading and Publishing's journal of book history research in translation, *Lingua Franca*.

JANE POTTER is Reader in Arts at the Oxford International Centre for Publishing Studies, Oxford Brookes University. Her publications include *Boys in khaki, girls in print: women's literary responses to the Great War* (2005), *Wilfred Owen: an illustrated life* (2014) and, with Carol Acton, *Working in a world of hurt: trauma and resilience in the personal narratives of medical personnel in war zones* (2015).

ANTHONY QUINN founded the magazine website Magforum.com in 2001. His career includes: Group Editor at Redwood/BBC Magazines; Head of Publishing at the School of Printing at West Herts College, Watford; Chief Production Journalist at the *Financial Times*. He is a graduate of the University of Warwick and a Fellow of the RSA. His book *A history of British magazine design* was published by the V&A Museum in 2016. He presently freelances for *The Times* and *Sunday Times*, and as a lecturer and external examiner.

PADMINI RAY MURRAY was head of the Digital Humanities Masters programme at the Srishti Institute of Art, Design and Technology, India. Her recent publications have focussed on intersectionality in the digital archive and feminist protest in India. She is currently Co-Investigator on the Two Centuries of Indian Print project run in conjunction with the British Library, an initiative digitising more than 400,000 pages of Bengali texts published between 1778 and 1914.

SAMANTHA J. RAYNER is a Reader at University College London, where she is also Director of the Centre for Publishing. She teaches and writes on publishing and book-related topics, with special interests in academic publishing, publishing archives and publishing paratexts, the culture of bookselling, and editors and editing. She is deputy editor of the *Journal for the International Arthurian Society*, general editor for a new series of publishing and book trade minigraphs with Cambridge University Press, and a member of the UCL Press Board.

CATHERINE SEVILLE, who died in 2016, was Reader in Law, and Vice-Principal and Director of Studies in Law at Newnham College, Cambridge. Her many publications include *Literary copyright reform in early Victorian England* (1999), *The internationalisation of copyright law: books, buccaneers and the black flag in the nineteenth century* (2006) and *EU intellectual property law and policy* (second edition, 2016).

IAIN STEVENSON, who died in 2017, had a distinguished career in publishing at Longman, Macmillan, Pinter, Leicester University Press, Wiley, and the Stationery Office. He founded the environmental publisher Belhaven Press in 1986. He created the award-winning MA in Publishing Studies at City University, London before joining UCL as Professor of Publishing in 2006, retiring in 2015. His publications include *Book makers: British publishing in the twentieth century* (2010).

CLAIRE SQUIRES is Director of the Stirling Centre for International Publishing and Communication at the University of Stirling. Her research focusses on contemporary book cultures, including literary festivals and book prizes, editorial, marketing and communication processes within publishing, and aspects of diversity and politics relating to book industries. Her publications include *Marketing literature: the making of contemporary writing in Britain* (2007) and, with Padmini Ray Murray, 'The digital publishing communications circuit' (2013).

SHAFQUAT TOWHEED is Senior Lecturer in English at the Open University where he directs the UK Reading Experience Database, 1450–1945, and the History of Books and Reading (HOBAR) Research Collaboration. He has written extensively on the history of reading and is co-editor of Palgrave's 'New Directions in Book History' series. Recent publications include (with Edmund King) *Reading and the First World War: readers, texts, archives* (2015) and *Austen and romantic writing* (2016).

JOHN WAGSTAFF enjoyed a long career as a music librarian in both the UK and the USA, and is now librarian of Christ's College, Cambridge. His music printing and publishing interests have involved research into the nineteenth-century London music publisher Robert Cocks, and have also resulted in a chapter on music printing and publishing for Lewis Foreman's *Guide to information sources in music*.

ANTHONY WATKINSON trained as a historian at the University of Cambridge. He was Senior Lecturer in the Department of Information Studies at University College London, now an honorary position, and previously had a visiting chair at City University. He now works mainly for CIBER Research as an independent academic researcher primarily on scholarly communication issues. He has written widely on academic publishing, especially changes in the digital scholarly environment. He was a scholarly publisher for forty years, including senior positions at Academic Press, Oxford University Press and Chapman & Hall.

ALEXIS WEEDON holds the UNESCO chair in New Media Forms of the Book at the University of Bedfordshire. She is author of *Victorian publishing: the economics of book production for a mass market* (2003), and with V. L. Barnett of *Elinor Glyn as novelist, moviemaker, glamour icon and businesswoman* (2014). She was editor of *The history of the book in the west* (5 vols., 2010) and, with Julia Knight, *Convergence: the international journal of research into new media technologies* (1995–2017).

HELEN WILLIAMS holds a PhD thesis on Scotland's regional print economy in the nineteenth century. She is the Secretary of the Scottish Printing Archival Trust, and was Programme Manager for the celebrations of '500 years of printing in Scotland' in 2008. She has written articles and chapters on the printing industry in Scotland and on Russian publishing in Britain. She holds an MPhil from the School of Slavonic and East European Studies, and an MA in Librarianship from the University of Sheffield. She has worked for the British Library and the National Library of Scotland.

I.R. WILLISON held several senior posts in the British Museum Library from 1955 until his retirement in 1987. As Senior Research Fellow in the Institute of English Studies, University of London, he has played a leading part in the development of book history as a field in the English-speaking world. He edited volume 4 of *The new Cambridge bibliography of English literature* (1972) and has authored numerous essays on bibliography, book history and librarianship in Britain and in a global context. He was awarded the CBE for services to the field in 2005. He is the benefactor of the Willison Foundation Charitable Trust, which was established in 2016 to promote the advancement of the history of the book in the humanities.

Acknowledgements

First and foremost we wish to thank all of our contributors for their hard work and forbearance over the long period of time it has taken for this volume to be completed. We are enormously grateful to David McKitterick and John Barnard, general editors of the *Cambridge history of the book in Britain*. Their advice, encouragement and wise counsel at every stage have been invaluable. Linda Bree, Bethany Thomas, Tim Mason, Sarah Lambert and other staff at Cambridge University Press have been patiently accommodating of our needs and circumstances. Frances Brown's attentive copy-editing improved the text in its final stages. Rachel Noorda provided helpful research assistance at an earlier stage of the project. For advice, assistance, information and support of various kinds we would also like to thank Christopher Cipkin, Simon Eliot, David Finkelstein, the late Jeremy Lewis, Jane Potter, the late Tim Rix and the late Iain Stevenson.

Editing is a team effort, but for his steadfast and sure-handed steerage of this volume from commission to publication, Claire Squires and I. R. Willison are extremely grateful to Andrew Nash. Finally, Andrew Nash and Claire Squires also wish to acknowledge I. R. Willison, both in his role as Co-Volume Editor and as General Editor of the series. He has been central to the development of book history as a discipline in Britain for much of the period covered by this volume, and his intellectual perspicuity, engagement and commitment have helped bring not one but seven volumes of the *Cambridge history of the book in Britain* to fruition, and the series to a conclusion.

Introduction

ANDREW NASH, CLAIRE SQUIRES AND I. R. WILLISON

Mapping the book in the twentieth and twenty-first centuries

When the *Cambridge history of the book in Britain* project was first conceived in the early 1990s it was acknowledged by D. F. McKenzie that, compared to the first six projected volumes in the series, 'the terms of reference' for the final volume – originally planned to cover the period 1914–2000 – 'remain disturbingly imprecise'. McKenzie offered three explanatory factors: 'partly because the book must now share its functions with other media with which it is complexly interdependent, partly because the archival resources are so much richer than for earlier periods, [and] partly because new technologies and the emergence of multinational publishing weaken the very premises of a national history'.[1] A quarter of a century on we might add a fourth factor. Compared to earlier volumes in the series the period after 1914 remains largely unmapped – or at best inconsistently plotted. With a much smaller body of existing research on which to draw, this volume should be seen as laying the groundwork for future exploration of the book in Britain since 1914 as much as the summation of current work in the field.

There is, of course, an additional, ever more conspicuous factor of imprecision, the scale of which was unanticipated when McKenzie set out the terms of the project. In the 1992 essay quoted above, there is mention of 'new technologies', and indeed the impact of the computer had been a factor in the making of books since the 1960s. The speed of the development of digital technologies since the early 1990s, however, and the scale of their impact on the production, distribution and consumption of textual matter, could not have been foreseen. The changes have led many to refer to the 'third

---

1 McKenzie, 'History of the book', p. 300.

1

revolution of the book', following the movement from orality to literacy, and from manuscript to print. It is a revolution through which we are living and its effects are changing before our eyes, making precise judgements about its impact on the *history* of the book a challenging if not impossible task. This volume makes no attempt to write the future but it does not refrain from addressing the changing present. The subtitle – 'the twentieth century and beyond' – has been deliberately chosen to allow contributors to address the latest developments, including the impact of digital technologies, to a greater or lesser extent. Some have chosen to adopt fixed end-dates to their coverage of individual topics as a way of exercising control over a picture that is forever shifting. In Part I of the volume we have included a dedicated chapter on 'The digital book' which explores specifically technological developments, an area where the changing historical map is more clearly delineated. The broader social, cultural and commercial impacts of digitisation, however, are themes that recur throughout.

To return to McKenzie's three factors which characterise the 'disturbingly imprecise' terms of reference. It is true that archival resources for the twentieth century are much richer than in earlier periods, but records are amorphous and far from complete. Substantial parts of the accumulated archive of printers, publishers and booksellers have been lost – destroyed through fire, enemy action or the transfer of company ownership, among other reasons. Records have been inconsistently preserved, are often difficult to navigate, and are frequently impossible to access for commercial reasons. The more recent the archive the harder it can be to unlock.[2] McKenzie's other two terms of reference, however, are persistent themes in this volume. The interdependence of the book and other media is visible not only in the changing structure of the trade and the rise of multimedia conglomerates, but also in the constant interpenetration between books and radio, television and digital media, whether viewed from the perspective of authors, publishers, booksellers and distributors, or of readers and consumers. The 'emergence of multinational publishing', which McKenzie warned 'weaken[ed] the very premises of a national history', is equally pervasive. Its roots lie in the transatlantic partnerships that emerged in the late nineteenth century, when US publishing houses established offices in London and British firms did likewise in New York. Emblematic of this growth of transatlantic cultural and commercial exchange in an expanding English language world was the purchase by Doubleday, Page & Company of

---

2 For a fuller discussion of all these issues, see Nash, 'Publishers' archives'.

William Heinemann – one of the enterprising new firms that had transformed British publishing in the late nineteenth century – following the death of the British publisher in 1920. But the international context of the book in Britain since 1914 also lays bare the distinctiveness of this national history. The system and culture of the British book emerge from these chapters as distinctive in many ways, not least because of the continued importance of imperial and post-imperial markets which, alongside the trade's absorption into global markets and business environments, make for a unique kind of internationalism.

The book is organised into four sections. Part I contains three chapters which address changing technologies of print and book production, and the design, look and material form of the book across the period. Among the topics covered in this section are the development of the illustrated book, changing taste and practice in typography, and the combined impact of photocomposition, computerised typesetting, and recent developments in digital technology in the twenty-first century. Chapter 1 also provides an account of the printing industry against the changing social and industrial background of the period.

Part II is devoted to the sociology of text production, circulation and consumption. Substantial chapters on 'Authorship', 'Publishing', 'Distribution and bookselling' and 'Reading and ownership' provide a comprehensive historical survey of the institutional structures of the book, and the social, cultural and economic factors underpinning its creation, transmission and use. Many of the points introduced in these chapters are explored in greater depth in other parts of the volume. Extensive cross-referencing allows the reader to trace the entire treatment of a topic from the different perspectives offered.

Part III considers different types of books covering a wide range of genres or subject areas. Substantial space is devoted to major sectors of the publishing trade, such as literature (fiction, drama and poetry), children's books, and schoolbooks and textbook publishing, as well as to smaller but equally distinct areas like academic publishing, learned journals, museum and art book publishing, and music publishing (a topic that encompasses both sheet music and performance material as well as books about music). The substantial chapter on religion addresses a subject that illustrates social and cultural change in the period. Other topics covered, such as popular science and popular history, deal with areas of the trade which became more distinct as the century progressed, and which owe part of that distinctiveness to the layout and organisation of bookshops. The chapters on 'Publishing for leisure', and 'Information, reference and government publishing' cover broader, less obviously discrete, areas of book production focussing on a representative sample of sub-topics. Though wide-ranging, this section of the book does not seek to be comprehensive and not all sectors or subject areas are represented. For topics not addressed here, such as law books and legal publishing, the reader is directed to the entries in relevant reference works.[3]

Also included in Part III is a chapter on magazines and periodicals, an area linked more closely to the newspaper industry than to the book industry in terms of production and financing. Like the previous volume in this series, this book does not present a separate account of the newspaper press – a huge topic that demands a history of its own – but its scope extends beyond the 'book' as narrowly conceived. Newspapers are frequently referred to, especially in the context of reading. From the consumer perspective, the reading of a magazine or newspaper and the reading of a book are patently part of the same activity, even if they can be viewed differently. The synergies between the 'book' and other kinds of printed matter, including magazines, periodicals, pamphlets and newspapers, are thus very much part of this volume's concerns, whether, as in the case of magazines, or comics and graphic novels, it represents an area of print production closely linked to the newspaper industry, or, as in Gail Chester's discussion of the radical, alternative and minority book trade, it epitomises the way diverse forms of print have circulated in society for particular cultural or political purposes. The chapters on 'Literature' and 'Popular science' (to select only two) also demonstrate the importance of the magazine market to authors as a site of cultural production and income, especially in the first half of the century.

Part IV offers a more conceptual approach to some of the main themes and issues raised throughout the volume. The chapters presented here, though frequently structured chronologically and responding to the changing world of the period, adopt a less strictly historical approach. They aim to articulate more explicitly the distinctiveness of the period through examining some of the cultural, political and socio-economic contexts of the book. Chapters on books and the media, copyright and intellectual property, the book in wartime, and imperialism and post-imperialism offer synoptic accounts of major topics introduced throughout the volume. Other chapters discuss changing cultural attitudes to the book in the context of broader

---

3 For example, Suarez and Woudhuysen (eds.), *The Oxford companion to the book.*

debates about class, democracy and value, and map the intersections between the book and civil society or political cultures and social movements.

Region and nation

The Cambridge history of the book in Britain has been written and produced alongside separate histories of the book in Scotland (scheduled for completion in 2019) and Ireland (ongoing), and a single-volume study of the history of the book in Wales.[4] When complete, these four projects will together amount to seventeen volumes – an indication not only of the size of the history of the book as a field of study but also of the complexities involved in producing a 'national' history of the British Isles in any subject. Like the previous volume in the *Cambridge* series, the existence of specialist histories dedicated to Scotland, Ireland and Wales has influenced the structure and approach of the present volume, and it should be read alongside the coverage of the post-1914 period in these separate projects. The founding of the Irish Free State in 1922 means that the larger part of the island of Ireland lay outside the United Kingdom for all but the earliest years of this history. The civic and cultural distinctiveness of Scotland, however, is visible in areas such as bookselling and, notably, education (see Chapter 10). Scotland also remained an important location of printing and a publishing centre of significance for certain areas of the trade, such as maps and cartographical publishing, where for much of the century Edinburgh was the largest centre of production in the UK (see Chapter 20).

Britain is a small island, and London and the south-east of England have proved an increasingly powerful magnet for components of the trade. As David Finkelstein and Alistair McCleery observe in Chapter 5, conglomeration in the 1980s hastened 'a process of geographical concentration as well as amalgamation of imprints, leaving London as the undisputed centre of publishing in the UK'. Nevertheless, as other chapters show, the 'regional' dimension of the book has continued to be felt in many ways. Small regional publishers (often local museums or newspapers) sustained the area of local history, while the dominance of the ancient universities in England meant that Oxford and Cambridge remained the most stable centres of academic publishing in the period, with other towns and cities outside London intermittently productive in this field. From the consumer perspective, the story is

---

4 *The Edinburgh history of the book in Scotland*, gen. ed. Bill Bell; *The Oxford history of the Irish book*; Jones and Rees (eds.), *A nation and its books*.

one of growth outwards from large cities to smaller urban, suburban and rural areas. In the inter-war period the spread of twopenny libraries to villages and suburban areas brought books within a closer reach of a large part of the reading public (see Chapter 7). Similarly, the story of the expansion of the public library system is one of growth outwards from metropolitan centres to greater provision via branch libraries and in rural and suburban areas, especially after 1945. The bookselling system was also for much of the century marked by a significant geographical reach. Although Q. D. Leavis complained in 1932 that 'shops existing solely to sell books are rare outside the university towns of Oxford, Cambridge, and Edinburgh, certain parts of London and a few big cities',[5] Iain Stevenson demonstrates in Chapter 6 how bookselling actually operated for much of the period via a 'model of local dominance'. Although London had the greatest concentration of book-selling, the independent town centre bookshop was as distinctive a part of the nation's consumer culture as were the ubiquitous chain stores of W. H. Smith and John Menzies: 'Virtually every town or city above a certain size possessed a privately-owned bookseller which often became synonymous with literary life in local society.' In the second half of the century, the growth of literary festivals (beginning with Cheltenham in 1949) and book towns (Hay-on-Wye was first designated as such in 1961) also introduced a markedly regional accent to the book environment. As explored in Chapter 30, such book-related activity 'attests to the values (social, cultural and financial) of such events to local economies and communities'.

Beginnings

Volume 6 of the *Cambridge history of the book in Britain* covered the period 1830–1914. While 1914 has obvious significance as a date in European history, in book trade history more significant dates occurred in the decade or so before the outbreak of war. For this reason, most chapters in this volume reach back to earlier foundational moments such as the introduction of the Linotype and Monotype composing systems in the 1890s, the establishment of the Net Book Agreement (NBA) in 1900, and the passing of the Copyright Act of 1911. Broader cultural and commercial shifts from the late nineteenth century, such as the enormous growth of the newspaper and magazine industry and the Victorian information revolution, also form the backdrop for the discussion of certain topics.

5 Leavis, *Fiction and the reading public*, p. 4.

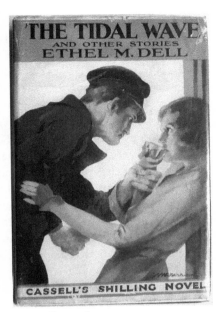

Intro.1 Cheap fiction from the 1920s published by Collins and
Cassell. (Private collection)

government calls for scrap metal led to the melting of huge stocks of stereotype
plates.[14] No longer able to rely on printing new impressions of old works from
plates, and confronted by an additional pressure 'to increase revenues dramatically' to meet 'steep rises in production costs',[15] post-war publishers were, in
Joseph McAleer's words, forced 'to accelerate the movement towards cheaper-
priced new books, and to accommodate more closely the tastes of the lower-
middle and working classes, the ever-expanding "new reading public"'.[16] Lower
profit margins encouraged the publication of fewer titles with larger print-runs
and a lower retail price. Cheapness and value for money became a noticeable
part of the marketing and visual appearance of books (fig. intro.1). However, the
price structure of British books was intimately connected with the supply chain.
Publishers built their lists around specific outlets: bookshops, bookstalls, non-
specialist retailers and, most importantly, libraries in all their varieties.

If the foundation of the NBA and the passing of the 1911 Copyright Act
provide the obvious starting points for an understanding of book trade

14 St Clair, *The reading nation*, p. 430. 15 McAleer, *Popular reading and publishing*, p. 54.
16 *Ibid.*, p. 48.

structures and business practices in this period, the outbreak of war in 1914 offers the first large social, cultural and political context which impacted upon those structures and practices. The problem of sourcing raw materials (especially paper), rising costs of production, labour shortages, and government strictures and censorship were matched by the opportunities provided by an increased demand for reading, new markets and distribution schemes, and partnership with the War Propaganda Bureau at Wellington House. A similar pattern occurred during the Second World War, when the effects of rationing and aerial bombardment were set against the enormous demand for reading matter. Especially important during 1939–45 was the propaganda work of the Ministry of Information which not only allowed commercial publishers to partner with a government office but also gave writing opportunities to authors (see Chapter 4). The chapters in this volume each discuss the impact of both World Wars on the topics they cover, demonstrating how wartime strictures impacted upon the look and feel of the book, the kinds of printed matter that circulated, and their channels of distribution. Part IV also includes a focussed account of the book in wartime by Jane Potter which provides a holistic view of the two World Wars and considers the impact of other political and military conflicts on books and the book trade.

'A nation of book-borrowers'

One way of identifying what is characteristic about the book in Britain in the twentieth century is to begin with perhaps its most iconic product – the Penguin paperback. Allen Lane's experiment in 1935 with sixpenny paperback reprints of recently published titles helps identify some of the distinctive aspects of the British book system as it developed over the course of the twentieth century and beyond, especially around price, format, distribution, and institutions of reading.

Lane's venture was first and foremost a challenge to the pricing structure of the British book, which for most trade titles (especially new works of fiction) was built around sales to subscription and public libraries. As evidenced throughout this volume, library borrowing and library reading remained throughout the century a central component of the trade, one which affected not only the reading public but also the practice of authorship and the policies of publishers.[17] For trade publishers of the inter-war period

17 See also Black and Hoare (eds.), *The Cambridge history of libraries in Britain and Ireland. 3. 1850–2000.*

the substantial market was not bookshops but libraries. New books in Britain in the inter-war period were published at a high price – 7s 6d for most new novels, more for a biography or work of history – and print-runs were set on the basis of anticipated sales to library markets. An illustration of how this pricing model precluded mass purchase is provided by the first edition of Lytton Strachey's *Queen Victoria* (1921). Published at 15s 6d, the printing and production cost of the first impression of 5,000 copies was 1s 6d per copy in quires, three times what it would later cost a reader to purchase a Penguin paperback.[18]

From the consumer's perspective, high retail prices naturally encouraged more borrowing than buying. As a 1932 report by the Joint Committee of publishers and booksellers noted, whereas a subscriber to a circulating library 'can get 50 or 100 books a year on a subscription varying from 10s. 6d. to 21s., he can only buy three new novels for the same sum'.[19] In an essay published in 1935, F. R. Richardson, the chief librarian of Boots Book-Lovers' Library, wrote: 'for better or for worse, we have become a nation of book-*borrowers*, and I foresee the day when the trade will at last awaken to this fact'.[20] The trade, generally, put up with the fact. When Harold Raymond of Chatto & Windus received from Henry Holt & Company the US sales figures of Rosamond Lehmann's *Dusty answer* (1927), a successful title on both sides of the Atlantic, he wrote in a resigned tone: 'You make us feel very jealous in this book-borrowing little island.'[21] Although this became a familiar refrain in the book world, other publishers profited from the book-borrowing habit, building their lists almost wholly around sales to libraries rather than direct to customers through bookshops. Mills & Boon developed its enormously profitable line in romance fiction in the inter-war period in precisely this way, capitalising on the new 'twopenny' libraries which spread rapidly in the 1930s, and later the public libraries (see Chapter 7). Significantly, the firm did not expand much into the paperback market until the mid-1960s when it at last began to target book-buyers.[22]

Allen Lane's experiment in 1935 was thus essentially about reaching a new market of book-buyers from across the spectrum of this book-borrowing public. With a lower profit margin on the 6d retail price, Penguins had to be issued in large print-runs and thus had to reach a market of purchasers to

18 Nash, 'Literary culture', p. 326.   19 Sanders (ed.), *British book trade organisation*, p. 144.
20 Richardson, 'The circulating library', p. 196.
21 26 July 1927. Chatto & Windus archive, University of Reading, M S2444/117.
22 McAleer, *Passion's fortune*, pp. 114–21.

recover the costs. This market Lane believed to lie outside as well as inside the dedicated bookshop. The distribution and bookselling component of the trade had hitherto been strongly demarcated in terms of the kinds of goods that circulated in different retail outlets. By setting out to bring 'intelligent books' to the 'vast reading public', Lane attempted to bridge the apparent class divisions underlying the means of access to texts.[23]

The revolutionary nature of Penguin, then, lay not in selling books cheaply, but in selling titles which had not previously been available at affordable purchasable prices. As discussed in Chapter 5, Lane, like others in the trade, believed in a 'new reading public' that had not been reached by a publishing system geared towards library sales and expensively priced titles in upmarket bookshops. Not all books were borrowed from libraries, of course. As noted above, in the inter-war period several publishers developed highly profitable lines in cheap fiction. Series such as Hodder & Stoughton's two-shilling Yellow Jackets, with Edgar Wallace, Baroness Orczy and 'Sapper' among the leading authors, were hugely successful (fig. intro.2). A history of Hodder & Stoughton claims: 'There was not a bookshop that did not open its doors to a traveller with the Yellow Jacket list to sell.'[24] But popular fiction of this period priced at two shillings down to sixpence was equally likely to be acquired via chain stores such as Woolworths, or other non-book outlets. As widely documented, the profitable sale of Penguins in Woolworths was crucial to Lane's success, and highlighted the inherently conservative nature of the publishing and bookselling trade.[25]

Nevertheless, as Chapter 7 shows, evidence from readership surveys suggests that, while Penguin Books generated a new attitude to bookbuying, it did not unlock a new class of readers. More accurately, it encouraged existing readers to purchase more books and to acquire their reading in different ways. Britain was not turned into a book-buying nation overnight. Indeed, after the Second World War, accelerated expansion of the public library movement further entrenched Britain as a 'bookborrowing little island'. Public libraries and library policy provided a powerful social and cultural infrastructure for the reading public's access to texts. A Mass-Observation report of 1942 underlined 'the importance of borrowing in shaping the whole book outlook of the individual'.[26]

23 Lewis, *Penguin special*, p. 122.   24 Attenborough, *A living memory*, p. 98.
25 Lewis, *Penguin special*, pp. 99–100.   26 Mass-Observation, *Books and the public*, p. 63.

(a)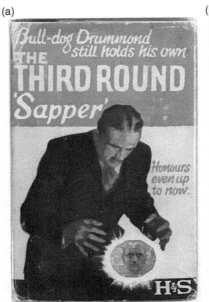

(b)

Intro.2 Titles from Hodder & Stoughton's Yellow Jacket series published in the 1920s and 1930s. (Private collection)

The various stakeholders in the book world – authors, publishers, book-sellers, librarians, readers – inevitably took up different, sometimes con-flicting, positions in the debates that proliferated throughout the century about the public library's role in the book system. In the context of author-ship, the multiple circulation of single copies of books for free led to the campaign for Public Lending Right (see Chapter 4), which after protracted debates in the 1960s was finally introduced via the Public Lending Right Act of 1979. Authors claimed that lending books to the public 'constituted an ancillary use of an author's property',[27] and the novelist John Fowles estimated in 1971 that 'for each single library royalty the writer gets, he is deprived, on a commercial basis, of another fifteen'.[28] The call for literature to be allowed to operate on 'a commercial basis' carried a perhaps unwit-ting irony.

27 Bonham-Carter, *Authors by profession*, vol. 2, p. 101.
28 Findlater, *Public Lending Right*, p. 101.

Paperbacks and the emergence of a mass market

Arguably, it was in the publication of original works of non-fiction, not reprints of fiction and biography, that Penguin Books really broke the mould of British publishing. The first Pelicans appeared in May 1937. Consisting of both reprints and newly commissioned works, the series covered all areas of science, history and archaeology, politics and economics, and the arts. It was not an entirely new concept. In 1927 Ernest Benn had launched 'Benn's Sixpenny Library', issuing well over 200 titles in the space of two years – Chapter 11 notes the prevalence of science topics in this series – but these extended only to eighty pages and, compared to Pelicans, were closer to pamphlets. Lane had envisaged Pelicans as 'a true Everyman's library of the twentieth century' which he hoped might bring 'the finest products of modern thought and art to the people.'[29] As Chapter 7 again shows, however, Pelican reading was 'very largely a middle class habit', and while it encouraged people to purchase more books, it is easy to exaggerate the extent to which it brought modern thought to 'the people'.

Pelicans had 'a definite educational impulse behind them' and early editors were closely involved with the adult education movement.[30] As Gail Chester notes in Chapter 27, the list also had 'a general impulse of social radicalism'. This was equally true in a more international context of the Penguin Specials, commenced in November 1937. Consisting of books of topical interest on contemporary political and social issues, the series was a response to the growing international crisis. The topicality required them to be 'printed and published at speed'[31] – Geneviève Tabouis's *Blackmail or war*, translated from the French, was reported to have been produced 'in record time'.[32] The series thus bridged the world of the newspaper and the hitherto expensively priced sphere of non-fiction publishing, issuing books of substantial length – the typical span of early titles was 256 or 288 pages – at little more than twice the price of a newspaper.[33] Benefiting from Penguin's high wartime paper rationing, the Specials series expanded greatly during the Second World War, with 145 titles produced between the outbreak of conflict and the end of 1945. Sales of individual titles regularly exceeded 100,000 copies. With famous titles such as R. A. Saville-Sneath's *Aircraft recognition* (1941), the books also crossed over into the 'information' publishing territory, popularising, as Susan Pickford

---

29 Lewis, *Penguin special*, p. 113.   30 Hare, *Penguin portrait*, pp. 51–2.
31 Lewis, *Penguin special*, p. 135.   32 Hare, *Penguin portrait*, p. 68.
33 *The Times* cost 2½d in 1937.

notes in Chapter 19, the 'how-to' category in a cheaper, more easily handled, physical form.

For all its success in introducing cheap paperback series into Britain, the triumph of Penguin Books did not lead to an immediate embrace of the softcover format for most books. Although the formation in 1944 of Pan Books – a consortium of publishers which included Collins, Macmillan and Hodder & Stoughton – represented a further stage in the stimulation of a mass market for paperbacks, in business terms the paperback model of publishing did not become fully developed in Britain until the 1960s. The expansion of the public library movement after 1945 nurtured the demand for hardbacks with their extra durability and prolonged the publishing model that had proved dominant in the first half of the century. According to the bookseller-turned-publisher Tony Godwin, 'paperbacks were still no more than a minor sideline in 1948, a promising trend in 1954. By 1960 they had come to be recognised as the most dynamic factor in the publishing world.'[34] In some respects the responsibility for developing that dynamism lay with publishers other than Penguin. Chapter 5 shows how in the 1960s new and rival paperback imprints such as Panther, Fontana, Corgi and Pan began to reach a truly mass market. It is highly revealing that of the 1.5 million paperback copies initially sold of Ian Fleming's *On Her Majesty's Secret Service* (1963), less than half were through conventional bookshops. Exploiting the market that Penguin had in part opened up, Pan made Fleming the first super-seller – it was claimed that ten out of the first eighteen million-sellers in Britain were James Bond novels.[35] As Chapter 8 notes, the success of rival paperback imprints in the 1960s forced Penguin to alter its publishing strategy, targeting the mass-market sector directly and breaking with its previously conservative policy over cover design.

As other chapters show, the growth of paperback publication in the 1960s altered the face of British books, bringing new kinds of product to the consumer. Penguin led the way in several areas, including art and architecture where Nikolaus Pevsner's English county architectural guides *The Buildings of England* 'appealed to enthusiastic amateurs and scholars alike' (see Chapter 15). Similarly, Kaye Webb's work at Puffin 'contributed to the dramatic expansion of paperback publishing for children' during the 1960s (see Chapter 9). Literature also took on a more extensive paperback form from the 1960s onwards. Penguin, and even more so Methuen, made

34 Bonham-Carter, *Authors by profession*, vol. 2, p. 94.
35 Sutherland, *Fiction and the fiction industry*, p. 176.

big advances in play publishing in the 1960s and 1970s, capitalising on new movements in British theatre, while the Penguin Modern Poets series widened the market for a traditionally niche area of output. Another area of growth was religion. Michael Ledger-Lomas shows in Chapter 13 how paperbacks offered a new direction for religious literature, widening the scope of the market beyond Bibles and sermons. Alongside its success with Agatha Christie's detective novels, Fontana developed a strong religious paperback list which was soon followed by other imprints, achieving considerable sales of titles ranging from translations of Paul's Epistles to spiritual books by television and entertainment celebrities.

As paperback publishing became the dominant mode of book production, diversity in form and business model began to emerge. Pan's introduction of its Picador imprint in 1972 represented the beginnings of a more variegated market, and paperback originals became more common in the fiction category. Chapter 8 outlines some of the changes in paperback publishing in the fiction market, noting how the rise of the 'best-seller' as a marketing strategy coincided with repeated fears over the future of the 'literary' novel. As the chapter goes on to show, when paperback advances became the determining factor in hardback publishing decisions it provided an impetus for hardback firms to acquire or develop their own paperback imprints. What Eric de Bellaigue has called the 'dawning realization' in the early 1980s that 'paperbacks held the key to financial soundness'[36] was felt in other sectors as well, including children's books where the paperback market expanded significantly in the 1980s.

State, government and education

The centrality of the public library to the reading nation for much of the period helped to sustain an institutional infrastructure for the book that was never wholly dependent upon the marketplace. It also points up another important aspect of the book in this period: the recurring discourse around the social mission of books and reading. Public funding for the provision of reading meant that debates over the civic and educative functions of the public library movement were frequently accompanied by anxieties about the public's overwhelming demand for what was perceived as recreational reading. Even with the major expansion of the public library movement after 1945 – part of the social fabric of post-war welfarism – statistical surveys

36 De Bellaigue, *British book publishing*, p. 14.

revealed that usage continued to be disproportionately middle-class in character and clustered around specific social groups, especially those in full- or part-time education (see Chapter 7). The growth of television and later the arrival of the internet intensified the debate over the library's function. When supermarkets began selling books cheaply in the mid-1990s following the demise of the NBA, it bred fears that public library visiting and borrowing would decline, as did the spread of the internet with its seemingly infinite gateway for information and reference. As Chapter 7 goes on to explain, 'discourses of anxiety around reading (implicitly about *not* reading, or reading non-literary works)' continued to inform policy-making at the start of the twenty-first century.

The public library movement is only the most conspicuous example of the intersection between state and market structures in the book environment. Kate Longworth's chapter on 'The book and civil society' offers a focussed account of this topic, discussing cooperative schemes between government and the book trade in the promotion of reading and literacy. Longworth traces in particular the enduring work of the National Book Council (later the National Book League and Booktrust), which emerged in the 1920s from the Society of Bookmen, and proved a catalyst for much of the book trade organisation in the 1920s and 1930s mentioned above. The aim of the NBC was not to promote the sale of books directly but to 'create the taste and habit of reading' through the promotion of reading and literacy schemes that were indirectly linked to commercial aims.

Among the core activities of the NBC was the provision of textbooks for schools, and educational publishing represents another area in which state and market structures have interpenetrated. In Chapter 10, Sarah Pedersen shows how the market for school textbooks has proved highly susceptible to political and socio-economic forces, with educational publishers having to respond quickly to changes in government policy. The sector became especially important during the depression years of the 1920s as one of the few guaranteed markets for books. A government report on *Books in public elementary schools* called for greater expenditure on textbooks, making education 'a captive market' for publishers like Nelson and Longman. The 'close, if not symbiotic, link' between educational reformers and educational publishing is strongly evident throughout the period. If the appointment of Henry Newbolt – author of the 1921 report on the teaching of English in schools in England and Wales – as editorial advisor at Thomas Nelson & Sons represented a smart piece of business on the part of the firm's director John Buchan, the Curriculum Development Project of the 1960s introduced a more formalised link between government-funded agencies and publishers, with firms competing for rights to produce, market and distribute educational materials. As Pedersen goes on to show, subsequent developments – including changes to the way schools were funded, the implementation of a new National Curriculum, and the introduction of more digital content into the classroom – further altered the size and character of the textbook market.

Links between the market and social and educational policy are further explored in the chapter on children's books. Peter Hunt and Lucy Pearson trace the peaks and troughs in the sector amidst the backdrop of changing government policy and funding for schools and libraries. High levels of public investment in the 1960s and early 1970s meant that publishers could rely on 'almost guaranteed sales'. Correspondingly, when public spending was cut in the 1980s and the number of books bought by state schools fell by 35 per cent, publishers shifted more towards sales to individuals, before new initiatives in the 1990s, such as the National Literacy Strategy (1998) and the National Year of Reading (1998), provided 'more funds and more focus on children's books'. Publishing for children was far from being a specialist enterprise, as to some extent it had been in the nineteenth century. Hunt and Pearson conservatively estimate that the period saw 'over 250 British publishing houses try their hand at children's books'. With such a fertile market it is unsurprising that these included firms, such as Oxford University Press, whose lists did not naturally extend into this area. The children's book sector also proved susceptible and responsive to the changing social, cultural and ethnic demographics of the nation. Hunt and Pearson point to the work of organisations such as the Children's Rights Workshop (CRW) and the National Committee on Racism in Children's Books, which encouraged publishers to respond to the challenges around diversity posited by the 1967 Plowden Report.

Government publishing in itself represents an area of increased importance in the twentieth century, its influence felt in many areas of print production and consumption, from telephone directories and the *Highway code*, through town plans and street guides produced by local authorities, to the practical guides on cookery and food management issued by the Ministry of Food in the Second World War. In Chapter 19, Susan Pickford surveys the 'massive expansion in the amount of government-issued information available for public consultation', focussing on the core activity of His/Her Majesty's Stationery Office, 'long among the largest publishers by volume in the UK'. Pickford demonstrates an overall trend towards 'increasing access to information and therefore government accountability'. Parliament's takeover in 1909 of the publication of Hansard (a commercial venture for much of the nineteenth century) was a foundational moment in this development. As Pickford's discussion demonstrates, however, governmental publishing activities frequently crossed over into the private sector, and became more closely structured on commercial business models in the later decades of the century.

Books, legislation and society

Government publishing, and the broader role of the state in the book environment, is part of a wider legislative framework which throughout the century has controlled – and in some instances curtailed – the production and sale of books. The law of copyright is crucial here. So, too, is the history of censorship and obscenity laws. Censorship of printed matter since 1914 has operated both directly – through the application of, and changes to, obscenity laws – and indirectly through the policies and practices of publishers, booksellers and libraries.[37] Well-known episodes from the first half of the century, such as the prosecution of Methuen over D. H. Lawrence's *The rainbow* (1915) and of Cape over Radclyffe Hall's *The well of loneliness* (1928), and the banning of Joyce's *Ulysses* in Britain between 1922 and 1936, are discussed in this volume. Against this culture of oppression, the inter-war period saw a rise in publishing initiatives that promoted a more radical alternative to the problems of society at home and abroad. For example, Chapter 9 cites recent research which shows a strong current of 'social/political radicalism' or 'aesthetic radicalism' in children's book publishing of the period. Among the publishers who advanced a left-wing ethos in this area was Victor Gollancz, whose more famous venture in politically committed publishing, the Left Book Club, is referenced widely in this volume. In Iain Stevenson's words, the Left Book Club, which ran from 1936 to 1948, was 'as much a political movement as a means of merchandising books'. Its decline and eventual demise after the end of the Second World War and the election of a Labour government in 1945 suggests that it served a particular purpose at a particular moment in history.[38]

The period after the Second World War witnessed a greater intensity in the opposition between forces of censorship and publishing ventures that sought to break through social and sexual mores. Chapter 8 relates how the

---

37 For a chronological survey of events and issues in censorship in England since 1850, see Bradshaw and Potter (eds.), *Prudes on the prowl*.
38 The Left Book Club was revived in 2014. See www.leftbookclub.com.

brief but spectacular era of the 'mushroom' publishers – firms that issued cheap American-style genre fiction from back-street premises – was brought to an end by a spate of prosecutions in the 1950s. Similarly, Chapter 22 shows how campaigns against the reprinting of American comics led to an effective banning of such imported material for a period and the setting up of a Comics Code Authority. The emergence of what became known as the permissive society from the late 1950s intensified the book industry's efforts to break free from legal constraints around the depiction of sexuality in particular. The prosecution, trial and acquittal of Penguin Books in November 1960 for its edition of D. H. Lawrence's *Lady Chatterley's lover* is discussed in detail in Chapters 5 and 8. The publication was in effect a test of the new 1959 *Obscene Publications Act*, and the outcome has come to be seen as a watershed in British publishing and society. Both chapters emphasise, however, that the acquittal did not put an end to prosecutions for obscenity in the ensuing years as a determination of what constituted the 'public good' continued to operate in the courts.

The 1960s witnessed an upsurge in book and publishing initiatives that promoted cultural and political movements and causes. In Chapter 27 Gail Chester offers a wide-ranging account of the 'radical, alternative and minority book trade' in the twentieth-century, which should be read alongside Chris Atton's focussed discussion of counter-cultural and underground publishing in Britain during the 1960s and early 1970s. Chester traces the publishing and book-related initiatives that promoted the rights and representations of women, minority sexual and ethnic groups, and oppositional political move-ments. As her discussion shows, the 1960s and 1970s witnessed some of the most influential moments in the history of feminist, Black British and radical publishing and bookselling which disturbed the predominantly conservative nature of the mainstream book market. Nevertheless, distribution to a larger market (especially surmounting the conservative stocking policy of W. H. Smith) remained an obstacle into the 1980s, as did reactionary attempts to contain or police the spread of the printed word, such as the raiding and seizure of stock in London's Gay's the Word bookshop in 1984.

Beyond changing attitudes to censorship, social change in the twentieth and twenty-first centuries can be traced in key sectors of the book trade, including the broad area of publishing for leisure. In Chapter 14 Susan Pickford concentrates on three sectors of the industry that were already established at the start of the period – cookery, gardening and sport – and also traces the later emergence of self-help books, or the mind, body, spirit (MBS) category, an area which connects to issues of lifestyle choice that 'play into the conceptualisation of leisure as a consumer category'. If the development of cookery books reflects changes in employment patterns, the social role of women and the impact of electrical appliances, the growth of the gardening sector is strongly linked to the rise of suburbia and increased home ownership. There is an obvious crossover between leisure and information publishing, and in Chapter 19 Pickford offers further examples of publishing initiatives which illustrate broader aspects of social history, such as changes in patterns of transport and car ownership.

Pickford's coverage of the growth from the 1980s of self-help/MBS books links with Michael Ledger-Lomas's discussion of religion, which traces the enduring importance of religious publishing (as broadly conceived) in an increasingly secular nation. Throughout the period, religious books and Bibles remained a substantial market. Indeed, it is often overlooked that just a few months after the trial of *Lady Chatterley* there was another 'publishing sensation' – the New Testament volume of the New English Bible – which also produced queues outside bookshops (W. H. Smith put in the biggest pre-publication order in the firm's history). Ledger-Lomas also shows how the 'declining intellectual authority and social presence of churches' nevertheless opened up a 'spiritual market' that was never wholly divorced from an apparently 'ailing Christian sector'. Even the growth in the twenty-first century of the 'New Atheism', typified by the writings of Richard Dawkins, has served to revive as much as to 'bury' religion.

If religious belief and secularisation provides one important index of social change in this period, class offers another. Class has never been far away from debates over books and culture in twentieth- and twenty-first-century Britain. As discussed above, it informed debates about the provision of books in public libraries, as well as developments in educational and children's book publishing. In Chapter 25 Ronan McDonald provides a critical overview of the intellectual debates about books and reading in relation to class, democracy and value, from the impact of Victorian educationalists, through the influence of Leavisite criticism in universities, and the rise of cultural studies. McDonald concludes with an assessment of the impact of the internet and social media on these questions.

Developments in format, design and technology

Much has been made of the paperback format of Penguin Books as breaking the mould of the previously hardback-dominated market. Paper-covered books existed in Britain long before 1935, although these were generally larger in format and more ephemeral in appearance and design. In addition to popularising the smaller format (which, as Chapter 8 notes, followed continental models), Penguin paperbacks accelerated the spread of a new development in binding. As Chapter 1 notes, mechanisation of the binding process facilitated from the 1930s onwards the rise of 'perfect bindings', where pages were glued into the covers. At first the method was crude, and the adhesive bindings on many early Penguins proved liable to cracking. As the process was improved, however, more books were bound in this way, including hardbacks, and perfect bindings had largely replaced the gathering and sewing of signatures by the 1980s (see Chapter 2).

Increased mechanisation in the binding process led to a revival of interest in decorative bindings among some small press publishers which extended to larger publishing concerns. The Folio Society, founded in 1947, issued books in large, unlimited editions as part of what Sebastian Carter terms 'the democratisation of fine book production' which took place in the years immediately after the Second World War. Later dispensing with dustwrappers, Folio used different binders and binding styles, 'with the board coverings often printed as well as blocked', to create an appearance that, while instantly recognisable, was never blandly homogeneous. It is noticeable that towards the end of the twentieth century mainstream commercial publishers became more willing to use elaborate binding designs as a feature on some of their hardback titles. For example, the artist-novelist Alasdair Gray successfully persuaded first Canongate and then Jonathan Cape to issue his hardback editions with elaborate metalling – a relatively inexpensive ornament – on the front and back covers as well as the spines of the bindings of his books.[39] As the digital twenty-first century progressed, production values of print books were perceived to be more rather than less important, making a 'vogue for beautiful books' and a revival of interest in book design.[40]

One example of the employment of different binding styles for different kinds of use is the Shell Guides. A series of guidebooks on the counties of Britain, the series began in 1934 under the editorial control of John Betjeman, who wrote the first guide on Cornwall. Initially published by the Architectural Press, the guides were produced in card covers and a comb binding. Since the series was aimed in part at the new generation of car-

39 Gray, *A life in pictures*, pp. 217–19.
40 Alex Preston, 'How real books have trumped ebooks', *Observer* 14 May 2017, www .theguardian.com/books/2017/may/14/how-real-books-trumped-ebooks-publishing-revival.

motoring tourists, a ring binding enabled easier reading on the road, and, as Sebastian Carter notes, 'allowed different papers to be used for text, maps and illustrations'. When the series was taken over by Batsford in 1937 the volumes were issued simultaneously in both a comb and a conventional sewn, cloth-covered binding. Under Faber from 1939 the series acquired more of the flavour of armchair reading and by the 1950s the spiral binding had been dropped.[41]

Binding techniques aside, the inter-war period witnessed some important changes in the internal and external appearance of the book, especially in the expansion of the number of typefaces available for book work, and a new adventurousness in the use of dust-wrappers. The outstanding example is Victor Gollancz, whose firm was founded in 1927. Aided by the type designer Stanley Morison, who in addition to being a director of the firm was also consultant for the Monotype Corporation, Gollancz evolved a form of typographical jacket design that has been judged as 'one of the most brilliant and successful innovations in publishing in the twentieth century'.[42] If Morison's design for the text pages of Gollancz's books observed what Sebastian Carter calls 'an austerely uniform standard', the jackets, printed on yellow paper in black and magenta, introduced a bold and entirely new visual design. Eschewing pictorial images, the Gollancz wrappers were emblazoned with a mixture of types and rule combinations, pointing fingers, and other devices, along with slogans, excerpts from reviews, or sales figures (fig. intro.3). Gollancz also made striking use of typography in his advertising, on which he expended large amounts of money, leading a rival publisher, Frederic Warburg, to observe retrospectively that 'the age of shouting, the period of the colossal and the sensational, had arrived'.[43]

Inside the covers of books, the introduction of new, more refined practices in typography and page design was slow to emerge. Carter points out that before 1914 decisions about design were normally left to printers, but the interwar period witnessed the rise of the publisher's designer who assumed responsibility for the choice of type and layout of the page. Critical here was the work of successive editorial and design directors at Penguin, who intro-duced new techniques and tastes from Europe, transforming what was widely perceived by outsiders as a book culture lacking any conspicuous standards. Carter points to the important role of Jan Tschichold, who joined Penguin in 1947 as design director and whose *Penguin composition rules*

41 www.shellcountyguides.co.uk. The use of comb binding for road maps was a much later development.
42 Hodges, *Gollancz*, p. 30.   43 Warburg, *An occupation for gentlemen*, p. 119.

Intro.3 A. J. Cronin, *The stars look down* (1935). Dust-jacket of the first cheap edition issued by Gollancz in 1936. (Private collection)

established 'a basic trade standard'. Tschichold's influence at Penguin, like that of his successor, Hans Schmoller, points to the wider importance of European influences on British book production discussed below.

Just as changes in typography could be said to have moved slowly, the most impactful developments in production technologies did not occur until the middle and second half of the century. The inter-war period saw improvements in printing machinery, with faster flat-bed and rotary presses and multiple-process machines. The widespread adoption of the Monotype composing system by book printing houses made typesetting quicker and brought greater economies of scale. Most Penguin paperbacks, with their large print-runs, were set in this way. But as Chapter 1 makes clear, the hot metal process was not displaced in book typesetting until the 1960s with the introduction of photocomposition and offset lithography. These technological advances enabled significant reductions in unit costs. Titles with large print-runs and multiple impressions could be produced more quickly and cheaply, facilitating greater paperback publishing, while at the other end of the production scale niche publishing ventures also benefited. The 1960s and 1970s may have been the era of the mass-market paperback but it was also the era of the British counter-culture, and the most significant innovation in the underground publishing movement was the use of offset litho printing which allowed the underground 'to experiment creatively and to be independent from at least one part of the printing industry' (see Chapter 28).

In comparison to the USA and continental Europe, photocomposition and offset litho were slow to develop in Britain. The need to reprint book stocks destroyed in the war held up the gradual conversion from letterpress, as did the cost implications of investing in new machinery and the consequent impact on employee relations (see Chapter 1). As Chapter 9 shows, when Heinemann's subsidiary The World's Work published children's books with four-colour offset litho the company had to use American duplicate film and print the books in Holland. When the process became more widely adopted, however, it brought about a revolutionary and belated development in book illustration. Existing techniques meant most illustrations in books were printed separately from the typesetting process, which prevented integration of text and image on the same page. In *The truth about publishing* (1926), Stanley Unwin noted how 'the "offset" process' was 'coming increasingly into vogue' as a method for reproducing illustrations, and as Chapter 10 notes, full-colour illustrations began to be used in school textbooks before the Second World War.[44] It was only in the 1960s, however, that the technique became widely used in Britain, and integration of text and image on the page became common. The effect was to dramatically alter the appearance of the page and, consequently, the reading experience. The impact of these changes is traced in Chapter 2 through an analysis of the Pelican History of Art series.

The introduction of phototypesetting had a social and commercial impact as well as a technological one. As Chapter 1 demonstrates, by the mid-1980s much of the initial preparation of text and illustration for reproduction no longer took place within the printing house. This had a negative effect on the printing industry, which was forced to change established work practices and retrain or dispense with specialist staff. However, as Bromage and Williams point out, many firms were reluctant to dispense with technology in which large amounts of money had been invested. The printing industry was also heavily unionised, and the move to dispense with expensive durable machines operated by skilled printers 'who had undertaken long apprenticeships and were protected by their unions, was not an easy obstacle for the industry to surmount'.

Photocomposition lasted a relatively short time and was soon replaced by computer technology, which proved cheaper and more flexible. While the impact of digital technologies on the consumer was felt mostly from the 1990s onwards, the use of computers in the production process reached back

---

44 Unwin, *The truth about publishing*, p. 152.

further into the century. Bromage and Williams trace the transition from photographic to computer composition to the late 1970s with the creation of digital typefaces stored as outline vectors. The increasing use of micro- or personal computers in the 1980s meant that designers could control every detail of a book's design, and much of the initial preparation of text and illustration was taking place outside the printing house, which had radical implications for the industry. Increasingly, it became more economic for the actual printing of British books to take place overseas, part of what Finkelstein and McCleery refer to as the 'decentralisation of activity' in the book industry (see Chapter 5).

The full impact of digital technologies on the production of books and the evolution of the digital book as a format are outlined in Chapter 3. Padmini Ray Murray traces the development and impact of the word processor and desktop publishing, citing the publication of Peter James's *Host* (1993), 'widely accepted as the first book to be published electronically in the UK and possibly worldwide'. While these developments brought changes to the way books were created and, eventually, consumed, it was not until the creation of e-reading devices at the end of the century, and in particular the development of mobile apps, that a crucial 'shift in the mediation of the book' took place.

Books and other media

The above sections have suggested that aspects of the British book in the twentieth century – the maintenance of price protection, the belated emergence of the mass-market paperback and the gradual adoption of new technologies – suggest a slow pace of change, at least in the period up to the 1960s. In other ways, however, the twentieth century can be seen as a period of intense change in the book market. The growth of other media – film, radio, television and latterly digital media – brought significant transformations to the structure of the industry and the character and form of its products. In her synoptic chapter 'Books and the media', Alexis Weedon refers to the absorption of publishing companies by transnational media organisations as 'the most radical change in the institutional structures of the book trade since the Stationers' Company's loss of control of the trade in the eighteenth century'. As Weedon demonstrates, from the news empires of the press barons Alfred Harmsworth (Lord Northcliffe) and Lord Beaverbrook, through companies such as Granada, which moved from the theatre and television into publishing, to the growth in the late twentieth century of transnational media companies, the period has witnessed a highly volatile relationship between book publishing and commercial media operations.

The business context of cross-media conglomeration in the book industry is discussed in Chapter 5. The volume as a whole, however, illustrates the ubiquity of the interpenetration between books and other media, showing how film, radio and television have both depended upon and helped to promote printed matter. If, as Weedon judges, the book 'lost its status as the primary medium for the communication of stories, ideas and knowledge', it was nevertheless 'to the book industry that the film, radio, television, and later media industries turned for stories, scripts, ideas, formats and all forms of creative content'. As noted above, the extension of copyright protection to adaptations of literary works proved a major boost to authorship, and as Chapter 4 demonstrates, the growth of the film industry offered huge financial rewards for some authors. Writing for stage and screen became a vital part of an author's commercial practice in the twentieth century and publishers increasingly judged manuscripts not solely as books but on their potential as a possible source of a film, or a radio or television serial.

What the chapters in this volume repeatedly show is that book publishing has worked in tandem with the wider media industry both in terms of its business operations and in the creation of its products. In the magazine market, books quickly took on aspects of the visual culture of cinema. Amalgamated Press issued numerous magazines about the early film industry, including the weekly comic *Film Fun* (1920–62) which included stills from films alongside comic stories depicting famous Hollywood actors. In the book market early film 'tie-ins' appeared via the book jackets that adorned the Readers Library and other popular series (fig. intro.4). Radio broadcasts led to increased demand in several areas, including sermons and religious titles in the inter-war period, and poetry in the 1940s and 1950s. Surveys from the post-war period referred to in Chapter 7 showed that, in spite of heightened fears that other forms of entertainment were reducing the reading habit, radio and television served to stimulate reading and library borrowing. Even when television emphatically became the principal leisure pursuit of the nation, successful programmes frequently produced best-selling book titles, a trend aided in recent decades by commercial integration in the publishing and media industries. For example, Chapter 9 notes how novelisations of the hit television series *Dr Who* in the 1970s achieved some of the highest sales in the children's book market (the books also helped boost the science fiction sub-sector of literature publishing). Similarly, Chapter 15

Intro.4 Titles from the Readers Library, including film tie-in editions. (Private collection)

records how Kenneth Clark's *Civilisation*, produced by BBC Publications and John Murray to accompany Clark's television series on European art and architecture, became the best-selling non-fiction title of 1969. Chapters 11, 12 and 14 on popular science, popular history and publishing for leisure point to many other examples where books published in association with television series have achieved enormous sales, particularly in the areas of cookery and the natural world. The appearance and growth of cookery sections in book-shops owes much to the success of television tie-ins.

Retailing is another area where the interdependence between the book and other media is strongly visible. The emergence of book superstores in the 1990s, notably the American company Borders, saw books increas-ingly being sold alongside other media products, a trend which other large chains, including Waterstone's, and latterly independents, soon followed. In the twenty-first century, the success of the Richard and Judy Book Club has boosted the sales of fiction, not simply, as Chapter 7 notes, by acting as 'a marketing device and a marker of literary tastes', but through co-branding and business cooperation with the dis-tributor and retailer W. H. Smith.

An enduring illustration of the synergies between print and other media is the *Radio Times*. Founded in 1923, the magazine was initially a joint venture between the BBC and the commercial publisher Newnes, but in 1925 the BBC took over editorial control and by 1937 'the entire operation was in-house'.[45] As Tony Quinn notes in Chapter 21, by the 1950s the *Radio Times* was the overall sales leader in the magazine market, reaching nearly 9 million copies per week in 1955. As Quinn states, this represents 'an astounding figure for a total population of about fifty million'. The BBC's long history of magazine production, from the *Listener* (developed mainly as a printed record of broad-cast talks) to the continued success into the new century of specialist maga-zines like the *BBC History Magazine* and the *BBC Music Magazine*, illustrates the enduring symbiotic relationship between print and broadcasting. Indeed, as Quinn's chapter goes on to demonstrate, BBC Magazines and BBC Enterprises became major players in the magazines market in the 1980s and 1990s, acquiring other titles when it needed to reduce its dependence upon the *Radio Times*.

Chapters 5 and 24 both draw attention to the biggest transmedia creation of the period: J. K. Rowling's Harry Potter books. The phenomenon is not unique, as Hunt and Pearson's reference to the marketing and merchandising

45 www.bbc.co.uk/historyofthebbc/research/general/radio-times.

of Enid Blyton's character Noddy demonstrates, but the scale and global penetration of Harry Potter is unprecedented. Finkelstein and McCleery note the crucial role of the literary agent in exploiting all available platforms for dissemination of the product, and Catherine Seville discusses some of the copyright and intellectual property complications that have arisen as a result. Of particular importance in this context is the existence of the internet as a platform not only for analysis of the books and films but for reworkings of their content in the form of imitations and fan fiction.

Compared to radio and television, it is less easy to see a mutually beneficial influence on the book of the rapid spread of online media, especially in the twenty-first century. The spread of personal computers in the home in the 1980s and 1990s did create a new market for printed guides and literature on computer use, including computer magazines – a 1984 survey recorded no fewer than forty-six titles issued by fifteen magazine publishers (see Chapter 21). The spread of the internet in the twenty-first century, however, and the ease with which information can be accessed and shared online, has altered the picture, although the potential for media to stimulate reading and the sales of books continues. In Chapter 15 Sarah Anne Hughes points to the success in 2010 of the BBC radio programme *A history of the world in a hundred objects*, which in addition to eliciting over 10 million downloads generated large sales of a subsequent book published by the Penguin Group. On a much larger scale, E. L. James's *Fifty shades of grey* trilogy – claimed in 2012 to have outsold even the Harry Potter books in the UK – began life as fan fiction and a self-published e-book before moving to print publication.[46] The complex interplay between print and digital media forms of this title is discussed in Chapter 4.

The internationalisation of the book

As David McKitterick writes in the preceding volume in this series, by the beginning of the twentieth century 'internationalism was the dominant defining characteristic of the book trade – at least in Britain, the United States, France, Germany and their respective global offshoots'.[47] In the opening section of Chapter 5 Finkelstein and McCleery point to the international trade organisations and agreements, the principle of international copyright, and the international communication structures, all of which made for the 'development of a stable international market' built around 'collaboration

46 Deller *et al.*, 'Introduction'.   47 McKitterick, 'Introduction', p. 20.

rather than competition'. Catherine Seville picks up on this context in Chapter 24, outlining the significant changes in copyright law made in response to growing pressure to harmonise internationally. At the start of the century that pressure mainly centred on relations with the United States, but Seville underlines the substantial influence later on of the European Union. Britain's shifting political and economic relations with continental Europe means that the internationalisation of the British book is characterised by European as well as transatlantic influences and exchanges.

In the early part of our period European influences on British publishing were most prominent in the areas of design and illustration. That the highly successful (and nationally celebratory) *Buildings of England* series should have been directed at Penguin by two German émigrés, Hans Schmoller and Nikolaus Pevsner, neatly encapsulates the importance of the far-reaching European outlook on the trade that developed in the middle of the twentieth century. The influence of Jan Tschichold at Penguin in the 1940s is noted above, but the first major development came in the 1930s when Stanley Unwin purchased the stock of the art book publisher Phaidon Press, which relocated to London in 1938. As Sarah Anne Hughes notes in Chapter 15, Phaidon's editors introduced into Britain the higher production standards found on the continent, 'bringing improvements in page design, typography, picture research and photographic reproduction'. European influences on photographic techniques were also imported into the magazine industry in this period (see Chapter 21). As Hughes goes on to show, after the war Thames & Hudson, founded in 1949 by two other refugees from Nazi Germany, Walter Neurath and Eva Feuchtwang, further advanced the international dimension of art book publishing via its links with American publishers and art museums.

The numerous other firms established after the war by European émigrés brought a transformational perspective to British publishing. Richard Abel identifies three qualities that the long list of new publishers brought to both the British and the American book trades in this period: a commitment to 'the highest standards of intellectual and ethical probity', an intimate and thorough acquaintance with the intellectual climates of the subject fields in which they published, and the entrepreneurial spirit necessary to 'launch new kinds of publishing ventures'.[48] One area where this entrepreneurial spirit was deeply felt was scholarly journals, especially in scientific, technical and medical (STM) publishing. In particular, the contribution of Robert Maxwell's Pergamon Press

48 Abel, 'Introduction', pp. 5–6.

developed new models for scholarly communication in an era of expansion in higher education in Britain (see Chapters 17 and 18).

So far as Britain's changing political and economic relations with the EU are concerned, in the late twentieth and early twenty-first centuries the imbalance of translation flows (in which substantially more rights were exported from the UK to the rest of the EU than imported) meant that business practices and lobbying, arguably, had a greater impact than inter-cultural exchange.[49] In the new digital age, the European Commission has worked on a raft of activities, including lobbying for a single digital market, interoperability (of devices and networks) across the EU, and the prevention of geoblocking (where consumers cannot buy a digital product from another member state).[50] How the withdrawal from such initiatives following the UK's 2016 referendum decision to leave the EU, as well as the right to work of the substantial numbers of EU citizens in the UK book-related trades, will unfold is, at the time of writing, unclear.

In a global context, the last third of the twentieth century was a period of dramatic restructuring in international publishing business. Chapter 5 traces the critical moments in the development of a global publishing industry 'dominated by a small number of transnational companies'. Finkelstein and McCleery emphasise how the emergence of transnational organisations brought a 'shift in the control and shaping of the Anglophone book market'. Where Britain had led the way in the nineteenth century, there was a noticeable shift from the mid-twentieth century onwards towards US and European rivals 'as significant players in the world market'. The sweeping away of 'family owned' publishing houses 'and small independent operations into a net of global corporate existence' meant that by the 1980s it was difficult 'to disentangle UK publishing from global publishing'.

A crucial factor in this shift was the loss of the British colonies as 'captive markets'. In the closing chapter of this volume, Caroline Davis provides a focussed discussion of the book in its imperial and post-imperial contexts, examining the cultural, educational and ideological dimensions – as well as the commercial factors – of the trade in books to the colonies and former colonies. Throughout the century, the importance of the colonial and Commonwealth markets provided the British book trade with a unique

---

49 Translation is regularly cited as around 3 per cent of production, although precise statistics are hard to establish. See Donahaye, *Three percent?*

50 Benedicte Page, 'EC white paper aims to level digital playing field', *Bookseller* 15 May 2015, www.thebookseller.com/news/ec-white-paper-aims-level-digital-playing-field.

international dimension. Davis shows how, at the beginning of the period, Britain had established a 'global distribution network' which stretched from Australia, New Zealand, India and South Africa to Canada. The export trade benefited from the 1842 and 1911 Copyright Acts which applied throughout the colonies, substantially expanding the market for home-produced books. India and especially Australia were major export markets for literature and school textbooks. The legal framework around copyright and the 'special commercial relationships' that were consolidated in the first half of the century allowed British publishers to continue to operate in, and profit from, colonial book markets in the period of 'rapid and widespread decolonisation' after 1945. Indian independence in 1947 pushed publishers to turn their attention to Africa, capitalising on the establishment by the Colonial Office of literature bureaux to stimulate the production of cheap books across the continent. The initiative allowed for British publishers to act as partners in the production of textual material in schoolbooks, a topic explored by Sarah Pedersen in Chapter 10.

Most importantly, for the continued importance of colonial and postcolonial markets, the formation of trade agreements – the British Commonwealth Market Agreement of 1946 and the Traditional Market Agreement (TMA) of 1947 – allowed British publishers to enjoy a form of monopoly in those territories which formed the Commonwealth. As Finkelstein and McCleery assert, the protected market afforded by the TMA 'was significant because of the dependence of the UK on its overseas markets', and publishers benefited hugely from protected sales until the abolition of the agreement following a successful challenge in 1976. The loss of such sales, in particular to Australia, changed the international outlook of British publishing. Nevertheless, both Davis and Pedersen demonstrate the continued importance of book exports to the Commonwealth into the twenty-first century. While the years 2009–14 saw a drop in export revenue for printed and digital books, with a pronounced decline in Africa, Davis quotes a statistic from 2013 which shows that, with 41 per cent of its book sales coming from exports, 'the UK is the largest exporter of books in the world'.

The internationalism of the British book is not solely a matter of exports, global markets and multinational ownership. Local writing from postcolonial countries was imported into Britain via successful ventures such as OUP's Three Crowns Series (1962–76) and Heinemann's African Writers Series (also founded in 1962) and Caribbean Writers Series (founded 1970).[51] Post-war

---

51 Low, *Publishing the postcolonial*; Davis, *Creating postcolonial literature*.

immigration from India and Pakistan and the British Caribbean, and the increased ethnic diversity of Britain, brought changes to the domestic market. In Chapter 27 Gail Chester traces the development of 'Black book publishing' from early periodicals of the first half of the century, through the publication of African and Caribbean writers by mainstream publishers in the wake of the first wave of immigration, to the establishment of newspapers and the first independent Black book publishers and specialist bookshops in the late 1960s. Independent publishers such as New Beacon Books and Bogle-L'Ouverture were deeply committed to Black radical politics, publishing the work of native Caribbean writers as well as influential investigations of the Black British experience, such as Bernard Coard's *How the West Indian child is made educationally sub-normal in the British school system* (1971). Chester goes on to note the increased demand for books about Black immigrants after the race riots of the early 1980s and the increasing focus by independent publishers on writers from minority ethnic and social groups. This topic is also explored in the conclusion to Michael Ledger-Lomas's chapter on religion, which shows how publishing by and for Muslims has grown in step with the rise of Muslim numbers in Britain. Beyond the primary focus of distribution of the Qur'an, Ledger-Lomas detects a rise in books for children and in self-help literature as Muslim publishers concentrate 'as much on helping British readers to live Islam as on defending or extending its frontiers'. As Chapter 4 indicates, however, in the twenty-first century issues remain about publishing's lack of diversity, and unequal access to publishing careers, authorship and representation.

The digital revolution

As noted above, the earliest effects of digital technologies were felt on the production side. The use of computers in the area of distribution and book-selling also came early but was slower to develop. In Chapter 6 Iain Stevenson points out that, although books were highly suitable for computer-controlled management in both wholesale and retail, particularly after the advent of the ISBN in 1966, 'the innate conservatism of the trade made the introduction of IT supported systems difficult and slow'. Teleordering – 'one of the first automated computerised stock control and supply systems in the retail trade' – was only introduced in 1979 'after many delays'.

One area of the trade where computerisation had an early effect was information and reference publishing. In Chapter 19 Susan Pickford shows how from the 1970s the impact of computers allowed for the creation of central databases which reduced publication schedules and enabled publishers to tailor their products to different markets. It is not surprising that in the 1990s many computer companies moved into reference publishing themselves. If, as has been argued, the Victorians 'knew they were living through a time of transformation in the provision of information',[52] then this is equally true of those living in the twenty-first century. Printed encyclopaedias have all but disappeared with the arrival of the internet, but Pickford shows how traditional reference publishers successfully responded to online content by refining and repositioning their products.

The first major impact of the digital revolution on the consumer was on purchasing patterns (see Chapter 7). The internet bookseller Amazon entered the UK market in 1998 and by the end of the next decade it and smaller online retailers had captured a substantial market share. With the spread of the internet to the overwhelming majority of the population, British readers moved from exclusively buying and borrowing books from physical outlets to a mixed economy of acquisition. The swift and continued expansion of Amazon as a business – to the point where books form only a small part of the company's operations – has energised movements to support and sustain independent bookshops, seen in the development of online guides and cooperative ventures such as Independent Bookshop Week, established in 2007, the Books Are My Bag campaign, and the online retailer Hive.co.uk, where a portion of each sale contributes to an independent bookshop.

Further into the new century, with the spread of electronic reading devices and the development of more optimised practices for reading on screen, texts were not only being acquired online, they were also being read electronically. In Chapter 3 Padmini Ray Murray outlines the technological features of e-readers and mobile reading apps in the context of the commercial growth of the e-book industry from the mid-2000s. As she and Claire Squires have argued elsewhere, the 'Device' upon which printed matter is accessed is a component of digital communication that sets it apart from print communication.[53] The spread of e-readers, along with the tablet and the mobile phone, has fuelled an appetite for 'new modes of reading instantly and conveniently'. Nevertheless, as outlined in Chapter 7, 'British readers at the end of the first decade of the twenty-first century still remained habitual buyers of material books.' Amidst all the revolutionary change in the production, distribution, selling and consumption of the 'book', the printed codex

---

52 Fyfe, 'The information revolution', p. 567.
53 Ray Murray and Squires, 'The digital communications circuit', p. 14.

has remained remarkably resilient. Industry figures suggest that, after reaching a peak in 2014 e-book sales have gone into decline,[54] prompting debates about the future of the format.[55] However, such statistics do not capture mass digital reading which has been enabled by online self-publishing platforms (see Chapter 4). Narratives about the resilience of print and the decline of e-reading should thus be treated with scepticism.

One area where the digital revolution has been keenly felt is academic and educational publishing.[56] In Chapter 18 Michael Mabe and Anthony Watkinson conclude by outlining the major developments in academic journal publishing since the mid-1990s, assessing the impact of new models of distribution and digital platforms for access on publishers, libraries and researchers. The continued growth of larger journal publishers in the new century has been accompanied by open access initiatives and directives which complicate and challenge the business models of traditional academic publishing. Mabe and Watkinson's discussion of this topic should be read alongside that of Samantha Rayner in Chapter 17. As both chapters make clear, debates over open access are ongoing, driven substantially by changes in government policy, and are far from clear at the time of writing.[57]

Debates over open access form part of the wider legislative context of digitisation explored in Chapter 24, especially the complicated question of copying. The widespread adoption of photocopiers in business and education from the 1970s onwards allowed texts to be copied more easily by users. In the new digital environment, with an 'increasingly ready access to texts', it has become even easier. Furthermore, as Seville emphasises, the ease with which digital copies can be distributed across national boundaries has challenged copyright law and made control on use more difficult. When Google began digitising books in libraries in 2002 and making copyright texts available on the internet it represented what Finkelstein and McCleery call 'a revolution in the delivery of content'. These developments have increased pressure for harmonisation of copyright law in the international sphere, and

---

54 '"Screen fatigue" sees UK ebook sales plunge 17% as readers return to print', *Guardian* 27 April 2017, www.theguardian.com/books/2017/apr/27/screen-fatigue-sees-uk-eboo k-sales-plunge-17-as-readers-return-to-print.

55 Simon Rowberry, 'Is the e-book a dead format?', *Bookseller* 24 July 2017, www .thebookseller.com/futurebook/ebook-dead-format-595431.

56 Thompson, *Books in the digital age*.

57 For a stimulating account of one side of this debate, see Eve, *Open access and the humanities*.

the European Union began developing policies for a 'Digital Single Market' in 2015, with a mid-term review reporting in 2017.[58]

The digital revolution has stimulated many scholars to rethink conceptual frameworks for understanding the book in the twenty-first century. One intervention into the debate, by Padmini Ray Murray and Claire Squires, redraws Robert Darnton's influential communications circuit of the book for the twenty-first century. The authors emphasise how the digital environment has disrupted the traditional relationships between author, agent, publisher, distributor, retailer and reader, facilitating in many instances a 'conflation of roles'.[59] Authors have forged business relationships directly with distributors and retailers; readers have become part of the marketing process and have developed closer links with authors via the spread of social media and online platforms for shared reading, such as Goodreads, and for self-publishing, such as Kindle Direct Publishing. In 'the battleground for control of the market-place', literary agents have become ever more powerful while publishers have responded by diversifying the kinds of services they provide, including services to other publishers.

A significant factor underpinning these and other changes in the book industry has been the spread of Print-on-Demand (POD), which allows single copies of a book to be printed from electronically stored documents. For publishers, print-on-demand has reduced costs and freed up cash flow, benefiting small business operations and facilitating niche market areas such as poetry (see Chapter 8). It has also allowed them to maintain and revive backlists. For authors it has increased opportunities to do without traditional publishers altogether by using platforms provided by retailers and distributors for the sale and delivery of both print and e-books.[60] For all the criticism levelled at the monopolistic growth of Amazon in the distribution and retail environment, it has supported the exponential growth of self-publishing in the second decade of the century. In 2016 it was reported that self-published titles constituted 22 per cent of the UK e-book market, a statistic which demonstrates that narratives about declining e-book sales might be false if non-traditionally published books are included.[61]

These developments should not lead us into predictions about the disap-pearance of the 'traditional' publisher or the printed book. Just as the spread

---

58 https://ec.europa.eu/commission/priorities/digital-single-market; https://ec.europa .eu/digital-single-market/en/policies/shaping-digital-single-market.

59 Ray Murray and Squires, 'The digital communications circuit', p. 4. 60 Ibid., p. 6.

61 Lisa Campbell, 'Self-published titles "22% of UK e-book market"', Bookseller 23 March 2016.

of home computers in the 1980s resulted in swathes of printed how-to guides, in the twenty-first century guidebooks on self-publishing and e-publishing abound, 'often, ironically, produced as books by conventional publishers'.[62] It has often been argued that the printed book retains many advantages over the digital product in terms of its portability, durability and archiving. As Angus Phillips comments, 'print solves the archiving problem of the modern age, when formats change with great rapidity, and the pages of websites alter or disappear overnight'.[63] It would be wrong to draw certain conclusions about the future, however. In a review of John B. Thompson's *Merchants of culture*, Jason Epstein observes: 'Technological change is discontinuous. The monks in their scriptoria did not invent the printing press, horse breeders did not invent the motorcar, and the music industry did not invent the iPad or launch iTunes.' For Epstein, book publishers, 'confined within their history and outflanked by unencumbered digital innovators', have missed yet another critical opportunity, 'seized once again by Amazon, this time to build their own universal digital catalog, serving e-book users directly and on their own terms while collecting the names, e-mail addresses, and preferences of their customers. This strategic error', he warns, 'will have large consequences.'[64] So while the digital revolution is still evolving – and the chapters in this volume demonstrate how it has emerged out of the continued importance of the technological, social, cultural and commercial power of print – it is simultaneously clear that a power shift is occurring in publishing's global markets, and in the control over those routes to market. Any conclusion offered here, then, on the future directions of the book will 'remain disturbingly imprecise', in McKenzie's words. But with such market knowledge in the grasp of technological giants, there is no room for complacency or certainty about the circulation, status and ongoing endurance of books, or the role of associated individuals, organisations and agencies.

62 Ray Murray and Squires, 'The digital communications circuit', p. 7.
63 Phillips, 'Does the book have a future?', p. 557.
64 Jason Epstein, 'Books: onward to the digital revolution', *New York Review of Books* 10 February 2011, www.nybooks.com/articles/2011/02/10/books-onward-digital-revo lution. Cited in Smith, *The publishing business*.

PART I

*

Materials, technologies and the printing industry

SARAH BROMAGE AND HELEN WILLIAMS

Until the middle of the twentieth century print production remained a labour intensive process. The traditional work practices that had existed since the mid-1800s remained largely unchanged and the workforce was strictly demarcated along work role and gender lines. Production processes and the material form of books continued to change throughout the twentieth century, which finally saw an end to the dominance of relief (letterpress) printing as the primary method for the production of text, with the shift to offset lithography in the second half of the century, followed by the rise of digital printing at the end of the century. Printing had long been a heavily unionised trade, but the period also saw the breakdown of union structures in the printing industry in common with other 'craft' trades such as engineering, steelmaking and coal mining. This chapter will explore the technical innovations and other changes in book production in the twentieth century, and consider the implications that these advances had for the workforce that produced the printed word.

Machinery and typesetting

The nineteenth century had been one of change and innovation in the printing trade.[1] At its beginning, wooden presses operated by hand, and familiar since the days of Gutenberg, were universal, and all type was set by hand and distributed by hand after use. Illustrations were produced from etched or engraved metal plates, or from wooden blocks; paper was produced by hand, limiting the maximum size of the sheet; printers made their own ink. In general the organisation and processes of the print shop would have been familiar to Gutenberg. By the beginning of the twentieth century, hand presses in book production, now made of iron, were used only for

---

1 McKitterick, 'Changes in the look of the book'.

proofing, and the application of water power and steam power and later electrical power to presses had increased the speed of output, as had the introduction of the rotary principle. It had become possible to print on the larger sheets of paper (or from the continuous reel of paper known as a web) because of the greater speed and the greater force that could be applied to the platen. This change (the production of a continuous web of paper which was then wound onto a reel) was the result of the mechanisation of papermaking, and reel-fed printers became especially common in the production of newspapers and magazines.

The era of hot metal

Despite the many attempts at mechanisation, the setting of type by hand remained the dominant process into the twentieth century, although printing firms had long known that it was impractical to continue setting type in this way. Compositors were highly skilled, but setting type by hand was time consuming and labour intensive. Inventors had made attempts throughout the nineteenth century to mechanise typesetting, but successful typesetting machinery first came into general use in the printing industry in the final quarter of the nineteenth century. The earliest of these was Ottmar Mergenthaler (1854–99), a German watchmaker who emigrated to the United States, who in 1872 began to work alongside an American engineer James Clephane (1842–1910) and by 1884 was successful in inventing the Linotype (line o' type) machine.

The Linotype machine was worked by a single operator who sat at a keyboard (similar to a typewriter). As a key was struck, a circulating brass matrix was brought into the line of type and automatically spaced. The face of the matrix contained the letter, number or punctuation mark which would form the impression. Whole lines of type were then cast in a single 'slug' of type metal. The matrices were returned to the magazines they had originally come from, to be reused. The use of hot metal casting, with type being cast specifically for the text being set, before being melted down for reuse, not only speeded up the pace of typesetting, which was particularly significant in newspaper production, but also did away, at a stroke, with the tedious and time-consuming business of distributing the type accurately for reuse after the text was printed.

Newspapers were the first 'consumer' printers to utilise this new technology and continued to be its predominant users. The first Linotype machine was installed in 1886 in the *New York Tribune*. Despite industry fears that there would be mass redundancies, the reality was that there was plenty of work for compositors as the mass consumer printing and publishing sector grew. Linotype composition was introduced into the British printing industry by the English Linotype Company in 1891.[2] Several typefaces were cut specially for the Linotype machine, the most popular ones being Granjon, Caledonia, Electra and Eric Gill's Pilgrim. Although used for book production elsewhere, in the UK a rival system was more common in book production.[3]

This alternative hot metal casting machine was the Monotype composing system (fig. 1.1), invented by Tolbert Lanston (1844–1913): the system's first US patents were granted in 1887, but the first commercially viable machines did not go into production for ten years. The first Limited Fount Monotype machines in Britain were installed at Wyman & Sons in London in autumn 1897.[4] The Monotype system comprised two separate units: the keyboard (which like the Linotype machine was similar to a typewriter) and the caster. The keyboard used compressed air to punch holes in a paper ribbon, according to the sequence of keys struck by the operator. The caster operated by blowing compressed air through the paper strip to select the letters and set lines out in a uniform width. Unlike Linotype, letters were cast individually, making it possible for the assistant supervising the caster to make corrections 'on the run', whereas Linotype corrections necessitated recasting the whole line of type. The use of the Monotype system enabled casting of some 6,000 characters an hour, more than double the capacity of a good hand compositor.

Child records that by 1914 'almost all news offices throughout the country were using Linotypes, and all the main book-houses were using Monotypes'.[5] Some printing purists disapproved of the quality of output from these machines, largely because of the uninspiring typefaces available. However, the various university presses and Francis Meynell's Nonesuch Press, part of the Private Press movement, enjoyed excellent results and economies of scale in the 1920s. For this reason, most paperback Penguins, which had large print-runs, were set on Monotype. Realising that it was important to offer a high-quality innovative service, the Monotype Corporation formally appointed Stanley Morison as typographic advisor early in 1923, although he had undertaken commissions from the company the previous year.[6] Morison set about recutting past 'classic' designs as well as commissioning new fonts from designers Bruce Rogers, Eric Gill and Frederic Goudy. Morison also had his

2 Glaister, *Encyclopaedia of the book*, p. 295.   3 Twyman, *Printing*, p. 63.
4 Slinn, Carter and Southall, *History of the Monotype Corporation*, especially pp. 17, 34.
5 Child, *Industrial relations*, p. 182.
6 Slinn *et al.*, *History of the Monotype Corporation*, p. 209.

Figure 1.1 Monotype keyboard. (Edward Clark Collection, Edinburgh Napier University)

most famous type cast here – Times New Roman, first used by *The Times* in 1932.[7] By the mid-twentieth century the Monotype composing machines were found in every book printing house in the world, and long-established British foundries were losing their markets. Miller & Richard of Edinburgh closed in 1952, and eventually, in the early years of the twenty-first century, Stephenson Blake of Sheffield closed its doors. The Monotype machines went

7 For a summary of the type repertoire associated with Monotype, see Carter, 'Typeface design'.

out of production in 1987, although spare parts and matrices were supplied for another five years.[8]

Developments in printing machines

As well as changes in the pre-press stages through which the text and other content of a book would pass, the machines on which books were actually printed changed unrecognisably during the course of the twentieth century. In the nineteenth century the invention of the rotary printing press in 1847 by Richard Mark Hoe had transformed the production of the printed word. The rotary press machine was fed by a web of paper and the printing surface consisted of curved stereotypes (printing plates cast in metal or plastic from a mould taken of metal type) mounted on cylinders. The paper then passed under a knife which cut the paper web into sheets. One example of the widespread use of the rotary press was Thomas Nelson & Sons in Edinburgh. Following a fire at their works in 1880 the firm established a separate printing and binding works in 1907 which was using six Bauer rotary presses capable of turning out 200,000 books per year,[9] producing cheap editions to reach a mass market.

However, by the beginning of the twentieth century the Miehle was the predominant printing machine, having largely replaced the Wharfedale. The Wharfedale was a 'stop cylinder design' consisting of a travelling flat bed holding the forme of type which passed under the inkers before passing under the cylinder to produce the impression. The Miehle (invented by Robert Miehle in Chicago in 1884) was more effective, as the impression cylinder never stopped. It continued to revolve at a constant pace as the machine contained a gear which was powerful enough to control the forward motion of the bed. The Miehle had great impressional strength, accurate register and durability and took the lead in machine printing. It was largely hand-fed at this time but later versions were automatically fed. The cylinder press makes two revolutions to each impression, rising slightly to allow the bed to pass under it on the second movement. In the large printing centres there was a desire to produce 'fine cut and registered colour work', giving rise to a need for a heavy-duty press which was easy to control at the point of reversal for the second impression. The 1921 Miehle Vertical had a speed of about 3,600 impressions per hour, later improved to 5,000 per hour. Between 1952 and 1968 this machine was manufactured in Goss Works in Preston.

8 Slinn *et al.*, *History of the Monotype Corporation*, p. 174.
9 SAPPHIRE Archive, Edinburgh Napier University. 1999/244. Bicentenary Thomas Nelson, p. 10.

Developments over the twentieth century included printing on both sides of the sheet and in more than one colour.[10]

Lithography

Hot metal typesetting remained as the standard process for book typesetting for more than half a century until the 1960s when letterpress was superseded by the method known as offset lithography (or offset printing). Offset litho was first patented in 1853 by John Strather of England. The principle was not practically applied until the 1870s, when rubber offset rollers were used on flat-bed presses for printing on metals. The photo transfer process enabled a photographic image on sensitized paper to be inked from the stone that was fixed to a bed which moved to and fro beneath a cylinder and transferred to the printing surface. Six years later the first lithographic halftone screen was used in Britain. Offset methods for printing on paper were developed in the United States shortly after 1900 and the first British offset lithographic printing machine was built by George Mann in 1906. The offset lithographic presses were cylinder machines for printing from the lithographic stone or plate and consisted of three continually revolving cylinders. The first, carrying the printing plates, has a damping and inking mechanism which makes contact with the rubber blanket moulded on the middle cylinder; the blanket offsets the design to paper, carried by the third cylinder.

Initially this development was employed in magazine publishing, though by the Second World War it became more commonplace in book production, leading to a reduction in the use of relief printing. Increasingly books were produced using offset litho, and for those texts with long print-runs and many new impression this became the only real option, as the rubber printing surface was much more durable than relief surfaces. Still more durable options became available with the introduction of polymer printing plates.[11] Lithographic printing on the rotary offset press started to print text from a flat plate produced photographically ('phototypesetting'), which enabled the presses to produce high-quality, finely detailed impressions at high speed, reproducing any material, text or image that could be photographed in the plate-making process. Offset litho presses were lighter and cheaper to run, and became more widespread from the 1950s. By the late 1970s and early 1980s they had become, and still remain, the dominant method of production with low origination costs, although digital presses had entered the market. Web offset litho, developed from the 1950s, is an

10 Moran, *Printing presses*, p. 159. 11 Luna, 'Books and bits', p. 383.

alternative production process. The press is fed by a reel (or web) of paper, and after printing the paper is cut into sections and folded for binding.[12]

Photocomposition

Photocomposition, which became widespread in the second half of the twentieth century, was well adapted to use with the offset printing process. Technological development meant that photocomposition had started to replace hot metal technology by the 1960s. The concept of utilising the art of photography and photographing letters to produce words was mooted as early as 1898. W. Friese-Green devised plans for a machine in which individual white letters on black background were released by hitting a keyboard and were subsequently photographed. This and other potential photocomposition machines were devised in the early 1900s, though it was not until the mid-1920s that potentially workable machines were conceived. These included Edmund Uher's 1927 glass cylinder model, the American 1929 Luminotype machine which claimed to be able to set 7,000 words an hour, and W. C. Huebner's 1939 glass disc machine, which was followed by R. Higgonnet's disc machine with electronic memory (1944). The first machine to go into commercial production was the Dutch Hadego machine (1948), which was designed primarily for display work,[13] and the Rotophoto launched concurrently with the installation of the first Intertype photosetter in 1950, which heralded the widespread use of photosetting.[14]

By the 1960s there were various different forms of photocomposition which were slowly being adopted into printing firms in the UK including Photon, Linofilm, Monophoto and Fotosetter. These all worked on the same basic principle of setting type by photographing characters on film from which printing plates were made. The characters were then developed as photographic positives on film or light-sensitive paper from a negative master containing all the characters; the film, carrying the completed text, would then be used for making a plate for printing.

Systems like Monophoto and Fotosetter used existing technology and adapted it to meet this new concept. The Monophoto was launched by the Monotype Corporation in 1954. This machine was a photocomposing machine and was the counterpart of the Monotype composition caster. Instead of casting columns of individual pieces of type from molten metal, it produced exposed photographic film or paper ready for development.

---

12 Steinberg and Trevitt, *Five hundred years of printing*, p. 221.
13 Clair, *A chronology of printing*, p. 186.   14 Larken, *Compositor's work in printing*, p. 172.

The character images were still carried on a matrix. However, instead of molten metal the characters were exposed to a photo sensitive film or plate to produce a photographic proof. The work to be produced was then made up on an illuminated glass screen, and either offset or etched plates could be produced from the resulting image. This gave the printer increased flexibility in terms of typefaces and spacing, which was limited in Monotype machines. However, in the first incarnations it was difficult to correct type. The whole line containing a single incorrect letter had to be re-keyed and re-exposed, and the new section of film taped to the original. This soon moved on and by the later 1960s the machines could be driven by keyboards producing correctable punched-paper type, which effectively streamlined the process.[15]

In the 1960s developments in hardware and software, and reductions in the costs and size of the machines, meant that the application of computers to the typesetting process became commercially viable for the printing trade. Developments in computer-aided typesetting were closely linked to improvements in the process of photocomposition (which produced a printing surface from a photographic image of the imposed page). The Fotosetter was introduced in the United States in 1945 and was a development of the hot metal line composing machine the Intertype. It retained the circulating matrix and the mechanism for matrix assembly and distribution, but in place of the metal pot there was an optical system for the projection of characters on film. Intertype installed the first Fotosetter machine in the UK in 1956 in the Printing Department of the Corporation of Glasgow, and one of the earliest phototypeset books produced in the UK, an edition of Eric Linklater's *Private Angelo*, was set on an Intertype Forrester machine and printed by McCorquodale & Co. of Wolverton in 1957.[16] These early systems relied on punched tape created at a keyboard: the tape was processed before being used to produce a relief printing surface with familiar hot metal technology. By 1968 the Compugraphic was able to perform line-end word division.[17]

Linofilm and Photon methods instead chose to adopt new technology rather than adapting to existing systems. The Linofilm was first exhibited at the 1958 DRUPA international printing exhibition in Dusseldorf. It consisted of a keyboard and a photographic unit. The keyboard produced a perforated tape and proof; the tape was used to control the photographic unit.

15 Slinn *et al.*, *History of the Monotype Corporation*, pp. 117–18.
16 Wallis, *A concise chronology*, pp. 28, 29.
17 Steinberg and Trevitt, *Five hundred years of printing*, p. 221; Bann, *The all new print production handbook*, pp. 12–14.

The benefit of the Linofilm system was that the two units were completely separate, which meant that the photographic unit could often manage the work of several keyboards. The Photon system alternatively was comprised of three units: a setting console, a relay rack which controlled the spacing and tabular settings, and a photographic unit. All three units were controlled by one operator who could make corrections during the process.

In parallel with these developments, changes in print production technology (printing surfaces and the offset litho process) and increasing use of micro- or personal computers meant that by the mid-1980s much of the initial preparation of text and illustration for reproduction no longer took place within the printing house at all. Thus, for the printing industry the introduction of phototypesetting was not necessarily good news, as although it eliminated storage of large formes of type and essentially produced film that was storable and reusable, it also involved large-scale expenditure in an industry that had not long invested in hot metal technology.[18] The technology developed quickly and many firms which had invested in the first phase of phototypesetting found it quickly superseded.

The use of photocomposition also meant retraining for a workforce which in some cases had only just adapted to the use of hot metal. Photocomposition required the compositor to undertake his make-up with pieces of film rather than type, and to work on a light table rather than an imposition surface (fig. 1.2). Although the basic job remained the same, the skills used to achieve this had changed markedly and required a new generation of composing skills. Further technological developments meant that the second generation of photosetters were able to vary the leading from line to line and make the first moves towards the computer-assisted page make-up.

Illustration, ink and binding

Illustrations in books had until the middle of the twentieth century been printed by a separate process from the text, and were often grouped together as a set of plates for binding. Developments in the typesetting process, however, facilitated the integration of text and images, although it was late in the twentieth century before this became common, with the widespread use of offset lithographic presses. In traditional page make-up the integration of images into a printing forme was a laborious process which involved making up the page using type and plates held in place by furniture (wooden

18 Wallis, 'Seven wonders'. Later developments are discussed below.

Figure 1.2 Positioning type. (Edward Clark Collection, Edinburgh Napier University)

or metal pieces used as spacing material). Lithographic images came to be employed, requiring the use of a particular limestone. The fundamental principles established in 1796 by Alois Senefelder, the inventor of lithography, remained unchanged in the twentieth century, although other substrates gradually came into use. By writing or drawing with a greasy ink on a specially prepared slab of limestone, the grease is absorbed by the stone and the image thus formed has an affinity for printing ink, while the remaining parts of the stone repel the ink as long as the surface is kept moist with water.

After the invention of photography in the mid-nineteenth century, the use of photographic techniques for reproduction allowed more visual images to be produced and led to dramatic technological innovations taking place. By the 1870s it became possible to use photography to produce line drawings and other black and white images. However, it was not possible to reproduce shades of grey. This was remedied by the use of a halftone screen, which broke down the tonal image of the photograph into a series of small dots. The dots varied depending on the amount of light passing through a mesh of lines engraved on glass. The negative was exposed onto the plate through the screen, resulting in a halftone block broken into raised dots of greater or smaller size in correlation to the light and dark areas of the photograph. When printed, the dots reproduce the light and dark area of the picture. This led to a change in the type of book produced as commercial printers could use art paper to produce books with many illustrations, usually inserted as a section in the centre of the book.

This method was also later used to reproduce colour photographs, initially using relief printing surfaces, stereotypes and electrotypes. Electrotypes moved to plastic materials for the printing plates in the 1930s, an innovation which gave book designers greater freedom to develop page layouts and made the production of books significantly cheaper. Colour printing, however – although made cheaper by these improved pre-press processes – remained relatively expensive, as printing in colour continued, and still continues, to require additional inks and more complex printing machines. However, with these innovations, publishers could utilise new technologies to produce vibrant and innovative books at affordable prices.[19]

Ink had traditionally been made of a combination of linseed oil and lamp-black. The changes in the technology of printing demanded different inks. Coloured inks had been employed mainly for the hand colouring of illustrations, but with the introduction of aniline dyes in the nineteenth century following advances in the chemical industry, especially in Germany, a wider range of tints became available. As print-runs increased, colouring images by hand was no longer viable, and experiments were made with engraved and lithographed images. Photography of the original image, using filters to separate out the colours, produced improved results, but the necessity to print each colour separately to produce the final image meant that colour printing continued to be an expensive process. It was only with the changes to offset litho as the dominant printing process in the latter part of the twentieth century that coloured illustrations, integrated in the text (not as a separate run of plates), became commonplace anywhere other than in children's books, although the addition of colour to the printing processes still added significantly to costs.

The form and process of binding also changed. At the beginning of the nineteenth century binding was almost entirely a hand process, and had changed less by the beginning of the twentieth century than most of the other aspects of book production. However, mechanisation of the process generated changes in the finished product, notably the rise from the 1930s

---

19 Feather, *A history of British publishing*, p. 211.

onwards, co-existent with the rise of paperbacks, of so called 'perfect bind-ings', where instead of the sheets being folded, collated and sewn, the pages are guillotined and glued into their covers.

The printing industry

In the early twentieth century, printing and publishing were still often undertaken within a single company. Print houses often combined the process of commissioning, printing, publishing and selling under one roof.[20] However, the separation of book production from the publishing process had begun early in the nineteenth century, and by the end of the twentieth century few book publishers other than the Oxford and Cambridge university presses still retained a printing operation. Well-known names survived as publishers, having sold or closed their printing operations. Some specialist book printing firms, such as Clays of Bungay in Suffolk, or R. & R. Clark in Edinburgh, had rarely if ever published under their own imprint, but focussed on book production for those publishing houses which had no production facilities of their own.

Printing processes involved a variety of work roles. Traditionally these had been strictly segregated, and print unions had come to control how many employees could work in a firm, how many apprentices could be taken on, rates of pay, and working conditions. In the pre-production stage, firms employed compositors and readers. In the machine room there were the pressmen (sometimes called machinemen) and their assistants and post production was the bindery, which was the only area of book production where women predominated. In addition there were semiskilled and unskilled workers, under the direction of the time-served journeymen, especially in the press-room, and in other aspects of the business such as stereotype foundries and warehouses. Each trade had its own individual work conditions, hours of work and rates of pay. In the twentieth century, entrants went through the Printers' Exam and their apprenticeships lasted seven years for males (later six) and four years for females, after which they became journeymen. Women's entry to traditional craft areas such as type-setting was strongly resisted by the men until the final third of the century.[21]

---

20 Finkelstein, 'The globalization of the book', p. 329.
21 For two accounts of this, see Reynolds, *Britannica's typesetters*, and Cockburn, *Brothers*.

The impact of war

Both the First and Second World Wars had a dramatic impact on the printing and publishing industries in terms of both manpower and the availability of raw materials. Not only were the metals required for typecasting and printing plates rationed by demand elsewhere, paper was also in short supply, because by this time much of it, or the raw materials used to manufacture it, was imported. During the First World War, in 1916 a government Royal Commission on Paper limited imports of paper and papermaking materials to two-thirds of those of 1914, and appointed a commission to oversee the licensing of imports and ensure that supplies of paper were allocated fairly throughout the trade.[22] In the Second World War, supplies were controlled by the 'paper controller', who decided what could be produced and where it would be allocated. These controls came into force on 12 February 1940 and paper producers were prohibited from supplying 'more than 60 per cent of the weight of paper consumed by any single user in the same three-month period (March–June) the previous year'.[23] By this period many papermills relied substantially on imported esparto grass from North Africa and Spain as the raw materials for pulp. In 1939 Britain imported 272,000 tons of esparto grass. By 1942 imports had 'fallen to zero'.[24] With no available imports, many mills struggled to find sources of cellulose and took to using potato haulms, tomato plants, rope or straw as their raw materials, which had its own impact on the quality of material produced. Holman records that by June 1943, 'twenty-eight mills in England and Wales were using straw, as were eleven in Scotland, while the Ministry of Supply was consuming 300,000 tons of straw a year in the manufacture of paper'. Paper control remained in place until 1956: this had a long-term impact on the industry and heralded the slow decline of papermills in the UK throughout the rest of the century.

In addition to problems with the source of paper there were issues with the availability of type and the metals used to produce printing plates. A large proportion of standing type which would have been used in reprints was increasingly donated by firms over the course of the war and melted down and used for weapons and other essential war work.[25] Zinc and metal, used for plate-making, were also essential to the war effort, meaning that illustrated books with screened halftone photographs were more difficult to

---

22 Howe, *The British Federation of Master Printers*, pp. 51–2; Gennard, *Mechanical to digital*, p. 75.
23 Holman, *Print for victory*, p. 14.   24 *Ibid.*, p. 63.   25 *Ibid.*, p. 80–1.

produce, and publishers began increasingly to use line blocks for illustration as these used less metal.[26]

Conscription during both wars led to manpower issues and contributed to 'dilution' of labour, or the employment of individuals without traditional craft training in craft roles.[27] During the Second World War 'nearly half of the Typographical Association's thirty-two thousand members were moved to munitions work or called up'.[28] Overall, there was a reduction of available labour and decline in output. However, dilution meant that in many large printing firms women undertook the 'traditional male role' of composing and printing during wartime, before transferring back to their traditional roles, for example in the binderies, during peacetime.[29] Printing firms also participated in the war effort. The Glasgow firm of Blackie gave over a third of the floor space in their Bishopbriggs works to armaments production and staff from their bindery transferred to the munitions labour force, and in Surrey the Monotype factory was producing machine gun components and Hurricane aircraft.[30]

There were problems with the supply of new machinery which had an impact on papermaking and printing machine manufacturers. For example, in 1934 the German printing machine manufacturer Heidelberg introduced a fully automatic high-speed cylinder press to the market and 60 per cent of the company's revenues from their base in the UK came from foreign sales. Trade with the USA and Germany was not possible in wartime conditions and the company accepted orders for precision lathes and hydraulic devices to supplement its income during this period. Other firms such as the Edinburgh papermaking machine manufacturer Bertrams suffered during wartime conditions as the resources of the company were directed largely to armament work. Only essential maintenance of papermaking machinery could be undertaken, and company records show that several papermaking machines sent overseas during wartime did not complete their perilous journey. One example is the replacement wet end of a papermaking machine sent to India to further the war effort, which went down when the ship was sunk so another had to be sent.[31]

---

26 Gennard, *Mechanical to digital*, pp. 138–40, sets out the various controls on raw materials, 1939–45.
27 On the First World War see Child, *Industrial relations*, pp. 220–2.
28 Holman, *Print for victory*, p. 82.   29 Child, *Industrial relations*, p. 287.
30 Blackie, *A. C. Blackie & Son*, pp. 60–1; Slinn et al., *History of the Monotype Corporation*, pp. 89–90, 100.
31 *Within a mile of Edinburgh town*, p. 18.

The availability of new machinery, however, did not pose a significant problem to the printing and publishing industry during wartime and beyond since most printing machinery was heavy-duty, durable and reparable. Large firms would often employ engineers and technicians to mend machines that could operate for decades rather than years with periodic in-house repairs. In the immediate post-war period, printing houses were slow to adapt to new techniques and many firms were uneasy about the implications that the fast pace of technology had in terms of investment, and also the impact that it had on the workforce.

The impact of new technologies

Until the mid-1970s, hot metal was still used in the majority of printing houses and the compositors/Linotype or Monotype operators still made up a significant proportion of the workforce. However, developments in technology, particularly the rise of offset litho and the disappearance of many of the specialist printing houses that printed books such as Thomas Nelson in Edinburgh (1967), led slowly to the specialist role of the compositor being completely eradicated. The introduction of computers to pre-press processes meant that the means by which the author produced the typescript and the typesetter set the type became one and the same process. Specialist typesetting staff were no longer needed and it became an economic necessity to dispense with this sector of the workforce.

The consequences of this technological shift had a wider significance because of the influence that the unions and the 'chapels' held within the printing industry in Britain.[32] Most printing firms operated a 'closed shop' policy, which meant that to work in the company you had to be a union member. Unions controlled entry to the trade by limiting the intake of apprentices and there was a strong sense of belonging through membership of the local 'chapel', usually synonymous with the workplace branch of a print union. The chapel was presided over by the 'Father of the Chapel', or 'Mother of the Chapel' in the bindery section, who would represent employees in disagreements with management, and undertook a social welfare function for union members. The Society of Master Printers (later the British Printing Industries Federation) and the Society of Master Printers in Scotland (later the Scottish Print Employers Federation) together represented the employers in the UK printing industry. The print unions fought for their members' rights, particularly with respect to working hours and holidays

32 Child, *Industrial relations*.

with pay and other benefits. In 1919 'a comprehensive set of National Agreements' was effected by all the major unions 'covering the basic terms of employment' and throughout the inter-war period printers' earnings remained 'very favourable in comparison with those of all Industries'.[33] The strength of the unions and their bargaining power with employers meant that by 1946 the Printers and Kindred Trades Federation had negotiated two weeks' holiday with pay, making print workers the first in the UK to achieve this.[34] Though this strength gave employees good working conditions, pay and holidays, it did not assist the print employers when they had to make significant changes to the workforce in direct response to changes in print technology.

In the nineteenth century, the majority of the letterpress trade societies, some of which had their origins in the latter part of the eighteenth century, had coalesced into the Typographical Association (covering England, apart from London, Wales and the whole of Ireland), the London Society of Compositors and the Scottish Typographical Association. The bookbinding and papermaking trades had likewise amalgamated into national unions. Workers in newer processes had been represented by sectional unions such as the National Society of Stereotypers and Electrotypers, the Society of Lithographic Artists and Designers (SLADE) and the Amalgamated Society of Lithographic Printers. By the turn of the twentieth century, unskilled workers were also organised into unions, having previously been excluded by criteria which included a seven-year apprenticeship. The unions representing the compositors in the letterpress trade in general succeeded in retaining control over the operation of 'hot metal machines' (Monotype and Linotype) and the rates of pay applying to them; they also succeeded in excluding women and 'unskilled' men from them more or less until the end of the 'hot metal' era. Proportionally more women were employed in binding and some areas of the papermaking trades than in other areas of printing and the kindred trades.

Issues such as wages, holiday entitlement, sickness and other benefits, and the ratio of apprentices to fully qualified staff were part of the National Agreement, arranged between the print unions' national negotiating committee and the representatives of the employers, the British Federation of Master Printers, later the British Printing Industries Federation. In Scotland separate negotiations were undertaken between the unions and the

---

33 *Ibid.*, pp. 226–9, 283.
34 Ibid., pp. 299–303. See also Howe, *The British Federation of Master Printers*, pp. 197–205.

organisation representing the Scottish employers. The interests of workers represented by the various competing unions led to 'demarcation' disputes, for example over who should work a particular machine. The situation was ultimately resolved by the amalgamation of the various unions, as technological advances showed the weakness of this state of affairs. The process of amalgamation took place throughout the twentieth century, and by the end of the century unions in the printing industry were much reduced in influence, and print workers were represented by a section of UNITE! The Union.[35]

The existence of durable machines which had cost firms a small fortune to purchase, and were operated by skilled printers who had undertaken long apprenticeships and were protected by their unions, was not an easy obstacle for the industry to surmount. Until the 1970s, in many printing firms books were still produced on letterpress rotary machines, with type composed using the Monotype system. The advent of offset lithography as a viable technology for reproducing text, and text in combination with images, rather than images alone, changed that. However, many firms had invested large quantities of money in technology that still worked and employed onsite engineers for maintenance, and were reluctant to change work practices brought by innovations such as photocomposition and offset printing which, by the last decade of the twentieth century, had become the dominant processes for book production.

Developments after 1970

Although the method of producing a book had completely changed by the 1970s, there was to be yet another revolution in book production. The third generation of phototypesetters and the introduction by the Linotype Corporation of the Linotron 202 in 1978 offered digital typefaces stored as outline vectors, that is dispensing with photographic images and moving towards a digital storage of images which heralded the end of photographic composition and the introduction of digital technology. With increasing use of computer technology bringing desktop publishing software, digital printing began to overtake offset litho at the beginning of the twenty-first century as the quality of the end product improved.

---

35 Gennard, *A history of the National Graphic Association*; Gennard with Bain, *A history of the Society of Graphical and Allied Trades*; Gennard with Hayward, *A history of the Graphical Paper and Media Union*.

The global economic crisis of the 1970s impacted significantly on the printing industry. Printing costs rose dramatically throughout the decade. In 1975 Collins reported experiencing increased costs of 60 per cent in paper and binding materials.[36] The heavily unionised workforce extracted high wage increases, putting added pressure on printing firms. By 1981 'compositors had become – after coalface workers – the second highest paid manual workers in the country'.[37] Between 1975 and 1981 the printing industry as a whole shrank: more than 1,200 companies disappeared, and the number employed in the industry was reduced by 66,000.[38] Book and periodical printers were the largest sector within the industry, and some of the remaining firms cut costs by moving out of town centres into the periphery, such as Collins which moved from central Glasgow to Livingston, outside Edinburgh. To cope with the change in the market and the cost of production, many publishers moved away from photocomposition to 'strike on' typesetting machines such as the IBM Selectic and electronic composers. These were not as high in print quality and their spacing was erratic in the initial stages. However, what they lost in quality they made up for in cost of production.

The main impediment to high-quantity production remained in the typesetting stage with the compositor, and the time needed to make up a page. By the mid-1980s many of these issues were resolved. Photo/imagesetters were now not simply concerned with laying out columns of type but were involved in the placing of images and text on the whole page, which was a radical departure and development. However, this development was soon to be replaced by the widespread adoption of computers. The use of personal computers allowed authors the freedom to type and edit text themselves and then save it to an external disc to be transferred to another machine for the next stage in the production process. It could then be reproduced multiple times, for example on a laser printer. These machines deposit toner as instructed by the computer which is then sealed by a heat process. The introduction of the Apple Mac and the IBM PC in the 1980s as 'computer compositors' had radical implications for all sectors of the printing industry. While previously a page with illustrations would be laid out by designers for a typesetter to implement by assembling text and images on the page, systems such as PageMaker could achieve this in one process.[39] The skill

---

36 Sutherland, *Fiction and the fiction industry*, p. 26.   37 Greenfield, *Scribblers*, p. 134.
38 [Printing Industries Sector Working Party], *The future of the printing industries*, p. 4.
39 Bann, *The all new print production handbook*, p. 14.

and craft of typesetting became increasingly blurred with the tools used by the author to create the book, and pre-press processes were conducted away from the printing plant.

Towards the millennium, the improvements in the quality of digital printing meant that it became an increasingly viable option for book printing, especially for reprints and the short-run and print-on-demand markets, which became more economical as the need for expensive printing plates was eliminated. OCR (optical character recognition) technologies made the production of reprints of obscure and out-of-print items cheaper and quicker, though the quality remains questionable. By the end of the twentieth century, pre-press processes for book production had become almost entirely digital, with only 'fine-press' books still produced by more traditional methods, using Monotype castings and letterpress printing surfaces. At the same time, it had become more economic to print United Kingdom publications elsewhere in the world, transferring camera-ready copy electronically and transporting back the finished (or part-finished) items, rather than producing them from scratch in the UK.

Conclusion

The twentieth century saw a range of technological changes which altered fundamentally the way books were produced. The century saw the disappearance of many firms that had been in existence for generations and the breakdown of the large skilled workforce which produced the printed word. Many who worked in the industry may agree with the line from J. M. Barrie's novel *Sentimental Tommy*: 'The printing press is either the greatest blessing or the greatest curse of modern times, one sometimes forgets which it is.'[40] Although the story of the material book in British publishing was one of development, technological advance and change, this did not always chime with the aims of the printing workforce, which often resisted both technological advance and alterations to work practices. For many firms the pace of change and the sheer proliferation of new technology made it very difficult to keep pace financially. The shift from hot metal to photocomposition and then to computerisation in the second half of the twentieth century completely bypassed the once crucial role of the compositor in the printing process. The introduction of the internet, e-books and online editions, which has

---

40 Barrie, *Sentimental Tommy*, p. 55.

characterised the last decade of the twentieth and continues to grow in the early part of this century, perhaps poses an even bigger challenge to book publishers and the nature of the material book than the technological advances of the previous century. These developments are discussed in Chapter 2.

2

Format and design

In reviewing the period covered by this volume, it should be borne in mind that although the means of composing words and printing them on paper have changed enormously, the internal appearance of the majority of books has altered less than one might expect. A sequence of upright rectangles of type paired on spreads, preceded and sometimes followed by prelims and endmatter in a traditional order, remains the norm. The most significant typographical changes have been a great increase in the typefaces available for use, and a greater freedom in mixing them within texts for literary or explanatory purposes, and many more title-pages ranged left rather than centred.

The greatest change between the covers has been in the treatment of illustrations. When most books were printed by letterpress, illustrations that were included in the text were printed by relief processes: traditionally by wood engravings, but by 1914 mostly by photo-etched line blocks. The reproduction of photographs by halftone blocks produced a poor result on text papers, and so they were usually printed on coated paper, either tipped in with the text or in a separate section bound in. This led to a separation of text and illustration which made reference time-consuming. If an argument in the text required constant verification in the illustration section, turning pages backwards and forwards became laborious. Even when halftone illustrations were printed by gravure, as they were in early Pelican illustrated books for example, and in art books from Phaidon and Thames & Hudson after the Second World War, this still meant the separation of text and image, although there were a few cases of books in which the text also was printed by gravure. The introduction of offset lithography in the last third of the century as the predominant print medium made possible the integration of text and illustrations, printed on less shiny paper. The design implications of this will be described below.

The external changes to the book's appearance have, however, been even more significant. Cased bindings are no longer sewn, except in a few examples. The first edition of the book you are reading, although it has head and tail bands and the appearance of gathered signatures, is adhesively bound: the Cambridge Histories made the change from sewing around the middle of the 1990s, and most trade hardbacks had already done so. The binding material is no longer predominantly cloth: imitation cloth is nearly universal. Elaborate jackets, their design given a great deal of attention and expertise, have become almost universal, and have replaced the ornately decorated bindings of the nineteenth century. But by far the greatest change has been the rise of the paperback. In 1914 many cheap editions were available, in cased editions with printed cloth or paper covering, but it was not until the launch of Penguins in 1935 that the modern paperback made its appearance in this country.

The changing look of the book

One of the most observable changes during our period is the expansion of the number of typefaces available for book work. Although the Monotype and Linotype machines were well established in 1914, the repertoire of faces was small. The printing trade relied on, and indeed demanded, recuttings of popular nineteenth-century foundry types, which perpetuated the broad division into Old Styles, much modified versions of the type family that went back via Caslon and Dutch types to Garamond and Aldus, and Modern faces, distantly derived from the types of Baskerville and Bodoni, with vertical stress and greater contrast between thick and thin strokes. The first two faces cut by Monotype at the beginning of the twentieth century were Modern, Series 1, and Old Style, Series 2, both modelled on types issued by existing foundries.[1]

But the type repertoire was beginning to change rapidly. Monotype had introduced Imprint, a heavier version of Caslon, in 1912, and Plantin the following year. The design of the latter was a marked advance on traditional procedures, in that the Monotype Drawing Office undertook historical research into sixteenth-century models in the Plantin-Moretus Museum in Antwerp, and then radically redrew the type, making it bolder and so suitable for printing on smoother papers without appearing weak.

---

1 Burke, 'The early years', p. 5.

During the First World War, Monotype made a more faithful version of Caslon, but it was not until the 1920s and 1930s that a great leap forward was made with recuttings from a wider range of historical models such as Bodoni, Garamond, Baskerville, Poliphilus, Fournier, Bembo, Bell, Ehrhardt, Times New Roman, Centaur, Walbaum and Bulmer, as well as the cutting of new designs by Eric Gill (Perpetua and Joanna, as well as the popular Gill Sans, used on all the early Penguin covers) and by the Dutch designer Jan van Krimpen (Lutetia and Romulus and, after the Second World War, Spectrum). A very late addition to the core repertoire was Sabon, designed in 1966 for both the Monotype and Linotype systems by Jan Tschichold, whose work at Penguin Books in the late 1940s is described below. Linotype had introduced their own Garamond version, called Granjon, in 1924, overseen by their typographical advisor George W. Jones, followed by Juliana, by the Dutch designer S. L. Hartz, in 1952, and a Gill face, Pilgrim, in 1953.

Nevertheless, buying sets of matrices for new designs in a full range of sizes was an expensive commitment, and the great majority of printers typically held only a handful of faces. Most common were Baskerville, Imprint, Modern Series 7, Plantin and Times New Roman. It was only printing houses with a serious interest in design, such as the Curwen Press and the Cambridge and Oxford university presses, which held a wider range. Even so, the May 1938 Curwen Newsletter stated, 'A Monotype machine was first installed at The Curwen Press in 1906; ten years later, our records show we possessed Monotype Caslon, Gloucester, Imprint and Old Style, supplemented by some half dozen type faces for hand setting.' In 1941 the Press still had only nine Monotype composition faces, the ones listed above as most common, with the exception of Modern and with the addition of Bembo, Caslon, Garamond, Lutetia and Walbaum. Eleven years later, the only additions to the repertoire were Ehrhardt and Perpetua.

Curwen had an untypically large number of display faces for hand setting, some from English and continental European foundries, and some cast on the Monotype Super Caster, a display-size casting machine introduced in 1928 which, augmented by a matrix hire scheme, enabled printing firms to have what was in effect an in-house type foundry. A large number of now familiar faces were soon cut for the Super Caster, such as many elaborations of the Gill Sans family, Berthold Wolpe's Albertus, seen on numerous jackets for Faber, and a wide range of faces aimed chiefly at the advertising and jobbing markets.

With the introduction of photocomposition in the late 1950s, the position was similar to the early days of hot metal setting, with familiar faces being adapted to the new system, and facing many technical obstacles to producing an acceptable result. Although Stanley Morison (1889–1967), Monotype's typographical advisor who had been responsible for much of the Corporation's type programme before the war, wrote favourably of the possibilities of the new technique, it was left to his successor John Dreyfus (1918–2002), who took over in 1955, to commission new faces for the Monophoto. The first was Apollo (1962) by Adrian Frutiger, a young Swiss/French designer who had also produced the very successful Univers sans-serif family, jointly issued in both metal and film form by Monotype and the Paris foundry Deberny & Peignot, which had an interest in the advanced electronic typesetter the Lumitype. A decade later Dreyfus commissioned another roman, Photina, from the French designer José Mendoza.

In the years that followed, Monotype yielded its position as the source of the most prestigious new typefaces. Until the 1960s, the technical superiority of Monotype casting machines, combined with an enterprising, extensive and imaginatively promoted type programme, made Monotype the favoured system for book work. While the primary means of composition was hot metal setting, printers were tied to the designs supplied by their typesetting machinery manufacturers, but as photocomposition machines and then digital typesetters became smaller and cheaper, the need for the same fonts to be available on different devices became more easily satisfied. At the same time, other type companies, notably Linotype, began more energetically to initiate type design programmes. The spread of faces also became more international as fonts and typesetting machinery became increasingly inter-changeable. Matthew Carter's Galliard (1978), for example, was designed for Linotype, but then licensed to the International Typeface Corporation of New York, which marketed fonts adaptable for a variety of typesetters. After the introduction of digital typefaces generated by personal computers, the proliferation of designs was made easier still, so that designers were presented with an unprecedented choice of fonts from across the globe. One of the most ubiquitous designs in current use, Minion (1990), was designed by Robert Slimbach for the Adobe company in California. The typeface used in previous volumes in the *Cambridge history of the book* series, Renard (1996), was designed by a Dutch designer, Fred Smeijers, for the Enschedé Font Foundry.

Increasingly sophisticated software meant that designers could not only become their own typesetters but make up pages on screen, controlling every detail of a book's design, including the integration of illustrations. A publisher like the Folio Society, which had worked in a traditional way with its printers since the Second World War and produced books with a traditional appearance, made the move from hot metal to photocomposition at the end of the 1970s, and in 1993 installed terminals in its office to handle typesetting and paging up, a change mirrored throughout the publishing industry.

Before the First World War, decisions about design were normally made by printers, but during the interwar years publishers, prompted by a growing awareness of the limitations of most printers in that field, gradually assumed this responsibility. In a lecture of 1936, Richard de la Mare of Faber said that this change 'should not be interpreted as a criticism of the printer, as one incapable of his own business; although, to judge by results, there must be many printing houses yet, where the design of the book is left to the compositor, who, except by happy accident, is clearly unsuited for the job'.[2] Jan Tschichold, writing shortly after his period at Penguin in the late 1940s, was even blunter:

> The shortcomings of English compositors – whose apprenticeship lasts a full seven years – are in sharp contrast with the opportunities offered by the splendid range of type-faces which have been available on English composing machines for more than twenty years. Fine type-faces, bad composition and appalling hand composition are the characteristics of the average printing house of today. The difference between the best English printing (e.g. Oliver Simon at the Curwen Press) and the average is very great – far greater than in Switzerland or the USA.[3]

In *Modern book design* (1958), Ruari McLean surveyed the 1920s and 1930s. He gave credit to those printers who did take typographical standards seriously. He described the work of Bernard Newdigate at the Shakespeare Head Press and Oliver Simon at the Curwen Press, and praised the Kynoch Press in Birmingham, Lund Humphries in Bradford, two long-established firms in Edinburgh, R. & R. Clark and T. & A. Constable, the Westminster and Chiswick presses in London and the two university presses at Oxford and Cambridge under a succession of capable university printers and their typographical advisors.

But he then addressed the rise of the publisher's designer. He began with Stanley Morison, who apart from his role as a scholar and an advisor to Monotype and Cambridge University Press, also worked for the publisher Victor Gollancz between 1928 and 1938, where he devised an austerely uniform standard for books, with text pages set in a limited number of sizes of Baskerville, and an equally severe binding style in Gill Sans. These were balanced by instantly recognisable jackets, printed on yellow paper in black

2 De la Mare, *A publisher on book production*, p. 11.   3 McLean, *Jan Tschichold*, p. 145.

and magenta in a wide variety of frequently jarring display types. These jackets also showed Gollancz's copywriting skills and became well known. McLean went on to discuss a number of other publishers' designers, who at that period were often senior directors of their respective firms, which gave them the necessary authority to push for improvements. He singled out Charles Prentice at Chatto & Windus, G. Wren Howard at Jonathan Cape and Richard de la Mare at Faber, who raised the standards of design and production of general trade publishing. They were followed by Desmond Flower at Cassell and Ian Parsons at Chatto, after Prentice's retirement in 1934.[4]

The work of these designers was sober and classical, aiming at an economy of means prompted by both budgetary and aesthetic considerations, though more gentle than Morison's severe rationality at Gollancz. It was a comfortable style which echoed the preferences of a generally conservative readership. There was a feeling that the revival of typography led by William Morris at the end of the previous century had raised awareness of the subject, but had also led to over-decoration. Describing the 1914 number of the *Studio* devoted to the book arts, Bernard Newdigate wrote:

> the influence of Morris, who had died in 1896, was predominant, and sumptuous decorated pages from the Kelmscott Chaucer, *The Tale of Beowulf*, and the *Note on his Aims in Founding the Kelmscott Press*, are the most noticeable of facsimiles in the book. In book-illustration the influence of Walter Crane may be noted; also that of Aubrey Beardsley and *The Yellow Book*.[5]

An example of the influence of the Kelmscott style on trade books was Everyman's Library, with heavily decorated title spreads and endpapers. But in the 1928 number of the *Studio*, the editor wrote of 'the return to typography in its clearest and simplest form . . . part of the general return to fundamental principles which is typical of the age'. By 1938, he was quoting de la Mare on 'the well-produced book that has character, and, hardly less important, the "house style"'.

The house style among the publishers described by McLean was fairly uniform. Text pages were generally set in the small range of Monotype faces outlined above and obeyed the rules of words-per-line and proportion described in the section on typographical instruction below. Title-pages were centred. The chief difference between the productions of different

4 McLean, *Modern book design*, pp. 42–93.   5 Newdigate, *The art of the book*, p. 3.

publishers, at least to the eye of the general public, lay in the jackets – described by the *Studio*'s editor in 1928 as 'a novel feature', although pictorial jackets were beginning to become commonplace.

McLean finished his chapter with a mention of 'the climax of the whole printing revival', the launch in 1935 of Penguin Books. The first production manager at Penguin, Edward Young, was responsible for the original three-band cover, and oversaw the design of all the books until he went into the Navy at the outbreak of the Second World War. During the war the company had to rely on its printers to do most of the typography that was needed, but after the armistice Penguin's founder Allen Lane felt that design standards needed refining, and he consulted with colleagues on who might best do the job. Oliver Simon at the Curwen Press suggested Tschichold.

Jan Tschichold (1902–74) was born in Leipzig, and his only book produced in Britain at that time had been the 1938 number of the printing trade journal the *Penrose Annual*, done on a brief visit to work at Lund Humphries, who printed it. Hitherto he had been known chiefly as a radical modernist, responsible for a series of New Typography manifestos and handbooks culminating in *Die neue typographie* of 1928. But after his flight to Switzerland in 1933 (he was not Jewish, but was considered a cultural Bolshevik) his modernism, though still observable in his *Penrose Annual*, had softened considerably, and he soon re-converted back to a refined classicism, shown in a series of books for the Swiss publisher Birkhäuser. It was this style he applied at Penguin.

His first act, even before his arrival in March 1947, was to look at a wide range of printed matter from the firm, books, pamphlets and ephemera, and to pencil comments on everything. He next drafted the Penguin Composition Rules, which are still referred to as setting a basic trade standard. He then single-handedly overhauled the design of the insides and the covers of not only the three-band Penguins, but Pelicans, Penguin Poets, the Penguin Shakespeare and other series. The King Penguins had been started before his arrival in imitation of the German Insel-Bücherei; they were small-format cased books with illustrations on subjects ranging from natural history to architecture. In Tschichold's hands the typography was transformed from the banal to the exemplary (fig. 2.1). His design for Alfred Fairbank's *A book of scripts* (1949) was described by the *Times Literary Supplement* as able to 'surpass the Insel-Verlag at its best'.[6]

6 Harley, 'The King Penguin series', pp. 143–50.

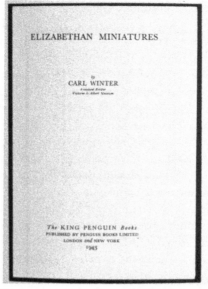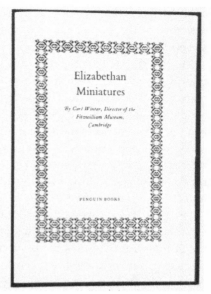

Figure 2.1 Two versions of a King Penguin title-page, 1943 (*left*) and as redesigned by Jan Tschichold in 1949 (*right*).

Tschichold left Penguin in December 1949. In twenty-nine months he had overseen the design of over 500 titles and left a lasting mark on British design. He wrote that, when he arrived, the books 'were then nearly all set in Times New Roman, a type outstandingly suitable for newspapers but much less so for books. Of the books I personally supervised, only about twenty per cent are still set in Times New Roman; the rest are set in Baskerville, Bembo, Garamond and Caslon.' Of his successor he wrote in *Typographische mitteilungen* (1950), 'my work is being well taken care of by H. P. Schmoller, a first-class book designer, and its fundamental lines can now hardly be altered'.[7]

Hans Schmoller (1916–85) was born in Berlin into a cultured Jewish family, and moved to Britain in 1937 to train at the Monotype Technical School. After spending the Second World War at a missionary printing works in Africa he returned to Britain and worked for two years at the Curwen Press with Oliver Simon, before joining Penguin. 'Books, covers, display cards, advertisements, company signs and stationery – all came under his watchful eye. He embraced Tschichold's dogmatic rules, and

7 McLean, *Jan Tschichold*, pp. 146–7.

added many more of his own. He allowed no lapses in his constant search for perfection.'[8]

Apart from hundreds of carefully designed individual titles, Schmoller was responsible for two notable series in the Penguin list. Both were under the editorial control of another German émigré, Nikolaus Pevsner, who had already been enlisted as editor of the King Penguins. The Buildings of England, which started to appear in 1951, were county-by-county paperback volumes in the basic format, with a standard brown livery. Maps and other diagrams in the text were printed from line blocks, the photographs in a separate section printed by gravure. The typographic style was carefully planned for maximum clarity, and shows Schmoller's characteristic sophistication. The other series was the Pelican History of Art, described more fully below.

While Schmoller's preference was for simple, mostly typographical covers (although Lane himself was undecided on the subject),[9] he was aware of the need for change. Penguin began to bow to commercial pressures and the competition from newer paperback imprints such as Pan. A telling contrast of Pan and Penguin covers was reproduced in *Fifty Penguin years* (1985). Both were film tie-ins. The Penguin edition of John Braine's *Room at the top* (1959) had the vertical orange band version of the standard cover with a monochrome cut out photograph of Laurence Harvey. The Pan edition of Alan Sillitoe's *Saturday night and Sunday morning* from the following year was in full colour, with a lurid painting of Albert Finney in front of a newspaper quote that said that the book (and by implication the cover) 'makes *Room at the top* look like a vicarage tea-party'.[10]

Penguin's attempt to outdo its rivals took various forms. In 1957 Schmoller invited Abram Games, best known for his posters and for the Festival of Britain device, to make proposals. Games's covers introduced full-colour illustrations which ranged from his own semi-abstract designs to drawings by Edward Ardizzone, together with standardised type panels, but despite their merits the covers were not a success: the public did not recognise them as Penguins.[11] In 1962 a more enduring overhaul was overseen by Romek Marber, strongly influenced by modern Swiss typography, with a regular ranged-left grid for the wording but considerable freedom for the graphic panels. The genre colour coding was maintained, and the style included the Pelican series.

Under Germano Facetti, appointed Penguin's new art director in 1961, covers became more colourful while an identifiable house typographical

---

8 Cinamon, *Hans Schmoller*, p.10.   9 Lewis, *Penguin special*, p. 280.
10 Lloyd Jones and Aynsley, *Fifty Penguin years*, plates 43–4.
11 Baines, *Penguin by design*, p. 87.

Figure 2.2 Arnold Bennett, *These twain* (Methuen, 1916). An early example of a full-colour jacket. (Photograph by Nicholas Redman.) Bennett was highly critical of the jacket rough: in a letter to his agent J. B. Pinker, he wrote protesting at its 'horrible ugliness' and misrepresentation of the look of his characters. (In the printed jacket, his objections had been addressed.)

style was maintained. But with the arrival of Alan Aldridge in 1965 pictorial covers were introduced which could be identified as Penguins only by the bird device in a small oval somewhere on the front. Under later design directors David Pelham, John Hamilton and Jim Stoddart the cover designs continued to be divided into one-off designs for the most commercial titles and standard styles for series such as modern classics.

The designs for the Penguin Shakespeare series can be seen as reflecting many of these changes. The first, introduced in 1937, was a version of Young's basic three-band covers with the addition of a portrait wood engraving by Robert Gibbings. After the war Jan Tschichold introduced an elegant design with a Renaissance-style border, a new engraving by Reynolds Stone, and the individual play titles in red. This lasted for two decades until the late 1960s, when Facetti commissioned David Gentleman to produce designs based on colour wood engravings; a version of the Marber grid was used for the typematter. In 1980, Paul Hogarth was asked by Pelham to supply full-colour drawings, combined with a series style with Shakepeare's name in calligraphic blackletter, followed by a much simplified series with woodcuts by Louisa Hare. At the very end of the century there was a film tie-in with a cinema-poster style cover for *Titus Andronicus*.[12]

The paperback cover, attached to the book as it is, when viewed in the context of general product design, is a rare example of display packaging, designed to encourage purchase, lasting for the lifetime of the product. By contrast, study of the early history of book jackets in the nineteenth century is made difficult by the lack of surviving examples. They were seen as protective packaging which could be thrown away once books were on the shelf. Even in the twentieth century, when their design was given greater attention, and in spite of growing awareness of their bibliographical importance as described by Anthony Rota and by G. Thomas Tanselle,[13] they were still often removed, even in many institutional libraries (fig. 2.2). Richard de la Mare of Faber did not like them:

> The wretched thing started as a piece of plain paper, wrapped round the book to protect it during its sojourn in the bookseller's shop; but it has now become this important, elaborate, not to say costly and embarrassing affair, that we know to-day, and of which we sometimes deplore the very existence. How much better had this mint of money, that is emptied on these ephemeral wrappers – little works of art though many of them may be – be spent on improving the quality of the materials that are used in the making of the book itself![14]

12 Yates, *William Shakespeare in Penguin Books*.
13 Rota, *Apart from the text*; Tanselle, *Book-jackets*.
14 De la Mare, *A publisher on book production*, p. 41.

He was writing in 1936, and yet a few years later his firm employed Berthold Wolpe (1905–89) to design jackets that became famous.

The jackets designed by Stanley Morison for Gollancz have already been mentioned. Many of them were printed at the Fanfare Press, where Wolpe was working after his arrival in England in the mid-1930s, and himself carried on the typographical style. He also designed the house typeface Tempest, and in 1938 Monotype commissioned his Albertus. After his move to Faber, where he stayed until his retirement in 1975, he used Albertus extensively on jackets, as well as his own hand lettering.

Among other designers who concentrated on hand-lettered jackets, often combined with stylised illustration, were Hans Tisdall, another German émigré, who produced many jackets, notably for *The Leopard* (1960) for Harvill and the novels of Hemingway for Cape; and Michael Harvey, working for a wide range of publishers, most notably the Bodley Head under its design director John Ryder. Many artists also designed book jackets: just a small sampling includes Edward Bawden, Vanessa Bell, Barnett Freedman, Edward McKnight Kauffer, Eric Ravilious and Rex Whistler. Some series of books were quickly identified with a particular designer, such as Brian Cook at Batsford, and Richard Chopping for the James Bond books at Cape. Thrillers seem especially to lend themselves to design branding: the covers by Raymond Hawkey for Len Deighton's books, with photographed still lives of the spy's armoury and travel documents, are a case in point. Indeed, photography in documentary forms, as for example the jacket for Colin MacInnes's *Absolute beginners* in 1957, and as elements in more creative designs, such as P. D. James's *Shroud for a nightingale* in 1971, has become the major pictorial source for jackets, although designers such as Andrzej Klimowski and Jeff Fisher continued to produce work with highly individual graphic styles.

As jackets and paperback covers became more brightly coloured, often with foil blocking and embossing, some publishers reacted by adopting a quieter, more early-Penguin-like style. In 1981 Faber asked the design agency Pentagram to restyle and to a degree standardise their titles, and other smaller independent publishers have followed their lead, usually for series such as Canongate's Pocket Canons.[15]

The development of the illustrated book

The separation of text and halftone illustrations in books printed by letter-press has already been referred to, together with the new possibilities for

15 Powers, *Front cover*.

integration offered by the general use of offset lithography in the last third of the century. An example of this transition can be seen in the Pelican History of Art series. When these first appeared in 1953, designed by Hans Schmoller, they were large quarto cased volumes with text and line illustrations printed by letterpress on wove paper, and photographic halftones also printed by letterpress in separate sections of coated paper. Although undeniably hand-some, they were perceived as out of date and too expensive almost from the outset,[16] and in the late 1960s the series began to appear as smaller-format paperbacks designed by Schmoller's successor, the American-born Gerald Cinamon, with the text and illustrations fully integrated. This involved a quite different approach to the layout of the page.

European modernism was slow to make an impression on British book design. Bernard Newdigate in the 1938 *Studio* reproduced one of the Shell Guides, edited by John Betjeman, where the plastic ring binding allowed different papers to be used for text, maps and illustrations, but the layout remained unaffected by Jan Tshichold's celebrated diagram in *Die neue Typographie* which banned typesetting on different measures to wrap around illustrations. Although some magazines in the 1930s dealing with art and architecture, such as *Axis* (1935–7), echoed the language of modernism, they would have been condemned by Tschichold as *Malerei mit Buchstaben*, or painting with type, for not obeying his rigorously logical laws of layout. *Circle*, published by Faber in 1937, was a collection of work by leading British and continental European constructivists, and included an article by Tschichold in his modernist vein. It was printed throughout on coated paper, yet the photographs still appeared in separate sections, and although Gill Sans was used as a display face, the title-page was centred.

In the *Penrose Annual* in 1949, Herbert Read wrote of British design: 'one might say that by 1930 bookcraft had caught up with the architecture of Mies van der Rohe, Gropius, Le Corbusier, etc. By 1945 it had gone back to the Parthenon.' He pointed to the work of Max Bill in Switzerland and Paul Rand in the USA as examples of models that should be followed.[17] While Read was overstating his case, his article was accompanied by an illustration in which Tschichold redesigned the *Penrose* volume title-page as a clear demonstration of his return to the classical fold – an apostasy for which he had been violently criticised by Max Bill in 1946. And with few exceptions book design took little notice of the logic of modernism until compelled to do so by the need to integrate text and illustrations in a way that would work editorially and also

16 Lewis, *Penguin special*, p. 256.   17 Read, 'The crisis in bookcraft', p. 13.

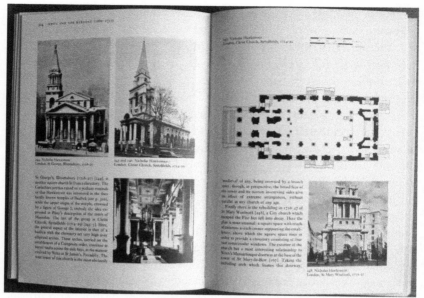

Figure 2.3 A spread from John Summerson's *Architecture in Britain: 1530–1830*, in the Pelican History of Art series as redesigned by Gerald Cinamon (1970). Cinamon manipulates the two-column text, with the large number of archive illustrations, of which the margins do not permit much cropping, so that the references are illustrated in the spread, and the result looks harmonious. John Summerson, *Architecture in Britain: 1530–1830* (Penguin, 1970), pp. 304–5. (By permission of Gerald Cinamon)

satisfy the eye. In the same year as Read's article, a writer in the first number of *Typographica* dealt with the subject in purely aesthetic terms, as a problem of reflecting the inner rhythms of a photograph in the accompanying typography in a spacious modernist layout.[18] He did not address the more mundane requirements of integration. The previous year, a Christmas book produced by Cambridge University Press was a book of photographs of the architectural wood carvings of Grinling Gibbons. Although it was printed by letterpress on coated paper throughout, the university printer Brooke Crutchley wrote later about the problems of integrating illustrations and text within a traditional typographic layout: 'The book ... served to answer the challenge of a reviewer in a Sunday newspaper who lamented that an age which could fire bullets between the blades of a rotating propeller had not discovered how to arrange illustrations on the same page as the text

18 Hale, 'The integration of photo and type', pp. 13–18.

to which they referred.'[19] The Press achieved this by instructing the photographer to leave plenty of background that could be cropped as necessary, and occasionally asking the author to tailor her copy. It was left to designers of the next generation in Britain to use the opportunities offered by the increasing use of offset lithography for the combining of text and image, and to employ more efficient modernist layouts.

In the redesigned Pelican History of Art volumes, combining the positioning of illustrations close to the point in the text that refers to them within a harmonious page layout in which the illustrations are neither crowded nor too assertive, and align with each other, took considerable skill. Gerald Cinamon achieved this by the manipulation of a two-column page, while not wasting space (fig. 2.3). As books with integrated illustrations became more widespread, the influence of magazine design, with a strong emphasis on the unity of a series of spreads, and the increased use of colour, became more noticeable. In 1971 *The world atlas of wine* was published by Mitchell Beasley, and was an early and successful example of a book in which large amounts of information were conveyed through illustration. Dorling Kindersley was another publisher specialising in such books, producing a wide range of educational works and guidebooks. By the end of the century the Pevsner architectural guides were published by Yale University Press in full colour.

Typographical instruction

While in the nineteenth century manuals of typography had been produced for printers, the twentieth century saw the growth of books written for the designers who now began to issue detailed instructions to printers, as well as for the interested reader.

The first one that has remained well known was Stanley Morison's *First principles of typography*, first printed in the final number of Morison's journal the *Fleuron* in 1931, and published in book form five years later. As its title says, it was a brief outline of the underlying disciplines of design, but it was also a manifesto for simplicity and tradition as against '"bright" typography', favouring 'an obedience to convention which is almost absolute – and with reason'. Morison acknowledged that this convention was broadly followed: 'In practical printing today, these details of imposition are on the whole adequately cared for; so that it is possible to report that the mass of books presents a tolerable appearance.'[20]

19 Crutchley, *A printer's Christmas books*, p. 10.
20 Morison, *First principles of typography*, p. 8.

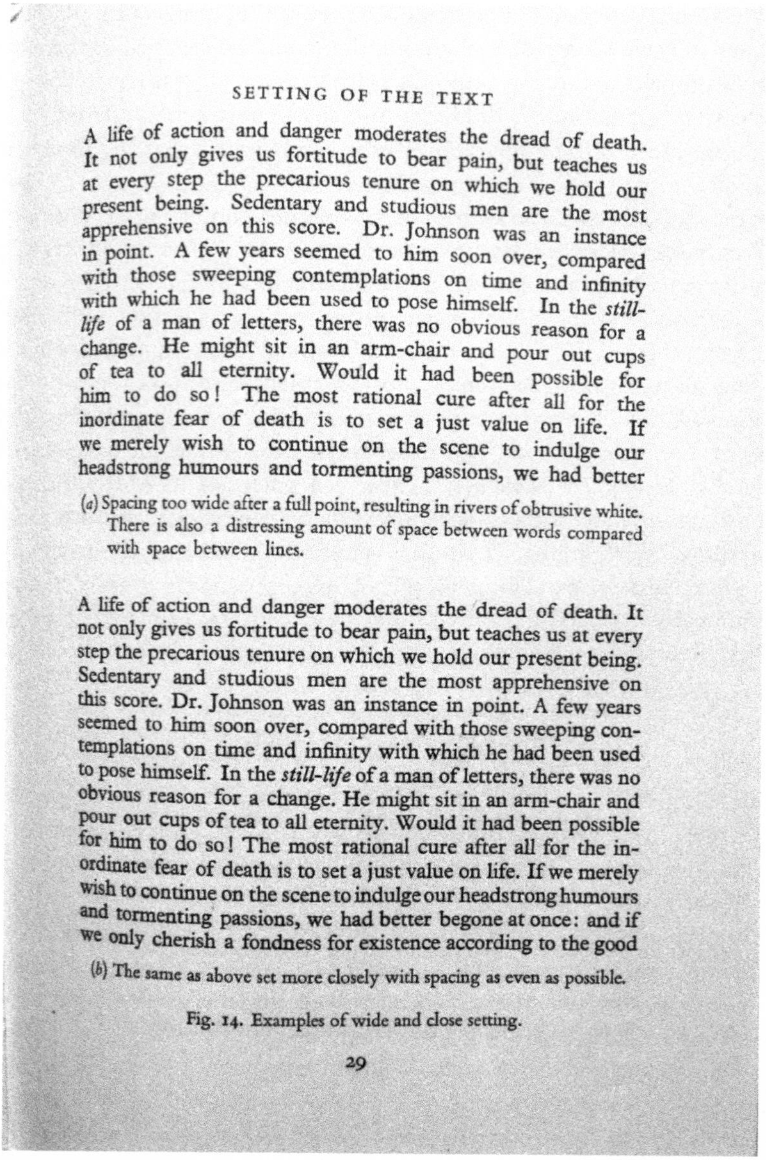

SETTING OF THE TEXT

A life of action and danger moderates the dread of death. It not only gives us fortitude to bear pain, but teaches us at every step the precarious tenure on which we hold our present being. Sedentary and studious men are the most apprehensive on this score. Dr. Johnson was an instance in point. A few years seemed to him soon over, compared with those sweeping contemplations on time and infinity with which he had been used to pose himself. In the *still-life* of a man of letters, there was no obvious reason for a change. He might sit in an arm-chair and pour out cups of tea to all eternity. Would it had been possible for him to do so! The most rational cure after all for the inordinate fear of death is to set a just value on life. If we merely wish to continue on the scene to indulge our headstrong humours and tormenting passions, we had better

(*a*) Spacing too wide after a full point, resulting in rivers of obtrusive white. There is also a distressing amount of space between words compared with space between lines.

A life of action and danger moderates the dread of death. It not only gives us fortitude to bear pain, but teaches us at every step the precarious tenure on which we hold our present being. Sedentary and studious men are the most apprehensive on this score. Dr. Johnson was an instance in point. A few years seemed to him soon over, compared with those sweeping contemplations on time and infinity with which he had been used to pose himself. In the *still-life* of a man of letters, there was no obvious reason for a change. He might sit in an arm-chair and pour out cups of tea to all eternity. Would it had been possible for him to do so! The most rational cure after all for the inordinate fear of death is to set a just value on life. If we merely wish to continue on the scene to indulge our headstrong humours and tormenting passions, we had better begone at once: and if we only cherish a fondness for existence according to the good

(*b*) The same as above set more closely with spacing as even as possible.

Fig. 14. Examples of wide and close setting.

29

Figure 2.4 Page from *Introduction to typography* with examples of wide and close setting. Oliver Simon, *Introduction to typography* (Faber & Faber, 1945), p. 29.

Nevertheless, *First principles* was short on specific recommendations. Morison favoured line lengths of ten to twelve words, a rule generally accepted, although broken in the 1936 edition of his text, which is a small-format book with an average of seven words per line. He went into some detail on leading, and made some recommendations for title-pages. He suggested making the overall page height less than the text page, to avoid a yawning gap in the middle, but stipulated that the title should not be in a size more than twice that of the body face.

Morison did not specifically indicate that word spacing within the line should be tight, saying only 'It is often argued that loose spacing is not admirable in itself', and later, 'it is obvious that the space between words composed in a condensed letter may be less than that between words in a round, wide form of letter'. He was more concerned with the relationship of word spacing to leading than the inherent virtue of close spacing. Nor did he condemn extra space between sentences outright.

In the same year, 1936, *A publisher on book production* appeared from Richard de la Mare of Faber, a lecture in the Dent Memorial series. It is a brief survey of the subject that deals with a wider range of practical issues than Morison's and, like Morison, de la Mare aired a few prejudices. He objected, as no other writer does, to the 'senseless' custom of repeating the book's title as a running head throughout the text. Morison's book was guilty as charged, and so are a vast number before and since. De la Mare's view of jackets has been referred to. And his printed text had extra space between sentences.

Jan Tschichold, on the other hand, specifically demanded the same space throughout the line, even after full stops, as well as close spacing. In a set of instructions written in 1937 for Swiss printers, he proposed 'three-to-em' spaces as the norm, which is actually quite wide. By the time he came to draft the Penguin Composition Rules in 1947, the norm was a mid-space, or the width of a lower-case i.[21] Later still, in 1956, back in Switzerland, he was still fighting against extra space between sentences, making the practical and obvious point that more space demanded extra work from keyboard operators.

Tschichold's Rules formalised best practice for the wide range of printers who worked for Penguin. They attempted to instil the need for close spacing at the keyboarding stage, since adjustment of Monotype setting by hand was costly. There was a celebrated case with the Nonesuch Press *Don Quixote*, printed at Cambridge University Press in 1930, when the publisher Francis Meynell criticised the galley proofs for wide word spacing. Walter Lewis, the

---

21 McLean, *Jan Tschichold*, pp. 94–5.

university printer, agreed with him, and the book, over 1,000 pages in two volumes, was respaced by hand. But in general the better firms in Britain were already setting to Tschicholdian standards, although even with word-break programs in computer-aided typesetting, tight spacing still needs an alert compositor with a trained eye, and loose spacing is common in much book printing to this day.

All the instructional texts described so far were short – de la Mare's was the longest at forty-six small pages, and Tschichold's the shortest at four pages – but in 1945 Oliver Simon produced *Introduction to typography*, a book-length manual. Simon's was the first thorough discussion of the subject for the British market, from sub-editorial details through to jackets, and was lavishly illustrated with examples, many in colour. Comparative settings in different typefaces and different leadings were shown, and there was even a comparison of wide and close setting (fig. 2.4). The liveliness of the illustrations and the clear style meant that the book had an appeal to an audience beyond professional designers, and it was reissued as a Faber paperback.

Although other books appeared as competitors, none rivalled Simon's until in 1956 Hugh Williamson's *Methods of book design: the practice of an industrial craft* was published by Oxford University Press. At 430 pages, this was an exhaustive account of design for letterpress production. Not only were Monotype and Linotype systems described in detail with diagrams, but there were extensive specimen settings of the available founts. It was intended as the last word for the fully qualified designer. Williamson even discussed the subject of legibility. The writers before him had dealt with the subject in a pragmatic way. Cyril Burt's 'A psychological study of typography' did not appear until 1955, and Williamson wrote, 'The chief obstacles to successful research have been the lack of science among typographers and the ignorance of typography among scientists. Legibility appears to be too subtle a quality for measurement and analysis.'[22] Although he then attempted a formulation of some general principles, his view, shared by designers in general, was that common sense prevailed over calculations and dogma.

However, soon after *Methods of book design* was published, much of the technical information associated with hot metal setting began to be redundant. The first Monophoto machine was introduced the following year, and although for a time many books, even when printed by offset lithography, were still set in hot metal and proofed for photographic reproduction, new techniques of pasting up camera-ready copy had to be learned. In a brief

22 Williamson, *Methods of book design*, p. 67.

section in his short *Typography: basic principles* (1963), John Lewis, who taught the subject at the Royal College of Art, compared pasted up reproduction proofs with photosetting, and pointed out the increased choice offered by the latter to the designer: 'he can set in 14½ point with ¼ point leading if he so wishes'.[23]

Throughout the rapid changes in typesetting and paging technology which followed, designers had to find their way with relatively brief handbooks such as Ruari McLean's *Thames and Hudson manual of typography* (1980). At the same time the growing sector of non-professional designers producing print-quality documents for business and social uses was addressed by John Miles's *Design for desktop publishing* (1987). And the increasingly internationalised world of design led to the leading manual of the next generation coming from Canada: Robert Bringhurst's *The elements of typographic style* (1992).

The twentieth century also saw a surge of periodicals devoted to the book arts and aimed at professionals and interested amateurs. In 1913, the short-lived journal *The Imprint* appeared, which dealt with a wide range of subjects from papers and inks, to staff training and costing, as well as typographical design and illustration. A new typeface, Imprint, was cut for it by Monotype, but not kept as a proprietary face. 'Our policy is sincerely to improve the craft of which we are so proud', the editors wrote in the first number. These editors included Gerard Meynell, manager of the Westminster Press, where it was printed, J. H. Mason, who had been a compositor at the Doves Press, and the calligrapher Edward Johnston.

There was already another trade publication, the *Penrose Annual*. It began life in 1895 as *Penrose's Annual* serving the process engraving industry, but gradually widened its scope. Under the editorship of, successively from 1934, R. B. Fishenden, Alan Delafons and Herbert Spencer it published articles by most of the names mentioned so far in this section. The other trade journal that achieved a reputation in the larger design world was the *Monotype Recorder*, under the editorship of Stanley Morison and later Beatrice Warde.

A decade after *The Imprint* came another venture. *The Fleuron* was edited first by Oliver Simon, and printed at the Curwen Press; then the editorship was taken over by Morison, and the printing moved to Cambridge University Press. Each number was a bound volume and most had a de luxe edition; seven numbers appeared at irregular intervals between 1923 and 1931. The subjects covered were type history and present-day typographers and

---

23 Lewis, *Typography*, p. 68.

graphic artists in Britain, the USA and continental Europe – of a traditional sort: no work by the designers of De Stijl or the Bauhaus or by Tschichold was shown. New types from Monotype and type foundries were reviewed, often with lavish tipped-in samples. Every number had an article by Morison, though two were co-authored, and the last had his influential essay 'First principles of typography', already described.

Four years after the end of *The Fleuron* Oliver Simon produced the more modest but also more regular journal *Signature*, printed at the Curwen Press. Appearing three times a year, in a smaller format than its predecessor and in limp covers, more standardised in layout – it was set in the recently cut Monotype Walbaum – its range was wider, and included articles by or about artists such as Paul Nash, John Piper, Graham Sutherland and Picasso. *Signature* was temporarily halted in 1940 by the war; a further eighteen numbers of the New Series appeared between 1946 and 1954, and included draft chapters of Simon's autobiography *Printer and playground* (1956).

The third of the inter-war journals, *Typography*, was edited by Robert Harling (1910–2008) and printed and published by the Shenval Press, whose managing director James Shand did much to support such periodicals. Looking back in 1980, Harling wrote:

> Morison and Simon started *The Fleuron*, probably the most influential printing journal ever to be published in the Western World, on a hopeful shoestring; *Signature* and *Typography* were readily subsidised by their eager founders and committed printers and sympathetically supported by indulgent advertisers.[24]

Eight numbers of *Typography* appeared between 1936 and 1939, running at the same time as *Signature*. Its coverage was wider, with articles on vernacular ephemera such as tram tickets and timetables, newspapers, film advertising (by Francis Meynell) and the work of Ashley Havinden (by Herbert Read). After the war, *Alphabet and Image*, from the same team, ran for another eight numbers from 1946 to 1948, with similar subject matter. This broader coverage, though it included books, was continued with Herbert Spencer's *Typographica* (1949–59, new series 1960–67) and Ruari McLean's *Motif* (1958–67), also published by Shand. A number of trade publications also appeared. *Book Design and Production*, which came out under the editorship of James Moran between 1958 and 1964, had articles

24 Shipcott, *Typographical periodicals between the wars*, p. xiv.

of broader appeal than professional technique. The most recent book arts journal is *Matrix* (1980–), published by the Whittington Press and still printed by letterpress.

Alongside these journals there were a number of substantial newspaper supplements devoted to printing, testifying to a growing interest in the subject among the wider public. Notable examples were in *The Times* in September 1912; in the *Manchester Guardian* in 1922 (printed at the Cloister Press under the control of Stanley Morison); and in the *Times Literary Supplement* in 1927, 1963 and 1973. In January 1940, to celebrate the half millennium of the invention of printing – at that time by an enemy national – *The Times* had a special insert. Public awareness of the subject after the Second World War was further promoted by exhibitions of the best-produced books of the year at the National Book League, which had premises in central London until the mid-1980s.

In 1963, the printing trade exhibition IPEX, held in London in Olympia and Earls Court, was made of wider interest by a display called 'Printing and the mind of man', organised by a number of the leading printing historians and book dealers of the day. This showed an extensive historical collection of typecasting and printing machinery, ending with some recent photocomposition machines, together with an exhibition of books which had influenced and advanced intellectual history. An accompanying exhibition of books selected more for their aesthetic appeal was held at the British Museum.[25]

Part of the public interest in 'Printing and the mind of man' – although sales of the catalogue were only a third of the print-run – was due to the historical display of technology. The development of composition machinery since 1963 has meant that print production has lost its romantic appeal. It is easier to interest people in a demonstration of hand typecasting, with the drama of molten lead, than a computer screen.

Fine printing

In the early years of the First World War, the Doves Press printed its last few titles: among them was an edition of Goethe's poems in German as a protest against the war, and the final *Catalogue Raisonné*. The Press had begun at the turn of the century, inspired by William Morris's Kelmscott Press but very different in style, using one size of a proprietary typeface with exemplary simplicity. In 1916, the founder, T. J. Cobden-Sanderson, threw the type into

25 Carter, 'Printing and the mind of man', pp. 172–80.

the Thames to prevent it ever being used again, an example of the lengths to which press owners can become obsessed by their endeavours.

The slightly older Ashendene Press was more nearly a true private press, in that its owner, St John Hornby, was a wealthy director of the bookselling chain W. H. Smith, and marketing the books was a secondary consideration. With two specially cut types and a typographical style based on Italian Renaissance models, Ashendene continued until 1935.

Both these two presses followed the Kelmscott example of printing on hand-made papers with hand presses, and employing professional printers. The Golden Cockerel Press, however, began in 1921 more as a classic small press, publishing new work, than as a fine one. Harold Taylor founded it as a cooperative venture with writers, but soon found that his own inexperience and that of his volunteer helpers made the Press uncompetitive. He was forced to print more established works on better papers, and to hire professional compositors and pressmen. When ill health forced him to sell the Press, it was taken over by one of his illustrators, Robert Gibbings, who during the later 1920s made it a showcase for wood-engraved book illustration, with work by Paul and John Nash, David Jones and, most significantly, Eric Gill, whose masterpiece, *The four gospels*, came out in 1931. Gill also designed a special type for the Press, which had previously used the small-press favourite Caslon. While the type was set by hand, and hand-made papers were used, printing was done on a powered platen press.

The Depression made it impossible for Gibbings to continue, and the Press was in turn bought by Christopher Sandford, a director of the Chiswick Press in London. The rural workshop at Waltham St Lawrence near Reading was closed, and the printing was done at Chiswick and other large firms until Golden Cockerel finally closed in 1959. In this third phase, much of the typesetting was done on Monotype machines. Begun at the same time as the Golden Cockerel Press, the Gregynog Press in Wales, supported by two wealthy sisters, also employed pressmen and compositors and, unusually among private presses, had its own bindery and a Monotype plant.

At these presses, while the production standards were high, and the books highly valued, the typographic style was in the straightforward classical style that was common in the printing trade at large. Gibbings, influenced by Gill, experimented with unjustified setting, but in general did not do experimental work. It was left to another enterprise, started in 1923, about the time that Gibbings took over Golden Cockerel, to show what could be achieved while working with trade printing firms. The Nonesuch Press, in spite of its name, was a publishing firm, whose guiding spirit was Francis Meynell. Many years later, in 1968, introducing the work of the Folio Society, Meynell wrote of his dislike of the uniform appearance of books from the Doves Press, 'sadly restricted by its one type-face', and added, 'the Folio Society – like (I hope) a venture of my own – has avoided this monotony of style by the use of many printing-houses and of many type-faces; many paper-makers; many different binders and binding styles'.[26]

This venture of his own used a number of printers, notably the university presses of Cambridge and Oxford, the Curwen and Kynoch presses, as well as Meynell's Pelican Press, and a few established firms such as William Brendon, MacLehose and R. & R. Clark. The editions were mostly limited and numbered, although often between 1,000 and 2,000 copies, and they were printed to a high standard on hand-made or mould-made papers. There were also a number of unlimited editions such as *The week-end book*, an anthology of poetry and games, which went through a large number of editions and impressions. Its first jacket was designed by McKnight Kauffer, who went on to contribute illustrations for three Nonesuch titles. The variety of Meynell's typographic style made it difficult to believe that one designer was responsible for them all. It had some of the allusiveness of the American designer Bruce Rogers, usually when setting seventeenth- and eighteenth-century texts, but was broader in its choice of models. Among the first thirty titles were an edition of Donne poems set in the seventeenth-century Fell types at Oxford; two Ernst Toller plays in unlimited editions, the second one with the first illustrations by Georg Grosz published in Britain; and an edition of *Genesis* with wood engravings by Paul Nash and the first use in Britain of a new sans-serif face, Neuland, by the German designer Rudolf Koch.

Nonesuch was outstandingly successful at first, and secured valuable distribution deals with Random House in the USA but, once again, the Depression showed up the high investment and small profit margins of fine editions. In 1936 the Press was taken over by George Macy, who had founded the Limited Editions Club in New York in 1929. After the war Macy returned the imprint to Meynell, but it did not recover its pre-war verve.[27]

In the years immediately after the Second World War the next step in the democratisation of fine book production was taken. The Folio Society was the brainchild of a recently demobilised young Charles Ede (1921–2002), a collector of fine editions who had briefly trained at the London College of Printing. The plan was for a series of classics, one a month, printed in large unlimited editions, to a higher, but not dramatically higher standard than

26 Folio Society, *Folio 21*, p. 8.   27 Dreyfus, *A history of the Nonesuch Press*.

trade books. In the early years, although a wide variety of printers were used – the first book was printed in Belgium, to get round the post-war paper shortage – Mackays were the most frequently employed. Illustration was paramount, and few book illustrators did not do at least one title for Folio. Plates originated in intaglio were usually printed by collotype, although two titles were actually printed from the plates by a security printer in Budapest. Those that originated as wood engravings were printed from the wood or from electros.

The Folio typographic style, as developed by Ede, was classical and used the resources of the Monotype repertoire; although, of the first ten books, five were set in Perpetua, the other five were in five different types. In the hands of Ede's successors as designer, Tim Wilkinson, Peter Guy and Joe Whitlock Blundell, the classical style was refined under the influence of Jan Tschichold, and layouts were also made more varied. The title for *The third crusade* (1958) was set asymmetrically in Libra with a picture across the spread. Folio books also dispensed with jackets, and concentrated on elaborate bindings in several colours, with the board coverings often printed as well as blocked; they are housed in slipcases.

While the Nonesuch Press and the Folio Society broadened the market for well-designed and well-produced books, using trade printers working at their upper limit, a few small presses continued producing books with low over-heads and only one or two owners doing the work. The Rampant Lions Press produced its first book in 1936 and the Whittington Press in 1972, and both were still working at the end of the century. A large number of other fine presses, including a significant proportion of part-time ones, were also active. At the Oxford Fine Press Book Fair in 1999, around thirty-five such presses exhibited, together with others from overseas. The collecting public can therefore be seen as having divided into a larger group, whose needs were satisfied by the Folio Society, and a smaller one that continued to demand books printed in small editions by letterpress on rag papers.

3

The digital book

PADMINI RAY MURRAY

The potential of the digital book, entertainingly explored by Douglas Adams in *The hitchhiker's guide to the galaxy* (1978), promised stores of infinite content, unhindered by the constraints of physical space. However, as the shift to digital became more ubiquitous in the late 1990s it was perhaps inevitable that the new format should inherit the conceptual shape of the printed book. Nowhere was this more evident than in the skeuomorphic design of e-books with 'pages' (albeit that one had to swipe, not turn) and book 'covers' represented by thumbnail images of the same. Nonetheless, this remediated reworking of an authorial manuscript extended far beyond mere reproduction of the text in digital form. As a different format, new rights regimes had to be constructed to take into account the relative ease of publishing e-books, and their facility to cross territorial boundaries due to their global home, the internet. Moreover, traditional business models for publishing have been put under pressure, and there have been new entrants to the publishing market (see Chapter 5). This chapter focusses on the evolution of the digital book as a format, from its earliest incarnations to the present day, although no commentary on the contemporary scenario can be definitive, given the publishing industry's state of flux.

The developments traced in this chapter disrupted the meaning of the 'book', which had hitherto referred to the codex form of pages between a front and a back cover, but whose definition has been increasingly challenged by its digital incarnations. It could be argued that these developments have made 'the book' an ontologically unstable category. The shift from a physical to a virtual entity is transforming our understanding of what a book can be, what it might contain, or even what it might be like to hold. The e-book mimics the material book in that it is a textual container, but the capabilities and use of digital devices used to access these texts extend far beyond this single purpose. As Ray Murray and Squires have argued in their reformulations of Robert Darnton's 'communications circuit', the

'Binder' of the original diagram has now been replaced by the 'Device'. While occupying the same position in relationship to the reader, e-readers and tablets also have a relationship to the technology companies, which thereby create 'walled gardens' in order to ensure the loyalty of the reader to both the device and the platform.[1]

Early attempts

The American engineer Vannevar Bush's vision of the Memex (1945) as an infinitely extendable storage device that could be used for rapid retrieval of linked documents was never realised in practice in his lifetime, though many of the features he imagined, such as the ability to annotate and transmit information, have now been implemented.[2] Bush's compatriot, Douglas C. Engelbart, showcased a number of technologies in his revolutionary 'Mother of All Demos' (1968) the impact of which can still be felt today, such as word-processing, hypertext and links, and the computer mouse.[3] Theodore (Ted) Nelson drew on the work of Engelbart, extending the potential of Bush's imagined device in his idea of the 'docuverse' (1980), a global distributed electronic library of interconnected documents.[4]

The British author Len Deighton is credited with being the first writer to compose a novel using a word processor. He purchased a machine weighing 200 pounds marketed by IBM as the MT72 in 1969 and used it to write *Bomber*, a novel about the Second World War, published in 1970.[5] The MT72, which was operated by Deighton's secretary Ellenor Handley, would convert keystrokes into data stored on a magnetic tape cartridge. As the personal computer grew in popularity in the early 1980s (and shrunk in size), publishers encouraged authors to submit manuscripts on disk as opposed to typewritten scripts. This allowed content to be directly read by computer-assisted typesetting devices, and also allowed for authors to have more power over the appearance of the text, given the growing range of fonts and formatting tools offered by programmes such as Microsoft Word.[6] However, it also

1 Ray Murray and Squires, 'The digital publishing communications circuit'.
2 Barnet, 'The technical evolution of Vannevar Bush's Memex.'
3 http://dougengelbart.org.   4 Nelson, *Literary machines*, pp. 5–6.
5 Matthew Kirschenbaum, 'The book-writing machine', *Slate* 1 March 2013, www .slate.com/articles/arts/books/2013/03/len_deighton_s_bomber_the_first_book_e ver_written_on_a_word_processor.html. See also Kirschenbaum's full-length treatment on the history of word processing, *Track changes*.
6 Feather, *A history of British publishing*, second edition, pp. 217–18.

meant that two versions of the manuscript were in existence – the electronic file and its printed counterpart.

As early as the 1960s, publishers began considering computers as an alternative medium for disseminating content. At Pergamon Press, Robert Maxwell entered into negotiations with Saul Steinberg of the Leasco Data Processing Corporation, in the hope that the company would help distribute Pergamon's scientific journals and its subsidiary ILSC's encyclopaedias electronically to libraries and professionals.[7] Despite the negotiations breaking down in 1969 when Steinberg realised that Maxwell had exaggerated the worth of his business, Maxwell's ambition anticipated by twenty years how publishers' content could be distributed through computer networks, and would be especially appropriate for education and reference books.[8]

Desktop publishing was heralded by the release of the Mac-compatible Aldus Pagemaker in 1985, which, used in conjunction with LaserWriter (Apple's own printer), could create professional-looking documents on home computers. The combination of these factors meant that it became cheaper to produce professional-looking books on a small scale, and also to have a file that could be distributed as a digital version. However, reading on screen was still not an optimised practice, and a number of developments such as managing screen reflectivity, as well as achieving contrast levels comparable to that of paper, had to be in place before stand-alone e-books became readily available as a commodity.[9]

The momentum of electronic publishing was sustained by academic publishers keen to embrace the possibilities of the new medium, which enhanced the potential of textbooks by making them easily searchable, and enabled cross-referencing via hyperlinks. Early electronic journals (pre-1994) were distributed by FTP or via email, but the coming of the web browser in 1993 allowed for hypertext publications that could be enhanced by images. The number of online journals and newsletters available, as documented by the Association of Research Libraries, leapt from 110 in 1991 to 6,000 in 1998.[10] The academic journal, access to which had hitherto been via the physical library, was now accessible through library databases in

7 Stevenson, *Book makers*, p. 221. See also Chapter 18 in this volume.
8 Dennis Barker and Christopher Sylvester, 'The grasshopper: obituary of Robert Maxwell', *Guardian* 6 November 1991.
9 'Digital ink meets electronic paper', *Economist* 7 December 2000, www.economist.com/node/442911.
10 Gould, 'Protocols and challenges'.

a distributed fashion, allowing for anyone who had subscription privileges to access these publications from anywhere.

Crime fiction author Peter James's *Host* (originally published by Gollancz in 1993) is widely accepted as the first book to be published electronically in the UK and possibly worldwide. The book's plotline deals with downloading a human consciousness onto a computer, and one of the students helping James suggested that an electronic version would be very appropriate given its subject matter. The suggestion was made during the editing stage, so did not influence James's writing of the book. Nonetheless, the use of hyperlinks allowed the text to be enhanced through, for example, the inclusion of photographs of real places mentioned in the book such as Alcor, a cryonics facility in the USA. The following year, Penguin's Marketing Director agreed to producing the book in print and electronically – the latter on a set of two floppy discs for both Mac and PC. The electronic edition was priced at £10, the same as the hardback, and was available at the bookseller Dillon's, which bought 10,000 copies each for Mac and PC for a thirty-day exclusive in the UK, after which it went on general sale. However, fear of piracy meant that Penguin only felt confident publishing the first five chapters electronically, which then sold about 20,000 Mac versions in the UK and Commonwealth. The PC version did not fare as well, due to technical problems. In interview, James recalled that one reviewer in *The Times* lugged his desktop computer, along with a portable generator, down on to the beach in order that he could read the 'electronic novel', as it was called at the time.[11]

The reading device

Reading books digitally only began to become more accessible to a wider public with e-reading devices (or e-readers), which were initially called e-books.[12] This taxonomic conflation of hardware and software continued until individual texts packaged and sold as e-books began to gain in ubiquity and be sold as an alternative format to the print book. The first of these was Stephen King's *Riding the bullet*, which sold in downloadable chapters over the internet in 2000. Some of the confusion over the definition may have been perpetuated by the advertising of the e-reading device as a commercial product, as in

11 Email interview between the author and Peter James, 17 July 2014.
12 The word 'e-book' entered the *OED* in 1988.

the case of 'Rocket e-book' which attempted to mimic the codex form by giving it a bulky plastic body.[13]

By the mid-2000s, the portable e-reading device had become a viable commercial reality and technological corporations were eager to capture the English-speaking markets in the USA and the UK. The Sony Portable Reader System (the PRS-500), which had an initial 'library' of eighty books and was priced at £189, was made available in the UK in September 2006 to '[o]verwhelming demand' and sold out online shortly afterwards.[14] Two years later, Waterstone's started to stock the Reader in-store, in a bid to compete with Borders' stocking of the iLiad, though the former was not nearly as much of a threat as Amazon's Kindle which had already been launched in the USA in 2007 and whose British launch followed in 2009. The Kindle's slim dimensions were almost a metaphor for the pared-down, single-function device whose USP was its dedicated use as an e-book reader, eschewing sustained connectivity (apart from that required to download books) thus gaining a strong following amongst avid readers.[15]

Despite Sony's headstart, and Amazon's teething problems due to the difficulty of obtaining wireless availability, Amazon's established relationship with publishers as an online bookseller gave it a distinct advantage.[16] This was borne out by the scope of Amazon's stock: at the time of its launch in the USA, the Kindle had 90,000 books to offer its readers, and at an Independent Publishers' Guild conference shortly before its launch in the UK, Amazon representative Genevieve Kunst encouraged participants to digitise their holdings further:

> We have 245,000 books available in the US, and are working every day with publishers around the world to grow that catalogue. If publishers have the rights to sell in the US, we would welcome their participation. The more publishers digitise in the UK, the better it is for everybody.[17]

Amazon's vision to dominate the market was evident from its adoption of a proprietary file format that could only be used with the Kindle itself, or with Kindle reading apps on other devices.

13 Shirley Keane *et al.*, 'UKOLN Public Library Research', www.ukoln.ac.uk/public/nsptg/e-books.
14 'Briefs', *Bookseller* 5,251 (2006), p. 7.
15 James Bridle, 'From books to infrastructure', *Domus* 4 June 2012, www.domusweb.it/en/design/2012/06/04/from-books-to-infrastructure.html.
16 Graeme Neill, 'Sony and Amazon in e-books battle', *Bookseller* 5,278 (2007), p. 3.
17 Catherine Neilan, 'Amazon urges indies to digitise', *Bookseller* 5,373 (2009), p. 9.

Formats

EPUB, the standard distribution format developed by the International Digital Publishing Forum (IDPF) in 2007, optimises text for reading devices and supports both reflowable text and fixed-layout content. Its open format allows for interoperability across a range of devices, and emerged out of the Open eBook format, which was first published by Microsoft in 1999. Microsoft decided to make EPUB available free of cost in order to grow the market for electronic reading. The company's vice president for technology development Dick Brass made this evident:

> Before we can make profits, we need to make an industry. And we need to avoid a catastrophic standards war that will alienate consumers ... It is critical for the success of the eBook industry to unite and provide publishers and consumers with a common standard by which all eBooks can be formatted.[18]

Despite the universality of the EPUB standard, consistent rendering across devices and apps is still a major issue, as, unlike the majority of web browsers, none of them is open source.[19] There have been some industry efforts to resolve this issue, such as the open source Readium project, which was initially spearheaded by the International Digital Publishing Forum to develop a reference system for rendering EPUB 3 publications. A number of publishers, technology companies and cultural organisations form part of the consortium that supports and helps develop the software that can be run in-browser and in-app. For illustrated and enhanced books, HTML5 has been a popular choice, though how to monetise books in-browser is still a challenge that publishers are trying to resolve, especially since cross-browser and version compatibility cannot be taken for granted, thus potentially shrinking the consumer base.

The transition from the print book to the e-book required a paradigm shift, especially since a sales and technology company, Amazon, rather than a consortium of publishers, led developments. Inevitably the question of pricing arose as publishers and technology companies struggled for power. While publishers accepted that the costs of producing e-books were not as much as for hardcovers, costs such as royalties, digitising, quality assurance and typesetting still meant that overall production costs were far from cheap,

---

18 'Paving the way for books of the future', Microsoft News Center, 21 September 1999, http://news.microsoft.com/1999/09/21/paving-the-way-for-books-of-the-future/#er QYrd7mqAei48bw.97.

19 Derrick Schultz, '99 problems', *ePUBSecrets*, http://epubsecrets.com/99-problems.php.

and still needed to be recouped from consumer sales. Moreover, while print books are zero-rated for VAT in the UK, VAT is charged on e-books. Major issues had to be addressed: when the release of the e-book should be timed with respect to the hardback and the paperback; how to manage expectations regarding author royalties; and, most importantly, how to handle relationships with Amazon and Apple.[20]

As soon as legitimate content could be downloaded from the internet, pirated content could be as well. E-books were no exception. As early as 2000, author Harlan Ellison filed a lawsuit against a fan, Stephen Robertson, who had posted unauthorised digital copies of Ellison's work on an internet newsgroup. The publishing industry was especially nervous in the aftermath of the lessons learnt by the music industry with the rise of peer-to-peer filesharing networks such as Napster. This meant that not only were e-books embedded with code by publishers to prevent copying, but also devices were developed in such a way that they were the only keys to the walled gardens created by proprietary software, such as Amazon's Kindle and its unique .azw format. These barriers also made it difficult for accessibility to be implemented, as the text-to-speech functionality that screen readers deploy is disabled by the Amazon Kindle or cannot be used for reading Kindle e-books.[21]

Such measures have often marred the user experience: preventing buyers from transferring files across their own devices easily or from lending e-books. Consequently a range of software solutions have been made available to enable users to strip digital rights management (DRM) from files downloaded from proprietary bookstores. Territorial restrictions, which were implemented in keeping with publisher contracts, also frustrated buyers who were keen to purchase titles that they had come across on social reading sites or elsewhere on the Web, but were prevented from buying from their local webstore. The Publishers Association argued that vendors such as Amazon needed to do more to prevent 'territorial flipping',[22] in which book-buyers can easily purchase books that were not intended for sale in their own country by using an international IP address.

Some publishers, however, have taken advantage of the open e-book format EPUB, which can be read across all devices. Tor Books, one of the

20 Ben Parr, 'Apple vs. Amazon: the great e-book war has already begun', *Mashable UK* 30 January, 2010, http://mashable.com/2010/01/30/amazon-macmillan/#KpbIn9eLyqqw.
21 Schiller, 'A happy medium'.
22 'Territorial controls greatly important, says PA', *Bookseller* 5,454 (2010), p. 4.

largest producers of science-fiction and fantasy in the world, decided that DRM was an unnecessarily punitive measure for their readers, and chose to do without it completely as of July 2012.[23] Since this decision, Tor have found that there has been no significant piracy of their books, and have been considered a standard-bearer for DRM-free publishing, although no other major publishers have adopted this approach at the time of writing.[24]

Interactivity and innovation

The digital reading market has not been completely dominated by the dedicated e-reading device, such as the Kindle. Publishers have been keen to optimise mobile reading apps and other alternative online reading opportunities, especially for their more visual and non-fiction offerings, which could not be rendered that attractively on the black and white devices previously available on the market.[25] Apple thus became another player in the e-reading market, though following a somewhat different trajectory to its competitors. Its App Store (launched in 2008) offered a marketplace for applications, and this included reading and book apps. As Peter Collingridge, formerly of digital publisher Enhanced Editions put it, the Kindle and the Sony Reader featured 'boring, monochrome, facsimiles of the printed book on . . . leaden dedicated devices – [then in 2008] the iPhone came out in its full technicolour multitasking wonderful app-store glory'.[26]

This increased multimodality offered by mobile apps inspired publishers to experiment, and Edinburgh-based publisher Canongate responded in its characteristically maverick fashion – working with Collingridge and his team to commission and package rock and roll legend Nick Cave's novel *The death of Bunny Munro* as an 'enhanced e-book' (2009). The text was complemented by an unabridged audiobook read by Cave, and punctuated by original music composed by Cave and Warren Ellis, which synched to the text, allowing the reader to switch between the aural and visual experience of the novel. The e-book also made the most of the device's wifi capabilities, enabling readers to use social media tools to share passages from the novel

23 'Tor/Forge e-book titles to go DRM-free', *Tor.com* 24 April 2012, www.tor.com/2012/04/24/torforge-e-book-titles-to-go-drm-free.

24 'One year later, the results of Tor Books UK going DRM-free', *Tor.com* 29 April 2013, www.tor.com/2013/04/29/tor-books-uk-drm-free-one-year-later.

25 Luan Goldie, 'UK publishers look at digital alternatives as Kindle launch suffers delays', *New Media Age* 19 February 2009, p. 5.

26 'The iPhone interviews: Peter Collingridge' (2010). Video available at https://vimeo.com/14431646.

and an updated list of Cave's upcoming gigs and appearances. Faber & Faber provided another model of digital innovation, working in partnership with Touch Press to create a number of high-end apps that made the most of its back catalogue and authors – from an adaptation of T. S. Eliot's *The waste land* (2011), to the award-winning *Solar System* app (2010), which was created by Marcus Chown, a Faber author.

App development represented a shift in the mediation of the book – rather than repurposing a pdf that was a by-product of the existing printed book workflow, it was a manipulation and enrichment of the text at the level of typesetting and markup. The iPhone itself, which could be considered a 'remediated telephone',[27] could also now function as a reading device, and the scaled-up version of the tablet responded to this affordance. Indeed, Apple optimised this potential by launching the iPad in 2010 and with it the iBooks store, thus intensifying the market frenzy around the digital book.[28] The Google Books store was also launched in 2010, increasing the competition in the e-book market.

Technology has had a considerable impact on children's publishing, despite the resilience of the print market for children's books, by using interactivity to enhance both classic and newly commissioned titles. This transformation was accelerated by the tablet, whose haptic graphical inter-face is easier for younger children to use and access than the personal computer. Egmont, for example, struck a deal with Apple to preload *Winnie the Pooh* onto the iPad when it launched, and Penguin launched the *Baby touch: peekaboo* app, which transformed Ladybird books into the first app of its kind for babies.[29] Newer publishers such as Nosy Crow established their reputation based on successful app releases ahead of print books.

Academic and educational publishing have also been profoundly altered by the possibilities offered by digital technologies. Functions such as search and hypertext are linked to online resources, enrich content and enhance usabil-ity, especially for reference books. However, academic publishers have had to respond to the challenges of renting out their textbooks on aggregating platforms such as CourseSmart rather than relying on guaranteed sales to students. Pressures on library budgets and space have meant that publishers

---

27 Anders Fagerjord, 'Toward app studies', unpublished paper, http://fagerjord.no/down loads/FagerjordAppstudiesIR13.pdf.
28 Charlie Jane Anders, 'Hard lessons that 2010 taught the entertainment industry', *Wired* (2010), www.wired.com/2010/12/hard-lessons-2010.
29 Smith, 'Book learning'.

have been experimenting with e-book platforms that can be sold direct to libraries, such as Bloomsbury Academic's 'Collections', which makes an archive of DRM-free front and backlist titles available to participating institutions.

Shifts in technology have also inspired authors and publishers to think differently about what fiction and narrative might look like in a digital age. The potential of the hyperlink as narrative mechanism in digital literature began to be explored in the 1980s, even before the coming of the World Wide Web in 1993. These texts included links but were self-contained, and Michael Joyce's *Afternoon, a story*, the first example of electronic fiction to be sold commercially, was published by Eastgate Systems in 1987. The coming of the Web allowed more authors the space to write, publish and share their own work, to link externally to content, and to push the boundaries of the form. While there is now an established tradition of electronic literature, it still has a limited audience.

Experiments such as Profile Books' *Frankenstein* (2012) by Dave Morris (a choose-your-own adventure style retelling of the classic, heavily inspired by the decision tree logic of videogames) or Random House's *Black crown* (2013), a 'narrative game' by Rob Sherman, have demonstrated the willingness of some publishers to take risks with digital that exceed adaptation, and instead extend to commissioning a new form of artistic product. Finding a business model that succeeds to support such innovation, however, has proved difficult – *Black Crown* had to be taken offline after eighteen months; despite 6,000 people signing up to play the game, only 5 per cent were willing to pay money for in-app purchases.[30]

The reading experience

The e-book, despite its inheritance of the print paradigm, rarely structurally replicates its print counterpart. Unlike a facsimile, which is a photographic reproduction of a printed page, e-book features such as reflowable and resizable text, and the frequent omission or distortion of paratextual material, can considerably alter the reading experience as compared to that of reading a physical book. These elements are shaped significantly by the proprietary reading ecosystems the digital book inhabits, which dictate the manner in which the text is rendered and navigated. Alan Galey demonstrates how the

---

30 Sarah Shaffi, 'PRH's Black Crown project to go offline', *Bookseller* 29 October 2014, www .thebookseller.com / news / prhs-black-crown-project-go-offline.

imposition of device affordances can interfere with authorial and publisher intentions in his case study on *The sentimentalists*, which was published (and printed) by small artisanal publishers Gaspereau.[31] As Galey notes, the back matter of the book contained a 'Note on the text' by the publishers, whose decision to use a digitally updated version of a typeface named by Eric Gill for his daughter Joanna resonates with the thematic preoccupations of the book. These are inspired by the author Joanna Skibsrud's father's own recollections of the Vietnam War. However, the limited set of default typefaces offered by the reading device (in this case the Kobo) means that the 'Note' (and indeed all of the book's text) is rendered in Georgia, making the Note itself irrelevant. Similarly, Simon Rowberry's comparison of the digital version of J. J. Abrams and Doug Dorst's *S.* to its physical counterpart, which makes the most of its materiality by packaging it with postcards, annotated napkins and other ephemera, also demonstrates how in such cases it is difficult for the traditional e-book to replicate the experience of engaging with the codex form of the book.[32]

The e-book reader or the application used to access the digital surrogate, then, alters rather than mimics the reading experience of the physical book by introducing elements imposed by these proprietary technologies. The networked nature of devices allows for public sharing of annotations; readers can 'gamify' their textual consumption by earning badges of achievement for the amount of content read. The weightlessness of the e-book, devoid of the physical heft of the codex, means that the only way readers can assess how far they are into the text is by referring to the feature that displays the percentage read. Page numbers can become irrelevant as what is seen on screen does not necessarily correspond to the physical page; users can alter their view using the settings built into the reading software, which can enlarge or shrink the type depending on the readers' preferences.

The relatively ephemeral nature of digital platforms and objects has raised some urgent questions regarding sustainability and storage. Major national and institutional libraries such as the British Library and the National Library of Scotland, as well as the Bodleian and others in the UK, now accept e-books and digital material under the remit of legal deposit. Websites such as the Wayback Machine also archive websites, but proprietary e-book content is always at risk as vendors license content for use, rather than allowing full ownership in exchange for payment. The lawsuit brought against Amazon by Justin Gawronski, a high school student whose annotated copy of *1984* was

31 Galey, 'The enkindling reciter'. 32 Rowberry, 'Ebookishness'.

remotely wiped by the company, exposed the risk inherent in these transactions.[33]

The challenges faced by the legal deposit system in collecting digital material are numerous: obsolescence of format and the disappearance of hosting websites, as well as the vast content of self-published material,[34] mean that libraries have had to take into account a number of considerations in order to guard against the futility of such efforts. As Marietjie De Beer *et al.* have pointed out (quoting Gibby and Green), this requires a constant revisiting of existing legislation, because issues such as territoriality are made more complex 'when the electronic book exists exclusively and geographically independently "in the cloud"'.[35]

Conclusion

Innovative forms of interactive narrative blur the lines between computer games and the book; content can be presented through rich media as well as text, and linked to the World Wide Web; anyone can now publish a book and reach the widest possible audience. Despite all of these shifts, the digital book is far from displacing the print book completely, and the popularity of reading electronically still varies dramatically between cultures and nations. The print book is still central to reading culture, and ironically the challenge posed by digital text has been responsible for nurturing new formats and incarnations of the material book. Compared to the coming of print, the evolution of the digital book is still in its early phases, and the twenty-first century is bound to witness developments that will alter the reading experience and the publishing landscape irrevocably for the foreseeable future.

33 Cory Doctorow, 'High school student suing Amazon over book-deletions which rendered his study-notes useless', *BoingBoing* 30 July 2009, http://boingboing.net/2009/07/30/high-school-student-1.html.

34 Lisa Campbell, 'Self-published titles "22% of UK e-book market"', *Bookseller* 23 March 2016, www.thebookseller.com/news/self-published-titles-22-e-book-market-325152.

35 De Beer *et al.*, 'Legal deposit of electronic books', p. 92. See also Gibby and Green, 'Electronic legal deposit in the United Kingdom'.

PART II

★

4

Authorship

ANDREW NASH AND CLAIRE SQUIRES

1914–1970s

By 1914 the legal and financial structures of authorship had never been more secure. The emergence of the literary agent in the 1870s and the founding of the Society of Authors in 1883 (whose membership had grown to 2,500 by 1914) had helped regularise contracts and make relations with publishers more transparent. The 1911 Copyright Act – 'the greatest single advance in the protection of authors' rights since copyright was first established by law in 1709'[1] – had enhanced the value of literary property and provided new protection for performance and adaptation. There are 'now more youths than ever eager to be writers', reported *The Times* on 2 June 1913. Authorship came to be seen as a craft that could be learned. Books such as Charles Platt's *Authorship as a career* (1926), R. A. H. Goodyear's *Money-making authorship* (1927) and Michael Joseph's series of help guides collected under *Complete writing for profit* (1930) instructed authors on literary techniques and the practical side of writing for a living. With a healthy periodical culture, an expanded market overseas (especially in America) and new openings in radio and film, the inter-war years were productive for the versatile writer. After 1945, however, it became increasingly difficult for the market alone to sustain professional authorship. A 1953 handbook commissioned by the Society of Authors opened with cautionary words: 'I do not advise any young man or woman to think of making a living by writing.'[2] Amidst increasing disquiet about the financial plight of authorship, the extent and nature of state support for writers became a persistent topic of debate in the 1950s and 1960s, generating a shift in authors' roles in the marketplace and in social attitudes towards authorship.

1 Bonham-Carter, *Authors by profession*, vol. 2, p. 19.   2 Strong, *The writer's trade*, p. v.

Writers at war, 1914–1918

The activities of authors during the Great War underlined the new public face of authorship that had arisen by 1914. Established writers, such as Arnold Bennett and Arthur Conan Doyle, took up war journalism: Bennett wrote political articles for the *Daily News*; Doyle produced commentaries on 'The British Campaign in France' for the *Strand*. Both writers were among those present at a conference organised early in the conflict by the War Propaganda Bureau.[3] Numerous authors were subsequently recruited to write officially sanctioned publications. In the same year that he published *The good soldier* (1915), Ford Maddox Ford wrote books on German and French culture; Bennett's *Over there* (1915) and Rudyard Kipling's *France at war* (1915), articles first published in the *Daily Telegraph*, were based on official visits to the Front; Mrs Humphrey Ward's *England's effort* (1916), syndicated in American newspapers, was written to mobilise pro-war sentiment in the USA. The author most embedded in the war effort was John Buchan, who became a director at the Ministry of Information. *The thirty-nine steps* (1915) established Buchan's reputation as a thriller-writer, but it was as author of *Nelson's history of the war*, issued in monthly and bi-monthly parts over 1915–19, as well as war reporting for *The Times* and the *Daily News*, that his popular profile was established.[4]

The conflict proved a ready subject for versatile writers. E. M. Delafield was persuaded by her publisher to suspend work on one novel to write another, *The war-workers* (1918), about women's labour; John Masefield used his experiences with the Red Cross for his best-selling romance *Gallipoli* (1916); William Le Queux, author of spy fiction and fantasies of foreign invasion, turned inexorably to anti-German popular fiction. For less compliant pens, however, the conflict brought restrictions. The most high profile among several instances of censorship was the withdrawal of D. H. Lawrence's *The rainbow* (1915) and subsequent prosecution of his publisher Algernon Methuen. The catalyst was a vituperative review by James Douglas in the *Star* which denounced Lawrence's novel explicitly in the context of war.

If the political climate alienated some writers, it rehabilitated others. Lawrence's erstwhile friend John Middleton Murry had gone into bankruptcy in 1913 following the closure of his modernist magazine *Rhythm*.[5] Like Lawrence, he spent much of the war in poverty. His first novel *Still life*

3 Waller, *Writers, readers, and reputations*, chapter 26.
4 Macdonald, 'Translating propaganda'.   5 Lea, *The life of John Middleton Murry*.

(1916) earned less than the £9 typing costs. A critical study of Dostoevsky was written to pay off a publisher's debt of £30. Salvation came when he was recruited by the War Office on £5 a week. He rose to become Chief Censor and was awarded the O.B.E. After the war, he took over editorship of the *Athenaeum* on a salary of £800 a year (worth around £30,000 in 2010).[6]

Range of markets and types of authorship

Immediate post-war economic conditions weakened the outlook for author-ship. Royalty rates fell and advances failed to keep up with rising production costs and retail prices. In a climate of increasing industrial unrest, printers and compositors secured wage increases, but authors had no such bargaining power. With publishers becoming more cautious over issuing new titles, Edmund Gosse stated, in a 1920 speech to the Royal Literary Fund, that 'the hope of living by writing books' was becoming 'forlorn'.[7] However, few authors made a living exclusively through books. Most who established a reputation after 1914 combined book authorship with journalism. The periodical market remained buoyant in the inter-war period (in 1922 alone thirteen new titles were launched), offering the prospect of a steady income through articles, short stories and reviewing. Aldous Huxley wrote reviews for the *New Statesman and Nation* and articles for the *London Mercury* before joining the editorial staff of the *Athenaeum* in 1919, which enabled him to give up teaching and get married. In the space of eight months he wrote twenty-nine signed articles and 171 anonymous notices and reviews. This, and subsequent work for *House and Garden* and *Vogue*, and as dramatic critic of the *Westminster Gazette*, he considered '[s]ordid journalism, but a screw of £400 which, at the moment, and in the circ[umstance]s, I can't refuse'.[8] In fact, it doubled his income. Over a twelve-month period in 1921–22 he earned just over £400 from royalties on four books (two novels, a story collection and a poetry volume) – the fruits of four years' work.[9]

Huxley's experiences were typical. When J. B. Priestley gave up his position as a university extension lecturer in 1922 with only £50 capital, he survived at first by writing articles and reviews for literary papers. Similarly, until 1925 literary journalism was Virginia Woolf's main source of income 'and her main job'; from 1909 to 1921 she earned only £205 from her books.[10]

---

6 Calculation taken from *Measuring worth*, www.measuringworth.com. Comparisons made throughout this chapter are with 2010 and are based on the Retail Price Index.
7 *The Times* 4 June 1920. 8 Bedford, *Aldous Huxley*, vol. 1, p. 112.
9 Information from the Chatto & Windus archive, University of Reading Library.
10 Lee, '"Crimes of criticism"', pp. 117–18.

George Orwell also began his writing career with periodical articles. His first book, *Down and out in Paris and London* (1933), appeared only after several rejections and much internal censorship.

Although journalism remained the most common entry-point into authorship, more writers were finding success initially with novels – a contrast with earlier periods. In the years immediately after the war publishers and readers clamoured for new talent.[11] Fisher Unwin and Collins both started a 'First Novel' series, and John Long ran a £500 first novel competition. Many young writers found that newspaper and magazine work followed on from fiction success. Storm Jameson's debut novel *The pot boils* (1919) – on which she was advanced just £10 – led directly to a job earning £50 a month as a sub-editor on the *New Commonwealth*.[12] On a larger scale, Evelyn Waugh received more offers than he could handle after the success of *Vile bodies* (1930). Regular reviewing for the *Graphic* was augmented by a 'money for jam job' of £30 a week for a series of thirteen 800-word 'light pieces' for the *Daily Mail*.[13] His subsequent trips to Abyssinia, which fuelled the writing of novels and travel books, were undertaken as correspondent for the *Mail* and *The Times*.

Joseph claimed in 1931 that 'Hard-working journalists and short-story writers may be able to produce excellent work, but it will not fetch the prices paid to their novelist rivals.'[14] The range from top to bottom was huge. In 1918 Arnold Bennett claimed to have 'beaten all journalistic records' when he accepted £100 (twice Jameson's monthly salary) for a weekly 1,500-word article in *Lloyd's Weekly News*.[15] Eight years later, Bennett's annual payment of £3,750 (£170,000 in 2010) for his 'Books and persons' column in the *Evening Standard* was almost five times the salary (fourteen guineas weekly) paid to Charlotte Haldane as gossip columnist of the *Daily Express*, and over thirty times the amount paid in 1930 to Geoffrey Trease who, before he established himself as a children's author, was employed by a magazine publishing company on £117 a year, ghostwriting four to six articles a day.[16]

In spite of the disparities in payments, the periodical market sustained many professional authors. Joseph estimated the average annual income of a 'well-known and active' freelance in the 1930s as between £400 and £1,000. Remuneration rates recorded in the *Writers' and artists' yearbook* show that in the inter-war period most technical, leisure and trade magazines paid between one and three guineas per thousand words. Rates for literary and

---

11 Hentea, 'Late modernist debuts'.   12 Birkett, *Margaret Storm Jameson*, p. 63.
13 Stannard, *Evelyn Waugh*, p. 215.   14 Joseph, *This writing business*, p. 13.
15 *Letters of Arnold Bennett*, vol. 3, p. 56.
16 Adamson, *Charlotte Haldane*, p. 24; Trease, *A whiff of burnt boats*, p. 156.

larger-circulation magazines varied. *John o'London's Weekly* advertised three guineas per thousand (the price given to Walter Allen for articles published as a schoolboy); the *Nation and New Statesman* four to eight guineas; *Punch* seven to twelve; and *Lilliput* (established 1937) up to fifteen.

The strong periodical market supported various specialist branches of authorship. Successful children's writers such as Richmal Crompton, whose *Just William* books were collected from stories published in magazines, and Enid Blyton, who was invited to run her own magazine by Newnes, developed their careers in the periodical market. Although established writers could earn substantial sums from volume publication, the magazine was essential for the beginner. In the 1920s and 1930s the *Writers' and artists' yearbook* concentrated only on periodicals in its section on 'Writing for the juvenile market'. Remuneration was low, from just one guinea per thousand words, but the *Yearbook* reported that 'the market can pay more than commonly thought'.[17] Trease earned fifty guineas from the *Boy's Own* for a 50,000-word story in 1931, a larger sum than his earnings from book publication.

The periodical market was equally important for science writers, who could supplement their professional incomes significantly. Peter Bowler estimates that a junior scientist in the first half of the century could earn £50 a year 'by writing a handful of articles; a professor or a well-known public figure could earn hundreds'.[18] The anatomist Arthur Keith claimed to have made £2,000 in a two-year period in the 1920s, 'almost the equivalent' of his hospital salary. The book market was less remunerative. Although J. B. S. Haldane allegedly earned £800 from *Daedalus* (1924), most of his other books sold only a couple of thousand copies, and his income from journalism was 'far more substantial'. The move towards mass-market publishing in the late 1930s increased the potential for book authorship, however. Along with Pelicans, launched in 1937, popular scientists were attracted to ventures such as Collins's New Naturalist series, commenced in 1945, which paid a minimum of £400 per title.[19]

For most scientists, writing was an aside from their professional work. Julian Huxley was unusual in abandoning an academic career for authorship. Even before resigning his university chair Huxley employed a literary agent to maximise his earnings. His work spanned both specialist publications and mass-market newspapers – he claimed that a payment of ten guineas from the

---

17 *Writers' and artists' yearbook* (1928), p. 54.   18 Bowler, *Science for all*, p. 252.
19 *Ibid.*, p. 233, 229, 267.

Daily Mail first 'gave him the idea that it would be possible to create a career based on popular science writing'.[20] From 1927 to 1935 his income depended entirely upon writing, with payments reaching as high as thirty guineas for a 1,200-word article for the *Daily Herald*. The range of his writing was wide, encompassing educational series and mass-market ventures such as Benn's Sixpenny Library and Pelicans, and he acted as Science Editor of the Home University Library.

History authorship was less dependent upon periodicals but, like science, was defined in part by a professional/popular dichotomy. While academic scholars pursued writing as a professional duty, mainly through the university presses, popular histories aimed at general readers made long and profitable careers for writers like G. M. Trevelyan – who refused commissions from Cambridge and made a fortune from his *History of England* (1926) with Longman – and John Ernest Neale, whose biography of *Queen Elizabeth* (1934) sold 10,000 copies.[21] An Oxford fellowship meant that A. L. Rowse did not have to worry about money, but he began making significant money from his books in the 1940s (his first volume appeared in 1927). His breakthrough was the autobiographical *A Cornish childhood* (1942) – which sold 7,000 copies in less than two years followed by 20,000 copies printed for the Readers Union – but his subsequent major historical books had first print-runs of 10,000 copies.[22] The century's most consistently successful author was Arthur Bryant, whose first publication, *King Charles II* (1931), was selected by the Book Society and sold 27,000 copies in eighteen months. Longman's advertisements triumphantly proclaimed: 'a historical monograph has become a best-seller'.[23] Over the next sixty years Bryant wrote around forty books. He claimed 'a curious little public of my own'[24] but the immense distribution of his popular histories through book clubs – which in the 1950s could escalate sales by over 200,000 copies – and the prominence of his voice in the media make him characteristic of the twentieth-century popular author. The third volume of his biography of Pepys was serialised in the *Sunday Times* in 1933; *The national character* (1934) was based on talks for the BBC; a trilogy of books on Anglo-French relations in the Napoleonic era, 'retold for the common man' and published during and immediately after the war, had total sales of over 800,000 copies in thirty years.[25] In 1936 he succeeded G. K. Chesterton as the highly paid columnist on the *Illustrated London News* and in the 1960s he

---

20 *Ibid.*, p. 223.   21 Howsam, *Past into print*, p. 100.   22 Cauveren, *A. L. Rowse*.
23 Stapleton, *Sir Arthur Bryant*, p. 58.   24 Howsam, *Past into print*, p. 113.
25 Stapleton, *Sir Arthur Bryant*, pp. 161–2.

went under contract with Beaverbrook newspapers, writing for much of the rest of his life for the *Daily Express*.

With such a range of options open to the writer capable of shifting from one branch of authorship to another, the period is best characterised by the 'miscellaneous' author, such as Beverley Nichols. Purely in terms of the business of authorship, Nichols was one of the most successful writers of the century.[26] Over 1919–21 he published three novels – the first while still a student – and sold articles to papers and journals for up to £4. After a period freelancing he became a 'cub' reporter on the *Sunday Dispatch* and published short stories in the *Daily News*. Adept at identifying shifts in popular taste, his impudent, best-selling autobiography, *Twenty-five* (1926), later one of the first Penguins, bred a host of imitations. Travel books and polemical volumes on religion and politics followed. All the time he was writing articles, fiction, plays, and music and sketches for revues. He could turn almost anything into a book – one of his novels was a fictionalised account of the writing and production of one of his revues. In 1931 he signed a contract with the *Daily Mail* to write an article a week for £18 (£950 in 2010). The following year he published the first of his enormously successful gardening books, *Down the garden path*, which established a new genre, the spread of suburbia having fuelled a widespread interest in gardening. After the war there were further forays into travel and politics, and new adventures in children's books, cats and flower arranging; in the 1970s three more autobiographical volumes appeared. He wrote for *Woman's Own* for over twenty years and his column in the *Sunday Chronicle* reportedly increased the paper's sales by 100,000 copies.

As a miscellaneous author Nichols was characteristic of the celebrity writer, whose name alone increased circulations and shifted books whatever the subject. The early twentieth century witnessed an intensification of the celebrity status of the author. Rosamond Lehmann's debut success with *Dusty answer* (1927) provoked a flurry of requests for photographs, interviews and personal information about her tastes, hobbies and superstitions.[27] Bennett jokingly remarked in 1928: 'If a prominent author uses his handkerchief in a public place he will read of the event next day in the press.'[28] The media interest surrounding Agatha Christie's mysterious disappearance in 1926 is only the most famous example of the life of an author becoming national news.

26 Connon, *Beverley Nichols*. 27 Hastings, *Rosamond Lehmann*.
28 Bennett, *The Evening Standard years*, p. 213.

Popular authorship

Beneath this kind of mainstream writing lay a huge market for anonymous and pseudonymous authorship. The many popular fiction magazines that flourished in the Edwardian period continued until the 1950s.[29] Geoffrey Cotterell, whose first novel *Then a soldier* (1944) sold 12,500 copies, began by selling anonymous stories to such magazines for £5, calculating that if he wrote a 4,000-word story a week he could earn £250 a year – 'an income beyond the avaricious dreams of many' in 1937.[30] Although the market contracted after the war, a new outlet for such writing briefly flourished with the 'mushroom publishers', who issued American-style gangster, western and detective pulp paperbacks in the forties and fifties. The market facilitated the careers of writers like Norman Firth, 'The Prince of the Pulp Pedlars', who in five years 'produced some five million words of fiction and articles'.[31] Such writing had to be produced very quickly since the rates of pay were small. One author reported in 1951 that he made a living by turning out '55,000 words of gangster fiction in five days', selling it all for £1 per thousand words.[32]

The most consistently remunerative market for popular authorship was women's romance, dominated from the 1930s by Mills & Boon. The firm's authors would commonly adopt pen-names to disguise their prolificacy; some wrote as many as seven novels a year. Joseph McAleer notes that most of the firm's regular authors 'were from solidly middle- or lower-middle-class backgrounds', and were 'either married and raising children, or single working women'.[33] Many graduated from journalism or magazine work. Jay Blakeney ('Anna Weale'), a reporter on a provincial newspaper, was advanced £150 for her first novel published in 1955, which, in addition to proceeds from serial rights, amounted to two-thirds of her yearly salary as a journalist. The highest-paid author on the inter-war list was Denise Robins, who received a form of salary. In 1932 she was paid £100 a month to write eight novels over three years. It was not unusual for authors to earn £1,000 a year before the war, and £2,000–£3,000 in the 1950s (£40,000–£50,000 in 2010). Some writers effectively became employees of the firm, receiving monthly payments and leaving subsidiary rights in the hands of the publisher. They rarely dealt directly with magazines, even though serial rights to their stories could fetch up to £1,000. In 1971 Mills & Boon had 'a record 109 authors

---

29 Ashley, *The age of the storytellers.*   30 Quoted in Leasor, *Author by profession,* p. 96.
31 Holland, *The mushroom jungle,* pp. 35–6.   32 *Ibid.,* p. 67.
33 McAleer, *Passion's fortune,* pp. 71, 101.

under contract', with annual earnings of some reaching £10,000 (over £100,000 in 2010).[34]

Literary authorship

The strong magazine market ensured a ready demand in the inter-war period for short stories, offering an important supplement to literary authors. Elizabeth Goudge, who came to prominence in the 1930s, was advised by her agent to '[l]ive by your short stories, and make your reputation from your books'.[35] For established writers the proceeds were considerable. P. G. Wodehouse was reportedly earning £475 (around £25,000 in 2010) for a single story. In view of the cultural divisions that have come to be associated with the literary market in the inter-war period, it is illustrative of the decisive importance of magazines that such divisions were frequently elided in the periodical context. A. E. Coppard's first published story appeared in *Pearson's Magazine* – 'to my dismay', he later wrote;[36] and D. H. Lawrence sold stories to the *Strand* and *Hutchinson's Magazine* for £30–£40.

Lawrence's career provides a telling illustration of the conditions of literary authorship in the first third of the twentieth century. Following the withdrawal of *The rainbow* he struggled to find a market for his novels and felt increasingly alienated from the literary and publishing culture. The potentially lucrative three-novel contract he had secured from Methuen was cancelled – though he kept the £300 advanced on *The rainbow* – and he spent the war in near poverty, securing small sums for poems, essays and short stories, and borrowing money from his agent J. B. Pinker, whose financial help kept him alive. With little prospect of publishing *Women in love*, and 'in some despair', he agreed to write a school history book, *Movements in European history* (1921), simply because the publisher 'will give me £50 when I give them the MS., so that will solve my financial difficulties for the moment'; popular authorship offered greater monetary reward than serious writing.[37] The turning point in his career came in the 1920s when he effectively abandoned the British commercial market for America (where he found larger remuneration and greater freedom from censorship) and for private publication. The £1,000 he earned on the first, privately printed, edition of *Lady Chatterley's lover* (1928) was more

---

34 *Ibid.*, p. 136. 35 Leasor, *Author by profession*, p. 147. 36 [Strong], *Beginnings*, p. 47.
37 Worthen, *D. H. Lawrence*, p. 76.

than he had received on any of his previous writings and 'effectively relieved him from financial cares'.[38]

For modernist authors like Lawrence, private publication and patronage became a refuge from a censoring market that both inhibited expression and offered little financial reward. Harriet Weaver, business manager of the *Egoist*, paid James Joyce more than £20,000 over a period of nine years from 1914 (the equivalent of over £1 million in 2010), allowing him to ride the inevitable failure of his writing to penetrate the mainstream market. The difficulties he and Lawrence experienced with censorship were not unique, however. In the inter-war period authors and publishers were constrained by a commercial market that was dominated by circulating libraries which either refused to stock books or forced authors to tailor their work to the perceived demands of readers.[39] The law of libel was another obstacle implicating both authors and publishers. When Heinemann was sued by the Duke of Windsor over Philip Gibbs's *Ordeal in England* (1937), which dealt with the constitutional crisis, the author paid half of the £3,000 court costs.[40] Libel actions and threats reached fever pitch in the 1930s and became, in Stanley Unwin's contemporary judgement, 'one of the main discouragements of the book trade'.[41] Gollancz withdrew Rosalind Wade's autobiographical first novel *Children be happy* (1931), when they were 'snowed under with solicitor's letters',[42] and reached an out-of-court settlement when threatened over Cronin's *The citadel* (1937). Graham Greene was forced to make changes to *Stamboul train* (1932) when Priestley threatened action, and writers like Orwell discovered that any hint of reference to real people, or in the case of *Keep the aspidistra flying* (1936) advertising firms, had to be removed. Although the pressure loosened after the war, libel remained an issue for writers of the 1950s, especially in the context of obscenity. The costs to authors, in loss of sales and publicity, could be considerable. In 1962 Heinemann withdrew the first edition of Anthony Burgess's *The worm and the ring* when a former teaching colleague of the author took action; and thousands of copies of the paperback edition of John Fowles's *The collector* (1961) were pulped when the publisher was sued by the Save the Children Fund.[43]

For authors whose work appealed directly to the mainstream commercial market of libraries and book clubs, the rewards in the interwar period were potentially enormous. Priestley's struggles were spectacularly arrested in 1929 when *The good companions* cleared £16,000 (over £750,000 in 2010) in two

---

38 *Ibid.*, p. 143.   39 Wilson, 'Libraries, censorship and reading patterns'.
40 St John, *William Heinemann*, pp. 279–80.   41 Unwin, 'Introduction', p. 3.
42 Hodges, *Gollancz*, p. 59.   43 Warburton, *John Fowles*, pp. 258–9.

years.[44] Georgette Heyer's historical novels sold up to 15,000 copies a year in the 1930s, with advances of £750.[45] The success of Cronin's first novel allowed him to give up his medical career. He was later given a three-novel contract with Gollancz with a combined advance of £10,000 and a flat royalty rate of 25 per cent. *The citadel* (1937) sold 100,000 in ten weeks.[46]

Such best-selling authors were, of course, exceptional. As Chris Baldick records, in the period 1910–40 '[m]ost novelists and virtually all poets failed to become self-supporting authors. They were part-time writers only, living on their salaries from other employments.'[47] It was common for such employment to be linked in some way to writing. As noted, journalism was the most common support, but many writers worked in the book trade itself, as manuscript readers (which had been a common occupation for nineteenth-century authors), editors or even company directors. Priestley read manuscripts for the Bodley Head in the 1920s for £6 a week; Frank Swinnerton was employed as reader by Chatto & Windus from 1913 to 1926, on an annual salary that never 'exceeded £550 a year' (£25,000 in 2010).[48] Juggling the creative and the day-to-day was never easy. Norman Collins, deputy chairman of Gollancz from 1934 to 1941, stuck regimentally to writing five pages of his novels each night before bed. His work in publishing, and later as a Controller of BBC radio and television, did not prevent him writing a book a year.[49] Working in the trade undoubtedly gave writers a privileged sense of the tastes and mechanisms of the market. For Virginia Woolf at the Hogarth Press, involvement in publishing provided a welcome control over her work, and company directors, like T. S. Eliot at Faber & Faber and Graham Greene at the Bodley Head, were able to shape literary culture directly.

One example among many illustrates the necessity of paid employment for most authors. In 1957, having published three novels, Paul Scott's life's income from authorship was £532. In comparison, he was earning £1,248 a year as a junior director of the literary agents Pearn, Pollinger & Higham.[50] Along with journalism and the book trade, twentieth-century literary authors typically combined writing with related employment, such as librarianship (e.g. Philip Larkin and Angus Wilson) or teaching (e.g. W. H. Auden, Cecil Day-Lewis and William Golding). The spread of higher education in the 1960s was a significant development. Poets, in particular, benefited from residencies and lectureships for new creative writing courses.[51] Prior to this,

---

44 Brome, *J. B. Priestley*, p. 101. 45 Kloester, *Georgette Heyer*. 46 Hodges, *Gollancz*, p. 72.
47 Baldick, *The modern movement*, p. 29. 48 Swinnerton, *Figures in the foreground*, p. 169.
49 Leasor, *Author by profession*, pp. 60–73. 50 Spurling, *Paul Scott*.
51 Crawford, *The modern poet*.

British authors had frequently found work in American universities. Walter Allen, who lived a 'hand-to-mouth existence' on £3–£5 a week before the war through journalism, broadcasting and reporting on film scenarios, received $800 for a summer's lecturing in 1935 at the University of Iowa. After the war he continued with what he described as 'all sorts of miscellaneous writing', before a further period in Iowa confirmed that he could support himself through combining journalism in Britain with college teaching in America. It was this that determined posterity would look upon him as a literary critic, rather than a novelist.[52]

What authors craved was a steady income while they wrote. A lucky few secured this through special financial arrangements with publishers. In 1923 Chatto & Windus agreed to pay Huxley £500 a year in exchange for two works of new fiction, and from 1930 Greene had a similar £600 arrangement with Heinemann. After the war the practice became more common. Lehmann, who had received a £750 advance for a novel published in 1944, secured a new arrangement from Collins in 1947 where she was allowed to run an overdraft of up to £1,250 set against the proceeds of her next three novels. Unfortunately for the publisher, she only wrote two further novels in the remaining forty-three years of her life. Angus Wilson left his job at the British Museum in 1955 when Secker & Warburg gave him a guaranteed salary of £600 a year for three years, a sum matched by the *Observer* in exchange for regularly book reviewing.[53] Scott gave up his agency work in 1959 when he was afforded a similar arrangement, first by his American publisher and then by Heinemann, who advanced £2,000 on two novels in the form of a quarterly payment of £500. Without this money, it was claimed, the 'enormous project' of *The Raj quartet* would not have been completed.[54]

Managing literary property

Throughout the period, the Society of Authors kept up its campaign to educate authors about the disposal of literary property. G. H. Thring's *The marketing of literary property* (1933) provided exhaustive advice on copyright and libel laws, contracts, methods of remuneration, subsidiary rights, and agents. There were four main ways of handling literary property: outright sale, profit-sharing, commission or, most commonly, the royalty system. Though easily abused, the profit-sharing agreement was not inappropriate for certain classes of publication such as academic books,

52 Allen, *As I walked*, pp. 112, 146.   53 Warburg, *All authors are equal*, p. 276.
54 St John, *William Heinemann*, p. 523.

where little profit might be expected, or textbooks and technical books which required regular updating. Commission agreements, where the author undertook the cost of production and advertisement and the publisher acted as a selling agent, were rare in mainstream publishing, though George Bernard Shaw and John Maynard Keynes were notable exceptions. Shaw had used Constable as a distribution agent since 1903 and retained an active interest in pricing and publicity. Keynes's early volumes with Macmillan were issued on a half profits basis, but *The economic consequences of peace* (1919) was published on commission because Keynes wanted a larger print-run (5,000 copies) than Macmillan was prepared to risk. With the publisher taking 10 per cent on receipts from sales, the success of the volume provided the author with a substantial income, helping him 'out of the disastrous consequences of his currency speculations' in 1920.[55] The arrangement, retained for the author's subsequent books, gave Keynes greater control over all aspects of production, pricing and publicity.

The Society's main directive to authors was always to lease, never to sell, a copyright or any subsidiary rights. James Hanley sold his first novel, *Drift* (1930), outright for a mere £5 and the practice certainly persisted at a lower level of the market. Thring asserted that some education and technical books were sold outright by authors 'ignorant of the probable sales' that could occur if a book was chosen by a school or educational authority, and that many publishers of children's books purchased copyrights for only £25 to £50 'for a work that may sell in its thousands'.[56] The juvenile market was notoriously bad and in the 1960s the Society launched a renewed campaign against the practice of selling copyrights. A questionnaire revealed that 91 out of 175 authors had been offered outright payment by publishers, with terms ranging from less than £2 per thousand words to £100 for a 2,000-word story published by Ladybird Books. Ladybird's publisher, Wills & Hepworth, maintained that 'the system of paying an author by means of a lump sum is the fairest and most satisfactory method',[57] but when the firm advertised sales of its Key Word reading scheme as 'beyond the million mark' the Society of Authors questioned how much of a projected £12,500 in royalties a Ladybird author had earned.[58]

The advantages of maintaining control over literary property was obvious in view of the increasing value and range of subsidiary rights. Allen noted in 1957 that publishers 'are tending to judge a manuscript not simply as a novel,

---

55 Moggridge, 'A risk-bearing author', p. 221.
56 Thring, *The management of literary property*, pp. 127, 131.   57 *Author* Spring 1964, p. 17.
58 *Author* Summer 1965, p. 28.

a biography or a work of history, but as the possible source of a film, a television or radio programme, a newspaper or magazine serial, or even as material for condensation in the digest magazines'.[59] The publisher claimed a share in these rights on the basis of having taken the initial risk in a work and helped establish its success, but the lack of regular agreements provoked disputes. Heyer signed an agreement in 1940 ceding half the income from film sales in her novels to Heinemann. This proved a mistake when in 1970 the rights in one novel were bought for £5,000 (£60,000).

The serial market, which had been crucial to Victorian authors, remained a potentially lucrative source of income and advertisement, though proceeds could vary significantly. At the top end, Hugh Walpole received £800 from his publisher Macmillan for serial rights in *Portrait of a man with red hair* (1925), while the *Daily Telegraph* paid £2,000 (£93,000 in 2010) to run T. E. Lawrence's *The revolt in the desert* (1927). By contrast, Richard Hughes received just £50 from the abridged publication of *A high wind in Jamaica* (1929) in *Life and Letters*. Increasingly the serial market catered for 'middlebrow' or genre fiction. The women's magazine market was high-paying. In the 1940s Heyer was paid £1,000 from the *Woman's Journal* for serialisation of her Regency novels.[60] Established authors generally sold serial rights through their agent, ceding only the normal 10 per cent commission on the proceeds. On first novels, however, publishers often insisted on retaining control over serial rights and taking a larger proportion of the sale. The Bodley Head took half of the £50 paid by the *Times Weekly* for Agatha Christie's first detective novel, *The mysterious affair at Styles* (1920). With success, however, Christie's serial earnings rose to £500 when the *Evening News* accepted her fourth book, *The man in the brown suit* (1924).

The introduction of book clubs in the 1930s provided a significant new market for literary and popular non-fiction authors. The Book Society selected its first monthly choice in 1929, and though membership was never as large as its American model the Book of the Month Club, it offered significant extra income for authors. Lehmann's *A note in music* (1930) earned over £800 in its first year, nearly half of which had been paid by the Book Society.[61] Authors were not unwilling to adapt their work to the Society's selection tastes. As noted above, the unexpected selection of Arthur Bryant's biography of Charles II contributed to that author's decision to write popular, rather than academic, history. Other book clubs soon followed, and though

59 Allen, 'Authorship', p. 21.   60 Kloester, *Georgette Heyer*, p. 267.
61 Nash, 'Literary culture', p. 333.

royalties were low compared to normal sales, the huge membership ensured substantial extra sales. Foyle's printed an extra 175,000 copies of Evelyn Waugh's *Put out more flags* (1942), adding £1,000 to his income.[62] In the 1950s Heyer was regularly earning an extra £1,000–£2,000 via book clubs.

Until the 1960s, money from paperback rights increased authors' earnings only moderately. The initial royalty rate for Penguin paperbacks in the 1930s was 5 or 7.5 per cent. With the expansion of paperback publishing in the 1960s, however, proceeds grew. Standard royalty rates rose to 10 or 12.5 per cent for some authors, and advances, hitherto around £100, rocketed. Paperback rights were frequently being sold before publication. Pan paid 'an English first novel record' of £3,500 (£60,000 in 2010) for Fowles's first novel *The collector* three months before the hardback appeared.[63] When Penguin made a strategic decision to pursue more popular genres in the 1960s, it led to advances of over £15,000 to authors like Len Deighton.

As paperback rights became more lucrative, the Society of Authors began a campaign to secure better terms for authors. Hardback publishers generally took 50 per cent of book club and paperback proceeds. There was increasing pressure, however, for authors to take 60 per cent. In 1956 Cronin held Gollancz to ransom and obtained a 70/30 split, and by the 1970s this ratio had become the norm. American hardback publishers could also insist on taking a 50 per cent share of subsidiary rights. Brian Aldiss ceded half the proceeds of US paperback and film rights in his science fiction work *Non-stop* (1958) but saw little of the money, and Golding complained bitterly when Harcourt Brace took half of the $20,000 advance paid by Pocket Books on the paperback edition of *The pyramid* (1967), claiming they had done nothing to earn it except sign the agreement.[64]

International rights were nevertheless crucial to maximising income. Translation rights and English-language continental rights added only small sums. Colonial and Commonwealth markets offered more, but because books were sold at cheaper prices overseas royalty rates were lower. The really big market lay in America, where, as noted in relation to Lawrence, British authors could also experience greater artistic freedom. Most authors dealt with American publishers directly or through an agent, although it was not uncommon for British publishers to handle American and other subsidiary rights on an author's behalf taking a share in the proceeds. In 1930 Gollancz took 25 per cent of American proceeds of Cronin's first

62 Stannard, *Evelyn Waugh*, p. 73.   63 Warburton, *John Fowles*, p. 226.
64 Aldiss, *Bury my heart*, pp. 78–9; Carey, *William Golding*, p. 316.

novel. Cronin later dealt directly with his American publishers and, like Maugham, came to look on America as his primary market, with British sales a subordinate concern.

The serial market was also much larger in America. In 1935 Cronin forced Gollancz to delay publication of a novel because he had been offered money for a US serial 'that it would be sheer insanity on my part to refuse'.[65] Waugh's *Brideshead revisited* (1945) was sold for £1,000. After the war, when the British serial market contracted substantially, success in the American magazines was more than just a welcome bonus. The $6,000 (over £2,000) paid by the *New Yorker* for Muriel Spark's *The prime of Miss Jean Brodie* (1961) was more than Spark had earned from any of her previous writings, and Golding's payment of $10,000 (£3,500) for a three-part serialisation of *The spire* (1964) in *Show* magazine was seven times the advance paid by Faber for the British volume rights.[66]

American book clubs offered a further lucrative market. The Book of the Month Club even in its infancy could generate enormous extra sales. In 1932 the Club paid Lehmann the equivalent of £4,000 for *Invitation to the waltz*. Maurice Collis gave up his job in the Indian Civil Service when the Book of the Month Club selected his travel book *Siamese white* (1936), and by 1944, when *Brideshead* was selected, the payment to Waugh was £10,000 (£337,000 in 2010).

Success in America could transform an author's career. When Joyce Cary's *The horse's mouth* (1944) was selected by the Book of the Month Club he earned more from his writing in a few months than he had in the previous fifteen years.[67] Like Waugh, Cary subsequently embarked on a celebrity tour across the USA, giving lectures, broadcasts and bookshop appearances. The money from these tours maintained his living. After the war, this aspect of the American market became more pronounced. When Fowles undertook a promotional tour after *The collector* he found himself at the centre of the American media, appearing in front of millions on chat shows. The cult of the celebrity author was more entrenched in American literary culture and impacted upon several prominent British writers. Golding's term as writer-in-residence at a small liberal arts college during 1961–62 'lifted him out of stagnation and brought him fame, wealth and the adulation of the young'.[68] *Lord of the flies* (1954), which had made little impact in America on first

65 Davies, *A. J. Cronin*, p. 127.   66 Carey, *William Golding*, p. 281.   67 Foster, *Joyce Cary*.
68 Carey, *William Golding*, p. 252.

publication, became the rage of college students; paperback sales rocketed to half a million by 1962.

With the rapid expansion of cinema in Britain and America, film rights – newly defined and protected by the 1911 Copyright Act – became the most lucrative, but also the most volatile, subsidiary right for novelists. As early as 1922 Shaw was telling members of the Society of Authors that cinema rights in a novel might be worth £10,000.[69] Contractual arrangements varied. The popular novelist Elinor Glyn sold her first film rights in America for a flat fee of up to $5,000; later she secured a one-third share of the profits.[70] In 1923 Maugham's share of the film of his short story *Rain*, which fetched $150,000, was 25 per cent; in 1944, however, he accepted a single payment of $250,000 (over £60,000), for rights to *The razor's edge*, money which helped establish the Somerset Maugham Award.

Because of the scale of the operations, however, film negotiations were invariably drawn out and frequently frustrated. It was nine years after the success of Ian Fleming's *Casino royale* (1953) that the first James Bond film was released. J. G. Ballard recalled that films based on his early novels from the 1960s 'were lunched, but never launched'.[71] Nevertheless, money could be earned simply by negotiating options or retainers, and sometimes outright payments, for films that might never be made. Hollywood paid $2,000 a week 'for approximately four weeks discussion with no obligation' on Waugh's *Brideshead*, but the discussions came to nothing.[72] Lehmann received a massive $250,000 (£60,000) for a film of *The ballad and the source* (1944) that was never made, and bought a new house with the money.[73] Most writers left adaptations of their works to others. Fowles wrote the script for the film of his first novel but so hated the experience that he settled for consultation and veto on the adaptation of *The French lieutenant's woman* (1969).

The arrival of television produced a further outlet. Cronin, whose sales had declined by the 1960s, received a huge boost with the success of the *Dr Finlay's casebook* series, based on short stories he had published and collected almost twenty years previously. Payments were initially £325 per programme, or £8,450 for a series. This later rose to just short of £10,000 (around £130,000 in 2010).[74] His input into the stories was almost non-existent; the income derived from the enduring strength of his literary property.

69 Bonham-Carter, *Authors by profession*, vol. 2, p. 250.
70 Weedon, 'Elinor Glyn's system of writing', p. 42.   71 Ballard, *Miracles of life*, p. 252.
72 Stannard, *Evelyn Waugh*, p. 179.   73 Hastings, *Rosamond Lehmann*, pp. 247–8.
74 Davies, *A. J. Cronin*, p. 234.

Writing for stage and screen

Most authors viewed films as little more than an additional source of income from having written and published a book. Some, however, were sufficiently attracted by the artistic and financial potential of the new medium to pursue screenwriting itself. Graham Greene wrote *The ministry of fear* (1943) as a 'good cinematic idea', selling the film rights for £3,250.[75] Several of his novels, including *The third man* (1950), grew out of film scripts, a practice that became more common. The best-selling *Where eagles dare* (1967) was one of several Alistair MacLean novels that was 'foisted' on him by 'film producers who originally commissioned them as screenplays'.[76] Frederick Forsyth's *The day of the Jackal* (1971) was derived from a film scenario which had already been sold before the author wrote a novelised version.

Before the arrival of talkies in 1929, a film script was 'often worked out on the spot' by a director.[77] As with books, scriptwriters could sell their work outright, or receive a share of profits or a royalty. Cecil Raleigh recorded in the *Author* in 1913 that the period of 'endless plots' being written for £2 or £3 was passing away. Raleigh considered £100 down on a 5 per cent royalty 'quite fair remuneration', and well-known names could expect £400 on 10 per cent.[78] With the arrival of sound, literary authors found they could earn more from scriptwriting than from books. A 1936 guidebook recorded annual earnings of scenario writers as between £500 and £1,500 (£26,000–£80,000 in 2010).[79] Christopher Isherwood was paid £125 for five weeks' work on a film script in 1933, substantially more than he earned on his first two novels. Even after the success of *Mr Norris changes trains* (1935) his earnings from scripts was still higher – he received £200 for four weeks' effort in 1937.[80]

When he emigrated to America Isherwood became a salaried scriptwriter in Hollywood, an example followed by several other high-profile authors. Walpole adapted his own works, and wrote the scenario and acted in a film of *David Copperfield*, earning £200 a week.[81] Huxley was paid $1,500 (£350) a week for adapting *Pride and prejudice*. Scriptwriting was not an easy profession to break into, however. Film studios in Britain and America generally employed scenario writers, and while hopefuls could send in 'treatments' of adaptations or original works, in 1936 it was estimated that only 5 per cent of films produced were based on stories bought from outside authors.[82] Success as a novelist or playwright was invariably a prerequisite.

75 Sherry, *The life of Graham Greene*, p. 147.   76 Sutherland, *Reading the decades*, p. 100.
77 Bonham-Carter, *Authors by profession*, vol. 2, p. 242.   78 *Ibid.*, p. 244.
79 Knight, *A guide*, pp. 7–8.   80 Parker, *Isherwood*, pp. 271, 350.
81 Hart-Davis, *Hugh Walpole*, pp. 348–51.   82 Knight, *A guide*, p. 146.

The formation of the Screenwriters' Association out of the Society of Authors in 1937 nevertheless indicated the growing status of film authorship. The outbreak of war brought further demand for both escapist and propaganda films. Scriptwriters nevertheless played a Cinderella role in film production. Only a percentage of their scripts might actually become films, and they retained little control over the eventual product. Rebecca West recalled that the largest sum she ever earned out of a single piece of work was from the sale of a story to a film corporation which 'used not a single incident nor a line of dialogue that was in my record'.[83] Screenwriters also received a tiny share of the profits and scant advertising of their authorship. The prolific T. E. B. Clarke recorded that his work for Ealing Studios brought him 'little in the way of hard cash'.[84] Outright payments were not unusual even after the war. Clarke received a single payment of £1,500 for *The Lavender Hill mob* (1951), and Forsyth sold *The day of the Jackal* outright, though he secured a percentage for his next film.[85]

The expansion of cinema weakened the earning potential of the theatre. The 1911 Copyright Act had secured protection for theatrical work by granting authors the sole right to dramatise a novel or novelise a play. This became an important component of literary property. At the end of his career Arnold Bennett was doubling his earnings by dramatising most of the novels he wrote. Successful stage versions could often spark demand for the original novel, as in the case of Margaret Kennedy's *The constant nymph* (1924). Dramatic authorship itself was an uncertain business, however, chiefly because of the amount of capital investment involved. In the inter-war years production costs rose 'by some 600 per cent' in London, and playhouse rents 'by as much as 1000 per cent', as the 'actor-manager' system gave way to an industry dominated by financial speculators.[86] The risks were high. Priestley's first play, *Dangerous corner* (1932), ran for five performances before the backers withdrew their support. Able to draw on substantial royalties from his best-selling novels, Priestley put his own money into the venture and the risk paid off. Beverley Nichols, by contrast, lost £3,000 on his revue *Floodlight* (1937) when a financial backer proved unworthy, forcing him to sell the country cottage which had inspired his series of gardening books. The Society of Authors was involved in numerous legal cases concerning unpaid royalties, management bankruptcies and copyright infringements. New authors were sometimes caught out. Terence Rattigan failed to spot

---

83 Findlater, *Author! Author!*, p. 82.   84 Bonham-Carter, *Authors by profession*, vol. 2, p. 271.
85 *Ibid.*, p. 281.   86 Gale, 'The London stage', p. 148.

a clause in the contract for his first (co-authored) play in 1933, which stipulated a threshold before royalties would be paid. Having paid £200 towards the expenses of the production themselves, all the collaborators received was a £100 advance when the production transferred to the West End.[87]

Unlike novels, plays depend upon a multitude of 'authorial' forces. In the 1928 *Writers' and artists' yearbook* Nichols advised would-be dramatists that what was needed to produce a play was not an agent or manager but a leading actor or actress. Agents were essential nonetheless because of the range of rights, including translation, touring, film and overseas rights. Though plays could be sold outright – which Nichols considered a 'crowning folly' – or on a profit-sharing basis, playwrights usually received a percentage of the gross takings. Rates could start from as low as 2.5 per cent, but 5 per cent gradually became the norm when fringe, provincial and repertory theatre expanded after the war. Throughout the period, the Society of Authors fought to regularise contractual arrangements and standardise methods of payment. In 1931 the League of Dramatists was founded out of the Society to protect the playwright's share of repertory, amateur, international and film rights. By 1947 most plays were produced on a sliding royalty scale, with 10 per cent on weekly takings over £1,500.[88] Cinema rights were commonly sold outright, with theatrical managers taking a share of the proceeds.

The biggest battle for dramatists remained censorship. A campaign of 1909 failed in its aims but 'helped liberalise the attitude of the Lord Chamberlain'.[89] The outbreak of war brought reaction, however, and the path to abolition in 1968 was a gradual one.[90] Few playwrights were unaffected. Noel Coward discovered that adultery depicted in *This was a man* (1926) was unacceptable, but drug taking in *The vortex* (1924) was not. In 1958 Samuel Beckett was forced to make changes to *Endgame* on grounds of blasphemy, even though the play had been performed complete in French the previous year. Only one of John Osborne's ten plays staged in London up to 1966 was presented without cuts or changes.

In spite of the risks and uncertainties, enormous sums could be earned from dramatic authorship. The original three-month run of Shaw's *Pygmalion* in 1914 earned the author around £2,600 (£195,000 in 2010); A. A. Milne was in the 1920s reportedly earning £200–£500 a week from his plays, with £2,000 a year from amateur rights alone.[91] R. C. Sherriff's war play *Journey's end*

---

87 Darlow and Hodson, *Terence Rattigan*, pp. 64–6. 88 *Writers' and artists' yearbook* (1947).
89 Bonham-Carter, *Authors by profession*, vol. 2, p. 170. 90 Findlater, *Banned*.
91 Thwaite, *A. A. Milne*, p. 224.

(1928) made the author over £50,000 (£2.3 million in 2010) in its first year, and in the 1940s Rattigan was regularly earning over £20,000 from each play, with similar amounts from sales of film rights.

Although guide books still warned authors that success in playwriting was freakish, the 1947 *Writers' and artists' yearbook* reported that 'the market for plays to-day is perhaps better than it has ever been'. In spite of threats from the growth of television, there was a surge in playwriting in the 1950s thanks to the introduction both of a Royalty Supplement Guarantee of 7.5 per cent and of state funding for theatres.[92] Bursaries, worth initially £500, were first paid to dramatists in 1952 and there were also theatre residencies. The growth of universities provided further new outlets. Harold Pinter's first play, *The room* (1957), was commissioned by the drama department of Bristol University. Increasingly, careers were being launched on the fringes, though, as Bonham-Carter notes, 'to make a fair living out of writing for the stage' an author still depended on commercial production.[93]

The success of John Osborne's *Look back in anger* (1956), a revolutionary moment in British theatre, coincided with a new professional culture and helped raise the status of the playwright above that of the leading actor or actress.[94] Whereas writers like Coward and Priestley had combined dramatic authorship with acting or other forms of writing, the backing of theatres enabled dramatists like Osborne to become full-time writers. Not everyone achieved overnight success, however. Tom Stoppard's first written play spent nine months unacknowledged in the hands of a theatre before an agent secured an option for £100. No production was made and the option ran out after a year. Adapted into a television play and broadcast in 1963, a further option on the play was sold but again came to nothing. It was not until 1968 that the play, *Enter a free man*, was produced, by which time *Rosencrantz and Guildenstern are dead* (1966), produced at the Edinburgh fringe festival and then in London, had made the author's name. Stoppard became one of the biggest-earning playwrights in the country (the advance from the National Theatre on *Rosencrantz* was £250) but had spent a dozen years struggling with journalism, radio and television work before making a breakthrough.

The arrival of BBC radio broadcasting in 1922 widened the market for dramatic authorship, and introduced a new subsidiary right for poetry and prose. The Society of Authors quickly agitated for standard minimum fees. An intensive, much publicised negotiation led at the end of 1923 to a table of

---

92 Bonham-Carter, *Authors by profession*, vol. 2, pp. 193–6.   93 *Ibid.*, p. 201.
94 Rebellato, *1956 and all that*, chapter 3.

minimum fees ranging from one to two guineas for poems, a guinea per thousand words for prose and six guineas for a full-length stage play.[95] Authors considered such terms paltry, and rates were even lower for children's programmes and overseas broadcasting. Walter Allen received just one-and-a-half guineas for broadcasting his children's stories in the 1930s, compared to five guineas for a 1,500-word article in the BBC's magazine *Radio Times*.[96] The rapid growth of radio in the 1930s was a boon to authors, however. Literary authors such as Eliot, Priestley, E. M. Forster and Harold Nicholson welcomed the exposure, whilst the successful Dartmoor novelist Eden Phillpots, whose first book appeared in 1890, made a new career for himself by mastering the medium and continuing writing up until his death in 1960. Allen argued that broadcasting had 'completely changed the lot of the professional author of modest financial success'. Being known to the public 'simply as the stalwart of the BBC's Sunday "Critics" programme' might be 'galling', but it was necessary for survival.[97]

As radio audiences expanded, the Society intensified the campaign for better terms. By 1942, payment for full-length plays had risen over fourfold to twenty-five guineas but the monopoly status of the BBC made bargaining difficult. The BBC also maintained a right to reject commissioned material. In 1947 the Society issued a manifesto complaining about low fees – five guineas for world broadcasting rights in a short story was cited; the practice of demanding all broadcasting rights; and the right to refuse commissioned work.[98] Threat of strike action (unprecedented in authorship but possible under the monopoly/service arrangements of the BBC) brought a response, as the corporation increased fees for most types of work from 20 to 50 per cent and set better terms for overseas and repeat broadcasts. A 1949 guidebook reported that, as a consequence, 'never has the field for the freelance broadcaster been wider'.[99] With nearly 1,000 plays broadcast in a year, the market for scriptwriting was especially rich. As L. A. G. Strong reported in 1953: 'radio of all kinds offers excellent chances to the new writer'.[100] By the mid-1940s Strong had himself sold over seventy 2,000-word stories, receiving on average fifteen guineas for each, plus four guineas for broadcasting the stories himself. For a minor novelist these rates were substantial: 'I have only once been paid a higher price by a British periodical for a story of that length',

95 Bonham-Carter, *Authors by profession*, vol. 2, chapter 10.
96 Allen, *As I walked*, pp. 50–1.   97 Allen, 'Authorship', p. 26.
98 Bonham-Carter, *Authors by profession*, vol. 2, pp. 225–6.
99 Jonsson, *Writing for broadcasting*, p. 7.   100 Strong, *The writer's trade*, p. 153.

he noted.[101] In the 1960s Stoppard's payments, before he became a famous playwright, reached £150 for radio and television plays, and £30 a week for writing a radio serial.[102]

The expansion of television after the war increased the broadcasting market further. In 1963 Richard Findlater noted that, '[i]nstead of living on essays, reviews and reading for publishers, the new-model freelance is more likely to write revue and cabaret sketches, advertising jingles or plays for television'.[103] For many writers, radio and screenwriting took over from magazine work. N. J. Crisp started writing for television in 1959, giving up the short story writing which had previously been his main sustenance as an author. Television was even more remunerative than radio work. Although the League of Dramatists and the Radio Writers' Association successfully pushed up payments for radio plays in the 1960s to 150 guineas for ninety minutes, this compared poorly with television rates which, at a base of six guineas per minute, could reach £750 for full-length plays. Nevertheless, a 1955 guidebook commented that a writer 'can scarcely make a living out of television', even if he sold ten plays a year,[104] and most television writers made up their living by script adapting and editing. A survey by the Television and Screenwriters Guild in 1963 recorded that 575 of its members earned up to £1,000 from television, 15 per cent up to £2,000 and only 6.5 per cent over £5,000.[105]

'Critical times for authors'

The Second World War had a more immediate effect on authorship than the earlier conflict as paper shortages and rising production costs cut into incomes. Robert Graves left Methuen when the company refused to match his pre-war rates of 25 per cent after the sale of 7,500 copies, and A. E. Coppard, who had received 20 per cent for his short story collections, reluctantly accepted a starting royalty of 12.5 per cent.[106] As in 1914, established authors were recruited by the government for their writing skills: Greene and Hanley were among many who worked for the Ministry of Information; Richard Hughes and Joyce Cary wrote scripts for propaganda films; Forster, Orwell and Priestley gave broadcasts on different branches of the BBC; and Maugham, living in America, was commissioned to write a novel – *The hour before the dawn* (1942) – 'to show America the effect of

---

101 Bonham-Carter, *Authors by profession*, vol. 2, pp. 222–3.
102 Nadal, *Double act*, pp. 159, 154.   103 Findlater, *What are writers worth?*, p. 289.
104 Bartlett, *Writing for television*, p. 71.   105 *Author* Spring 1963, p. 4.
106 Duffy, *A thousand capricious chances*, pp. 116, 119.

the war on a typical British family'.[107] H. E. Bates was recruited into the Air Force solely to write short stories about pilots. Initially published in the *News Chronicle* under the pseudonym Flying Officer 'X', these were collected as *The greatest people in the world* (1942) and sold 16,000 copies. Though he took no royalties (his remuneration was his pay as a serving officer), the book's success transformed Bates's career, leading to a £750 advance on his next novel *Fair stood the wind for France* (1944).[108]

After 1945, the economic conditions of authorship became precarious. With retail prices of books failing to keep up with escalating costs of production, publishers needed to print and sell more copies of a book to break even. As a consequence, advances and royalty rates fell. In 1951 the Society of Authors resisted an attempt by the Publishers Association to impose a fixed reduction in royalties, but the decade still witnessed a 'steady, stealthy and unrelenting campaign on the part of publishers to push down the royalty rates of authors'.[109] Jameson was well served by Macmillan, who in 1950 gave her a £1,000 advance in the form of a loan, but by 1952 was still 'pessimistic about the prospects of her writing ever providing a reasonable living'.[110] First-time authors could expect only low advances. Golding received just £60 on *Lord of the flies*; Burgess £50 on *Time for a tiger* (1956). J. G. Ballard did better, but considered the £100 advanced by Gollancz for *The drowned world* (1963) 'barely enough to keep a family afloat for a month'.[111]

Media interest in the economics of authorship intensified after the war. In 1946 the periodical *Horizon* reported on a questionnaire sent to writers on 'The cost of letters'.[112] Respondents included Orwell, Stephen Spender, Robert Graves, Laurie Lee and Rose Macaulay. Among the questions asked were how much an author needed to make a living, whether a 'serious writer' could expect to earn this sum from writing alone, what other employment was appropriate, and whether the state 'or any other institution' should do more for writers. The final question was significant given the timing of the report, shortly after the election in 1945 of a Labour government committed to the creation of a welfare state. To the first question, Elizabeth Bowen suggested £3,500 a year net; Cyril Connolly around £1,800. Spender and Herbert Read thought £1,000 the requirement for a married author with children; Orwell considered this the '*best*' possible income and £312 (£6 a week) the minimum for an unmarried man. Few respondents thought it possible to earn their estimated sums by writing alone, not even those who

---

107 Morgan, *Somerset Maugham*, p. 494.   108 Eads, *H. E. Bates*, pp. 46–7.
109 Allen, 'Authorship', p. 20.   110 Birkett, *Margaret Storm Jameson*, pp. 290, 292.
111 Ballard, *Miracles of life*, p. 191.   112 Reprinted in Davison (ed.), *Literary taste*, pp. 241–78.

considered £400 as the minimum. Connolly reckoned it was only possible to meet his requirement of £5 a day if a writer sold a novel or play to Hollywood or had it selected by 'one of the American book societies'. An ancillary job in journalism, reviewing, broadcasting – what Henry Reed called 'subsidiary literary work' – was generally preferred. Most considered that work outside literature widened a writer's sphere of experience but was nevertheless a diversion of energy. For Spender the more journalism he wrote the more 'irritable' he became, the less he read, and the less he wrote poetry.

Responses to the question of state support varied widely, often according to political opinion. Some feared the imposition of censorship: to Orwell there were 'invariably strings tied to any kind of organized patronage', and to Graves the state was 'a dangerous patron of literature'. Reed, by contrast, believed 'emphatically' in state help, but only if administered independently (he suggested the universities). The entitlement to a state pension; temporary maintenance for young writers; changes to systems of taxation; and more state funding for libraries and reading were recurrent themes among the responses. Most agreed that old-style patronage, which had supported Joyce in his later career, was not viable, and that government had to be involved. Robert Kee proposed that the state 'should make £400 a year available to anyone who wants to be a writer', a sum that would be insufficient 'to tempt the crook', to make it 'possible for him to write'. There was agreement that poets were a special case, unable to make a living from their work and therefore more in need of support from the state.

Significantly, respondents complained about the activities of publishers and the commercial structures of the trade – Julian Maclaren Ross was alone in proposing a minimum royalty advance. It was accepted that market conditions alone could support only certain types of writing, and therefore certain types of author. One respondent considered an author could survive only if 'he happens to write in one of the genres or styles which are commercially subsidized'. Cecil Day Lewis, a poet and translator who wrote crime novels under a pseudonym, proposed that such 'literary hack-work' at least honed the technique of writing.

Over the next fifteen years the Society of Authors undertook a campaign to raise awareness of the financial state of authorship. In 1953 Walter Allen published a commissioned pamphlet *Critical times for authors* which predicted 'the end of professional authorship as we have known it in the past'. In 1955 the Society set up a committee under Priestley to investigate existing financial relations between author and publisher with reference to royalties, book club and overseas sales, and paperback rights: 607 authors responded to a questionnaire – a small but representative sample; 405 earned under £250 per annum, 58 per cent under £500 and 73 per cent under £1,000. The conclusion was that 'the majority of professional authors earn from their writing of all kinds well below the national average wage'.[113] Only a quarter claimed to rely wholly on writing for their living.

A significant factor in making the times critical was the decline in opportunities for journalism and freelance writing. A 1940 guidebook could still argue that 'writing articles for the popular and trade press is certainly the easiest of all branches of this writing business', but things would soon change.[114] Established writers could still earn reasonable sums. Orwell's rates for reviews of 800–900 words in the *Observer* and the *Manchester Evening News* during 1943–44 was seven to ten guineas; he received less from literary and political papers, *Horizon* and *Tribune* paying only two to three guineas per thousand words.[115] New writers would have found it hard to survive even on these terms.

The newspaper press became less remunerative. After the war the number of national and provincial newspapers dropped, and many general magazines disappeared. In 1954 Tom Stoppard's weekly wage as a seventeen-year-old cub reporter on the *Western Daily Press* in Bristol was £2 10s 8d (£54 in 2010).[116] When the Bristol papers consolidated in 1960 Stoppard went freelance, writing two columns and several articles a week, earning three guineas per article. A £30 payment for an article on John Steinbeck for *Men Only* was a significant amount in the circumstances. He spent seven months as theatre critic for *Scene* over 1962–63, earning £20, surviving afterwards on columns and sports reporting earning £40 a week while he waited for his breakthrough in the theatre.[117]

Throughout the 1950s the *Writers' and artists' yearbook* noted that in spite of a sharp rise in the cost of living, and an increase in the price of most magazines, 'many are still paying pre-war rates' as low as 'a guinea or less a thousand words'. Reasonable payments could still be secured by wide-circulation magazines – Jameson received fifty guineas for a short story in *Good Housekeeping* in 1952 – but remuneration rates for technical and leisure journals did not begin to creep up until the end of the decade, when the number of publications in those areas increased. In 1952 James Leasor compared the position of the pre-war writer to the current situation:

---

113 Findlater, *What are writers worth?*, p. 283.   114 Boyce, *This writing business*, p. 7.
115 Orwell, *I belong to the left*, Appendix.   116 Nadel, *Double act*, p. 58.
117 *Ibid.*, pp. 78, 83, 105, 123.

The young man who wanted to produce one novel a year and had no full-time job could easily make his bread and butter (with some jam as well) by reviewing for the Sunday papers and literary weeklies; by writing essays, and if need be, by straight reportorial journalism for a newspaper.

Now there was 'nothing much doing in any of these fields'.[118] Strong, although he still considered freelance journalism 'the best chance to the beginner', reckoned that an unknown writer would 'have to do pretty well to make £100 a year' (less than £7,000).[119] There were also fewer opportunities for reviewing and literary journalism. Strong considered that if a beginner made thirty shillings a week from reviewing 'he ... would be deliriously lucky'.[120] Looking back on the 1960s, Walter Allen recorded that he 'belonged to the last generation of the old type of literary journalist'. The traditional literary and political weeklies were declining in numbers and most high-profile reviewers were academics.[121]

The disappearance of literary and fiction magazines had a significant effect on literary authorship. Of the thirteen new magazines launched in 1922, only one remained in 1962. The market for stories had so declined that N. J. Crisp concluded it was 'practically impossible to make a living from writing short stories alone'. The market 'to all intents and purposes' was entirely women's magazines, and payment was 'disgracefully low'.[122] In the 1950s *John Bull* would pay between thirty-five and seventy-five guineas, and the top women's magazines forty to sixty. Rates had remained stagnant whilst the cost of living had increased 40 per cent. Calculating that even a short story of 'wide appeal' may earn only a hundred guineas, Crisp compared this to the $1,000 to $2,000 (£350 to £700) commonly paid in America, but noted that it was extremely difficult to sell to that market – 'few manage it with any regularity'. Crisp was one of the lucky ones. During his peak years he was 'grossing between £3,000 and £4,000 a year' from short stories, 'but only because of American sales'. A table of one writer's earnings recorded in the *Author* of 1963 confirms the trend. Over a three-year period, 1960–62, the author sold thirty-two stories to UK magazines, receiving around £1,860, an average of £58 per story. In America s/he sold just five stories (four in one year), but this yielded £2,962, an average of £590 per story.[123]

These statistics underline how the writing market had become more extreme, with a few authors receiving vast sums and the majority earning

---

118 Leasor, *Author by profession*, pp. 72–3.   119 Strong, *The writer's trade*, p. 39.
120 *Ibid.*, p. 36.   121 Allen, *As I walked*, p. 259.   122 Crisp, 'The short story scandal', p. 16.
123 *Author* Summer 1963, p. 7.

less than in previous decades. Until *Lord of the flies* became a cult classic on American university campuses, Golding earned less in royalties than he did from his teacher's salary. His novels in the 1960s were delayed by his having to take on more reviewing. By contrast, Fowles was able to give up his teaching post on the back of substantial advances on his first novel and John Braine's earnings on *Room at the top* (1957), which cleared £10,000 in two months, far exceeded the £600 he earned annually as a librarian.[124] The trends were underlined by further investigations undertaken by the Society of Authors in the 1960s. Two pamphlets by Richard Findlater, *What are writers worth?* (1963) and *The book writers: who are they* (1966), assessed the range and earnings of authorship. Findlater estimated that the total number of professional authors, 'in the sense that they had written full-length books and would be eligible to full membership of the Society of authors', was between 6,500 and 7,000.[125] The findings were bleak. Of those authors who did not combine authorship with an outside occupation (56 per cent of the total respondents), nearly half earned less than £500 a year (half the national wage) from 'all sources of literary income (books plus journalism, scriptwriting etc.)'. At the top, one-sixth of respondents earned over £1,000 a year, while the bottom two-thirds earned less than £6 a week (£300 per year).

Although income from subsidiary rights was substantial for top authors, nearly three-quarters of respondents earned nothing at all from this source. Nor was income from journalism, broadcasting and lecturing as substantial as had been thought – over a quarter received no money from such sources and only half earned more than £70 a year. Once again it was the top authors who benefited, with the same one-sixth who earned more than £1,000 a year from books earning an extra £1,000 from 'other literary earnings'. Findlater concluded that the book industry was 'booming' but 'book writing' was not:

> In plain terms, it doesn't pay enough. It doesn't pay as much as it *ought* to, in a country with a growing appetite for books. The British public wants, increasingly, to read: it does not, on the whole want to *pay* for reading . . . A golden nucleus of book authors, not necessarily the best, build up small fortunes in ways denied to the pop novelists of the past. But hundreds more – and these by no means flops or failures – squeeze only a miserable dole from their work. Britain is getting its books at the expense of its authors.[126]

As discussed below, when the survey was repeated in 1972 Findlater concluded that the findings were worse and wrote of the situation as

---

124 Sutherland, *Reading the decades*, p. 35.
125 Bonham-Carter, *Authors by profession*, vol. 2, pp. 93–7.   126 Quoted in *ibid.*, pp. 95–6.

a 'national scandal'. By framing the findings in terms of the nation, Findlater's conclusions brought into perspective the writer's relation to the state. Two issues preoccupied authors in the post-war period: taxation and Public Lending Right. Taxation was a contentious subject for several reasons. The chief complaint was that income tax was assessed on a strictly annual basis and an author's income could fluctuate wildly from year to year. Many authors arranged to have royalties and lump sum payments paid in instalments. It was not until 1953 that 'the Government finally conceded . . . that for tax purposes a writer could spread back earnings from a sudden success over three years instead of having to pay a high rate on what was the result of many year's work'.[127] In 1952 Bates reported that if an author earned £25,000 in one year, he could expect to keep just £2,000 of it.[128] Double taxation was another obstacle. When Elizabeth Goudge won a novel prize in America worth £30,000 in 1944, the money was taxed in Britain and America, reducing the payment to just £5,000.[129] A 1945 agreement between the two countries resolved the issue, but money from literary prizes was not ruled exempt from taxation until 1978.[130]

A further problem was that copyrights were treated as income, not capital, and were thus taxable. In 1940, to help clear her overdraft, Georgette Heyer sold the copyrights in three of her best-selling titles to her publisher Heinemann for £750. She declared the money a capital sum, but when she received a tax demand and fought the case in the courts, she lost and was ordered to pay over £1,000 in taxes and costs.[131] The issue came to a head in 1952 when Compton Mackenzie sold the copyright in twenty of his books to his publisher Macdonald for £10,000. Taxed £6,000, he pursued and lost the case in the courts. The publicity raised public awareness of the issue, however, and in 1967 a new ruling was introduced 'which, in certain circumstances, made it possible to spread *forward* over six years any lump sum received for the sale of copyright'.[132]

The introduction of high levels of surtax after the war hit big-earning authors. In 1950, with the top rate reaching 85 per cent, Heyer quickly wrote a crime novel to clear back-surtax of £6,000 (£160,000).[133] A. L. Rowse arranged with his publishers Macmillan in 1949 to be paid an annuity of £10,000 'in forty quarterly instalments of £250'.[134] In 1955 some £7,000 of his

127 Findlater, *What are writers worth?*, p. 284. 128 Greenfield, *Scribblers for bread*, p. 281.
129 Leasor, *Author by profession*, p. 152.
130 Bonham-Carter, *Authors by profession*, vol. 2, pp. 80, 83.
131 Kloester, *Georgette Heyer*, p. 253. 132 Bonham-Carter, *Authors by profession*, vol. 2, p. 81.
133 Kloester, *Georgette Heyer*, p. 289. 134 Ollard, *A man of contradictions*, p. 330.

earnings was being held by his publisher simply to avoid 'losing it practically all to the government'.[135] Cronin and Greene were among many writers who became tax exiles on the continent. The conditions had a demoralising effect on some authors. In 1968, with a top rate of 90 per cent, Fowles was advised by his accountant 'to be on the move, resident nowhere, thus avoiding all tax liability'.[136] Eventually, he followed the example of others, including Christie, in setting up a company, J. R. Fowles Ltd, that owned his work and paid him a salary and expenses. The complicated arrangement required him to defer his income over five years, thus avoiding the 90 per cent class. However, the 'pressure to defer, in fact *not* to earn', contributed to his 'apathy about finishing work or publishing anything'.[137] Heyer, who had created a similar venture in 1946, still felt the taxation pinch, until in 1968 her company was purchased by Booker Bros. Ltd – who owned the copyrights of Fleming and Christie among others – for £80,000 (over £1 million), with Heyer paying only £100 in tax.[138]

In 1970, Richard Findlater reflected in the *Author* on the prospects for authorship in the new decade. With a pressured commercial environment '[t]he odds against the writer [were] high', but other factors gave hope.[139] The prospect of Public Lending Right, the campaign for which had gathered pace in the 1960s, loomed large; the growth of education at home and abroad, the opening up of new markets overseas, the continued expansion of state and civic aid for the arts, and the increase in grants and prizes were also identified as positive factors. It was increasingly clear that the commercial market, which had sustained professional authorship at the beginning of the century, could offer security to few; the future of authorship was to depend increasingly on state policies as well as market trends.

1970s to the twenty-first century

The period from 1970, as the previous section suggested, found authorship affected by a seemingly paradoxical yoking: on the one hand, that of state policies and institutionalisation, and on the other, of commercialisation and market trends. This was the period of the rise of the mega-seller, the Booker Prize, and the very public author mediated by events and (latterly) social media. The same period also saw the establishment of Public Lending Right (PLR), the Arts Council's Literature Panel, and increasing concerns around

135 Ollard (ed.), *The diaries of A. L. Rowse*, p. 185.   136 Warburton, *John Fowles*, p. 302.
137 *Ibid.*, p. 311.   138 Kloester, *Georgette Heyer*, p. 370.   139 *Author* Winter 1969, p. 158.

diversity, access and inclusion. Distinctions between the state and the market quickly break down under analysis of authorship in the period, with, for example, the growth of university creative writing programmes fuelled by and in turn feeding the desire of individuals to become published writers, to win book prizes and to sustain literary careers. By the end of the period under study, opportunities to get published – assisted by digital technologies and self-publishing platforms – gave unprecedented access to the title of 'author'. At the same time, the income earned by writers became increasingly stratified into marketplace successes and the vast majority of other writers who struggled to make a living. For those commercially successful writers, their placings on best-seller lists and through multimedia adaptations confirmed their location at the centre of a global creative economy, with a substantial dealing in rights sales for their work and its subsidiaries around the world. For the remainder, authorship remained an attractive proposition despite its financial difficulties, aided by the continued presence of authors in the media, and by their increasing visibility through events, festivals and social media. The remainder of this chapter explores authorship in the most recent historical period from 1970 to the present day, examining the economics and institutionalisation of authorship, the trends of celebrity and invisibility within the marketplace, and the twenty-first-century iteration of the 'author unbound'.

The economics of authorship

By 1984, Victor Bonham-Carter produced the second volume of his work in association with the Society of Authors, *Authors by profession*.[140] From this vantage point, he tracked how the Society had armed itself through statistical surveys to gain knowledge of the financial situation of its members, and a sense of the economic positioning of authorship more broadly. He gave particular credit to Richard Findlater's two volumes from the 1960s, *What are writers worth?* (1963) and *The book writers: who are they?* (1966), which, as articulated earlier in this chapter, clearly set out the position and economic fate of the author at the dawn of the period scrutinised here. Findlater's statement that the 'book industry is booming' but 'book writing is not' was a rallying call for authors. A further survey conducted in 1972 by the Society of Authors yielded similar commentary from Findlater in the pages of *The Author*. Noting that '*Everything* has gone up' (annual production of titles;

---

140 Bonham-Carter, *Authors by profession*, vol. 2.

the value of export trade; library borrowing; the increase of paperback sales; the prices of books; and the profits of publishers), he asked:

> surely the author's income from his book has gone up too? ... On the contrary: this year's survey reveals that the situation is *worse*. After six years the national scandal persists. Our society has more reason than ever to be ashamed of the way in which it rewards most living authors of its books.[141]

One of the chief criticisms to emerge from Findlater's commentary, according to Bonham-Carter, was 'the scandal of massive public lending of copyright works without remuneration of any kind to the author beyond the royalties deriving from the purchase of copies required for library use'.[142] Bonham-Carter charts the campaign for Public Lending Right (PLR) beginning in 1951, with a letter from the novelist John Brophy to *The Author*. This opening sally, however, drew ire from public librarians as it proposed that readers should pay one penny for each in-copyright title borrowed, thus undermining the principles of free public library use.[143] The first parliamentary Bill (an amendment to the Public Libraries Act 1892) was presented to the House of Commons in 1960. Its lack of success would lead to over two decades of campaigning, information finding (including Arts Council-sponsored trips to Denmark and Sweden to report on Scandinavian initiatives and processes), argumentation, proposals, and test runs.[144] A Department of Education and Science working group was set up in 1971 to examine proposals, and produced a 1972 report which gained traction with both the Society of Authors and the Publishers Association. However, five writers (Brigid Brophy, Michael Levey, Maureen Duffy, Francis King and Lettice Cooper) objected to the proposed ideas (surcharging on the published price of a book, or blanket licensing). The Writers' Action Group (WAG) they formed instead argued for a form of PLR which was based on actual lending statistics, not library purchases.[145] Debates and arguments rumbled on, with WAG's attack on the Society of Authors' position creating a schism among authors. It was not until 1979 that a Bill was finally passed in parliament based on the principle of actual lending of titles.[146]

It would still take until 1982 before authors saw any payment from PLR, but the principle was established in law, premised on book borrowing via libraries and a transaction underpinned by copyright. The money delivered by PLR was, however, limited: in 1985, £2 million was shared among 9,000

141 Cited in *ibid.*, p. 98.   142 *Ibid.*, p. 97.   143 *Ibid.*, pp. 101–2.   144 *Ibid.*, pp. 104–5.
145 *Ibid.*, pp. 107.   146 *Ibid.*, p. 109.

writers, with £5 million shared between 24,000 a decade later. The maximum amount any writer could receive was capped at £6,000, with only 135 writers granted more than £5,000 in 1995.[147] The annual collation of lending data by public libraries enabled the assemblage of 'most borrowed' lists, providing stimulating data for historians of reading. For authors, these figures largely reflected those in the commercial marketplace, with popular fiction being the most heavily borrowed. By the end of the period under study, in 2017, £6 million was distributed to authors for borrowing, with the cap of £6,600 received by 205 authors. The same year, PLR was extended to e-book lending under the Digital Economy Bill, with the first payments to be made in 2020.[148] The establishment of PLR was an important principle, but, as one observer put it, 'PLR on the scale at which it will be awarded in Britain can only be a supplement to income; welcome enough, doubtless, as a token of goodwill but not of substantial value as an instrument of patronage.'[149]

As the 1970s progressed, the 'Americanisation' of the British publishing industry (or, at least, the trade sector of the industry), and a shift towards a best-seller culture, had its impact on author advances.[150] John Sutherland depicted the 'impatience with the pettiness of the British scale of doing things' in the 1970s, with the illustration of Anthony Burgess refusing a 'paltry £1,000' advance from a British publisher: 'I'm fed up with being humble when Mario Puzo can get two and a half million dollars for 500 pages and characters saying things like, "I knew he was full of shit".'[151] The deregulation of the financial markets enabled the intensification of UK publishing through the 1970s and 1980s, enabling rising advance levels, for some authors at least.[152] The clamour for high advances from both mass-market and more literary writers reached its apogee in the case of Martin Amis's *The information* (1995), for which Amis's new US agent Andrew Wylie (popularly nicknamed 'The Jackal') negotiated a substantial advance of £500,000 from HarperCollins UK.[153] This financial transaction led to a substantial marketing campaign for a novel about literary rivalry, and a backlash from other writers led by A. S. Byatt, whose comments in the *Guardian* introduced a gendered critique to the debate about 'Americanisation' and large advances, seeing them as 'a kind of male turkey-

---

147 Stevenson, *The last of England?*, pp. 153–4.
148 'Remote ebook lending and UK PLR', www.bl.uk/plr/plr-news.
149 Sutherland, *Fiction and the fiction industry*, p. 129.
150 Sutherland, *Bestsellers*, chapter 1; Squires, *Marketing literature*, chapter 4.
151 Sutherland, *Bestsellers*, p. 27, citing a *Guardian* article of 29 September 1978.
152 Squires, *Marketing literature*, p. 21.   153 *Ibid.*, pp. 115–18.

cocking which is extremely bad for the industry and makes life hard for young authors'.[154]

The number of literary agents in the UK rose in the post-war period, and accelerated rapidly from the 1970s. Legat's *An author's guide to literary agents* notes a doubling of agents from 1946 to 1975 (thirty-nine to eighty), and ever upwards to 138 in 1995.[155] The 1980s in particular was a period in which the literary agent came to reign over trade publishing in the UK, although Murray argues that these 'brokers' of world literary rights were not the 'prime mover' of change but 'a serendipitous beneficiary of structural industry realignments'.[156] Nonetheless, literary agents have been central to the business of authorship in the latter part of the twentieth century, exploiting a multitude of intellectual property rights for their author-clients, and simultaneously protecting and diversifying their interests in the global and increasingly digital literary marketplace.

Alongside some high advances, the opportunities for additional rights revenue negotiated by literary agents from translation, subsidiary and multimedia rights developed in this period (see Chapter 29). Yet a more typical narrative of authorship in the latter period confirms Sutherland's assertion in 1978 that 'Authorship has always been a badly paid profession.'[157] In 1998, in association with bookseller Waterstone's, an update of the 1946 *Horizon* survey discussed above revealed as disheartening a picture of the economics of authorship as its predecessor. 'Anyone looking in this survey of literary living standards', wrote the editors, 'for lurid tales of sky-high advances and lotus-eating lifestyles may get something of a shock when reading the responses of our contributors.'[158] Similarly, the periodic surveys made by the Society of Authors and the ALCS (Authors' Licensing and Collecting Society) into the lot of writers successively and repeatedly revealed financial difficulty and sometimes penury, alongside the much rarer high-earner. From the 1960s, the Society of Authors surveys showed a consistent downward trend in the number of writers who could support themselves solely through their writing (half in 1966; a third in 1971; a sixth in 1981; and by the end of the 1990s one in seven).[159] At the turn of the century, the average annual salary derived from freelance writing was £16,600. While 5 per cent earned over £75,000, 75 per cent earned under

---

154 'In the pay of the Jackal', *Guardian* 7 January 1995, cited in Joe Moran, *Star authors*, p.151.
155 Legat, *An author's guide*, p. 36.   156 Murray, *The adaptation industry*, p. 51.
157 Sutherland, *Fiction and the fiction industry*, p. 107.
158 Holgate and Wilson-Fletcher (eds.), *The cost of letters*, p. vii.
159 Stevenson, *The last of England?*, p. 157.

£20,000, and 46 per cent under £5,000.[160] By 2015, the financial situation for writers deteriorated further, with advances declining or not being received at all. An ALCS survey further revealed that, compared to 2005, when 40 per cent of professional writers earned their income solely from writing, by 2013 the percentage had dropped to 11.5 per cent. Moreover, the median income of writers had dropped from £12,330 to £11,000 in 2013.[161] The proliferation of broadsheet newspapers and relatively well-paid arts journalism sustained many writers in the 1980s to the mid-1990s. D. J. Taylor comments that 'A freelance critic with an annual contract for the *Sunday Times* who, additionally, reviewed for a daily newspaper while keeping his, or her, hand in with the weeklies, could earn between £15,000 and £20,000 a year from literary journalism.'[162] The slump of newspaper sales thereafter, however, curtailed a once steady source of income. The institutionalisation of authorship via forms of state support and creative writing programmes in universities, as well as additional fees earned from author appearances at events, became a crucial additional financial support structure, as subsequent sections of this chapter detail.

With the introduction of Amazon's Kindle to the UK in 2010, e-book royalty rates became a point of contention between authors, their agents, literary estates and publishers, with renegotiations needed for existing contracts which had not envisioned e-book rights. The initial low rates offered by publishers pushed some authors and estates into alternative arrangements. Ian Fleming's estate, for example, licensed e-book rights to Ian Fleming Publications in 2010, rather than Penguin, the print publisher of the James Bond books.[163] The same year, Andrew Wylie set up Odyssey Editions to publish his agency's authors directly with Amazon, with a list including Salman Rushdie and Philip Roth as well as Martin Amis.[164] In 2011, Catherine Cookson's agent made a deal to publish her e-book backlist direct with Amazon, arguing at the same time that Transworld had been doing little

160 Kate Pool, 'Love, not money: the survey of authors' earnings', *Author* III:2 (2000), pp. 58–66, cited in Squires, *Marketing literature*, p. 36.
161 The Authors' Licensing and Collecting Society, 'What are words worth now? further findings' (2017), https://wp.alcs.co.uk/app/uploads/2017/07/Authors-earning-further-findings-2017-download-version.pdf.
162 Taylor, *The prose factory*, p. 426.
163 Robert McCrum, 'Fleming estate cuts out Penguin as James Bond goes digital', *Guardian* 8 November 2010, www.theguardian.com/books/2010/nov/08/fleming-estate-james-bond.
164 Richard Lea, 'Wylie's Amazon deal brings the end of the publishing world nigh', *Guardian* 23 July 2010, www.theguardian.com/books/booksblog/2010/jul/23/authors-amazon-deal-publishing.

to promote the saga writer's brand.[165] In 2013, mountaineer Joe Simpson rejected the 25 per cent e-book royalty deal offered by Random House to publish directly.[166] Some of these ploys ended up as negotiating tools rather than 'curtains for conventional publishing', as one headline put it.[167] Fleming's estate negotiated a new print and e-book deal with Random House in 2012 (although with the merger of Penguin and Random House in 2013 the licences came under the same corporate ownership again). E-book royalty rates remained a point of contention at the end of the period, allowing Amazon's e-book split of up to 70 per cent for the author seem an attractive proposition for self-publishers, and disrupting the relationships between authors and publishers. The economics of authorship, then, remained contentious and a cause of strife through the period, with sporadic high-earners only serving to increase feelings of exploitation and precarity among others.

The institutionalisation of authorship

Using the case of J. B. Priestley's 1951 comic novel *Festival at Farbridge* (the plot of which involves a provincial South Midlands town in the year of the Festival of Britain), D. J. Taylor makes the case for Priestley's (not entirely positive) perception of the future of English literature lying in both its 'professionalisation' and 'institutionalisation'.[168] Aspects of this future were already well established by 1970: the place of English literature within universities, and the beginnings of the campaign that would eventually see authors' rights enshrined in PLR, as discussed above. From 1970 onwards, the trend of professionalisation and institutionalisation would develop further, through the establishment of the Arts Council's Literature Panel, in the growth of creative writing within the academy, and in an events-based book culture.

The Labour Minister Jennie Lee's 1966 white paper *A policy for the arts* noted that 'painters, poets, sculptors, writers and musicians are sometimes lost to art for lack of a comparatively small sum of money which would support their start in life'.[169] The paper thus established a principle of supporting individual writers, and of artistic labour as work, thereby extending cultural subsidy's focus on institutions to patronage of individual artists.

---

165 'Catherine Cookson estate goes direct in e-book deal', *Bookseller* 28 March 2011, www.thebookseller.com/news/catherine-cookson-estate-goes-direct-e-book-deal.
166 Alison Flood, 'Joe Simpson dumps "bullying" publisher over ebook royalties', *Guardian* 10 January 2013, www.theguardian.com/books/2013/jan/10/joe-simpson-publisher-ebook-royalties.
167 Lea, 'Wylie's Amazon deal brings the end of the publishing world nigh'.
168 Taylor, *The prose factory*, pp. 333–4.
169 Cited in Sutherland, *Fiction and the fiction industry*, p. 131.

Two years previously the Publishers Association had encouraged the Arts Council's existing Poetry Panel to expand into a full 'Literature Panel', which duly began its business in 1966.[170] In its first year (1966–67), it granted almost £18,000 of its approximately £50,000 budget to bursaries for writers.[171] By the mid-1970s, however, statistics reproduced by Sutherland bear testament to an 'apparent meagreness of literature's slice of state patronage': the Arts Council's funds was only three-quarters of 1 per cent of the budget of the Department of Education and Science; of which 1 per cent went to literature; and of which approximately 15 to 20 per cent went directly to writers. In 1973–74, for example, the total budget for the Arts Council was £17,541,961. Of this, £146,278 was allocated to literature in England, of which £41,500 was grants to authors.[172]

Sutherland argues the 'apparent meagreness' of state patronage was to some degree mitigated by literature support in the form of libraries which were funded by local authorities, as well as having a 'large, commercially successful sector adjacent to it which has hitherto been willing to subsidise literary merit out of book-profits'.[173] Perhaps in the face of such claims about the commercial nature of publishing, and also as a criticism of the decisions the Literature Panel made in heavily funding the literary journal the *New Review*, the book club the New Fiction Society, and literary tours outside of the metropolitan centres, it struggled to sustain an argument for state funding. By 1984, in the wake of the Arts Council's *The glory of the garden* report, funding for literature was halved from £1 million to £500,000, on the basis that the impact of literary funding was 'highly marginal' in terms of enlarging audiences, and that whereas opera and the theatre could barely survive without funding, literature would survive through its commercial underpinning.[174] The argument about state subsidy versus publishing as a commercial business would continue to arise in funding literature, with the amounts allocated to it continually well below that of other art forms. The 2017 Arts Council England report *Literature in the 21st century: understanding models of support for literary fiction* re-emphasised the continuing, and worsening, financial difficulties of non-commercial writers, their need for cultural funding, and for a supportive and supported ecosystem (including independent publishers and bookshops).[175]

Reflecting on his foundation of the first Creative Writing degree in Britain at UEA (the University of East Anglia) in 1970 with fellow novelist Angus

---

170 Taylor, *The prose factory*, p. 339. 171 *Ibid.*, p. 340.
172 Sutherland, *Fiction and the fiction industry*, p. 132. 173 *Ibid.*, p. 133.
174 Taylor, *The prose factory*, p. 348. 175 *Literature in the 21st century*.

Wilson, Malcolm Bradbury wrote that 'a course of this kind, conducted from the distance of an academic environment, distinct from the commercial marketplace, could have some impact on the state of serious fiction in Britain'.[176] As earlier sections of the chapter indicate, before 1970 universities had offered writers security against the economic pressures of the marketplace by offering them lecturing posts and hence a source of regular income. However, it was not until this later period that universities turned to another aspect of 'Americanisation' in the form of the creative writing programme. Before then, as Sutherland notes, 'Britain had no boom equivalent to America's', even a 'British boycott of campus writers'.[177] The development of creative writing within the US academy had been early, with the University of Iowa programme established in 1936, following more informal classes from 1897. By 1975, there were already over fifty formal American programmes.[178] UEA's establishment of its MA in Creative Writing in 1970 was therefore a departure, although the University of Stirling's English Department had written into its constitution from its foundation in 1967 'a commitment to creative writing . . . as part of a radical revision of the usual British degree'. Stirling's (then) unusual coursework assessment enabled this, with students allowed to submit creative writing rather than traditional academic dissertations at the end of their degree.[179] But it was with the UEA programme that creative writing made its name in the UK. Bradbury and Wilson were fortunate in their first (and only) student, Ian McEwan, whose first story collection *First love, last rites* (1975) established his name, and the reputation of the course. Indeed, by 1992, Bradbury's reflection on the growth of creative writing turned somewhat sardonic:

> In the past few years, British universities, polytechnics, schools and even kindergartens have seen a massive growth occur in a subject that not too long ago was regarded as a suspect American import . . . It is called Creative Writing, and, along with other latter-day or postmodern activities like Media Studies or Women's Studies, has turned into one of the subjects of the season. Besides achieving academic recognition, it has spread freely through the broader hinterland. Farmhouse seminars, weekend courses, evening writing workshops, postal courses and handy mercantile handbooks encourage all of us to develop the obscure quality known as creativity or stimulate

176 Bradbury, 'The bridgeable gap', p. 7. Cited in Dawson, *Creative writing and the new humanities*, p. 19.
177 Sutherland, *Fiction and the fiction industry*, pp. 150, 151.
178 McGurl, *The program era*, pp. 24–5.
179 Rory Watson, 'History of creative writing', https://creativewritingstirling.wordpress.com/about.

the belief that we can all soon be running off with the Booker Prize, or writing scripts for *Casualty*.[180]

Bradbury's comments position the desire for creative writing across the literary and commercial divides (gestured towards by his mention of the Booker Prize and the BBC's hospital TV drama). The period from 1970 upholds his perspective. By 2017, NAWE (the National Association of Writers in Education) counted more than eighty universities offering creative writing in taught undergraduate or postgraduate programmes, and more than fifty PhDs in creative writing.[181] Such programmes are staffed by professional writers, providing steady employment, particularly in the face of the decline of income from literary journalism. The workshop – in which students with tutors read and critique work in development – is central to the pedagogy of creative writing programmes. As avenues for short story publication also declined, the workshop nonetheless sustained the genre.

Outside the formal framework of university courses, there was also a growth of informal writing teaching, with Arvon – a network of residential writing programmes around the UK – setting up in 1968 with the original aim of providing poetry teaching for school children by poets John Moat and John Fairfax, 'as a place where individuals, and in particular young committed writers, could be given a sanctuary away from . . . the creative deprivation imposed by the system of standard education – and there offered . . . the guidance of writers'.[182] Arvon grew into a national creative writing network, including from 1975 Lumb Bank, the former Yorkshire home of Ted Hughes.

Additional income sources, and opportunities for promotion, arose over the period with the growth of book festivals and other literary events (see Chapter 30). In the wake of post-war festivals and events including the Cheltenham Literature Festival and Edinburgh's International Writers' Conference, the Arts Council's Literature Panel organised writers' tours around the country. The first was held in 1969 in North Wales, and led by Angus Wilson, who was the Literature Panel's new chairman, along with authors Nell Dunn, Christopher Logue and Margaret Drabble. Drabble commented that the tour was 'hectic, non-glamorous and very stimulating'.[183] This and subsequent tours were done in the name of increasing access to literature, but led some writers to question the purpose and their

---

180 Bradbury, 'The bridgeable gap', p. 7.
181 NAWE, 'Writing courses', www.nawe.co.uk/writing-in-education/writing-at-univer sity/writing-courses.html.
182 Arvon, 'History of Arvon', www.arvon.org/about-us/history-arvon.
183 Cited in Taylor, *The prose factory*, p. 346.

interactions with their audiences. Shiva Naipaul's frustration on tour in Humberside in 1978 was particularly critical, commenting that 'The ignorance I have so far encountered – and not simply of cultural matters but of the world lying beyond the borders of daily experience – has an almost medieval quality.'[184] Taylor comments that the perceived success of the tours lay in the 'temperament of the participants', but also was hindered by 'the piecemeal nature of the enterprise', with no concerted engagement plan or understanding of local audiences.[185] A fuller history of the Arts Council's dealings with literature is yet to be written, but the writers' tours of 1969 onwards were a stage in the ever more public role of the writer, which is discussed in more detail below.

Marketplace presence, celebrity and invisibility

Writers would be thrust into the literary spotlight, and literature itself further organised and canonised in the post-1970 period, through the growing number, and importance, of book awards. Britain had literary awards before the end of the 1960s (including the James Tait Black Memorial Awards and Hawthornden Prize, both established in 1919), but it was not until the establishment of the Booker Prize in 1968 that Britain could claim to have a prize with the profile of the US's National Book Awards, or France's Prix Goncourt – both of which were used as potential models. The prize was initiated by two different organisations: the Publishers Association, spearheaded by Tom Maschler (Publishing Director at Jonathan Cape), and the food distribution, marketing, engineering and shipping company Booker McConnell.[186] Maschler's aim was to generate the kind of 'excitement [and] intellectual fervour' around books that he had seen in France over the Prix Goncourt.[187] The press release announcing the award made a claim for the promotional role the organisers hoped the prize would play in authors' careers:

> Although the sum of £5000 will be a generous award to the winning author, we hope that his real success will be a significant interest in the sales of his book and that this will to some extent be shared by not only the authors who have been short-listed, but, in the long run, by authors all over the country.

184 Cited in *ibid.*, p. 333.   185 *Ibid.*, pp. 347–8.
186 Squires, 'Literary prizes and awards'. For further histories and accounts of the Booker Prize, see Todd, *Consuming fictions* and English, *The economy of prestige*. See also Chapters 8 and 30 in this volume.
187 Tom Maschler, 'How it all began', p. 15, cited in Squires, 'Literary prizes and awards', p. 295.

A substantial literary prize should mean that a writer does not need to be censored, imprisoned, or labelled outrageous and controversial before hitting the headlines and will, we hope, help to narrow the all too frequent gap between artistic and commercial success.[188]

Written against the background of the censure and imprisonment of authors in the Soviet Union (and a gender bias in the perceived sex of a writer), the Booker Prize intended to bring critical acclaim and commercial success to British and Commonwealth writers. (The eligibility remit remained until 2014, when the prize opened out to any author writing in English published via the UK, thereby enabling US novels to compete.) Further book prizes were created in the wake of Booker's success, including the Whitbread (later Costa), which has the winners of various genre categories (including poetry, auto/biography and the novel) competing for an overall book of the year award, and, from 1996, the Orange Prize for Fiction, for novels by women. The latter was born in the wake of the 1991 Booker shortlist of six, which did not contain a single female writer, passing over – among others – Angela Carter and her final novel *Wise children* (1991).[189]

Issues of diversity and access to the literary marketplace remained a theme from 1970 onwards. The second-wave feminist publisher Virago was set up in 1973 to publish books by and about women (both new titles by authors such as Carter, Pat Barker and Margaret Atwood, and rediscovered classics), and to publish *by* women, a mission it still fulfils at the end of the period, although with a conglomerate owner.[190] Virago operated alongside magazine publisher *Spare Rib*, which was started in 1972 as a voice for the Women's Liberation Movement.[191] Both magazine and book publisher, along with presses including Onlywomen (which focussed on lesbian writers) and Sheba (writing by black, working-class and lesbian authors) would give exposure to female writers, opening up the gatekeeping processes of the publishing industry (see Chapter 27).

In the 2010s, however, issues of access and value still remained in regards to gender as well as other forms of intersectionality. The novelist Kamila Shamsie called for a 'Year of Publishing Women' in 2018, in response to the continuing dominance of male writers over literary prize submissions,

188 Publishers Association, Press Release, 4 October 1968, Box BP/BK1, Booker Prize Archive, Oxford Brookes University, Oxford. Cited in Squires, 'Literary prizes and awards', p. 296.
189 Women's Prize for Fiction, 'History', www.womensprizeforfiction.co.uk/about/history.
190 Murray, *Mixed media*.
191 The British Library has digitised Spare Rib at www.bl.uk/spare-rib.

shortlistings and winners, in World Book Night books, and (via Nicola Griffith's work) in the protagonists of prize-winning books.[192] Shamsie also pointed out all-male line-ups in festival panels, and the disproportionate space given to men in reviewing columns, as counted annually by the organisation VIDA: Women in Literary Arts.[193] The *London Review of Books* was a particular target of VIDA's statistics, with only 22 per cent of bylines by women, 18 per cent of their book reviewers female, and 26 per cent of reviewed books written by women in 2016, a pattern it had sustained since 2010. In the same year, the *Times Literary Supplement* had only 27 per cent of bylines from women, 38 per cent of its book reviewers, and 29 per cent of its reviewed authors. While the journal *Granta* had marginally more women than men published in 2016, a severe imbalance in the coverage given to female writers (both as literary journalists and as book authors) still remained forty years after *Spare Rib* and Virago began their work.[194]

VIDA's move to a greater intersectional analysis indicated gender was not the only demographic or identity form with restricted access to authorship. At the time of writing, the access of people of colour to authorship and publishing remains a serious concern, as a 2015 report commissioned by writer development agency Spread the Word evidenced.[195] This report, along with a year in which the children's CILIP Carnegie Medal's longlist was exclusively white, pushed writers Sunny Singh and Nikesh Shukla to set up the Jhalak Prize for Book of the Year by a Writer of Colour in 2016. As the announcement of the prize argued:

> the prize exists . . . to celebrate the achievements of British writers of colour. That we live in a mono-cultural literary landscape has been proven time and again, with the Writing the Future report . . . the backlash following last year's all-white World Book Night booklist and frustrations echoed by writers of colour who feel that their work is often marginalised unless it fulfils a romantic fetishization of their cultural heritage.[196]

192 Kamila Shamsie, 'Let's have a year of publishing only women – a provocation', *Guardian* 5 June 2015, www.theguardian.com/books/2015/jun/05/kamila-shamsie-20 18-year-publishing-women-no-new-books-men. Nicola Griffith, 'Books about women don't win big awards: some data', https://nicolagriffith.com/2015/05/26/books-abo ut-women-tend-not-to-win-awards.
193 www.vidaweb.org. VIDA initially began by counting gender in literary reviews, but has extended its survey data to various forms of intersectionality.
194 'The 2016 VIDA count: the big picture gets bigger: commitment to intersectionality', www.vidaweb.org/the-2016-vida-count.
195 Spread the Word, *Writing the future*.
196 Media Diversified, 'The Jhalak Prize for Book of the Year by a writer of colour', https:// mediadiversified.org/about-us/the-jhalak-prize. Cited in Squires, 'Publishing's diversity deficit', p. 3.

As the final section of this chapter indicates, digital technologies have enabled approaches to the market and to readers which have the potential to sidestep the traditional gatekeeping processes of publishing.

The increasingly commercial pressure of the literary marketplace, alongside diminishing financial returns for many (if not all) writers, has made an intensely competitive environment for authorship.[197] While Wylie achieved a large advance for Amis, and indeed Amis's antagonist Byatt revealed that she had spent her Booker Prize winnings for *Possession* in 1990 on a swimming pool for her house in the south of France, other 'midlist' writers have struggled to achieve sales and marketplace presence, and to convince publishers to continue offering them contracts, particularly after sales data became more readily available to publishers with Nielsen BookScan.[198] Alongside the manifold possibilities for authors to appear in the public via promotional events including book festivals, author events in bookshops, appearances on television, radio and (latterly) social media – the 'journalistic capital' observed by James English – there is a concomitant invisibility, what Karl Miller called a 'painful soundlessness in the utterance of writers'.[199]

Celebrity of a very different kind confronted Salman Rushdie, in the most visible, and contested, example of authorship in the period. His novel *The satanic verses* (1988) was deemed blasphemous to Islam by the Iranian Ayatollah Khomeini, who issued a fatwa. The fatwa forced Rushdie to live in hiding for many years, a period of time he chronicled in his memoir *Joseph Anton* (2012). Others involved in the book's publication were also under threat, with the Japanese translator killed, the Italian translator stabbed and the Norwegian publisher shot. The book was burned on the streets of Bradford (an event later satirised in Zadie Smith's novel *White teeth* (2000)), British bookshops which stocked the book were bombed, and hundreds were killed in protests against the book in countries including India and Turkey.[200] As a consequence, discussions about freedom of speech, censorship and authorial self-censorship became part of the fabric of literary life in the twenty-first century.

---

197 Squires, *Marketing literature*, pp. 34–9.
198 Boyd Tonkin, 'The books interview, A S Byatt: sun stroke and inner lights', *Independent* 7 November 1998, www.independent.co.uk/arts-entertainment/the-books-interview-a-s-byatt-sun-strokes-and-inner-lights-1183283.html. See also Squires, *Marketing literature*, p. 30.
199 English, 'Winning the culture game', p. 123; Miller, *Authors*, p. 192, cited in Squires, *Marketing literature*, p. 37.
200 Andrew Anthony, 'How one book ignited a culture war', *Guardian* 11 January 2009, www.theguardian.com/books/2009/jan/11/salman-rushdie-satanic-verses.

Very different types of invisibility and marketplace presence were apparent at the end of the twentieth and beginning of the twenty-first centuries in the use of ghostwriters and brand-named fiction factories, particularly for books purportedly written by celebrities, sports people and politicians.[201] Glamour model Katie Price 'authored' a series of children's books, footballer David Beckham an autobiography, and YouTube vlogger Zoella the book *Girl online* (2014). The most discussed case of ghostwriting arose with the autobiography of Wikileaks' founder Julian Assange, which was contracted to be secretly ghostwritten by novelist Andrew O'Hagan. After Assange and his publisher arrived at irreconcilable differences, O'Hagan published a lengthy article about his experiences.[202]

The writing life continues to have an allure into the twenty-first century, both for those who want to write, and for those who contract others to write for them. The polling company YouGov reported in 2015 that one of its surveys had 'Author' as its most popular desired job, with 60 per cent of respondents saying they would like to write for a living.[203] Despite all the financial difficulties of the writing life, the enormous marketplace presence of writers as diverse as literary novelist Ali Smith, erotic fiction author E. L. James with her *Fifty shades of grey* trilogy, J. K. Rowling with her Harry Potter series of children's books, and Lee Child and his thriller protagonist Jack Reacher, make authorship both visible and attractive. Child enabled remarkable insight into his creative process by allowing academic Andy Martin to sit with him while he was writing his 2015 novel *Make me*, and to discuss with him his processes and decisions.[204]

The author unbound?

The increasingly digital twenty-first century has, like many aspects of the book in Britain, brought change to authorial life, and altered relationships between authors, publishers and readers.[205] Social media have enabled authors to speak directly to their readers via a multitude of platforms, including Facebook, Twitter, Instagram, with blogs and on YouTube. Rowling's reach on Twitter is vast (over 13 million followers by 2017), replicating her fanbase and her potential to communicate news, respond to

---

201 Knapp and Hulbert, *Ghostwriting*, pp. 126–45.
202 The article initially appeared as 'Ghosting' in the *London Review of Books*, and was subsequently republished in O'Hagan, *The secret life*.
203 Will Dahlgreen, 'Bookish Britain: literary jobs are the most desirable', https://yougov .co.uk/news/2015/02/15/bookish-britain-academic-jobs-are-most-desired.
204 Martin, *Reacher said nothing*.
205 Ray Murray and Squires, 'The digital publishing communications circuit'.

fans, engage in political debate and promote causes she aligns with. When Rowling introduced Pottermore, the series' online presence, she called it her 'magical corner of the internet', with a direct address in the second person to fans: 'Pottermore is a place where you can unleash your imagination and allow it to lead you on adventures; if you need a little extra magic in your life, well, you've come to the right place.'[206] The appeal to her readers creates an intimate relationship with the author, and her books and characters as textual creations also housed, and extended, on the internet. Author–fan relationships in the digital environment can also create discord. The rebranding of the Pottermore site in 2015 created consternation among some fans with the loss of messageboard functionality and aspects of the site's previous iteration (including its sorting hat). Fans expressed their unhappiness on social media, forcing Rowling and Pottermore to respond. Rowling's huge fanbase also generated unofficial websites such as Steve VanderArk's The Harry Potter Lexicon. When a print publisher in the USA planned to produce a book based on VanderArk's website, however, Rowling initiated and won a court case for breach of copyright.[207]

Other texts with their origins in fandom have fared better. E. L. James, author of the *Fifty shades* series (2011–17), began writing online fan fiction of Stephenie Meyer's young adult vampire books, *Twilight* (2005–8), under the pseudonym 'Snowqueens Icedragon'. James's fan engagement turned the burgeoning teen romances of *Twilight* into something much more explicit, publishing erotic instalments on FanFiction.net as *Masters of the universe*. After rewriting the texts to remove the Twilight references, James published the book with a small Australian print-on-demand company, The Writers' Coffeehouse, before eventually being picked up by Random House and selling many more copies than its original inspiration, *Twilight*.[208] Fan fiction might normally be categorised as an activity by readers, but the generative possibilities of online publication led to James's titles becoming huge international mega-sellers, spawning film franchises, and a range of merchandise including branded wine and sex toys.

Avenues for self-publishing have developed from the vanity press of print culture to easy-to-use digital platforms, such as Amazon's Kindle Direct

206 'J K Rowling welcomes you to the brand new Pottermore', 22 September 2015, www .pottermore.com/news/j-k-rowling-welcome-message.
207 Tom Leonard, 'J K Rowling wins copyright battle over Harry Potter lexicon', *Telegraph* 8 September 2008, www.telegraph.co.uk/news/celebritynews/2707165/JK-Rowling-wins-copyright-battle-over-Harry-Potter-lexicon.html.
208 Kirschenbaum and Werner, 'Digital scholarship', pp. 449–50.

Publishing and Wattpad. Some writers remain on the platforms, but others use their self-publishing success to springboard writing careers with traditional publishers. The crime writer James Oswald is one British example; despite his first two unpublished novels being shortlisted for the CWA (Crime Writers' Association) Debut Dagger Award, he could not find a publisher, so uploaded his books to Amazon. His initial sales were very low, but after making the title free he achieved downloads of 1,500–2,000 copies a day, top place on the Kindle free chart, and a mainstream publishing deal with Penguin.[209] Self, or 'indie', publishing has enabled authors to get published without the filter of traditional gatekeeping processes, drawing instead on networks of digital influencers.[210] Other authors and new publishers have used digital platforms to crowdfund books. Nikesh Shukla's edited collection *The good immigrant* (2016), featuring essays by BAME (Black and Minority Ethnic) writers, was funded via the publishing-specific Unbound. Edinburgh-based 404 Ink used Kickstarter to fund *Nasty women* (2017), a collection of essays on intersectional feminism, as did Liverpool's Dead Ink, whose title *Know your place* (2017), a book of 'essays on the working class by the working class', found its origins on Twitter.

Authors with well-established mainstream track records have turned to social media for creative purposes. In 2014 the novelist David Mitchell published the short story 'The right sort' on Twitter in advance of the publication of his new novel *The bone clocks* (2014).[211] The timing meant that the story was seen as promotional rather than an aesthetic experiment in its own right, and Mitchell openly stated his publisher had developed the idea for the story. Yet Mitchell went on to develop the story as a full novel, *Slade house* (2015), with one of its characters tweeting from @I_Bombadil, showing the interplay of traditional authorship with that mediated by the digital.

As the technologies of the book have proliferated and exploded in the twenty-first century, making them more available to authors who can choose to sidestep the intermediaries of literary agent, publisher, printer or bookseller, it remains a question as to whether those technologies have emancipated the author. Is the author now beyond gatekeeping processes, with digital platforms offering unfettered and instantaneous access to global

209 Writers and Artists, 'Interview with James Oswald', www.writersandartists.co.uk/w riters/advice/401/self-publishing/interviews-on-self-publishing.
210 Ramdarshan Bold, 'The return of the social author'.
211 Ian Crouch, 'The great American Twitter novel', *The New Yorker* 23 July 2014, www .newyorker.com/books/page-turner/great-american-twitter-novel.

markets? In theory this is the case, and many thousands of authors have indeed unbound themselves (with the help of various technology companies) from the traditional structures – and strictures – of the publishing industry. And yet others desire to transfer from their status of indie author to mainstream, or traditional authorship, while others retain strong relationships from the foundations of their career with legacy publishing. The 'unbound' author of the early twenty-first century is both a fact and a persuasive narrative fiction, which demonstrates (alongside the increasing hold of technologies companies) a continuing aspiration to authorship. The economic pressures and cultural values that this entails across the period addressed by this volume are historically specific, contingent upon commercial, sociological and technological change. Wherever it may go in the future, the proliferation of authorship online proves an ongoing desire to write and communicate in the digital age.

5

Publishing

DAVID FINKELSTEIN AND ALISTAIR MCCLEERY

By 1914, British publishing was embedded in professional structures that would sustain business success for much of the century.[1] Associations representing key players in the field were firmly in place, including the Society of Authors (founded in 1884), the Publishers Association (founded in 1896) and the Associated Booksellers of Great Britain and Ireland (founded in 1895). Similarly, the entrance of the literary agent as mediator between creators, producers and distributors of textual material ensured that print material was recirculated in a growing variety of media (from periodicals, newspapers and books through to theatre, film and, later, radio). The US Chace Act of 1891 allowed some measure of protection for British authors seeking remuneration from their transatlantic publications, while the 1911 UK Copyright Act updated practices to extend copyright protection in published works to an author's lifetime plus fifty years. Further stability in book prices emerged after a period of unsustainable, cut-throat pricing practices following the demise in 1894 of the three-volume format for the publishing of most new works of fiction. Retailers eventually agreed to the Net Book Agreement (NBA), a consensual fixed pricing arrangement for new works implemented in January 1900 (fiction remained outside the agreement until the First World War). The NBA, which set minimum price and discount levels for all books sold in the UK, remained in place until 1997 (although it had been undermined from 1995) and provided a level of stability in price margins that benefited booksellers and publishers alike.

International trade organisations and agreements aimed at standardising and monitoring world trade in general and the book trade in specific matched such national activities. The Berne Convention of 1886 established the principle of international copyright that was subsequently built on in treaties negotiated at key points throughout the twentieth century. Issues such as

---

1 For the pre-history, see McKitterick, 'Introduction'.

international communication structures found expression in the creation of standardised measurements of time (via agreeing the International Date Line of Greenwich Mean Time in 1884); standardised weight authorities (creation of the International Bureau of Weights and Measures in 1875); standardised postal rates (establishment of the Universal Postal Union in 1874) and the development of the Universal Radiotelegraph Union in 1906. These ensured 'the establishment of regulatory regimes for, in principle, the predictable and orderly conduct of pressing transnational processes'.[2] The new structures enhanced international, particularly UK/US, collaboration rather than competition, through the development of a stable international market protected by the legalities of international copyright law, and represented the initial foundations for the emergence of a global industry, dominated by a small number of transnational companies, by the end of the twentieth century.

Such changes in nineteenth- and early twentieth-century legal statutes, technology and business practices also worked in general to create opportunities for printed texts to be manufactured more quickly and cheaply, advertised more widely, and sold and distributed more extensively, and served as sources of increasing profits for authors, printers, publishers and distributors. Economic integration of goods and capital markets was exemplified in particular by the dominance by British publishers of colonial markets, what one might categorise as an initial wave of globalisation that would give way later in the century to the rise of transnational conglomerates led by North American and European competitors. New figures entered publishing after each World War and in the generation afterwards, adding fresh vigour to the industry, reforming its practices and introducing innovations designed to capture new or neglected markets. Publishing was regarded by many of them as a vehicle for encouraging social change, reflecting liberal, socialist or, later, feminist perspectives, often through challenges to the last remaining legal restrictions upon publishing, namely, those statutes or procedures that enshrined particular views of sexual morality or social behaviour. As the twentieth century closed, individual entrepreneurship did not sit well within the corporate publishing structures that had emerged from the 1970s onwards. Publishing conglomerates increased both vertical and horizontal integration while often consolidating around educational publishing, a trend that had begun after the First World War. No new generation appeared from within publishing to shake up its practices; yet the entrepreneurs behind companies such as Apple, Amazon and Google, from outside

2 Held *et al.*, *Global transformations*, p. 43.

publishing, created a revolution in the delivery of content and in the business relationship between publisher, distributor and reader that by the time of writing had not yet concluded.

1914–1918

When war was declared on 4 August 1914, the British publishing and print industry was steering a generally sedate course, depending on a steady flow of sales from long-worn if comfortable print formats and price structures.[3] The onset of war brought with it challenges that many publishers struggled to cope with. Not least was the immediate struggle to source the raw material needed to produce printed work. Paper proved one of the most difficult commodities for which to obtain a steady and consistent supply, with its importation severely rationed as the war effort progressed. In December 1917, for example, the British government reduced levels of finished paper and raw material importation for business use for 1918 from 540,000 to 390,000 tons, of which less than 14,000 tons was utilised for book publishing.[4] Stanley Unwin reflected in later years that such paper rationing severely restricted the industry's ability to meet increased public demand for reading material, with prices rising accordingly and to the publishers' detriment. 'There were times when we paid as much as 1s 7d a pound for paper greatly inferior to what we could have bought at 2¼d before the war', he complained. 'In brief, as in the Second World War, paper was priority number one.'[5]

Copper for block making, electrotyping and type foundry proved equally scarce, requisitioned for bullets and war machinery. By 1916 use of new metals in publishing such as zinc and lead was being prohibited unless exchanged for an equal amount of blocks and electrotypes from publishers' surplus stock. Similarly, strawboard used for the binding of books rose exponentially in price from £4 10s per ton pre-war to over £35 per ton in 1917, and used Monotype lead fetched an astonishing £36 per ton.[6]

Scarcity in raw materials was accompanied by scarcity in skilled labour. Despite the lobbying efforts of key publishers such as Heinemann, Stanley Unwin and others, printing and allied trades were not declared trades of national importance, so leaving them without protection against rationing of raw material and the conscription of men in the second half of the war. By the

3 See also Chapter 23.   4 Kingsford, *The Publishers Association*, p. 56.
5 Unwin, *The truth about a publisher*, p. 141.
6 Kingsford, *The Publishers Association*, p. 57; Howe, *The British Federation of Master Printers*, p. 57.

end of 1917, for example, military service had claimed over 7,000 of the 23,000 members registered with the Typographical Association, the main union representing compositors and journeymen printers in England and Wales.[7] This was accompanied by a general decrease over the decade in employment of labour across the paper, printing, books and stationery trades, which fell from a total of 397,000 in 1911 to 314,000 in 1921.[8] The depletion of trained male printing, publishing and allied trade workers, on the other hand, enabled an influx of women into areas previously closed to them. A small example, a survey of sixty-two out of eighty-two members of the Publishing Association in June 1918, serves to illustrate the effect of this shift in gender balance in the workplace. Members surveyed recorded a workforce in 1918 of 1,559 men of military age or over in their service, and 1,522 women and boys under age. This was in contrast to four years previously, when 2,891 men and 658 women and boys were recorded in employment.[9]

The effect of wartime privations on the look, feel, substance and quantity of published material was substantial, ranging from the imposition of a grey, harsh texture to paper due to restrictions on bleach for its softening and whitening, to the elimination or substitution of standard leather and gold tooling for inferior-quality material in book binding. When J. M. Dent's Everyman series of classics was forced to replace gold leaf with imitation gold on its spine, one commentator would later lament: 'The war had literally taken the glitter from Everyman's Library, just as it had tarnished everything else.'[10] Book output declined over the war period, even while reading demand soared: in 1913, the number of books published totalled 12,379, of which 9,451 were new titles; by 1918 book output totalled 7,716, of which 6,750 were new titles, a drop of 62 per cent and 28.5 per cent respectively.[11] Individual publisher's accounts reflect such precipitous drops, as in the case of Edward Arnold, which saw their new books listings fall from 130 titles in 1912 to just sixteen in 1918.[12]

Government strictures aimed at controlling and channelling the type of material produced for wartime readers at home and on the front added to publishing challenges. The 1914 Defence of the Realm Act (DORA), passed shortly after the outbreak of hostilities, made it an offence to issue material deemed to be of potential use to the enemy. To monitor publishing output in

7 Musson, *The Typographical Association*, p. 319.   8 Eliot, *Some patterns and trends*, p. 154.
9 Kingsford, *The Publishers Association*, p. 58.   10 Rose, 'J. M. Dent and Sons', p. 88.
11 Mumby, *Publishing and bookselling*, p. 371.
12 Bennett and Hamilton, 'Edwin Arnold', p. 21; Potter, 'For country, conscience and commerce', p. 14.

both book and periodical form, an official press censorship office was established. The Press Bureau (or as some waggishly renamed it, the 'Suppress Bureau') worked closely with the Admiralty and the War Office to control the type of material issued to the front, with secret lists drawn up of books and periodicals prohibited for export.[13] As the war dragged on, censorship became more intrusive: by 1917 all material initially approved for issuing in periodical form, for example, was subject to a second round of inspection if reissued in book format. Such was the case with a proposed 1917 reprinting by the Edinburgh publishers William Blackwood and Sons of 'Airman's outings', Officer Alan Bott's tales of flying exploits on the front first serialised in *Blackwood's Magazine*. The Press Bureau curtly informed the firm that approval for its republication, despite having passed the censors the first time round, was now dependent on a submission of two copies of the work in its proposed new form, with no guarantee of avoiding a second encounter with the dreaded censor's blue pencil.[14]

In alignment with this, several schemes were developed to engage readers actively with appropriate texts at home and on the front line. These included the British War Library, which initially sent used books to serving troops in France and the Middle East before focussing on supplying reading material to wounded and convalescing soldiers on home leave. It would ultimately be responsible for issuing over 6 million volumes in this fashion.[15] In addition, networks of camp and mobile libraries provided reading material to servicemen in the Royal Navy, the Flying Corps and the Army, while a Newspapers for the Fleet Scheme, administered by the London Chamber of Commerce, distributed newspapers, journals and literary periodicals to naval servicemen. At home, publishers organised National Book Fortnight in 1915 and 1916 to inspire home readers to buy and read new books and then send them to troops stationed overseas.

The results of such organised campaigns and strategic focussing on the direction of publishing was a stasis of textual production geared towards avoiding particularly sensitive issues – political, military, social – in favour of escapism or consensus-building support for the war effort.[16] Much of the best-selling fiction of the war period tended to be escapist in nature (see Chapter 23). By the end of the war, many firms were keen to branch out into new directions, and several smaller firms seized opportunities to restructure and redevelop their lists and interests appropriately.

---

13 Finkelstein, 'Literature, propaganda and the First World War', p. 94.   14 *Ibid.*, pp. 94–5.
15 Mumby, *Publishing and bookselling*, p. 376.   16 Potter, *Boys in khaki*, especially pp. 88–94.

1918–1939

After the end of the war, the print and publishing industry began to regroup within larger social and cultural contexts. On the one hand, the number of people employed in printing and allied trades in England and Wales rose as skilled workers demobbed and returned to their former employment: from 138,000 in 1911 to over 190,000 in 1931. On the other hand, the spread of Linotype and Monotype machinery throughout the print trade saw a displacement of traditional hand compositors in favour of machine operators: machine operator numbers in England and Wales rose from 3,156 in 1911 to 11,833 in 1931, while hand compositor numbers dropped precipitously from 26,487 in 1911 to 11,954 in 1931.[17] Letterpress printing saw great developments in technology that increased speed and efficiency in the printing process, including new and faster flat-bed and rotary presses, multiple process machines for cutting, scoring, folding and binding texts, and new processes for handling halftone, colour and photogravure imaging processes. Such improvements in efficiency enabled the costs of publishing and printing to drop, as did the relaxing of import duties on raw materials and a corresponding drop in paper prices from wartime highs.

Thomas Nelson & Sons, based in Edinburgh, was typical of the family-led publishing houses such as Macmillan, Blackwood's and John Murray, that had prospered before the First World War in conditions of stability at home and expanding markets overseas, but which now faced new challenges to its reprint business in the post-war period. John Buchan, one of its Directors, had written in retrospect in his autobiography *Memory hold-the-door* (1940) of the pre-1918 period in the history of the firm:

> We were a progressive concern, and in our standardised Edinburgh factories we began the publication of cheap books in many tongues. On the eve of the war we must have been one of the largest businesses of the kind in the world, issuing cheap editions of every kind of literature not only in English, but in French, German, Magyar and Spanish, and being about to start in Russian.[18]

Yet the war itself, through the denial of foreign markets, the loss of manpower and the general exigencies of wartime, led to the temporary rundown of Nelsons and initiated a change in its publishing strategy from reliance on reprint production to a focus on educational material. After the death of Thomas Nelson III in 1917, commemorated by Buchan in the dedication to

17 Musson, *The Typographical Association*, pp. 348–9. See also Chapter 1 in this volume.
18 Buchan, *Memory hold-the-door*, p. 87.

The thirty-nine steps, Ian Nelson, his cousin, became head of the family firm. The takeover of the publishing house of T. C. & E. C. Jack in 1915, with its strengths in children's titles, had consolidated the direction to which the company was to commit itself. Buchan brought in Sir Henry Newbolt, with whom he had worked in the Ministry of Information during the war, to act as editorial advisor in the educational field. Various series along the lines of its reprints were produced, such as the Nelson School Classics. The Royal Readers series, followed by the Royal School series, eventually extending to seventy titles, sold in vast quantities throughout the British Empire and later the Commonwealth. Among other educational works published by the firm, *Highroads of history*, *Highroads of literature* and *Highroads of geography* were to remain on Nelsons' backlist for more than forty years. In part response to Newbolt's own 1921 report on the teaching of English in schools in England and Wales, Nelsons produced in 1922 'The Teaching of English' series (eventually running to some 200 titles) under the editorship of Newbolt himself and Richard Wilson. The latter also introduced a new type of school reader in *Reading for action* and *Read and remember*. A further series, 'The Teaching of History', also grew out of Buchan's and Newbolt's collaboration. Thus much of the effort expended during the inter-war period, particularly in expanding the education list and reducing the dependence on reprints, represented Nelsons' attempt to maintain its turn-of-the-century pre-eminence. The company had moved away from the uncertain business of publishing for a general reading public to the securer business of publishing for the captive market of education. Others followed this trail, including Longman and Oliver & Boyd, while others already established in this field, such as Oxford University Press, expanded their lists to complement academic interests with educational innovation.[19]

Many established companies did adapt to changing circumstances in the years that followed the First World War, of which key examples included Thomas Nelson, Longman, Macmillan and George Allen & Unwin. This often entailed the pursuit of more specialised markets, including the distinction between categories of fiction often termed lowbrow, middlebrow and highbrow. Publishers such as Geoffrey Faber, building principally on the nursing list of Faber & Gwyer, sailed on the tide of modernism to establish a key presence in literary fiction and poetry, particularly of T. S. Eliot who became the first in a line of poet-directors of the company. The success of Mills & Boon, founded in 1908, was based on the move away in the 1930s from

19 For a discussion of this in relation to history textbooks, see Howsam, *Past into print*.

general fiction to focus on the lucrative field of romance fiction, initially sold as hardbacks and the staple content of twopenny libraries (see also Chapter 8).

Other publishers stagnated, as in the case of the Bodley Head discussed below. Significantly, new publishing houses were formed by younger men anxious to respond to a much changed world. George Orwell noted that

> at that time there was, among the young, a curious cult of hatred of 'old men'. The dominance of 'old men' was held to be responsible for every evil known to humanity, and every accepted institution from Scott's novels to the House of Lords was derided because 'old men' were in favour of it.[20]

Young men thought that they could do better and, in the circumstances of the postwar period, many such as Jonathan Cape, Victor Gollancz and Allen Lane seized the opportunity to do so. They shared a hunger for commercial success, a desire to change the nature of publishing and its markets, and an ambition to change the character of the society inherited from the pre-war 'old men'. Jonathan Cape was forty when he sought to found his eponymous publishing house in 1919 (it began publishing in 1921) but he had served a long apprenticeship with Duckworth, making his way upwards from delivery boy at the bookseller Hatchards, before service in the war. With the financial support of his partner, Wren Howard, and the acumen of his reader, Edward Garnett, 'a Trojan of energy and conscientiousness', Cape moved beyond the reprints of Elinor Glyn that he brought with him from Duckworth to create a list of the most notable authors of the period from T. E. Lawrence to Arthur Ransome.[21] Cape's recurrent visits to the USA, seen as the epitome of all that was modern in publishing, resulted in the strongest list of American writers of any British publisher.

However, Cape was also to publish Radclyffe Hall's novel *The well of loneliness* in 1928, a decision which almost killed off the young company. Cape's original proposal, along familiar lines for controversial titles, had been for a limited edition of 1,250 copies at twenty-five shillings. Hall resisted this scheme, just because it was redolent of other prurient titles, and Cape changed tack to 1,500 copies of a trade edition selling in a large format in a sombre black binding with a plain wrapper. The immediate reception of the book ranged from lukewarm to indifferent: it was generally criticised as boring and tedious as a novel, but brilliant and restrained as a discussion of the psychiatric condition of 'inversion' (lesbianism). Cape had influenced this

20 Orwell, *The road to Wigan pier*, pp. 170–1.   21 Moore, *The intelligent heart*, p. 131.

reading by commissioning Havelock Ellis to provide a brief introduction. Yet a damning review by James Douglas in the *Sunday Express* on 19 August 1928, 'exposing' the novel's obscenity and corrupting nature, demanded its immediate ban by the Home Office. Cape asked the advice of the then Home Secretary, Sir William Joynson-Hicks, and offered to withdraw the novel if the latter judged it obscene. The Home Secretary referred the question of the novel's obscenity to the Director of Public Prosecutions and a report was forthcoming which was in turn referred to the Lord Chancellor who confirmed its view that *The well of loneliness* was indeed obscene. The Home Secretary then wrote to Cape asking him to withdraw the book as Cape had intimated he would, including the undertaking that the second impression, then with the printers, would be destroyed. Cape wrote to *The Times* and other newspapers to confirm that he had done so. However, in reality he arranged for the book to be reprinted in Paris under another imprint (Pegasus) and imported into the UK for continuing sale. The authorities uncovered this ploy, and in the resulting trial Cape's devious-ness was exposed, and he was prosecuted and found guilty of the possession of obscene material with intent to sell and distribute it to others. Cape lost not only the income from a best-seller but also much of his reputation.

The case demonstrated the potential for prosecution if the 'young men' pushed the establishment too far in their challenge to social conventions as well as to publishing practice. It also illustrated the tools available to that establishment if there were to be a conflict with publishers. Obscene litera-ture could be handled in three ways. Firstly, private prosecutions could be brought by concerned citizens or bodies such as the Society for the Prevention of Vice. Secondly, the Director of Public Prosecutions could decide to bring an action on behalf of the state under the 1857 Obscene Publications Act as happened in the case of *The well of loneliness*. A judgement under this Act, in the *Regina* v. *Hicklin* case of 1868, had defined obscenity for all time as 'the tendency . . . to deprave and corrupt those whose minds are open to such immoral influences, and into whose hands a publication of this sort may fall'. One passage could condemn a whole book; there was as yet no defence of literary merit. D. H. Lawrence's *The rainbow* had been destroyed in 1915. The judgement against *The well of loneliness* in 1928 had been made by a magistrate who felt that a sentence referring to two women – 'And that night they were not divided' – would induce impure thoughts and horrible tendencies.

The third method of handling obscene literature was even more draco-nian. The Customs Consolidation Act of 1876 allowed an order to be issued banning the import of an obscene book produced abroad; no justification needed to be given and the right of appeal was very limited. Indeed, the books were usually destroyed before any protest could be heard. The books could be seized at port of entry, in the post, or anywhere in the UK. This was the initial procedure used in the case of *The well of loneliness* before the authorities decided to expose Cape through a public trial. It was also the procedure used in the case of Joyce's *Ulysses*, first published in Paris in 1922, and judged by Customs and Excise to be obscene. The Director of Public Prosecutions, to whom the case was referred, judged that *Ulysses* was indeed obscene; it should be impounded and destroyed where found by the Customs.

These cases created an environment in which many British publishers exercised self-censorship rather than challenge the establishment. *Ulysses* did not appear in the UK until 1936 after Allen Lane, on behalf of the Bodley Head, signed a contract with Joyce in 1934 and ran the calculated risk of a limited edition hard on the heels of a favourable judgement in the US courts in 1933. The obvious candidate for the honour was, however, Faber & Faber, and indeed Joyce first entered into negotiations with Faber. The firm had agreed to publish, and was publishing, *Work in progress*, later to become *Finnegans wake*. In 1933 Faber produced Joyce's *Pomes Penyeach*. The presence of T. S. Eliot as editorial director lent the firm the respectability and standing Joyce craved. Yet that very respectability and standing led to a pusillanimity within Faber. Faber looked to the government for a reassurance that no prosecution would result from publication of *Ulysses*. As in the case of *Lady Chatterley's lover*, some twenty-seven years later, that was a guarantee no law officer, in this case the Solicitor General, could give. Without it, Faber would not publish Joyce's novel. The Bodley Head limited edition attracted no prosecution and this emboldened the company to publish a trade edition in September 1937, some fifteen years after it had first appeared in Paris. This hardback edition was to remain the only one available in the UK, and therefore a valuable literary property for the Bodley Head, until Allen Lane issued the first UK paperback edition in 1967, thirty years later and with the confidence derived from the successful defence of *Lady Chatterley's lover* seven years previously.

Not all the challenges to the establishment were moral; some were political. Victor Gollancz had, like many of the other 'young men', served in the war and, after a brief period of public school teaching, found his vocation in publishing.[22] He entered the business through a post with the

22 Edwards, *Victor Gollancz*.

established family firm of Benn Brothers before setting up a company under his own name in 1927. Victor Gollancz Ltd successfully published the work of a number of novelists, including Dorothy L. Sayers, George Orwell and Edith Sitwell, and earned a reputation for risk-taking. This calculated recklessness, and particularly his dedication to the pursuit of a socialist agenda, was balanced by a keen commercial acumen and the promotion of a number of best-selling authors. He was aware of the importance of branding and adopted the yellow and magenta book jackets (with strikingly typographical devices on the front covers) that became the hallmark of the firm.[23] Gollancz shared with others of the 'young men' a concern to publish for a wider reading public. In 1930, he established a paperback imprint, Mundanus, anticipating the Penguin imprint, and in 1936, as developed below, he also founded the Left Book Club 'to help in the struggle for world peace and against fascism'.[24] This was one of the first book clubs in the UK, setting a pattern for many subsequently, and again represented a balance between conviction and commerce. Where Gollancz had anticipated an initial membership of 2,500, the LBC gained 40,000 subscribers within its first year of operation, rising to 57,000 by the outbreak of war in 1939.[25] The LBC also stimulated the growth of reading groups; by 1939 there were over 1,500 Left Discussion Groups throughout the UK. These, and the individual subscribers, received a book each month that had been chosen by a panel consisting of Gollancz himself and two other well-known figures of the Left, Harold Laski and John Strachey. The books were branded with distinctive plain orange or red covers and available in this edition only to subscribers. This emphasis on visual branding owed much to the presence of Stanley Morison on the Gollancz board and can be seen also in the company's general publications with their characteristic yellow covers and magenta typography. Through the success of the LBC and its general publishing, the firm grew considerably during the 1930s but Gollancz himself refused to delegate many decisions, a more general and recurring weakness as the 'young men' themselves became the 'old men' of the period after the Second World War.

The 1920s witnessed the start of a wider shift in reading practices and expectations. The key drivers reacting to and directing such expectations included the commercial twopenny libraries, which provided access to the fiction of publishers such as Mills & Boon or the lowbrow lists of Hodder & Stoughton, publishers of the prolific Edgar Wallace, in a way that the

---

23 Hodges, *Gollancz*.   24 Laity, *Left Book Club anthology*, p. ix.
25 Lewis, *The Left Book Club*.

moralistic public libraries with their mission to educate and improve did not.[26] The development of new subscription book clubs, such as the Book Society (established in 1929), the LBC or the Readers Union, founded in 1937, and the Book Club, run by London-based booksellers Foyles, which offered and promoted texts directly to readers, began undercutting traditional subscription libraries such as C. E. Mudie. Competition from mail order clubs, and from rival libraries such as W. H. Smith and Boots, was one of many reasons Mudie closed down in 1937, though it claimed overproduction and oversaturation in the book market as the rationale for its commercial demise.[27] A more accurate assessment was that disruptive interventions linked to new models of selling rather than lending books to readers were at the root of such closures.

However, the publishing industry was haunted from the late 1920s by the perception of a wider reading public to match the audience for the new broadcasting services of the BBC. In September 1934, Allen Lane, perhaps most prominent of the 'young men', was a participant in a weekend conference on 'The New Reading Public' held at Ripon Hall, Oxford, attended by some fifty publishers and booksellers, and initiated by the then presidents of the Publishers Association and the Associated Booksellers. The conference was itself prompted by an article by Philip Unwin in the *Bookseller*. Unwin drew an analogy with the creation of a new newspaper-reading public at the end of the nineteenth century and asked where the equivalent of Northcliffe and his papers were in the book trade. 'Another new reading public has arisen, but the Book Trade has not yet been able to secure its support as did newspaper proprietors a generation ago.'[28] He highlighted the growth of public libraries and their use, the buoyancy of the market for non-fiction material made accessible to non-specialist readers, and the large audience for 'talks' on the BBC (radio). The potential of this market was not being exploited by publishers. Unwin argued that 'there is nothing wrong with either the quality or price of the product which the book trade offers to the wide public' and illustrated this with the examples of Everyman's Library and the Home University Library, a series of short books for the autodidact.[29] For Unwin, the fault lay with booksellers who had not made their shops sufficiently attractive or indeed made much effort to attract 'the new reading public'. A general awareness of the existence of a reading public at the cheaper end of the market was therefore being articulated, but few, if any,

26 McAleer, *Popular reading and publishing.*   27 Griest, *Mudie's Circulating Library.*
28 Unwin, 'A new reading public?', p. 184.
29 Glasgow, 'The origins of the Home University Library'.

conclusions were drawn as to the best methods of reaching that market. Lane determined to fill that gap and, in so doing, to reach out to the 'new reading public' discussed at the Oxford conference. He was to take 'a gamble on the existence of a far larger critical and appreciative public than the book trade was at that time prepared to believe in' through the creation of Penguin Books in 1935.[30]

Yet other publishing houses were attempting, and had attempted, to create publications aimed at this very readership. The context into which Penguin appeared in 1935 was not one devoid of competitors; the market was full of rival sets of cheap reprints and the struggle for dominance was intense. Indeed, Nelsons had, as discussed above, tried to reduce its dependence on reprints by moving into the educational market. Harold Raymond of Chatto & Windus could write (dismissively) in 1938: 'The sixpenny paper-covered book is at least three-quarters of a century old.'[31] Collins had entered the field at the beginning of April 1934 with the announcement of a new series of reprints priced at sevenpence per volume.[32] The titles included Somerset Maugham's *The painted veil* (about to be released as a film starring Greta Garbo), several detective novels by Agatha Christie, Edgar Wallace, Freeman Wills Croft and Philip Macdonald, and Rose Macaulay's *Staying with relations.* Collins was followed by Hutchinson in May 1934 but the latter quickly withdrew – the front-page headline of the *Bookseller* of 16 May read 'We avert a sevenpenny "war"' – when faced with hostility from booksellers concerned about shrinking margins on low-priced titles and declining sales of higher-priced editions.

These sevenpenny editions were cloth-bound, but sixpenny novels in paper covers already existed in editions of genre fiction and the (non-copyright) classics. In July 1936, only one year after the first Penguins, Pearson was selling a sixpenny series, in striking orange and black covers, of genre novels including detective, western, romance and adventure by lesser-known authors such as Harold Ward, Victoria Cross and Ernest Goodwin. Newnes was also advertising sixpenny phrasebooks in the 'What you want to say and how to say it' series in a similar format. Of particular interest was the publisher's promise that 'booksellers stocking this series during the summer season will have the benefit of a national advertising campaign reaching weekly over a quarter of a million people in the right market'.[33] The Martyn sixpenny library for children, 'beautifully printed on

30 Young, 'The early days of Penguins', p. 210.
31 Raymond, *Publishing and bookselling*, p. 23.   32 Unwin, 'A new reading public?'
33 *Bookseller* 8 July 1936, p. 36.

good paper complete with three colour jacket', offered reliable out-of-copyright titles such as *The coral island, Black Beauty, Little women* and *The water-babies*.[34] Collins persisted in the earlier 'war' and by February 1935 was advertising nineteen titles in its sevenpenny library, including twelve available in a box or case for seven shillings, 'less than the price of one 7/6 Novel' as the advertising copy read.[35] The promotional material was aimed at both booksellers and the private, often twopenny, libraries, 'Both Lend and Sell!' At the same time, Collins was also selling over 140 titles, with jackets and full-cloth bindings, in its one-shilling novel series. This latter reprint venture included all of the authors, and some of the titles, issued in the sevenpenny format.

However, a general hostility, based on the book trade's innate conservatism, of its 'old men', re-emerged on the issue of the first Penguins. To be fair, Penguin was also issuing fairly recent titles which might otherwise be expected to go through a 3s 6d reprint rather than appear as a sixpenny paperback (which had hitherto largely been restricted to out-of-copyright classics or more lowbrow genre fiction). Key fiction publishers like Cape, Chatto and Secker & Warburg had each introduced uniform 3s 6d series in the late 1920s which proved very successful. They stood to lose out if the Penguin experiment succeeded.[36] Harold Raymond gave the J. M. Dent Memorial Lecture on 21 October 1938 at the Stationers' Hall in London. That lecture, published by Dent in November of the same year, crystallised the doubts and fears of the book trade related to Penguin in particular and cheap reprints in general. The detractors of Penguins were characterised as 'open-minded critics who are anxiously wondering whether the booktrade can afford to cut its profits to the fine point which a sixpenny novel nowadays involves'.[37] He was not alone in these views; even that promoter of the 'young men' George Orwell had been scathing in his public reaction to the appearance of Penguins. He viewed the cheap book as a boon for readers but a disaster, in terms of reduced revenue, for authors, publishers, printers and booksellers.[38]

There had been opposition also within Allen Lane's parent firm, the Bodley Head. The latter had been resting on its pre-war reputation when, under the direction of its founder, John Lane, it had published successfully both avant-garde and middlebrow authors. In order to ensure its succession

34 *Bookseller* 29 July 1936, p. 57.   35 *Bookseller* 20 February 1935, p. 9.
36 Nash, 'The production of the novel, 1880–1940'.
37 Raymond, *Publishing and bookselling*, p. 24.
38 George Orwell, 'Review of Penguin Books', *New English Weekly* 5 March 1936.

within the family, John Lane had invited a (comparatively distant) young relative, Allen Williams, to change his name and join the company. John Lane died in 1925 and control of the Bodley Head then lay in the hands of a Board of Directors, all rather conservative 'old men' with the exception of Allen Lane himself. The resulting stagnation led to a poor financial state of health by 1934. By the end of June of that year, the firm was carrying a cumulative deficit on its Profit and Loss Account of £42,367 18s 5d; by the end of June 1935, a further loss for the year of £4,968 18s 11d had to be added to that. Even then, the auditor was careful to note that the valuation of the stock on hand was that of the Directors of the company and therefore presumably an over- rather than an under-estimate of its worth, particularly the £2,749 2s 11d for work in progress. The true losses of the Bodley Head, in other words, were possibly even greater than the available sources would suggest.[39] No dividend had been paid on Bodley Head Preference Shares since 1927 and concern about the company's financial health had been voiced since 1932, particularly in regard to its large carry-over of indebtedness. Allen Lane's solicitor wrote to him in February 1936, having seen the accounts for 1935, to assert that 'there is no doubt that the Company is hopelessly insolvent, even when credit is given for the very questionable items of goodwill, copyrights, etc. There is, too, a substantial sum owing to you as the proprietor of Penguin Books.'[40] His solicitor advised Lane to resign immediately from the Bodley Head and to place the company in receivership. This is the context out of which his fellow-directors refused Allen Lane the authority to create Penguin Books as an imprint of the Bodley Head, regarding it as a 'make-or-break' enterprise more likely to shatter the already fragile company. Allen Lane, with supreme confidence in his own abilities, went ahead anyway to found Penguin Books as an independent company launched on his personal security and that of his two brothers, none of whom were at that time wealthy, and what they owned they stood to lose if Penguin failed. Penguin became a private limited company in early 1936. The Bodley Head went into receivership before being taken over by a consortium of other publishers in 1936. Penguin in the meantime prospered.

The planning for the launch of Penguins, and the need to focus upon their marketing within bookshops and other retail outlets, as opposed to trade magazines and newspaper reviews, was underpinned by a short news item on the front page of the *Bookseller* of 17 April 1935. Using information taken from

39 Research File 1930s, Penguin Archive D M1294, University of Bristol Library, Bristol.
40 Percy J. Davis to Allen Lane, 17 February 1936, Penguin Archive D M1819, folder 5d.

the US-based *Publishers' Weekly*, the article confirmed, and highlighted in its sub-head, that reprint publishers in the USA reached 60 per cent of the total population, 'a far greater percentage than that reached by the publishers of original editions', and were therefore both creating a new reading public as well as servicing the existing one. Moreover, 'the sale of reprints [was] to a large extent left to the department and drug stores' who did not necessarily know what the books contained but did know how to sell them in an attractive and non-threatening setting.[41] While the *Bookseller*, 'organ' of the establishment, may have concluded by emphasising the parasitic nature of the reprint trade upon 'new-book' business, others such as Allen Lane drew other conclusions from the North American experience.

Like Gollancz before him, Lane realised that marketing and distribution were the keys to making Penguin a success. The tale of the origin of the penguin has been repeated through most accounts of Penguin's history. Edward Young, the original artist, tells it in his reminiscence of the early days of the company: editorial discussions had reached a stalemate when a secretary, Joan Coles, piped up from behind a partition; Young was dispatched to London Zoo and 'the following morning produced, at first shot, the absurdly simple cover design which was soon to become such a familiar sight on the bookstalls'.[42] Young also tells the familiar story of Mr Prescott, buyer for Woolworths, being persuaded by his wife to place an order for the first Penguins at a point when bookseller resistance to the reprints had resulted in very few orders through the trade. The creation myth emphasises the serendipity of this and takes no account of the US precedent. For Woolworths itself, the sale of Penguins was not altogether a pioneering act: the company already sold cheap books and, in addition, had a link to the Boots Book-Lovers' Library – which offered preferential subscription rates to existing subscribers to the Woolworths twopenny magazine *The New Bond*.[43] Lane wished to gain access to 'the new reading public' through as many outlets as possible, including established bookshops. He had written in the *Bookseller* in May 1935 that the new reading public 'is being catered for largely by Woolworths and other chain stores and the 2d. libraries . . . the bookseller is getting a very small share, if indeed he is getting any at all'.[44] Lane wished to sell his brand of books to that public where it went, Woolworths and other chain stores, and in those places where it feared to enter, the bookshops: '"Penguin Books" are designed primarily to reach these people, where they

41 *Bookseller* 17 April 1935, p. 1.   42 Young, 'The early days of Penguins', p. 210.
43 *The New Bond* 1:1 (December 1935).
44 Allen Lane, 'All about the Penguin books', *Bookseller* 22 May 1935, p. 497.

congregate on railway stations and in chain stores, with the hope that when they see these books are available in the regular bookshops, they will overcome their temerity and come in.'[45]

The key element was the brand rather than the individual title.

In making what amounted to the first serious attempt at introducing "branded goods" to the book trade, we realized the cumulative publicity value of, first, a consistent and easily recognizable cover design, and, secondly, a good trade-mark that would be easy to say and easy to remember.[46]

(Lane was perhaps a little disingenuous here as other companies had similarly branded lowbrow fiction series. Where Lane was correct was that this was the first occasion on which serious literature had been marketed like this.) To encourage new readers to enter bookshops, Penguin provided huge quantities of brand-orientated display materials, centring on Young's 'absurdly simple' design and extending the characterisation of the penguins. In April 1936, Hudson's bookshop in Birmingham won a company-sponsored prize for the best window display of Penguin(s) while in May the whole of the front page of the *Bookseller* was given over to an advertisement for Penguin's 'Great Summer Sales Drive', and a sales promotion competition offering cash prizes to booksellers at seaside resorts and holiday towns for the most effective and original selling displays of Penguin books. Showcards were available in two colours; streamers in three colours; penguin cut-outs fifteen inches high; and long window strips – all advertising the brand, not specific titles.[47]

Not that the choice of titles was unimportant. On the contrary, to sell the brand entailed convincing the public of the rightness and reliability of the Penguin selected titles. The initial ten issued were a judicious mix of detective fiction, such as Collins was producing in its sixpenny Crime Club series, of the 'naughty but nice' autobiography of Beverley Nichols, of the light, deft humour of Eric Linklater, and of the accessible seriousness of *Ariel*, the biography of Shelley by André Maurois. In the first year of operation: 3 million books were sold, creating a turnover of £75,000 and using 600 tons of paper; the best-sellers were Dorothy L. Sayers, *The unpleasantness at the Bellona club*, Margot Asquith, *Autobiography*, Beverley Nichols, *Twenty-five*, Liam O'Flaherty, *The informer*, and Mary Webb, *Gone to earth*. From his share of the profits Allen Lane bought a nine-ton cutter, launched as the 'Penguin'.[48]

45 *Ibid.*   46 Lane, 'Penguins and Pelicans', p. 42.
47 *Bookseller* 8 April 1936, p. 3; 20 May 1936, p. 1.   48 *Bookseller* 15 July 1936, p. 3.

Not that Penguin had a free choice of titles from hardback publishers other than the Bodley Head itself. Harold Raymond of Chatto & Windus reacted in a very prickly manner when Allen Lane first approached him in late 1934.[49] When Ralph Pinker, the literary agent, made an approach on behalf of two of his authors whose books, first published by Chatto, Lane wished to reprint as Penguins, Raymond replied in the same vein as his 1938 Lecture quoted above:

> Concerning Lane's Sixpennies, I think I told you in conversation the other day that he tried to bring me in on the scheme at its outset, but after consultation with my Partners we decided to stand out of it, because we thought it was neither good for the booktrade as a whole nor for individual authors, except in very rare instances ... Practically all London booksellers are stocking these Sixpennies, and that means if you went into a shop and asked for a copy of "Twenty-Five", the book seller would not dare to sell you a 2/- or 3/6d. edition of that book without pointing out to you that you could get if [sic] for 6d.[50]

By October of that same year, the businessman in Raymond had relented and he made Lane an offer of nine Chatto titles.[51] Such a concession was made only reluctantly – Lane 'is obviously getting away with the series and there seems to be little point in individual publishers or individual authors trying to hold out against the scheme'.[52] These attitudes were widespread. Jonathan Cape only released some of his titles to Penguin because he felt that the company would not survive and, in the meantime, he might as well take its money.[53] Penguin not only survived but also became the most prominent British publisher of the twentieth century and, in doing so, established from the 1960s onwards the paperback as the predominant form of book until the challenge of the e-book some seventy years later.

1939–1945

On 3 September 1939, war was declared against Germany and its allies.[54] The British government swung swiftly into administrative action, setting in place wartime legislation covering aspects relevant to the book trade, such as

49 Harold Raymond to Allen Lane, 1 November 1934, Research File 1930s, Penguin Archive DM1294.
50 Raymond to Ralph Pinker, 30 August 1935, Chatto & Windus archive, MS2444/148.
51 Raymond to Lane, 4 October 1935, Chatto & Windus archive, MS2444/149.
52 Raymond to Pinker, 8 October 1935, Chatto & Windus archive, MS2444/149.
53 Morpurgo, Allen Lane, p. 87.
54 Chapter 23 for more detail on the book trade during the Second World War.

restrictions and prohibitions against trading with businesses classed as enemy organisations, paper rationing and control, and War Risks Insurance, which required all traders carrying stock worth over £1,000 to insure against losses due to enemy action. The latter proved most controversial for publishers on implementation. It required relevant publishers compulsorily to insure their stock at an insurance premium of 1.5 per cent for the first three months of holding, and 0.5 per cent thereafter. Because of slow stock turnover, many publishers faced high premiums. Methuen, for example, by no means the largest of companies, estimated at the time it would have to bear a premium cost of £12,000 per annum under this arrangement.[55] Many publishers lobbied against this levy, but on 29 December 1940 many had cause for thanking its existence, when a German Blitz attack on London ripped apart the publishing and wholesaling district centred on Paternoster Row. The entire stock of Simpkin Marshall, main wholesaler for the London publishing industry, estimated at 3 million titles, was burned to cinders, while twenty other publishing houses saw their premises reduced to rubble, including venerable and long-standing firms such as George Allen & Unwin, Methuen, Hurst & Blackett, and Ward Lock. Publishing titles lost in this and subsequent bombing raids across the country ultimately ran to an estimated 20 million volumes.[56] War Risks Insurance paid back handsomely in many cases, and while it could not restore lost material, it enabled several publishers to recapitalise, rebuild and revitalise their publishing lists. Such was the case of Longman, who emerged from the devastation with only twelve titles out of its backlist of over 5,000 available for immediate sale, yet over the coming years successfully rebuilt its lists and expanded its range and reach post-war into colonial markets, and African nations in particular.[57]

Wartime rationing of raw materials such as paper, like that endured during the First World War, was exacerbated by loss of access early on in the conflict to key supplies: of wood pulp from Norway, invaded by Germany in April 1940; and esparto grass, key ingredient in much of the paper produced by Scottish paper mills, lost as the result of the defeat of France in June 1940 and the subsequent barring of access to supplies from French North Africa. Paper rationing was fixed at this stage at 60 per cent of what firms had used in the year prior to commencement of hostilities. As Holman notes, subsequent paper and board consumption was ruthlessly squeezed in the period 1939–44, with ratios unfavourable to book publishing interests. In 1939, out of a total

55 Stevenson, *Book makers*, p. 109.   56 Unwin, *The truth about a publisher*, p. 278.
57 Briggs, *A history of Longmans*.

tonnage of 1,452,500, newspapers consumed the lion's share at 1,100,000, periodicals utilised 250,000, the HMSO and government sources appropriated 40,000, and book publishing consumed 62,500. By 1944, out of a tonnage of 519,000, HMSO and government sources accounted for 34 per cent at 179,000 tons, newspapers accounted for 262,000, periodicals for 50,000, and book publishing for 28,000, the latter a drop of 45 per cent in five years.[58]

Of similar concern was the unceasing demand, as in the First World War, for type metal for uses other than print production. Frequent calls for the donation of old type for weaponry meant that, by 1942, the shortage of metal for type, blocks and plates, and zinc for line blocks in particular, was so acute as for new titles to be almost wholly dependent on the recycling of old material in publishing and printing warehouses. By January 1943 it was estimated that members of the Publishers Association had contributed over 5,000 tons of type metal to the war effort, equivalent to 11,000 titles of standing type.[59]

Labour shortages also dogged publishing efforts. Whereas in 1939 the total number of workers employed in printing, publishing and bookbinding stood at 304,300 (of whom 105,400 were female), by 1945 the workforce had decreased by 57 per cent to 173,400 (of whom 76,400 were female).[60] In the autumn of 1945, the Federation of Master Printers worried that even with demobilisation and transfers from war industries after cessation of hostilities, the estimated number of skilled operatives in the printing and binding industry available for work was some 10,000 less than its 1939 workforce figure of 70,000. This posed a problem for an industry that intended to bring back into print 43,000 lapsed titles and had in hand ready for production 9,000 new titles: a long and ambitious production queue of 52,000 titles.[61]

The wartime scramble for raw materials and skilled labour proved challenging yet also contradictorily beneficial for publishers, particularly in the face of a significant rise in demand for reading material. Stanley Unwin would later write that the tension between demand and supply ensured that the war years were extremely profitable for publishers. Almost any book succeeded due to the reduction in number of titles publishers could issue, and so 'there was no need for a publisher to take risks if he did not want to'.[62] Some categories fared better than others: books on naval and military matters rose exponentially, from sixty-two issued in 1937 to 229 in 1943; books on wireless telegraphy (nineteen in 1937, thirty-four in 1943) proved popular, and texts

58 Holman, *Print for victory*, p. 264.   59 Kingsford, *The Publishers Association*, p. 177.
60 Holman, *Print for victory*, p. 251.   61 Kingsford, *The Publishers Association*, pp. 185–6.
62 Unwin, *The truth about a publisher*, p. 272.

published on agriculture, animal husbandry and veterinary science doubled as Victory vegetable gardens were dug with increasing fervour. Other genres saw major slumps in interest, such as illustrated gift books, a staple of Christmas book purchasing for several decades, which dropped from sight and failed to re-emerge after the war had ended.[63]

Long evenings without much in way of entertainment may also have been one of the reasons why libraries witnessed an unprecedented rise in book borrowing (see Chapter 7). Price rises throughout the period (between 1938 and 1942 book prices rose 30 per cent, while binding costs rose 50 per cent) did not halt book buying or borrowing, but rather from 1942 onwards began shifting 'the type of object and location of reading from the many-times borrowed hardback in a public library to the less durable paperback that could be bought for a few pence'.[64] Penguin Books, particularly with the help of W. E. Williams, a key intermediary between the publishers and the government, was the major beneficiary of this shift, much to the general industry's chagrin, not least because of Allen Lane's attempts to ensure the firm acted as a major supplier of paperbacks for the Armed Forces, via such schemes as supplying works to prisoners of war and initiating the Forces Book Club in October 1942, with the aim of supplying ten new Penguin titles a month to military subscribers at a third of list price. The scheme lasted only a year, having attracted 5,000 subscribers against a forecast figure of 75,000.[65] Trade resentment towards Penguin was further fuelled by the fact that its allocation of paper, based on tonnage used pre-war, boosted by the success of the Penguin Specials, was set at a more generous level than most; its efficient production methods and economical use of raw material enabled it to continue operations fairly unscathed, with output consequently almost unchecked throughout the war period.[66]

Penguin, however, was not the only firm seeking to make its production more cost-efficient. The Book Production War Economy Agreement, negotiated by the government with the Publishers' Association and coming into force in 1942, imposed low production standards on all participants, including raising levels of words per page, minimising page margins and typefaces, and reducing paper quality and maximum weight for binding boards by 20 per cent. At the same time, the re-imposition of the Defence of the Realm Act of 1914 caused publishers to exercise caution in the types of material published, and, as had occurred during the First World War, the

---

63 Feather, *A history of British publishing*, pp. 194–5.   64 *Ibid.*, p. 51.   65 *Ibid.*, pp. 119–20.
66 Morpurgo, *Allen Lane*, pp. 156–7.

Ministry of Information operated a Press and Censorship Bureau to which publishers submitted manuscripts to prevent later placement on a prohibited list. Censorship was less heavy handed than in the previous war period, and the Bureau seems to have operated efficiently (turning round manuscripts within weeks if not days of submission), and in as supportive a fashion as possible. As the *Publisher's Circular* noted at the time, their 'Technical Censors' had past links with the industry, and were 'anxious not to prevent the publication of books, but rather to advise publishers how their books can be modified if need be'.[67]

Certain publishers also played key roles in disseminating government-supported propaganda, such as Oxford University Press, whose long-running Oxford Pamphlets on World Affairs series, backed by the Ministry of Information (MOI), was launched in September 1939 with a short text by R. C. K. Ensor on *Hitler's self-disclosures in 'Mein kampf'*. Over the next five years the series would encompass seventy-two pamphlets and sell over a million copies in the UK, Canada, Australia, India and elsewhere. The series, which offered short historical essays on contemporary issues in a form that understatedly confirmed the democratic and intellectual tenor of the government's stance against fascism and the Axis alliance, chimed with the MOI's indirect methods of persuasion. As the Secretary to the Delegates of OUP informed Oxford University's Vice Chancellor:

> The principle has been determined, that is that the Ministry *does* wish to disseminate this kind of information, and experience has shown that by using a semi-official channel they are relieved of the necessity of getting various Government departments to pass anything, a procedure which is almost paralysing.[68]

It was not the only work undertaken with the active backing of the MOI, and OUP's key role in publishing and printing similar work on behalf of government political agendas led it to be dubbed 'Printing House Number One' by the Admiralty.[69]

1945–1970

The methods by which businesses coped with the complexities of wartime production, and the rebuilding and restructuring that accompanied the industry's emergence from disruption, destruction and rationing, ensured

---

67 Quoted in Holman, *Print for victory*, p. 93.   68 Quoted in *ibid.*, pp. 259–60.
69 Squires, 'The history of the book in Britain from 1914', p. 190.

that the war became, as one commentator has noted, 'an essential catalyst crystallizing and fixing the new directions made in the previous years, and preparing the way for the great changes that were to come'.[70] Recovery, however, was slow and painful. Wartime controls over raw material remained in place for several years under the newly elected Labour government (paper rationing did not end until 1949), though supplies gradually increased and improved. In 1945 the industry issued 5,800 new titles; by 1950 this had risen to 11,600, joined by most of the 43,000 back titles queued in production at war's end.[71] As British publishing slowly re-engaged and expanded its lists, so too did the number of firms increase: 1950 trade directories, for example, recorded 572 firms operating in Britain, significantly up from the 320 listed in 1939. Many new firms were the result of an influx of refugees from continental Europe, newly resurgent, outward facing and prepared to experiment and challenge set practices and norms. They were the 'young men' of this part of the century. This general buoyancy enabled other risk-takers in the literary marketplace to thrive, such as John Calder, who in 1949 began publishing continental playwrights and authors including Ionesco, Alain Robbe-Grillet and Samuel Beckett.

A key feature of the period 1945–70 is the growth of paperback publication, to the point where it became the predominant form of print publishing. Paperbacks were no longer reprints of existing hardbacks, but features in their own right. For example, building on its earlier successes, by the 1950s Allen Lane's Penguin had achieved a commanding presence in paperback publishing, selling overall 10 million copies of titles a year, half of them in overseas markets. In the 1960s, new imprints such as Panther Books, Fontana, Four Square (owned by a cigarette company) and Corgi moved forward with innovative paperback series. Panther drew attention to their products with titles in brightly coloured paper covers, Fontana garnered success in crime fiction, including high levels of sales of Agatha Christie, while Corgi specialised in children's fiction. Other British publishers, recognising the potential market reached by such means, followed suit in developing paperback series of their own. Pan was founded in 1944 as an independent subsidiary of the Book Society and became a consortium of publishers including Macmillan, Collins, Hodder & Stoughton, Heinemann and Cape. It had a major success with its paper editions of Ian Fleming's *On Her Majesty's Secret Service* (1963); originally published by Cape in hardback, in paperback it sold initially 1.5 million copies (but only 45 per cent through conventional bookshops)

70 Stevenson, *Book makers*, p. 10.   71 Feather, *A history of British publishing*, pp. 196–7.

while Grace Metalious's *Return to Peyton Place* (1959) sold 700,000 copies. By 1969 UK book market sales totalled 77 million copies, valued at 145.7 million pounds, with four paperback publishers accounting for 80 per cent of those sales (Penguin, 27 million copies; Fontana, 13 million copies; Corgi, 13 million copies; Panther, 9 million copies).[72] This tracked alongside similar upward trends in the twentieth century global book economy: in 1850 annual world book production totalled 50,000 titles; in 1952 it had risen to 250,000 titles; by 1963 it equalled 400,000; and in 1970 it soared past 521,000.[73]

George Weidenfeld represented the positive aspect of the fresh energy and European outlook brought to British publishing after the war by the refugees from Nazi Germany. He embodied the transformational perspective shared by André Deutsch, Paul Hamlyn and Paul Elek, in founding their own companies; it was to be seen too in the achievements at Phaidon of Bela Horowitz and at Thames & Hudson of Walter Neurath. In 1948, Weidenfeld co-founded the publishing firm Weidenfeld & Nicolson (with Nigel Nicolson, the son of Harold Nicolson and Vita Sackville-West). Nicolson, later a Conservative MP, largely provided the funding as well as a list of contacts both pre- and post-war that complemented Weidenfeld's own extensive networks within émigré communities and left-wing politics. The company developed a list that was innovative and commercially successful, including key historical and political works as well as Nabokov's *Lolita* noted below. (The latter, published in 1955, sold 200,000 copies in hardback.) One of the first titles was *New deal for coal* (1945) by the future Prime Minister, Harold Wilson, while the initial survival of the company was ensured by the publication of a series of illustrated children's classics under contract from Marks & Spencer. Weidenfeld employed Sonia Orwell, the widow of George, as an editor and she brought notable American authors such as Saul Bellow and Mary McCarthy onto the list. The company largely grew organically, though it did take over J. M. Dent and Everyman in 1988, and retained its independence until acquired by the Orion Group in 1991, itself to be the object of a successful takeover by Hachette Livre in 1998.

Robert Maxwell's name is missing from the list of refugees and 'young men' above. The twists and turns of his career, reflecting at times the experiences of Weidenfeld but also diverging strongly from them at others,

---

72 Rose, 'Modernity and print I', p. 352; Clark and Phillips, *Inside book publishing*, fourth edition, p. 16.
73 Escarpit, *The book revolution*, pp. 57–8; Milner, *Literature, culture and society*, p. 70; Zaid, *So many books*, p. 21.

represent another aspect of the transformational effects upon post-war British publishing. His proficiency with languages had resulted in his employment by the British Forces of Occupation in Berlin as a censor, and this in turn provided him with a key network of contacts that he was able to deploy in post-war scientific and academic publishing.[74] He became the UK and US distributor for Springer Verlag, a key source of German scientific material since the mid-nineteenth century, and exploited this position in creating a subscription model for access that would come into its own with the expansion of the British higher education system in the 1960s.[75] Maxwell's role as intermediary, particularly with countries now lying behind the Iron Curtain, was consolidated in 1951 when he bought the company Butterworth-Springer in partnership with Paul Rosbaud, a relationship dissolved in 1956. Rosbaud, a scientist of note in his own right, added reputation to the company, renamed the Pergamon Press, as well as his own network of scientists, editors and publishers. The access that both partners had to these networks enabled them each to build up his own journals list as well as acting as agents for European material from both sides of the Iron Curtain. Pergamon developed from six journal titles in 1951 to fifty-nine in 1960 and 418 in 1992 by which time it had been taken over by Elsevier.[76] The 'new universities' of the 1960s had to build up library collections in a very short period to provide their staff and students with (print) access to the archive of world scientific knowledge. Pergamon supplied this service, often reprinting back volumes of journals to which they had acquired rights cheaply, and tied their clients into highly lucrative contracts for complete series or bundles. The consequent mixture of resentment and impotence felt by the new universities may have sowed the seeds of the contemporary 'open access' movement.[77]

The revenues from this period fuelled Maxwell's ambitions within publishing and within politics. In 1969 he tried to sell the 'golden goose' of Pergamon to underwrite further acquisitions, but the sale to Leasco, a US company, fell through when it was discovered that Maxwell had manipulated Pergamon's share price in order to negotiate a larger sum. Maxwell lost control of Pergamon, and his stewardship of a publicly quoted company (as Pergamon had been since 1964) was criticised in a DTI (Department of Trade and Industry) report. Maxwell reacquired Pergamon in 1974 and continued to build on its success. He took over the ailing British Printing Corporation in 1981 and it metamorphosed from the British Printing and

---

74 Haines, *Maxwell*.   75 See also Chapter 18.   76 Cox, 'The Pergamon phenomenon'.
77 See comments by the bookseller Bill Bauermeister in McCleery *et al.*, *An honest trade*.

Communications Corporation to the Maxwell Communications Corporation. The expansion continued as Maxwell tried to build a transnational conglomerate straddling books and journals, newspapers, and other media. In 1988, however, he over-reached himself in the purchase of the US company Macmillan, for the greatly inflated price of $2.6 billion. This was an unsustainable debt and so resulted in the sale of Pergamon and Maxwell Directories to Elsevier for £440 million in 1989. Maxwell's failed attempt to build a multimedia empire, based around the 'secure' profits of Pergamon's academic and educational publishing, prefigured much of the development of the sector in the closing years of the twentieth century. On Maxwell's death by drowning in 1991, his companies were discovered to be deeply in debt. Their survival up to that point had depended on both large bank loans and the unauthorised use of pension funds without the knowledge of shareholders, pensioners or government. The remaining companies collapsed or were sold off at relatively low valuations. At that point, this left Pearson, by then owner of both Penguin and Longman, as the only British-owned conglomerate in a globalised publishing industry.

Maxwell's twin careers in publishing and politics seem to have been relatively compartmentalised; however, other publishers continued to address social and political issues through their lists. It seemed appropriate to post-war experimentation, such as represented by Calder's list, and to further expansion of readership, not least through those 'new universities' targeted by Maxwell, that efforts should be resumed to create greater freedom for publishers in the UK. The pre-war challenges to forms of censorship made by Cape and Lane, in the examples of *The well of loneliness* and *Ulysses* respectively, seemed to many 'unfinished business', with a guilty verdict in the case of the former and restricted sales through price in the latter creating dissatisfaction and frustration among publishers young and older. The key moment in legal challenges to censorship in this period occurred with the prosecution of Penguin for its paperback publication of *Lady Chatterley's lover* in 1960. There had been signs of a thawing of official views on such matters prior to this landmark trial. Thus in the case of *The philanderer* by Stanley Kauffmann, who was prosecuted and acquitted in 1954, the trial judge emphasised that the tendency to deprave and corrupt had to be seen in a contemporary context. Books had to be judged, and obscenity defined, by the standards operating at the time rather than in the past.[78] In 1959, Nabokov's *Lolita*, published as noted

---

78 *Regina* v. *Secker Warburg Ltd. and Others*, Central Criminal Court, 2 July 1954, 2 All ER 683, [1954] I WLR 1138, 118 JP 438, 38 Cr App R 124.

above by Weidenfeld and Nicolson, had not been prosecuted. That decision had been taken at a meeting between the Home Secretary, the Attorney General and the Director of Public Prosecutions.[79] Only the Attorney General dissented from the decision. He was overruled partly because a new statute was making its way through the parliamentary process that would itself reform the treatment of banned books. The 1959 Obscene Publications Act grew out of a reaction to the disproportionate propensity to prosecution, exhibited by successive Conservative Home Secretaries, particularly Sir David Maxwell-Fyfe. The 1959 Act altered the framework of obscenity trials so that literary merit, the common good, could be taken into account and attested to by expert witnesses. It contained a new definition of obscenity including a stress upon the work as a whole (rather than selected passages) and a significant qualifier – 'having regard to all relevant circumstances' – in terms of the book's availability. However, two negative changes were introduced: the work no longer had to be sold, with more often than not the police acting as bogus customers or agents provocateurs, but merely likely to be sold; and the right to trial by jury was discretionary.[80]

Penguin's prosecution under the new Act is discussed in Chapter 8 of this volume. Customs officials seized copies of the newly legal American edition of *Lady Chatterley's lover* arriving from the USA in late 1959, including twelve sent to Lawrence's step-daughter. Dr Alan Thompson MP stated in the House of Commons at the time: 'It is absurd that in 1959 Customs officials should be rummaging through the luggage of British or foreign citizens looking for copies of *Lady Chatterley's lover*.'[81] As C. H. Rolph points out in his introduction to the transcript of the trials: 'The decision to prosecute was a great surprise to many in the world of publishing, and of the law.' However, a momentum built up and, as Rolph again notes, once the legal procedure had started 'there was nothing and no-one in the legal machine able or willing to stop it'.[82] On the other hand, a prosecution of Penguin was welcomed by many as an opportunity to clarify a muddied and muddled area of law enforcement. The *Observer* editorialised: 'if the decision to prosecute is wrong-headed, we may in the end be thankful for the first full-scale literary trial in our legal history'.[83] The trial of Penguin Books in 1960 helped to clarify the status of the novel, to test the operation of the new Obscene Publications Act, and to settle the question whether the manner of publication – in this

---

79 Sir Theobald Mathew to Sir Austin Strutt, 19 April 1960, TNA DPP 2/3077.
80 Obscene Publications Act 1959 [U.K.], Crown Office.
81 Hansard fifth series Parliamentary Debates Commons 1959–60, Vol. 614, cs.365–6.
82 Rolph (ed.), *The trial of Lady Chatterley*, p. 2.   83 *Observer* 21 August 1960.

case, sold in volume at a relatively low price – in addition to the nature of the book was relevant to its legal status.

The eventual judgement in Penguin's favour in November 1960 contributed strongly to the company's balance sheet. The cost of the trial to Penguin was £12,777 11s 6d. The calculated risk brought commercial success. Penguin sold 2 million copies of *Lady Chatterley's lover* in the six weeks up to Christmas 1960. A further 1,339,631 copies were sold in 1961. No bonus was paid to the company's reps as a result of the tremendous sales but the novel had a knock-on effect on sales generally, which increased from 13 million in 1959 to 15 million in 1960 (not including *Lady Chatterley's lover*) so that they benefited from it anyway.[84] Penguin Books became a public company in April 1961 and the press linked the share issue to the trial by referring to the shares as 'Chatterleys'. The offer for sale of 750,000 of the company's 2,500,000 four-shilling shares at twelve shillings each (the remainder was held by family trusts) was oversubscribed: 150,000 people applied and 3,450 were successful in a ballot for 200 shares each. Penguin employees were given preferential treatment for the balance of 60,000 shares. At the close of the first day of trading, the shares were being bought and sold for seventeen shillings, a premium of five shillings each, and the value of Allen Lane's stake in the company rose to £1,147,500.

The 1960 trial seemed also the final victory of the 'young men' of the inter-war generation, like Cape and Lane, that would open the doors for others to publish and promote texts that challenged social and sexual mores in a more open fashion. This was true, but only to a limited extent. When the next generation such as John Calder and the one after that such as the editors of *Oz* magazine tried to open those doors wider, they met with continued resistance as much as their predecessors had done. In particular, the trial in 1964 in Sheffield of Alexander Trocchi's *Cain's book* demonstrated a new set of boundaries. Magistrates there had judged the novel, first published in the UK by John Calder in 1963 following the American edition from the Grove Press, obscene within the terms of the 1959 Obscene Publications Act and ordered the book's destruction. Despite the precedent of *Lady Chatterley's lover*, and the same line of defence, including the calling of expert witnesses, the novel was banned. The provincial verdict in Yorkshire was upheld by the Lord Chief Justice and two of his judicial colleagues on appeal to the Queen's Bench. The decision of the Lord Chief Justice and his two fellow judges made it clear that, while there was no precedent for obscenity being defined in

84 Penguin Archive DM 00.1484 5. *Lady Chatterley's lover* Editorial File.

anything other than sexual terms, it could apply to any aspect of social behaviour that tended to deprave and corrupt, thus including drug taking, violence, racism, religious offence and all forms of moral obscenity. This ruling paved the way for 'lifestyle trials' of books such as *Last exit to Brooklyn* (1966) by Hubert Selby Jr, police seizure of copies of William Burrough's *The naked lunch* in 1967, and calls for the prosecution of Salman Rushdie's *The satanic verses* in 1988 and 1989 on moral grounds. On the issue of determining the 'public good' in terms particularly of literary merit, the judges agreed that evidence of 'public good' presented by expert witnesses could be taken into consideration when making a judicial decision but did not pre-empt it. This conclusion clearly preserved the role of judges, including magistrates, in making that decision and their right to come to a decision contrary to the expert opinion presented. It also took much of the force as precedent out of the process of the Chatterley trial and its outcome. Prosecutions of publishers by individuals also remained a threat. Mary Whitehouse successfully brought a case in 1977 against *Gay News* on the grounds that its publication of a poem by James Kirkup portraying a gay Christ constituted a 'blasphemous libel'. An appeal to the House of Lords failed. Lord Scarman argued in his judgement that publishers should be pursued if any of their publications gave 'grave offence to the religious feelings of some of their fellow citizens or are such as to tend to deprave and corrupt persons who are likely to read them'.[85] The language was a clear restatement of the pre-1959 definition of obscenity. However, in terms of political rather than moral challenges to publishers, the UK government was humiliated, in its ineptness and its ignorance of the distinct Scottish jurisdiction, in its attempts to ban Peter Wright's behind-the-scenes account of the UK security services, *Spycatcher*, in 1987. It could be argued that, in an age of broadcast news and documentary, the print media had lost their power to reach a wide public and were regarded by government and courts alike as of only minor importance in the information ecumene.

While these social challenges were still being framed in a fashion familiar to the 'young men' from the inter-war generation, in addition to the already noted paperback revolution, the 1960s saw another trend in publishing that would dramatically alter the publishing landscape, namely the sweeping of family-owned and small independent operations into a net of global corporate existence. Some examples include the Edinburgh-based Thomas Nelson & Sons, taken over by the Anglo-Canadian media corporation Thomson in

85 *Whitehouse* v. *Gay News Ltd* [1979] AC 617, HL, 664.

1962, then systematically dismantled and amalgamated with other media acquisitions, and Longmans, bought out and amalgamated in 1968 with the multinational conglomerate Pearson, who in turn took over Penguin in 1970. Mergers and acquisitions marked the decade in a manner that would have implications for how British publishing interests were subsequently viewed, often as mere cogs within transnational media clusters. Indeed, the mass-market strategies that had marked Allen Lane's entrance into the British market gathered momentum as British book publishing began grappling with the fact that previously lucrative and captive colonial markets were no longer passive recipients of British texts but now required new strategies in face of the decolonisation process and an incipient growth of indigenous publishing interests.

A stepped process of reorganisation saw UK publishers move from dependency on representation in overseas territories by independent agencies, to the establishment of wholly owned overseas branches carrying out the agency functions of import and distribution, and finally to an evolution of these overseas branches from import agents to autonomous commissioners and publishers of locally focussed titles, as noted below. Throughout this, the Traditional Market Agreement (TMA) was used by UK publishers from 1947 to 1975 to consolidate commercial control over those territories that were seeking greater cultural and political autonomy, ultimately leading to independence, beginning with India in 1947 itself. The TMA was a non-statutory concordat arrived at in 1947 between UK publishers.[86] Until its termination in 1975, after an Anti-Trust suit brought in the USA in 1974, the TMA divided the markets for English-language books into those that were exclusive to one or other of UK or US editions, and those that were 'open' where both editions competed against one another. UK publishers tended to exercise their monopoly in those territories, with the occasional exception of Canada, which formed the new Commonwealth. So New Zealand, South Africa and, to a greater extent, Australia were among key protected markets for UK publishing. No British publisher would buy or sell rights in a particular title unless a monopoly was ceded over sales in the Traditional Markets.

Contracts for the publication of specific titles would condense the TMA as 'British Commonwealth and Empire as constituted in 1947'; or by the early 1960s as 'British Commonwealth and Empire as constituted at the date of this agreement together with the Republic of South Africa, the Irish Republic,

---

86 Bryant, 'English language publication and the British Traditional Market Agreement'; de Bellaigue, *British book publishing*.

Burma, Egypt, Iraq, Israel, Jordan and the British Trusteeships with the rest of the world an open market except the USA, its dependencies and the Philippine Islands'. From the mid-1960s some UK contracts omitted Israel; while others, in the face of aggressive US competition, clarified the position of Canada by specifying 'UK and Commonwealth including Canada'.[87]

The TMA was significant because of the dependence of the UK on its overseas markets. Exports accounted for 40 per cent of the total British books manufactured in 1961; 25 per cent of these were destined for Australia alone.[88] Even after the demise of the TMA, and a consequent slump in UK exports, Australia represented significant sales for publishers: in 1984 it and New Zealand still accounted for 11.8 per cent and 1.6 per cent respectively of Penguin's turnover.[89] The TMA protected those sales from US encroachment for the best part of thirty years. For some time, moreover, publishers could depend on a common legal framework within most of the territories specified within the TMA, in terms of both a foundation of English legal principles and practices and a tendency, even after independence, to look to precedents set in the courts of London.[90] The desire of the markets in the TMA territories was increasingly for educational material, both formal textbooks and other reading that came informally into that category.

From 1947 onwards, publication of textbook and educational works for emerging Commonwealth markets became a primary focus of the UK industry. So for Thomas Nelson & Sons, with its strong presence in the home educational market noted above, overseas markets for textbooks became key areas of concentration, with spin-off branches established to ensure representation of its products: in 1949 the Canadian branch became an independent company; in 1960 the Australian firm was established; in 1962 the South African branch was registered as a distinct company; a Nigerian company was set up in 1961; a Kenyan company followed in 1963. Nelsons moved swiftly to consolidate its indigenous targeted material, publishing a wide range of textbooks in Kiswahili, Yoruba, Ewe, Twi and Ga, while specialist schoolbooks such as West Indian histories and Malayan arithmetics illustrated the company's determination to retain its hold on important but vulnerable markets. In 1962 Thomas Nelson & Sons was absorbed into the Thomson Organisation, in an effort to sustain these academic and educational publishing interests on a global scale. The production plant remained in Edinburgh until its demolition six years later, while the editorial offices

---

87 Clark, *Publishing agreements*.   88 Johanson, *Colonial editions in Australia*.
89 Field, *The publishing industry*.   90 McCleery, '"Sophisticated smut"'.

moved to London. (In 1969, the successful US division was sold off to a Tennessee-based religious publishing firm that retained the name Thomas Nelson & Sons. In 2012 it was, in turn, taken over by HarperCollins.) The move to London represented the first in a number of changes of address indicative of the imprint's role as a building block in international merger and acquisition strategies. Thomson merged the imprint with its acquisition of Pitman and it moved to Walton-upon-Thames. Thomas Nelson & Sons made a further migration to Cheltenham as a result of its sale by Pearson, which had only just bought it from Thomson, to the Dutch conglomerate Wolters Kluwers. Kluwers merged the imprint in 2000 with Stanley Thornes to form a new division, Nelson Thornes. In 2012, Nelson Thornes was part of Infinitas Learning, an international company specialising in multimedia educational publishing. All this movement from 1962 onwards was itself a local consequence of global realignments in publishing.

Nelsons was not the only company to shift emphasis in textbook publication to Commonwealth countries. Firms such as Evans Brothers and Longman worked hard to expand their educational textbook lists in new ways, liaising with local authors and publishing houses to create material specific to target audiences, and in both cases having great success in Nigeria. Both were to suffer significant losses in 1980 when Nigeria imposed currency restrictions and the flow of funds out of the country ceased. Longman, for example, saw turnover from Nigerian interests that year go 'from 10 million pounds to nothing', with resulting mass redundancies of almost half the staff of their African division of seventy. As its then joint managing director Tim Rix noted, while redundancies would become a common thing in the second wave of mergers and acquisitions that marked the 1980s and 1990s, at this early stage 'nothing like that had ever happened in Longman – neither had it happened much in British publishing'.[91]

Even Penguin felt it necessary to move into educational publishing. However, this was consistent with the firm's overall cultural mission, in particular its emphasis upon informal education – as opposed to the provision of school and academic textbooks for formal education. The democratisation of knowledge was the more obvious goal of a number of specialist series – Pelicans, Penguin Specials, Penguin Classics, and others such as the Penguin Shakespeare – but was also fundamental to all of Penguin's endeavours. This meant not that the commercial imperative took second place to educational,

---

91 Bradley, *The British book trade*, p. 45.

cultural and political ambitions but that the two co-existed within the company, yoked together by the stubborn vision of Allen Lane. The eventual move by Penguin into more formal educational publishing followed an agreement with the then Longmans, Green for Commonwealth exploitation of the Penguin lists in 1959. Longmans, rather than Penguin, was the more eager suitor with most to gain from access to Penguin's list and brand identity. Mark Longman stressed his company's large overseas network for educational and academic publishing on a global scale: in Africa, India, the Far East, Australasia, the West Indies and Canada.[92] Penguin realised the advantages of this expansion of its markets and signed, rather tentatively perhaps, an agency agreement with Longmans, Green. The latter would hold Penguin stock locally in its overseas offices and pass orders to Penguin in the UK. Such stock was held on the basis of a 7.5 per cent commission for the first year and 10 per cent for the further four years the contract was to run. The USA, Canada, Australia and New Zealand were initially excluded from this agreement, as Penguin felt relatively secure in those territories in terms of its own representation and market intelligence.

By the early 1960s, a more formal entry into educational publishing had been decided on: 'a highly competitive and specialized area of publishing', as Jeremy Lewis notes in his biography of Lane.[93] It represented 'dangerous waters' that demanded a specialised sales force, specialist suppliers, and specialist marketing and promotion – but was seductive because it seemed to be simply an institutionalisation of Penguin's prior role in informal education. Lewis also quotes 10,000 copies of the Penguin Classics edition of Vasari's *Lives of the artists* being sold in a year after its adoption as textbook by the new UK Open University.[94] Change was in the air in education and Penguin felt it was entitled, as much as Robert Maxwell, to catch the tide of expansion in the UK and overseas.

In 1964, Penguin was appointed, again with Longmans Green, as publisher for the Nuffield Foundation's Science Teaching Project, providing a set of innovative teaching materials for a five-year secondary course in physics, chemistry and biology. The stability and repetitive nature of the market indicated a very profitable business model over a period of time. However, the move into education generally had demanded an investment of £500,000: Penguin's educational endeavours had therefore to generate high levels of profit in order to recoup that initial investment. Profit margins had to be managed. The *Sunday Times* noted at the time that the school textbook

92 Penguin Archive D M1663/2.   93 Lewis, *Penguin special*, p. 374.   94 *Ibid.*, p. 375.

venture was 'currently squeezing Penguin's margins but should reach the break-even point next year' (that is, in 1969).[95] Optimisation of profits from 1964 to 1969 required also the maximisation of overseas sales in its TMA-protected markets. Penguin was capable of this success without sacrificing its mission. *Lord of the flies* and *Animal farm* sold in vast numbers to schools in the UK and overseas; the latter had sold 700,000 copies up to 1962.[96] Examples like Penguin demonstrate how the move into formal educational publishing and its need to exploit overseas textbook markets often put a strain on the governance, the management structures and the level of independence of publishing firms during this period.

1970–2010

Allen Lane, the last of the inter-war 'young men', died in 1970. Penguin Books had been incorporated, distinct from the Bodley Head, as a private limited company on 15 January 1936, with all the shares held by Lane and his two brothers. In 1961 the status of the company was changed to that of a public limited company with its shares available to trade in the stock exchange. Lane gave two reasons for this in a memo to all Penguin staff in April 1961: firstly, 'to assure, as far as is humanly possible, that the future conduct of the firm will be on the lines which we have followed since our earliest days' – in other words, he was very conscious of the distinctive Penguin mission and wished somehow to build it into the structure of the company rather than having it depend on his personal vision; and, secondly 'to protect my family after my death' through the establishment of a share-owning Trust.[97] The share issue was, as noted above, very successful: it provided to many who bought the shares a large instant return and, when sold for this quick profit, enabled a consolidation of holdings that defeated the initial rationed allocation of 200 shares per applicant. There were two consequences of this public flotation: other publishers began to build up a share in Penguin (such as McGraw-Hill, the US educational publisher, owning eventually 17.3 per cent) and through these holdings could influence the policies and direction of the company. Lane placed too much faith in his own 51 per cent holding. Even the value of the shares on the Stock Market was an intangible, but nonetheless potent, influence upon the company mission. Small sales of shares after an unpopular or uncommercial venture could bring the share value down and inculcate

---

95 *Sunday Times* 10 November 1968, p. 36.   96 Penguin Archive D M1294/4/2/1.
97 Memo dated 19 April 1961 from Allen Lane to all staff, Penguin Archive D M1819 Box 16.

a reluctance to do anything like that again. The pressure to provide healthy dividends to keep up the share value could curb innovation and result in market-chasing rather than market-leading.

The takeover by (though presented as a merger with) Pearson Longman when it did take place in a precipitate fashion after Lane's death was based on chasing the formal educational market – prefigured over a decade earlier in the initial agency agreement with Longmans Green. It was also a reaction to a threatened takeover by McGraw-Hill, whose shareholding was seen as a platform for a fuller bid. Better a British corporate takeover than a North American one seemed to be the xenophobic rationale. Some of the rhetoric in support of the merger with Longman as part of the Pearson Group was very over the top: Christopher Dolley, then Managing Director of Penguin, forecast a 50 per cent increase in profits due to the merger based on increased sales generated through the entry into educational publishing.[98] However, it was the sort of rhetoric designed to appeal to the anonymous figures of the Stock Market. Lord Boyle, formerly Edward Boyle, a Conservative MP, then acting Chairman of Penguin, claimed in a letter to all shareholders that the Longman deal 'was the best prospect for maintaining the company's independence, integrity and tradition for offering good reading at acceptable prices'.[99] The new company was 60 per cent Pearson, 40 per cent Penguin.

For the rest of UK publishing, takeover became more difficult to avoid. Victor Gollancz died in 1967 and his company passed into the hands of his daughter Livia. In 1989 she sold it to the American publisher Houghton Mifflin; in 1992 Houghton Mifflin sold it to Cassell; and in 1998 Cassell was taken over by the Orion Group, within which Gollancz remains as an imprint. The publishing firm of Jonathan Cape had survived the Second World War with a strong list of fiction and poetry. In the post-war period, its most profitable author was Ian Fleming; the revenue from the James Bond novels enabled Cape to take risks on unknown literary fiction. Jonathan Cape himself died in 1960. In the late 1960s, the firm combined with three other publishing houses (Chatto & Windus in 1969, the Bodley Head in 1973, and Virago Press in 1982) to form a consortium, preserving the editorial independence of the individual companies, but intended to stave off the threat of conglomerate acquisition. However, this ploy was ultimately unsuccessful, and the whole group became part of Random House in 1987 and therefore by 2013 an imprint of Bertelsmann, with the exception of Virago, which, after a management buyout, had been sold to Little, Brown. From the 1980s, it

98 Penguin Archive DM1819 Box 21.   99 *Ibid.*

became difficult, as in the case of Cape, to disentangle UK publishing from global publishing. The international industry stabilised in terms of its overall structure: a small number of very large, cross-media global conglomerates and a large number of smaller companies operating at national level. For the latter, their domestic markets represented the primary focus and source of titles and revenue. The UK publishing industry itself became increasingly concentrated. By 2004, it consisted of more than 15,000 publishers, covering 48,000 imprints. Of these, approximately 2,700 (the number registered for VAT [Value Added Tax] and therefore claiming a minimum level of turnover of £61,000) were publishing on a regular basis. The top ten of these accounted for 65 per cent of all bookshop sales; the top five 55 per cent; and the three largest publishers – Bertelsmann, News Corporation and Pearson – controlled 45 per cent of the consumer market alone.[100]

However, the 1970s also saw the rise for a period of a wave of independent publishing companies that challenged corporate developments and focussed on under-represented groups and interests. These were, in the main, new, start-up firms whose founders explored, and made successful headway in opening to the mainstream, previously ignored agendas and work in feminist, Scottish literature and gender areas. The 'young men' of this generation were being overtaken by an increasing number of women, who used their autonomy from corporate structures in order to innovate in publishing and to influence social change, as previous generations of publishers had done. There had been influential female players in the decision-making processes in UK publishing, including successful literary agents such as Christine Campbell Thomson (1897–1985), active as writer, editor of the influential 'Not at Night' horror anthologies for Selwyn & Blount and Hutchinson from 1925 to 1937, and later founder of the influential literary agency that would evolve into Campbell Thomson and McLaughlin Ltd, and later amalgamate with the Marsh Agency in 2006. Others such as Norah Smallwood had started from the bottom and worked extremely hard to become powerful arbiters. Smallwood commenced her publishing career as a secretary in Chatto & Windus in 1936, and thirty-nine years later in 1975 became its Managing Director, a role she retained until retiring in 1982. Eunice Frost worked under the shadow of Allen Lane at Penguin: she joined the company as Lane's secretary in 1936, a year after its creation, rose to the post of Executive Editor, and, before her retirement in 1960, had become one of Penguin's Board of Directors. But the early 1970s saw more determined pushes by

---

100 *UK publishing industry statistics yearbook 2006*, p. 2.

women to redefine old publishing certainties: in Scotland, Stephanie Wolfe-Murray co-founded Canongate publishing in 1973, which would go on to enjoy significant success in issuing ground-breaking work by Alasdair Gray and Lady Antonia Fraser. In the same year, Virago Press was set up in London by an expatriate Australian, Carmen Callil, and her colleagues Harriet Spicer and Ursula Owen. Initially dedicated to republishing neglected works by female writers, it expanded to feature distinctive works 'for women by women', and by the end of the 1970s was producing sales of half a million pounds on its initial slender investment.[101] Its success led to its takeover by and absorption into the Chatto, Bodley Head and Cape Group in 1982, with Callil becoming joint managing director of Chatto as part of the merger. Virago's unique branding of its paperback titles in distinctive green covers echoed the successful format of Penguin, and proved equally as influential. As Philippa Harrison, first female president of the Publishers Association 1998–99 and co-founder of the firm Little, Brown, explained: 'Many people of my generation were affected by the concept of Virago . . . the idea of the list, excellent, occasionally great literature by women . . . coming back into the mainstream, gave us a sense of our own history . . . Gradually we all began to publish the sorts of books that would have gone to Virago.'[102] Such successes emboldened other women to follow, particularly as key support networks sprang up to promote the status of women in publishing, such as the London-based Women in Publishing organisation, founded in 1979 with input from Liz Calder and Ursula Owen. Small yet nimble independent publishers focussed on women's writing were started in the wake of Virago's success, such as the Women's Press, founded in 1978 to publish feminist fiction and non-fiction titles, Honno, founded in 1986 with support from the Welsh Book Council to promote Welsh women's work, and Persephone Books, founded in 1999 to revive interest in out-of-print popular 'middlebrow' titles by women. Throughout the 1980s and 1990s there was also a significant influx into the higher echelons of British publishing of talented women, including Liz Calder, who would become editorial director of Gollancz and Cape and later Bloomsbury. Marion Sinclair took over editorial direction of the Edinburgh-based, formerly student-run, Polygon Books in 1990 and proved fleet-footed in securing work by notable authors such as James Kelman and Alexander McCall Smith, turning Polygon into a cultural leader in Scotland, recognised in 1993 by the *Sunday Times* as best small publisher of the year.

101 Stevenson, *Book makers*, pp. 241–2.   102 Bradley (ed.), *The British book trade*, p. 215.

The twenty-first century publishing landscape suggests that opportunities for women to engage productively in UK print and publishing circles have expanded exponentially since the early 1970s, when the general workforce in editorial and management sectors of publishing had been overwhelmingly male. By 2007, key UK trade publishing firms could boast large female workforces, with women running some of the UK's largest publishing houses, such as Helen Fraser at Penguin, Gail Rebuck at Random House and Victoria Barnsley at HarperCollins. In 2007, female staff across the Penguin Group as a whole totalled 75 per cent of the workforce; HarperCollins reported a gender balance across most sectors of the firm of 70 per cent women and 30 per cent men, while women made up twelve of Hodder & Stoughton's senior editorial team of three publishing directors and thirteen commissioning editors.[103]

What becomes clear when looking at such issues in particular, contextualised within the trajectory of publishing in general after the war, is that the pace of change in publishing has accelerated as global forces have borne down on British firms. As Richard Ohmann accurately summarised in relation to the global book trade: 'Publishing was the last culture industry to attain modernity. Not until after World War II did it become part of the large corporate sector, and adopt the practices of the publishing and marketing characteristic of monopoly capital.'[104] The general traits and practices of British family-run and family-focussed publishing houses gave way to the force of international corporate interests. One can see this in the way the Net Book Agreement, a system in place since 1900 whereby books were retailed at an agreed, fixed price, was eventually dismantled in the mid-1990s under concerted pressure from bookselling chains such as Waterstone's and key publishing conglomerates like HarperCollins and Random House. While the collapse of the NBA led to shifts downwards in retail prices for popular and best-selling books, it also exerted pressure on small, independent publishers of niche material, whose profit margins were substantially reduced to the point where many were either forced out of business or acquired and absorbed by larger competitors.

The process of globalisation gathered pace from the 1970s onwards, and clearly reveals a changing pattern of ownership. As book market dominance by transnational organisations increased, there was a corresponding shift in the control and shaping of international book markets, particularly in the

---

103 Alison Bone, 'Men – an endangered species?', *Bookseller* 18 May 2007, p. 46.
104 Ohmann, *Selling culture*, p. 22.

Anglophone world. Whereas in the nineteenth century Britain led the way in terms of creating, defining and exporting book trade initiatives, in the mid-twentieth century, with the loss of its colonies as captive markets and the takeover and merger of many of its family-based firms, there was a noticeable shift towards US and European rivals as significant players in the world market. What becomes clear in examining these shifts is the emergence of two types of multinational firms with distinctive foci. Firstly, there was the development of primarily print-based operations working in a number of different countries (for example, the German-based Bertelsmann and Oxford University Press); and secondly, there was the evolution of multi-media organisations in which book publishing was only one and not necessarily the most important of information outlets (for example News Corporation, the owner of HarperCollins, and Pearson, owner of Penguin). The large corporations operated (and operate) multi-stranded imprints within the UK targeting different market segments. Thus, under the French-based Hachette corporate umbrella, which in 2007 was the largest trade (consumer) publisher in the UK with an estimated UK trade revenue of £298.8 million, one finds listed the following UK imprints: Hodder & Stoughton, John Murray, Headline, Octopus, Orion, Weidenfeld & Nicolson, Gollancz, Phoenix, Little, Brown and Virago. Random House, itself owned by Bertelsmann, which in 2007 occupied second place in terms of UK trade revenue (£263.4 million), operates over thirty separate imprints in the UK, including Jonathan Cape, Chatto & Windus, William Heinemann, Harvill Secker, Bodley Head, Century, Hutchinson, Transworld, Doubleday and BBC Books.[105]

The distinction between forms of corporate organisation remains, however, less clear-cut than the above division implies, as companies that grew as a result of horizontal integration began also expanding through vertical integration of activities upstream and downstream from the core publishing business. The ongoing transition (driven partly by digital technologies) from publishers producing only books and, for example, studios producing only films and television programmes, to conglomerates doing both (and more) has blurred the distinction between the two types of conglomerates from the 1990s onwards. The original publishing conglomerates shared the characteristics of other contemporary media industries: large capital investment, mass production for mass markets, and the creation of marketable products that also formed a globalised cultural asset. These players have instituted

---

105 Thompson, *Merchants of culture*, pp. 120–4.

significant technical developments that have shaped contemporary book markets. Thus we have seen an important shift away from fiction to non-fiction titles as the commercially dominant part of a publishers' list, with what Robert Escarpit has called 'functional books', particularly textbooks, providing 'powerful testament to the commercial significance of the captive market delivered to the book trade by the systems of higher and secondary education'.[106]

The ability to exploit digital material, whether text, sound or image, across a number of media has also increased the dependence on what has been termed 'synergy'. Many media conglomerates were fired by the 'dotcom mania' of the 1990s to acquire interests in the new digital technologies and products with which to complement, and cross-promote, existing interests in analogue services and products, again including book publishing. Over 80 per cent of the material available online is in English, a further factor consolidating the hegemony of the English language. The synergy sought by these companies was based on a clear model of integration itself dependent on the ability to translate the value of intellectual property from medium to medium under international protection of its rights.

The book products of the media conglomerates find an international market that was in previous centuries the achievement only of sacred books, such as the Christian Bible. The example of J. K. Rowling's series of books about the young wizard Harry Potter is instructive in this instance. In this case, however, the media clustering around the book has been accomplished through the robust mediation of Rowling's literary agent, the Christopher Little Agency. Their parcelling up and canny negotiations of international book and film rights, commercial tie-ins, podcasts, audio books and other media outputs has created a nexus of activity spread across a variety of media platforms, and drawn together a variety of media organisations and publishers with the aim of controlling the process of dissemination and distribution.[107] These books have achieved an immense international success initially in the English-speaking world and then, as the series progressed, in over forty translations. (The time-lag between English-language publication and French translation of *Harry Potter and the order of the phoenix* led to the English version becoming the number one children's best-seller in France in the interval – a phenomenon repeated in Germany in 2007 with the publication of *Harry Potter and the deathly hallows*.) That success has been

106 Milner, *Literature, culture and society*, p. 70.
107 Patterson, 'J. K. Rowling and Harry Potter'.

enhanced by the making of the novels into films, and the consequent re-promotion of the titles; it has been strengthened by crossover sales between the children's and adult markets encouraged by the books' publishers, for example in the provision of separate jackets or covers for each; and it has been optimised by the manipulation of hardback and paperback publishing schedules to ensure maximum purchase of the more expensive format before the cheaper is issued on a fresh wave of publicity and expectation. Such an international outreach, particularly from the making of the films onwards, might constitute evidence for the homogenisation of international culture, or more likely is evidence of control exerted on behalf of an individual author by a committed representative.

On the other hand, such cross-border activity has been accompanied by a devolution and rationalisation of tasks and activities that once were the domain of centralised, in-house units, but since the turn of the twenty-first century have increasingly been outsourced to independent operators. Freelance editors and marketing specialists become tasked with working on individual titles on a piece rate basis; typesetting from digital files is now undertaken in centres far from central offices, as is the production and printing of titles. The key point is a decentralisation of activity that seeks to ensure all parts of the production process are undertaken wherever labour costs are cheapest.

The same could be said for the way the publishing industry is facing a slow displacement of physical spaces for displaying and promoting works (book-shops, libraries) by the digital realities of twenty-first-century commerce. The World Wide Web has become an established resource for retail selling and purchasing of all sorts since the turn of the twenty-first century. It has also become a powerful tool for promoting goods, and a space where sales of both hard copies and digital versions of texts are adding complexities to the publishing model. This situation was partly due to the success of Amazon, launched as an online bookshop in 1995 (and introduced into the UK in 1998) with a user-friendly interface, the use of 'intelligent agents' to replace the bookshop assistant, a range of contemporary and out-of-print 'stock' out-stripping any constraint by a physical building, and the launch in 2007 of its e-book reader, the Kindle, which has created new revenue streams from digital content. Its founder, Jeff Bezos, was named *Time* magazine's 'Man of the Year' in 1999 for the manner in which he had transformed online shopping. Larger publishers, such as Penguin, began at this time to build up websites that not only gave bibliographical details of their titles but provided complementary material of all kinds, ranging from author interviews to reading guides for book groups. Smaller publishers tried to follow suit, but, given their restricted resources and tight margins, tended to produce static web pages that aged quickly and were not revised or updated.

Conglomerates represent an absorption of individual entrepreneurial initiative, including the absorption of independent talent, such as Victoria Barnsley, discussed below, developed within the remaining independent sector. It could also be argued that this can lead to a loss of social or moral vision in publishing, particularly in cases where principles conflict with profit. HarperCollins itself was the result of an arranged marriage in 1987 by News Corporation between two publishers in which it had stakes. At the time this amounted in the case of Collins to some 41 per cent of its shares, but in a hostile bid in 1988 News Corporation bought the balance, giving it complete control. Collins had been one of the last of the family publishing businesses from the nineteenth century to succumb to takeover (as Nelsons had before it). The News Corporation purchase was not without acrimony, particularly in the light of broken promises not to move editorial posts out of Scotland to London.[108] This, like Nelsons, Oliver & Boyd, and later Chambers, was also indicative of a process of geographical concentration as well as amalgamation of imprints, leaving London as the undisputed centre of publishing in the UK when at one time, in the nineteenth century, Edinburgh might have been seen as its peer.[109] HarperCollins in 1998 withdrew its commitment to the publication of *East and West*, Chris Patten's memoir of his period as final British Governor of Hong Kong, in the light of its parent company News Corporation's ambition to expand in the virgin market of the People's Republic of China.[110] The editor who had commissioned the autobiography, Stuart Profitt, resigned as an act of principle, moving on to another job at Penguin, but the corporate juggernaut trundled on in its pursuit of commercial gain, and Patten's book was published by another publishing conglomerate, Macmillan, which was less perturbed by the political issues.[111] Not that Rupert Murdoch, the owner of News Corporation, did not also have political intent within the UK as well. Robert Maxwell may have set a precedent in using his companies, particularly his newspapers, to wield political influence, but News Corporation was more blatant in aspects of this such as using HarperCollins to pay large advances to political figures for books that were unlikely to recover these advances through sales. Many of the works

---

108 Finkelstein, 'The globalization of the book', pp. 323–5.
109 Nash, 'The changing face of the publishing house', p. 197.
110 McKnight and Hobbs, '"You're all a bunch of pinkos"'.
111 Squires, *Marketing literature*, p. 22.

commissioned were memoirs by politicians who during their careers had promoted, or at least not obstructed, the onward march of News Corporation's commercial expansion, such as Peter Carrington (1988), Margaret Thatcher (1993) and John Major (1999). Intervention in civil society by publishers was no longer a matter of fighting for freedom of expression or pursuing a progressive agenda; it was purely to protect the ability of the corporation to make profits by increasing its oligopolistic outreach.

The manner of operation of conglomerates – seen in the case of Penguin after 1970 – focusses on the paramount need to maintain a level of profit appropriate to the expectations of shareholders and stock exchanges. When the Bertelsmann conglomerate took over the Random House conglomerate in 1998, the new owners expected Random House to make a 15 per cent profit and to increase turnover by 10 per cent annually. This would have entailed a leap in profits from \$1 million to \$150 million on annual sales of roughly \$1 billion; it would also have involved a concurrent growth in those sales of \$100 million. André Schiffrin sums up the conclusion to this process: 'The logic of the profit center began to be counterproductive. The need for each entity [within the conglomerate] to achieve an annual increase in sales and profit forced every part of the publishing house to duplicate the other's efforts and to compete for the most lucrative titles.'[112]

One result of this logic was further closure of long-standing imprints. Oliver & Boyd had been founded, like Nelsons, at the end of the eighteenth century. From the middle of the nineteenth century, its educational and medical lists dominated and provided the basis for strong export revenues. This position persisted until the second half of the twentieth century when the company retrenched to serve the distinctive Scottish educational market. The company was sold to the Pearson Group in 1962. The university and general publishing departments were immediately closed but the schools division continued to thrive. Its textbooks designed for the then new Scottish Standard Grade examinations anticipated the change from O-level to GCSE in England and Wales and captured some of the market south of the border. However, Oliver & Boyd was closed down completely by the then Pearson Longman in 1989 with a turnover of £2.75 million and a net profit level of 10 per cent. Its closure left Scotland at that point without an educational publisher to supply the needs of its distinctive schools system. The Oliver & Boyd list was transferred to Longman in Harlow and allowed to expire in time.

112 Schiffrin, *The business of books*, p. 76.

Another result of conglomerate logic was the stress on minimising risk and optimising the security of the company's investment in content. This in turn led to both an increased emphasis upon the secure educational market, noted already and seen in the Pearson takeover of Oliver & Boyd, and, in the case of trade publishing, an increasing blandness and homogeneity of publication. Pearson has moved from horizontal integration by taking over other educational publishers to vertical integration across education by taking over education and training providers themselves. Such opportunities were previously available through ownership and integration of hardback and paperback imprints, or of book publishing companies and film production studios, or of film and TV production, or of production companies and TV networks, or of all of these (in the case of News Corporation).

While the independent sector continued to exist – and on occasion to thrive, as in the case of Bloomsbury, founded in 1986, powered by the global success of its sales of the Harry Potter novels – the talent it possessed, whether of authors, editors or ideas, could easily fall prey to the stronger financial muscle of the conglomerates. Fourth Estate, established by Victoria Barnsley in 1984, acquired a strong reputation for publishing new fiction that achieved critical and commercial success. It was taken over by HarperCollins in 2000. Barnsley became CEO of HarperCollins itself and Fourth Estate survived within the larger group as an imprint 'licensed' to take risks on new writers, though whether this has resulted in expected innovation is not certain. The firm of Hamish Hamilton had from its beginnings in 1931 also built up a record of publishing innovative fiction. It was taken over by the Thomson Organisation in 1965, which then sold it on to Pearson in 1986. It performs similar roles within Pearson's trade publishing to those of Fourth Estate within HarperCollins: to appeal to new talent and readers in terms of a brand identity distinct from that of its parent and to be more speculative in terms of that new talent (in the hope of finding another J. K. Rowling).

'Young' men and women, those expected to innovate and provoke change in publishing, no longer found their own way, as in the earlier cases of Cape, Gollancz, Lane, Weidenfeld, Maxwell and Callil, but were harnessed to the need to maintain the dividends of investors and owners. The same could be said of the entrepreneurs powering Apple, who have pioneered methods of selling online digital products, Amazon, who have dominated online sales and distribution of books, and Google, who are dominating data gathering and searching and digitisation of texts. Perhaps it was that there were no new battles to fight in the name of social progress. Apple and Amazon in particular concentrated on the consolidation of virtual monopolies in hardware, software and delivery of digitised content. The business models they introduced, while on occasion heralded as libertarian in the sense of freeing authors from the evil of intermediaries such as agents or publishers by offering them direct access to the marketplace, sought to ring-fence markets through hardware and software exclusivity. In the case of Apple and Amazon, sheer size and volume of sales, whether of the iPad or the Kindle, provided the leverage; in the case of Amazon, this also included the purchase of ancillary businesses such as AbeBooks and LoveFilm while opening online stores, including Kindle stores, in a number of language regions (other than English). Google, while promising to 'do no evil', began a process of digitisation of texts both in and out of copyright, in collaboration with major academic libraries such as the Bodleian and Harvard, with the results only available through Google services. This professed to be another exercise in the liberation of the digital consumer from archaic and restrictive practices pursued by publishers; but it may well be seen by future generations as the foundation of a new monopoly over the digital text. From this one can see a particular repetitious cyclical pattern of development, expansion, conglomeration and attenuation. A cynical view might see also a relentless focus on economic and financial factors at the expense of the more socially inclined goals that might have inspired earlier generations of print and publishing families and workers.

6

Distribution and bookselling

IAIN STEVENSON

During most of the twentieth century, the distribution and retailing of books in Britain appeared a remarkably stable business. Although many of the trends that would transform the trade had already begun, before the expansion of chains and, above all, the collapse of the Net Book Agreement in 1995, a small-town bookseller and its customers would have found the experience of merchandising, selecting and buying a book had hardly changed from that of their counterparts of 1914. While the retail environment for food, clothing and household goods had been transformed by new techniques of presentation and selling and the emergence of new forms of outlet such as self-service supermarkets and out-of-town stores based on models imported from the United States, most book-buyers would still typically make their purchases from an owner-managed high street shop which was often dowdy, poorly stocked and meagrely staffed. Many of these occupied the same site and sometimes even possessed the same shop-fittings and décor they had at the century's beginning. While some customers found such conservative surroundings reassuring, others chafed at the poor service and limited choice with which they were presented.

By the end of the period under consideration, the distribution and selling of books and other publications has been radically transformed. Virtually all the old, established bookselling names have disappeared and the options available to purchasers in 'bricks and mortar' locations, and latterly in cyberspace, are bewilderingly complex in format, price, availability and capability. Predictions abound that the purveyors of what have become known as 'p-[for 'print'] books' are at least critically endangered, more likely terminally ill, and the future for the sale of fashionably described 'content' is emphatically digital.

Neither of these generalisations – stability through most of the twentieth century and then rapid change at the century's end – is overwhelmingly, or even partially, true. The long period of supposed stability contained much change and development and the 'continuous revolution' of the century's end retained many features of the old system, suggesting an exaggerated narrative of the decline of the bookselling trade. This chapter provides a detailed account of book wholesaling and retailing, adopting a thematic narrative approach. It provides a chronological description of how booksellers, their suppliers (publishers and wholesalers) and their ultimate customers (individuals and libraries) reacted to new opportunities and constraints of the twentieth and twenty-first centuries.

A useful concept for interpreting this history is that of the 'supply and value chain'. In reality, these are two distinct but closely related ideas. The supply chain in bookselling links the original creator (the author) with the publisher (the packager) to the wholesaler (the distributor), the retailer (the bookshop) and eventually the customer (the reader) by the sequential movement of physical objects (books). The main direction of travel in this chain is from left to right, but in bookselling, more than any other branch of retailing, there are feedback loops in which the objects move in a reverse direction. This occurs notably in the 'returns process', a feature unique to the bookselling ecosystem and which, as this chapter explores, can be a crippling disadvantage. The articulation of the supply chain is complicated, since it has progressively become longer and its functions have become the prerogative of commercial operators whose interests are often at odds with each other. The supply chain, therefore, is concerned with the logistics of the physical movement of books, but it is closely shadowed by the value chain, which is concerned with the movement of money, again broadly in a left to right direction, but with complicated reverse flows, in the form of discounts (which transfer value from publishers to retailers and wholesalers) and royalties (from publishers to authors and literary agents). While the dominant flows within these chains are well established and understood by the participants, it has tended to be the reverse feedbacks that have caused dissension and tension between those involved, and the story of most of bookselling in this period has been dictated by attempts to control and regularise this tension, and to reach an uneasy common ground between suppliers and distributors whose interests have often been at variance. An ironic observation of the current turbulent digital model for bookselling is that the old disagreements have powerfully re-emerged, albeit with different protagonists and emphases, but with the supply and value chain concepts still clearly operational.

'The magna charta of the book trade'

At the close of the nineteenth century, there was a general perception that the book trade was in crisis.[1] Despite an enormously enhanced level of literacy, book sales were sluggish, and although there had been a number of new publishing businesses established, like Heinemann and Methuen, the output of books was dominated by firms whose origins (and business practices) were rooted in the early years of the century, or even the previous one. A large part of the trade was devoted to supplying three-volume novels to the circulating libraries like Mudie's. Once they had been circulated, these used publications were often 'dumped' on the retail market at very cheap prices. Some book-sellers, most notably W. H. Smith, which had grown from a single railway bookstall to a nationwide chain of shops selling cheap editions of popular authors ('the railway novels') and a wide range of non-fiction, had success-fully extended the market, particularly outside London, although for many their businesses to a substantial degree also comprised stationery, periodicals and dry goods.[2] Many booksellers, especially the single-owner-managed shop, felt excluded and battered by a market they felt was weighted unfairly against them.

Some of the concerns of the book trade dated to 1852 when in a landmark judgement Lord Campbell declared that the fixing of book prices was illegal.[3] This had been welcomed by entrepreneurial retailers like John Chapman as a liberation (although as a publisher himself he could exercise some control in his favour) but the onset of a deep economic depression in the 1880s, which led to the emergence of 'cutting booksellers' and vicious competition on price, drove many less resilient shops out of business. By the 1890s, book-sellers again felt that price regulation and an 'orderly market' was the only way in which their trade could survive. They argued that if they were to maintain an adequate stock from which customers could select, while keep-ing overheads under control, then price control must be eliminated and publishers should supply all retailers (through intermediaries or directly) on identical terms, no matter the size of order or enterprise, and with the consequence that the eventual purchasers had no option but to pay the same retail price no matter where the book was purchased. Retailers wished to retain some of the concessions that they had enjoyed from publishers like the 'odd-copy' system (which supplied thirteen copies for the price of twelve) and an additional 10 per cent discount for cash, but overall booksellers

---

1 Stevenson, *Book makers*, chapter 1.   2 Colclough, 'Distribution'.   3 Ashton, *146 Strand*.

agitated to withdraw within the bulwark of fixed prices and a 'level playing field' for all scales of operation. This was a remarkable demand in an age of deregulation and was justified by the claim that 'books are different', which was to resound throughout the period and long after.

The immediate consequence of this movement was the creation of a trade association, the United Booksellers of Great Britain and Ireland (now the Booksellers Association or BA) in 1895, but it was left to publishers to devise a workable model for what became known as 'net pricing'. Its initial advocate was Sir Frederick Macmillan, who as early as 1890 proposed to publish books on 'net terms' at a fixed price and discount. At this point, booksellers were still undecided and fearful of this development, but slowly the movement gained momentum and by 1895 Macmillan was publishing 140 new titles per year on net terms – 30 per cent of his firm's output. To keep its options open, Macmillan continued to distinguish between 'net' and 'subject' titles: these were popular books 'subject to no regulation as regards price and might be sold at a discount [to the bookshop customer] at the discretion of the dealer'.[4] Thus he rather cautiously confined net terms to relatively expensive non-fiction and luxury illustrated or finely bound books, with which it might be concluded price competition was a relatively unimportant feature.

It took other newer and more adventurous publishers to prosecute the introduction of net pricing more energetically into the wider marketplace. William Heinemann, who had set up his firm only in 1890, aggressively applied net prices to his list. However, the real breakthrough came when the relative newcomer J. M. Dent launched his cheap reprint series the Temple Classics at net prices in 1894. He faced down opposition from the major bookseller Stoneham, and won the support of the wholesaler Simpkin Marshall, bringing net books to a mass market.

The United Booksellers were impressed by these successes but they failed to agree on a generally acceptable framework for net pricing across the trade. Instead, a group of fifty-eight publishers combined to form the Publishers Association (PA) in 1895 with the specific objective to create an agreed implementation of a new pricing regime.[5] Negotiations with the Booksellers were by no means smooth, but eventually, on 1 January 1900, the Net Book Agreement (NBA) came into force, with virtually all books published for the next ninety-five years subject to its controls.

---

4 Macmillan, *The Net Book Agreement*, p. 5.
5 Kingsford, *The Publishers Association*, chapter 1.

The principle of net pricing was that publishers who adhered to the Agreement would supply member booksellers with stock at fixed discounts across the trade. 'Standard' (later known as 'A') terms were one-third off the regulated retail price. (Later 'C' terms, 25 per cent discount, and 'B' terms, 30 per cent discount, were introduced for specialist categories.)[6] In return, retailers agreed to sell to customers at not less than the minimum net price fixed by the publisher. There were a number of exceptions which allowed for special short-term promotional pricing and the sale of 'excess stock' at remainder prices, and publishers could always opt to publish certain types of books 'non-net', mainly educational titles and other publications like prize books which tended not to be sold through retail booksellers. As discussed below, works of fiction remained 'specially exempted' from the system until World War I, after which they became 'almost universally published at net prices'.[7] Some publishers and a few booksellers like Stoneham refused to sign up to the Agreement but the overwhelming majority of the trade participated and found the new system welcome and beneficial.

The NBA did not receive such a warm reception from an important interest group which had been largely overlooked during the negotiations. The Society of Authors, led by Walter Besant and George Bernard Shaw, opposed the Agreement as against their interests since they believed it would be detrimental to their incomes. Shaw in fact remained intransigent throughout his long literary career and sought on many subsequent occasions to subvert or circumvent net pricing.[8] The agitation of the authors did have one important unforeseen consequence. To resolve their objections, the ownership of the NBA was vested in the publishers, who thereby had the sole right to determine prices, fix discounts and mete out punishment to defaulters. The booksellers, who had imagined that they were equal partners in the Agreement, were thus deprived of any significant influence in its operation.

Reaction to the NBA was not universally positive outside the book world. Press criticism was strident and suspicious. It was not surprising therefore that the first major challenge to it came from a newspaper, although this was launched for commercial rather than ideological reasons in what became known as 'the Book War'.[9] By 1905, the General Manager of *The Times*, Charles Moberly Bell, was seeking to reverse decreasing circulation of his paper, and used the services of a shady American advertising man, Horace Hooper, to create circulation-building promotions. Hooper's earliest scheme,

6 Stevenson, *Book makers*, p. 14.   7 Macmillan, *The Net Book Agreement*, p. 30.
8 Bonham-Carter, *Authors by profession*, vol. 1, chapter 9.
9 Macmillan, *The Net Book Agreement*, pp. 31–77.

to provide *Times* readers with cheap sets of (out-of-date) *Encyclopaedia Britannica*, had been a moderate success, selling over 20,000 copies, and this encouraged Hooper and Bell to extend their scheme to the opening of a Book Club whose membership would be free to the newspaper's annual subscribers.

Early in 1905, Hooper approached the leading members of the PA, outlining a scheme in sketchy detail and asking to be supplied on 'best trade terms'. He assured them that he was aware of the NBA and planned to observe its terms. He even prevailed upon Moberly Bell to sign it on behalf of *The Times* in July. Publishers were a little suspicious when Hooper made a condition of his business that they should guarantee to take advertising in the paper for a minimum of five years (on which Hooper would receive a commission). Despite these misgivings, most publishers saw this as a useful extension of sales and happily supplied Hooper with the books he wanted.

When the Club was publicly announced in September 1905 with full-page advertisements, publishers abruptly realised the extent of Hooper's duplicity. It was to be both a bookshop and a lending library (thus directly challenging the circulating libraries which had supported the introduction of the NBA and remained major customers of both publishers and retailers). Subscribers could buy not only new books at a discount of up to 25 per cent but also 'nearly new' titles (which had been lent out only twice) with up to 50 per cent discount. A catalogue listing all the books available was distributed in an edition of 100,000 copies. It offered 'clean uninjured copies ... virtually as good as new' at half net price.[10] Booksellers erupted in fury and publishers claimed they had been duped (but continued to sell books to the Club). Hooper was not to be knocked off his course. By April 1906 he claimed with characteristic hyperbole to be 'the largest buyer of books in the world' and in May opened a large building in Oxford Street in London accommodating a stock of 60,000 titles for sale or loan to Club members (and it was assumed to casual customers).[11]

Hooper (or possibly Moberly Bell) then turned on the NBA itself and on 1 May 1906 directly criticised the fixed price regime, as exploiting the book-buyer to produce 'the enormous balance ... [which] goes in profit to the publisher, author and bookseller', in an unsigned *Times* leading article.[12] This, and the fact that the new Oxford Street shop was besieged by eager customers buying three-guinea biographies at 7s 6d, and six-shilling novels at

---

10 *Ibid.*, p. 43. 11 Kingsford, *The Publishers Association*, p. 31n.
12 *The Times* 1 May 1906, p. 15.

ninepence, finally prompted the PA to action. An extraordinary meeting was convened by John Lane (whose Bodley Head imprint did little business with the Club) in July which proposed to amend the NBA to forbid the sale of new or second-hand books at less than published price until six months after publication, and to allow no net titles to be sold to the public at discounts greater than 25 per cent. This amended NBA came into force on 1 October 1906 but Moberly Bell refused to sign it, citing the terms of the previous agreement with Club members. Hooper gleefully pointed out that his two largest suppliers, the publisher Longman and the wholesaler Simpkin Marshall, had signed binding five-year contracts to supply on old terms. *The Times* continued to fan the flames in its leader columns with increasingly bitter and hysterical accusations thrown at publishers as monopolists of 'real evil'.[13]

Skirmishing continued through the early months of 1907, but the initial enthusiasm of customers for the Book Club waned as they found that neither the titles they wanted nor their condition lived up to promises. *The Times* began to lose subscribers and more and more publishers declined to supply. The paper used its recently established *Times Literary Supplement* to criticise uncooperative publishers in reviews and to point out which books were unavailable in the Club. A catharsis came in the closing months of 1907 when a pseudonymous letter in the paper (probably written by Moberly Bell) described John Murray's refusal to supply *The letters of Queen Victoria* to the Club as 'the act of Judas Iscariot'.[14] Murray sued for libel and won £7,500 damages.

Despite a few further successes (Shaw licensed a special edition of *John Bull's other island*), the Times Book Club was in retreat during 1907, and whereas it had earlier contributed to profits and circulation, it was now losing money and beginning to destabilise the continued survival of the paper itself. Predators in the shape of C. A. Pearson of the *Standard* and Lord Northcliffe of the *Daily Mail* saw the Book Club as a weakness of *The Times* and secretly negotiated with leading publishers an undertaking to modify the Club's operations to meet the new NBA if they were successful in a takeover. In May 1908 the Council of the PA agreed to support an anonymous 'Mr Bates' to implement the NBA with a prospective new owner of *The Times*. Northcliffe duly bought the paper two weeks later, sacking Hooper within days, and although Moberly Bell remained he quickly lost all taste for combat. In September, the Times Book Club signed the NBA, and although

13 *The Times* 26 September 1906, p. 5.   14 Macmillan, *The Net Book Agreement*, p. 59.

it survived for many years, with upwards of 30,000 members, it behaved impeccably within its terms. Macmillan, writing in 1924, saw this outcome as having 'saved the Retail Book Trade throughout Great Britain from bankruptcy and the virtual extinction from which it was threatened, owing to the suicidal system of underselling'.[15] The Book War firmly entrenched the NBA in its revised form as the governing regime of the book trade for the next eighty-five years, and for most of that period publishers held all the levers of control.

Despite or perhaps because of its turbulent first decade, there was little call to re-examine the structure of book pricing and supply until after the Second World War. Booksellers were generally content to function in a price-controlled environment where there was certainty about terms of trade. Publishers preferred to see prices standardised and uniform across their customer base, while book purchasers (if they were at all aware of the special market conditions they experienced) believed the confident assertion that the NBA kept small booksellers in business and maintained a breadth of choice. The stability of the NBA depended, however, on a low-inflation economy, and by 1948 questions had begun to be raised with regards to its continued viability in post-war inflationary conditions. A joint Book Trade Committee was established by publishers and booksellers to examine how the NBA functioned, and in 1952 produced a report of 'pulverising tedium' which concluded that, while it might have faults (the lack of flexibility on discounts was highlighted), its loss would cause the trade damage.[16] In 1956 the focus of enquiry changed significantly. Restrictive practices in business generally, and specifically the then common practice of resale price maintenance (RPM) of which the NBA was a prominent example, came under government scrutiny. The NBA was referred to the new Restrictive Practices Court to determine whether it was in the public interest. The PA mounted a spirited defence, although not all publishers agreed. The law publisher Butterworth (not then a PA member) used its expertise to produce 'an elegantly reasoned opinion' that the NBA was indefensible.[17] The court took almost seven years to deliberate, and eventually decided in 1962 that the Agreement served the public well, although many other examples of RPM in other retail trades were struck down.[18] The NBA then seemed immortal and unchallengeable and, as discussed below, would not come under serious question again for over thirty years.

15 *Ibid.*, p. 77.   16 Norrie, *Mumby's publishing and bookselling*, p. 93.
17 Jones, *Butterworths*, p. 261.   18 Barker and Davies (eds.), *Books are different.*

'A settled trade'

The immutability of the NBA seems to suggest that bookselling remained changeless and fossilised. However, while the NBA brought stability to pricing, bookselling did experience rapid and fundamental change after 1914. The immediate impact of the First World War was to enhance demand and restrict supply. In 1910, 8,468 new books had been published (one third more than in 1900) and this total was equalled and exceeded in 1914 and 1915. Thereafter output fell steadily until the end of the war, from 7,537 new titles in 1916 to 6,750 in 1918.[19] As has been shown, these circumstances 'helped to extend the net system'.[20] Booksellers, with little incentive to cut prices, were persuaded to limit the discounts on subject books (i.e. books not subject to the net system) to twopence in the shilling. Furthermore, by the end of the war most works of fiction were covered by the net system, a consequence of the rising costs of production which made it impossible to sell new works at 4s 6d, the standard retail price of a six-shilling novel before the war.[21]

Although there was high demand for reading matter for military 'Camp Libraries' (much of which was charitably donated by 'book drives'), a combination of supply shortages, especially paper and type metal, and the absence of male publishing and bookselling staffs on active service meant that fewer books were available. Reprints of popular titles suffered particularly since much standing type was requisitioned for scrap. Newspapers and periodicals which flourished during the war (and which were stocked by many booksellers) filled some of the gaps, but wartime bookshops were notably drab and sparsely stocked spaces, made worse by the poor quality of bindings and absence of dust jackets.

Bookselling profitability, which had averaged about 9 per cent pre-war, fell to under 2 per cent by 1916.[22] Surprisingly few bookshops closed during the war, or in the period of inflation and economic disruption that characterised the aftermath. In fact, as with publishing, there was a remarkable post-war renaissance of new companies as returning servicemen spent gratuities and savings on opening shops. Typical of these was Austicks in Leeds, which, from a small general shop founded in 1928, eventually became the dominant book retailer in West Yorkshire, with substantial library and school supply businesses and specialist branches for medical and academic books near the city's university and St James's University Hospital. By 1940 it had become the

19 Stevenson, *Book makers*, p. 39.   20 Taraporevala, *Competition and its control*, pp. 57–8.
21 *Ibid.*, pp. 59–60.   22 Norrie, *Mumby's publishing and bookselling*, p. 20.

region's leading bookseller but, despite opening branches in Harrogate and Huddersfield, it never ventured outside its local catchment.

This model of local dominance was replicated throughout the country. Virtually every town or city above a certain size possessed a privately owned bookseller which often became synonymous with literary life in local society. Basil Blackwell estimated that every town with a population above 40,000 could support a stock-holding bookseller, although many smaller towns, generally in affluent areas, also sustained quite large booksellers, like The Ibis in Banstead in Surrey.[23] A few surprising exceptions to this rule existed, such as Leicester, which, despite a thriving university and economy, never had a 'local' bookseller. George's of Bristol, William Smith of Reading, Hudson's of Birmingham, Thorne's of Newcastle-upon-Tyne, Hartley Seed of Sheffield, Heffers of Cambridge, Wheaton's of Exeter, Parry's of Liverpool, Boddy's of Middlesborough, Willshaw's of Manchester and Over's of Rugby, among many others, formed a litany of now nearly forgotten names which defined what became known as 'English provincial bookselling'. Many were founded during the 1920s (although several had significantly older origins) and were family owned and managed, with most surviving until the 1990s in the hands of their founder's children or grandchildren. A few cities by their size or high concentration of students (such as Manchester with Sherratt & Hughes, and Cambridge with Bowes & Bowes and Galloway & Porter) supported competing retailers, but elsewhere a single bookseller enjoyed a complacent monopoly in a staunchly defended local fiefdom.[24]

All adopted remarkably similar commercial models. A town-centre shop provided a general stock-holding retail front, often with a large antiquarian department and sometimes a subscription lending library, while peripheral branches near colleges or hospitals supplied textbooks and specialist monographs. Many were publishers in a small way, producing books of a staunchly local nature, frequently on a commission basis. Stationery and jobbing printing were also key parts of the business and sometimes became very substantial as at Wheaton's or Over's, who specialised in the manufacture of dust-jackets for publishers. The profitable core of the business for virtually all, however, came from lucrative contracts held from local authority library and

---

23 *Ibid.*, p. 79.

24 Leicester was the first university to open its own campus bookshop in the 1950s because it could not induce a commercial retailer to do so. Later Sussex and Warwick did the same.

educational administrations which guaranteed constant and predictable cash flows. The prominent social position of bookselling families within their communities meant that the negotiation of such arrangements was rarely openly tendered. While many of these businesses, especially during the expansion of universities and growth of local government in the 1950s and 1960s, expanded their number of branches and occasionally diversified by opening concessions in local department stores (which were equally loyal to their home towns), they rarely expanded beyond their zones of political influence and never overlapped geographically. By a tacit agreement, provincial booksellers left each other alone to till their local markets untroubled by much competition.

The archetypical and only surviving example of this once widespread type of enterprise is B. H. Blackwell of Oxford, perhaps because it alone expanded out of its protected environment and embraced a more testing and diversified business model, especially after it became apparent that the NBA would not survive. Founded in 1879, it began as a small academic shop mainly supplying textbooks. It absorbed a number of other small retailers throughout the twentieth century,[25] but under the energetic management of its founder's son, Basil Blackwell, who ran the business from 1924 until his death in 1984, it began a rapid expansion in new areas, first in global retail mail order and then in specialist library supply, particularly academic and scientific journals. In 1999 it eventually took over its only main competitor in this sector, Heffers of Cambridge, paradoxically just as terrestrial mail order was giving way to internet sales. In the 1980s, in association with Oxford University Press, Blackwell set up an academic bookselling chain University Bookshops Oxford (UBO) with campus shops throughout the country, and then began a sustained programme of expansion, including a major new shop in Charing Cross Road in London, opened in 1995. In 2013 it had over forty branches from Aberdeen to Portsmouth, employing over 700 staff during term time.[26] While still nominally under family control, its ownership was transferred to a trust with its shares owned by its employees in 2010. It has been a consistent supporter of new technology, and although its initial online retailing operation in 1995 was not a success,

---

25 Norrie, *Mumby's publishing and bookselling*, p. 80.
26 http://bookshop.blackwell.co.uk/stores; Rebecca Burn-Callender, 'Blackwells bookshop back in the black', *Telegraph* 18 January 2015, www.telegraph.co.uk/finance/news bysector/retailandconsumer/11350937/Blackwells-bookshop-back-in-the-black.html.

it was a pioneer of in-store print-on-demand, installing the first Espresso Book Machine in Europe in 2009 in its Charing Cross Road branch.[27]

London had the greatest concentration of bookselling in Great Britain. Norrie estimates 400 shops in 1914, increasing to 500 in 1929 and falling again to 400 in 1945.[28] Unlike the provinces, competition in London was fierce and the market was segmented by subject and clientele. The 'carriage trade' retailers, which served affluent purchasers and provided bespoke service echoing their often eighteenth-century origins, occupied fashionable and expensive sites, such as Hatchards in Piccadilly. Paradoxically it is only the most recently founded of these, Heywood Hill of Mayfair, which opened its faux-Georgian bow-fronted premises as late as 1937, that survives. The West End continued to support a few specialist booksellers related to the fine art trade, like Thomas Heneage, but the business district of the City of London, which was the original locus of bookselling in the capital, progressively lost its once numerous retail outlets after 1945, with the only survivors being a few law specialists clustered round the Royal Courts of Justice on its western boundary. The combination of high rents and a changing clientele rendered bookselling an unprofitable option in both areas.

Since 1914 London bookselling had concentrated in the relatively low-rent district of Charing Cross Road and comprised a mix of general and specialist shops. Nearby, the British Museum and the University of London with its colleges and hospitals attracted specialist shops of national importance. Medicine and science were served by Henry Kimpton, opposite the (now demolished) Middlesex Hospital, and H. K. Lewis which was actually incorporated into the building of University College London. The latter generated more than half its business from a subscription lending library supplying medical textbooks and monographs to a global customer base of practitioners. Social science was the specialty of the Economist Bookshop, owned and operated by the London School of Economics in Clare Market and opened in 1946. Collet's, established in 1934 in Charing Cross Road, concentrated on radical left-wing literature and exclusively stocked imported Soviet titles. It came under official suspicion during the Second World War but was never closed, although many years later it was fire-bombed during the controversy over *The satanic verses* in 1989. It never recovered and was wound up shortly afterwards. More general but still primarily academic

---

27 Alison Flood, 'Revolutionary Espresso Book Machine launches in London', *Guardian* 24 April 2009, www.theguardian.com/books/2009/apr/24/espresso-book-machine-launches.

28 Norrie, *Mumby's publishing and bookselling*, p. 77.

shops were opened by Una Dillon in Store Street opposite the new University of London Senate House, and the Modern Book Company adjacent to St Mary's Hospital in Paddington during the 1930s. When students were evacuated to Wales and Hertfordshire during the Second World War, Dillon opened small satellite shops on the temporary campuses. Her London shop nearly foundered, but the great influx of demobbed student servicemen after 1945 and the expansion of college libraries revived her business greatly, enabling her to move to the marvellously turreted chateau-like five-storey premises that occupied the south frontage of Torrington Place, opposite University College London.

Elsewhere in London, a large number of highly specialist outlets, like Probsthain for books on oriental history and language, Stanfords for maps and travel, SPCK for Christian literature, the Building Bookshop for architecture, Schott for music, and J. A. Allen for equine books, not only served local customers but had extensive international mail order business. Most survived until the 1980s but several went out of business because of unsympathetic rent reviews. Nevertheless, the concept of specialist retailing attracted new entrants like 'Murder One' which sold only thriller fiction during the 1990s and early 2000s until a rent rise saw it off as well.

Two particular specialist retailers operated on a distinctive business model. They were Samuel French, which concentrated on the theatre, and Stainer & Bell on music.[29] Both maintained small retail bookshops in Fitzrovia but their main business was and remains the hire of play scripts and scores for performance. Stainer & Bell moved out of central London in the 1970s (French remained) but both conduct much business remotely by renting and selling digital downloads.

Despite these varied forms of retail, the best-known and most iconic London bookseller of the twentieth century was Foyles, which was established as a second-hand business by brothers William and Gilbert Foyle on Charing Cross Road in 1904. William Foyle was a natural entrepreneur who seized new opportunities and always had an imaginative eye for unusual ways to merchandise. He sold books by weight and allowed customers a 'trade-in' allowance on old books (provided they bore the Foyles sticker), and established book clubs for regular readers and literary lunches. In 1929 he acquired a freehold site adjacent on Manette Street and erected a four-storey purpose-built shop which claimed, with justification, to be 'the world's largest bookshop'. An extensive international mail order business led to the

29 On Samuel French, see Chapter 8.

establishment of a 'philatelic department' to sell the stamps from the envelopes from overseas enclosing orders, and a 'Speakers' Bureau' provided professional experts and entertainers for ladies' lunch clubs. When William died in 1963, the business passed to his daughter Christina and her husband Ronald Batty who supervised the huge antiquarian department. Initially they ran the business well and energetically (a major extension was opened in 1966), but after a bitter strike by assistants and Batty's death, Christina's management became wayward and erratic. Staff were only hired on short-term contracts, stock levels became unsustainably high, and the mail order business was unreliable and slow. The retail environment deteriorated into gloomy, uninviting and frequently filthy spaces with shelving piled dangerously high. Shoplifting was rife and rumours circulated of fraud among senior staff. Christina's style was notoriously capricious, with even long-serving staff (of which there were decreasingly few) often suffering instant dismissal on a whim. A bizarre attempt to organise the stock by publishing imprint rather than subject resulted in steeply declining sales and puzzled customers.[30] When Christina died in 1999, it was widely believed that the shop was insolvent and the valuable site would be sold for non-bookselling redevelopment, particularly since Blackwell's had just opened a large and glamorous new shop opposite.

In fact, the business enjoyed an amazing rebirth. What Christina's heirs, her nephews Christopher and Anthony Foyle and Bill Samuel, found was truly dreadful. Sales had fallen from over £19 million to just under £10 million in five years and a notoriously sullen and underpaid workforce were in revolt. Rather than sell up, they decided to refurbish the entire building, employ trained bookselling staff on decent terms, invest in modern technology, and create a very attractive retail environment. They also provided homes for old-established nearby retailers, like Ray's Jazz and Silver Moon feminist bookshop, dislodged by unsustainable rents. A café and a gallery space were created. By 2007, Foyles was named as 'independent bookseller of the year' and began for the first time to open branch outlets at cultural venues and shopping centres, although a false move with a branch in the City's New Change development among fashion boutiques and jewellers was swiftly reversed. In 2011, it was announced that the Charing Cross Road site was indeed to be sold, but only to enable the purchase and development of

---

30 John Walsh, 'Still driving customers up the wall after 100 years: Foyles, the bookshop that time forgot', *Independent* 23 January 2003, http://web.archive.org/web/200302100 71945/http:/enjoyment.independent.co.uk/books/news/story.jsp?story=371917.

the much larger and now redundant Central St Martins College next door to provide even more bookselling space in 2014.

Scottish bookselling possessed characteristic features.[31] Some of these derived from relative sparseness of population which meant that outside of Glasgow, Edinburgh and Aberdeen the trade was often combined with other forms of retail. However, even quite small towns like Dumfries could support surprisingly large shops which drew on an extensive rural hinterland. Edinburgh, while not challenging London in numbers, had an array of specialist shops, including the first Government Bookshop for official publications in the country, and the foreign language specialist Bauermeister which was first established in Glasgow but moved to Edinburgh in 1924. Bookselling was often combined with printing, as with the Edinburgh firm of George Waterston who also manufactured currency notes for the Scottish banks. Because of Scotland's distinctive legal, educational and religious systems, specialists emerged to fulfil their requirements like Grant Educational in Glasgow and law specialists W. Green in Edinburgh. Academic and scientific businesses, including Bisset's in Aberdeen and James Thin in Edinburgh, grew in association with the four ancient Scottish universities, with both original shop sites now occupied by Blackwell's branches. John Wylie in Glasgow set up in 1935 in the surprising location of the less salubrious end of Sauchiehall Street, a shop resembling 'the hall and library of a country house'.[32] It had a uniquely close relationship with customers, having initially been capitalised by ten prospective customers pledging £100 each against future purchases. The manager would select and deliver monthly orders for account holders who trusted his taste.

John Menzies grew from its single shop in Edinburgh established in 1833 to create a chain of railway bookstalls and subsequently town centre branches throughout Scotland, developing from five shops in 1945 to 150 in 1965, including some in northern England. To meet the requirements of the far-flung scatter of small shops throughout Scotland, which publishers' representatives could not afford to visit, they operated a wholesaling service with depots in Edinburgh, Dunfermline and Motherwell. By 1980, their turnover had exceeded £233 million, with profits of almost £7 million and a diverse portfolio which included broadcasting and photographic equipment as well as books.[33] Unfortunately their exit from bookselling was almost as precipitate as their earlier growth. The purchase of newsagency chains like Martin's

---

31 Ward, 'The development of the bookshop'.
32 Norrie, *Mumby's publishing and bookselling*, p. 191.   33 *Ibid.*, p. 195.

in an attempt to consolidate their reach into England proved expensive and unsuccessful, and during the 1990s they disposed of all their book and periodical retail and wholesale businesses. At the end of our period, they survive only as a freight and logistics business, with the only remaining link with the former core business in news distribution, which, as print periodical circulations dwindle, faces an uncertain future.

One Scottish bookseller which successfully reinvented itself and broke out of its traditional heartland to ensure its independent survival was John Smith & Son of Glasgow. Founded in 1751, and claiming to be the 'oldest bookselling company in the English speaking world',[34] until the last quarter of the twentieth century it was very much a traditional provincial retailer with a large general and rather old-fashioned city-centre shop (which included a significant second-hand and antiquarian trade) and an academic branch close to the University of Glasgow in the city's west end. Competition from newly arrived chain booksellers, and changes in the city's retail structure, made its future look uncertain. Instead, it abandoned two centuries of tradition and created a new business model. The city-centre shop was closed and the site sold. Smiths decided to concentrate on the student market in higher education by creating a chain of small campus outlets selling not only textbooks but also leisure goods and other student 'necessaries'. This eventually grew to over twenty-five branches mainly on the smaller campuses of 'new' universities throughout Britain, but also in Ireland and Botswana.

Some other innovative retail models elsewhere in Britain proved less durable. Landsman Bookshop operated a small retail outlet in the 1970s and 1980s deep in the Herefordshire countryside but for many years its main business came from a fleet of specially fitted 'mobile bookshop' vans that carried carefully selected stock on rural and farming topics to agricultural colleges and shows. A combination of increasing fuel costs, pressure on margins and competition from alternative sources made the travelling bookseller uneconomic and they eventually succumbed during the 1980s.

Circulating subscription libraries persisted late into the period. Mudie's, the dominant nineteenth-century library, occupied a large central London site and enjoyed an upmarket clientele who would pay an annual guinea (£1 1s, later £1 17s) and a sixpenny borrowing fee to read the latest fashionable fiction and general literature from 'Mudie's Select Library'. From a dominant trade position where they could dictate terms and prices (and even genres and subjects) to publishers in 1914, and despite opening provincial branches in

---

34 www.johnsmithinternational.com/live/about-us/history.

Manchester, York and elsewhere, Mudie's failed to keep up with changing reader tastes. With free public 'county libraries' stocking a wider range of material, they eventually went out of business in 1937, a casualty of both economic recession and poor management. The resulting market gap was taken up to some extent by the book sections of department stores like Harrods and Army and Navy which established lending libraries to cater for their upper-class clienteles. However, the dominant position in the sub-scription library market was taken over by the Nottingham-based pharmacist Jesse Boot (Boot's Pure Drug Company), which began a book lending library in 1898 to make use of the often empty first-floor spaces of their rapidly expanding chain of high street shops. By 1920 Boots had over 200 libraries attached to their high street pharmacies, and by 1938 there were 460 branches.[35] Annual subscription rates were lower than Mudie's. In the 1920s, the cheapest option, which entitled readers to borrow all but the newest books from one library one volume at a time, was 10s 6d. The rate was lowered in the 1930s.[36] The stock appealed to a middle-class, largely female readership. By the end of the Second World War there were over a million subscribers and in 1950 Boots libraries were issuing approximately 50,000,000 volumes a year.[37] The library continued into the 1960s, with the last branches closing only in 1966.

In the 1930s Boots introduced a new 'pay as you read' scheme in an effort to compete with the increasingly popular twopenny libraries. Aimed at working-class tastes and pockets, these libraries were run as adjuncts to small independent enterprises.[38] They were touted as ways in which a diverse range of shops, including groceries, butchers, haber-dashers and tobacconists, could usefully add to their trade. Ronald Batty of Foyles even wrote a practical manual, *How to run a twopenny library* (1938), and several wholesalers provided pre-selected stock of light romances, westerns and thrillers which were regularly refreshed every few weeks. For many retailers, the provision of a paid library service was a useful way to circumvent the Shops Acts, as it enabled them to remain open for book loans when the sale of foodstuffs alone was forbidden. For many others, however, they became sizeable freestanding enterprises producing good income during the recession of the 1930s and employing their own staffs.

35 Wilson, 'Boots Book-Lovers' library', p. 430. 36 *Ibid.*, p. 429. 37 *Ibid.*
38 Hilliard, 'The two-penny library'. See also Chapter 7 in this volume.

Another retail book lender was W. H. Smith, who for most of the period operated as the only English bookselling chain.[39] Originating as a chain of railway bookstalls (an echo of which is still preserved in the division of the retail business into 'travel' and 'high street' divisions), they developed a network of outlets at stations and airports, and in town and city centres, that eventually amounted to almost 600 locations. Although enormously influential and important for book sales, book retailing was never the sole or sometimes even principal focus. Until a demerger in 2006, the newspaper and magazine wholesaling operation (now Smiths News plc) was their largest operation, and during the 1970s and 1980s they embarked on a frantic and largely unsuccessful series of attempts at diversification, including acquiring interests in commercial television, DIY retailing, travel agency and, closer to home, book publishing (they owned Hodder Headline between 1999 and 2004) and music retailing. They also pursued broadly unremunerative ventures overseas, including in Canada. Nevertheless, they straddled the middle market for retail book sales up to the end of the NBA in 1995, and their decision to select and 'scale out' (that is, to authorise its stocking in their branches) a particular title was almost always crucial to determining its success or failure. For many book-buyers, particularly in small towns, Smiths was the only option, and although often excoriated by customers and publishers for their poor selection, occasionally bizarre ordering policies and weak merchandising,[40] they introduced many of the innovations that would enable the later development of the bookselling chain as a dominant model, from the introduction of the International Standard Book Number (ISBN) in 1966 to the invention of centralised 'hub' distribution in which a standardised stock is provided to each branch of a chain.

Wholesaling and 'trade intelligence'

Wholesalers played an important role in the distribution of books to bookshops and libraries over the period. Until the Second World War, the dominant company was Simpkin, Marshall, Hamilton and Kent Ltd. Formed from the amalgamation of three small wholesalers at the end of the nineteenth century and occupying a warren-like warehouse in Stationers' Hall Court in the City of London, it carried a widely varied stock and also

39 Smiths were effectively excluded from Scotland by Menzies until they acquired the latter in 1998. They still only have one high street branch in Northern Ireland.
40 The publisher Anthony Blond playfully mocks 'the much-satirized, near-monopoly W. H. Smith' in *The publishing game*, p. 48.

acted as an agent for non-metropolitan and overseas publishers. It was also a publisher on its own account. For small booksellers, Simpkin Marshall offered a quick and efficient service which freed them up from holding too much stock, but even larger retailers found the consolidation opportunities provided by the wholesaler a useful way of managing their cash flow. Simpkin Marshall had a very close relationship with the Associated Booksellers and were trusted for their fair dealing and integrity. They were staunch defenders of the NBA and defied the attempts of the 'cutting book-seller' Stoneham to sell net books at reduced prices by denying them supply in the 1900s. Ironically, they bought Stoneham's business when it went bankrupt in 1907, and successfully operated their seven London shops until 1941 when they were sold to Hatchards, eventually becoming part of the Menzies group.[41]

Simpkins also built up an extensive export wholesale business, including in India and Canada. For London booksellers, its cramped Dickensian premises provided an additional service, the 'trade counter', where the retailers sent their 'bagmen' every morning to collect required titles. Many of the London publishing houses also maintained their own trade counters (the last of which at John Murray only closed when they moved out of their Clerkenwell warehouse in 1966) but most of the London trade went through Simpkins. Until 1940 the sight of brown-coated envoys from Charing Cross Road bicycling energetically up Ludgate Hill en route for Simpkin Marshall was a familiar London scene.

The stable and measured intermediary role of Simpkin Marshall came to an abrupt end in December 1940 when one of the last mass bombing raids on the City of London all but destroyed the historic publishing and bookselling district round St Paul's, although the Cathedral itself miraculously survived. Simpkin Marshall lost over 3 million books in that night (probably 20 million in total were destroyed in the immediate area) and its building was obliter-ated. For a time it looked as if it would not recover, but a consortium of publishers, led by Sir Isaac Pitman and Company, reconstituted the company as Simpkin Marshall (1941) Ltd and within months it was open again, based in Pitman's warehouse in north London. It never regained its previous influ-ence and in 1949 it was acquired in one of the first deals by the émigré Robert Maxwell.[42] It collapsed for good in 1954, leaving a large gap in the market only partially filled by smaller, provincial wholesalers like Wymans or Menzies.

---

41 Norrie, *Mumby's publishing and bookselling*, p. 91. 42 *Ibid.*, pp. 96–7.

Outside of London, a number of local wholesalers filled a multi-purpose role, supplying local retailers and also providing a library supply service to local authorities. Typical of these was William Dawson & Sons, based in Folkestone in Kent. They specialised in technical and professional literature and also imported foreign-language books. After 1950, they increasingly concentrated on the supply of scientific and scholarly journals and by the 1970s were leading subscription agents for journal supply to many university libraries at home and abroad. Their services included the chasing up of lost and late issues and binding. Like many firms in this sector, they fared badly as journals converted to digital delivery, and they went out of business in the early 2000s.

Another specialist form of wholesaling was provided by educational contractors, like E. J. Arnold of Leeds. Founded in 1863 as a printer and stationer in Barnstaple in Devon, Arnold transferred to Yorkshire in 1870 and for several decades operated as a general bookseller. After obtaining a contract to supply textbooks to their local education authority, the company developed this business as its main focus. After the 1944 Education Act made secondary education free for all and local authorities instituted a regime of 'central buying', school supply became an enormously lucrative business. Arnold also sought markets overseas, particularly in Africa. During the 1980s, the company employed over 1,000 staff and sold educational equipment, stationery and books to schools throughout the world. However, the abrupt deregulation of schools, and the end of local authority buying, as well as an emphasis on information technology to the detriment of books, saw Arnolds driven out of business in the 1990s.

Although books were highly suitable for computer-controlled management in both wholesale and retail, particularly after the advent of the ISBN in 1966, the innate conservatism of the trade made the introduction of IT-supported systems difficult and slow. As late as 1980, the wholesaler Bertrams of Norwich, founded in 1968 and renowned for its responsive and speedy service, was still using hand-written invoices generated by a team of clerks. Bertrams survived a disastrous association with the Entertainment UK division of Woolworths, which bought it in 2006 and then went spectacularly bust in 2008, which had an adverse effect on many independent booksellers in the key pre-Christmas peak-selling season. Bertrams was then acquired by Smiths News who invested strongly in its development, employing by the second decade of the twenty-first century over 400 people. As well as book wholesaling, it provides distribution services for publishers.

The largest British book wholesaler by the end of the period was Gardners of Eastbourne. Founded in Bexhill in Sussex in 1955 to take up some of the market left by the collapse of Simpkin Marshall, they focussed initially on the South of England but have subsequently built up an extensive nationwide operation. As well as serving independent booksellers, they provide a bespoke stock service to chains including Waterstones and internet sellers. One innovation has been a service whereby customers can order books online via Gardners who then deliver them to a local bookshop for collection.

For effective selling, both retailers and wholesalers relied on what in the early part of the period was referred to as 'trade intelligence': details of authorship, title, publisher, availability, price, and terms of supply of all books in print and forthcoming titles. Bertrams, for instance, published a regular catalogue *Buyer's Notes* which carried paid advertising from publishers and recommended selections by the wholesaler's staff. However, the most trusted and comprehensive sources of information about new publications was supplied by weekly trade periodicals, the *Publishers' Circular* and the *Bookseller*, which listed these bibliographic details and which were subsequently collated into a reference title *(British) Books in Print*, as an annual printed catalogue.[43] The two titles briefly merged during the Second World War, and although *Publishers' Circular* survived until 1959, it was the *Bookseller*, owned and published until 1999 by the reference publisher J. Whitaker & Sons, that became the main source of book trade information. Under the editorship of Edmond Segrave, who oversaw it from 1933 until his death in 1971, and later by Louis Baum and Nicholas Clee, the *Bookseller* developed a reputation for fairness, accuracy and lively investigative journalism. It was also an early supporter of the application of new technology to solving information issues in the book trade. *British Books in Print* was one of the first reference publications to appear on microfiche and Whitakers was a part-owner of Teleordering, which was introduced in 1979, after many delays, as one of the first automated computerised stock control and supply systems in the retail trade. It was, however, never universally used or accepted by booksellers (although publishers were keen), and as late as 2004 the magazine was still printing a categorised list of new 'Titles of the Week' in every issue.

By the early twenty-first century the *Bookseller* had been acquired by the American market research company Nielsen, who since 2001 had been developing the online information system BookScan. Using electronic point

---

43 *Ibid.*, p. 180.

of sale (EPOS) equipment, which began to appear in the 1990s and is now universal in bookshops, to scan the bar codes on the reverse of all books, the system records and collates sales information about every transaction, including price and category. These data are used to prepare charts of sales on a weekly basis, for best-sellers, category leaders and 'heat seekers', titles which have begun to show surges in sales but are not yet obvious best-sellers. BookScan reports from a wide range of outlets and divides its findings into the 'General Retail Market' (GRM), which comprises mainstream book-shops, and the wider 'TCM' (Total Consumer Market), which includes supermarkets and other non-traditional sales markets. Publishers and book-sellers can have access (for a subscription) to detailed title-by-title, or subject-by-subject, compilations of sales as well as geographical information. Bookselling via BookScan probably has the most detailed and accurate sales information of any retail commodity, although its coverage has been under-mined in the most recent period by e-book sales, which, as of July 2013, were not included in BookScan figures.[44]

The people of the trade

Bookselling has always attracted eccentric and interesting employers and employees. A notoriously badly paid but relatively well-educated profes-sional, the stereotypical twentieth-century bookseller could be exemplified by the fictional Gordon Comstock in George Orwell's *Keep the aspidistra flying* (1936). A shabby, resentful poet with a neurotic streak, Comstock sees book-selling as an escape from the rat race, where he can concentrate on his own writing while avoiding customers in a dusty, poorly organised, old-fashioned shop presided over by a lazy, often absentee owner. Comstock is perennially short of money and can rarely afford to buy himself even a packet of cigarettes or a pint of beer.

Orwell's picture is certainly a caricature but is based on his own real experience as a bookseller and reflects the poor conditions and rewards of British bookselling for much of the twentieth century. In 1927, Norrie records that a fifteen-year-old assistant in a Belgravia bookshop could expect to be paid only twelve shillings per week, rising to £1 in 1935.[45] Wages were even lower in outer London and the provinces. Even in the late 1950s, a senior bookseller would be earning less than £1,000 a year. A female assistant might

---

44 Philip Jones, 'Ranking e-book sales', *Bookseller* 30 July 2013, www.thebookseller.com/blogs/ranking-e-book-sales.
45 Norrie, *Mumby's publishing and bookselling*, p. 77.

receive as little as £4 5s per week. When the Charter Group of Booksellers (an elite consortium of independent retailers) investigated bookselling wages in 1970, they found that fewer than 10 per cent of senior managers earned more than £2,000 a year, whereas a publisher's sales representative at the same time would expect to receive 50 per cent more as well as a company supplied car, and only one bookshop employee in the entire country earned over £3,000. There was a considerable gap between male and female wages: a man would earn an average of £12 per week, a woman £10. By 1980, after inflation had taken a serious toll, weekly wages were still only £48 per week, very close to the lowest available in the retail sector, although the gender gap had narrowed.

Hours were long, including all day on Saturdays, and pension schemes and other benefits were virtually unknown. Although the Book Trade Benevolent Society founded in 1812 (subsequently the Book Trade Charity) provided support for book trade people in financial difficulties and retirement accommodation, its resources were never equal to all the demands made on it. Its founding benefactor was, perhaps tellingly, not a publisher or a bookseller, but a papermaker, John Dickinson. Job security was also poor, and although employment conditions at Foyles under Christina Foyle's management were an extreme example, turnover among bookselling staff was comparatively high, and many took their knowledge and skills to work as representatives for publishers where conditions and rewards were marginally better.

Despite this, labour unrest and trade unionism were remarkably low in bookselling. A study in 1928/29 entitled *British book trade organisation* found that book trade employers had experienced little in the way of industrial action even during the General Strike of 1926. A fall in wages had precipitated strikes among packers and warehousemen at Simpkin Marshall, W. H. Smith and Wymans in the early 1920s, but the employers locked the strikers out and, after a three-month stand-off, the strikers returned to work and accepted reduced pay. Trade unions only began to recruit noticeable numbers among bookshop workers in the 1960s, but even then the main unions represented were not the shop workers but organisations such as the Association of Scientific, Technical and Managerial Staffs (ASTMS) and the National Union of Journalists (NUJ). Since most bookshops were small owner-managed enterprises for the majority of the twentieth century, opportunities for training and career progression were limited and many shops relied on part-time, often female, staff who had other sources of income. As chains emerged, however, a more professional staff arose.

Nevertheless there were moves in the 1920s to establish formal training schemes.[46]

Some of the roles in book retailing were very distinctive. The armies of cycling 'bagmen', collecting orders and replacement stock from trade counters, persisted until the late 1950s. Many also doubled as delivery men for account customers, although Foyles invested in a fleet of delivery vans and drivers in the 1930s. As bookshops developed specialist departments there emerged a middle managerial group of department heads whose principal role was as 'buyer'. They would see publishers' representatives or 'travellers' (as they were generally known until the 1950s), receive presentations of new titles, and place orders which enabled the publisher to build up advance orders ('dues') before publication. Many buyers of long experience built up great knowledge of their markets and they were often consulted by publishers evaluating new projects or draft cover designs.

Book clubs

The idea of a book club as an effective alternative means of selling books was in such disregard with publishers and booksellers from the Times Book Club affair that it was not until the 1930s that the concept re-emerged. The Times Book Club had in fact continued to operate in a modest fashion and many publishers found its small discounts and elite membership a useful additional sales channel, and booksellers did not see it as drawing away their custom. They were much less sure when a number of new organisations began to emerge to challenge their businesses.

The Book of the Month Club was founded in the United States in 1926 and was shortly followed by the Literary Guild. As their names suggest, their business model was to 'inertia-sell', with one book per month being sent to its membership by mail order. The 'selection' was to be of special merit and offered at a special price. Such merchandising suited the American environment well as it served a widely scattered customer base which often had no access to a retail bookseller.[47] When Alan Bott introduced the concept into Britain in 1929 he called it the Book Society, and he was careful not to alarm booksellers by undertaking to sell only at full price and to stress that the selection was chosen with care by distinguished literary judges, including Hugh Walpole and J. B. Priestley. The Society prospered, and although it ostensibly pursued a 'no undercutting' policy, in effect it did force the prices

46 Rayner, 'A new spirit of hope'.   47 Radway, *A feeling for books*.

of books down, since it would decline to select a title unless the publisher would agree to a low net price. It also purchased at a larger discount. Nevertheless, booksellers were in the main untroubled by the Society's activities.

They were less happy when John Baker announced the formation of Readers Union in 1937. Baker was an enthusiastic merchandiser whose Phoenix Book Company had sold books on an instalment plan basis since the mid-1920s, and he was convinced that he had discovered a class of book-buyer who would not visit bookshops because they found them intimidating and their merchandise expensive. He felt that by offering to his members reprints of good recent books at 2s 6d (sometimes as much as five-sixths off the normal retail price) he would greatly extend the market. Publishers were enthusiastic since he was predicting large additional quantities, but book-sellers were uncertain as they saw this as a direct frontal attack on their trade, despite many acting as agents for the scheme. Authors too were uncertain, as their royalties were to be paid on the low club prices. Readers, however, loved the idea and within weeks Baker had signed up 17,000 members and was selling large quantities of new books identical to what were available in bookshops apart from their title-pages and reduced prices.

Booksellers called 'foul' and invoked the NBA.[48] Baker countered by stating correctly that he was not selling net books but special editions to a closed membership. Publishers uneasily prevaricated; they liked Baker's mass selling but did not wish to alienate their principal and established customers. A bizarre proposal was made by the Booksellers Association that Readers Union should deliver its members' books through local bookshops and give booksellers a cut. The booksellers' case was undermined when Foyles announced that it was setting up a club of its own to provide its customers with discounted titles by mail order and its vans displayed the phrase: 'Join the Book Club.' In the end booksellers, although remaining officially against them, learned to live with book clubs and even cooperated with them by accepting membership proposals (for a commission) on their behalf. They never quite accepted the claim that the clubs were finding customers that booksellers could not reach. By 1958 Readers Union had sold in excess of 8 million books across 417 titles from sixty-four different publishers.[49]

---

48 For a full discussion of the trade's response to book clubs in the context of the NBA, see Taraporevala, *Competition and its control*, chapter 10.
49 Baker, *Low cost of bookloving*, p. 11.

The most famous and influential book club of the inter-war years was the Left Book Club (LBC), founded and operated by the publisher Victor Gollancz. Gollancz was a radical by conviction but also a shrewd business-man who saw a large market for selling politically engaged literature to readers worried by the growing problems of society and polity at home and abroad. Gollancz was inspired by Baker's plans for Readers Union and he launched the LBC even before Baker made its first choice in September 1937.[50] From the beginning the LBC was serious, committed and very successful. A distinguished panel, including Harold Laski, the director of the London School of Economics, the leading left-wing intellectual John Strachey and Gollancz himself, selected appropriate titles, mainly (but not exclusively) from Gollancz's own list, and offered them in orange or red limp cloth covers at 2s 6d, promoting them through the club's magazine *Left Book News*.[51] Membership grew from an initial 9,000 in 1936 to over 50,000 by 1939,[52] and its activities soon diversified to include 'The Left Book Theatre Guild', which produced plays on suitably radical themes, and the organisa-tion of evening classes and rallies.[53] As much a political movement as a means of merchandising books, LBC even had its own member of parliament in Vernon Bartlett, who won the Bridgwater by-election of 1938 as an 'Independent Progressive', overturning a Conservative majority of over 10,000.

Gollancz recognised from the beginning that he needed to get booksellers on his side if he was to succeed. Although LBC books could only be sold to registered club members, who were required to wear a circular enamel badge (the famous 'lefty bottle top') for identification, they were sold mainly through bookshops. Gollancz had studied the operation of the Crime Club, established by Collins in 1930 to sell thrillers and detective fiction through retailers who received 'incentive discounts' to stock these titles, and shame-lessly copied their procedure. Unlike Readers Union, relatively little was sold by mail order, although there were always substantial sales made at events and rallies where book stalls, often staffed by local booksellers, did a roaring trade. Unlike many book clubs, which were suspended or much reduced in activity during the Second World War because of paper rationing, the LBC continued strongly during the conflict and the list diversified to include novels, poetry and memoirs as well as non-fiction. Although the LBC came under official scrutiny more than once, it was in the main seen as a positive

50 *Ibid.*, p. 9.   51 Hodges, *Gollancz*, pp. 126, 310.
52 *Ibid.*, p. 127. Stevenson, *Book makers*, p. 93.   53 Hodges, *Gollancz*, pp. 132–5.

contribution to the war effort and Gollancz occasionally received an extra paper ration for particularly important titles. One such was *Guilty men*, published in June 1940, a searing attack on pre-war appeasement which was widely regarded as bolstering Churchill's leadership. It was probably the first book to be sold by London street newsvendors facilitated by one of its (pseudonymous) authors, Frank Owen, who was editor of the *Evening Standard*. It eventually went through forty-three printings and sold over 220,000 copies.[54]

Most booksellers supported the LBC since it brought them reasonable income and profits, but a few resisted on ideological grounds. A competing Right Book Club never prospered, and religious retailers, particularly those with a Roman Catholic clientele, objected to the atheism of many LBC titles. Gollancz saw such recidivism as a challenge to be robustly countered and he wrote in a press advertisement in August 1940: 'If any bookseller refuses to supply any of these volumes, *insist*, on grounds of public policy. If he still refuses (but *only* if) send 2/9 direct to us for each volume required – and let us know the name of the recalcitrant bookseller.'[55]

Gollancz viewed the LBC as a patriotic duty to enhance the war effort, and after the peace and the post-war Labour election victory, it rather ran out of steam. The production of new titles became fewer and eventually in 1948 stopped altogether. The final title sold fewer than 6,500 copies. Membership had fallen from the height of 50,000 in 1939 to around 15,000 in 1946.[56] Nevertheless, the LBC had been during its dozen years of existence both a great financial success and a significant intellectual movement of enormous influence.

General book clubs revived in the post-war period but paper rationing and austerity production limited both the quantity and quality of their output. The Reprint Society had begun as a consortium of publishers in 1939 and was directed by Alan Bott as a development of his experience with the Book Society.[57] At the end of the war it had a membership of just 2,000, but an able promotional campaign and attractive cheap books saw its numbers increase to over 200,000 by the mid-1950s. It concentrated mainly on middlebrow fiction and history and, trading under the name World Books, it carved out a large market niche. In 1956 it was claimed that book clubs in the UK were distributing over 10 million books a year, catering for 'a vast new reading public ... that did not go into bookshops'.[58] The standard price of 2s 6d for

---

54 *Ibid.*, pp. 153–4.   55 *Ibid.*, p. 154.   56 *Ibid.*, pp. 157–8.
57 Stevenson, *Book makers*, pp. 90, 162; Hodges, *Gollancz*, p. 56.
58 Greenfield, *Scribblers for bread*, p. 234.

a buckram-bound hardback against the standard retail NBA-fixed price of six shillings led to considerable bookseller concern, and eventually, in 1967, the PA and ABA negotiated new book club regulations which tightly controlled the pricing, timing and availability of book club editions.[59]

The Reprint Society was noted for the quality of its manufacture and presentation, and once rationing and control of materials loosened towards the end of the 1940s there emerged a new type of club which deliberately celebrated high-quality design and production to be sold at a premium price. This was the Folio Society, founded by Charles Ede in 1947 to bring the aesthetics of fine press printing and craft binding to a wider public. Titles were originally out-of-copyright 'classic' fiction and included specially commissioned artwork from artists of the calibre of Edward Ardizzone and Joan Hassall. Later, non-fiction and modern fiction appeared, and expensive limited-edition projects including a letterpress edition of the works of Shakespeare and a full-scale reproduction of the Hereford Mappa Mundi selling for several hundred pounds were added. The Folio Society continues to flourish in the twenty-first century, although it is noticeable that their production standards are less refined than previously. Nevertheless, they are estimated to have a membership of 120,000.

In 1966, the Reprint Society was sold to a partnership of W. H. Smith (which had already experimented with some limited book club activity) and the American publisher Doubleday and renamed Book Club Associates (BCA). Readers Union was in turn acquired by the non-fiction publisher David & Charles in 1971 and its character became more specialised, focussing on special interest non-fiction topics like transport, cookery, crafts and photography. Extensive media advertising attracted many members to BCA who were, so it was generally claimed, not regular book-buyers. The 'offers' (of which members had to accept four per year) were made at prices of between one-half and one-third of the retail price and supported by 'loss-leading' premiums. BCA increasingly began to produce its own titles not available elsewhere and created some innovative channels, like the Softback Preview which offered new novels in paperback when they were only available in the trade as hardbacks. Membership peaked in the mid-1990s, and BCA began to receive increasing criticism for its aggressive marketing and poor customer service. In the meantime it had been sold to German media conglomerate Bertelsmann, which successfully operated book clubs throughout Europe. Bertelsmann invested in BCA but failed to halt its slide,

59 *Ibid.*, pp. 233–4.

culminating in its disposal in 2008 to another German company which in turn sold it on in 2011. By that time, book club sales in the British book market were minimal.

A variant of the book club model was operated by the American magazine publisher Reader's Digest, which was first introduced into Britain in 1938.[60] Reader's Digest used aggressive mail order promotion to obtain subscriptions by offering a limited range of lifestyle and leisure interest books, often lavishly produced, as premiums often associated with 'competitions' and supported by television advertising. It also produced a series of abridged novels ('Condensed Books') on a subscription basis. The rights to publish the British edition of the magazine were sold in 2010 and it announced its withdrawal from book publishing in 2012.

The changing bookshop

The retail environment of the bookshop has arguably changed much less since 1914 than many other categories of shop. Whole species of retailer like haberdashers, creameries, tobacconists and confectioners have virtually disappeared or only survive in the protected environments of 'heritage' sites. Others classes, like music recording retailers or high street electrical dealers, have risen and declined almost to invisibility within the period. Essentially a bookseller now, as then, displays a selection of titles arranged on shelving units, mainly 'spine-out' and in alphabetical order by author and divided into categories such as 'new fiction', 'crafts and pastimes' or 'children's'. A few leading titles may be shown 'face-out', although to many in the book trade, a large number of 'face-out' titles denoted poor stock levels and space being used up to disguise gaps on shelves. The introduction of book superstores in the 1990s reversed this tendency, with large surface areas for stock-holding as well as non-book products.[61]

Earlier in the period some booksellers did not even allow their customers to handle titles, displaying them in locked cases. A variant of this form of customer-unfriendly display persists when a 'reading copy' of a title, often dog-eared and tattered, is available for browsing while the 'sale stock' is sealed in unopenable shrink wrapping. Gradually, however, more imaginative merchandising and presentation techniques were introduced. As noted above, Foyles even sold books 'by weight' and introduced 'literary luncheons' during the 1930s to promote authors and their books. Under the

60 See also Chapter 7.   61 Squires, *Marketing literature*, p. 34.

guidance of Christina Foyle, these became fashionable and newsworthy events attracting international attention and greatly heightening the profile of writers as celebrities. Foyles used their lunches to celebrate not only novelists but also significant non-fiction writers and commentators like Winston Churchill and Mahatma Gandhi.

Although some shops had always hosted gatherings of literary-minded people for poetry readings and the like, it was not until after the Second World War that bookshops developed a significant social function as arts venues and even performance spaces. The pioneer was Better Books which, under the ownership of Tony Godwin (who later would work as Editor-in-Chief at Penguin Books), took over the decrepit Charing Cross Road shop of Miller & Gill in 1946. Godwin had the poky Dickensian shop gutted and replaced the dark wooden shelves with modern units, introduced good lighting and employed bright and fashionably dressed young staff. The shop quickly became the destination of choice for a much wider artistic and cultural clientele than simply book-buyers, and a lively programme of events, readings, art exhibitions and recitals drew in fashionable crowds. In 1959 Godwin took over the venerable and fusty Bumpus on Oxford Street and employed similar tactics. It became famous for its display of books as art objects. Some traditionalists bridled: Norrie snorted about 'the snaky aluminium stands . . . [a]nd everything . . . painted silver'[62] but Godwin undoubtedly caught the mood of the age in which youth culture and a fashionable aesthetic demanded much more of a bookshop than just books on shelves. Better Books hosted artistic events every evening and became a rendezvous for 'hip' individuals. Among its innovations were comfortable seating, gallery displays on walls and, probably for the first time in a bookshop, a café selling espresso coffee in clear glass cups and saucers. Although Better Books eventually failed in 1974 when it was no longer in Godwin's hands, there is little doubt that it blazed the way for new models of bookselling.

One of the major inheritors of Godwin's vision was Tim Waterstone, who had pursued a varied business career until joining W. H. Smith in 1973, where he developed some of the merchandising ideas like 'bookseller picks' that later became synonymous with his name. Made redundant in 1981, he set up a revolutionary new shop in Kensington, London, in 1982. He employed well-educated staff who engaged positively with customers in a well-lit, comfortable environment. New ideas like 'staff picks' (recommendation cards on

---

62 Norrie, *Mumby's publishing and bookselling*, p. 206.

shelves), even more author events and attention-grabbing publicity quickly made the shop successful, and especially popular with a younger clientele. More branches opened elsewhere in London and later throughout the country, and Waterstone's was widely hailed 'as a new kind of bookseller' which made customer service, wide stock range, local interest and unstuffy atmosphere the heart of its retail offering, creating for the first time in bookselling a nationwide chain of branded shops that enjoyed great customer loyalty and wide recognition. Waterstone's fate, both personally and as a brand, suffered later, but when he sold his company to W. H. Smith for £9 million in 1993 he had demonstrated how his approach could revive what was elsewhere an ailing trade.

Similar, but on a smaller scale to Waterstone's, was the chain Ottakar's, set up by James Heneage in 1987. They also concentrated on high-quality customer service and range but their shops tended to be smaller than Waterstone's, although they too provided comfortable 'browsing spaces' and cafés, and recruited well-educated book-loving staff. They often had large children's departments which hosted after-school events and reading clubs for under-fives. The business model was to open in small, affluent market towns like Trowbridge (the site of their first store), Banbury and Bishop's Stortford. Their aim was to become the focus of local cultural life and they forged links with schools and local voluntary groups to promote book sales and interest in author events. They also supported 'reading groups', which spread widely in store and to other venues like libraries during the 1980s and 1990s, by providing space and publicity. Their in-store events became legendary, particularly in association with the launch of each successive volume of J. K. Rowling's Harry Potter series which involved late openings, fancy-dress parties, 'readathons' and imaginative shop dressing.

Books were, of course, not only sold by booksellers. Several large department stores in London, such as Harrods, Army and Navy Stores, and Selfridges, and in the provinces Lewis's in Liverpool and Binns in Newcastle-upon-Tyne, operated book departments, although their range of stock was limited and they tended to atrophy towards the close of the century, as indeed did the more traditional stores. Waterstone's eventually occupied the building of one of the most iconic of the department stores, Simpsons of Piccadilly. At the other end of the scale, the once almost ubiquitous small CTNs (Confectioners, Tobacconists and Newsagents) sold a range of books, mainly cheap genre fiction paperbacks. Wholesalers provided selected stocks for these shops, and the publishing lists of Mills & Boon and Hurst & Blackett were largely channelled through these outlets. Since 1985 independent CTNs have declined almost to invisibility in the face of the fall of the sale of tobacco products due to health concerns and price competition from supermarkets. Another key non-traditional outlet was Woolworths, which expanded after 1918 to have a cheap and cheerful presence on virtually every high street, and was a major factor in the initial success of Penguin Books in 1935 when more traditional retailers were suspicious of, or downright hostile to, cheap paperbacks. Later they also were decisive in the success of Paul Hamlyn's highly illustrated and colourful books on cookery, fashion, art and other subjects that were dismissed by some in the book trade as 'Council House Coffee Table Books'.[63] Cheap reprints of classic children's books by Dean & Son were also a staple of Woolworths' business during the 1960s and 1970s. Despite owning the book wholesaler Bertrams, Woolworths later marginalised the retail selling of books in favour of music and home entertainment, but books always remained an important element of their range until the retailer's sudden demise in 2009.

Merchandising, advertising and publicity

Merchandising was regarded as *infra dig* by many booksellers but successful bookselling has gone hand-in-hand with imaginative promotion, from Foyles' events to Waterstone's helpful sales assistants. One of the fundamental measures of retail success is the concept of 'stock turn', which is the amount of time it takes for the inventory held to 'turn over' and be completely replaced. In fast-moving retailing, like food or clothing, this can be a matter of days, but in bookselling, with its vast range of lines, stock turn is often measured in years, with undesirable consequences for costs and profitability.

The most obvious merchandising device is the book jacket or cover.[64] Originating in the late nineteenth century, 'dust-jackets' were originally simply paper wrappers whose main functions were to keep cloth book bindings clean. If they bore any printing it was restricted to title and author. From the 1920s, publishers began to see the potential of using covers to promote sales by printing attractive artwork on them, often commissioning cutting-edge graphic designers working in fashionable styles from Art Deco to Punk (later in the century). Artists accomplished and perhaps better known in diverse fields like poster design, woodcut, cartoon and caricature, and theatrical design did some of their finest work as book jackets. Robert

63 De Bellaigue, *British book publishing*, p. 94. 64 See also Chapter 2.

Gibbings, David Gentleman, Jacqueline Duhême, Charles Mozley and Sidney Nolan are only some of the many prominent designers important in book jacket art.[65] The purpose of a book jacket became increasingly to catch the eye of a prospective purchaser by an arresting image, and as the century progressed book exteriors became more elaborate, with the use of colour, lamination, foils and 'cut-outs'. Distinctive visual tropes to identify genres and target readerships emerged, such as the use of pastel colours, cursive print and cartoonish high-heeled female legs to denote 'chick-lit'. Although most books were displayed 'spine-out', great efforts were expended on the faces of jackets; 'cover meetings' became important decision-making events at publishers, and major booksellers were often consulted (and sometimes had the power of veto) over cover design.

Allied to the elaboration of jacket design was the development of the 'blurb', the printed description of the book and its author on the jacket flaps or cover reverse which appeared in the 1890s but became essential in the 1920s and 1930s. Originally a simple, factual description of content and authorship, these became increasingly strident and important to book sales, aiming to cement the sale to the prospective purchaser who had picked the book up on the strength of its jacket design.

Press advertising was once a major element in bookselling but has declined steadily in importance. Publishers in general believe that it is unproven in creating sales, and most booksellers believe that in-store events and the books themselves are the most effective advertisements. Gollancz believed other-wise and was in mid-century famous for his typographically inventive and witty print advertisements. Advertising in other media is rarely applied to books, but Waterstone's and W. H. Smith have mounted television cam-paigns in the critical Christmas period, where as much as one-third of their annual sales can occur. It is difficult, however, to assess their success.

In-store merchandising has mainly been confined to arranging the stock accessibly and logically with clear signage and information. Publishers of specific series would supply booksellers with 'spinners', which contained quantities of their titles that made efficient use of space (and generated quicker stock turn), and especially important titles would be supplied in 'dump bins' paid for by the publisher and containing quantities of a (potentially) fast-moving title. They were often unwieldy, however, and their effectiveness as a sales tool was open to question. By the second decade

65 For examples of dust-jacket art in the twentieth century see Bertram Rota, Catalogue 306, www.bertramrota.co.uk/rota%20cat%20306.pdf.

of the twenty-first century, they had virtually vanished as a merchandising tool. After the end of the NBA, and the advent of price competition, space utilisation in bookshops dramatically changed with a restricted selection of price-promoted titles being displayed on tables in piles and face-out at the front of the shop.

The need for booksellers to reduce stock turn has resulted from the 1930s in one of the most contentious supply arrangements between publishers and retailers. The 'returns' or 'see safe' system, which allows booksellers to return for full credit unsold stock to the publishers, was introduced as a temporary measure to help retailers over a recession. The system has been perpetuated and was open to abuse; until the 1970s retailers only had to return torn-out title-pages to obtain credit, which accounts for many books still surviving (and apparently sold) without title-pages. Returns were sometimes made before the invoice for them had been paid. The pointless circulation of thousands of books between bookshops and publishers' warehouses (and increasingly landfill) is a wasteful and environmentally reprehensible system that is unique to the book business, and its resolution has defied the earnest attention of many joint trade committees.

Various indirect methods of increasing book sales were introduced in the century. One of the most successful was Book Tokens, invented by Harold Raymond of Chatto & Windus. First suggested in 1926, the idea of book-shops selling stamps of various values which could be affixed to attractive cards and then sent as gifts to be redeemed at any outlet was at first treated with suspicion, but by 1935 most booksellers adhered to the scheme and it eventually became the model for similar voucher schemes among other retailers. A variation, the Book Tally scheme operated by Rupert Hart-Davis, involved children buying low-value 'savings stamps' towards their book purchases which could be redeemed, but the system died out in the 1950s.

Book sales were promoted by many other mechanisms like published reviews, outdoor advertising and events, the growth of literary prizes and festivals, and the important role of broadcasting (the 'Richard and Judy Book Club' on daytime television in the 1990s and early 2000s created many best-sellers), but for many bookshops it was the advent of the author tour and 'signing session' from the 1970s onward that became their key publicity and sales events. As noted above, Foyles and Better Books had earlier pioneered in-store events, but the idea of authors meeting their readers and signing their purchases presented major sales opportunities. The costs were mainly met by the publish-ers (who liked these events since signed books could not be returned for credit), but booksellers would provide staff, catering and space. These sessions undoubtedly increased sales and cemented reader loyalty to favourite authors.

The second-hand book trade

The sale of second-hand books was an integral part of the traditional bookseller's business in the nineteenth century and continued to be so in the twentieth.[66] Many shops had substantial antiquarian departments offering rare and out-of-print titles, while the recycling of discarded library stock and special classes of books like paperbacks was a general business element. Used books would be bought for cash or part-exchanged, and academic booksellers would buy back used textbooks from students at a fixed percentage to sell on to the next generation. A few retailers, like John Smith & Son, issued catalogues and actively built up a collector clientele with special services like 'book search' for elusive titles. Most, however, sold used books alongside new, and did not see that by doing so they were often undercutting themselves with the same titles.

Although there had always been second-hand book dealers, the emergence of the specifically antiquarian merchant catering to a collector market was codified with the creation of a professional body (The Antiquarian Booksellers Association) in 1906.[67] At the higher end of the market, dealers like Henry Sotheran and Maggs Bros. dealt in an international market for rare books like incunabula, 'association copies' (books from the libraries of authors and famous people) and manuscripts. During the twentieth century, a substantial collector market emerged for 'modern first editions', often signed by their authors and dedicated to other prominent members of the literary scene. The leading dealer in this field was Bertram Rota, although the market was pioneered by Gilbert H. Fabes, Foyles' antiquarian manager, who published limited-edition bibliographies of 'modern' authors like D. H. Lawrence and John Galsworthy in the 1920s, thereby establishing prices and rarity factors.

The condition of these books (whether or not they retained unblemished jackets was a key factor in establishing value) and their popularity was more relevant than their literary importance. The first editions of the James Bond novels of Ian Fleming and later the Harry Potter books by J. K. Rowling would achieve remarkably high prices; although they were not 'rare books',

66 McKitterick, 'Second-hand and old books', pp. 637–9.
67 Mandelbrote (ed.), *Out of print and into profit*.

high demand and scarcity made them collectable. The rare book and literary manuscript market was also served by the major London auction houses, such as Christies and Spinks, and a specialist house, Bloomsbury Book Auctions, held a number of notable sales, particularly of individual libraries and early and rare scientific, medical and natural history titles. The market was for many years driven by the desire of well-endowed American research libraries, like the University of Texas at Austin, to acquire substantial literary archives which saw many manuscript collections leave their home country.

The middle and lower end of the market was served in almost every town by a large number of owner-operated 'second-hand shops', which became a byword for chaotic organisation and a honey pot for 'runners' to discover treasures for instant resale to upmarket customers. There was even a handbook for such entrepreneurs entitled *Drif's Guide* which described the stock and idiosyncracies of each shop and its owner. Some small towns, like Hay-on-Wye and Wigtown, possessed such a concentration of second-hand bookshops that they became tourist attractions in themselves as 'book towns' and established highly successful and popular literary festivals on this reputation.[68] An important outlet for second-hand sales from the end of the twentieth century became the 'charity retailer' which solicited donations of unwanted books and resold them, often using volunteer staff. Used books are probably the largest single component of charity sales, and many charities, led by Oxfam, established 'book only' shops. In 2012, Oxfam declared itself the third largest book retailer in the UK.[69] The BA, worried by what they saw as 'unfair' competition, petitioned local councils to control the growth of charity shops.

The greatest recent transformation in second-hand bookselling was the creation of the online marketplace Abebooks in 1996. Originally the 'Advanced Book Exchange', and created by a consortium of small Canadian book dealers to help book search, it deploys a simple yet powerful business model. Book dealers place their stocks on the website which can be searched by customers seeking a particular title, author or edition. The scope is global and the service is free to buyers (sellers pay a commission once a title is sold). The site provides a simple and secure payment procedure via credit card. The service diversified into selling new books as well as digitised 'print on demand' titles. The internet retailer Amazon also offered a 'book

68 See Chapter 30.
69 'State of donation: Oxfam takes over the high street'. *Telegraph* 9 January 2012, www.telegraph.co.uk/culture/books/8995389/State-of-donation-Oxfam-takes-over-the-high-street.html.

226

marketplace' for second-hand titles but recognised the success and potential of Abebooks, with 100 million titles from 12,880 booksellers in fifty-seven countries, by buying the company in 2008.[70] The functionality offered by Abebooks has allowed the emergence of large online used book retailers like Book Barn, based near Bristol.

A variation of the second-hand trade is remainder bookselling. Publishers are left with surplus stock and they dispose of this, often through intermediate brokers, at very low prices to free up warehouse space. 'Bargain book' outlets, often ephemeral, sell exclusively remainders at a small fraction of the original prices but they can confuse the 'retail offer' of booksellers selling new books. It was the mixture of new and remainder stocks that harmed the image of the chain British Bookshops and probably contributed to its eventual collapse in 2011.

Conclusion

As we have seen, the development of bookselling chains pre-dated the collapse of the NBA in 1995 but its demise greatly foreshortened and intensified these processes of concentration and transformation. The primary factor in the NBA's disestablishment was the desire of supermarkets, particularly Asda, to sell books at unregulated prices, and the willingness of the largest publishers to sell to them. Equally vociferous in condemning fixed prices was the rapidly growing chain of Dillon's shops, owned by the aggressive entrepreneurial company Pentos, who might have gathered more support among publishers had they paid their bills on time. Under their energetic owner Terry Maher, they opened dozens of new bookshops throughout the country, often on sites with unsustainably high ground rents.[71]

In 1995 almost two-thirds of bookselling was done by independents; ten years later, 60 per cent was through chains.[72] Although several inefficient independents foundered as the NBA went, the unexpected consequence of its disappearance was an actual increase in book sales and book outlets. Waterstone's had begun to develop as a nationwide chain and opened many new branches in towns in direct competition with Dillons. In 1995, it was acquired by W. H. Smith and with joint sales of £300 million occupied almost 10 per cent of the market. Dillon's suffered under the pressure and were acquired by music retailer HMV in 1998, which promptly bought

---

70 www.abebooks.co.uk/docs/CompanyInformation/factSheet.shtml.
71 Maher, *Against my better judgement.*   72 Stevenson, 'The book trade', p. 319.

Waterstone's and put the former bitter rivals together under the Waterstone's brand, making a 20 per cent market share.

New merchandising techniques like the '3 for 2' offer appeared, and virtually every title sold was discounted from the publishers' recommended retail price. Reducing prices was counter-intuitively seen as the only way of expanding the market and, for a time, it seemed to be working. By 2005 the total retail market for books achieved £2,850 million, over 20 per cent more than in 1995.[73] Most of this gain was achieved by relentless erosion of publishers' margins by booksellers' demands for ever-increasing discounts. New chain superstore entrants like the American Borders, which offered a 'destination bookstore experience' of coffee shops and sofas to a fashionable and young clientele, briefly flourished, offering a new, more mass-market version of the Better Books experiment discussed above. But most significant among the newcomers was the internet bookseller Amazon which by discounting, slick customer service, massive stock-holding and innovative possibilities for customer comments and recommendations was by 2005 selling one in ten of all books supplied in the UK. A few larger bookselling chains like Blackwell's and Waterstone's set up competing book sales websites but none managed any significant market share.

Waterstone's moved far from its roots as an upmarket range bookseller, and although it had a chequered business history, by absorbing rivals like Ottakar's it emerged as the largest and only national chain of bookshops with over 200 branches in 2010, and over 30 per cent market share. Potential rivals like Borders (which, separated from its US company, went into receivership in 2009) and British Bookshops (acquired disastrously by Irish retailer Easons) withered. Supermarkets, despite precipitating the end of the NBA, found books as a commodity troublesome and their suppliers not as docile as they were used to. Asda and Tesco maintained a small book range but only Sainsbury's offered a reasonable selection, even becoming the 'Chain bookseller of the year' in the *Bookseller* awards in 2010. Until 2009, book sales from terrestrial outlets had continued to grow year-on-year and bookshops seemed set for a secure future as a stable element of the retail structure of British towns and cities.

The very end of this period saw intense change, following the relatively settled patterns of bookselling. The international banking crisis of 2008 severely mauled business confidence and decimated personal discretionary spending, on which bookselling depends. Despite notable successes,

---

73 *Ibid.*

especially in the crucial Christmas product of celebrity memoirs and cookery books, the overall sale of what became known in an increasingly digital environment as p-books began to decline, and electronic books began to assume significant importance. E-books and their reading devices had been available since 2000, but it was not until the introduction of Amazon's Kindle device to the UK in 2010 that e-reading grew rapidly. Amazon had an irresistible incentive to promote its system, since it saw this as the way it could reduce its crippling terrestrial stock-holding and wrest control of pricing from publishers. Although their success was by no means complete – Kindle has a patchy reliability record and Amazon's attempt to avoid the 'agency model' where prices are set by the publisher has failed – their simple, convenient reader, selling in 2012 at £89, with its enormous range of titles, has made a very significant breakthrough into the book market.

At the end of 2011, the sales of p-books continued to fall and their digital counterparts increased by some 500 per cent, although by 2016 sales first plateaued then dipped. The impact of the more sophisticated but more expensive and multi-purpose iPad from Apple did not have as dramatic an impact as Kindle, but its colour screen and multi-media capability makes it a formidable competitor. Kindle was initially limited by its black and white screen which is unsatisfactory for many illustrated and non-fiction titles, but a colour-screen tablet version with enhanced functionality was launched as 'Kindle Fire' in 2012, with colour e-ink versions in development from 2016.

Amazon has pioneered the sale of very cheap novels as e-books at 99p and has enabled the massive growth of 'self-publishing' by providing aspiring authors unable to break through to conventional publishers' lists with a cheap and convenient platform. Most self-published books sink without trace, but in 2012 this platform provided conventional publishing and book-selling with its greatest sales success for a decade, the so-called 'Mummy Porn' trilogy, *Fifty shades of grey*, which began life as 'fan fiction' and, despite its leaden prose and unlikely plot, sold in excess of 40 million copies, albeit in the hands of a mainstream publisher, Random House.

By the middle of the new century's second decade, Amazon has become probably the largest player in bookselling, both for the direct sale of p-books and for the download of e-books. By 2015, Amazon accounted for above 30 per cent of most publishers' business, with digital sales continuing to grow beyond then in volume if not always volume terms. Whether or not the growing dominance of one commercial organisation in retail book supply is of concern, does this ineluctably mean the end of 'bricks and mortar' bookselling? Prediction is unwise in such a volatile market but there are some interesting pointers. Waterstone's was sold by HMV early in 2011, and in a surprising but widely applauded move the new owners, a Russian-backed investment business, appointed James Daunt, the owner of a small and much-admired upmarket bookselling chain, as managing director. He immediately announced the end of general price discounting and '3 for 2' and a return to range bookselling and enhanced customer service. An even more surprising development, especially after denouncing them as 'the Devil', was Daunt's agreement with Amazon to sell their devices in his shops in 2012, an arrangement that continued for three years. By 2019, the chain's future seems much more assured than under its previous owners. Under Daunt's stewardship, Waterstones have gained market share while maintaining a diverse range.

Elsewhere, perhaps more significant pointers to the book trade's future come from the success of upmarket shops like Topping & Company in Bath, Ely and St Andrews, Lutyens & Rubenstein in West London, and most of all Foyles. They have abandoned cheap and cheerful in favour of carefully chosen, often quirky stocks, welcoming atmospheres and informed staff. They have made their shops fashionable and desirable venues with regular events, performances and gatherings, providing space for reading groups and literary soirées. Publishers are responding to this movement by providing beautifully designed and superbly produced books that become objects of desire (and at premium prices). Some may see this as a forlorn hope and a mere delay of the inevitable electronic colonisation of the book trade, but for others it looks remarkably like bookselling returning to its roots where the bookshop once again becomes a salon rather than a supermarket.

7

Reading and ownership

ANDREW NASH, CLAIRE SQUIRES AND SHAFQUAT
TOWHEED

'It is as easy to make sweeping statements about reading tastes as to indict a nation, and as pointless.'[1] This jocular remark by a librarian made in *The Times* in 1952 sums up the dangers and difficulties of writing the history of reading. As a field of study in the humanities it is still in its infancy and encompasses a range of different methodologies and theoretical approaches.[2] Historians of reading are not solely interested in what people read, but also turn their attention to the why, where and how of the reading experience. Reading can be solitary, silent, secret, surreptitious; it can be oral, educative, enforced, or assertive of a collective identity. For what purposes are individuals reading? How do they actually use books and other textual material? What are the physical environments and spaces of reading? What social, educational, technological, commercial, legal or ideological contexts underpin reading practices? Finding answers to these questions is compounded by the difficulty of locating and interpreting evidence. As Mary Hammond points out, 'most reading acts in history remain unrecorded, unmarked or forgotten'.[3] Available sources are wide but inchoate: diaries, letters and autobiographies; personal and oral testimonies; marginalia; and records of societies and reading groups. All lend themselves more to the case-study approach than to the historical survey. Statistics offer analysable data but have the effect of producing identikits rather than actual human beings. The twenty-first century affords further possibilities, and challenges, with its traces of digital reader activity, but the map is ever changing.

Book historians of this period are confronted by a further problem. More so than other chapters in this volume – and more so than in equivalent chapters in previous volumes in the series – there is a paucity of extant

---

1 'The reading tastes of the "under forties"', *Times Literary Supplement* 29 August 1952, p. 572.
2 For a recent summary, see Hammond, 'Book history in the reading experience'.
3 *Ibid.*, p. 240.

research for the topic of reading and ownership. In particular, assembling and interpreting evidence about the habits and experiences of actual readers – what Jonathan Rose has called 'the history of audiences' – has only just started.[4] While research projects like the Reading Experience Database (which ends at 1945) and the Reading Sheffield project have begun to organise and preserve source material, a large part of the period remains unmapped, with research questions still to be formulated.[5] Writing a definitive history of reading in the twentieth century and beyond is thus at present an impossible task. What follows is no more than a preliminary sketch of the period. It focusses mainly on institutions of reading and on changing social and cultural attitudes to reading practices. It also draws on statistical and sociological surveys from the period which attempted to tabulate and evaluate changing reading habits.

1914–1945

First World War

As noted throughout this volume, the First World War intensified public interest in books and reading. In the early months of the war in particular, public appetite for information led to 'newspaper rushes' at stalls and shops.[6] After an initial period of slump, publishers and booksellers quickly found that sales of books were also increasing, especially of cheap publications such as Nelsons' sixpenny classics series.[7] With fewer alternative outlets for leisure, reading became an important form of distraction. Public libraries recorded increases in fiction borrowing as 'romantic tales and detective thrillers' offered readers an escape from wartime living conditions.[8] As Jane Potter remarks, there was a 'fine line between so-called "light-reading material" and propaganda', but there was also a greater appetite for more instructive reading.[9] At a conference of the English Association in 1916, members of the book trade observed how the war had generated new interest in 'the best books, and especially for poetry', a trend which a reporter in the *Times Literary Supplement* attributed to 'the heightened sense of values brought about by seeing life, liberty, and

---

4 Rose, 'Rereading the English common reader'.
5 The Reading Experience Database, www.open.ac.uk/Arts/RED/. Reading Sheffield, www.readingsheffield.co.uk is an oral history project gathering evidence mainly from readers born before 1945.
6 Colclough, 'No such bookselling', pp. 29–31.
7 Towheed and King, *Reading and the First World War*, pp. 7–8.
8 Potter, *Boys in khaki*, p. 89. 9 *Ibid.*, p. 53.

country daily at stake before all eyes'.[10] Books dealing with the immediate causes of the war and 'the history of Europe out of which it came' were also cited as popular; and author and publisher John Buchan and bookseller J. G. Wilson were at one in claiming that 'there never was a time when more books of the best sort were being read in England, especially if we include that greater England which is now in France'.[11]

That expanded – or displaced – market created new reading audiences in trenches and war hospitals, and among prisoners of war.[12] Voluntary organisations such as the Camps' Library collected books through local post offices for distribution to the trenches and prisoner-of-war camps. The Red Cross and St John Ambulance War Library sent reading matter to the sick and wounded in hospitals, while the YMCA provided tent-based reading rooms for soldiers.[13] First-hand reports record that trench-bound soldiers mainly read for escapism or out of boredom, but reading was also an important way of staying in touch with home, whether factually or imaginatively, and thus sustaining 'a degree of civilian identity'.[14] Books and newspapers were passed around and in some prisoner-of-war camps readers formed study groups 'centred on a small library of vocational texts'.[15]

Schemes like the Camps' Library attempted to guide soldiers in their reading and to encourage personal improvement, but the most popular kind of reading was fiction. E. W. Hornung, who operated a YMCA library for British soldiers at Arras for two months in early 1918, recorded that 87 per cent of books borrowed were works of popular or classic fiction.[16] Hornung nevertheless observed an eclectic taste among the readers, from 'romance readers' who devoured Charles Garvice, to 'rough poor lads' who demanded Ruskin and Carlyle.[17] To judge from distribution figures, religious texts constituted a substantial part of reading in the trenches. Oxford University Press alone supplied 4.5 million copies of the New Testament for the battlefield, and one estimate suggests some 40 million Bibles, prayers books and other religious texts were distributed to servicemen.[18]

---

10 John McCann Bailey, 'Literature and the war', *Times Literary Supplement* 1 June 1916, p. 253.
11 *Ibid.*
12 Towheed and King, *Reading and the First World War* for a range of recent approaches and perspectives. See also Imogen Gassert, 'In a foreign field: what soldiers in the trenches liked to read', *Times Literary Supplement* 10 May 2002, pp. 17–19.
13 King, '"Books are more to me than food"'.   14 *Ibid.*, p. 264.   15 *Ibid.*, p. 263.
16 King, 'E. W. Hornung's unpublished "diary"', p. 373.   17 *Ibid.*, pp. 377, 379.
18 See Towheed and King, *Reading and the First World War*, p. 13.

Inter-war reading

Joseph McAleer argues that, as well as perpetuating existing reading habits, the First World War newly encouraged reading among war workers, 'either in the Forces or on civilian duty', whose appetite for 'lighter forms of reading' represented 'the principal growth area in the reading public' after the war.[19] This growth was abundantly visible to inter-war cultural commentators like Q. D. Leavis. In her book *Fiction and the reading public* (1932), Leavis began with the line: 'In twentieth-century England not only every one can read, but it is safe to add that every one does read.'[20] A dramatic increase in the sale of national daily newspapers – from 3.1 million copies a day in 1918 to 10.6 million twenty years later[21] – was only the most conspicuous indicator of the growth of the reading public. The expansion of library systems brought books to within a wider reach of the population, while in the 1930s the spread of book clubs and sixpenny paperbacks increased book ownership. Periods of depression and unemployment brought greater surplus time for reading. At the height of the Depression in 1931 the *Publishers' Circular* reported 'an amazing increase in the amount of reading done by the general public'.[22] The inter-war period was also marked by a preoccupation with investigating and measuring the activity of reading. Alongside Leavis's academic study, Mass-Observation surveys, commenced in 1937, attempted to capture information about what, why and how people read.

Leavis proceeded from the premise that reading activity was strongly determined by class contexts and Mass-Observation findings largely endorsed her views. Major modern studies of reading by McAleer and Rose have underlined how changes in reading practice in this period were strongly linked both to social and economic factors that influenced literary taste and to institutional contexts that determined the acquisition of reading matter. Working-class readers generally borrowed books from public libraries and purchased reading matter from newsagents, stationers or market stalls. Middle- and upper-class readers were more likely to subscribe to circulating libraries or purchase from bookshops, which, as Leavis noted, were sparse outside London and the university towns. By the 1930s this pattern was beginning to break down as class and institutional barriers became more blurred. McAleer argues that the one significant change in the 'size and complexion of the reading public' was 'the addition of the new "leisured

19 McAleer, *Popular reading and publishing*, p. 72.
20 Leavis, *Fiction and the reading public*, p. 3.   21 Lewis, *Penguin special*, p. 79.
22 McAleer, *Popular reading and publishing*, p. 73.

class" . . . drawn largely from the lower-middle and working classes'.[23] It was this group of readers whose needs and demands were serviced by the cultural and commercial changes in the period.

Library expansion

More than anything else, growth in reading after 1918 was facilitated by expanded public library provision. A Mass-Observation report of 1942 declared it 'impossible to overestimate the importance of the library in determining the reading habits of Britain'.[24] In 1915, however, it had been estimated that 38 per cent of the population of England and 54 per cent in Wales lived outside a library area.[25] The total number of books in UK public libraries rose from 11 million in 1911 to 27 million in 1935 and an estimated 42 million in 1950.[26] The catalyst was the Public Libraries Act (1919) which allowed county councils in England and Wales to become library authorities (a separate Act of 1918 introduced changes in Scotland) and abolished the 'penny in the pound' rate limitation which restricted spending.[27] Provision could now be extended to smaller urban and rural areas where branch libraries were often set up in local schools or village halls. By 1935 the counties of England and Wales could boast 'a total stock of five and a half million books and a reading public of over two million people who had had no library service before 1919'.[28] The expansion became a source of national pride. A 1927 report by a committee of the Board of Education proclaimed 'a remarkable progress, much accelerated of recent years in the library movement as a whole'; the public library was now 'an indispensable element in the life of the community' and 'recognised as an engine of great potentialities for national welfare'.[29] Such rhetoric needs to be qualified by statistical evidence which shows that, if there was a new reading public, it consisted of the middle and artisan classes more than unskilled workers. The 1942 Mass-Observation survey discovered that 76 per cent of unskilled workers did not use any form of library.[30]

Change was also discernible in the public library's physical environment. As open access became more standard, most libraries consisted of a reading room (and sometimes a newspaper room), and separate reference and lending departments. Provision for children increased significantly after 1918 with more libraries operating separate lending facilities. In the mid-1930s

23 *Ibid.*, p. 76.   24 Mass-Observation, *Books and the public*, p. 63.
25 Carnell, *County libraries*, p. 22.   26 Munford, *Penny rate*, p. 86.
27 Black, *The public library*, p. 18.   28 Stockham, *British county libraries*, p. 19.
29 *Ibid.*, p. 37.   30 Mass-Observation, *Books and the public*, p. 64.

Walthamstow opened 'the first dedicated teenage library'.[31] The legacy of this expanded provision for young readers is visible in Mass-Observation surveys of the 1940s which found that public library borrowing was 'appreciably more frequent among younger people than among older people'.[32]

The public library movement had always been informed by a civic ideal which promoted reading and literacy as a means rather than an end. Libraries continued to be conceived of as guardians of national education and often served as spaces for adult education classes and University Extension lectures. Preoccupation over the library's recreational role had in the early years of the century provoked the 'Great Fiction Debate', and guiding reading continued to be a central aim of library authorities. Rural expansion offered a particular challenge in this regard. An advice manual on setting up a village library from 1918 emphasised the need to provide readers with the 'rubbish' they ask for: 'There is only one answer to the question: "what do village people want to read?" They want to read what interests them quickly and easily, not anything which presupposes both a wide education and an untired body and mind.'[33] In public libraries readers were generally allowed to borrow one fiction and one non-fiction title at a time, yet fiction was by far the most borrowed category. A 1924 investigation revealed that while 63 per cent of books stocked in urban libraries were non-fiction, 78 per cent of issues were fiction.[34] Statistics like this encouraged the objective outlined in the 1927 Board of Education report to supply 'recreational literature of as good quality as [the] public can digest', and 'if the proportion of indifferent fiction is high ... to lead people to discriminate between the better and the worse, and to arrive at a higher standard'.[35]

The range of books stocked in public libraries was limited, however. As a 1933 commentator noted, readers couldn't expect to find 'an ample supply of the popular biographies and novels as soon as they are published. It is impossible for the public library to cater for such immediate popular demands.'[36] To be certain of sampling the most recent books, readers needed to subscribe to one of the commercial libraries such as Boots, Mudie's or W. H. Smith's. By the mid-1930s Boots Book-Lovers' Library, which has come to be viewed as a powerful instrument in the emergence of middlebrow reading culture, had over 400 branches and half a million subscribers. In 1926 it cost forty-two shillings to get books on demand, 17s 6d to choose from

31 Denham, 'Public library services for children', p. 108.
32 Mass-Observation, *Books and the public*, p. 64.   33 Sayle, *Village libraries*, p. 113.
34 Leavis, *Fiction and the reading public*, p. 4.   35 Munford, *Penny rate*, p. 39.
36 McColvin, *How to use books*, p. 70.

books in circulation, and 10s 6d for the standard service. The most expensive option thus allowed subscribers to acquire a new novel a week for less than tenpence; the cheapest meant books could be borrowed for around 2½d weekly. For Q. D. Leavis the structures of borrowing and the 'strict moral censorship' of the libraries created a situation where readers – especially that majority taking the cheapest subscription option – were 'prepared to have their reading determined for them'.[37] The majority of circulating library readers were women. According to Nicola Beauman, 'Boots catered more for suburban shoppers than for fashionable ladies' and 'only one quarter of the library customers were male'.[38] This was confirmed by the 1942 Mass-Observation survey which also found that borrowers were more likely to be aged over thirty.[39]

Mass-Observation also recorded that subscription libraries were 'hardly used by poorer people'.[40] Readers from the lower-middle and working classes were more likely to acquire books from twopenny, or 'no-deposit', libraries which spread rapidly in the 1930s. Twopenny libraries were mostly run as adjuncts to newsagents, tobacconists or department stores, and their ubiquity led the President of the Library Association to remark in 1938: 'it would seem the lending of reading matter is becoming an auxiliary of every business'.[41] Twopenny libraries probably added to the reading public because of their wide dissemination. As the publisher Harold Raymond observed, circulating libraries were in the main confined to towns, whereas twopenny libraries were to be found 'in villages and in suburbs' and thus more easily accessible to those living outside urban centres.[42]

It would be wrong to suggest that twopenny libraries served a working-class readership only. George Orwell recalled that the library attached to the Hampstead bookshop in which he worked in the mid-1930s was 'frequented by all types from baronets to bus-conductors' and that subscribers were probably 'a fair cross-section of London's reading public'.[43] The restricted range of reading available in twopenny libraries, however, does allow for some conclusions about what the majority of the working-class public read. Economics dictated that most books stocked were works of popular fiction, predominantly romance, westerns, thrillers and detective stories. Orwell wrote with barely disguised contempt of the insatiable demand among men for detective stories and among women 'of all kinds and ages' for the

---

37 Leavis, *Fiction and the reading public*, p. 6.
38 Beauman, *A very great profession*, pp. 174, 11.
39 Mass-Observation, *Books and the public*, p. 67.   40 *Ibid.*, p. 64.
41 McAleer, *Popular reading and publishing*, p. 58.
42 Raymond, *Publishing and bookselling*, p. 20.   43 Orwell, 'Bookshop memories', p. 275.

novels of Ethel M. Dell.[44] In his advice manual *How to run a twopenny library* (1938), Ronald Batty advised that 'no efficient service for the supply of non-fiction titles can be given, whether juvenile, or any other type of book except popular fiction'.[45] New novels priced at 7s 6d 'barely pay for themselves at a loan fee of twopence weekly'.[46] The commercial basis of the operation ensured that choice was limited. Would-be librarians were advised to 'please the majority, which means a profit, and discourage the small minority of readers whose reading is specialised'.[47]

Batty's advice may paint a partial picture of the typical twopenny library. He acknowledged that while 'Intellectual writers are not so popular in twopenny libraries at present ... there are some slight signs of an improvement in the public's taste in this direction.'[48] Christopher Hilliard has recently argued that the availability of middlebrow fiction in twopenny libraries 'problematizes the distinction between a middle-class public for new hardcover novels and a working-class readership of fiction that appeared in cheap papers and magazines'.[49] The key factor here is that by the end of the 1930s the works of contemporary authors were more readily available in cheap editions. Batty's 1938 checklist of the most popular authors in twopenny libraries included D. H. Lawrence, Aldous Huxley and Evelyn Waugh, none of whom had appeared in earlier lists covering 1933–35 compiled by the *Library Association Record*.[50]

While it is hard to assess how far such libraries altered reading tastes, it is clear that they increased the reading habit. John Boon, whose firm Mills & Boon profited enormously by the twopennies, recalled how 'commercial libraries needed a tremendous supply of books to keep their customers happy. Some of them would read a book in, say, three days.'[51] Once again evidence suggests use was strongly gendered. Mass-Observation found that women used twopenny libraries twice as much as men (though this may not correlate with reading habits) and that the space was often 'a social meeting ground' for young working-class mothers.[52] The typical borrower read purely for relaxation and was mostly influenced in the choice of books by an author's name, although the appearance – notably the dust-wrapper – and weight of a book, the number of date-stamps inside it, and the influence of cinema were also factors in selection.[53] Pay-as-you-go libraries declined after

44 *Ibid.*   45 Batty, *How to run a twopenny library*, p. 77.   46 *Ibid.*, p. 17.   47 *Ibid.*, p. 29.
48 *Ibid.*, p. 31.   49 Hilliard, 'The two-penny library', p. 201.
50 McAleer, *Popular reading and publishing*, p. 88.   51 *Ibid.*, p. 104.
52 Mass-Observation, *Books and the public*, p. 67.
53 McAleer, *Popular reading and publishing*, pp. 83–7.

the war but remained attractive to readers in search of certain types of fiction. In 1957 Richard Hoggart pointed to the importance of 'stationers' fourpenny libraries whose main function is to hold a large stock of the kinds of fiction ... of which the public libraries never have enough copies'.[54]

Working-class reading of the inter-war period was not restricted to commercial and rate-paying libraries. In industrial areas – notably South Wales – institute and welfare hall libraries served local communities. Chris Baggs estimates that there were between 150 and 200 reading facilities in the miners' libraries of South Wales, funded through a combination of payments by the miners themselves and, from 1921, via the Miners' Welfare Fund, the product of a levy imposed on coal owners to provide amenities for the miners. While the size and stock of individual libraries varied considerably, 'scarcely any mining community went without a library or reading room provided largely by themselves, for themselves'.[55] Stock was controlled by the miners, but as with public libraries, the promotion of serious and politically committed reading struggled against the overwhelming demand for popular fiction, which in many cases constituted over 90 per cent of book loans.[56] Research has pointed to a 'neglect of politics': Marx and Lenin appeared on the bookshelves but miners and their families were more likely to borrow Dickens, Mrs Henry Wood and Edgar Rice Burroughs.[57] Surviving collections, such as that of the Tylorstown library in the Rhondda, include 'almost a complete set of Left Book Club editions' but are dominated by 'light fiction'.[58]

Institute libraries went into decline in the 1930s following the economic Depression. Acquisition of stock was cut back and the spread of county libraries drew readers away. Declining revenues led to the closure of many libraries after the war. It may be an overstatement to argue that the 'dramatic contraction' of the coal industry after 1959 and the rise of alternative forms of entertainment, such as television and bingo, suggested that 'reading was [no longer] one of the major recreational pursuits in the coalfield',[59] but the decline of the institute libraries certainly points to the disappearance of a distinct reading community created and nurtured by an industrial way of life.

54 Hoggart, *The uses of literacy*, p. 250.
55 Baggs, 'How well read was my valley?', pp. 287–8.   56 *Ibid.*, p. 289.
57 Rose, *The intellectual life*, p. 248.
58 Francis, 'Survey of Miners' Institute and Welfare Hall libraries', p. 31.
59 *Ibid.*, pp. 29–30.

Book ownership

The class divisions evident in library trends were also conspicuous in book buying and ownership, although once again the period witnessed change. One historian has argued that after 1918, 'many more books, periodicals, newspapers were to be seen in ordinary homes',[60] and recent research by Jonathan Rose has traced the many ways in which men and women of the working class accessed and read books of all kinds. A 'spirit of mutual education'[61] underlay the formation of informal groups for intellectual exchange, and reading in working-class homes was often a collective activity with books circulating among friends and co-workers. Rose detects a 'promiscuous mix of high and low' culture among 'working-class readers of all regions, generations, and economic strata' and concludes that by the 1930s and 1940s 'a large personal library was no longer a rarity in the slums'.[62]

Increased ownership of books among poorer households was facilitated by the availability of cheaper editions of 'classics' or 'standard' works. Series such as Dent's Everyman's Library became a 'standby' of the Workers' Educational Association.[63] Educative books were also within reach of a wider spread of the population. The Home University Library, commenced in 1911, issued books on science, religion, history, geography, literature and philosophy written by academic experts, priced initially at one shilling. Although production dropped during and after the war, by 1935 176 volumes were available at the still cheap price of 2s 6d.[64] In the 1930s and 1940s the Thinker's Library (published by C. A. Watts & Co.) offered two-shilling reprints of books by Darwin, J. S. Mill, Thomas Huxley, H. G. Wells and others. Once again, statistical evidence should warn against generalisation: Mass-Observation reported in 1940 that 66 per cent of working-class adults never bought books.[65]

Personal libraries became more widespread in the 1930s across all class groups as readers came to acquire books in new ways. Circulation wars led daily newspapers to begin selling books via coupons cut out from the paper. These were typically encyclopaedias, reference works, and complete sets of authors like Dickens and Shakespeare. Mass-Observation recorded that libraries in many low-income households consisted entirely of such books, along with prize books. Mail order was an effective way of reaching readers physically or psychologically distanced from bookshops. In 1928 the Phoenix

---

60 Roberts, *The classic slum*, p. 228.   61 Rose, *The intellectual life*, p. 83.
62 *Ibid.*, pp. 371, 230.   63 *Ibid.*, p. 135.   64 *The Times* 27 May 1936, p. 12.
65 Mass-Observation, *Wartime reading*, pp. 21–2.

Book Company began selling books on an instalment plan. Readers were offered a selection of around 5,000 titles with the payment spread out at 2s 6d a month (one penny a day). An early publicity slogan declared 'a liberal education at the price of a daily newspaper'.[66]

The spread of book clubs in the 1930s served a more middle-class audience. Mass-Observation reported that membership was higher among younger people and much higher among the better educated and better off: 'among the great mass of people their impact is negligible'.[67] The Book Society, founded in 1929 and modelled on the American Book of the Month Club, came to epitomise middlebrow literary culture, representing for Q. D. Leavis a standardisation of taste.[68] More far-reaching in terms of reducing the price of books and thus encouraging book ownership was the Readers Union, commenced in 1937, with 17,000 members by the following year.[69] The club's aim was to 'select an important book of general interest each month, a book of unusual merit, published at a price beyond the reach of most book buyers' and make it available for 2s 6d.[70] Selections included some works of non-fiction ordinarily priced as high as sixteen shillings. The claim that 'many members had not seriously bought a book until they joined Readers Union' is hard to prove, especially since 'very large numbers' were enrolled through booksellers.[71] But in offering recently published titles at huge reductions the club participated in the increased democratisation of reading. An early advertisement declared: 'What a penny a day will bring you.'[72] As Nicola Humble notes, this and contemporaneous ventures such as the Book Club, one of many clubs run by Foyles bookshop, used a promotional language 'designed to evoke a life of cultured gentility – "splendid books", "a first class library"', whereas the most likely lure for readers was the heavily reduced prices on offer.[73]

It is the nature of book clubs to appeal and respond to special interest groups, helping to construct reading as a communal activity. Significant in this context was the Left Book Club, launched by Gollancz in May 1936.[74] It issued a newly published book each month at 2s 6d (around a quarter of the price of most new works of non-fiction), and membership reached nearly 40,000 within ten months and peaked at 57,000 in 1939.[75] Demonstrating the increased level of social and political commitment to reading, the club's

---

66 Baker, *Low cost of bookloving*, p. 9.   67 Mass-Observation, *Books and the public*, p. 53.
68 Leavis, *Fiction and the reading public*, p. 22.   69 Baker, *Low cost of bookloving*, p. 15.
70 *Ibid.*, p. 9.   71 *Ibid.*, p. 14.   72 *Ibid.*, p. 28.
73 Humble, *The feminine middlebrow novel*, p. 44.   74 See also Chapters 5 and 6.
75 Lewis, *The Left Book Club*, pp. 22–3.

success spawned ancillary activities including political rallies, summer schools and discussion groups, which numbered 1,500 by the war years.[76] Partly in an attempt to capture industrial workers, Gollancz introduced an allied series 'The New People's Library', publishing introductory books at sixpence to club members.[77] Nevertheless, membership remained predominantly middle class: 'It was estimated that 75 percent of the members were white-collared workers, black-coated professionals, and newly converted Left intellectuals.'[78]

The arrival of Penguins and Pelicans in the late 1930s signalled a shift in attitude towards book buying and ownership. In books and essays of this period reading is often compared in terms of opportunity cost to attending the cinema or smoking. Allen Lane's decision to price his Penguin paperbacks at sixpence and market them as 'something that could be bought as easily and as casually as a packet of cigarettes'[79] was an attempt to promote ownership of books as part of everyday living. His other important innovation was to bring recently published works into the hands of a larger public more quickly. He judged that in the 1930s a successful book 'probably didn't get through to the suburbs for ten years'.[80] By selling his books through general outlets such as Woolworths and even a vending machine, the Penguincubator, he aimed to capture those readers who still perceived bookshops to be the preserve of different classes, convinced that there was 'a vast reading public for *intelligent* books at a low price'.[81] He was right. Mass-Observation detected a new attitude to book-buying, claiming that 'those who practically never buy books in the ordinary way will buy Penguins quite frequently, and those who are very careful and critical in buying more expensive books will buy them on spec'.[82] When Lane added the non-fiction Pelicans, new and recently published books on politics, religion and the whole range of the arts and sciences were available to 'the lay reader'.[83]

At the other end of the scale, book collecting underwent a dramatic history in the inter-war period. In the 1920s prices rocketed for both antiquarian books and limited editions of contemporary authors as books were turned into investment objects. George Bernard Shaw allegedly remarked that a publisher's first strategy in deciding what edition to issue was to begin by 'plundering the collectors, who never read anything'.[84] When the stock-

---

76 *Ibid.*, p. 12.   77 *Ibid.*, pp. 80–1.   78 Samuels, 'The Left Book Club', p. 75.
79 Lewis, *Penguin special*, p. 87.   80 Hilliard, 'The two-penny library', p. 200.
81 Lewis, *Penguin special*, p. 122 (original emphasis).
82 Mass-Observation, *Books and the public*, p. 29.   83 Lewis, *Penguin special*, p. 270.
84 Carter, *Taste and technique*, p. 58.

market collapsed the book-market followed and, as John Carter recalled, 'collectors of the investment-minded kind had their paper profits wiped out inside a few months'.[85] The *Book Collector's Quarterly* welcomed the disappearance of the 'artificial and unreasonable increases', commenting in 1930: 'It is to be hoped that those who benefited by the dizzy rise have suffered from the giddy fall . . . and the field is now open to those whose aim it is to collect and read books, and not simply to hold them for a rise.'[86] New tastes did emerge. A 1934 exhibition at Bumpus booksellers entitled 'New Paths in Book-Collecting' revealed new interests in cheaper or more ephemeral forms such as yellowbacks, detective fiction and serial fiction.[87] In addition, eighteenth-century literature, war books and modern literature were identified as sought-after subjects. To John Carter, the 'most important of all [trends] to the historian of taste', was that 'modern and even contemporary authors could now be collected without the suspicion of faddism or eccentricity'.[88]

While the inter-war period witnessed a decline in the number of private collectors whose purses and proclivities allowed collecting on a massive scale, there was a corresponding growth of the smaller collector. P. H. Muir argued in 1952 that in the first half of the twentieth century book collecting became 'a pursuit not only for rich men . . . but for those of modest incomes also'.[89] The period also witnessed a growth in societies devoted to book collecting. The First Edition Club, formed in 1922, claimed to be 'the first English organization of bibliophiles to maintain a meeting-place for its members'.[90] Its activities included 'exhibitions illustrating special aspects of book-collecting'[91] and in 1930 it inaugurated the *Book Collector's Quarterly*.

Second World War

As has been widely documented, the biggest challenge for the book trade during the Second World War was supplying the remarkable demand for reading matter. Statistical evidence suggests that reading activity declined on the immediate outbreak of war in September 1939. A 1940 Mass-Observation report noted a 'big drop'[92] in the reading of books and magazines in the first week of conflict, along with fewer issues from public libraries and a downturn at booksellers. In the same year the National Book Council lamented: 'It is an indictment of the nation that only about fifteen per cent

85 *Ibid.*, p. 46.   86 *Book Collector's Quarterly* I (1930), pp. vi–vii.
87 Carter (ed.), *New paths.*   88 Carter, *Taste and technique*, p. 37.
89 Muir, *Talks on book-collecting*, p. 7.   90 *Book Collector's Quarterly* I (1930), pp. v–vi.
91 *Ibid.*, p. 129.   92 Mass-Observation, *Wartime reading*, p. 1.

of the population use public libraries.'[93] The situation soon changed, however. According to Valerie Holman, 1940 was a 'turning-point in reading: books borrowed and books bought both began to show a significant increase in numbers, and encouragement of reading became a matter of [government] policy'.[94] The Board of Education issued a circular to authorities urging extension of the public library service, and temporary branches and mobile libraries were introduced to encourage more reading. In 1940 a 20 per cent increase in book issues was the norm nationwide. One mobile library in a housing estate in Manchester increased its issues from 4,000 to 10,000.[95] The Library Association's 1940 report proclaimed:

> Remarkable figures have come from counties and towns in the Midlands, where towards the end of the year, monthly issues in some cases showed a fifty per cent increase over the corresponding period in the previous year, and one or two instances of doubled issues. With a very few exceptions, the tale is one of record use of the public libraries in all parts of the country.[96]

The demographics of borrowing shifted. Child evacuation was a notable factor in the rise in library issues in county districts. The 1942 Mass-Observation report revealed that in city borough libraries fiction and non-fiction borrowing had declined, as in the case of the London-based Bermondsey public library, where lending levels dropped from 25,353 in March 1938 to 18,592 in March 1942. In contrast, rural town libraries registered increased lending levels. In the small south-west town of Bridgwater, fiction and non-fiction borrowing rose from 8,483 in March 1938 to 11,415 in March 1942.[97]

By 1943 the wartime surge in reading was visible to booksellers, who reported having 'extended sales tremendously among the working classes'.[98] Christina Foyle, the leading London bookseller, spoke of 'a tremendous boom in books' which she put down to various factors: 'books aren't rationed, there's no purchase tax, and they don't require coupons, and then people have so much more time for reading'.[99] In the early years the most noticeable sales increase was for popular reprints of the classics, notably Everyman's Library. Fiction remained the most popular genre but there was also demand for books on war and international affairs, and an increased interest in technical books as war workers sought quick knowledge on unfamiliar tasks. The daily press expanded to what Raymond Williams in

---

93 Holman, *Print for victory*, p. 48. 94 *Ibid.*, p. 49. 95 *Ibid.*, pp. 49–51.
96 Quoted in Holman, *Print for victory*, p. 49. 97 Quoted in *ibid.*, p. 50.
98 Rose, *The intellectual life*, pp. 233–4. 99 McAleer, *Popular reading and publishing*, p. 74.

The long revolution called 'something like the full reading public . . . reaching over 15,000,000 in 1947'.[100] Mass-Observation reported that people were undertaking 'more purposeful, planned reading, and less purely recreational reading',[101] a trend observed by George Orwell in 1942 when he argued that the 'enormous sale of Penguin books, Pelican books, and other cheap titles' meant that 'the average book which the ordinary man reads is a better book than it would have been three years ago'.[102]

Reading was a cheap and convenient activity for wartime living conditions. Blackouts and transport restrictions meant more time was spent at home. In October 1940 the *Publishers' Circular* claimed that 'reading had supplanted the wireless in most homes as the principal leisure activity'.[103] Mass-Observation recorded that, in choosing a book, 'one of the most important qualities' readers looked for was 'its suitability for reading in bed'.[104] Outside the home, reading spaces were strongly determined by availability of lighting. Tubes, trains and railway stations were the most popular spaces, ahead of parks, teashops and cafes, and buses. Inevitably, reading proved a popular activity in air-raid shelters, where libraries were often run by wardens or volunteers. The unused underground station at Bethnal Green 'boasted a library of four thousand volumes serving six thousand borrowers'.[105] Concerted arrangements on the part of government and publishers also ensured that servicemen, the wounded and prisoners of war were also supplied with reading matter.[106] As Holman judges, 'Through the vast network of camp libraries and book distribution schemes, many servicemen were introduced to literature and reading for the first time.'[107]

1945–1979

Surveying the post-war (non)-reader

Although the Second World War is often viewed as marking the arrival of a new and hungry reading public, immediate post-war investigations into reading habits suggested that older trends endured. In 1946 Mass-Observation undertook a survey of reading and book ownership, drawing on interviews with 1,000 members of the public as well as investigations into retail outlets, libraries and homes. This was two years after the 1944 Education Act, which introduced compulsory free secondary education for all, and the year after

100 Williams, *The long revolution*, p. 199.
101 Mass-Observation, *Books and the public*, [p. 201].   102 Lewis, *Penguin special*, p. 156.
103 McAleer, *Popular reading and publishing*, p. 75.   104 Holman, *Print for victory*, p. 53.
105 Ibid., p. 29.   106 See Chapter 23.   107 Ibid., p. 46.

the election of a Labour government committed to the introduction of a welfare state, and the social concerns of the period were strongly evident in the survey's summary finding that, 'at the heart of the potential reading public, there is a core of the illiterate, the indifferent and the antagonistic', indifference and antagonism being 'found chiefly among unskilled working class people and, more commonly, among the over-forties'.[108] Post-war debates about reading were strongly inflected by a discourse of social welfare and educational provision, reflective of wider debates about the role of the state in the provision of culture and entertainment. As public library usage continued to grow, librarians agonised over how to reconcile the educative ideals of the movement with the overwhelming demand for 'recreational' reading. The expansion of further and higher education in the 1950s and 1960s increased the appetite for instructional reading, but at the same time the impact of radio and television heightened fears that other forms of entertainment were reducing the reading habit.

Although the main purpose of the 1946 Mass-Observation survey was to assess the impact on the reading public of Penguin paperbacks, the report produced general findings about the habits of readers and non-readers. Reading was found to be the favourite leisure pursuit of just one-sixth of the population. While only 3 per cent of respondents declared that they never read anything at all (an unreliable guide in view of the stigma attached to such an admission), 34 per cent never read books. The report put the total book reading public – those for whom book reading was 'an accepted habit'[109] – at 51 per cent, but it was a public sharply defined by educational and class difference: 44 per cent of unskilled workers and 29 per cent of the skilled working classes did not read books, compared to only 7 per cent of middle-class people; and book readers were 'almost twice as likely to have had a secondary as an elementary education'.[110]

The most common reason for not reading books was lack of time, followed by fatigue, lack of interest, bad eye-sight, and an inability to read well. Unsurprisingly, working-class readers were most likely to complain about a lack of time for reading, and long working hours no doubt contributed to the finding that an 'inability' or 'lack of desire' to 'concentrate' was 'a very real reason' for not reading.[111] Acquisition of books was also

---

108 Mass-Observation, *A report*, p. 3.   109 *Ibid.*, p. 16.
110 *Ibid.*, pp. 7, 17. The survey used the NRS social grade system for classifying class groups: 'B' represented middle-class occupations; 'C' lower-middle and skilled manual workers; 'D' unskilled manual workers.
111 *Ibid.*, p. 120.

characterised by class trends. Book-buying was significantly greater among the higher-education groups, with those of lower educational attainment more likely to borrow from libraries or from friends.

In 1950 a different survey was undertaken in three London boroughs – Bermondsey, Tottenham and Wandsworth.[112] With a small sample of just over 500 respondents, the survey was designed principally as an exercise in statistical method. It nevertheless produced a strikingly detailed analysis of the tastes and demand for different kinds of books among different class, gender and educational groups. Fiction remained by far the most popular reading matter, accounting for two-thirds of the books currently being read by respondents. Detective and mystery stories were the most popular genre overall, with 66 per cent of men and 49 per cent of women reporting a 'special interest'. Education was a strong marker of taste, with those with higher levels 'significantly less interested in detective, mystery, adventure, Western, love and happy-ending stories, and more interested in novels about political and similar problems, character and psychological stories, and, particularly, historical stories'.[113] Non-fiction books were also read more extensively by those educated beyond elementary levels. When confronted with eighteen different subject areas the trends were even more distinct. Very few men read anything about 'running a house'; very few women reported an interest in 'politics and economics', 'problems with our society', or 'sport and recreation'. Perhaps the most revealing statistic was that while only 2.5 per cent of women expressed particular interest in 'scientific and technical books to do with your job or hobbies', compared to 16.5 per cent of men, the figures were higher and the trend reversed for 'scientific and technical books *not* to do with your job or hobbies', a clear reflection of employment demographics in the period.

The survey made little attempt to account for these trends. Although it reported that over 80 per cent of reading was done in the home, the importance of different reading spaces and environments, for example, was not otherwise considered. Evidence in the Mass-Observation report, however, suggests that personal taste was not the only contributing factor in determining choice of reading. When asked why they read, men were more likely to stress 'the educational side of their reading' and women more inclined to say that they 'read for pleasure'.[114] Reading among men emerged as a more active pursuit, whereas women more commonly stressed it as a means of escapism. It was also noticeable that both occupied and

112 Stuart, 'Reading habits'.   113 *Ibid.*, p. 45.   114 Mass-Observation, *A report*, p. 30.

unoccupied women were the most 'time-conscious' about reading as an activity. Women were 'over three times as likely as men' to say that they had no time for reading, reflective, perhaps, of a less clearly marked distinction between work and leisure.[115]

Revealingly, both surveys indicated that *book* reading was more prevalent among younger age groups. Mass-Observation found that 56 per cent of people over forty did not read books, compared to 42 per cent of those aged between twenty-one and forty and only 20 per cent aged between sixteen and twenty.[116] While reading for educational purposes might in part account for these figures, they do suggest an emerging generational shift, with those born after 1918 much more likely to read books than their parents and grandparents. It was significant, too, that it was 'the younger generation of working class men' who most conveyed a conscious 'striving after knowledge through books', more so than older groups and working-class women.[117]

It would be tempting to link these findings with the arrival of Penguin paperbacks in 1935. For many commentators the immediate success of Penguin signalled the emergence of a new reading public. In 1938 Margaret Cole concluded her Hogarth Press pamphlet *Books and the people* with the words: 'there *is* a new public, a vast new public', one that had hitherto been 'affected by the snobbery about books and reading' and, in possession of only 'very low incomes and pensions', had been unable to 'afford anything more than 6d for a book'.[118] Mass-Observation suggested, however, that the Penguin public consisted chiefly of those already buying and reading the most books. Among existing book readers, 41 per cent of the middle classes read Penguins, compared to 17 per cent of the artisan classes, and only 8 per cent of the working classes. Readers with secondary education were five times as likely to read Penguins as those with elementary education only.[119] Statistics were even more marked for the non-fiction Pelican volumes. Secondary education was found to influence Pelican reading 'even more decisively' than Penguin reading, with only 2 per cent of book readers with elementary education reading Pelicans.[120] Buying Pelicans was 'very largely a middle class habit', with working-class readers apparently not buying them at all, and artisan classes 'only rarely'.[121]

115 *Ibid.*, p. 13.
116 In the London survey the figures were comparable: 59 per cent of respondents aged over fifty never read books compared to less than 25 per cent aged under thirty.
117 Mass-Observation, *A report*, pp. 32–3.　118 Cole, *Books and the people*, p. 38.
119 Mass-Observation, *A report*, pp. 39–40.　120 *Ibid.*, p. 42.　121 *Ibid.*, p. 85.

Rather than opening up a new reading public, then, Penguins and Pelicans were filtering off the public that was already reading, borrowing and buying the most books. Typical Penguin buyers read and bought more books generally; they kept more books in the home and were less inclined than non-Penguin readers to sell, exchange or give them away; they were more conscious of the value of reading and 'more likely to believe that their ideas and opinions [had] been affected by the books they read'.[122] They were also more likely than non-Penguin readers to belong to public and subscription libraries and to consider reading their favourite leisure activity. What Penguins had done, however, was engender a new attitude of adventurousness towards books. Readers were reportedly more willing to experiment with new authors and new subjects when parting only with sixpence. Compared to hardbacks, which readers looked upon as books to re-read and to keep permanently, the purchase of paperbacks was 'something essentially more casual'.[123] With hardbacks the buying process was often begun 'long before the bookshop is entered'. Paperbacks, by contrast, were frequently bought on impulse: 'people tend far more often to go to the bookshop with no particular book in mind – often to have a look at the new Penguins – look through the stock, and select a book which interests them'. When purchasing from railway stalls, in particular, readers – and especially women – were more likely to buy 'on sight' and to come away with titles they had 'no intention of buying'.[124]

These attitudes to buying influenced trends in book ownership. Home libraries were still more likely to consist of hardbacks and reference volumes. The survey concluded that 'ownership of paper-covered books is, for 89 per cent of working class people, 74 per cent of artisan class and 51 per cent of middle class people essentially a casual kind of ownership. These people give away, exchange or throw away their books when they have read them.'[125] In 'average working class and artisan households', Penguins and paper-covered books were 'heavily outnumbered by cloth books', many of which had been passed down through generations or acquired as gifts.[126] Most artisan households contained a 'skeleton' library consisting of 'a few essential reference books', some 'light' fiction, and 'a little non-fiction', but 'feelings of possessiveness and delight in the acquisition of books' and the 'systematic planning' of home libraries was found to be the preserve of the middle classes. Lack of space and 'proper' bookcases and shelving meant that in working-class households books were often found on

122 *Ibid.*, p. 43.   123 *Ibid.*, p. 87.   124 *Ibid.*, p. 91.   125 *Ibid.*, p. 100.   126 *Ibid.*, p. 130.

sideboards or dressers and, more commonly 'shared and passed round from household to household, without anyone expecting their return'.[127] Fiction was most frequently passed on, with some 'more serious' books kept for reference.[128]

Later surveys undertaken in the 1960s gave some insight into daily patterns of reading.[129] Unsurprisingly, most reading was done during evenings and at weekends: 87 per cent of respondents to a 1965 survey reported that they read in the evenings and at night, with a notably high proportion coming from the lower socio-economic groups and those aged between thirty and forty-four. More weekend reading was undertaken by those in higher socio-economic groups, while the youngest age-group of sixteen to twenty-nine were the most likely to read while travelling. A different survey from 1962 reported that, on average, the public spent just thirty minutes reading out of a total of nine hours eighteen minutes of waking time spent at home on weekdays. As with surveys from the 1950s, women were reported as reading for less time – twenty-two minutes on average compared to forty-five for men. Those aged fifty-five and over spent on average three times as much reading as the youngest age group, sixteen to twenty-four.

Newspaper reading

In contrast to books, newspaper reading was part of the everyday life of the nation. Mass-Observation produced an additional report in 1949, *The press and its readers*, drawing both on its own investigations and on the annual Hulton surveys of newspaper reading begun in 1947.[130] The findings showed that daily newspapers were read by all but 13 per cent of the population, and Sunday papers by all but 8 per cent.[131] Newspaper reading was more common among men, younger people and the middle and artisan classes than among women, older people and the working classes. Men not only read newspapers more often than women, they also read them for longer, and were more likely to read 'most' of the paper, rather than just 'glance at the headlines' or read only 'some' of it. Leading articles and, in particular, sport were much more popular among men, with only the Letters section liked significantly more by women. Book reading and newspaper reading could sometimes be

---

127 *Ibid.*, p. 124.   128 *Ibid.*, p. 139.
129 Information in this paragraph is drawn from the research notes of Peter H. Mann, preserved in the Mills & Boon archive, University of Reading Library, MB ADM/4/1.
130 The Hulton readership surveys ran until 1956 when they were succeeded by the National Readership Surveys.
131 [Mass-Observation], *The press and its readers*, p. 12.

mutually exclusive. Some working-class readers reported that time spent reading newspapers restricted the opportunity to read books, and marriage was found to decrease book reading (among both men and women) as it increased the tendency to read newspapers.

Bare statistics tell us little about actual reading experiences, but the report made some attempt to observe readers in different environments, showing how newspapers were put to varied reading use. In libraries, where readers were more likely to consult the 'Situations Vacant' columns, the average reader spent just four to five minutes on each daily paper read; in trains and buses the average was six minutes in the morning and eight in the evening. Most of the time was spent reading the front page news, though often this amounted only to 'the briefest headline reading'. The report concluded ruefully that, 'although the majority of people look at the political news, it is only to glance at it'.[132]

The newspaper industry was, of course, extremely diverse, and the loose formulation 'newspaper reading' disguises considerable variety in reading material. Daily papers ranged from those like *The Times* and the *Daily Telegraph* with small readerships and a 'pronounced emphasis on the older and higher income groups' to the 'picture-papers' – the *Daily Mirror* and *Daily Graphic* – whose predominantly working-class readership was least interested in 'serious news'.[133] Although readerships of some papers were fairly evenly distributed among different income groups, choice of paper was in general strongly influenced by class, income and political outlook. This inevitably influenced what people actually read. Concentration on news items was found to increase with educational level, the 'less well-educated' spending more time on pictures and 'gossip'.[134] Conversely, readers of the 'picture-papers' were least interested in editorials and political news and the most likely to read comics and cartoons.[135]

Sunday papers were more widely read than dailies. Scarcity of time during the working week was suggested as one reason for the greater popularity, but they were also consumed for different purposes. Whereas dailies (more likely to be bought by 'the better-off') were read by those wanting 'more serious news', the main attraction of the Sunday papers was 'feature and gossip'.[136] Sunday newspaper reading was found to be more casual, 'not only at all sorts of odd times of the day, but also with a feeling of relaxation rather than of

132 *Ibid.*, p. 22.
133 For a summary of the newspapers published at the time of the survey, see *ibid.*, pp. 110–17.
134 *Ibid.*, p. 35.   135 *Ibid.*, p. 41.   136 *Ibid.*, p. 12.

duty'.[137] By 1953 it was reported that two out of every three adults read more than one Sunday paper. The most popular of all, the *News of the World*, had a circulation of over 8 million in 1950 and was read by every second adult.[138] Found to be 'especially popular amongst people of the unskilled working classes', the luring attraction of crime and sensation was directly referenced by George Orwell in his essay 'The decline of the English murder' (1946).

A view of reading in the 1950s

The readership of newspapers – especially Sunday newspapers – was a leitmotif of Richard Hoggart's widely reprinted study of working-class culture and entertainment, *The uses of literacy* (1957).[139] For Hoggart, 'the Sunday smell of the *News of the World*-mingled-with-roast-beef' was one of the recognisable details of working-class domestic life.[140] Impressionistic in its perception and use of sources, *The uses of literacy* was more a study of popular cultural products than reading and readers. It nevertheless illustrates how views of reading habits in the 1950s reflected wider preoccupations with social welfare, commerce and common culture.

As both Collini and Hilliard have argued, *The uses of literacy* was a book deeply influenced by F. R. Leavis and the *Scrutiny* movement.[141] Hoggart's concern was not the lack of reading – he drew attention, for example, to surveys that indicated book reading was more widespread in the UK than in the USA and Sweden[142] – but the lack of intelligent reading. Like Q. D. Leavis, Hoggart sought reasons in the commercial structures of publishing. The 'popular Press', he argued, imposed a narrow uniformity and restricted access to culture. Newspapers and magazines had become 'the products of large-scale commercial organizations' which worked 'to ensure that their customers want no other reading . . . millions each week and each day see the same paper and see few other publications'.[143] In addition to the sensational Sunday papers, Hoggart referenced the picture dailies; threepenny story magazines for 'adolescent girls and unmarried women'; and the crime, science fiction and '"blood and guts" sex novelettes' that filled magazine shops found in 'every large working-class shopping-area'.[144] The overwhelming characteristic of this literature was 'fragmentation' and 'bittiness':

137 *Ibid.*, p. 27.   138 *Ibid.*, p. 113.
139 In its Pelican edition (first published in 1958), the book was reprinted eight times during the 1960s. See also Chapter 25.
140 Hoggart, *The uses of literacy*, p. 39.
141 Collini, 'Richard Hoggart'; Hilliard, *English as a vocation*, chapter 5.
142 Hoggart, *The uses of literacy*, p. 332.   143 *Ibid.*, pp. 242, 237, 243.
144 *Ibid.*, pp. 257, 122, 250.

newspapers and magazines, for example, were filled with short, unconnected anecdotes that could be consumed 'in a very easy gear', and 'one minute stories' that kept reading at 'the two- or three-syllabled word and the seven-word-sentence level'.[145] Such publications belonged solely to the sphere of 'entertainment'. They held down taste and kept readers at a level of 'passive acceptance'.[146]

As has been argued, *The uses of literacy* was 'a book that spoke to, and was shaped by, the adult education movement'.[147] University extramural departments and voluntary bodies like the Workers' Educational Association grew substantially after the war, supported by the Labour government. As Hilliard has shown, Hoggart's methods as an extramural teacher in Hull after the war were strongly influenced by 'the currency of left-Leavisism' and promoted a discriminating close reading in pursuit of '"appreciating real literature"'.[148] Hoggart the educationalist fundamentally distrusted and dismissed reading for entertainment. He was motivated by a conviction that individuals should '*work* on their reading', and that commercialism prevented the working classes from even recognising this. In language strongly reminiscent of Q. D. Leavis, he concluded his sketch of popular publications by arguing: 'purely on this evidence, the situation looks dreadful: sensation, fragmentation, over-simplification, unreality; "never a real or a good thing read", to paraphrase D. H. Lawrence'.[149] Hoggart's conclusions were nevertheless less hyperbolic and pessimistic than *Fiction and the reading public*. Hilliard has persuasively argued that his critical procedure differed from Leavis's.[150] Writing post-Penguin, Hoggart could not avoid pointing to the availability of cheap high-quality books to the 'earnest minority' of working-class readers, in addition to the promotion of educative reading via the expansion of adult education. Furthermore, there was already evidence that the very divisions in culture and reading practices he detected were changing and narrowing. That 'blood-and-guts' novelettes and 'sex-books' mingled with Penguins and Pelicans and '"hobbies" and "handicrafts" magazines' on railway bookstalls suggested a less atomised reading culture, and that the former was 'ceasing to be even slightly furtive reading'.[151]

One successful publication which demonstrated Hoggart's point about the popularity of 'fragmented' reading was the *Reader's Digest* magazine. Founded in the USA in 1922, *Reader's Digest* contained article-length excerpts from new books and special book features. International sales of the

---

145 *Ibid.*, p. 202.   146 *Ibid.*, pp. 242, 237.   147 Hilliard, *English as a vocation*, p. 166.
148 *Ibid.*   149 Hoggart, *The uses of literacy*, p. 240. Emphasis added.
150 Hilliard, *English as a vocation*, p. 167.   151 Hoggart, *The uses of literacy*, p. 257.

magazine expanded in the late 1930s when the Reader's Digest Association began soliciting material from British publishers. In 1939 the new London office reported to Allen & Unwin a 'substantially increased sale' in Britain 'during the past year',[152] and a separate British edition soon appeared. By 1962 *Reader's Digest* was claiming in its advertisements and on the cover of its magazine UK sales of 1.25 million and an actual readership of 8 million.

The 'bittiness' of the *Reader's Digest* magazine extended to many of the company's book publications. Reader's Digest Condensed Books were introduced in the UK in 1954. The previous year the New York editorial office had sent a report to leading British publishers entitled 'How the Reader's Digest book condensations affect book sales', claiming that 'in many cases, READER'S DIGEST condensations have skyrocketed books to best-sellerdom'.[153] Each condensed book contained three or four works of current fiction or non-fiction in abridged form in 500 pages, issued quarterly, at ten shillings net, sold principally to subscribers of the magazine. In a memorandum, the publisher Mark Longman noted that Kenneth Wilson, the American organiser of the Condensed Books, 'admitted that he would never willingly read one himself' but had explained to Longman 'very convincingly . . . that there was a genuine market for them which was quite different from the ordinary book-reading market'.[154] When the company expanded its book operations in the 1960s, its special brand of condensed and reference reading material – notably the *Reader's Digest atlas of the world* (first published in 1961) – became a ubiquitous feature of many British households.

Along with the expansion of public libraries and the advance of paperbacks, the impact of *Reader's Digest* contributed to the decline of the book clubs which had flourished before the war. The Left Book Club had ceased in 1948 and the Readers Union went into 'steady decline' in the 1950s.[155] There remained, however, a number of smaller operations, 'with memberships ranging from three to ten thousand', devoted to subjects such as the countryside, gardening and science.[156] Serving disparate reading communities, usually by mail order, these niche clubs helped promote virtual reading communities around loosely defined genres of books.

152 Reader's Digest Association to Allen & Unwin, 19 May 1939. Allen & Unwin archive, University of Reading Library. AUC 70/12.
153 Allen & Unwin archive. AUC 610/13.
154 Memo dated 8 March 1954. Longman archive, University of Reading Library. MS 1393/2/265/38.
155 Baker, *Low cost of bookloving*, p. 24.   156 Baker, *Book clubs*, p. 122.

The post-war library reader

In the conclusion to *The uses of literacy*, Hoggart lamented the high percentage of borrowing in public libraries of 'worthless fiction' or non-fictional books that were 'of little value'.[157] The politicised concerns about reading that underpinned his study also informed post-war debates over public library provision. Alistair Black has argued that in this period the public library 'increasingly defined itself, notwithstanding some librarians' suspicion of state planning, less in terms of civic society and more according to the principles of welfarism'.[158] In 1942 Lionel McColvin produced a report for the Library Association which conceived of libraries as 'a great instrument and bulwark of democracy'.[159] McColvin became a leading spokesman for the idealistic vision of public libraries after the war, confidently predicting in 1950 that the service would become more 'active' and 'purposive' and less concerned with satisfying 'recreational demand'.[160] Seven years later he reiterated his conviction that public libraries 'can afford to neglect the books readily available in commercial libraries and in cheap editions'.[161] However, the overwhelming demand for 'recreational' reading meant that debates in this period repeatedly returned to the public library's role in the shaping of reading tastes.

Until the spending cuts of the 1970s and 1980s severely reduced expenditure, the public library service enjoyed continued expansion after the war. Between 1949 and 1959 the number of service points rose from 23,000 to 34,000, and volumes in stock increased from 42 million to 71 million.[162] Membership remained around one quarter of the national population throughout the 1950s, but increased markedly in the 1960s with the growth in higher education. By 1964 the number of registered users was over 13 million, compared to 2.5 million in 1924.[163] Total book issues doubled from 300 million in the 1950s to 600 million by 1968–69.[164]

The most notable area of expansion was in branch services. In the county service the number of branch libraries almost trebled in the twenty years after the war. As one librarian wrote in *The Times* in 1956, 'there are few villages, nowadays, which are not within easy reach of a branch of the County Libraries system'.[165] Mobile services also increased, bringing books closer to

---

157 Hoggart, *The uses of literacy*, pp. 332–3.   158 Black, *The public library*, p. 111.
159 *Ibid.*, p. 98.   160 Quoted in Kelly, *A history*, p. 380.
161 McColvin, 'Public, national and other libraries', p. 169.   162 Kelly, *A history*, p. 352.
163 Groombridge, *The Londoner*, p. 87.
164 See the annual *Statistics of public (rate supported) libraries in Great Britain and Northern Ireland* published by the Library Association.
165 'Realism about readers', *The Times* 21 August 1956, p. 9.

people in both rural areas and the new suburban housing developments. In 1949 fourteen authorities were known to use mobile libraries, carrying about 2,000 books and visiting each site once a week; by 1960 there were over 270 such libraries in the country.[166] Surveys undertaken over 1971–72 found that the mobile service was used overwhelmingly more by women – 'housewives' – than men, and was especially important for older readers: 28 per cent of mobile library users were aged sixty-five or over, compared to 14 per cent of 'static' library users.[167]

In the immediate post-war period, there was evidence that tastes in library borrowing, and thus reading, were becoming more diverse. Readership surveys from provincial towns and cities revealed significant increases in the borrowing of non-fiction. One librarian in 1952 observed an 'astonish[ing]' demand for 'highly specialized knowledge of technical literature' to do with 'hobbies such as radio and photography', and a more advanced level of reading among women 'in the literature of childcare, management and psychology'.[168] The library in Stockport reported a 222 per cent increase in issues of science books over 1936–56.[169] These trends coincided with increased expenditure on commercial and technical departments to support local industries, 'a reflection of the public library's commitment to economic modernisation'.[170] The most popular non-fiction subjects throughout the period, however, were travel, biography and history.[171]

The spread of higher and further education in the 1960s had a major impact on library borrowing and reading habits. In the twenty years following the war, the number of university students rose from 52,000 to 113,000 and those in further education (excluding teachers in training) from 54,000 to 202,000.[172] The significance of this enlarged reading group is witnessed by a survey at Manchester Central Library in 1964, which showed that on a single day 1,450 out of 3,681 users were students.[173] Such a statistic tells us little about actual reading habits – many students would use the library simply as a place to work – but expansion of education undoubtedly brought 'an enormously increased demand for reference and study books'.[174] A 1966 study of thirty-three reference departments found that students made up 53 per cent of all

---

166 Kelly, *A history*, p. 362.   167 *Public libraries and their use*, p. 26.

168 'The reading tastes of the "under forties"', *Times Literary Supplement* 29 August 1952, p. 572.

169 Kelly, *A history*, p. 384.   170 Black, *The public library*, p. 121.

171 Ward, *Readers and library users*.   172 Kelly, *A history*, p. 343.

173 Luckham, *The library in society*, p. 56.   174 Kelly, *A history*, p. 371.

users. Another survey showed that students spent twice as long in the library as adults generally.[175]

In spite of these developments, public libraries remained predominantly a vessel for the consumption of fiction. In March 1947, the county of Middlesex undertook a survey of public library usage on one sample day: 84,000 volumes out of a total stock of 173,000 were out on loan, of which 60.7 per cent were fiction. The fiction volumes were broken down into eleven categories, with romance (26.2 per cent) the most popular. In 1957, in Keighley, West Yorkshire, fiction was reported to account for 75 per cent of loans, in spite of efforts to boost 'serious' reading by giving readers an additional non-fiction-only ticket.[176] With continued demand for popular genres in particular, there was a revival of 'the old and sterile controversy about the provision of fiction'.[177] The debate turned on how far public libraries were responding to demand and how far they were responsible for perpetuating it. In August 1956 *The Times* ran an article by a librarian which cautioned against the assumption that increased library borrowing meant 'the public are becoming more intelligent [and] more conscious of the cultural (in its broadest sense) value of reading'.[178] The librarian reported that approximately two-thirds of books borrowed from public libraries were fiction, and with greater organisation of books by genre, readers were making selections by 'kind' and at random, rather than by 'any of the recognized literary standards'. Predictably, the article drew much correspondence, the debate again raising the dilemma of how public libraries could marry an idealist ethos with what one correspondent called 'the constant vocal pressure of a body of ratepayers crying, one might say quite literally, for blood'.[179] In a leader *The Times* questioned why libraries supplied light fiction at all: 'No one expects the local council to supply him with free sweets or tobacco', a view which demonstrated how far these debates were embedded in a welfare state discourse.[180] Later surveys recorded a continued demand for fiction. In a 1971–72 report, it was estimated that two-thirds of all adult library users who were borrowing books for themselves were looking 'for any novel of interest'.[181]

For all the civic expansion, usage of public libraries continued to be disproportionately middle class in character. Surveys undertaken in London in 1959 and 1962 suggested that 'nearly half the adult population'[182] had never

175 *Ibid.*, p. 434; Luckham, *The library in society*, p. 113.   176 Kelly, *A history*, p. 125.
177 *Ibid.*, p. 380.   178 'Realism about readers', *The Times* 21 August 1956, p. 9.
179 Letters, *The Times* 28 August 1956, p. 9.   180 Leader, *The Times* 28 August 1956, p. 9.
181 *Public libraries and their use*, p. 21.   182 Groombridge, *The Londoner*, p. 21.

been enrolled in a public library anywhere, and a more extensive study of seven London boroughs undertaken in 1962–63 by the Research Institute for Consumer Affairs (RICA) reached a similar conclusion. From a sample of 1,306 adult Londoners, 593 (46 per cent) had never been members while 317 had allowed their membership to lapse.[183] While total membership was spread fairly evenly across the different occupational groups, this did not correspond with relative numbers in the population as a whole. Non-members were more likely to belong to 'the three least skilled occupational groups',[184] while members of the three highest socio-economic groups, which constituted just 17 per cent of the population, accounted for 45.8 per cent of library membership. Educational background and attainment was also a strong indicator of usage. The survey concluded that people were 'more likely to join a public library, at some time in their lives, if they stay on longer at school or in full-time education' or if they attend 'a grammar-type or public school'.[185]

Surveys throughout the period and in different geographical areas produced comparable trends.[186] In the 1970s commentators were still concluding that, while the public library captured 'a broader social cross-section of the general public than the bookshop', it 'still does not get very far with the bulk of the ordinary manual occupations'.[187] The 1970s was a decade of intense analysis of public library usage, much of it government sponsored, and everywhere the findings were the same: library users were 'more than proportionately drawn from persons with extended education, non-manual occupations and younger in age'.[188] One report from 1978 found that while the middle classes made up less than 20 per cent of the population, they accounted for 50 per cent of library membership.[189]

Of course membership or non-membership of a library does not automatically correspond with usage or non-usage. But the 1962–63 RICA survey found that only 28 per cent of members reported visiting a library once a week, and that 'the great majority' of non-members made no use at all of public library facilities, although some (around 15 per cent) read books borrowed by other people.[190] Over a third of respondents agreed with the suggestion that they preferred doing other things with their time, and newspapers and magazines continued to be the sole reading of many. In all the surveys conducted in the 1960s and 1970s, lack of time was the main reason

183 Ibid.   184 Ibid., pp. 42, 43, 110.   185 Ibid., p. 40.
186 Kelly, A history, p. 385; Ward, Readers and library users.
187 Mann, Books: buyers and borrowers, p. 147.   188 Luckham, The library in society, p. 24.
189 Black, The public library, p. 147.   190 Groombridge, The Londoner, pp. 23–4.

given for not joining or using a public library. Lapsed membership was often attributed to moving home or getting married (among both men and women), but most commonly it was prompted by leaving education. A series of surveys in the North-West of England undertaken over 1964–69 found 'no one who had joined a library for the first time after normal school-age'.[191] Once beyond school, the lives of many adults were bookless.

With the expansion of public libraries, subscription libraries went into decline in the post-war period. The two largest, W. H. Smith and Boots, closed in 1961 and 1966 respectively. The subscription library reader did not disappear altogether, however. Some smaller ventures struggled on into the 1970s. The Manchester-based Allied Libraries continued to supply small shopkeepers (mostly newsagents) with lending stock (mostly fiction) until 1975,[192] and another wholesaling firm, South Counties Libraries, based in Bath, was still operating in 1981. At its peak after the war, this consortium of suppliers had 'an estimated six or seven thousand agents', which had declined to 'eleven or twelve hundred' in the 1960s and just 150 in 1978.[193] Over half of the agents were newsagents and confectioners, with post offices, food and general stores, and wool shops and hairdressers making up the rest. The 'vast majority' of the books loaned were 'light fiction', with Mills & Boon and Robert Hale the largest suppliers. The clientele was mostly female and in the upper age groups, and an investigation into sample libraries in 1978 found that membership could still reach as many as 900 registered borrowers, with anything from fifteen to 300 'fairly regular' users.[194] Distance from a public library was cited as the main reason why readers preferred to acquire their reading from rental libraries, but these small establishments also served specialist reading groups: a haberdashers in Southsea had 'a constantly chan-ging naval clientele', while a bookshop in Worthing rented books to holidaymakers.[195]

Reading and the impact of radio and television

In the post-war period in particular, the spread of radio, cinema and television proved an important influence on the printed word, serving both to challenge and to stimulate reading as a leisure activity.[196] The first publication of *Radio Times* in 1923 demonstrates the symbiotic relationship between sound or visual media and print. Initially a joint venture between the BBC and the publisher Newnes (the operation became entirely in-house in 1937), *Radio*

191 Luckham, *The library in society*, p. 45.
192 Long, 'The commercial circulating library', p. 187. 193 *Ibid.*, p. 188.
194 *Ibid.*, p. 190. 195 *Ibid.*, p. 191. 196 See Chapter 14.

Times combined radio and later television listings (initially occupying just two pages at the back of the magazine) with articles, special features and high-quality illustrations. Competition arrived in 1955 with the launch of Independent Television (ITV) and the rival *TV Times*.[197]

Another long-standing print publication inspired by radio was the *Listener*, a weekly magazine established by the BBC in 1929. Developed mainly as 'a medium of record for the reproduction of broadcast talks', the magazine also previewed broadcasts and reviewed new books.[198] The cultural pretensions of the magazine were asserted on the front cover of the first issue, declaring the *Listener* to be 'a medium for the intelligent reception of broadcast programmes by way of amplification and explanation of those features which cannot now be dealt with in the editorial columns of the "Radio Times"'.[199] The *Listener* ceased publication in 1991.

The post-war expansion of radio and television was generally seen as providing a stimulus to reading rather than a threat. A librarian writing in *The Times* in 1952 reported that the 'very great popularity' of the book review programme 'Books by the Fire' had proved an 'effective means of stimulating demand for books' among younger readers.[200] In the early 1950s the BBC undertook a series of experiments to determine the effects of radio serials on subsequent buying and borrowing. The findings showed convincingly that broadcasting boosted reading, especially of 'classic' works. Out of a sample of nearly half a million, 90 per cent of readers attributed borrowing of serialised books entirely to broadcasts.[201] Weekly demand for Trollope's *The last chronicle of Barset* increased by 60 per cent during its eleven-week serialisation on Sunday evenings, and Cecil Day Lewis's translation of the *Aeneid* 'produced a demand for the book far exceeding that previously recorded for all other translations put together'.[202] Another survey assessed the effects of television, revealing only 'a slight shift in habit', with a small percentage of viewers reporting that their reading had declined as a result of acquiring a television set.[203] These findings led Joseph Trenaman to conclude in 1957 that 'There is as yet no serious threat to reading.'[204]

In the 1960s, however, the spread of television provoked concerns over the decline of reading as a leisure pursuit. The number of television licence

---

197 Currie, *The Radio Times story.*   198 *Ibid.*, p. 27.   199 *Ibid.*
200 'The reading tastes of the "under forties"', *Times Literary Supplement* 29 August 1952, p. 572.
201 Ward, *Readers and library users*, p. 24.
202 Trenaman, *Books, radio and television*, pp. 202–3.   203 *Ibid.*, p. 204.   204 *Ibid.*, p. 205.

holders doubled from 6.4 million in 1954 to 12.8 million in 1964,[205] and while the 1962–63 RICA survey had found television to have negligible effect on public library use – only 3 per cent of respondents mentioned it as a reason for having ceased to use the library[206] – by the end of the decade the picture had changed. A 1968 survey showed that while radio and television could stimulate those already reading, it had no effect on increasing the size of the reading public as a whole.[207] As public library borrowing rates dropped in the 1970s, a sample survey of urban areas from 1973 showed that 'watching television' was the most popular leisure activity, followed by 'reading newspapers' and 'relaxing', with 'reading books' trailing in at seventh.[208] In general, evidence suggested that while few existing readers were drawn away from reading by the lure of television, those who watched most television were also those who read least.

A view of reading in the 1960s and 1970s

Academic investigations into books and reading took a different turn in the 1960s with the expansion of higher education research. Assisted by a grant from the Booksellers Association, the sociologist Peter Mann undertook a series of investigations at the end of the decade into 'social aspects of book reading'. Mann evolved a sociological model for reading built around a 'work–leisure continuum', dividing reading into three main categories: 'utilitarian', 'social' and 'personal'.[209] The categories could never be discrete but Mann's aim was to use them to distinguish the 'general functions' of books and assess how readers 'actually *use*' them.[210]

'Utilitarian' reading, at the extreme 'work' end of the continuum, involved the use of books for their relevance to other interests and purposes. This encompassed books used in the workplace (textbooks, manuals and reference volumes) and in the home (e.g. cookery books, car manuals and books on hobbies). Such reading satisfied extrinsic interests and purposes, although sometimes in the case of books on particular hobbies (which reached over to the 'leisure' end of the continuum) it might lead to the building up of personal libraries with an intrinsic value of their own. Since such books needed to be close at hand, they were more likely to be bought than borrowed. They were also popular as gifts, and Mann's investigations

---

205 Black, *The public library*, p. 127.   206 Goodbridge, *The Londoner*, p. 62.
207 Ward, *Readers and library users*, p. 24.   208 Kelly, *A history*, p. 436.
209 Mann, *Books: buyers and borrowers*, p. 9.   210 *Ibid.*, p. 8. Original emphasis.

demonstrated how often book tokens were used to acquire such reading, particularly student textbooks.[211]

'Social' reading involved books upon which value or status had been conferred by 'opinion leaders', for example newspaper reviews. Such reading involved a conscious element of 'self-improvement' and a greater readiness on the part of readers to have their attitudes or beliefs challenged. Because books of this kind had been identified as 'important' or 'serious' by social forces, they were more likely to be kept and re-read, and to be given as a 'status present'. By contrast, personal reading, at the extreme 'leisure' end of the continuum, was characterised as reading for 'distraction', and typically involved genre fiction (romance, mystery, detective), paperbacks that were bought and sometimes thrown away, or borrowed from friends. These books were rarely given as gifts since they did not confer status on giver or receiver, and were likely to be read only once. Importantly, such reading was undertaken not to challenge a reader's attitudes or beliefs but to have them reinforced.

Mann emphasised that his work–leisure distinction was, 'at best, merely a helpful device for setting up polar types which allow for considerable overlap between them'.[212] It nevertheless offered a useful model for understanding how readers might use different books for different purposes, especially when considering personal reading. His extensive study of the 'romantic' novel demonstrated the importance of evaluating different *kinds of reading* rather than *kinds of readers*. The function of such fiction was intrinsic rather than extrinsic – to give pleasure 'at the time of reading' and not for any external reason such as the conferral of status or the extension of knowledge. The actual reading experience was thus likely to be different from the experience of reading a book which social forces had conditioned a reader into thinking he or she *ought* to read for self-improvement, or which was being read for strictly educational or occupational purposes.

Mann produced two reports on romance reading, in 1969 and 1974. For the initial survey, questionnaires were distributed to over 9,000 readers who regularly received the Mills & Boon romance catalogue, and Mann's report was based on 2,788 replies. Analysis of age and of occupational and educational trends showed that there was no typical Mills & Boon reader, and that the books were read by a cross-section of society. The myth that romance appealed only to 'factory girls' or 'ancient spinsters' was exploded. The results gave 'a fairly "flat" age distribution, with proportions above the

211 Mann, *Books and reading*, p. 60. 212 *Ibid.*, p. 55.

national average in the age groups between 25 and 54'.[213] One-sixth of the sample had experienced further or higher education, and among employed women the most common occupations were office or clerical jobs. Romance readers were also surprisingly eclectic in their reading tastes and leisure activities as a whole. Newspapers that were more popular with female romance readers than women readers as a whole included several of the more 'serious' titles such as the *Sunday Times* and *Sunday Telegraph*. Conversely, the *News of the World* was conspicuously less popular compared to the national average.[214] Mann was also surprised to find that 21 per cent of the sample said that they viewed television '"not very much" or "never", which seems quite a high proportion'.[215]

What was really important about Mann's research was how it suggested that romance fiction was more about the *experience* of reading than about reading *tastes*. Although one married woman with a job as a bookseller considered the books 'most educative', and believed that they were capable of reaching 'a more intellectual audience',[216] romance reading more commonly emerged as a therapeutic activity undertaken in the evening, after work or domestic duties had been completed. A housewife undertaking adult education claimed the books were her 'only means of relaxation'; another with children and a part-time job described them as 'an excellent vehicle for forgetting the strains of modern living'.[217] Women pursuing high-level careers were also reporting a desire for the same reading experience. Mann recorded how a 'graduate computer programmer' found the romances 'excellent relaxation after her day's work', and several 'women who ran businesses of their own expressed similar views'.[218]

The fact that 46 per cent of respondents claimed to re-read Mills & Boon novels 'very often' supported Mann's claims about the importance of intrinsic reading practices to everyday behaviour.[219] His focus on uncovering different types of reading experience among individual users, and the varied ways in which readers might actually use books, demonstrated the truth underlying an observation in Raymond Williams's *The long revolution*:

> I think there are certain circumstances – times of illness, tension, disturbing growth as in adolescence, and simple fatigue after work – which are much too easily overlooked in sweeping condemnations of 'reading as an addiction'. I doubt if any educated person has not used books – any books – in this way.[220]

213 *Ibid.*, p. 168.   214 *Ibid.*, p. 170.   215 *Ibid.*   216 Mann, *A new survey*, p. 21.
217 *Ibid.*, p. 9.   218 Mann, *Books: buyers and borrowers*, p. 169.   219 *Ibid.*, p. 171.
220 Williams, *The long revolution*, p. 193.

While matters of class, education and politics provided the main lens through which reading habits were assessed and analysed in the post-war period, the unique tastes of individual readers should caution against sweeping generalisations about the habits and practices of the reading public.

1979–present

Readers in the free market

In 1979, British readers acquired or purchased books and reading matter from a regulated retail market with fixed prices, and through a large network of publicly funded local libraries. By the end of the century, readers enjoyed the benefits of a competitive retail environment for books, with a substantial reduction in ownership costs. At the same time, however, the decline in funding for local libraries significantly reduced free access to reading matter. As such, the closing decades of the twentieth century witnessed an unravelling of many of the structures surrounding reading in the earlier years of the century, and would also usher in some of the changes of the twenty-first.

Economic deregulation in the era of Thatcherite Britain was central to these changes. As Chapter 5 charts, the deregulation of the financial markets enabled mergers and acquisitions, conglomeration and cross-media synergies, and encouraged a culture of entrepreneurialism and growth. These led to an increasingly competitive (and increasingly global) literary marketplace, affecting readers in terms of the types of books produced and the manner of their marketing. Concurrent with the conglomeration of publishing houses during the 1980s and 1990s were shifts in the book retail environment. The growth of selling via bookshop chains, supermarkets, US-style 'big-box' bookstores, and, by the end of the twentieth century, online, meant that book consumers were increasingly buying books in ways different from the preceding decades of the century.[221] Readers in the book superstore would encounter in its vast floorspace the 'bookshop as social club', with 'author and discussion events, with musical entertainment, late opening hours, serving food and drink, and holding a range of other stock including newspapers, magazines, stationery, toys, CDs and DVDs'.[222]

The competitive environment of this period led to the demise of the price-fixing Net Book Agreement (NBA) at the end of the 1990s.[223] From the

---

221 Miller, *Reluctant capitalists*, pp. 117–39; Squires, *Marketing literature*, pp. 27–34.
222 Leon Kreitzman, 'Shop around the clock', *Bookseller* 26 March 1999, p. 36; Squires, *Marketing literature*, p. 34.
223 See Chapter 6.

perspective of book consumers, this meant books were then heavily discounted, making them substantially cheaper. Price promotion became the primary book marketing mechanism, ushering in 3-for-2s and similar offers. A book consumer walking into a large chain bookshop would be assailed by discount offers (co-funded by publishers), attractively displayed on front tables, or piled high in dump bins. Massification was not new in the publishing industry (the sales of Penguin Books via Woolworths in the mid-twentieth century was an earlier example), but the abolition of price regulation brought a wholly new emphasis on competition. The impact on book consumers was access to heavily discounted books sold in large and welcoming spaces.

Prior to the demise of the NBA at the end of the 1990s, the public library offered readers access to otherwise high-price books for free. The rise of supermarket and discount selling cheapened books, leading to 'people who may have been frequent library users in the past being more able to purchase books', and thus less likely to visit their public library.[224] In the previous decade, public libraries had been defunded during a period of cuts to local government, and had also been confronted with an ideological interrogation of public sector provision. The *Ex Libris* report (1986) from the free-market Adam Smith Institute advocated the extension of competitive tendering into library services, and even paid-for subscription services offering privileged lending rights to those willing to pay for them.[225] The recommendations were not, in the end, taken forwards, but engendered hostility among librarians and – as evidenced via Mass-Observation documentation from 1988 – some library users, who were already angry about public library cuts. As one commented, '"On the whole, my library withdrawals are merely political acts. I use my library to defend the principle against those philistines in the government who would say that a public library system is not being used by sufficient numbers to warrant public subsidy."' Another commented that '"Our libraries are our great heritage and I do hope that the Thatcher revolution will not do anything to remove universal free libraries."'[226] In his analysis of the Mass-Observation archive, Alistair Black also noted an opposing distaste of public libraries becoming politicised. One correspondent,

> commenting on the libraries run by the radical council in his area of London [in the late 1980s], wrote that librarians selected 'too many feminist and pseudo psychology books . . . the place is plastered with leaflets on people's

---

224 McMenemy, *The public library*, pp. 14–15.   225 Snape, 'Libraries for leisure time', p. 54.
226 Black, 'The past public library observed', p. 443.

rights, etc., and campaigning-type posters. On the counter there is always some petition they want you to sign – Sign of the times I suppose.[227]

The public library's increasing transition into community hub was both a politicised act with access and notions of diversity at its heart, but also a reaction to a more consumer lifestyle orientated culture that bookshops were displaying. The bookshop may have become a 'social club' in the 1990s, but the public library attempted to be a more socially conscious version of that club.[228]

Towards the end of the twentieth century, the ideological leanings of the New Labour government elected in 1997 reshaped cultural policy, with reading as a tool of social inclusion becoming a key strand through third-sector agencies such as Booktrust and the National Literacy Trust.[229] Building on, as Fuller and Rehberg Sedo phrase it, 'a belief in reading as an individually transformational, educational, therapeutic, creative, and even "civilising" experience', this cultural policy approach inflected an 'ideal of shared reading as a way of building community and improving of cross-cultural understandings'.[230] The development of successive 'National Years of Reading' (in 1998/99 and 2008) and activities such as the Bookstart programme (which gave out free books to babies) promoted reading as an agent of social change.[231] Books and the activity of reading were incorporated into the neoliberal agenda, in which 'public good' was transmuted to 'public value'. In the late 1990s and early twenty-first-century Britain, softer benefits such as social inclusion, employability and an emphasis on creativity were perceived as the primary values of reading rather than in terms of hard economics. Nonetheless, the construction of reading as an agent of social change potentially overburdened it, while – at least for a short period – ploughing money into its support, before a later period of twenty-first-century austerity curtailed funding.[232]

The introduction of Public Lending Right (PLR) in 1979 meant that, from the 1980s onwards, comprehensive records were kept of library lending in order to disburse money to authors.[233] The records provide evidence of the most popular genres, authors and individual titles. The fiction list for 1991–92 was dominated by popular fiction authors such as Catherine Cookson, Barbara Taylor Bradford, Dick Francis, Danielle Steel and Wilbur Smith,

227 Ibid., p. 444.   228 McMenemy, The public library, p. 15.
229 Squires, 'Too much Rushdie, not enough romance?', p. 105.
230 Fuller and Rehberg Sedo, Reading beyond the book, p. 3.   231 See Chapter 26.
232 Fuller and Rehberg Sedo, Reading beyond the book, pp. 133–4.   233 See also Chapter 4.

while Roald Dahl comprehensively led the children's list. Non-fiction titles were more diverse, but had a leaning towards celebrity auto/biographies and TV tie-ins, as well as Peter Mayle's Provençal travel books, *The diary of Anne Frank* and the Department of Transport's *Driving manual*.[234] Ten years later, the adult fiction list looked very similar, but the children's list had come to be dominated by the Harry Potter series, and books by Jacqueline Wilson. The non-fiction titles showed a similar mix of celebrity-led titles, travel books (from Bill Bryson and Chris Stewart), *The official theory test for car drivers and motorcyclists* and a book on Windows 98, and the newer genre of 'misery memoirs'.[235]

Indeed, as well as the import of the US-style book superstore, the British publishing market was also affected by another US import from the 1970s onwards: the mass-market fiction best-seller, or, as Sutherland puts it, 'An American kind of book'. This version of the best-seller brought together a more commercial and supranational approach to publishing, an increase in levels of consumption, the importance of best-seller lists (which only really began in Britain in the 1970s), marketing hype, and cross-media synergies such as film tie-ins and novelisations.[236] As the PLR lists reveal, celebritisation was also an important factor in the range of genres which were successful in library lending in the period. Anxieties about the continued place of books in society arose because of competing forms of leisure consumption (films, TV, video and DVD), but in practice books and the publishing industry worked with other cultural forms to create multimedia products.[237]

The literary, as opposed to the mass-market, novel had a promoter of growing significance in the Booker Prize. Founded in 1968, the prize achieved great international prominence over the subsequent decades, not least in substantially pushing sales of literary novels, and creating expanded markets for 'quality' books, as was the founding intent of the award, with a seasonal, event-based approach to its marketing.[238] As such, the more literary end of the marketplace was also commercialised over the course of the 1980s and 1990s, creating a competitive environment and opportunities for bookshop promotion. Readers responded by buying winners – and indeed shortlisted books – in great numbers.[239]

234 PLR, 'Most borrowed titles July 1991–June 1992', www.plr.uk.com/mediaCentre/mo stBorrowedTitles/top20Titles/1991-1992Top20Titles.pdf.
235 PLR, 'Most borrowed titles July 2001–June 2002', www.plr.uk.com/mediaCentre/mo stBorrowedTitles/top20Titles/2001-2002Top20Titles.pdf.
236 Sutherland, *Bestsellers*, pp. 10–30.   237 See Chapter 29.
238 Squires, 'Literary prizes and awards'. See also Chapter 30.
239 Squires, 'Book marketing and the Booker Prize'.

In the late 1990s, reading groups became another way in which readers organised their practices, and by which publishers and other media organisations could interact with them. As Jenny Hartley details in her study of the phenomenon, social and organised reading groups have a long history in Britain (and an international history elsewhere, particularly in the Anglophone world), but the last decade of the twentieth century witnessed an explosion of their numbers and activities. Hartley traces the 1990s development via organisations such as public libraries, the University of the Third Age and the Women's Institute, but also in 1997 in the mobile telephone company Orange's Reading Group pack, and subsequent reading groups set up by the *Mail on Sunday* and *Good Housekeeping* magazine. Largely female in membership, such groups would meet on a regular basis to discuss books, but also to perform other socialising activities.[240] Publishers saw these reading groups as an opportunity for promotion, and explicitly marketed books towards them.[241] By the early years of the twenty-first century, the phenomenon led to the TV comedy series *The book group*, which ran for two seasons in 2002–3.

Alongside reading groups and the Booker Prize, mediatised book clubs (such as the US's Oprah Winfrey and the UK's Richard and Judy, the latter discussed below), educators, book reviewers and literary festivals have worked, in Beth Driscoll's argument, to create a 'new literary middlebrow' at the turn of the twentieth and twenty-first centuries. One of Driscoll's key features of the middlebrow is that it is 'middle class', and certainly patterns of cultural consumption would corroborate this statement, even if – as Driscoll herself admits – varying patterns of cultural practice occur within broad sociological categorisations.[242] Reader demographic statistics confirm this: in 2005, for example, Mintel reported that while 71 per cent of ABs (the highest social demographic classification) had visited a bookshop, only 30 per cent of Es had. Similarly, 53 per cent of ABs had purchased one or more books in the last month, while only 22 per cent of Es had. The same set of statistics showed women to be more engaged with books and reading than men, with the heaviest book-buyers and bookshop visitors being the forty-five to fifty-four age bracket.[243] A further 2005 study found that 45 per cent of people 'rarely, if ever, buy books', while 25 per cent 'read very little, if at all', demonstrating a stratification of reader – and non-reader – behaviour.[244]

---

240 Hartley, *The reading groups book*, p. 6.   241 Fuller *et al.*, 'Marionettes and puppeteers?'
242 Driscoll, *The new literary middlebrow*, pp. 17–21.
243 Cited in Clark and Phillips, *Inside book publishing*, fourth edition, p. 172.
244 *Expanding the book market*, p. 5.

Reading in the digital age

The first decade of the twenty-first century saw fundamental changes in the acquisition and reading of books in Britain brought about by the digital revolution in the world of print, a phenomenon often referred to as the 'third revolution of the printed book'. This ongoing digital revolution is both a global and a local phenomenon, with significant impact on both modes of access and reading, and methods of distribution and acquisition. In 2000, only a minority of British readers (26.2 per cent) were using the internet on a regular basis, and the overwhelming majority of the population would still need to buy or borrow a material copy of a printed book in order to read it; however, by 2011, 82.5 per cent of Britons had internet access at home.[245] Amazon entered the UK market on 15 October 1998 as an online book broker/retailer, and the first major impact of the 'third revolution' was on purchasing patterns rather than on format or reading practices; by the end of 2010, online retailers had captured 27 per cent of the volume and 31 per cent of the value of total book sales, with Amazon alone accounting for more than 70 per cent of all online book retailing.[246] With the launch of its Kindle e-reader in the UK market in November 2009, Amazon repositioned itself as a retailer and distributor of both printed and digital reading material, with online access becoming both a means of acquisition and a mode of delivery. In the space of a decade, British readers moved from exclusively buying and borrowing books from physical outlets (bookshops and libraries), to a mixed economy of acquisition, primarily ordering books online, and occasionally downloading digital content to a range of internet browsing devices, including 3G and 4G mobile phones, tablets, laptops and proprietary e-readers such as Amazon's Kindle. Amazon.co.uk was recording a higher volume of digitally downloaded books than online purchases, with new-release hardback books particularly eclipsed; by April 2011, less than eighteen months after the launch of the Kindle in the UK, e-books were outselling hardback books by a ratio of 2.4 to 1.[247]

The increase in online retailing and subsequently of digitally distributed content certainly had a negative effect on some of the traditional favourites of

---

245 Figures taken from the *International Telecommunications Union* (ITU), www.itu.int/IT U-D/ict/statistics/explorer/index.html.
246 Amazon UK corporate timeline, http://phx.corporate-ir.net/phoenix.zhtml?c=25119 9&p=irol-corporateTimeline. Market share figures from the Booksellers Association deposition to the Office of Fair Trading, 18 July 2011, www.booksellers.org.uk.
247 Adam Gabbatt, 'Amazon and Waterstones report downloads eclipsing printed book sales', *Guardian* 19 May 2011, www.guardian.co.uk/books/2011/may/19/amazon-wat erstones-ebook-sales.

the British reader, the high street bookshop and the independent bookshop, with the number of independent bookshops nearly halving in the five years from 2005 (4,000) to 2010 (2,178).[248] At the same time, leading supermarket chains heavily discounted books, often offering them as loss leaders to consumers. However, despite the increasingly deregulated and competitive free market for book purchasing described in the previous section, and with multiple options for acquiring reading matter, British readers at the end of the first decade of the twenty-first century still remained habitual buyers of material books. While book sales were impacted by fewer bookshops and pressures on disposable income, British readers in 2010 bought 225.5 million volumes (an average of 4.5 books per person per year), spending some £1.69 billion, higher than the equivalent participation figures for cinema attendance (169.2 million tickets sold, an average of 2.7 visits per person per year).[249]

Despite the rise of digital media and new modes of access in this decade, more established forms of cultural consumption of the book continued to hold importance. Replicating the tested formula of magazine and radio book clubs from earlier decades, and cashing in on the contemporary vogue for reading groups, in 2004 the doyens of middlebrow cultural consumption, television chat-show hosts Richard Madeley and Judy Finnigan, launched the Richard and Judy Book Club as part of their Channel 4 show.[250] Translating the trusted American formula of Oprah's Book Club for British readers, each year they promoted ten books, with reviews, discussions and author interviews embedded within their hour-long show, which aired every week-day at 5pm; the first book featured was the 2003 Man Booker Prize winner, Monica Ali's *Brick Lane*, and viewers could vote for their book of the year from the shortlist. Effectively, the Richard and Judy Book Club operated as both a marketing device and a marker of literary tastes, and had a strong impact on book sales. After moving off Channel 4 and temporarily to a cable TV channel, it then was sponsored by Thorntons (the largest British-owned chocolate manufacturer) and co-branded with one of the most established

---

248 James Hall, 'Internet and supermarket kill off 2,000 bookshops', *Daily Telegraph* 2 September 2011, www.telegraph.co.uk/culture/books/booknews/8738701/Interne t-and-supermarkets-kill-off-2000-bookshops.html.

249 Philip Stone, 'Book sales in 2010 fall by more than 3%', *Bookseller* 5 January 2011, www .thebookseller.com/news/book-sales-2010-fall-more-3.html; Ben Keen, 'BSAC Conference UK movie market update', www.bsac.uk.com/files/uk_movie_marke t_update_2011.pdf.

250 Ramone and Cousins (eds.), *The Richard and Judy Book Club reader*; Fuller and Rehberg Sedo, *Reading beyond the book*, pp. 50–90.

firms in British book retailing, W. H. Smith. Books selected by the book club are bundled and sold through the 1,000-plus branches of W. H. Smith's bookshops as well as online through e-readers such as the Kobo, foregrounding associations with both established and emerging modes of consumption. Paralleling the changing preferences of audiences from analogue mass broadcast media to personally optimised, digitally delivered online content, the Richard and Judy Book Club moved from being a slot on their own daytime television show, to an interactive online website exclusively delivered by W. H. Smith, complete with video author interviews, podcasts, a blog, and a social media presence.[251] Despite this move to online delivery, the Richard and Judy Book Club continues to champion readers' preferences for the novel as a genre, and the material book as an established means for consuming it. In late 2013, they launched 'Richard and Judy's search for a bestseller', a competition with a £50,000 prize, designed to showcase first-time novelists, while earlier that year, Madeley became a first-time novelist himself.[252]

Despite the continuing emphasis on the material book – and the continuing shared reading practices of book clubs and what Fuller and Rehberg Sedo have termed 'Mass Reading Events', or MREs – the impact of technology has also had a substantial effect on reading in the digital twenty-first century. Social media have provided platforms for authors, publishers and readers to communicate about books, share reading lists, and network. Amazon's Customer Comments, book blogs, vlogs and 'BookTubes', Twitter hashtags used for digital and in-real-life literary festivals, the sharing of reading lists and recommendations on Goodreads, virtual browsing via Google's 'snippet view' and Amazon's 'look inside', gamification – with reading 'awards' – via Kobo's Reading Life, and annotation tools such as the 'highlights' function on the Kindle all provide opportunities for socially networked reader activity.[253] Such technologies and the practices they generate can provide traces for the historian of contemporary reading which have already been taken up by scholars; they can also give data to technology companies on customer behaviour or – as some might see it – surveillance opportunities.[254]

As Chapter 3 details, digital technologies have also radically enabled self-publishing, via platforms such as Amazon's Kindle Direct Publishing and Wattpad. As well as providing large hinterlands of text, digital self-publishing platforms respond to readers' tastes in a much more immediate way than the

251 http://richardandjudy.whsmith.co.uk.
252 http://richardandjudy.whsmith.co.uk/search-for-a-bestseller.
253 Ray Murray and Squires, 'The digital publishing communications circuit', pp. 14–18.
254 Rowberry, 'Ebookness', p. 12.

traditional gatekeeping model of publishing does. One of the biggest-selling series of the second decade of the twenty-first century, E. L. James's *Fifty shades* trilogy, started life as fan fiction before transitioning to traditional publication. A new publishing sub-genre for erotica, flavoured with BDSM (bondage, discipline, dominance, submission, sadomasochism) scenes, was reborn for the mainstream market, thereby – at least for a short while – shaping best-selling reading tastes.

Perhaps because of the increasing complexity of readers' engagements with books and other forms of reading matter in a highly competitive multi-media environment, discourses of anxiety around reading (implicitly about *not* reading, or reading non-literary works) still circulated in popular discourse and informed policy-making at the start of the twenty-first century. The locus of these anxieties – whether substantiated by statistical evidence or not – has invariably been the reading habits of children, especially teenagers, who constitute a new generation of 'digital native' readers, for whom traditional models of acquiring, owning and reading books might be challenging, or even alien. An online survey in November 2010 by the National Literacy Trust of 18,141 schoolchildren aged between eight and seventeen found a direct correlation between the number of printed books owned and kept at home, the enjoyment derived from reading as a pastime, and educational achievement. They found that young people who owned books were twice as likely (26.6 per cent) to like reading very much compared to those who did not own books (13.1 per cent), while children who did not own books of their own were nearly four times more likely not to enjoy reading at all (23.7 per cent) than those who did own books (6.7 per cent).[255] Nearly one in ten children who didn't possess books of their own (9.4 per cent) also reported that there were no books of any kind at home, while a further 29.8 per cent estimated that there were fewer than ten books at home, starkly indicating that the paucity of printed books at home reinforced a negative attitude to reading. However, while this cohort grew up as digital natives, they proved to be discriminatory in their leisure (as opposed to curricular) reading habits, with printed fiction (56.6 per cent) the third most popular type of material (after magazines and SMS text messages) and well ahead of websites, blogs, e-mails, and even e-books (6.1 per cent) which surprisingly proved to be the least popular form for leisure reading. Anxieties over the role of public libraries and the decline in bookshops were also evident in the National Literacy Trust survey; 5.2 per cent of children who owned books

255 Clark and Poulton, *Book ownership.*

and 12.6 per cent of those who did not own books had never visited a library, while the numbers who had never visited a bookshop were even higher (8.3 per cent and 21.5 per cent respectively).

While these figures might indicate the decline in a reading culture amongst twenty-first-century young people (an anxiety continuously aired and reinforced in public discourse), statistics collected by the PLR suggest just the opposite; for the period from July 2009 to June 2010, no fewer than seven of the ten most borrowed authors were children's writers, with Jacqueline Wilson's books having been borrowed at least a million times in every single year (2000–10) of that decade.[256] The pattern continued later into the century, with 2014–15 statistics showing six out of the ten most heavily borrowed authors being a writer for children.[257] PLR figures contradict predictions of the demise of the habit of children acquiring and reading printed books from the public library system in the face of the onslaught of digital media, and indeed tangibly demonstrate the appetite of young people for readily accessible, free material that they want to read – something not always offered by distributors of online content.

Beyond the printed book?

By the start of the second decade of the twenty-first century, then, British readers were fully enmeshed in the effects of the third revolution of the printed book, witnessed by the mass digitisation of the back catalogue of printed books and new modes of reading instantly and conveniently enabled through a range of e-reading devices delivering content downloaded from online retailers, such as Amazon and iTunes. Increasingly, twenty-first-century consumers of reading matter are being presented with information in the form of online structured content, with text accompanied by audio-visual or other interactive material. Often, text is presented not in the standard sequential arrangement familiar to readers through many centuries of engagement with the codex, but rather through a series of interlinked objects that can be accessed, viewed or interrogated in relation to one another, either continuously or discontinuously. While e-readers have consciously mimicked the material conventions of the codex (successive

---

256 Maev Kennedy, 'Children's authors dominate list of favourite UK library books', *Guardian* 18 February 2011, www.guardian.co.uk/uk/2011/feb/18/children-top-library-books-authors?INTCMP=ILCNETTXT3487.

257 Public Lending Right, 'Most borrowed authors July 2014–June 2015', www.plr.uk.com/mediaCentre/mostBorrowedAuthors/top20Authors/2014–2015Top20AuthorsRevised.pdf.

iterations of the Kindle, for example, have kept the proportions of the most popular paperback formats as well as its portrait orientation), the reading practices that are possible include both linear and non-linear reading, both turning pages and scrolling, in either or both directions. Nowhere is this flexibility of possibilities more evident than in the rise of e-magazines, often delivered through apps and attached to brands promoting other forms of leisure consumption such as travel, online shopping or use of social media. This kind of discursive reading may indicate new practices analogous to those that accompanied earlier developments in ephemeral reading during the era of print.

But while e-books and other more sophisticated forms of interactive, text-based, multimedia content have potentially fostered a wide range of different modes of acquisition and possible consumption, it is debatable whether this will in fact increase either the amount of time spent reading or the range and diversity of material being read. Ironically, ease of access is sometimes inversely proportional to breadth of coverage or availability of choice; whether e-readers and digital content actually foster a demand-driven, infinitely long tail, or merely promote a succession of short-lived best-sellers, remains to be seen. Studies of book borrowing from public and subscription libraries in earlier periods in British history have demonstrated that the availability of books does not by itself guarantee their use, nor is the cost of access determined only by library membership charges or the price of books. In the nineteenth century, the cost of access to books was determined as much by the development of the railways (and therefore the cost of travel) as by the price structures of circulating libraries; indeed, it was the falling cost of public transport that both facilitated particular reading practices and made possible the distribution of new genres and formats for books. In the twenty-first century, the cost of access to books and other reading matter is increasingly determined by the price of internet access (especially data download and roaming mobile access through 3G and 4G capable devices) and cumulative data storage (such as reliable Cloud networking), as well as by costs that are often surreptitiously passed on to consumers, such as VAT charged on electronic content (but not on printed books), optional individual customisation of books (such as electronic skins in lieu of dust-jackets), and the acquisition, maintenance and energy (recharging) costs for e-reading devices. The business models behind digital books have also changed how book ownership operates. Digital book readers no longer own copies on platforms such as the Kindle and Apple's iBooks library, but instead have licences to them. Moving British readers from the tax exempt world of printed books to taxed digital content with optional add-ons generates new revenue streams for both distributors and government, while passing on invisible costs to consumers. It also exposes readers (as consumers) to far higher levels of scrutiny, content control and direct commercial marketing than ever before.

Despite the inexorable rise of digital content, readers have so far remained more than merely sentimentally attached to printed books in a digital age. Indeed, the ubiquity and ease of access to e-books might even encourage a new bibliophilia for material books, for while downloading an e-book is an immediate and convenient method of accessing information, it is both anonymous and discreet: a Kindle cannot visibly articulate and display the cultural capital, literary tastes and social standing of the owner the way books on a shelf can, so instantly and tellingly. Indeed, by the middle of the 2010s, e-book sales started to plateau and even decrease in popularity. IKEA has sold 41 million units of its iconic 'Billy' book case since its introduction in 1979 (the same year as the first demonstration of the now already largely obsolescent CD), with current global sales of around 3 million units a year and still rising, despite the rapid growth of e-readers and downloaded content in the last decade.[258] Of course, not all 'Billy' book cases are used solely to house books, but with each having the capacity to hold some 250 standard format paperback books, this suggests that (potentially at least) the shelf space to display over 10 billion books (significantly more than the equivalent of one book per human on the planet) has been sold to householders across the world in the last thirty years.

This extraordinary sales phenomenon demonstrates more than merely aesthetic preferences (book-lined shelves promoting domestic conviviality, or the material culture of gift-giving around books), or the inculcated habits of reading printed books ingrained in a pre-digital childhood. Rather it strongly indicates that twenty-first-century readers are still committed to printed books for their durability, cost of acquisition, ease of use, portability, and stability of format, despite their enthusiastic recent adoption of electronic media. Indeed, it is the printed book's low technology (it needs no mediation or reading device to access and incurs no fixed costs beyond domestic storage and lighting) that is the main reason for its resistance to obsolescence – unlike, perhaps, the majority of the different e-readers and e-book delivery systems currently competing for market share (there are well over 100 different devices available for sale, *not* including smart phones and tablets),

258 Lucy Mangan, 'The Billy bookcase: 30 and still going strong', *Guardian* 5 October 2009, www.guardian.co.uk/lifeandstyle/2009/oct/05/ikea-billy-bookcase; Pyne, *Bookshelf*, pp. 94–8, 104.

most of which will invariably be superseded long before the end of the century. Far from simply replacing one mode of acquiring and reading books with another, perhaps twenty-first-century readers might prove to be adept and proficient at accessing and engaging with reading matter (including the printed book) in a range of different ways.

PART III

*

8

Literature

ANDREW NASH AND JANE POTTER

At the beginning of the twentieth century the publishing of literature was characterised by widening readerships and falling retail prices.[1] New novels were priced at six shillings and reprints of recent titles two shillings or under. Older works still in copyright were available in large-format sixpenny paperbacks, or smaller cloth-bound sevenpenny editions popularised by Nelson and Collins. Classic works could be purchased for one shilling or less in Everyman's Library and other series. The outbreak of war in 1914 halted the cheapening trend. Higher production costs pushed up retail prices of new works and reprints; the sevenpennies largely disappeared from the market. Fiction also for the first time fell under the Net Book Agreement, meaning readers could no longer readily purchase at discount prices.

War presented the book trade with enormous challenges as well as opportunities to respond to a changing literary climate.[2] Although the number of books published gradually fell from 12,379 in 1913 to 7,716 in 1918,[3] the demand for reading material that informed, reassured and amused was high amongst a public for whom the 'Victorian classics, light novellas and complacent tales of imperial derring-do that had dominated pre-war lists' no longer appealed in light of the cataclysm of war.[4] Yet much popular fiction adapted the formulae of such writing to suit the current conflict, and many novels merely substituted the imperial hero or heroine for the British Tommy or the Red Cross Nurse. Memoirs by those on active service augmented the controlled newspaper accounts of battles and their aftermath and were surprisingly graphic, especially those written by medical personnel, who did not spare the reader descriptions of gas gangrene or amputated limbs.

1 Eliot and Nash, 'Mass markets: literature'. 2 See also Chapter 23.
3 Mumby, *Publishing and bookselling*, p. 20. 4 Stevenson, *Book makers*, p. 41.

Such accounts used these descriptions to bolster support for war, for winning the battles that had wreaked so much destruction on the bodies of British soldiers. Thus they escaped the censor. Other books did not. D. H. Lawrence's *The rainbow* (1915) was prosecuted under the Lord Campbell's 1857 Obscene Publications Act. Over 1,000 copies of the novel, seized from the publisher Methuen's warehouse, were ordered to be destroyed by the judgement of Sir John Dickinson at Bow Street Magistrates Court on 13 March 1915. Algernon Methuen offered no defence of the novel, branded 'a mass of obscenity of thought, idea and action', and claimed Lawrence had twice refused to rewrite offending passages. The judgement meant Lawrence lost his copyright and was effectively stigmatised as a writer, 'practically unable to publish fiction'.[5] It took him three years to pay back his £300 advance to Methuen. Lawrence was not the only author to suffer under censorship. The journalist who instigated the prosecution of *The rainbow*, James Douglas, turned his sights to Rose Allatini's novel *Despised and rejected*, which under her pseudonym A. T. Fitzroy was published by C. W. Daniel in 1918. Its sympathetic portrayal of pacifism, conscientious objection and homosexuality led to its prosecution under the Defence of the Realm Act (DORA), its content deemed 'likely to prejudice the recruiting of persons to serve in His Majesty's Forces'.[6] Fined £400 and ordered to pay £40 costs, Daniel represents the undercurrent of protest that struggled against the tide of patriotic stoicism.

Fiction, 1918–1939

Although book production levels did not recover their pre-war high until 1924, output of new fiction increased during the 1920s. The number of new novels published rose from 1,220 in 1924 to 1,828 in 1932.[7] With increased costs of production, however, publishers had to sell more copies of individual titles to recover their outlay. As a consequence, there was an upsurge in cheaply produced books aimed at a mass market.[8] Hodder & Stoughton led the way with its two-shilling Yellow Jackets, recycling iconic fictional characters such as Sapper's Bulldog Drummond and Baroness Orczy's Scarlet Pimpernel in successive titles. The pictorial wrappers, with catchphrases for individual novelists and 'H&S Yellow Jacket' printed at the foot of the spine, became

5 Worthen, 'D. H. Lawrence and the "expensive edition business"', p. 106.
6 Atkin, *A war of individuals*, p. 156.   7 Faber, *A publisher speaking*, p. 95.
8 McAleer, *Popular reading and publishing*.

instantly recognisable, leading a rival publisher to describe W. H. Smith bookshops as 'Hodder & Stoughton depots'.[9]

Price and colour became key marketing tools in the sale of popular fiction. Like the Yellow Jackets, series such as Collins's '1/- Novels' (with 'Detective', 'Romance' and 'Wild West' lists) and Cassell's 'Shilling Novels' displayed the price prominently on coloured dust-wrappers. Heinemann also marketed its backlist in this way, with a colourful '2/- library' which in the 1930s included older titles by John Galsworthy and Somerset Maugham. As more series emerged, distinct market sectors began to form. Mills & Boon, which also had a 'Westerns' list, began to specialise in romance fiction in the 1920s, developing a low-risk publishing strategy that marketed the brand as much as the author. In the 1930s the firm was issuing two to four hardback titles every fortnight in print-runs of 6,000 to 8,000.[10] Most sales were to libraries, and like other popular fiction publishers Mills & Boon benefited from the emergence of twopenny libraries (see Chapter 7) which, because they depended upon books being returned quickly, increased the demand for shorter works.

Outside the familiar names were publishing operations about which little is known. The Modern Publishing Company, for example, specialised in buying up surplus sheets from other publishers at low cost. In the 1920s it seems to have been a dumping ground for Nat Gould's racing novels. More wide-ranging was the Readers Library, issued by the Readers Library Publishing Company from 1923 to 1935.[11] These were sixpenny hardbacks, printed on low-grade paper with coloured jackets, sold mainly through Woolworths. Claiming sales of up to 10 million a year, the series initially consisted of out-of-copyright classics by British, American and European authors, but contemporary writers including Arnold Bennett and H. G. Wells were also included. A sub-series entitled the 'Readers Library Film Edition' featured ghostwritten novelisations of films, an early example of crossover between books and screen media. The dust-wrappers carried stills from the films along with the actors' names, and a manifesto printed inside the volumes claimed that the series met 'a real modern demand' from cinema-goers who wished to read the book of the film (which was itself often the film of a book).

It was books like the Readers Library that were displaced from the shelves of Woolworths by Penguin paperbacks when they appeared in 1935 (see below). Allen Lane's venture was distinctive as much for the type of book

9 Attenborough, *A living memory*, p. 98. 10 McAleer, *Passion's fortune*, p. 63.
11 Hammond, 'The multimedia afterlives of Victorian novels'.

281

published as for the format. Works of fiction had long been issued in soft covers. Many firms continued to produce the large-format double-column paperbacks that had flourished in the late Victorian period. The Bodley Head issued reprints of its early Agatha Christie titles in this way several years before it made *The mysterious affair at Styles* one of the first ten Penguins. In the late 1920s Hodder turned some of its hardback 'Yellow Jackets' into ninepenny paperbacks and Hutchinson followed suit with its ninepenny 'Red Jackets'.

For a large sector of the reading public, however, the main format was the magazine. The profusion of monthly fiction-carrying magazines inspired by the success of the *Strand* in the 1890s continued during and after the war, in spite of an increase in retail prices from 4½d to ninepence or one shilling. Conan Doyle's Sherlock Holmes made his last appearance in the *Strand* in 1927. Other survivors from the pre-war era included *Cassell's Magazine*, which continued until 1965, and the *Windsor Magazine* which boasted the prolific Dornford Yates. More specialist genre titles appeared in the 1920s such as Hutchinson's *Adventure-Story Magazine* and *Mystery-Story Magazine*, which became 'Britain's top-selling popular fiction magazines'.[12] Modelled on American pulps, both titles offered 96–128 pages of original material and stories drawn from American titles.

Most magazines were in 'standard' format (9½ × 6½ inches) and printed on cheap newsprint or pulp paper. They sold in huge numbers, reaching a much larger market than books. The most consistently best-selling title, *Nash's Magazine* (1909–35), 'peaked in early 1918 at 240,000'.[13] The *Premier Magazine*, launched in 1914 at 4½d, claimed sales of 242,720 for its first issue, which contained a number of war-related stories.[14] With the rise of cinema and radio, however, the market contracted. In 1929 Hutchinson, later an important player in the paperback market, 'closed down its magazine division and concentrated on book production'.[15] By 1950 almost all of the magazines launched in the 1920s had disappeared.

The story magazines gave birth to some of the century's most iconic fictional characters, including P. G. Wodehouse's Jeeves and Wooster and Christie's various fictional detectives. Although they specialised in popular genres and targeted a mass audience, the range of writers included demonstrates their market importance. The *Story-Teller* counted Wells and Rudyard Kipling among its contributors, while in the *Strand* D. H. Lawrence and

---

12 Ashley, *The age of the storytellers*, p. 128. 13 *Ibid.*, pp. 92, 134. 14 *Ibid.*, p. 170.
15 *Ibid.*, p. 93.

Aldous Huxley rubbed shoulders with Wodehouse and Ethel M. Dell. Lawrence also published three stories in *Hutchinson's Magazine* where Joseph Conrad's final uncompleted novel *Suspense* (1925) appeared. Conrad's *The arrow of gold* (1919) had earlier been serialised in *Lloyd's Magazine*.

These sorts of associations suggest that the market divisions in this period identified by contemporary commentators such as Q. D. Leavis should be treated with caution.[16] Leavis's construction of the reading public as fractured along class lines nevertheless has some validity. If newsagents and twopenny libraries furnished working-class readers with story magazines and cheap hardbacks, middle-class readers generally were served by the big subscription libraries: Boots, W. H. Smith and Mudie's. Britain remained essentially a book-borrowing culture for much of the century. Boots' chief librarian F. R. Richardson judged in 1935 that the majority of circulating library borrowers were 'people who would never pay seven shillings and sixpence for a new novel [and] would very rarely buy books in any case'.[17] In the 1930s 'the average subscriber borrowed two novels a week',[18] sustaining vast sales for authors like J. B. Priestley and A. J. Cronin, whose *The citadel* (1937) sold 100,000 copies in just six weeks, mostly to libraries.[19] The subscription libraries asserted a powerful hold on the market for fiction. Chatto & Windus told Rosamond Lehmann that 'the success or failure of a novel depends on whether the demands of circulating library subscribers are sufficiently insistent to force the libraries to increase their orders'.[20] Virginia Woolf discovered this when she attributed a 'rapid fall in subscriptions sales' of *The waves* (1931) to borrowers returning copies of the novel unread.[21] The libraries also exercised a form of censorship. Hall Caine, Compton Mackenzie and Aldous Huxley were among many whose work was banned or removed from circulation. This sometimes forced authors into pre-publication censorship. Lawrence rewrote a love passage in *The lost girl* (1920) – which he himself had considered 'quite fit for Mudie's' – when the libraries refused to stock it with the first edition already printed. His publisher, Martin Secker, reckoned that library sales would account for half of the first edition of 4,000 copies.[22]

16 Leavis, *Fiction and the reading public*. See also Nash, 'Literary culture'.
17 Hampden, *The book world*, p. 196.
18 Wilson, 'Libraries, reading patterns, and censorship', p. 47. See also Wilson, 'Boots Book-Lovers' Library'.
19 Davies, *A. J. Cronin*, p. 145.   20 Nash, 'The production of the novel', p. 12.
21 Wilson, 'Libraries, reading patterns, and censorship', p. 46.
22 Worthen, *D. H. Lawrence*, p. 93.

The subscription libraries were gradually undercut after 1945 by the spread of public libraries, book clubs and paperbacks. In 1957 Gollancz informed Cronin that the Times Book Club, 'which used to repeat anything up to a thousand copies in the week of publication if a book had a good press, now normally repeats 25'.[23] The last W. H. Smith library closed in 1961, the Times Book Club followed in 1962, and Boots (citing the influence of television) in 1966.

The emergence of book clubs in the inter-war period is covered more fully elsewhere in this volume (see Chapters 6 and 7). The Book Society, founded in 1929, became an important market for fiction writers, guaranteeing a substantial extra sale for monthly selections. Authors and publishers sometimes tailored the content of their novels to appeal to the selection committee and a club's perceived audience.[24] Book clubs helped demarcate readerships, even if, like Collins's Crime Club commenced in 1930, they were no more than exercises in branding. Membership of the Crime Club was free and readers joined by filling out a coupon printed on the rear flap of Collins's detective novels. The *Crime Club Bulletin* gave members advance notice of forthcoming books which could then be ordered in the ordinary way from booksellers or libraries. In effect Collins was simply issuing a catalogue. Whereas early Christie novels contained lists of other Collins titles on the dust-wrapper, these were replaced from 1930 by advertisements to join the Crime Club. The venture helped solidify detective fiction as a leading subcategory of literature publishing.

The dominance of book clubs and circulating libraries, along with the threat of censorship, was among the reasons why many of the canonical works of literary modernism appeared outside the main commercial marketplace.[25] After the banning of *The rainbow*, Lawrence struggled to find a market for his most ambitious works of fiction. *Women in love* was first issued in a private edition in America in 1920 and *Lady Chatterley's lover* was privately printed in an expensive limited edition in Florence in 1928. The publication of James Joyce's fiction follows a similar pattern. Twenty-two publishers read and refused *Dubliners* (1914) before it was taken by Grant Richards, who, on advice from his printers who feared prosecution for obscenity, refused to print one story. *A Portrait of the artist as a young man* (1916) was issued by the little magazine now turned book publisher the Egoist

23 Davies, *A. J. Cronin*, p. 200.
24 Wilson, 'Libraries, reading patterns, and censorship', pp. 48–50.
25 Wexler, *Who paid for modernism?*; Willison *et al.* (eds.), *Modernist writers and the marketplace*.

Press, while *Ulysses* (1922) appeared in Paris in a limited, de luxe edition by the specially created Shakespeare & Company. The market for limited editions boomed in the 1920s and it was not just small or private presses that exploited the demand. Chatto & Windus made profits on signed editions of Wyndham Lewis and Norman Douglas, writers whose commercial value in the library-dominated 7s 6d market had proved negligible.[26]

Virginia Woolf published her early novels through the firm of her half-brother, Gerald Duckworth. In 1917, however, she and her husband Leonard established the Hogarth Press, primarily as therapy for Virginia who was recovering from a nervous breakdown. The Hogarth Press published some of the key texts of literary modernism and the 1930s, including Katherine Mansfield's *Prelude* (1919), and an edition of T. S. Eliot's *The waste land* (1923), as well as Woolf's own work and Christopher Isherwood's Berlin novels. Designs and illustrations by Vanessa Bell, Dora Carrington and Roger Fry marked the Press's unique visual style. The first intention was to print and publish small books and pamphlets which could not be placed with commercial publishers, and the Hogarth Press initially operated on a private subscription basis. By 1923, however, the business had expanded and books were being sold in the ordinary way through booksellers. Though fiction was only a small part of the press's output, the successful sale from 1929 of the five-shilling uniform edition of Woolf's fiction generated considerable income. In 1937 the publication of *The years* helped earn the press 'profits of £2,442/18s/5d'.[27]

The transformation of the Hogarth Press into a commercial publisher exemplifies how from the late 1920s modernist fiction became absorbed back into the mainstream marketplace. Secker began a 3s 6d edition of Lawrence's novels in 1926; Cape acquired Joyce's early titles in the 1920s and issued them in cheap editions, and in 1937 *Ulysses* finally appeared in a trade edition from the Bodley Head (see Chapter 5). By the time *Finnegan's wake* was published in 1939, Joyce and other modernists could benefit from having T. S. Eliot on the editorial board of Faber & Faber.

The rapprochement between modernism and the marketplace was part of a slow shift towards a more book-buying culture. From the late 1920s, leading fiction publishers began issuing 3s 6d reprint libraries such as the Travellers' Library (Cape), which by 1932 had sold one million copies of 180 titles,[28] the Phoenix Library (Chatto) and the New Adelphi Library (Secker). Printed on

---

26 Nash, 'Literary culture', pp. 333–5.
27 Marcus, 'Virginia Woolf and the Hogarth Press', p. 128.
28 Howard, *Jonathan Cape*, p. 136.

thin paper, with a uniform binding and wrapper, the difference between these libraries and existing 3s 6d editions lay in the conspicuous branding, as well as the target audience and the nature of the books on the list, which included works by Lawrence, Joyce, Proust and Wyndham Lewis.[29]

Penguin and the growth of paperbacks

By targeting a book-buying market for quality literature the 3s 6d series anticipated the arrival in 1935 of the Penguin paperbacks which effectively destroyed them. The initial impact of Penguin Books is hard to imagine. In the midst of the Great Depression, in an era when bookshops were intimidating for all but the academically minded, and readers borrowed rather than bought new works of fiction and non-fiction, the stylish, colourful, inexpensive and modern texts that burst on the scene were a revelation. Publishing legend has it that Allen Lane, a young director at the Bodley Head, conceived the idea at Exeter railway station on his return from a weekend gathering at Agatha Christie's home in Devon. Finding nothing at the bookstall but old Victorian reprints, romance novels and popular magazines, he questioned whether the country was not full of people like him who wanted recent, high-quality fiction in a well-designed yet affordable format. As noted above, paperbacks were not new; neither was colour-coding by genre nor the animal logo, all features that would come to characterise Penguin Books. Tauchnitz and Albatross, for instance, well known on the continent for their distinctive soft-cover editions, provided an obvious model.[30] Lane's innovation was a combination of numerous elements that had been tried and tested before. The distribution channels were more unorthodox: the books were sold at Woolworths and other chain stores as well as bookshops and railway bookstalls. They were sold at sixpence, the same price as a packet of cigarettes. Much to the trade's surprise – and indeed alarm at what the cheap format might do to the market – they were phenomenally successful. By March 1936, one million had been printed and Lane was able to set up Penguin Books as an independent publisher.

Hutchinson and Collins quickly attempted to emulate Penguin by issuing their own backlists at sixpence in similar format. Collins introduced White Circle Novels in 1936, with sub-series devoted to Crime Club and Mystery Adventure. The first volume was Christie's *Murder on the Orient Express* (1934).

29 Nash, '"Sifting out rubbish"'; Jaillant, *Cheap modernism*.
30 McCleery, 'The paperback evolution'.

In contrast to Penguins, Collins's titles carried advertisements on the inside and outside of the back covers, as did Hutchinson's Pocket Library which also printed publicity slogans and statements of sales on the front, commercial tactics which Lane considered vulgar. Hutchinson focussed on genre fiction, adding 'Romantic', 'Wild-West' and 'Crime Novel' series in the same format. More clearly designed to rival Penguin's emphasis on quality was Guild Books, set up by a consortium of nine publishers including Heinemann, Chatto and Cape 'to beat the paperback firms at their own game'.[31] Backlist titles by Maugham, Huxley and Graham Greene appeared at ninepence or one shilling. After the war there were over twenty-five participants, but when Heinemann dropped out in 1947 Guild Books dissipated. Soon after, Penguin signed an exclusive contract with five main firms, including Heinemann, to publish the first cheap reprints of their books, effectively monopolising the upper end of the paperback market.

The Second World War firmly embedded Penguin Books into the national psyche. At a time when other publishers were cutting their output due to paper rations, Penguin expanded. Paper rations for publishers were initially set at 40 per cent of output in the twelve months preceding the outbreak of war (August 1938 to August 1939). Penguin's enormous sales meant that Lane's firm enjoyed the largest ration in the trade. Penguin received further paper supplies for government work, supplying troops with books via the Forces Book Club. The size and light weight of the paperbacks meant they fitted easily into soldiers' knapsacks or coat pockets and were sent in their millions by the Post Office to the Forces and to prisoners of war. Nostalgic symbols of home, they provided the distraction of reading at a time of war with its alternating periods of intense action and intense boredom.

Fiction, 1939–1970

Like other parts of the trade, fiction production suffered during the Second World War from rationing and destruction of stock. By the end of 1941 36 per cent of the titles in print in 1939 were unavailable.[32] Annual output of fiction fell from over 4,000 titles in 1939 to fewer than 2,000 in 1942 and around 1,200 in 1945. As before, war conditions encouraged publishers to issue fewer titles in longer print-runs. The formation in 1944 of Pan Books signalled a new approach to mass production. Founded as an independent subsidiary of the

---

31 St John, *William Heinemann*, p. 366.   32 Bartram, *Publishing in wartime*, p. 2.

Book Society, Pan grew out of a consortium including Collins, Macmillan and Hodder, and sold 2 million books in the first year. As Stevenson notes, its 'editorial and marketing strategy was radically different from Penguin'.[33] Books were cheaper, were printed on inferior-quality paper acquired on the continent, and used full-colour cover designs, reflecting the growing influence of American paperback publishing.

Pan's products were not far removed from those of the 'mushroom' publishers that proliferated in the 1940s.[34] Small, often disreputable back-street operations, these firms issued various types of American-style genre fiction, including racy romance (with eroticised cover images), westerns, gangster, and early forms of science fiction. Specialist distribution firms were employed, but titles were sold through the chief book chains, including W. H. Smith, as well as other retail outlets. The books were short – around 128 pages and 40,000 words (half the length of an ordinary novel) – and usually retailed at 1s 6d or lower. The 'mushroom' era was spectacular but brief. A spate of prosecutions against publishers for issuing illicit material hastened its end in the 1950s. Its enduring product was Hank Janson (pseudonym of Steve Frances), the 'king of 1940s and early 1950s pulp fiction'.[35] Janson was both hero and putative author of the many books that carried his name (in later periods they were written by others). From 1949 these novels appeared monthly, and in 1952 initial print-runs were 100,000, with total sales 'approaching five million copies in under five years'.[36] In 1954, however, the publishers and distributors of the novels were brought to trial and sent to jail for obscenity. The brand endured until 1971, with later covers pronouncing Janson 'England's best selling author'.

One genre that graduated from magazine and cheap paperback to the mainstream was science fiction. Early publications were American in origin. The first home-produced magazine was *Tales of Wonder* (1937–42), a shilling pulp published by World's Work Ltd, which issued early stories by Arthur C. Clarke. Paper rationing gradually shrunk its size from 128 to 72 pages and it folded after sixteen issues.[37] More epoch-making was *New Worlds*, which helped develop the careers of Brian Aldiss and J. G. Ballard.[38] The magazine (128 pages at two shillings through the 1950s) grew out of a fanzine, and from its fourth issue was self-published by the specially created Nova Publications. In 1956, another Nova magazine, *Science Fantasy*, printed a version of Aldiss's *Non-stop*, later published as a novel by Faber. Aldiss

---

33 Stevenson, *Book makers*, p. 163. 34 Holland, *The mushroom jungle*.
35 Sutherland, *Reading the decades*, p. 22. 36 Holland, *The trials of Hank Janson*.
37 Tymn and Ashley, *Science fiction*, pp. 652–4. 38 Ibid., pp. 423–37.

recalls that Faber was the only book publisher interested in science fiction at that time.[39]

In the 1960s the science fiction magazine went into decline. *New Worlds* became increasingly associated with underground cultural movements and was withdrawn from leading newsagents in 1968. Paperbacks filled the void. A successful reprint of John Wyndham's *The day of the triffids* (1951) led Penguin to detect a new market. Aldiss was recruited to edit a list and produce an anthology, *Penguin science fiction* (1961), which was still in print in 1990.[40] The boom in science fiction in the 1970s and 1980s can be attributed in part to a symbiosis between books and other media, as the success of television series such as *Dr Who* generated a wider readership for the genre.

The rise of science fiction and other popular genres coincided with growing commercial pressures on 'literary' fiction.[41] Although total book production rose after the war, output of new fiction declined. In 1955, a record year for overall production, the number of fiction titles (including reprints) dropped from 4,404 to 3,702. It was not until the 1960s that the 1937 record of 5,099 annual titles was approached. Escalating cost of production was the cause. By 1949 printing costs had trebled compared to 1939, and the price of paper and binding more than doubled. By contrast, the retail price of novels had risen more slowly, narrowing profit margins. In 1956 Rupert Hart-Davis reported that, whereas before the war a publisher could break even by selling 1,000 copies of a 1,500 edition of a 7s 6d novel, now 'the first print must be 4,000 at round about 12s 6d with sales of 3,000'. This made gambling on unknown authors 'more hazardous'.[42]

The commercial pressure on novel publishing led to repeated fears that 'literary' fiction was under threat. With hardback fiction relatively more expensive throughout the 1950s and 1960s, bookshops cut back on orders. In a newspaper article from 1963, Philip Unwin identified an 'urgent need for some economic method of printing [a] small experimental edition'.[43] Publishers developed various strategies to support new writing in this period. In 1957 Hutchinson founded New Authors Ltd, a profit-sharing venture that launched the careers of Stanley Middleton, Maureen Duffy, J. G. Farrell, Barry Unsworth and Beryl Bainbridge. The first title, Jay Gilbert's *The skinner* (1958), sold 3,600 copies within a fortnight, which Hutchinson's chairman, Robert Lusty, judged 'about three times' the usual figure for a first novel.[44]

39 Aldiss, *Bury my heart*, p. 57.   40 *Ibid.*, p. 81.
41 Nash, 'The material history of the novel I'.   42 *The Times* 9 February 1956.
43 *The Times* 23 August 1963.   44 *The Times* 17 September 1958.

The growth of public libraries after the Second World War meant that much fiction continued to be borrowed rather than bought. The library market was crucial for some best-selling authors whose work appeared almost exclusively in hardback. Catherine Cookson only became a paperback phenomenon towards the end of the 1950s, and A. J. Cronin, a consistent best-seller from the 1930s, was not published in softcover until 1961.[45] The huge expansion of paperbacks from the late 1950s, however, changed the face of fiction publishing. Collins launched Fontana in 1953, flooding the market with Agatha Christie. Pan, boosted by Ian Fleming's James Bond titles, 'achieved sales of over 8 million' from just 150 titles in 1955.[46] In the 1960s it moved into the more literary end of the market, publishing John Fowles and selling a million copies of Alan Sillitoe's *Saturday night and Sunday morning*.[47]

Penguin, under the new direction of Tony Godwin, was forced to respond. Allen Lane had been extremely protective of the Penguin brand, and famously loathed what he called the 'bosoms and bottoms' approach to covers of American paperbacks.[48] When Godwin entered the firm in 1960, he faced a generational war with the founder. The typographical look of Penguins had become tired and Godwin sought to bring design and output more up-to-date. He hired Germano Facetti, who in turn employed Romek Marber to design a new Penguin cover template. What became known as the 'Marber Grid' defined the look of the paperbacks in the ensuing decades.[49] The admission of colour and the active pursuit of best-sellers bore fruit. Penguin's first paperback printing of Len Deighton's *Funeral in Berlin* (1964) was 250,000 copies. But Godwin's efforts to modernise the content of Penguins came to a dramatic end when Lane seized and destroyed copies of Siné's infamous collection of anti-clerical cartoons entitled *Massacre* in 1967.[50] Godwin was fired and Lane, despite claims he would retire, never really left his company until his death in 1970, shortly after Penguin was acquired by Pearson.

The triumph of the paperback is best illustrated by Mills & Boon's decision in the early 1970s to shift to predominantly paperback publishing, generating 'a 33 per cent increase in sales between 1972 and 1974'.[51] Compared to 1935, however, paperbacks were now more expensive relative to hardbacks, chiefly because more titles were being printed and print-runs were lower. By 1968

45 Greenfield, *Scribblers*, p. 27; Davies, *A. J. Cronin*, p. 171.
46 Stevenson, *Book makers*, p. 163.   47 Bradford, *The life of a long-distance writer*, p. 159.
48 Lewis, *Penguin special*, p. 280.   49 Baines, *Penguin by design*, pp. 97–103.
50 Hare, *Penguin portrait*, pp. 319–27.   51 Sutherland, *Bestsellers*, p. 85.

the average Penguin sold for five shillings – a tenfold increase from 1939. By contrast, hardbacks had increased only fourfold. With more paperbacks in bookshops, in addition to the traditional outlets of newsagents and super-markets, and a shorter time-gap between hardback and paperback publica-tion, the distinction between the two forms began to break down. In 1973 Hutchinson launched 'Midway Books' – new novels in soft covers at a cost roughly half the normal hardback price. Though unsuccessful, the experi-ment showed how the book trade was, as Stevenson suggests, beginning to realise that the markets for hardbacks and paperbacks were not 'fundamen-tally different' and 'implicitly class-divided'.[52]

Censorship and de-censorship

The 1950s saw publishers faced with numerous challenges from the Director of Public Prosecutions over books with 'obscene' content.[53] Swear words and graphic descriptions of sexual acts were just some of the material that contravened the Obscene Publications Act of 1857 which lasted, unrevised, for over a century, governing publication despite changing mores and attempts by authors to push the boundaries of literary expression. As noted above, D. H. Lawrence, whose novel *Lady Chatterley's lover* was to be the test case that ushered in the 1960s, had already felt the sting of the censor in 1915 with *The rainbow* and did so again in 1928 when *Lady Chatterley*, published in Florence, was banned in Britain. Lawrence, who died in 1930, never lived to see his work become celebrated as a landmark case in a new era of more liberal approaches to sex and sexuality in literature. For over thirty years, the novel was legally available only in expurgated versions, but in the 1950s publishers began to challenge the spate of prosecutions for literary obscenity. Some publishers and printers censored content, withdrew books from the market and/or paid fines in order to avoid court. Frederic Warburg was one who refused to buckle under the pressure. Prosecuted for publishing Stanley Kaufmann's *The philanderer* in 1954, Warburg opted to face a jury trial at the Old Bailey, and was eventually acquitted of all charges. In doing so, he paved the way for a new, more modern Obscene Publications Act, which came into effect in 1959. Its main tenet was that a work had to be taken as whole and on the grounds of literary merit – words or passages could not be singled out as evidence of obscene content.

---

52 Stevenson, *Book makers*, pp. 154–5.   53 See also Chapter 5.

The trial of *Lady Chatterley's Lover* (*Regina* v. *Penguin Books Ltd*), tested this new law. Allen Lane had already published Lawrence's entire oeuvre, except for *Lady Chatterley*, under the Penguin imprint and wanted to bring out a 'Complete Works' for the thirtieth anniversary of Lawrence's death. The new law was his opportunity, and although a favourable verdict was by no means assured, as with many of his other ventures Lane felt confident he had judged the public mood correctly. In order that no bookseller would be prosecuted for attempting to sell the title, twelve copies were 'seized' at the Penguin offices in High Holborn by Scotland Yard police on 16 August 1960 and submitted to the Director of Public Prosecutions.

The jury trial began at the Old Bailey on 20 October 1960. The opening statement for the prosecution by Mervyn Griffith-Jones, QC, has gone down in history as indicative of the worn-out ideas of an earlier privileged age: 'Is this a book you would have lying around your own house? Is it a book you would even wish your wife or your servants to read?' It has also been argued that the low price of the novel, 'a price the merest infant could afford', to use Griffith-Jones's words, was a significant factor in the prosecution. As Feather notes, Vladimir Nabokov's *Lolita* was in fact published before Penguin's edition of *Lady Chatterley*, but was never prosecuted, ostensibly because 'Weidenfeld and Nicolson published it in hardback at £1.12s.6d., and not in provocative paperback at an accessible 3s.6d.'[54] The six-day trial made headlines not least for the many high-profile figures who testified for the defence, including Dame Rebecca West, Cecil Day Lewis, E. M. Forster, the publisher Sir Stanley Unwin, the Bishop of Woolwich, and rising academics such as Richard Hoggart. No witnesses testified for the prosecution. Lane and Penguin Books were acquitted on 2 November 1960 to enormous headlines and public interest. Not only was Lane seen as a champion of free speech but the 200,000 copies he had ready in anticipation of acquittal were soon sold out and his projected profit of £5,000 was surpassed by an actual profit of £112,000.

Stevenson argues that 'it is easy to claim too much for the Chatterley trial' as a harbinger of a new permissiveness.[55] The acquittal did not put an end to prosecutions for obscenity in the ensuing years. The firm of Calder & Boyars, which published Samuel Beckett and a host of unconventional and daring writers such as Henry Miller, William S. Burroughs and Alexander Trocchi, found itself in court in 1966 when it published Hubert Selby Jr's novel *Last exit to Brooklyn*. Two trials at the Old Bailey found the book obscene, but the

---

54 Feather, *A history of British publishing*, second edition, p. 205.
55 Stevenson, *Book makers*, p. 174.

ruling was overturned in 1968 on appeal, thanks to the efforts of the barrister and dramatist John Mortimer on behalf of John Calder and Marion Boyars. It was that final acquittal that Stevenson argues 'definitively broke the stranglehold of official censorship, at least as far as sexual content was concerned',[56] although attempts to censor the written word did not truly die out until after the trial of *Inside Linda Lovelace* in 1978, a book also defended by Mortimer.

Fiction 1970–2000

Like other areas of the trade, the publishing of new fiction in the 1970s was badly affected by the escalating costs of production and retail prices that accompanied the global recession.[57] Between 1972 and 1980 the price of paper rose by 600 per cent and printing costs by 30 per cent annually.[58] Major publishers like Faber and Collins cut back on new titles. Cape, 'noted for its support of new novelists, accepted only one first novel in the autumn of 1975'.[59] Cuts in public library budgets were another crucial factor in this period, severely contracting a market sector which had largely sustained the 'literary' novel. Tom Rosenthal of Secker & Warburg commented in 1977 that, where a publisher used to rely on a 'safe library sale' of 1,500 copies of 'a good literary first or second novel', now only 300 or 400 could be expected.[60] While new writers struggled to get their work accepted, publishers concentrated on 'name' authors and sure sellers. Established names like Fowles, William Golding, Anthony Burgess and Iris Murdoch regularly headed hardback best-seller lists.

The 'crisis' of the literary novel in the 1970s coincided with intensified marketing strategies around the 'best-seller'. Best-seller tables began to appear in Sunday newspapers in the early 1970s, encouraging retailers like W. H. Smith to introduce 'best-seller' sections and displays of 'Top Ten paperbacks' in its shops.[61] Dominated by writers of genre fiction such as Frederick Forsyth and Alistair Maclean, the displays confirmed the change in Smith's retail environment. In the 1950s, advertisements in literary publications such as the *Spectator* had promised that every book reviewed in the pages of the magazine was obtainable from any branch of a W. H. Smith shop. By the 1970s only best-selling genre fiction remained a staple line.

56 *Ibid.*
57 For a fuller account of this period, see Nash, 'The material history of the novel II'.
58 Stevenson, *The last of England?*, p. 145. 59 Greenfield, *Scribblers*, p. 128.
60 Sutherland, *Fiction and the fiction industry*, p. 8. 61 Sutherland, *Best-sellers*, p. 28.

Against the rise of 'bestseller-dom', the 1970s witnessed a new diversity in the paperback field as publishers began to experiment with different formats. In 1972 Pan began its Picador imprint, publishing more upmarket titles in a slightly larger 'B' format to differentiate the product from the normal 'A' format.[62] The spread of the 'B' format, and in the 1980s the even larger 'C' format, helped establish conspicuous market sectors. The 'C' format was an attempt to bridge the gap between hardbacks and mass-market paperbacks. Faber experimented with the form in 1986 when it issued P. D. James's *A taste for death* in hardcover at £9.95, followed, in less than five months, by an identical edition in soft covers at £5.95. A mass-market paperback edition followed from Sphere twelve months after original publication, at which point Faber withdrew its 'C' format from the market.[63]

The new formats increased the visibility of high-quality fiction. One commentator judged in 1993 that 'up-market paperback fiction has experienced enormous growth, the more so over the last few years, whereas mass-market fiction ... has declined by around 20–25 per cent'.[64] Paperback originals became more common, and by the end of the century 60 per cent of new fiction titles were issued in soft covers, compared to 30 per cent in 1975.[65]

General trends in publishing and bookselling, such as conglomeration, had a significant effect on fiction publishing from the 1980s. When paperback advances became 'the determining factor in hardback publishing decisions',[66] hardback firms were encouraged to acquire or develop their own paperback imprints. Growing verticalisation in the trade meant that paperback reprints were often issued by the same publisher rather than being leased to another firm. When Random House acquired Chatto, Bodley Head and Jonathan Cape (three firms which had entered a partnership in 1973 but remained separate editorially), it launched a paperback imprint, Vintage, which became 'massively important' to the firm, publishing reprints of the old group's backlists and picking up rights reversions on authors like Graham Greene, whose books had previously been licensed to Penguin.[67] Specialist paperback firms like Penguin responded by originating more books in hardcover and taking over publishing houses with hardback lists.

The rise of bookselling chains also had a major influence on the publishing and marketing of fiction. Promotional events, such as Waterstone's 'Book of the Month', encouraged new approaches to marketing and publicity. In 1985

---

62 Straus, 'Format', p. 69.   63 Greenfield, *Scribblers*, p. 160.
64 Chapman, 'Paperback publishing', p. 54.   65 Stevenson, *The last of England?*, p. 137.
66 De Bellaigue, *British book publishing*, p. 14.   67 Bradley, *The British book trade*, p. 154.

Hodder & Stoughton outsourced its marketing, furnishing the advertising agency Saatchi & Saatchi with a budget of £250,000 'to run special promotion campaigns' for seven leading novelists.[68] By 1993 Jacqueline Graham could claim that publicity had become 'integral to the whole publishing and editorial process in a way that would have been considered unnecessary and even undesirable twenty, or even ten, years ago'.[69] New works were often divided into 'lead' and 'non-lead' titles, with only the lead titles 'allocated a substantial marketing and publicity budget'.[70] Many of the most successful titles of the decade, such as Louis de Bernière's *Captain Corelli's mandolin* (1994), were marketed in this way with substantial pre-publication promotion.[71]

With the collapse of the Net Book Agreement in 1995 (precipitated by the sale of popular fiction in supermarkets at dramatically reduced prices), stock in bookshops became more uniform as chains focussed on fewer and faster-selling titles. Chains like Waterstone's were able to secure an even higher discount for featured titles on the argument that promotions amounted to free advertising. In the new century, publishers could pay as much as £8,000 to £10,000 to participate in special promotions and secure prominent book-shop space for their titles.[72] Promotional activities were not the sole domain of publishers and booksellers, however. In 1983, *Granta*, which three years earlier had judged the structures of publishing and bookselling 'anachronistic' and at odds with 'the actual state of British fiction',[73] teamed up with the Book Marketing Council to launch a promotional campaign 'Best of Young British Novelists'. Fiction by twenty established or emerging writers, includ-ing Martin Amis, Julian Barnes and Graham Swift, appeared in a special number. The promotion 'proved of real benefit in getting books and authors more widely known'.[74] It was reported that the three main paperback publishers involved in the promotion sold 'an additional 230,000 copies as a result of the marketing exercise'.[75] Best of British was repeated in 1993, 2003 and 2013.

The most influential promotional phenomenon of the closing decades of the century, however, was the literary prize, notably the Booker Prize.[76] Set up in 1968, the Booker did not have a substantial effect on fiction sales until the 1980s. In 1978 Sutherland observed: 'Almost every year commentators wonder at the fact that the Booker . . . adds only some 5,000 to 10,000 to the

---

68 Greenfield, *Scribblers*, p. 153.   69 Graham, 'Publicity', pp. 148–9.
70 Todd, *Consuming fictions*, p. 97.   71 Squires, *Marketing literature*, pp. 110–11.
72 *Ibid.*, pp. 28–9.   73 Buford, 'Introduction', p. 13.   74 Graham, 'Publicity', p. 148.
75 Nash, 'The material history of the novel II', p. 413.   76 See also Chapters 4 and 30.

winner's sales.'[77] In 1980, however, Golding sold an additional 17,000 copies of *Rites of passage*.[78] The following year, Salman Rushdie's career was transformed when *Midnight's children* won the prize. Having sold only 639 copies on subscription, sales reached 4,353 within two days of the award being announced and broke 10,000 in less than three weeks. When the paperback edition appeared in April 1982 the initial print order of 20,000 copies was quickly augmented by an additional 30,000 on the day of publication.[79] The Booker came to have a seismic influence on authors' sales and reputations. As Todd argues, its success has helped make 'both the promotion and reception of serious literary fiction ... more consumer-oriented'.[80]

'Classics' of English literature

Publishing literary works in series intensified in the late nineteenth century.[81] The World's Classics, commenced by Grant Richards in 1901 and taken over by Oxford University Press in 1905, and Everyman's Library, published by J. M. Dent, were the two most successful examples at the turn of the twentieth century. Such series were often deliberately positioned in the marketplace. In 1914 Dent added the Wayfarer's Library to Everyman's. Devoted, as an early advertisement declared, to 'all that is brightest and best in the modern field of literature', it included authors such as Arnold Bennett, Hillaire Belloc and Mrs Humphrey Ward, deliberately excluding any 'controversial or pessimistic texts' or any work that might compromise the seemly bookshelf of a middle-class household: 'there was nothing too risqué to shock the vicar'.[82]

Penguin turned its attention to classics of the past in 1944 when Allen Lane commissioned E. V. Rieu to edit a series of English translations of Greek and Latin works. Rieu aimed to 'break away from that academic idiom in which so many of the world's classics have been put before the general reader, and to present them in contemporary English without any transgressions of scholarship or textual accuracy'.[83] His translation of *The odyssey* (1946), the launch title, sold three-quarters of a million copies within ten years.[84] Notable authors, such as Robert Graves and Dorothy L. Sayers, were engaged as translators,[85] and European as well as Middle and Far Eastern works were added. Sixty-five titles appeared in the first ten years.

---

77 Sutherland, *Fiction and the fiction industry*, p. 23.   78 Carey, *William Golding*, p. 414.
79 Straus, 'The use and effect', pp. 159–64.   80 Todd, *Consuming fictions*, p. 128.
81 Eliot and Nash, 'Mass markets: literature', pp. 439–42.
82 Jaillant, *Cheap modernism*, p. 15.   83 [Williams], *The Penguin story*, p. 19.
84 *Ibid.*, pp. 19–20.   85 Hare, *Penguin portrait*, pp. 186–209.

In 1963 Penguin English Library was established. Planned as a complement to Penguin Classics, the volumes contained critical introductions and explanatory notes. The first four titles were *Wuthering Heights*, *Middlemarch*, *Great expectations* and *The pilgrim's progress*. Non-fictional works by writers such as Samuel Johnson, Edmund Burke and Gilbert White were also included. As with other Penguin series, the distinctive visual design – orange spine and a black and white portrait of the author on the inside front cover – became a hallmark of the series. The expansion of the university system in the 1960s provided a ready market, but like Penguin Classics the series was also aimed at 'the intelligent general reader'. Penguin's editor, Charles Clark, saw the aim of the series as the 'Pelicanization' (a reference to the company's hugely successful non-fiction imprint) 'of expert knowledge about the novels'. This demanded 'the will and ability to get expert knowledge over (and the feeling that such knowledge is relevant to the layman) without either pedantry or talking down'.[86] The initial print-runs – 20,000–30,000 copies – made an appeal to the 'layman' essential, but a dispute over the academic pitch of the introductions led to the forced resignation of David Daiches as General Editor before the first volume had appeared.[87]

As with Penguin Classics, which underwent a change of emphasis in the 1960s to meet the growing demands of university students (especially in the United States),[88] the Penguin English Library became closely identified with the discipline of English literature in higher education.[89] Penguin merged the two series in the mid-1980s. In the same decade, OUP relaunched its World's Classics series, previously issued as pocket-sized hardbacks. Declining sales in the 1970s persuaded the Press to challenge Penguin head-on with paperbacks.[90] The first twenty-four titles appeared in 1980. Penguin Classics and Oxford World's Classics (as they became in 1998) maintained ascendency over the market into the new century, surviving a challenge in the 1990s by Wordsworth Classics, which undercut its rivals by selling classic works, without introductions and notes, at £1 per copy. Oxford was forced to cut the price of some of its more popular volumes and Penguin introduced a short-lived £1 series of its own – Penguin Popular Classics. The endurance of the relatively more expensive 'classics' series, however, owed much to the strength of the brand as well as the dual importance of the general and educational (especially overseas) markets.

86 *Ibid.*, p. 122.   87 Donaldson, 'Penguin English Library'.
88 Hare, *Penguin portrait*, pp. 300–6.
89 For a personal view, see Sanders, 'Hatching classics'.
90 Phillips, 'Trade publishing', pp. 344–6.

Poetry, 1914–1945

Punctuated as this period was by conflict, much of the poetry published between 1914 and 1945 was consumed, inspired or written in opposition to war and political or social unrest. Yet in the first decade of the twentieth century the main difficulty was the marketplace. While poetry was ubiquitous in newspapers, magazines and volumes in ways unmatched in the late twentieth century, 'English readers bought very little new verse, and with a few exceptions living poets were not considered by publishers as a commercial proposition.'[91] For many, 'Tennyson was still the defining example of poetic greatness';[92] anthologies such as *Palgrave's golden treasury* (1861) and Quiller-Couch's *Oxford book of English verse* (1900) retained currency, even as the new London publishers of the 1890s (among them the Bodley Head, Heinemann, Grant Richards and Gerald Duckworth) 'carved out a market niche'[93] for a new generation that sought to forge different paths. Literary magazines such as the *English Review* (founded by Ford Madox Hueffer in 1909), *Poetry Review*, *Poetry and Drama* and the *Egoist* showcased writers such as H.D., Richard Aldington, F. S. Flint and Wyndham Lewis. Chris Baldick has argued that '[t]he parlous state of poetry at the turn of the century is evident from the number of groups dedicated to rebellion and reform'[94] and by 1914 two poetic movements, Georgian and modernist, had come to represent what was new in the genre.

Contrary to later critical assessment, the Georgians and the modernists were not antagonistic coteries and co-existed in the small world of literary London. Each sought a radical departure from the stuffiness and high rhetoric of Victorian verse. While in later decades Georgian verse came to be seen as the conservative, sentimental, lesser counterpart to modernism, it was far from parochial or traditional. Although steeped in the pastoral, Georgian poetry was concerned with the elements of everyday life, expressed in plain language. The epithet was coined by Edward Marsh via his anthology *Georgian Poetry*, published by Harold Monro at the Poetry Bookshop in 1912. This first volume (others were to follow in 1915, 1917, 1919 and 1922) featured, among others, Rupert Brooke and D. H. Lawrence, who at the time 'seemed to be the vanguard of a revolution'.[95] Yet Monro, as a publisher and promoter of poetry, refused to align himself with any particular coterie, later decrying the label 'Georgian'. He was 'careful to balance the first *Georgian*

91 Ward, *Twentieth-century English literature*, p. 172.
92 Baldick, *The modern movement*, p. 79.   93 Rose, 'Lady Chatterley's broker', p. 188.
94 Baldick, *The modern movement*, p. 14.   95 Hibberd, *Harold Monro*, p. 97.

Poetry by publishing Ezra Pound's anthology, *Des Imagistes*'[96] in 1914, which also featured Lawrence. Monro also published the Imagist chapbooks by Aldington (*Images (1910–1915)*) and Flint (*Cadences*) in 1915.

The First World War ensured modernism's ascendancy, however. The movement's insistence on fragmentation and its experiments with form, sound and imagery seemed most suited to the cataclysm. Although significant modernists like T. E. Hulme were killed in the war, it was the Georgians who lost many of its most accomplished voices: Edward Thomas, Rupert Brooke and Wilfred Owen. It has often been speculated that had they survived they might have challenged the supremacy of the modernists, shaping English poetry in ways very different from what it became in the inter-war period and beyond. Indeed, when Pound's *Des Imagistes* was published in March 1914, it received poor reviews in both Britain and America, 'and in London many returned their copies to the Poetry Bookshop, who published it'.[97] With no preface to explain the new forms and techniques, readers were puzzled – 'the title seemed too precious and cryptic'.[98] Arguments between Pound and Flint, one of the key proponents of Imagism, led to Pound aligning himself with the more radical and dynamic Vorticism, led by Wyndham Lewis and articulated through his short-lived magazine *Blast* (1914–15). Three further Imagist anthologies were published over 1915–17. Characteristically acerbic, Pound deemed these volumes 'flabby'.

Like Pound, his fellow American ex-patriot, T. S. Eliot remained a civilian during the First World War, carrying on the literary movement in London and elsewhere as others, such as Aldington and Lewis, saw action on the Western Front. Eliot joined H.D. on the editorial board of the *Egoist* in 1917 as Aldington left for the war, and the Egoist Press published his *Prufrock and other observations* that same year, the periodical *Poetry* having published the individual poem 'The love song of J. Alfred Prufrock' in 1915. At the same time, poetry interpreting the war more directly was finding popularity. Monro published Robert Graves's *Over the brazier* and Charlotte Mew's *The farmer's bride* in 1916, while Sidgwick & Jackson, one of the premier poetry and drama publishers of their day, issued Rose Macaulay's *Two blind countries* (1914), Rupert Brooke's *1914 and other poems* (1915) and Ivor Gurney's *Severn and Somme* (1917), as well as volumes by John Drinkwater, Herbert Asquith and F. W. Harvey. Siegfried Sassoon's *The old huntsman and other poems* was published by William Heinemann in 1917.

---

96 *Ibid.*, p. 5.   97 Jones (ed.), *Imagist poetry*, p. 19.   98 *Ibid.*

The reputations of the two main voices of Great War poetry, Wilfred Owen and Isaac Rosenberg, were, however, built on posthumous post-war collections. Edith and Osbert Sitwell dedicated *Wheels 1919* to Owen, including seven of his poems in the anthology. In 1920, *Poems by Wilfred Owen*, edited by Edith Sitwell and introduced by Sassoon, was published by Chatto & Windus, with a second edition appearing the next year. Another poet and war veteran, Edmund Blunden, edited *The poems of Wilfred Owen* in 1931, adding notes and a memoir. *Poems by Isaac Rosenberg*, edited by Gordon Bottomley, with a memoir by Laurence Binyon, was published in 1922, to be followed in 1937 by *The collected works of Isaac Rosenberg: poetry, prose, letters, and some drawings*, edited by Bottomley and Denis Harding, with an introduction by Sassoon. Neither of these attracted the same notice as the volumes by Owen and it was not until the 1970s that Rosenberg was recognised as one of the most important voices of the war.

In the immediate post-war years, Monro's *The Monthly Chapbook (Poetry and Drama New Series)*, published in July 1919 and renamed from January 1920 *The Chapbook: A Monthly Miscellany*, featured a broad range of contemporary English verse: 'Imagist poems by H.D., Aldington and Flint, and more "modern" work still by Read and the Sitwells, to Georgian poems by Lawrence and de la Mare'.[99] Forty issues of the *Chapbooks* were published in all, but as Hibberd argues, they 'fell between two markets, appealing neither to the sort of readership catered for by the Poetry Society nor to the intellectuals who were to support *The Criterion*, the journal Eliot was to launch with [Monro's] help' in 1922.[100]

The 1920s was the apotheosis of high modernism: Pound's *Hugh Selwyn Mauberley* was published in 1920, *The waste land* in 1922, and W. B. Yeats's *The tower* in 1928. But modernism did not go unchallenged in the inter-war period. J. C. Squire was its staunchest adversary. Described as 'vehemently anti-modernist and anti-realist',[101] Squire edited the *London Mercury* from 1919 to 1934. Writers like Eliot and Virginia Woolf referred to his reign in the literary world as 'Squirearchy', denoting his conservatism and populism. Yet as Jonathan Rose and others have pointed out, while '[d]efensively, modernists styled themselves as uncommercial artists ... that pose was itself a marketing device: readers could purchase a sense of distinction by patronizing elite literature'.[102]

---

99 Hibberd, *Harold Monro*, p. 204.   100 *Ibid.*, p. 205.
101 Baldick, *The modern movement*, p. 91.   102 Rose, 'Lady Chatterley's broker', p. 184.

Eliot's role as editor of the poetry list of Faber & Faber from 1925 was a key factor in solidifying modernist poetry's hold over the literary landscape with the appearance of his own work and Pound's *Selected poems* (1928). In a speech of 1931 Geoffrey Faber laid the blame for the small market for poetry at the doors of the bookseller, asking: 'How many booksellers . . . make any effort at all to sell the verse of any modern poet except the half dozen or so whose names are universally known?'[103] His firm was nonetheless successful in making new names known and enhancing the profile of existing poets in cheap series such as the 'Ariel poems', illustrated pamphlets issued in card covers over 1927 to 1931.

Faber was especially instrumental in bringing to prominence the key voices of the 1930s, those who 'combined a modernity of subject matter, tone, and diction with an obvious respect for established verse forms both popular (ballad and song) and literary (sonnet, sestina, and villanelle)'.[104] The 1930s saw the publication of 'the last great monuments of high modernism',[105] including Yeats's *The winding stair* (1933) and *Full moon in march* (1935), issued by Macmillan, and Eliot's *Ash Wednesday* (Faber, 1930) and *Collected poems 1909–1935* (Faber, 1935), which featured the first of his *Four quartets* cycle (published 1945), *Burnt Norton*. Yet anthologies such as *New signatures* (1932) and *New country* (1933) and the journal *New Verse* (1933–39) helped to solidify an alternative 'Thirties' poetry, one that was more political, urgent and socially engaged, marked as the period was 'by economic depression, ascendant Fascism in Europe, and the alignment of young intellectuals with Communism and Popular Front movements',[106] especially played out on the battlefields of the Spanish Civil War (1936–39). *Poems for Spain* (1939), edited by Stephen Spender and John Lehmann, included many of those who volunteered in the International Brigades supporting the Spanish Republicans against General Franco. Although Yeats famously excluded Owen from his edition of the *Oxford book of modern verse* (1936) on the grounds that 'passive suffering is not a subject for poetry', poets of the 1930s, including Spender, Day Lewis, Louis MacNeice and W. H. Auden 'accorded him the status of saint and martyr'[107] – representative of all the innocent young men cut down by politicians and generals.

Through key works such as Auden's *Poems* (Faber, 1930), Spender's *Twenty poems* (Blackwell, 1930) and *Poems* (Faber, 1933), MacNeice's *Poems* (Faber,

103 Faber, *A publisher speaking*, p. 38.   104 Baldick, *The modern movement*, p. 103.
105 *Ibid.*   106 *Ibid.*, p. 105.
107 Jon Stallworthy, 'Wilfred Owen', *Oxford Dictionary of National Biography*, www .oxforddnb.com/index/37/101037828.

1935) and *Autumn journal* (Faber, 1939), and Day Lewis's *Collected poems 1929–1933* (Hogarth Press, 1935), the so-called Auden group stamped its authority on the 1930s scene partly by the force of the poets' prolific outputs and partly, as Adrian Caesar notes, by mutual critical appraisal: 'Spender, Day Lewis and MacNeice in their books, *The destructive element, A hope for poetry*, and *Modern poetry* respectively, all wrote in praise of Auden and of each other.'[108] Recent commentators have argued for a more nuanced understanding of the period. Caesar points to those who published in periodicals such as *Left Review* and *Poetry and the People*, including Montagu Slater, Edgell Rickword and Christopher Caudwell. Jane Dowson also challenges the 'orthodox accounts' centred on a 'generation of young men aged about thirty, joined by a common zeal to use poetry as a political loud hailer', and laments how women poets such as Elizabeth Daryush, Anne Ridler and Frances Cornford have been left out of the Auden generation narrative.[109]

As Auden's early publishing history attests, however, the role of Faber in shaping this narrative was crucial. His first Faber volume, *Poems*, issued in an edition of 1,000 copies at 2s 6d, was published on the same day (18 September 1930) as two other titles, *The ecliptic* by J. G. Macleod and *Pursuit* by P. P. Graves.[110] Faber advertised the three books as 'by the coming men' but this was to be Graves's only book of poetry, and while Macleod would go on to publish eight further volumes, none was issued by Faber. Auden's *Poems*, by contrast, reached a second edition in 1933 (with seven poems replaced by new verses). Though priced at five shillings, twice as much as the original edition, by the end of the decade it had sold some 4,000 copies, and by the end of the war over 6,000.[111] These are significant numbers considering the volume was in competition with a *Selected poems* issued in 1938 at just three shillings, which itself sold over 6,000 copies by 1944.[112] By the 1950s Auden was firmly established as one of Geoffrey Faber's 'universally' known names. Faber printed 12,000 copies of the *Collected shorter poems* across that decade, a figure that was nevertheless small compared to later poets whose appeal reached beyond the immediate audience for 'serious' poetry.[113]

The poets of the Second World War looked to those of the First for their models. But for many, especially Keith Douglas, who was killed in Normandy in 1944, the anxiety of influence was great: 'hell cannot be let loose twice: it was let loose in the Great War and it is the same old hell now . . . Almost all that a modern poet on active service is inspired to write, would be

---

108 Caesar, *Dividing lines*, p. 26.   109 Dowson, *Women's poetry of the 1930s*, pp. 3, 9.
110 Bloomfield and Mendelson, *W. H. Auden*, p. 5.   111 *Ibid.*, pp. 6–7.
112 *Ibid.*, pp. 33–4.   113 *Ibid.*, pp. 62–3.

tautological'.[114] Yet the Second World War produced poets of high calibre supported by several publishers other than Faber. Douglas's reputation as the pre-eminent poet of 1939–45 rests on *Alamein to Zem Zem* (1947), which was published by Editions Poetry London, an offshoot of the magazine *Poetry London: A Bi-Monthly of Modern Verse and Criticism*. Among titles published during the conflict, Hogarth issued Roy Fuller's *The middle of a war* (1942) and Allen & Unwin – more renowned for books on politics and social science – published Alun Lewis's *Raider's dawn* (1942) followed by the posthumous *Ha! ha! among the trumpets* (1945).

Sidney Keyes's volume *The iron laurel* (1942) suggested a promise that was solidified with the publication of *The cruel solstice* in 1943, the year of his death aged twenty-one in North Africa. His books were issued by Routledge, which also published Keidrych Rhys's *Poems from the Forces* (1941) and *More poems from the Forces* (1943), anthologies that featured both experienced and amateur poets, including serving members of the navy, army and air force. There were numerous other Forces anthologies, including *Poems of this war by younger poets* edited by Patricia Ledward and Colin Strang (Cambridge University Press, 1942); *Poems from the desert* by members of the Eighth Army (Harrap, 1944); *Air force poetry*, edited by John Pudney and Henry Treece (John Lane, 1944) and other titles from Forces stationed in Italy and India.

Periodical and small press publishing remained vital to poetry production, notwithstanding the economic pressures of wartime. *Horizon*, edited by Cyril Connolly, ran from 1940 to 1949 publishing poetry, fiction and essays on the arts. With a circulation that peaked at 9,500, it was originally priced at two shillings, dropping to 1s 6d in 1943. Reaching a wider circle of readers, however, was John Lehmann's *Penguin New Writing* which, it has been argued, 'did more than any other single agency to make war poems accessible to those involved in the war'.[115] Though in name (and to some extent in content) a continuation of the biannual 7s 6d hardback *New Writing* edited by Lehmann for John Lane from 1936, *Penguin New Writing* was in market terms entirely different. Issued monthly as a sixpenny paperback, the first number (December 1940) was 'a startlingly swift success', 80,000 copies having been sold by March 1941.[116] About half the magazine consisted of reprinted material from issues of *New Writing*, the rest was original work. Lehmann reported that Allen Lane was 'jubilant' at 'having found that what he had originally

---

114 Douglas, 'Poets in this war', p. 352.   115 Currey, *Poets of the war*, p. 37.
116 Lehmann, *I am my brother*, p. 105.

envisaged to some extent as a "prestige" publication was in fact making him a profit'.[117] Healthy payments were made to authors, and many of the leading writers of the thirties, including Auden, MacNeice and George Orwell, contributed. Spender wrote a monthly review article 'Books and the War'. Given the scarcity of raw materials, the success of the magazine was extraordinary. Five tons of paper was set aside to produce approximately 75,000 copies of each number. Although publisher and editor were faced with 'rapidly increasing difficulties of production and paper supply'[118] the magazine survived and an anthology, *Poems from New Writing*, was published in 1946.

Poetry, 1945–1970

As Robin Skelton has pointed out: 'Many of the contributors to the overseas anthologies and the many little magazines that appeared during the war never achieved anything but amateurish near-poems, and it seems that when the war was over a good many of them never wrote again.'[119] The poetry boom of the 1930s and 1940s quickly diminished. In 1946 the revamped twenty-seventh number of *Penguin New Writing* was issued in a print-run of 100,000 which, Lehmann estimated, 'could easily mean a readership of at least 250,000'.[120] That readership soon fell away, however as print-runs dropped to 80,000 in 1947 and 40,000 in 1949 – still, as Lehmann recalled, a figure most magazine editors would find 'intoxicating'.[121] *Penguin New Writing* ceased publication in 1950. Other important magazines of the inter-war period, including *Poetry Quarterly* and *Poetry London*, folded in the same decade.

Poetry publishing after the war nevertheless benefited from the expansion of media. Radio, television and gramophone records provided new outlets expanding the market for writers like Dylan Thomas. The first printing of 3,000 copies of Thomas's fourth collection *Deaths and entrances* (1946) sold out within a month, while his *Collected poems* (1952) sold 10,000 copies in the year that remained of his life, more than Auden's *Collected shorter poems* (1950) sold in a decade.[122] His success indicated a growing popular market for poetry which publishers began to exploit. John Betjeman was another poet whose media profile helped generate in his case quite spectacular sales. Like many others, Betjeman relied as a young writer on support from a close friend in publishing, Jock Murray of John Murray, who reportedly contributed £53 to

---

117 *Ibid.*   118 *Ibid.*, p. 160.   119 Skelton (ed.), *Poetry of the forties*, p. 23.
120 Lehmann, *The ample proposition*, p. 69.   121 *Ibid.*, p. 70.
122 FitzGibbon, *The life of Dylan Thomas*, p. 337.

the failure of Betjeman's first commercial volume *Continual dew* (1937).[123] Betjeman's early collections were small, elegant productions, reflecting the author's interest in Victorian book design, and usually appeared in two formats: an ordinary edition priced between five shillings and 7s 6d, and a more expensive limited edition printed on special paper. Although *New bats in old belfries* (1945) 'had to be reprinted after only a few months',[124] and *A few late chrysanthemums* (1954) had a print-run of 6,000 copies with 1,000 sold before publication[125] (significant figures for poetry), Betjeman's immense popular appeal did not arise until the *Collected poems* became the 'publishing phenomenon of 1958'.[126] The initial run of 9,000 copies sold out within a week, and the book was selling 1,000 a day in the early months, exceeding 50,000 after eight months.[127] Its success led the critic A. Alvarez to complain that 'a huge proportion of the English poetry-reading public' was 'living in some hazy pre-Prufrock Never-Never Land'.[128] (By 2008 the book had reached 2 million.) Betjeman's subsequent volumes now had a ready market and regularly appeared in lists of non-fiction best-sellers.

Betjeman's case was exceptional, but in the same year as *Collected poems* appeared Geoffrey Moore wrote in a British Council pamphlet: 'more poetry is being published in the nineteen fifties . . . than at any time since the war, despite the fact that the outlets are still so small'.[129] An important development was the Poetry Book Society, founded by T. S. Eliot in 1953 and supported, until 2011, by Arts Council funding. Subscribing members received four 'choices' per year, and it was estimated that between 1954 and 1978, when membership varied between 700 and 1,000, the Society distributed nearly 100,000 volumes of poetry.[130] Though tiny compared to fiction book clubs, the promise of guaranteed sales was an encouragement to poetry publishers.

Moore also pointed in his 1958 pamphlet to the importance of established literary magazines, such as the *Spectator*, *Encounter*, the *Listener* and *Time and Tide*; the 'numerous' prizes available; and the 'various small presses unconnected with the commercial publishers and established for the specific purpose of publishing poetry'.[131] The Hand and Flower Press, the Marvell Press, the Fantasy Press and the University of Reading Art School – 'which publishes mainly the young Oxford poets' – were among those cited. When Elizabeth Jennings was asked to update the pamphlet two years later,

123 Carpenter, *The seven lives*, p. 249.   124 *Ibid.*, p. 266.
125 Hillier, *New fame, new love*, pp. 493, 498.   126 *Ibid.*, p. 605.
127 Petersen, *John Betjeman*, p. 100.   128 Hillier, *The bonus of laughter*, p. 594.
129 Moore, *Poetry to-day*, p. 67.   130 White, *Poetry Book Society*, p. 7.   131 *Ibid.*

however, she noted how 'the last three years' had been marked 'by the virtual silence and standstill of a number of small presses which did much to establish the reputations of Thom Gunn, Thomas Blackburn, Charles Causley, and many others'. Several of those mentioned by Moore had disappeared, although the Marvell Press, which had had 'a tremendous critical and public success' with Philip Larkin's *The less deceived* in 1955, continued.[132]

Larkin's publishing history is characteristic of post-war poetry, beginning with small presses before being taken up by a larger publisher. His poems were not published by Faber until *The Whitsun weddings* in 1964, seventeen years after the firm had issued his second published novel. His first poetry volume appeared in 1945, priced at six shillings, by the Fortune Press, a shady outfit that refused to draw up an agreement. His second, *The less deceived* (1955), was issued by the Marvell Press, again at six shillings, on the ancient method of half-profits and initially sold on subscription. The volume was nevertheless widely reviewed and the 700 copies printed were quickly sold. The text had to be reset because the printers had broken up the type but a new paperback edition of 1,320 copies was printed (still priced at six shillings) and sold out within a year.[133] The success gave Larkin an entry into important poetry circles, as new outlets in magazines, anthologies and broadcasting opened up, along with American publication and eventually the move to Faber, where he could benefit from larger, swifter distribution. *The Whitsun weddings* sold 7,000 copies in little over a year; *High windows* (1974) over 12,000 in six months.[134] These two volumes did not appear in paperback until, respectively, seven and five years after hardback issue, and in print-runs that were not much greater than the hardback editions, suggesting that Faber perceived little market difference between the two formats. Nevertheless, *The Whitsun weddings* would sell over 100,000 paperback copies in Larkin's lifetime. After his death in 1985 a *Collected poems* (1988) sold over 40,000 copies before appearing in paperback in 1990.[135]

Outside of those few poets whose sales made them a commercial proposition to book publishers, the main market for poetry publishing continued to be small presses, magazines and anthologies. The range was immense. A recent study has revealed the diverse scale of the magazine market and the importance at different phases of time of the regions of England, as well as Scotland, Northern Ireland and Wales.[136] Anthologies have played an important part in establishing poetic movements. For example, the 'New

---

132 Jennings, *Poetry to-day*, p. 33.   133 Bloomfield, *Philip Larkin*, pp. 21–2.
134 *Ibid.*, pp. 27, 41.   135 *Ibid.*, pp. 64, 67.   136 Miller and Price, *British poetry magazines*.

Apocalyptic' poets were anthologised in *The new apocalypse* (1940) and other publications, and Robert Conquest's *New lines* (1956) helped launch the 'Movement', which included Larkin, Jennings, Kingsley Amis and Donald Davie. A second 'Movement' anthology appeared in 1963, the same year when poets of 'The Group' were collected in *The Group anthology* (1963). While such assemblages may do scant justice to the range and variety of British poetry, they demonstrate how perceptions of changing fashions and trends owe much to the contexts of publishing.

Poetry publishing flourished in the 1960s. Leading firms such as Faber, Oxford University Press, Routledge, Macmillan and Chatto (which started the Phoenix Living Poets in collaboration with the Hogarth Press) expanded their lists. The market was broadened by a widening school and university readership. Faber's 1962 joint paperback selection of Ted Hughes and Thom Gunn proved highly popular in schools, selling 'well over 100,000 copies' by 1981.[137] Perhaps the most adventurous publisher was Cape, which in the early 1960s published Derek Walcott's *In a green night* (1962) and volumes by the politically outspoken Adrian Mitchell. In 1965 the firm 'determined to invest' in poetry. Under the direction of the American poet Nathaniel Tarn, it 'conceived the notion of a little press within the framework of an established house', entering into partnership with the Goliard Press, which specialised in hand-set volumes of mostly avant-garde poetry.[138] The Cape Goliard Press was incorporated in 1967 and was a partnership of equals. As Howard recalls: 'we proposed that they should form an equal partnership with Cape which would give them the benefit of our sales organization, without hampering their independence'.[139] Alongside British poets like J. H. Prynne, Cape Goliard published the Americans Charles Olson and Allen Ginsberg as well as translations of European and Latin American poets. Published simultaneously in hardback and paperback, the success of the series 'helped to inspire' the series of large-format Cape Poetry Paperbacks which appeared from 1969.[140]

The most striking development in the 1960s, however, was Penguin's aggressive move into the market in 1962, signalled both by A. L. Alvarez's polemical *The new poetry* – which sold 10,000 copies in the first month and became 'a canonical schoolroom text for at least a quarter of a century'[141] – and by the inauguration of the Penguin Modern Poets series. Consisting of three poets, each represented by thirty poems, these paperback volumes

137 Morrison, 'Poetry and the poetry business', p. 102.
138 Howard, *Jonathan Cape*, p. 316.   139 *Ibid.*, p. 317.   140 *Ibid.*, p. 318.
141 Sheppard, *The poetry of saying*, p. 28.

were priced cheaply at 2s 6d. The first two sold out their initial print-runs of 30,000 copies within a few months. The tenth, subtitled *The Mersey sound* (1967), became a brand in its own right, popularising the Liverpool poets Adrian Henri, Roger McGough and Brian Patten. Lifted by Beatlemania, the volume 'brought "poetry down from the dusty shelf and onto the street"' with sales approaching a million by 2008.[142]

The 1960s also witnessed a significant increase in numbers of poetry magazines, facilitated by improved print technology. During the boom years of 1966–72 as many as forty or fifty new magazines appeared each year. A proliferation of titles from Cambridge contributed to the emergence of The 'Cambridge School' of poets, and the demographic range of production amounted to a 'radically decentralised form of publication', giving voice to the regional accents of British poetry.[143] Leading magazines of the decade, such as *Agenda* and *New Departures* (both commenced in 1959 and enduring into the twenty-first century) and the older *Stand*, promoted a renewed interest in modernism, embracing European and American poetic styles, often in explicit opposition to a perceived establishment tradition of 'English' poetry rooted in Larkin and the Movement. The British Poetry Revival, as it became known, 'readily took on the aura of an underground or subversive literature ... as likely to be sold on a street corner as through a conventional outlet'.[144] More crucial to the flowering of such poetry, however, was the spread of upmarket or alternative bookshops in London, such as Compendium, Indica and, especially, Better Books, which 'in its heyday was staffed by a number of poets, writers and editors associated with little magazines'.[145] Better Books was managed during the 1960s by the concrete poet Bob Cobbing, who in 1966 helped establish the Association of Little Presses, helping to coordinate methods of production and avenues of distribution.

Poetry post-1970

Wars over prevailing traditions and styles in the period led to accusations that modernist and postmodernist strains in contemporary poetry were being 'largely ignored by the agents of information and distribution', reviewers, universities and schools and 'the big controlling presses'.[146] These were exacerbated in the 1970s with claims of bias in Arts Council funding decisions.

142 Bowen, *A gallery to play to*, p. 1.
143 Miller and Price, *British poetry magazines*, p. 124.
144 Stevenson, *The last of England?*, p. 180.   145 *Ibid.*, p. 121.
146 Mottram, 'The British poetry revival', pp. 18, 15.

A publication entitled *Poets and the Arts Council of Great Britain* (1978) protested at how magazines such as *New Departures* and *Poetry Information* had repeatedly had their applications turned down, whereas an 'archetypal establishment' magazine like the *New Review* had received grants of up to £35,000 annually.[147]

Although the number of new magazines continued to rise in the 1970s, albeit at a reduced rate, global depression inevitably impacted on poetry publishing. The bankruptcy of Better Books in 1974 removed an important outlet for poetry, not just in stock of titles but in the regular hosting of events. In 1976 Penguin Modern Poets, now numbering twenty-six volumes, suspended publication (one further volume appeared in 1979). By the 1980s poetry publishing, like much of the trade, was perceived to be in crisis. In a 1981 issue of *Granta* subtitled 'Beyond the crisis', Blake Morrison observed that in 1980 there were fewer poetry books published than bibliographies. Most large publishers had reduced their lists, some relying on a single poet such as André Deutsch with Geoffrey Hill. Cape had moved into the 'popular and fashionable' with Clive James, while others including Allen Lane, Macmillan and Eyre Methuen published only anthologies – 'the one kind of poetry book which can normally be relied on to receive reasonably good sales and which has also some possibility of a deal with a book club'. Only three major publishers – Faber, OUP and Secker – had 'anything that could be called a poetry list', and Secker's output was only around eight books a year, with an average print-run of 500 and the bulk of sales to libraries. Of the £25,000 a year expended on poetry, the firm recouped about £15,000.[148]

Several smaller presses established during the boom years of the late 1960s managed to thrive in this period, however. John Fuller's Sycamore Press, which 'published more than fifty pamphlets and broadsheets between 1968 and 1992', became a forum for Oxford poets such as James Fenton.[149] Other presses established in the late 1960s, notably Anvil (founded 1968) and Carcanet (founded 1969), grew into larger operations and exerted a lasting influence on contemporary poetry into the new century. Anvil, which issued Carol Ann Duffy in the 1980s, produced around a dozen books annually in the 1970s 'with print runs of between 500 and 1,000 copies'.[150] Carcanet became a strong supporter of Scottish poetry. It sold 2,274 copies of Edwin Morgan's

---

147 *Ibid.*, p. 47.   148 Morrison, 'Poetry and the poetry business', pp. 100–1.
149 Sperling, 'Books and the market', p. 197. See also Roberts, *John Fuller and the Sycamore Press.*
150 Stevenson, *The last of England?*, p. 262.

From Glasgow to Saturn (1973) in just over a year (including 1,000 via the Poetry Book Society), a figure which publisher Michael Schmidt judged 'incredible'.[151] In 1980 Carcanet was publishing eighteen to twenty poetry titles a year.[152]

Like the Newcastle-based Bloodaxe, the success of Anvil and Carcanet largely depended upon Arts Council support which, it has been argued, 'was fundamental to poetry's survival during a period of particular difficulty in the 1970s and 1980s'.[153] Carcanet's publication of Morgan's 450-page *Poems of thirty years* (1982) was substantially underwritten by a grant of £950 from the Scottish Arts Council. Public funding allowed publishers like Carcanet to develop educational initiatives. In 1985 the firm launched the Poetry Signatures series with volumes by Morgan, Les A. Murray, Elizabeth Jennings and others. The series was 'partly aimed at the schools market' and included an introductory essay by the poet and an accompanying cassette of readings.[154] 'Accessibility to a young audience was a key factor' and influenced the chosen selection of the Morgan volume.[155]

A different kind of popular dissemination occurred in 1986 with the introduction of London Transport's 'Poems on the Underground' (with resulting anthologies), an example of poetry's printed life beyond the book. Whether such ventures had a direct effect on the market or not, it has been argued that poetry readership 'almost doubled' in the 1990s, with 2,700 volumes published annually by the end of the decade, a fourfold increase on the two previous decades.[156] New lists such as Picador (an imprint of Pan Macmillan) emerged, and in 1995 Penguin briefly revived its Modern Poets series. Success was spread very unevenly, however, with only a few poets achieving substantial sales. An Arts Council report at the end of the decade found that contemporary poetry made up only 3 per cent of the nearly 2 million poetry books bought each year. Furthermore, 90 per cent of the 3 per cent came from one imprint (Faber) and 67 per cent from one author (Seamus Heaney).[157] For all its apparent dominance of the market, Faber actually published only a handful of new volumes of contemporary poetry each year, relying mainly on its backlist of Eliot, Larkin, Ted Hughes etc. – the canonical face of twentieth-century poetry.

Trade publishers continued to show a wavering commitment to poetry. When OUP dropped its poetry list in 1998 it generated widespread media

151 McGonigal, *Beyond the last dragon*, p. 241.
152 Morrison, 'Poetry and the poetry business', p. 102.   153 *Ibid.*, p. 263.
154 McGonigal, *Beyond the last dragon*, p. 292.   155 *Ibid.*
156 Stevenson, *The last of England?*, p. 266.   157 Sperling, 'Books and the market', p. 192.

attention. Other trade imprints endured, however, notably Cape and Picador. The latter's poet-editor Don Paterson has reported that Picador's poetry volumes need to sell on average 1,500 copies to be commercially viable. Those that fall short can be cross-subsidised by bigger-selling titles, but as an imprint of a trade publisher without Arts Council support Picador must operate within 'the "strict economic constraint" of the "in-house account"',[158] and must pursue some titles that will make a profit.

Over the course of the period under review, the history of poetry publishing bears out Paterson's assertion that the activity is concerned more with a 'readership' than a 'market'.[159] As such, it continues to be affected more than other areas of literary publishing by state funding policies. In the 2011 Public Spending Review, Faber & Faber controversially received Arts Council funding of £40,000 to support its New Poets programme of pamphlets, readings and mentorship – controversial because it could easily fund such a programme from its own profits. The grants to Carcanet and Bloodaxe were barely changed but a number of small presses had their funding cut entirely.[160] So too did the Poetry Book Society, which received £105,000 annually during the 1980s. Further controversy followed when the Society turned to an investment company to fund the administration of its T. S. Eliot prize, inaugurated in 1993 and now the most prestigious poetry prize in the country.

If the terrain of poetry publishing remains subject to the vagaries of both market forces and funding policies, advances in digital technology have offered small presses more workable business models. The development of print-on-demand has enabled publishers to cut costs and expand the number of titles published. As Tony Francis of Shearsman Books described in 2006, in poetry publishing 'sales tend to occur in dribs and drabs over a longish period'. Thus in the traditional small-press model, where a print-run of 500 copies involves investment upfront, 'having stock sitting in boxes is tantamount to tying up large amounts of cash. In the p-o-d, or short-run-digital model, you spend only at the outset for what you need . . . The fact that the cash flow is freed up means that one can produce far more titles than would otherwise be possible.'[161] With chain bookshops stocking very little poetry, publishers like Shearsman rely chiefly on direct sales through their own websites and large online retailers like Amazon and the Poetry Bookshop Online (run by the Poetry Book Society), which claims to sell all the poetry

158 *Ibid.*, p. 206.   159 *Ibid.*, p. 208.   160 *Ibid.*, pp. 201–2.
161 'Tony Frazer Interview', *The Argotist Online*, www.argotistonline.co.uk/Frazer%20int erview.htm.

titles in print in the UK. As a niche product, poetry is well served by internet selling and what has become known as 'the long tail' in modern retailing.

Drama and theatre publishing

For much of the twentieth century there was a division in drama publishing between reading and acting editions. Samuel French (which can trace its origins to 1830) was the main supplier of acting editions for amateurs and professionals and also licensed performing rights.[162] A bookshop, which for long operated more like a library, survives in central London. The increased interest in amateur acting at the turn of the twentieth century led to an expansion in business when French claimed to be printing 50,000 plays a month.[163] A 'Guide to selecting plays', with advice on subject-matter and intended audience, was revised annually. In 1933 over 2,500 titles were available, at prices ranging from a guinea to 2s 8d. In addition to the text, older French editions contained extensive sections on scenery ('furniture and property plot'), effects and lighting. This often led to the page becoming cluttered with technical information and illustration, and over time the amount of practical material was cut back. In the 1960s, when trade editions were providing stiff competition, prices had risen to six shillings. Harold Pinter's *The caretaker* and *The birthday party* were issued in 1962 and 1965 in editions of 2,000 copies and reprinted thereafter as demand required.[164]

French's near monopoly on acting editions was briefly rivalled in the 1960s when the educational publishers Evans Brothers issued Evans Plays, including titles by John Osborne and Alan Ayckbourn. French took over Evans's list in the 1970s. By 1991 the French catalogue listed 4,000 plays. This figure declined in the new century but in 2015 the firm still handled around 2,000 titles and had nearly 1,600 acting editions in print.[165] With offices in London, New York and Hollywood, it continues to provide licences and copyright advice for amateur and professional performances via its website, which offers a 'search-a-play' facility.

Outside these acting editions lay a largely separate market for reading editions of plays. Most of the major dramatists of the first half of the century, such as Maugham, Priestley and Galsworthy, were also novelists and their plays were printed by their fiction publishers. Duckworth issued Galsworthy

---

162 Michel, 'Samuel French'.   163 *Truly yours*, p. 9.
164 Baker and Ross, *Harold Pinter*, pp. 6, 14.   165 www.samuelfrench-london.co.uk.

in hardback and paperback, and in the late 1920s Hodder & Stoughton produced J. M. Barrie's plays in a uniform edition alongside his fiction.

A new development in play publishing was introduced by Victor Gollancz, who inaugurated the Contemporary British Dramatists series at Ernest Benn in 1923, publishing several Noel Coward plays including *The vortex* (1925). Printed in duodecimo format in paper or card covers at 3s 6d or cloth at five shillings, the series numbered over fifty within three years. Shortly after he established his own firm, Gollancz secured the rights to R. C. Sherriff's war play *Journey's end* (1929) – a huge box-office success in the theatre – selling it in paper and hard covers at the same price as the Benn series. Its success convinced Gollancz of a substantial market for contemporary drama.[166] In the same year his firm began a series of omnibus volumes of six of the most successful West End plays of the previous twelve months. Priced at 7s 6d (equivalent to a novel), the first, *Famous plays of to-day*, included *Journey's end*. The second was entitled *Six plays* (1930) before the series name took root with *Famous plays of 1931*. In the 1932 volume Gollancz announced that the printing of the original title was into its thirty-eighth thousand. The series was suspended after 1939 and only resumed in 1953 with *Famous plays of 1951–1952*, which proved to be one of only three further volumes; it ended in 1954 with a volume that included Agatha Christie's *Witness for the prosecution*.

The Gollancz initiative was followed to lesser effect by Elek Books which launched *Plays of the year* in 1949. Two volumes of four plays appeared annually. Edited by J. C. Trewin, the series featured largely minor dramatists, although two titles by John Mortimer appeared in the seventeenth volume (1958). The books offered good measure – some running to over 500 pages – but were expensive at twenty-five shillings. In spite of considerable success in 1972 with the scripts of the television play-cycle *The six wives of Henry VIII*, production dropped to a single annual volume and ended in 1981.

Along with Gollancz, the main mid-century publisher of drama was Heinemann, which began the Drama Library in 1948. Consisting of reprints of classical and modern plays, and, later, new work by contemporary authors, the series featured Robert Bolt's *A man for all seasons* (1960) which 'sold over two million copies in the UK version'.[167] Over fifty titles were available by the mid-1960s, but at 10s 6d they were expensive compared to rival paperback series like Penguin's New English Dramatists, which in 1963 was offering Bolt's play as part of a collection for just 4s 6d.

---

166 80,000 copies had been sold by 1970. Hodges, *Gollancz*, pp. 47–8.
167 St John, *William Heinemann*, p. 382.

The growth of paperbacks suited the shorter length of drama publications. In 1939 George Bernard Shaw's *Back to Methuselah* became the two-hundredth Penguin. Seven years later Penguin celebrated the playwright's ninetieth birthday by publishing ten of his plays in editions of 100,000 copies. The entire million sold out within six weeks.[168] Paperback play publishing did not really take off until the late 1950s, however, when the expansion of drama teaching in schools and universities enlarged the market for cheap texts. Although output remained small – Stevenson claims that only 'around 100 titles appeared annually in the 1960s and 1970s'[169] – the 'revolution' in the theatre that followed the production of John Osborne's *Look back in anger* in 1956 fuelled wider public interest. Penguin's launch of the New English Dramatists in 1959, developed by the influential editor Tom Maschler, was a landmark event. The first volume, priced at 3s 6d, contained plays by Doris Lessing, Bernard Kops and Arnold Wesker, and eventually sold over 200,000 copies.[170] 'In those days', recalls Giles Gordon who edited Penguin's list in the late 1960s, 'the sale of plays was reasonably big business.'[171]

Maschler's close friendship with emerging dramatists (notably Wesker) ensured that ground-breaking new drama became available at cheap prices. In 1960 Wesker's early titles could be bought in single volumes in the Penguin Modern Playwrights series for just 2s 6d, and half a million copies of his *Trilogy* were eventually sold in the Penguin Plays series.[172] Maschler was not the only important sponsor of drama in this period. At Faber, Charles Monteith established a list that included Osborne, Ayckbourn and Samuel Beckett, while at the more expensive end of the market John Calder started his Playscripts series in 1967, issuing the work of British and European playwrights in hardback and paperback.

The leading publisher of drama since the 1950s, however, has been Methuen, which entered the field with Brendan Behan's *The quare fellow* (1956) and Shelagh Delaney's *A taste of honey* (1958), a paperback original.[173] The list expanded rapidly in the 1960s, and the Methuen Modern Plays series, which published original work in paperback and hardback as it appeared in the theatres, numbered fifty by the late 1960s and over a hundred by 1979. A combined edition of 7,500 copies of Pinter's *The caretaker* (1960) appeared in hardback at 10s 6d and paperback at 3s 6d. Sales of the latter soared, with over

168 Hare, *Penguin portrait*, p. 76.   169 Stevenson, *The last of England?*, p. 152.
170 Maschler, *Publisher*, p. 48.   171 Gordon, *Aren't we due a royalty statement?*, p. 85.
172 *Ibid.*   173 Duffy, *A thousand capricious chances*, p. 138.

25,000 copies printed in 1966 alone, fuelled by the university market and a general readership.[174]

From the 1970s Methuen concentrated on paperback publishing, and over the ensuing decades issued a bewildering number of series. The omnibus volumes of individual playwrights which began in the mid-1970s have appeared variously as the Master Playwrights series, Methuen World Dramatists and Methuen Contemporary Dramatists. In addition there was Methuen Theatre Classics and Methuen World Classics containing plays by classical, European, and British and Irish dramatists from Euripides to Synge. In the 1970s there was briefly Methuen Young Drama, while Methuen Student Editions, with commentary and notes, appeared from the early 1980s. When the Methuen Drama imprint was acquired in 2006 by A. & C. Black, a subsidiary of Bloomsbury, it had over 700 titles in print. In 2012 the imprint's website listed around 150 omnibus volumes in the Contemporary Dramatists series and almost 500 individual titles marketed under Modern Plays. In addition to the Arden Shakespeare (see below), other series included Modern Classics (key twentieth-century plays), Classical Dramatists, and World Classics (containing American and European plays), as well as anthologies and student editions, making it the largest performing arts list in Europe.

Methuen participated in an important development in play publishing in 1981 with the launch of the Royal Court Writers series. Under its influential new artistic director Max Stafford Clark, the Royal Court Theatre issued cheap editions of the texts of its productions which, as early covers explained, fulfilled the 'dual role of programme and playscript'. Methuen had experimented with this form in 1965 with the Methuen Playscripts series and Methuen's New Theatrescripts, which listed over 100 titles by the mid-1980s. These series, printed in double columns with a flimsy paper cover, aimed 'to bridge the gap between the appearance of a new play in the theatre and its appearance in script form' (cover blurb). The Royal Court series, however, which was soon followed by the National Theatre, brought print and performance even closer together, raising the profile of contemporary dramatists, especially women playwrights such as Sarah Daniels and Caryl Churchill. The practice of publishing play texts in editions which double as programmes (and appear in theatre bookshops) is now common throughout British theatres. In these editions the name of the publisher and copyright information often appears at the end of the book, or after the preliminary

---

174 Baker and Ross, *Harold Pinter*, pp. 9–10.

programme matter. With texts of the plays needing to be printed in advance of final rehearsal, some editions carry a statement that the script sold as a programme might not correspond fully with the acted performance.

Methuen's main rivals in the twenty-first century have been the independent firms Oberon and Nick Hern. Both publish modern plays, omnibus volumes, classics, children's drama and books on theatrical topics. Hern, formerly drama editor at Methuen, set up his own imprint under the aegis of Walker Books in 1988.[175] The imprint was taken over by Random House but became a fully independent company in 1993 when Hern purchased the list. In 2012 the website listed over 1,000 plays and theatre books. Like Methuen, the company also provides licences for amateur performance via a 'Plays to perform' website.

The advent of digital media has begun to transform play publishing. Bloomsbury's acquisition of Methuen led to the development of online publications making imaginative use of interactive media. In 2012 the Publishers Communications Group launched Drama Online, a new resource for teaching and study that brought together the lists of Methuen Drama, the Arden Shakespeare and Faber & Faber. Nick Hern joined the platform in 2014. Aimed principally at the school and university markets, Drama Online publishes annotated texts, scholarly notes, critical analyses, contextual information, and acting and backstage guides, along with additional interactive media to aid the reading experience.[176] With this new electronic initiative, acting and reading editions of plays have been drawn even closer together.

Shakespeare publishing

As with fiction and poetry, much drama publishing in the twentieth century consisted of new editions of older dramatists. Shakespeare publishing was an industry in itself. Several cheap Shakespeare editions from the nineteenth century proved remarkably enduring. Cambridge's Pitt Press Shakespeare, dating from 1890, lasted beyond the 1960s – 100,000 copies of *A midsummer night's dream* were issued between 1917 and 1936, and 60,000 copies of *Macbeth* were printed in the series in 1965 alone.[177] Another 1890s product, the Temple Shakespeare, was revived by its publisher Dent as the New Temple Shakespeare in 1934, with volumes priced at two shillings. The schools market

175 www.nickhernbooks.co.uk.   176 www.dramaonlinelibrary.com.
177 Murphy, *Shakespeare in print*, p. 186.

became increasingly important. Nelson issued individual plays at sixpence in its paper-covered Teaching of English series.

More scholarly was the first Arden series published by Methuen. Commenced in 1899, this was almost complete by 1914, when volumes were priced at 2s 6d. The outstanding seven titles were published by 1924. When a second series was launched in 1951 at the relatively more expensive price of fifteen to eighteen shillings, Shakespeare publishing had been transformed by developments in bibliography and textual editing. Cambridge University Press's New Shakespeare (1921–66), edited by Arthur Quiller-Couch and John Dover Wilson, was the first series to be rigorously edited according to the standards of the 'New Bibliography'.[178] The initial price was a relatively expensive six shillings, and by the 1960s volumes cost twenty-five shillings, the same as a new novel.

There were cheaper options. Penguin's entry into the market in 1937 offered a bridge between scholarly and popular Shakespeare. Priced at sixpence, the volumes in the Penguin Shakespeare were aimed at a wider audience than Arden and the New Shakespeare, but with brief but informative introductions and a section on Shakespeare's theatre the series fulfilled Allen Lane's mission of educating the masses. Eighteen titles appeared in the first year but the series was interrupted by the war and not resumed until 1947. It was completed in 1959.[179]

It was not until 1957 that Cambridge responded to Penguin's challenge when it began the Pocket Shakespeare. Texts were based on the New Shakespeare but shorn of the scholarly apparatus. At five shillings they were around a quarter of the price of the academic editions but still twice as expensive as Penguin, which retailed at 2s 6d at this time. With the expansion of paperback publishing throughout the book market, however, Methuen and Cambridge were soon forced into changing their policies. When Ardens began appearing in paperback at 7s 6d from 1966, Cambridge quickly followed, slightly undercutting its rival with editions at five shillings and six shillings.

The launch of the New Penguin Shakespeare in 1967 indicated how the gap between popular and scholarly editions had narrowed even further. Like Arden and the New Shakespeare, Penguin's new series was produced with close attention to current developments in textual scholarship. Introductions and notes were lengthened and the initial price of six shillings was a significant increase in real terms from its predecessor, though still

178 Ibid., chapter 10.   179 [Williams], The Penguin story, p. 119.

fractionally cheaper than Arden. In the 1980s, Penguin editions carried an endorsement from the Royal Shakespeare Company.

The range of Shakespearean audiences led individual publishers to produce multiple series aimed at different market sectors. The Oxford School Shakespeare began in the late 1970s. It was joined in 1991 by the Cambridge Schools Shakespeare, which in the new century developed to include visual, multimedia and web content. One of the most commercially successful single volumes of the century was *The Complete Works of Shakespeare* issued by Collins in 1951, edited by Peter Alexander. At fifteen shillings (the same as a single Arden title) the book was remarkably cheap, albeit printed in double columns on a cramped page. Sales were boosted in the late 1970s when the text was used for the BBC television performance of the complete plays. The Alexander Text, as it became known, was widely adopted in universities, and in 1978 was reported to be selling 'roughly 10,000 copies a year'.[180]

Since the 1980s the publishing of Shakespeare in single-volume and collected format has been heavily influenced by – and has helped to influence – developments in textual theory and authorship attribution. Radical new versions of Shakespeare such as that presented by OUP in single volumes from 1982 and in *The complete works* (1986) and its accompanying *Textual companion* volume (1987) sparked complex and controversial debates.[181] The ever-changing scholarly landscape repeatedly drove publishers into producing new or revised editions. In 1984, shortly after the first volumes in the Oxford series emerged, Cambridge launched a rival series, the New Cambridge Shakespeare. A third series of the Arden edition commenced in 1995. In 2017 the New Oxford Shakespeare was published.[182] Marketed as 'an entirely new consideration of all of Shakespeare's works', it appeared as three interconnected print publications: a single-volume *Modern critical edition* 'for undergraduates, lecturers, actors, play-lovers'; a two-volume *Critical reference edition*; and a separate *Authorship companion*. In addition, marketed as 'for all users', all of the print materials were made available in 'one integrated online home': the New Oxford Shakespeare online. The future development of digital publishing environments promises to keep the proverbial and ubiquitous 'new' safely attached to Shakespeare publishing.

---

180 Murphy, *Shakespeare in print*, p. 242.
181 For a helpful summary, see *ibid.*, chapter 11.
182 See information on OUP website: http://global.oup.com.

9

Children's books

PETER HUNT AND LUCY PEARSON

Introduction

On 1 April 1914, Oxford University Press took full control of their joint venture in children's publishing from Hodder & Stoughton. This was an incongruous departure for a prestigious university press (and was still being questioned by the university authorities in 1967) but one that was characteristic of the paradoxes of a century which saw (at a conservative estimate) over 250 British publishing houses try their hand at children's books.[1] These included many whose contemporary lists have nothing to do with children's fiction – for example, Basil Blackwell's prestigious 'annual' *Joy Street* (1923–35) was briefly in competition with Longman's *Children's play-hour book*.

Although children's books are virtually invisible in histories of publishing – John Feather's *A history of British publishing* has only two direct references – their cultural and commercial importance through the period was enormous. They tend to track adult preoccupations, but because of their symbiotic relationship with adulthood have had a strong strain of conservatism: George Orwell's famous condemnation of boys' weeklies in 1940 as perpetuating the social and political attitudes of 1910 maintained its truth for many children's books well into the 1960s.[2] However, they also provide a site for subversion for adult writers, and have been at the cutting edge of political radicalism and multimedia experimentation. Commercially, they have been the mainstay of many companies – notably Penguin – and by the end of the century, with more than 8,000 new titles each year, and J. K. Rowling's Harry Potter series smashing all publishing records, children's books had become a dominant part of the book market.

---

1 Sutcliffe, *The Oxford University Press*, p. 147. See also p. 282.   2 Orwell, 'Boys' weeklies'.

They also differ significantly from adults' books: the distinction of high-, middle- and lowbrow lists is less clear, different types (picture books, movable books, cross-media texts, the annual) and genres (fantasy, animal stories, family stories) are more important, and gender distinctions are much more fundamental. The price of children's books has traditionally been kept low, and the market is strongly influenced by government policy, as with the growth of school libraries in the 1960s, or reports such as Plowden's *Children and their primary schools* (1967) and Bullock's *A language for life* (1975).

1914–1939

In 1932 Lionel McColvin wrote in the *Library Association Record* that there were 'a few admirable books [for children] ... submerged in an ocean of terrible trash ... books written by hacks, slovenly, often ignorantly ... And the publication equals the matter. In every respect – paper, printing, illustrations – most of these juvenile books are disgraceful.'[3] This view of children's publishing in the first part of the twentieth century was to dominate many of the accounts which came after; Marcus Crouch's assertion that the exigencies of war and its aftermath produced books which were 'derivative and stale' is characteristic of the general tone of criticism on this period.[4] As Dennis Butts has observed, this consensus is rather belied by the number of 'classic' titles published during this period, which included such iconic figures as Winnie-the-Pooh, Bilbo Baggins, Dr Dolittle, Little Grey Rabbit, the Swallows and the Amazons, William Brown, Milly-Molly-Mandy and Mary Poppins.[5] While conservative, poorly produced books for children were certainly prevalent, there was also space for radical innovation.

One area which has been widely recognised as thriving during this period is periodical publishing: such was the dominance of comics and family magazines in the children's story market that 'in the article "Writing for the Juvenile Market" in the 1930 edition of *The Writers' and Artists' Year Book*, the author does not bother to mention traditional book publishers – only comics, magazines and annuals.'[6] Comics were well established by 1914, and were dominated by Amalgamated Press titles such as *Puck* (1904–40) and *The Rainbow* (1914–56); their main rivals were D. C. Thompson of Dundee whose 'big five' story papers for boys, *Rover, Wizard, Hotspur, Adventure* and *Skipper*, appeared from 1922, followed by *Dandy* (1937) and *Beano* (1938). As far

3 Ellis, *A history*, p. 160.   4 Crouch, *The Nesbit tradition*, p. 17.
5 Butts, *Children's literature*, p. 120.   6 Wace, *From Carroll to Crompton*, p. 251.

as books were concerned, the 'rewards' and the 'annuals' dominated the market: Collins had published their first *Children's annual* in 1914 – 'forerunner of a long series of similar publications'.[7] Some, like *The Felix annual: the comic adventures of Felix the film cat* (Hulton, c. 1920) were derived from the cinema; others featured characters from newspaper strips, like Pip, Squeak and (in separate volumes) Wilfred from the *Daily Mirror*, or Rupert Bear. Rupert appeared in the *Daily Express* from 8 November 1920 as a rival to Teddy Tail (the first British newspaper strip, in the *Daily Mail* from 1915), and featured in annuals from 1936 onwards, selling over 1.5 million copies each year. (Rupert was drawn by Mary Tourtel to 1935 and Alfred Bestall to 1965.)

The ubiquitous 'rewards' were a curious phenomenon, printed as they were on 'featherweight antique' paper (70 per cent air) or on what amounted to thin card. Publishers (of a kind) liked this paper 'because it made a 100-page book look like two hundred, and printers hated it because its loose composition meant that fluff and dust constantly clogged their machines, which necessitated slower running and additional washing-up'.[8] It was not only the mass-market publishers, such as Dean & Son and the Amalgamated Press, who produced these bloated books: one of the major players was Oxford University Press (that is, Humphrey Milford in London), under the editorial eyes of 'Herbert Strang' and 'Mrs Herbert Strang', pseudonyms of the two editors of the old joint venture – the 'heavenly twins', Herbert Ely and C. J. L'Estrange – who ruthlessly recycled both text and images.[9] A typical example might be *The great book of school stories for boys* (1932) which advertises thirteen others in the Great Books series. This, a modest volume by the standards of the day, was nearly 5 cm thick, and contained 144 (unpaginated) pages (four 36-page gatherings plus one single-sided semi-gloss three-colour sheet bound in for each gathering). By comparison, *Harry Potter and the deathly hallows* (2007), of virtually the same thickness, has 605 pages. Given the age of some of the stories in these books, many dating back to at least 1918, it is unsurprising that many critics felt that children's books had a curiously ambivalent relationship to real life. Left-wing writer and critic Geoffrey Trease observed that novelists writing for adults

> did not depict war as glorious or the British as a superior race. Children's books had kept the pre-war outlook. There must be many 'progressive parents' (blessed phrase) who had acquired children somehow, in spite of the current vogue for contraception and abortion, and who felt uneasy at

7 Keir, *The house of Collins*, p. 232. 8 Wace, *From Carroll to Crompton*, p. 251.
9 Hogarth, 'Children's publishing in the 1930s', p. 55.

putting them to bed with Herbert Strang or Percy Westerman while they went off to a meeting of the I.L.P. [Independent Labour Party] or the League against Imperialism.[10]

On the other hand, some of the most lasting best-sellers of the period were produced in a spirit of pacifism and retreatism in the wake of the Great War, such as Hugh Lofting's Dr Dolittle series, brought from the USA by Cape in 1922. One of the biggest sellers was A. A. Milne's *When we were very young*, 'an astounding success' in 1924, lifting Methuen's profits to a new record.[11] Milne was in fact only one of Methuen's stable; books such as Rose Fyleman's *Gay go up* (1929) illustrated in the Shepard style by Decie Merwin (1929) or E. V. Lucas's *Playtime and company* (1925) illustrated by Shepard, were virtually indistinguishable from each other. Other publishers, however, were offering more diverse fare. Kimberly Reynolds has shown that Geoffrey Trease was far from alone in seeking more radical books for children: one notable actor in this area was Victor Gollancz. One of the founders of the Left Book Club for adults, Gollancz extended the same left-wing ethos to his publishing for children; indeed, two of his children's titles were offered for sale through the Left Book Club.[12] Gollancz was not alone in publishing children's books with a radical bent: Reynolds lists over seventy titles published in the period 1910–39 which she classes as demonstrating 'social/political radicalism' or 'aesthetic radicalism', including many from mainstream publishers including J. M. Dent, Routledge and Heinemann. Far from seeking to perpetuate the attitudes of the past, these radical children's books, Reynolds suggests, 'sought to play down ideas of nationhood, empire, military might, and individual achievement, and to instil in readers a sense of connection between the peoples of the world and an awareness of the benefits of sharing resources and solving problems collaboratively'.[13]

Periodicals also offered some more radical fare: Arthur Mee's *The Children's Newspaper* (1919–65) reported on such issues as the rise of fascism, the Spanish Civil War and Stalinism.[14] Mee's other major achievement (also with the Amalgamated Press) was *The children's encyclopaedia*, which has been described as 'the wonder book of the twentieth century in the history of book-publishing'.[15] It was first published in fifty fortnightly parts (1908–10) and was an immediate success; by 1946 it had sold in book form well over 5 million copies. Despite challenges from Cassell's *Children's book of*

10 Trease, *Tales out of school*, p. 21.   11 Duffy, *A thousand capricious chances*, p. 77.
12 Reynolds, *Left out*, p. 13.   13 *Ibid.*, p. 199.
14 Avery, 'Popular education and big money', p. 241.
15 Hammerton, *Child of wonder*, p. 121.

knowledge (seven volumes, 1924–26) and Odham's *The wonderland of knowledge* (twelve volumes, 1933) and others, it survived to be reissued in 1953 and 1964, but by then it had been superseded by newer formats such as the *Oxford junior encyclopaedia* (1949–).[16]

Just as the emergence between the wars of primers such as the Beacon Readers (1922) depended on government literacy policy, so the considerable output of non-fiction for children was initially stimulated by reports such as Sir Henry Hadow's *The education of the adolescent* (1926). This recommended that 'children should be trained not only to appreciate good general litera-ture, but also to read books relating to such subjects as engineering, garden-ing, housecraft, physical education and games', and educationalists felt that 'unless that habit of consulting books for information became automatic it could not be claimed that children had been taught to read'.[17] Publishers such as Evans, Pitman, Collins, Cassell and Batsford responded enthusiastically: one of the most successful series was Dent's Modern Science (from 1930), including books such as Eric Holmyard's *Chemistry for beginners* (1930). Possibly the most influential book of all was Victor Gollancz's *An outline for boys and girls and their parents*, edited by Naomi Mitchison in 1932. Marcus Crouch comments: 'for the first time in factual literature children were treated as sensible, responsible beings', and the expert writers included W. H. Auden, Hugh Gaitskell and Richard Hughes.[18] Crouch's evaluation overlooks the controversial nature of the *Outline*, however, which was far from universally lauded at the time of publication. The flagship title for Gollancz's left-wing publishing for children, it aimed to show 'how power and knowledge and order are organised, and how the organisation can be altered', and it was the target of much criticism from conservative institutions.[19] Nonetheless, under the influence of the School Library Association and the Schools Section of the Library Association (both founded in 1937), the quality and attractiveness of non-fiction increased; the distinction between school and home reading materials was eroded to the point that three Carnegie Medals, for the best children's book of the year, were won by non-fiction titles. All three also reflected a more politically radical or at least future-orientated outlook: Eleanor Doorly's *Radium woman: a life of Marie Curie for the young* (1939) emphasised both feminist ideals and Polish nation-alism; Agnes Allen's *The story of your home* (1949) not only traces the devel-opment of homes throughout history, but asks its young readers to imagine

16 Hancock (ed.), *A guide*, pp. xviii–xix.   17 Ellis, *A history*, pp. 152, 154.
18 Crouch, *Treasure seekers and borrowers*, p. 81.   19 Quoted in Reynolds, *Left out*, p. 24.

how homes might respond to the demands of the future; and Edward Osmond's *A valley grows up* (1953) shows the value of change as well as continuity in its fictional history of an English valley.

The movable, or the pop-up book as we now know it, was introduced in 1929 when S. Louis Girard and Theodore Brown patented a 'folded paper device' in which models sprang upwards from the pages of a book by themselves. (Movable books of the pre-war period, characterised by the work of Lothar Meggendorfer, and the publishers Ernest Nister and Dean & Son, had been generally two-dimensional, or had to be erected by hand.) Girard provided the pop-ups for some of the first of the *Daily Express* annuals (1929–30) which featured Rupert Bear. From 1936 until his death in 1950 Girard independently published the Bookano series, with print-runs of between 10,000 and 50,000; the books were ingeniously engineered, but used 'coarse, absorbent paper [and] crude photolitho printing'.[20] Since the 1940s, when approximately ninety movables were published, the numbers have rapidly increased (passing 800 in the 1980s), with the help of outsourcing production to third world countries.[21]

There were important changes in the production of picture books; apart from some involvement with the small-press, fine-art movement during the 1920s 'most children's book illustration was prepared for printing by letter-press – line drawings were converted photomechanically into line blocks to print with the text, colour was reproduced by three or four-colour halftone, or by colour line-blocks, all printing from a raised surface'.[22] The groundbreaking work of William Nicholson, notably with *Clever Bill* (1926) which combined illustrations and handwritten script, was developed in what was perhaps the first mass-market lithographed book, Edward Ardizzone's *Little Tim and the brave sea captain*, published by Grace Hogarth at Oxford University Press in 1936. The book was produced as a 64-page folio which 'had both the hand-lettered text and colour pictures printed on one side only of each leaf, so that, like the Potter books, there were blank pages at regular intervals'; this was partly to justify its price of 7s 6d, as well as helping the drying of the ink in the 'hot, humid summer of New York in 1935'.[23]

British artists were influenced by books by European, Russian and American artists – for example, Marjorie Flack's *Angus and the ducks* (1933), and Dr. Seuss's *And to think I saw it on Mulberry Street* (1937) which was admired by Beatrix Potter in 1938. Kathleen Hale, Jean de Brunhoff and

---

20 Dawson, 'S. Louis Giraud', p. 90.　21 Fox, 'Movable books', p. 87.
22 Alderson, 'Some notes on children's book illustration', pp. 55–6.
23 Whalley and Chester, *A history*, p. 189; White, *Edward Ardizzone*, p. 134.

Ardizzone, all working with laborious and intricate hand-separation, 'can be said to have pioneered the full-colour picture books we know today'.[24] Hale's *Orlando the marmalade cat*, de Brunhoff's *Babar* (both 365 × 265 mm) and *Little Tim* were all 'oversize' books: *Babar* was taken by Methuen, 'rather against their will, because they didn't think books that shape were a very good idea. For that reason *Orlando* ... was turned down, only to become a bestseller elsewhere.' That 'elsewhere' was *Country Life*: its editor, Noel Carrington, 'the pivotal figure in children's publishing in the 1930s, fell in love with it but realized that in seven colours it was a totally uneconomic proposition. He showed it to Geoffrey Smith of Cowell's [the printers] who said the colours must be reduced to four. They were.'[25]

The financial situation of authors can be gauged by two examples. Blackie had published Percy F. Westerman's first book, *A lad of grit*, in 1908, and Westerman had gone on to be possibly the most popular children's writer between the wars, turning out an average of thirty-eight books per decade in the 1920s and 1930s. In 1927 Blackie pulled off an unlikely coup by persuading him to sign a lifetime contract, specifying single payments of £150 for books of 83,000 words, £100 for 70,000, and £70 for 42,000. In contrast, at the upper end of the market, Cape gave Arthur Ransome an advance of £100 for his idea for a children's book – *Swallows and Amazons*. It was sold to Lippincott for $600 in 1931, and by March had sold 1,656 copies: 'Wren Howard [Cape's partner] regarded this as satisfactory. Ransome did not. "Until I can get into the 3,000 sales there will be small chance of making a living out of books. Once you get among the people who sell 3,000 regularly things are all right, and you have only to hold your mouth open for windfalls."' Ransome's income from writing first exceeded £1,000 in 1934 and rose to £2,066 13s 6d in 1938.[26]

Ransome's books were part of a fashion for 'camping and tramping'; other notable examples were Garry Hogg's Explorer novels (1938–40) and M. E. Atkinson's Lockett series (1936–49). There were well over 200 guiding books from publishers such as Epworth, Partridge, Sheldon Press, J. F. Shaw and Chambers published in the 1920s and 1930s, and this was also the 'heyday of schoolgirls' fiction' and the beginning of the pony book.[27] Numbers of new titles declined steadily in the 1930s, from 1,490 in 1934 to 1,303 in 1939 but, paradoxically (and possibly because of the success of libraries),

---

24 Moss, 'Kathleen Hale and Orlando the Marmalade Cat', p. 123; Duffy, *A thousand capricious chances*, p. 104.
25 Duffy, *A thousand capricious chances*, p. 104.
26 Brogan, *The life of Arthur Ransome*, pp. 305, 316, 317, 350.
27 Thomas, *True to the trefoil*, pp. 183–92. See also Cadogan and Craig, *You're a brick, Angela!*

'the market would have become glutted if the Second World War had not broken out in 1939, for by then the supply was just beginning to outrun the demand'.[28]

1939–1945

The war is often seen as a turning point for children's literature: vast stocks were destroyed by enemy action and afterwards publishers (generally) chose not to reprint outdated books. In fact, children's books did rather well. In figures given in the *Bookseller*, in 1939 there were 4,222 volumes of fiction published (the first of its thirteen categories), and 1,303 children's books (a third of its categories, after education). By 1944 the figures were 1,255 and 785, and children's books were the second-largest category.[29] The same impulse that made 'comforting' adult books popular applied to children's books: sales of A. A. Milne's five children's titles rose from 29,764 in the first six months of 1940 to 41,660 in the first six months of 1941; when, later, Methuen was rationed to binding 500 copies a week, it estimated that it could easily have sold 1,000.[30]

Paper rationing imposed in 1940 as 60 per cent of publishers' 1938–39 consumption was reduced on 1 January 1942 to 37.5 per cent, although under the Book Production War Economy Agreement of 1 January 1942, children's books were allowed to continue to use heavier papers than adults'.[31] And it was not only paper that was a problem: Ransome noted in 1942 that Cape had the paper for 25,000 copies of *The Picts and the martyrs* – 'and they have also (even more difficult) got the zinc for making the blocks'.[32] Perhaps the most ingenious way of saving paper was found by Ernest Roker, manager of the Brockhampton Press, an imprint set up by Hodder in 1938 to dispose of overstocks of theological works. He was given permission in 1940 to publish children's books; he bought off-cuts from the magazine *Picture Post*, and commissioned Enid Blyton to write texts for two-colour picture strips to fit three-inch by six-inch pamphlets. By 1942, 10,000 copies of *Mary Mouse and the doll's house* had been sold at one shilling each, and the series went on to sell over 4 million by 1970.[33] Blyton was one of the success stories

28 Ellis, *A history*, p. 160; Liveing, *Adventure in publishing*, p. 89.
29 Edwards, *British children's fiction*, p. 649.
30 Duffy, *A thousand capricious chances*, pp. 116, 119.
31 Holman, *Print for victory*, Appendix 2, pp. 268–71.
32 Brogan, *The life of Arthur Ransome*, p. 398.
33 Stoney, *Enid Blyton*, pp. 175–6; Ray, *The Blyton phenomenon*, p. 27.

of the war. Although, because of her prodigious output, accurate figures are difficult to come by, she seems to have had at least five publishers at the beginning of the war, and possibly seventeen by the end. Between 1939 and 1945 she published around ninety-five works of fiction and over fifty non-fiction, and 220 issues of *Sunny Stories*.

Picture Puffins were also successful: 'Most significant of all was Noel Carrington's discovery of photo-lithography applied to mass-produced children's books in the Soviet Union, which led him to put up the idea of a similar enterprise to Allen Lane.'[34] With print-runs of 10,000 and artists preparing their own plates, 'the rather improvised, emergency appearance of several of these Puffins added to their charms'.[35] A revealing account of the difficulties of the printing process is given by Sheila Jackson, illustrating Prudence Hemelryk's *Music time* for Noel Carrington's Picture Puffins in 1947, who writes of the difficulty of drawing directly onto heavy zinc plates: 'There was no way of making corrections on the plate – any errors had to be cunningly interpolated into the design. Blots were a total disaster!'[36]

The other great success was Puffin Books, after a shaky start. When the first batch was published in 1941, Eleanor Graham, the editor, was depressed:

> When I saw the finished copies my heart sank, for I could see the booksellers' dilemma. You couldn't make a show of five thin little books, however good ... Our real difficulty lay in getting booksellers to show Puffins properly. They did not want to sell 'wretched paperbacks' instead of the old reward types: and who would buy hard-cover editions if the same books could be got for about a shilling each?

Some indication of Puffin's rapid success was the quota in 1943 that Allen Lane gave to Collet's Bookshop: of one hundred volumes, thirty-four were Penguins, thirty-three Puffins and thirty-three Pelicans or Specials.[37]

As to the subject matter of the books, Arthur Ransome was warned by his publishers to 'steer clear of the war at all costs' and other authors, such as M. E. Atkinson, simply ignored it.[38] Some attempted to square the circle of empowering child characters in a disempowering world, notably Kitty Barne with a holiday adventure modified by evacuees, *Visitors from London* (1940), and Mary Treadgold's pony-and-Channel-Islands *We couldn't leave Dinah* (1941) (Treadgold was advisor to the Cape list).[39] Both titles were awarded

---

34 Alderson, 'Some notes on children's book illustration', pp. 56–7.
35 Feaver, *When we were young*, p. 24.
36 Jackson, 'A Puffin illustrator of the forties', pp. 41–2.
37 Graham, 'The Puffin years', pp. 118–19; Holman, *Print for victory*, p. 238.
38 Brogan, *The life of Arthur Ransome*, p. 379.   39 Howard, *Jonathan Cape*, p. 155.

the Carnegie Medal. The Chalet School went into exile and encountered Nazis, while Enid Blyton had two (slightly uneasy) forays into wartime settings – *Children of Kidillin* (as Mary Pollock (1940)) and *The adventurous four* (1941). Patriotic war stories were provided by, among many others, Capt. W. E. Johns: Oxford University Press had been Johns's publisher since 1935, but after they refused to move to a royalties deal, he defected to Hodder.[40] However, radicalism also continued: Kitty Barne's evacuee novel combines its reassuring return to the pastoral with a vision of a more democratic, forward-looking community forged out of the pressures of war, and Eric Linklater's *The wind on the moon* (1944), another Carnegie winner, uses fantasy to critique tyranny and war.

1945–1960: post-war recovery

In the immediate post-war years children's books shared two things with adult books – the essentially nostalgic attitudes of authors (as in C. S. Lewis, Lucy M. Boston and Philippa Pearce) and material shortages. Collins initially printed their *Collins' Magazine for Boys and Girls* in Canada, shipping it each month to Britain.[41] Heinemann's subsidiary, The World's Work, published books from 1957 using four-colour offset litho from American duplicate film and printed in Holland, because 'the British printing industry was so busy reprinting stocks destroyed in the war it was slow to convert from letterpress, whereas in the US what amounted to a whole new children's publishing industry had grown up based on first-class artwork and sound litho colour printing'.[42] The heyday of the novel with line illustration was approaching, with illustrators such as Shirley Hughes and C. Walter Hodges.

In terms of comics, the post-war years saw a large number of 'small publishers who issued scores of titles. Many were one-shots; all of them had short runs' until Marcus Morris's *Eagle*, then the only comic published by Hulton Press, revolutionised the form in 1950.[43] (See also Chapter 22.)

Meanwhile, Puffin was expanding, although things did not always go smoothly. The hardback picture book series Porpoises failed in 1948 after four titles, including two classics, Ardizzone's *Paul, the hero of the fire* and Vera Drummond's *The flying postman*. 'To keep prices low, yet using the expensive process of photolithography ... it was necessary to print 100,000 copies of each – which proved far too many' – although Eleanor Graham reissued

40 Ellis and Schofield, *Biggles!*, p. 191.   41 Kier, *The house of Collins*, p. 279.
42 St John, *William Heinemann*, p. 379.   43 Clark, *Comics*, p. 38.

them when she was at Constable.[44] Baby Puffins and Puffin Cut-Out Books were also short-lived. However, the number of children's books published rose steadily from 715 in 1945 to 2,500 in 1965. Children's book departments proliferated, and in the 1950s 'editors specialising in children's books were first generally recognised as a separate species'.[45] This move towards more specialist children's editors owed much to the efforts of a few dynamic women who had trained in North America, notably Grace Hogarth at Constable, who became well known for fostering the careers of many in children's publishing. While children's editors were to continue to be recruited on a rather ad hoc basis for some years to come, the shift towards more trained, specialist editors helped to support further developments in children's publishing.

In mass-market books, once again Enid Blyton led the way. In 1949, 'Purnell, with one of the largest printing presses in Europe (at Paulton, Somerset), were seeking a Disney-style figure to "fuel" it. J. C. Gibbs of Purnell sent the work of Dutch artist Harmsen van der Beek to Sampson Low (owned by Purnell). David White showed Beek's work to Blyton.'[46] Two days later Blyton returned with two stories, and firm ideas about the design of the series:

> Now about the general title – at the moment this is 'All Aboard for Toyland,' and I imagine we might have as a 'motif' a toy train rushing along crowded with passengers – all going round the jacket top, sides and bottom or something like that – to give the books a 'series' look. The specific titles . . . will each contain the name 'Noddy'. In the end, if they are very successful, they'll probably be referred to and ordered as the 'Noddy' books.[47]

Backed up by heavy marketing and merchandising – there was a daily strip for the *Evening Standard*, a *Noddy in toyland* play (1955) and Noddy was the first puppet series on ITV – 'Noddy' books sold (and sell) millions.

By the 1950s, though, a new wave of talent was emerging, and the 'quality' end of the market was gaining momentum. Oxford University Press was a leader in this area – between 1950 and 1959, Oxford won the Carnegie Medal for the best children's book of the year no less than eight times, and published fifteen of the thirty commended books. Despite the view of the OUP publisher John Bell in 1957, that 'the children's book publisher has a very slender

44 Margaret Clark, introduction to Jackson, 'A Puffin illustrator of the forties', p. 37.
45 Ellis, *A history*, p. 170; Wace, *From Carroll to Crompton*, p. 247; Reynolds, 'Publishing practices', p. 28; Goldthwaite, 'Notes on the children's book trade', pp. 396, 398.
46 Rudd, *Enid Blyton*, p. 64.   47 Stoney, *Enid Blyton*, p. 158.

profit margin indeed . . . his publishing risks are great . . . and only a publisher with a happy mixture of idealism and capital can keep his children's books going', the foundations had been laid for a phenomenal expansion and remarkable achievements by authors, illustrators, publishers and book makers in the 1960s and beyond.[48]

1960–1975

The social and economic climate of Britain in the 1960s and early 1970s provided a fertile ground in which children's publishing could grow. There was a new focus on childhood, education and literacy, high levels of investment in schools and libraries, and increasing specialisation in the area of children's literature. The Library Association's two-year full-time course in librarianship, launched in 1964, offered optional papers in children's literature and librarianship, and five new specialist journals on children's literature appeared between 1960 and 1971.[49] As a result, children's publishers not only enjoyed almost guaranteed sales – 75–80 per cent of Oxford University Press's output was bought by libraries – they were also selling to a well-informed, specialist market and were able to take more artistic and commercial risks.[50] The years 1961–63 saw the prestigious Kate Greenaway Medal awarded to debut books, notably Brian Wildsmith's *ABC* in dazzling colour (OUP, 1962). Seeking to capitalise on the popularity of *The lord of the rings*, Sir William Collins took a chance on a novel by a new young author, Alan Garner: *The weirdstone of Brisingamen* (Collins, 1960) was well received, and Garner went on to win the Carnegie Medal with *The owl service* (Collins, 1967). An original take on historical fiction came from Leon Garfield and Joan Aiken. The excitement generated by this activity led John Rowe Townsend to state in 1965 'the second golden age is now', and both the volume and the prestige of children's publishing continued to increase throughout the 1960s.[51]

Efforts to improve the quality and recognition of children's books gathered pace throughout the 1960s. In 1962, Grace Hogarth founded the Children's Book Circle (CBC) as a forum for children's editors to share expertise and ideas. In 1965 the group established the Eleanor Farjeon Award, which aimed

---

48 Bell, 'Publishing for young readers', pp. 94–5.
49 Lonsdale and Ray, 'Librarianship', p. 617.
50 'Interview with Paul Binding', 10 March 1997, in Reynolds and Tucker (eds.), *Oral archives*, p. 60.
51 Townsend, *Written for children*, p. 151; Pearson, *The making of modern children's literature in Britain*, pp. 15–72.

to recognise 'an outstanding contribution to the world of children's books', celebrating the work of librarians, critics and authors as well as of editors.[52] One such contribution was that of Kaye Webb at Puffin Books, who founded the Puffin Club for child readers in 1967. Membership was by subscription, and included quarterly copies of the Club magazine *Puffin Post*, which encouraged creative contributions from children. Puffin Club activities and events, such as the annual Puffin exhibition, helped to generate excitement about children's books. The Club promoted a strong sense of identification with the Puffin brand, but also served to raise the profile of children's books more widely; the Eleanor Farjeon committee also credited it with helping to ensure that 'reading and owning of books is seen as a source of excitement and pleasure by the children themselves'.[53]

Kaye Webb's work at Puffin from 1961 also contributed to the dramatic expansion of paperback publishing for children during this period. Paperbacks had initially been greeted with suspicion, and some high-profile authors such as Arthur Ransome were reluctant to allow paperback editions of their titles. The work of Eleanor Graham, the first editor of Puffin Story Books, had helped to establish that paperback publishing need not be synonymous with low standards. This laid the foundation for Kaye Webb to expand the firm's activities; she observed, 'I think paper-backs should be looked at rather like a magazine: they can buy and read and then if they fall in love with the book they can get themselves a permanent copy.'[54] Thus, in a period of economic prosperity, Webb rapidly increased Puffin's output, from just twelve new titles in 1960, to 127 by 1977.[55] In addition, she worked hard to make Puffins more prominent in the marketplace, introducing bright colours with wraparound illustrations, branded display units, and even an advertising jingle played in W. H. Smith stores around the country.[56] Her success at Puffin encouraged other publishers to compete, notably Brockhampton's Knights from 1967: more downmarket series included Pan

---

52 Children's Book Circle, 'Eleanor Farjeon Award', *Children's Book Circle*, www .childrensbookcircle.org.uk/farjeon.asp.

53 'Children's Book Circle Eleanor Farjeon Award: winner of the 1969 award: Kaye Webb', press release (1970). Kaye Webb Collection, Seven Stories, the National Centre for Children's Books, KW/11/01/06.

54 Kaye Webb to Noel Streatfeild, 26 July 1961. Penguin Archive, University of Bristol, DM1107 / PS 157.

55 Kaye Webb, 'A red letter day for children (or the rewarding road to the 1000th Puffin)', typescript draft of article, c. 1977, Kaye Webb Collection, KW/07/01/05/09/03.

56 Kaye Webb, 'On being a children's editor', typescript draft, Kaye Webb Collection, KW/15/32, f.4.

Piccolo, Armada and Granada's Dragon Books.[57] Webb also published paper-back originals, including William Mayne's *A parcel of trees* (1963) and Clive King's *Stig of the dump* (1963), which had been rejected by a host of hardback publishers.

A wave of innovation in picture books was stimulated by Mabel George at Oxford University Press, who recognised the possibilities of photo offset lithography for reproducing vibrant, painterly colours: Brian Wildsmith's *ABC* was followed by innovative books by Charles Keeping, Victor Ambrus, Shirley Hughes, Quentin Blake, Jan Pienkowski and Pat Hutchins.[58] At the Bodley Head, Judy Taylor published Maurice Sendak's *Where the wild things are* (1964) in 1967, despite the misgivings of some of her colleagues over the controversy it had aroused in the United States.[59] The risk of shocking parents and teachers was not the only deterrent: the cost of publishing Sendak's large-format, full-colour book would have been prohibi-tive had not Taylor's co-editor Margaret Clark negotiated an international co-edition, an arrangement which was to become increasingly important to the picture book market over the years to follow.[60] Such deals were often brokered at the Bologna Children's Book Fair, which was founded in 1963, providing a forum for publishers to market their own titles and acquire new ones.

Imports were particularly important to the emerging teenage market, which relied heavily on books from America and Scandinavia. The emergence of 'teenage' culture in the UK and the extension of the school-leaving age to sixteen in 1971 had focussed attention on the needs of adolescents as a specific group.[61] Kaye Webb launched the Peacock list 'for older boys and girls' in 1961. However, with a few notable exceptions such as Beverly Cleary's *Fifteen* (1962), an American import, Peacocks never really prospered, in part because their branding allied them too closely to Puffin. As a response to the Newsom Report of 1963, which had drawn attention to the 'unrealised potential' of children in secondary modern schools, Heinemann's Pyramids and Macmillan Education's Topliners appeared to serve the 'reluctant reader'.[62] The Bodley Head led the way in mainstream

---

57 Croome, 'A million a month', p. 1; Chambers, *The reluctant reader*, p. 137; Brockhampton Press, Knight Books promotional leaflet, 1967, Chambers Archive, Box 110/111 02, Aberystwyth University.

58 Graham, 'Picture books', pp. 65–70.

59 Lambert and Ratcliffe, *The Bodley Head*, p. 321.   60 *Ibid.*

61 Bell *et al.*, *Education in Great Britain and Ireland*, p. 112.

62 John Newsom, *Half our future*, the Newsom Report (1963), p. 1. Available at www .educationengland.org.uk/documents/newsom.

hardbacks, publishing the Bodley Head New Adults list, launched in 1969 with Paul Zindel's *The pigman*, and by the mid-1970s teenage fiction was well established as a genre, although it was to take much longer for it to find its identity within the marketplace.

By the 1970s, most of the major publishing houses had well-developed children's lists with specialist editors, and new imprints were appearing each year. The increasing diversification of the children's market was diluted, however, by a move towards increasingly large conglomerates in the publishing world. Penguin was purchased by the international media group Pearson in 1970, a merger which brought with it Constable Young Books and its editor Patrick Hardy, who was to become editor of Kestrel, Penguin's new hardback imprint for children. Macmillan consolidated its status as an international company in 1971 with the establishment of Macmillan International Ltd, and split its UK publishing endeavours into three, while the Bodley Head formed a publishing group with Jonathan Cape and Chatto & Windus. Such mergers played an important role in consolidating financial support for smaller imprints. As children's publishing headed towards a difficult period in the second half of the decade, such support was badly needed.

1975–1995

Recession through the second half of the 1970s and into the 1980s was accompanied by massive cuts in public spending: the number of books bought by British state schools fell by 35 per cent during the 1980s.[63] As a result, many children's publishers began to rationalise their lists: there were cuts at Piccolo, Macmillan and Chatto, and the Puffin Club was reduced to a school bookclub.[64]

Despite these challenges, children's publishing as a whole continued to expand. Elaine Moss notes that 'in 1976, twenty-five per cent more children's titles were published than in 1971', and between 1980 and 1992 the number of new titles doubled, although very short print-runs were to become a permanent feature.[65] The end of the 1970s saw the establishment of several significant new imprints: Klaus Flugge founded Andersen Press as a semi-autonomous imprint of Hutchinson, and Sebastian Walker founded Walker Books in association with Methuen in 1978 and branched out as an

63 'BfK News – July 1990', *Books for Keeps* 63 (July 1990), p. 27.
64 'BfK News – January 1983', *Books for Keeps* 18 (January 1983), p. 24.
65 Moss, *Part of the pattern*, p. 143; 'BfK News – July 1984', *Books for Keeps* 27 (July 1984), p. 26; Elkin, 'Trends in publishing', p. 104.

independent in 1987; both lists were to publish notable new picture book artists such as Tony Ross and Satoshi Kitamuri.[66] Many new paperback imprints were also established, and vertical publishing became common, with Kestrel/Puffin, Collins/Fontana Lions, Methuen/Magnet and Abelard Schulman/Grasshopper all ensuring that they benefited from paperback as well as hardback sales.[67] It was a market well worth targeting: 'between 1983 and 1987, children's paperback fiction sales by UK publishers rose by 139.4%'.[68]

The increasing focus on marketing direct to the individual led to the appearance of more novelty and mass-market books. Series and tie-in publishing thrived: Tandem's Target Books enjoyed some of the highest sales of the 1970s with its novelisations of *Doctor Who*, while Transworld's Corgi published American imports such as Sweet Valley High, and series based around popular toys such as Sindy and Transformers.[69] Puffin cashed in on the popularity of the Rubik's Cube with *You can do the cube* (1981), and in 1982 launched the Fighting Fantasy series, a 'choose your own adventure' format based on the role-playing game Dungeons and Dragons. New venues for sales also emerged: the School Bookshop Movement was launched in 1976, and in 1985 Sebastian Walker caused controversy by launching a series of books with Sainsbury's.[70]

During the 1960s, movable books had begun to reappear, largely thanks to Leopold Schliesser, who had introduced the innovative pop-up books of Czech artist Vojtech Kubasta to the UK.[71] Kubasta's books caught the eye of American advertising man Waldo Hunt, who was keen to introduce them to the American market; when Hunt found that it was difficult to procure them in large enough numbers, he was inspired to coordinate a 'package' of people to create and assemble the physical book which he could sell to a publisher, or several publishers in different countries, making production much more economical. The result was intricately designed and assembled titles such as Robert Crowther's *The most amazing hide and seek alphabet book* (Kestrel, 1977) and Jan Pienkowski's *Haunted house* (Heinemann, 1979), which were assembled overseas. Another innovation was Sebastian Walker's introduction of board books for babies, and Martin Handford's *Where's Wally?*

---

66 Pat Triggs, 'The man behind the books – Klaus Flugge', *Books for Keeps* 24 (January 1984), p. 18; Cecil, *Sebastian Walker*, p. 95.

67 Moss, *Part of the pattern*, p. 143.   68 Elkin, 'Trends in publishing', p. 102.

69 'BfK News – November 1985', *Books for Keeps* 35 (November 1985), p. 24.

70 Cecil, *Sebastian Walker*, p. 112.   71 Fox, 'Movable books', p. 93.

(1987), based around the simple but appealing concept of finding the distinctively attired Wally in a busy scene.[72]

Children's publishing of the 1970s and 1980s was heavily influenced by the societal focus on issues of sex, race and class, and the work of organisations such as the Children's Rights Workshop (CRW) and the National Committee on Racism in Children's Books. Specialist imprints, often housed within education rather than children's imprints, were particularly active in addressing the concerns of such groups: one early example was Macmillan Education's Nippers series, launched in 1971. Edited by the social activist Leila Berg, Nippers was an early reading scheme designed to reflect the ordinary lives of working-class British children. More books featuring working-class characters and female protagonists began to appear on mainstream lists, as did non-white characters and authors. Independent black publishers such as Bogle-L'Ouverture, founded in 1968 by Guyanese activists Jessica and Eric Huntley, led the way in producing books which represented the lives and culture of Black Britons.[73] In mainstream publishing, the Bodley Head was one of the first to publish a British picture book with a black protagonist: *My brother Sean* (1975) by the Jamaican illustrator Erroll Lloyd and Surinamese author Petronella Breinburg. Macmillan Topliner commissioned Indian-born writer Farrukh Dhondy to write a collection of short stories, *East End at your feet* (1976), and more titles came from America, including books by Mildred Taylor, Julius Lester and Rosa Guy.

The 'problem novel' was particularly dominant in teenage publishing, which continued to grow: 1987 saw the launch of six new teenage imprints.[74] American author Judy Blume, notable for her frank approach to adolescent concerns such as periods, wet dreams and sex, was published by Gollancz. By 1990 Julia Eccleshare was complaining that 'the message has far too often outweighed the medium'; nevertheless, the emphasis on social realism did expand the range of possibilities for children's books.[75] Jacqueline Wilson was one of those who became established in the teenage problem genre during the 1980s, before turning her attentions to books for slightly younger children.[76] Her lively book about a looked-after child, *The story of Tracy Beaker* (Doubleday, 1991), is one of the best examples of British social realism: Wilson was the most-borrowed author in the first decade of the new

72 Cecil, *Sebastian Walker*, pp. 80, 136.
73 O'Connor, *Children's publishing and Black Britain*.
74 Pat Triggs and Jessica Yates, 'Puffin plus', *Books for Keeps* 49 (March 1988), p. 8.
75 Eccleshare, 'Introduction', p. 6.   76 Pearson (ed.), *Jacqueline Wilson*, pp. 1–15.

millennium, and is one of the most prominent authors in contemporary children's literature.[77]

The introduction of the National Curriculum in 1988 provided a temporary buoyancy in the schools market, particularly benefiting non-fiction lists, although overall it largely served to redirect school spending to new titles rather than producing an increase in the overall number of titles sold. Changes in school funding also changed the education market, diminishing sales via specialist providers such as Schools Library Services, but increasing the opportunities for publishers to sell direct to schools.[78] The Book Trust suggested that annual levels of funding for books in 1992 fell short by at least £6 per pupil; as a result, the importance of sales to individuals rather than to schools and libraries continued to increase, and heavily branded titles began to dominate the market. American series fiction such as Scholastic's Babysitters' Club, Goosebumps and Point Horror were top sellers, while publishers' catalogues were increasingly dominated by 'character' titles such as Thomas the Tank Engine, Spot the Dog and Babar the Elephant, along with associated merchandise. The second half of the 1990s, however, was to produce an entirely different climate for children's publishing.

Post-1995

In 1997, Bloomsbury accepted a manuscript from an unknown author. The manuscript was *Harry Potter and the philosopher's stone*; a decade later, the Harry Potter series had sold more than 400 million worldwide, and Bloomsbury's annual turnover had increased from £11 million to over £100 million.[79] Nor was *Harry Potter* the only children's book to make headlines: Philip Pullman's *His dark materials* (Scholastic, 1995–2005) also enjoyed unusually high sales, at times toppling Rowling from the best-seller lists. Notably, it also garnered critical attention, and *The amber spyglass* (2000) became the first children's book to win the Whitbread Award.[80] It 'came at

77 Benedicte Page, 'Wilson tops decade as most borrowed author', *Bookseller* 14 February 2012, www.thebookseller.com/news/wilson-tops-decade-most-borrowed-author.html.
78 Elkin, 'Trends in publishing', pp. 111–12.
79 Guy Dammann, 'Harry Potter breaks 400m in sales', *Guardian* 18 June 2008, www .guardian.co.uk/books/2008/jun/18/harrypotter.news; 'The Harry Potter economy', *Economist* 17 December 2009, www.economist.com/node/15108711.
80 John Ezard, 'Harry Potter toppled in sales charts', *Guardian* 2 June 2006, www .guardian.co.uk/uk/2003/jun/02/books.pressandpublishing; Fiachra Gibbons, 'Epic children's book takes Whitbread', *Guardian* 23 January 2002, www.guardian.co.uk/ uk/2002/jan/23/whitbreadprize2001.costabookaward.

a time when international conglomerates were already turning their atten-tion to the lucrative youth market'.[81] The social context was also propitious for children's books, with initiatives such as the National Literacy Strategy (1998), the National Year of Reading (1998), and Booktrust projects such as Bookstart and the Children's Laureate providing more funds and more focus on children's books (the NYR was allocated £4 million for promotion and funding initiatives through local authorities, and an extra £115 million of funding for books in schools).[82] All this focussed attention on the children's market and helped to produce a flood of new children's authors, leading some commentators to make claims for a 'third golden age' of children's literature.[83]

The massive success of Rowling and Pullman has promoted a shift towards treating children's books more like adult titles, with high-profile 'celebrity' authors and large advances. The change has not been entirely positive, however: whereas the children's publishers of the 1950s and 1960s espoused the doctrine that it took ten years to make a children's book, in today's industry new books are often dropped if sales fail to reach a minimum value.[84] The demise of the Net Book Agreement in 1997 also enabled unprecedentedly large discounts on the *Harry Potter* books, which many large retailers treated as loss leaders. The supermarket chain Asda sold *Harry Potter and the deathly hallows* (2007) at a phenomenal 78.2 per cent discount, securing 80 per cent of UK sales but causing the *Bookseller* to disqualify the book from its best-seller lists.[85] While publishers emphasise the importance of best-sellers in today's children's market, however, the *Bookseller* reports that 'the percentage of sales accounted for by the top authors has actually lessened over the past decade' and midlist sales remain healthier than they are perceived to be.[86]

There is a growing number of successful independent houses and semi-autonomous imprints within the large publishers. Jane Nissen founded her own publishing imprint, Jane Nissen Books, following her retirement from

81 Crandall, 'The UK children's book business 1995–2004', p. 3.
82 National Literacy Trust, 'Executive summary of "Building a nation of readers: a review of the National Year of Reading (1998–1999)"', *National Reading Campaign* (2009), www.literacytrust.org.uk/campaign/execsummary.html.
83 Dina Rabinovitch, 'The greatest stories ever told', *Guardian* 31 March 2005, www.books.guardian.co.uk/news/articles/0,6109,1448965,00.html.
84 Crandall, 'Children's authors', p. 119.
85 Philip Stone, 'Why Harry missed out', *Bookseller* 18 July 2008, www.thebookseller.com/blogs/why-harry-missed-out.html.
86 Caroline Horn, 'In depth: children's mid and backlist', *Bookseller* 18 November 2011, www.thebookseller.com/feature/depth-childrens-mid-and-backlist.html.

Penguin: the imprint is dedicated to reprints of twentieth-century children's classics. Barry Cunningham left Bloomsbury to found independent Chicken House in 2004 (now a semi-autonomous imprint of Scholastic), while Philip Pullman's editor David Fickling departed from Scholastic and set up David Fickling Books in 2000 (now an imprint of Random House). Nadia Crandall, writing in 2006, cites more than twenty independent or semi-autonomous imprints established in the preceding decade, arguing that collaborations between small, individualised imprints and larger, well-financed conglomerates allow for individual vision within children's publishing without sacrificing the financial support and large-scale distribution which can be provided by larger outfits.[87]

The crossover phenomenon has also contributed to the buoyancy of the young adult market, which grew by 170 per cent between 2005 and 2010.[88] Sales to fans in their late twenties and early thirties were an important component in the success of the American series by Stephenie Meyer, *Twilight* (2005–8), which has achieved sales of almost £52 million worldwide. Publishers have emphasised the importance of this demographic in their plans for developing their young adult lists, which have proliferated in the last decade.[89] While such expansion threatens over-saturation, so far the teenage market has continued to thrive.

New developments in technology have always affected children's publishing, and publishers have made sporadic attempts to produce digital content, beginning with CD-Roms such as Broderbund's Living Books in the 1990s. The growing popularity of e-readers and the advent of devices such as the iPad, which are capable of displaying full-colour, interactive material, present new possibilities for children's publishers. While e-books which mimic the experience of reading a printed book have proven to be less popular with children than with adults, the interactive qualities of 'book apps' which blend reading and play are particularly relevant to the children's market.[90] Book apps have become increasingly popular, with adaptations of picture books including Rod Campbell's classic lift-the-flap book *Dear zoo* (1982, digital edition Macmillan 2012), and original content by companies such as Nosy

---

87 Crandall, 'Children's book publishing', p. 216.
88 Felicity Wood and Philip Stone, 'Genre focus: teenage kicks', *Bookseller* 22 July 2011, www.thebookseller.com/feature/genre-focus-teenage-kicks.html.
89 Julia Eccleshare, 'New teenage lists', *Books for Keeps* 132 (January 2002), p. 3.
90 David Kleeman, 'Tracking global kids' reading habits', *Publishers' Weekly* 25 January 2016, pp. 24–5; Sargeant, 'What is an ebook?'

Crow and Hot Key Books.[91] Both companies emphasise the potential of technology as a means of producing new kinds of narratives, rather than as simply a new tool for transmitting traditional content.[92] Hot Key's iBook edition of Sally Garner's Carnegie winner *Maggot moon* (2012) uses interactive elements to add context to the narrative, inserting images and other information relevant to the story (for example, a section on twentieth-century genocide), and animating text in order to demonstrate how her dyslexic protagonist might see it. Interactivity is also a key selling point of J. K. Rowling's Pottermore, which was described at its launch as 'the world's biggest enhanced e-book'.[93] The site, which was greeted as a 'gamechanger' for the children's market, blurs the boundaries between text and marketing platform, offering new content relating to Harry Potter, social networking features and interactive elements alongside a marketplace for Rowling's e-books.[94] While print still holds sway over digital in the children's market, the advent of new technologies has undoubtedly altered the way books are marketed and consumed. Teenage readers have carved out their own position in the marketplace: blogs and vlogs have become an important part of the reviewing landscape, and YouTube stars such as Zoe Sugg have crossed over into print.[95]

Children's publishing can no longer be described as invisible: since the 1950s both its cultural and its economic importance have become more prominent. The onset of recession and the arrival of widespread cuts in public funding dissipated the optimism generated by the growth of the industry around the turn of the millennium: 2008 and 2009 saw the industry in a pessimistic mood, with cuts to acquisitions and royalties and redundancies in a number of houses, including HarperCollins, Macmillan and Walker.[96] However, this pessimism proved to be ill-founded: children's

91 Caroline Horn, 'New app route for Macmillan children's', *Bookseller* 19 December 2011, www.thebookseller.com/news/new-app-route-macmillan-childrens.html.
92 Tom Bonnick, 'Not simply books squashed into smartphones', *Bookseller* 22 May 2015, www.thebookseller.com/futurebook/tom-bonnick-0. See also O'Connor *et al.*, 'Digital developments'.
93 Philip Jones, 'Pottermore: the world's biggest enhanced e-book', *Bookseller* 23 June 2011, www.thebookseller.com/futurebook/pottermore-worlds-biggest-enhanced-e-book.
94 Caroline Horn, 'Pottermore a "game changer"', *Bookseller* 22 August 2011, www .thebookseller.com/news/pottermore-game-changer; Charlotte Williams, 'Pottermore defends selling e-books directly', *Bookseller* 27 June 2011, www .thebookseller.com/news/pottermore-defends-selling-e-books-directly.html.
95 Alexis Burling, 'Book publishing comes to YouTube', *Publishing Weekly* 16 February 2015, pp. 22–6.
96 Caroline Horn, 'Children's publishers cutting acquisitions and advances', *Bookseller* 16 September 2009, www.thebookseller.com/news/childrens-publishers-cutting-acqui

books have retained their dominance in the publishing industry as a whole, and the first quarter of 2016 saw the UK children's book market grow more than 7 per cent.[97] An area of publishing which has been particularly adept at adjusting to social, cultural and commercial changes over the years, it is likely to continue to thrive.

sitions-and-advances.html; Horn, 'Walker trims staff and list', *Bookseller* 19 June 2008, www.thebookseller.com/news/walker-trims-staff-and-list.html; Horn, 'First cuts at HarperCollins children's after restructure', *Bookseller* 9 June 2009, www .thebookseller.com/news/first-cuts-harpercollins-childrens-after-restructure.html; Benedicte Page, 'Jobs go at Macmillan children's books', *Bookseller* 15 June 2009, www .thebookseller.com/news/jobs-go-macmillan-childrens-books.html.

97 Caroline Horn, 'Recession fails to bite children's market', *Bookseller* 23 January 2012, www.thebookseller.com/news/recession-fails-bite-childrens-market.html; Charlotte Eyre, 'Children's book market up 7% in first quarter', *Bookseller* 14 April 2016, www.thebookseller.com/news/uk-children-s-book-market-7-327130.

Schoolbooks and textbook publishing

SARAH PEDERSEN

During the nineteenth century the schoolbook market in Britain responded to the rise of both formal schooling and public examinations, which created regular demand for books in specific areas.[1] The 1870 Education Act and the 1872 (Scotland) Education Act had made elementary education compulsory for children between the ages of five and thirteen, and in 1902 another Education Act introduced some state-supported provision of post-elementary or 'secondary' education. By 1913–14 the new grant-aided secondary schools in England and Wales were annually admitting just over 60,000 children.[2] However, it was not until the end of the First World War that some form of secondary education became compulsory for all children. In 1911 the parliamentary report of the Consultative Committee on Examinations in Secondary Schools noted that more than 80 per cent of fourteen- to eighteen-year-olds received no education at all and recommended that children take public examinations at the age of sixteen.[3] To facilitate this, the Examinations Council was established in 1917 to administer School Certificate exams. However, when the Fisher Education Act (and the Scottish Education Act in Scotland) were passed in 1918 they only raised the school-leaving age to fourteen – with provision for it to be raised to fifteen on a yet-to-be-fixed date.

Even this limited expansion of schools was good news for British educational publishers such as Nelson, Longmans, Macmillan and Blackie after the traumatic years of the First World War. The war years had meant the loss of lucrative foreign markets, reductions in manpower, shortages, and the deaths of some potential future leaders of the industry, for example Thomas Nelson III, who died at the Battle of Arras in 1917. The difficult economic conditions of the 1920s and early 1930s meant that plans to raise the school-leaving age

---

1 Stray and Sutherland, 'Mass markets: education'. 2 *Ibid.*, p. 379.
3 Report of the Consultative Committee on Examinations in Secondary Schools London: HM Stationery Office 1911 (Cd 6004).

were postponed indefinitely while cuts in government budgets were urgently sought. This led schools and publishers to focus on financial prudence, which meant that many textbooks were closely printed on poor-quality paper with few illustrations. Yet the educational market was particularly important for publishers during the years of the Depression, being one of the only guaranteed markets for books. It was therefore important for educational publishers to react quickly to any changes in government education policy in order to continue to sell their products into schools. At Thomas Nelson & Sons, for example, John Buchan (who, in partial mitigation of Thomas Nelson III's death, had become a company director in 1915, as well as an author and editor) brought Sir Henry Newbolt, with whom he had worked at the Ministry of Information during the war, into the company to act as editorial advisor in the educational field. Newbolt's 1921 report on the teaching of English in schools in England and Wales had called for the raising of the status of the subject and emphasised a love of English literature.[4] In response, Nelson initiated new series under the editorship of Newbolt such as the Nelson School Classics and the 1922 Teaching of English.

In a similar way, the six reports produced by the Consultative Committees chaired by Sir William Henry Hadow between 1923 and 1933 were influential in the development of education and hence on the output of educational publishers. The 1926 report on *The education of the adolescent* recommended the separation of primary and secondary education (and the use of the term primary rather than the previous 'elementary') at the age of eleven and the establishment of two types of secondary school – 'modern' and grammar schools, with a more vocational and skills-based focus in the former – while the 1931 and 1932 reports recommended the division of primary school education into infant and junior schools. Some publishers responded in a most literal way to these reports, with W. & R. Chambers producing a No Lumber educational series in direct response to a call in the Hadow Report of 1931 to rid the curriculum of useless 'lumber'. Of most significance to the historian of educational publishing is the 1928 Hadow Report, *Books in public elementary schools*. The report listed forty-three recommendations, including greater expenditure on books in schools, the need for each school to have at least one library and that pupils should be encouraged in their reading and use of books. Recommendation 33 stated:

> every pupil should be allowed, at least in school, to retain possession of all
> the books which he is constantly using, and that they should remain in his

4 Newbolt, 'The Newbolt Report'.

keeping until the end of the term or year in which he requires them ... older scholars from the age of 11 and upwards should in addition be encouraged to take books home ... books on certain subjects in which individual pupils have displayed special aptitude or interest might, towards the end of their school life, be given to them as a privilege or reward.[5]

From 1918 onwards the introduction of School Certificate and Higher School Certificate examinations helpfully established the core subjects that textbooks needed to cover. In addition, the curriculum of grammar schools was governed by Regulations issued by the Board of Education. For example, these Regulations established the requirement for both theoretical and practical science in secondary schools. The inter-war years saw much debate about the order and manner in which separate science subjects should be taught, and also attempts to widen the science curriculum by schoolmasters-turned-authors such as Frederick W. Westaway (Blackie) to include subjects such as astronomy, the history and philosophy of science, and palaeontology.[6] Science textbooks for those in the 'modern' secondary schools, meanwhile, tended to focus on the occupations it was assumed pupils would take up when they left school.

Despite the recommendations of the Hadow Reports for a child-centred and progressive curriculum, the majority of teaching between the wars was conservative and old-fashioned. In one way this was beneficial for publishers because they were able to reprint established titles with little revision. As the economic situation improved during the 1930s, however, textbook quality began to improve markedly. Developments in printing brought in important changes in illustration, typography and layout. The introduction of the lithographic printing process meant that illustrations no longer had to be printed on separate specially coated and expensive 'art' paper, but could be printed alongside text.[7] During the 1930s, under the guidance of E. W. Parker, Longmans built up a list of textbooks aimed at the public and grammar schools markets that were able to dominate their subject areas into the 1950s and 1960s.[8] These new titles had good production values, were competitively priced and were written by scholars such as G. M. Trevelyan, whose *English social history* (first published in North America and appearing in Britain two

---

5 Derek Gillard, 'The Hadow Reports: an introduction', in *The encyclopaedia of informal education* (2006), www.infed.org/schooling/hadow_reports.htm.
6 Brock and Jenkins, 'Frederick W. Westaway and science education'; Jenkins, 'E. J. Holmyard'.
7 Yglesias, 'Education and publishing in transition'.
8 Briggs, *A history of Longmans*, pp. 391–4.

years later in 1944) sold out its 15,000 printed copies before publication day.[9] The inter-war years were a particular boom time for geography and history textbooks, with an increasing popularity for both subjects at secondary level leading to a larger number of textbooks available, plus improvements in quality of illustration and the influence of a more 'scientific' approach from the universities.[10] The so-called 'new history' took a more 'bottom-up' approach, focussing on local and social history and the use of original sources. Magraw's *Stories of early modern times* published by Oxford University Press in 1932, for example, offered fifty illustrations in one hundred pages and included contemporary sources, with questions at the end of each chapter to be answered by the pupils' own investigations.[11] There was also an attempt at catering for the less able child with the editing from some textbooks (for example the No Lumber series mentioned above) of a certain amount of factual detail.

The growth of overseas markets

The years between the wars were important for the consolidation of overseas markets for educational publishers, particularly in the British colonies. To be successful in these regions publishers needed to adapt their products for local conditions and be willing to publish to the guidelines of individual governments. Oxford University Press produced textbooks strictly designed for the individual Departments of Education in the various provinces of India, with books being produced in Gujarati, Marathi, Hindi, Kannada, Malayalam, Punjabi, Tamil, Telagu and Urdu.[12] Such overseas business was of a growing importance for OUP, which increasingly relied on its educational sales to colonial markets in Asia and later Africa to subsidise academic publishing at home.[13] In these regions OUP competed with companies such as Longmans and Macmillan. By the 1930s many companies had moved from the use of travelling sales staff to the establishment of complete branches in the colonies undertaking original publishing aimed at individual markets. Branches of Blackie & Son, the British India Publishing Company, Butterworth & Co. (India) and Longmans could be found in Calcutta while the entire business of producing schoolbooks in the four vernaculars in Bombay (Gujarati, Kannada, Konkani and Sindhi) had been awarded to

9 *Ibid.*, pp. 408–9. 10 Marsden, *The school textbook.*
11 Scotland, *The history of Scottish education*, p. 54.
12 Sutcliffe, *The Oxford University Press*, p. 200.
13 Davis, 'Histories of publishing under apartheid'.

Macmillan by government order.[14] By the 1930s indigenous textbook committees and boards of studies had been set up throughout India. It was largely
to deal with such committees, and associated copyright problems, that the
British Publishers Association set up its India Group in 1924.[15]

The inter-war period was also an important time for the development of
English-language teaching (ELT) publishing. Although educationalists
stressed primary instruction in the mother tongue, in Africa in particular it
was simply not possible to produce suitable educational materials in every
language and dialect. Moreover, there was a belief amongst some in the
colonies that education in the vernacular merely aimed at producing
a subordinate workforce, and in order to succeed children needed to be
educated in English.[16] There was thus a growing market for both educational
textbooks in English and books teaching English as a foreign language.
Longmans worked with Michael West, an educator in Bengal who stressed
the importance of reading for learning the English language, to produce their
New Method course from 1926 onwards. Laurence Faucett, a former missionary in China, worked with OUP to produce the Oxford English Course
from 1933. This series and OUP's 1935 Rapid English Readers, also edited by
Faucett, were well illustrated but tended to emphasise English culture,
making few concessions to the culture of other countries.[17] A different
approach was taken by the Longmans series Essential English for Foreign
Students (1938–42). Written by Charles Ewart Eckersley, a teacher at the
Regent Street Polytechnic, who was dealing with the growing number of
refugees arriving in Britain during the 1930s, the series stressed 'real' English,
focussing on the immediate needs of those who were already in Britain and
wanted to conduct conversations in everyday English.[18]

Impact of the Second World War

As the economy improved, a new date was set in 1936 for the raising of the
school-leaving age to fifteen – September 1939. The outbreak of the Second
World War meant that this plan was quickly shelved and the education
system suffered great disruption until 1945. Educational publishers' profits
were damaged by the national emergency and related paper rationing, but in
addition many found themselves physically on the front line – not only on the
battlefield but also in their offices. Part of Blackie's Bishopbriggs works in

14 Holman, *Print for victory*, p. 167.   15 *Ibid.*   16 *Ibid.*
17 Briggs, *A history of Longmans*, p. 394; Holman, *Print for victory*, p. 184.   18 *Ibid.*

Glasgow was turned over to the Ministry of Supply for the manufacture of twenty-five pound shells and aircraft radiators. The worst damage occurred on 29 December 1940 when the Luftwaffe's bombing during the London Blitz destroyed the area around Paternoster Row, including many firms' head offices and warehouses. Seventeen publishing firms were totally destroyed and the entire stock of 3 million books owned by the wholesaler Simpkin Marshall was burned (see Chapter 6). Overall it was estimated that 20 million books had been destroyed in the raid.[19] While Longmans had evacuated its editorial and administrative offices to the suburbs in 1939, the warehouse for all bound stock and the trade counter remained in Paternoster Row and thus overnight its catalogue of 6,000 titles was reduced to only twelve. There was one positive outcome from the terrible destruction for the publishers – books that had been slow to sell could be allowed to go out of print and were not reprinted, which meant that there was no longer the requirement to pay War Risks Insurance on sluggish backlist titles taking up space in warehouses. Instead, publishers were able to make a fresh start, using the insurance money to reprint titles that were still in demand. As Longmans stated in the introduction to their catalogue of educational works produced within three months of the raid: 'it contains no book which . . . did not on its recent and current sales justify immediate reprinting. Normally a Publisher's school catalogue includes very many books which are slow sellers. There are no such books in the pages of this list.'[20]

Paper rationing was a problem for all publishers during the war, although educational books could be given priority by the Paper Controller and the Moberly Advisory Committee if the Publishers Association Educational Advisory Panel certified that a particular work was educational. Moberly was the Vice-Chancellor of Manchester University and his advisory committee mainly came from educational, academic and professional publishing, meaning that the committee tended to favour those sectors.[21] Despite such support, the Publishers Association's Education Group spent the war arguing for a greater allocation of paper for educational publishers. By May 1944 it was warning that demand for textbooks was higher than ever, particularly as evacuated schools started to return to the cities.[22]

19 Stevenson, *Book makers*, p. 110.
20 Copy of the reprint of the Introduction to Messrs Longmans' catalogue of educational works, c. 1942, 55/33. Longman archives, University of Reading.
21 Stevenson, *Book makers*, p. 117.   22 Holman, *Print for victory*, p. 212.

A vocational trend

Once peace had been declared, attention turned once more to planning for the future. The Butler Education Act of 1944 repeated many of the provisions of the 1918 Act, but went further. The school-leaving age was to be raised to fifteen as soon as possible – which happened on 1 March 1947 – and then, when it was deemed advisable, to sixteen. Secondary education was divided into three: grammar schools, taking around 20 per cent of all pupils; technical schools, taking around 5 per cent; and the new secondary modern schools, which would take the rest. Pupils took an examination at the age of eleven to decide which school they should attend. These changes offered new opportunities and challenges for educational publishers who had to offer a wider range of titles to cater for both an older age group and three different types of school.

As a result of the changes, post-1945 education became far more vocational in slant, although there was still an open market for publishers with no specifically approved or compulsory textbooks. There was a reaction against the traditional idea that certain subjects, such as Greek or Latin, were necessary as essential training for the mind and, as universities started to drop Latin as an admission requirement, emphasis on the Classics was reduced in favour of more 'relevant' subjects. This vocational trend was reinforced in 1963 by the Newsom Report *Half our future*, which looked at the education of average and below-average children, and the Scottish Brunton Report, *From school to further education*, both of which had a strongly vocational bias and urged the expansion of the curriculum.[23]

Publishers of reading schemes also found themselves challenged by the Plowden Report of 1967, which focussed on primary schools. Series such as the Janet and John books, published in the UK by James Nisbet & Co. since 1949, and the Peter and Jane books, published by Ladybird from 1964, used similar 'look-and-say' key word schemes which relied on the memorisation of words through repetition. However, the Plowden report criticised the white, middle-class worlds of such schemes, which ignored the lived experiences of both working-class children and the growing numbers of children from immigrant families in British schools. Publishers such as Macmillan and Longmans responded to this criticism with series such as Macmillan's Nippers, produced in collaboration with children's author Leila Berg, and Longmans' Breakthrough to Literacy series. Karen Sands-O'Connor points

23 Scotland, *The history of Scottish education*, p. 180.

out, however, that both the Plowden Report and the reading material that resulted from it consistently regarded both working-class and Black British readers as problems to be solved by the education system.[24]

Changes in overseas markets

After the Second World War, publishers had to transform their old links with the colonies of the British Empire into new links with the emerging states of the British Commonwealth and beyond. Relationships with newly independent governments had to be established in order to keep access to these vast and lucrative markets, of which Africa's growing market for textbooks was key. From the late 1940s onwards, multinational companies in African countries began increasingly to change from the situation of merely selling textbooks produced outside Africa to one in which there were established branches or indigenised companies within individual countries. Thus Macmillan established itself in countries such as Swaziland, Lesotho, Botswana and Ghana – where it signed an agreement to manage state educational publishing, an outcome hotly resented by its competitors.[25] Meanwhile Longmans concentrated on Nigeria, praising that country's leaders for eschewing the idea of state publishing, and establishing an 'indigenous company' in 1965 using local managerial and editorial talent.[26] It followed this model in establishing companies in Kenya, Malawi, Tanzania and Zambia.[27] After 1962 Longmans identified four specific policy objectives: to obtain a larger share of the British market; to create a new generation of book titles for overseas markets, including books by indigenous authors writing in their own language; to expand and develop ELT materials; and to employ indigenous staff whenever possible in all overseas establishments.[28] However, as a special edition of the *Times Educational Supplement* pointed out in 1974, while sales and distribution departments were comparatively easy to indigenise, major editorial decisions still tended to be taken in London, and although there was a commitment to increase the amount of African and Asian authorship for books on these continents much of the copy-editing was undertaken by freelances in London.[29]

24 Sands-O'Connor, *Children's publishing and Black Britain*, pp. 27–51.
25 Norrie, *Mumby's publishing and bookselling*, p. 139.
26 Briggs, *A history of Longmans*, pp. 413–16.   27 Stevenson, *Book makers*, p. 191.
28 Briggs, *A history of Longmans*, p. 423.
29 Michael Church, 'Turning the tables', *Times Educational Supplement* 14 June 1974, p. 36.

Tim Rix, who coordinated Longmans' overseas publishing, admitted to the *Times Educational Supplement* that they had particular difficulty balancing the need to have African names on the covers of textbooks with a problem in sourcing African textbook illustrators.[30] The success of these indigenised companies depended on being able to work closely with each government's ministry of education to produce materials specifically tailored for national markets. Davis explores what this might mean for a company in her analysis of OUP's relationship with the National government in South Africa.[31] In 1953 the Bantu Education Act established government-controlled, separate black schools. While books for white schools were provided free, in black schools parents had to buy the books themselves. This offered a very lucrative market for OUP's Cape Town branch, which had converted from a sales office to a publishing branch in 1946. While it faced strong competition for the white schools market from Afrikaner publishers, there was less competition for the publishing of textbooks for the black schools. These books had to be approved by the Education Department and were subject to a number of restrictions relating to 'objectionable' material. Davis points out that the wider organisation of OUP called for the support of the academic publishing centre based in Oxford by the sales of the London-managed educational publishing wing, and particularly by OUP's overseas branches.[32] Thus OUP found itself in the situation that its academic publications at home, including liberal, anti-apartheid writings, were subsidised by sales within South Africa, a situation that became a growing PR problem in the UK until the dismantling of apartheid in the 1990s.

By the start of the twenty-first century several educational publishers were heavily invested in Africa. For example, in July 2011 it was reported that Macmillan owned or had a stake in companies in fifteen African countries, including Ethiopia, Gambia, Ghana and Mozambique, although Macmillan Kenya was sold as part of a management buy-out at the end of 2010.[33] However, both Macmillan and OUP were forced to reassess their involvement in this market in 2011 in the wake of accusations of bribery and corruption concerning tenders. This was related to the introduction in the UK of the Bribery Act in July 2011, making UK companies liable for corrupt acts committed by agents or representatives anywhere in the world, with or without their knowledge. Both companies were investigated and fined by the

---

30 *Ibid.* 31 Davis, 'Histories of publishing under apartheid'. 32 *Ibid.*
33 Benedicte Page, 'Macmillan Education to move out of Africa', *Bookseller* 29 July 2011, www.thebookseller.com/news/macmillan-education-move-out-africa.html.

Serious Fraud Office, and in July 2011 Macmillan announced that it was walking away from its education business in East and West Africa.[34]

The Curriculum Development movement

Prior to the Curriculum Development movement of the late 1950s and 1960s, change and innovation in the school curriculum had occurred gradually, sometimes at the instigation of a government or other body and sometimes in response to formal reports or publications such as *The teaching of general science* by the Science Masters Association in 1932.[35] However, a more conscious attempt to 'renew' the curriculum emerged in the late 1950s, initially fuelled by concerns that children were turning against mathematics and science in schools because of the way in which these subjects were taught. Starting with the work of the Physical Science Study Committee in the USA and moving to the UK through organisations such as the Nuffield Foundation and the Schools Mathematics Project, the aim was to emphasise learning by discovery. The teaching of science and maths should become a process of enquiry where 'learning' would replace 'being taught'.

In the UK the Curriculum Development project was led from the early 1960s by the Nuffield Foundation, the Schools Council, the Scottish Education Department and local education authority groups. The aim and, to a certain extent, achievement was that curriculum renewal would become a constant process led by such agencies. The impact of such developments on publishers was far-reaching, particularly with reference to the author–publishing relationship. Instead of textbooks written by individual authors, curriculum development occurred through teams, primarily established and funded through the agencies mentioned above. As the Educational Publishers Council indicated in 1977, if the research and development costs had been funded by publishers, the published price of the resulting materials would have been too high.[36] Instead, after initiating and testing a project's materials, the development agency would invite publishers to tender for the production and publication of the materials on a national scale. The publisher would then fund the production, marketing and distribution of the materials and pay a royalty to the development agency, which usually retained copyright. Publishers such as Chambers, which published the Nuffield Mathematics Project for the Nuffield Foundation, or Blackie, which joined

---

34 *Ibid.*   35 Educational Publishers Council, *Publishing for schools*, p. 41.   36 *Ibid.*, p. 6.

with Chambers to publish Modern Mathematics for Schools for the Scottish Mathematics Group, had to learn to work within these new parameters.

The Curriculum Development movement, with its stress on personal experience and learning by discovery, soon spread to all subjects. Marsden discusses its impact on the teaching of geography and history in schools, noting a trend towards prioritising content less and process more.[37] In history this led to the 'era' or 'patch' approach as an alternative to traditional chronological history, focussing on particular periods in depth, such as the reigns of the Tudors or the Vikings, rather than attempting to present pupils with an overview of the whole coverage of history. As Marsden notes, there was a new emphasis on developing pupils' historical skills, the use of original sources and the promotion of empathetic attitudes towards people in the past. In geography there was a movement away from statistical approaches and towards a 'more humanistic welfare geography' focussing on issues and case studies.[38] Textbooks began to contain a wide range of data sources such as maps, diagrams, graphs and photographs, to encourage pupils to create their own interpretations.[39]

A second phase of organised curriculum change commenced in the latter half of the 1960s. This phase focussed on the notion of compensatory education. The Newsom (1963) and Plowden (1967) reports, which emphasised child-centred learning, had suggested that equality of educational opportunity was not enough to raise the educational attainment of all pupils. Underprivileged children needed to be given more help in the classroom. This led to the creation of mixed-ability groupings, with cooperation rather than competition stressed. The old teaching methods, based on one teacher using a set of thirty textbooks with a whole class of students, were replaced. Now classes might contain separate groups or even individual students working at different rates through a range of activities. There was an emphasis on independent study, projects and discussions. As Becher and Young argue, in such a situation classroom materials attained a position of central importance as essential resources and offered new opportunities for publishers.[40] In addition, publishers were required to produce a wider range of learning materials. Not only were individualised work books, worksheets and activity books needed, but the introduction of new technology to the classroom meant that publishers needed to produce material to be used on video and sound recorders. Thus teams of teachers and authors were joined by sound

---

37 Marsden, The school textbook, p. 46.   38 Ibid., p. 89.
39 Graves and Murphy, 'Research into geography textbooks'.
40 Becher and Young, 'Planning for change'.

recordists, camera operators and film-makers. Full-colour printing for school materials was introduced in the early 1970s – just as colour television arrived in many children's homes – and publishers began to facilitate information skills development, providing indexes and glossaries to help users navigate information. In a highly competitive market, attractive presentation started to count much more than it had done previously.

During the late 1960s much research was undertaken into readability, with an emphasis on the need for educational materials to be targeted at the child. Interest in legibility in schoolbooks was not new: in 1913 an influential report by the British Association for the Advancement of Science on schoolbooks and eyesight had offered advice on appropriate type size, typeface, line length and spacing between lines. In the 1960s, the amount of text was again reduced and more design and typographical features were introduced into school-books. Marsden notes the ubiquity of the use of the two-page illustrated spread in history and geography textbooks, with suggestions for activities, for a timetabled double lesson.[41]

Curriculum development proved to be a mixed blessing for publishers: it required investment either to develop the materials or to tender to publish those developed by the curriculum development agencies. The employment of the right people could also be important – for example, after the publication of the Newsom Report, John Newsom left his post as Director of Education in Hertfordshire to become a chief advisor at Longmans.[42] The Educational Publishers Council (EPC) was established in 1969 to raise the profile of school publishing and to lobby government and local councils for more spending on books. However, two reports on the state of educational publishing which appeared in *Education and Training* to coincide with the formation of the EPC warned that curriculum development offered opportunities that only publishers with large resources could embrace, and that the number of mergers between educational publishers might increase because of current pressures.[43] These rather downbeat accounts of the state of educational publishing also warned that continuous development and the enthusiasm of teachers for change meant that the average life of a textbook had now been reduced from the comparative security of twenty to forty years before the war to less than seven or eight years. The reports drew a picture of a small group of innovative and wealthy houses benefiting from collaboration with the agencies leading curriculum development, with sizeable

41 Marsden, *The school textbook*, p. 50.   42 Briggs, *The history of Longmans*, pp. 422–7.
43 Barlow, 'Educational publishers: enquiry 2'; and Beard, 'Educational publishers: enquiry 1'.

backlists and overseas markets enabling them to support the 'almost inevitable loss on new products in the first year',[44] and a larger group of vulnerable, older, medium-sized houses 'enslaved by ageing backlists they should sell while less committed newcomers steal in on a confused market'.[45] Such houses were described as not having sufficient money or marketing techniques to benefit from curriculum development, and being too deeply entrenched in educational publishing to move fully into more general publishing. The reports also pointed out that such publishers were competing not only with the larger houses, but also with newcomers to the field drawn by the possibility of financial reward, such as Macdonald Educational, which focussed on the production of reference and topic books and held the Nuffield Junior Science contract.

Educational publishers also faced challenges from other sectors: a particularly successful product that emerged at this time was the Jackdaws, launched by the literary publisher Cape in 1963. These were collections of facsimiles of historical documents such as broadsheets, maps and visual materials contained in flapped foolscap wallets. These became so successful by 1966 that Cape established a separate company to publish them.[46] However, the content of Jackdaws was criticised as being of variable quality, with the reproduction of documents sometimes indecipherable and the quality of artwork poor.[47]

Thus educational publishing was completely changed by the Curriculum Development movement and associated changes in teaching methods. By 1975 the Bullock Report described a situation where schools had moved away from a reliance on basic course books, which could be printed in large quantities and so were comparatively cheap. Schools needed to purchase a greater variety of materials (not only books) to support individual and group work. These new materials tended to be more expensive since individual print-runs were lower. The EPC attempted to make these challenges clear in its 1977 *Short guide to educational publishing*, which set out to answer questions such as 'why are "topic" books often proportionately more expensive than the "complete" textbook?' and 'why is there considerable variation in the price of books of similar dimensions, length and appearance?' and to convince its readers – school authorities, teachers and the government – that educational books still offered value for money.

---

44 Barlow, 'Educational publishers: enquiry 2', p. 270.   45 *Ibid.*
46 Stevenson, *Book makers*, p. 187.   47 Marsden, *The school textbook*, p. 68

Growing criticisms of the textbook

One of the motivations behind the publication of the EPC's pamphlet was the fact that from the late 1960s onwards textbooks – and indeed all teaching materials produced by publishers – were under attack. They were criticised by many proponents of curriculum reform for being irrelevant, if not positively harmful for the learning experience. They were also attacked for promoting a white, middle-class and patriarchal ideal. Critics argued that textbooks omitted to consider important issues of race, class and gender, thus reinforcing establishment ideologies.[48]

There had been complaints throughout the twentieth century about bias in textbooks, particularly the presentation of the point of view of the victor over that of the conquered, for example in the use of national and racial stereotypes. In the 1920s the Catholic Education Council protested about the 'unsatisfactory' character of history textbooks used in London County Council schools that over-emphasised the cruelties of 'Bloody Mary' whilst ignoring Tudor persecution of Catholics.[49] While the more obvious stereotypes had been removed from textbooks in the years after the Second World War, more subtle ones remained, particularly in the forms of bias, stereotyping and under-representation.[50] Hicks analysed geography textbooks available in schools in the late 1970s and found a distinct Eurocentric bias which meant that other people and places were measured (and found wanting) against Western European norms.[51] The depiction of ethnic minority groups as problem people living in problem places was increasingly condemned as negative stereotyping that did not take into account the responsibility of developed nations for their situation.[52] Unfortunately, as the EPC pointed out in its 1983 pamphlet *Publishing for a multi-cultural society*, outdated textbooks with their 'defunct imperialist views of other cultures' were still available in schools because budget cuts meant they could not be replaced by newer, better materials.[53]

Gender bias in textbooks began to be discussed in the early 1970s. Feminist activists used content analysis to document both the under-representation of females in textbooks and gender stereotyping. Lobban's 1974 study of six popular British reading schemes found that women and girls were almost solely involved in domestic activity and were not shown as active, inquiring

---

48 Graves and Murphy, 'Research into geography textbooks'.
49 Marsden, *The school textbook*, p. 136. 50 *Ibid.* 51 Hicks, *Bias in geography textbooks*.
52 Marsden, *The school textbook*, p. 142.
53 Educational Publishers Council, *Publishing for a multi-cultural society*, p. 2.

individuals, while a 1981 study of illustrations in geography textbooks found that men outnumbered women four to one.[54] Critics argued that, since reading schemes were children's first introduction to the written word and presented in an authoritative manner, such depictions would influence the attitudes of the child. Reading schemes were also criticised for presenting a middle-class, suburban idyll far from the experience of working-class, urban children.[55] Criticisms focussed particularly on the gendering of examples and illustrations in science textbooks, which tended to exclude female scientists from descriptions of the history of science and used fewer females in illustrations depicting active scientific investigation. It was argued that such bias was particularly problematic for developing countries, where school laboratory facilities might not be satisfactory and therefore textbook depictions were particularly relied upon.[56] Some defenders argued that to show male and female figures equally in the history of physics in a textbook would be to misrepresent science as it had been and still was.[57] Critics responded that publishers of science textbooks should show science both as it was and how it *should* be.

Publishers responded to such criticisms in a number of ways, for example by producing books of poems and songs drawing on Caribbean, African and Indian cultures; more use of non-standard English dialects in storybooks; moving from a Eurocentric to a world perspective; and the development of books on subjects such as comparative religion. Guidelines and reports were issued by both publishers and professional associations,[58] for example the previously mentioned EPC pamphlet *Publishing for a multi-cultural society* and its earlier pamphlet *Sex stereotyping in school and children's books* published in 1981, two years after the formation of a working party on the subject.[59] The aim of these pamphlets was to encourage publishers, writers and illustrators to review their approach in order to 'reflect more truly the social situation'. In both pamphlets, the EPC was keen to emphasise the need for more spending on schoolbooks to remedy the situation, pointing out that less than 1 per cent of the total education expenditure was allocated to books and that such low levels of spending meant that books that reflected outdated attitudes were retained in schools rather than being replaced by more suitable ones. The difficulty of finding suitable authors and translators with the

54 Taylor, 'Sexist bias in physics textbooks'; Marsden, *The school textbook*, p. 142.
55 Davies, *Books in the school curriculum*, p. 79.
56 Whiteley, 'The gender balance of physics textbooks'.   57 *Ibid.*
58 Blumberg, *Gender bias in textbooks*.
59 Educational Publishers Council, *Sex stereotyping*.

appropriate background and experience was noted, as was the need for the examination boards to examine their racial and gender coverage. There were also suggestions that schools with a small intake of ethnic minorities tended to ignore these issues. The issue of presenting society both as it *was* and as it *should be* was also discussed, with the EPC suggesting that publishers had actually published books ahead of demand and that there was a need for more cumulative social change before society caught up with them. This view was supported in 1986 by a report for the National Book League on books in the school curriculum, which stated that many schools continued to use materials published over twenty years ago and that there was a reluctance to buy the more recent and less prejudiced books available.[60]

By the 1990s, according to the Education for All Monitoring Report of 2007, there had been some improvement in the representation of gender in textbooks worldwide.[61] However, as the report pointed out, 'second generation' studies noted the persistence of gender bias in some areas, particularly stereotyping, and increasingly gender initiatives were marginalised by newer concerns, including the increased testing of pupils, a growing concern with 'the boy problem' (for example, poorer reading performance, lower high-school graduation rates, declining enrolments in post-secondary education), and a belief that gender equity had been achieved.[62]

Such criticism of textbooks, plus the earlier curriculum reform movement, led many teachers to dismiss the textbook as a useful educational tool. By 1986, Florence Davies's report for the National Book League on books in the school curriculum described a situation where textbooks had become thoroughly discredited with many teachers, as a result both of the criticisms outlined above and of changing teaching methods brought about by curriculum development, which emphasised teacher-produced materials rather than material 'bought in'.[63] The arrival of the photocopier in schools from the 1960s onwards meant that teacher-produced materials were easier to make and to distribute in class. Davies's report describes the national projects for curriculum development run by organisations such as the Nuffield Foundation and the Schools Council as being antagonistic towards textbooks, seeing them as representing an 'authority' view that threatened the provision of opportunities for children to use their imaginations. Textbooks were criticised as necessary evils and poor compromises between educational desirability and financial viability.[64] Marsden describes this as a specifically

---

60 Davies, *Books in the school curriculum*, p. 77.   61 Blumberg, *Gender bias in textbooks*.
62 *Ibid.*   63 Davies, *Books in the school curriculum*.
64 Sheldon, 'Evaluating ELT textbooks and materials'.

British anti-textbook ethos, comparing Britain to the United States where the focus was on teachers making informed choices of textbooks.[65] Davies's survey found that extremely limited use was made of books in the classroom, as opposed to other resources. She related this to both a lack of funds and teachers' negative perceptions of textbooks. Reading was perceived as a passive process and pupils in both primary and secondary schools had limited access to books apart from materials such as graded readers. Instead, classes relied on photocopied worksheets and pupils' own notes either made from the teacher's dictation or copied from the blackboard. The anti-textbook ethos identified by Davies illustrated why textbook sales might be affected, leading to attempts such as the EPC's pamphlet *A short guide to educational publishing* to promote the good work of educational publishers and to campaign for more spending on books in schools.

A declining market

By the mid-1970s publishers were also contending with the impact of inflation and the loss of some overseas markets. In June 1974 the *Times Educational Supplement* (*TES*) published a special edition to celebrate the 250th anniversary of Longman. While part of the supplement celebrated the success of Longman, with its turnover of £15 million a year, of which two-thirds came from overseas sales, the rest of the supplement was more pessimistic about the future of educational publishing, particularly in the UK, stating that 'something is rotten in the state of educational publishing', and warning that any boom that had accompanied curriculum development might well be over.[66] Galloping inflation and a serious shortage of raw materials had meant that the cost of paper most commonly used for schools publishing had risen by about 50 per cent over the previous year and was expected to rise by a further 50 per cent in 1974. Printers' costs had also risen by about 25 per cent. In addition, publishers faced competition both from abroad and within the UK. US publishers were competing for a share of British educational publishers' overseas markets. The establishment of indigenous publishing companies, some of which were state monopolies, in the former colonies also offered competition. Problems were also caused by the adoption of the Paris revisions to the Berne Convention on Copyright in 1971, under which developing nations were allowed to relax copyright laws to allow publication with permission of works for educational purposes. While the 1977 edition of

65 Marsden, *The school textbook*, p. 55.   66 Church, 'Survival of the fattest?', p. 34.

the EPC's *A short guide to educational publishing* stated that 40 per cent of British book sales were made overseas, with some educational publishers exporting over half their output, when the second edition was published in 1982 this figure had shrunk to 33 per cent.[67] At home, school and local authority resource centres had started undertaking their own publishing, undercutting educational publishers, and television companies were also now seen as major competitors. In 1972–73 the BBC and ITV produced over 14 million copies for the schools market.[68] Such publications tended to be cheaper than those of educational publishers and associated with television programmes viewed in schools – although it was noted that this fact also gave them a built-in obsolescence.[69] The *TES* also noted the recent and controversial closure of Penguin Education, established in the mid-1960s and praised for its innovative series such as Connexions and the Penguin English Project, which aimed to break down the barrier between textbooks and 'real' books. Despite the support of eighty-seven leading figures who wrote to the *TES* deploring the closure, the textbook list was not making money and was abruptly closed down by Penguin's new parent company Pearson Longman in 1974.[70]

The *TES* made the point that even Longman had only survived economic problems by merging with the Pearson group of companies, and commented that any real identity that the company might claim to have had disappeared, symbolised by the death in 1972 at the age of fifty-six of Mark Longman, the last direct link with the founding family. Noting that the Pearson financial empire also included Westminster Press and the *Financial Times* as well as interests in fields as diverse as the Château Latour vineyard and Chessington Zoo, the supplement concluded that Longman 'have chosen to develop a multiplicity of interests at the cost of their individuality'.[71] Longman joined with Pearson in 1968 and the period between then and 1976 has been described as one of restructuring for the company, when it ceased to be thought of as a family concern and aimed to become more professional and competitive. In July 1970 Penguin merged with Pearson Longman.[72]

The example of Longman demonstrates, as with other sectors, the growing role of large corporations in educational publishing in the second half of

67 Educational Publishers Council, *Publishing for schools*, second edition.
68 Church, 'The survival of the fattest?', p. 35.   69 *Ibid.*
70 Jonathan Croall, 'Bound to succeed', *Times Educational Supplement* 9 June 1995, www .tes.co.uk/article.aspx?storycode=10539.
71 Brian Alderson, 'At the sign of the ship', *Times Educational Supplement* 14 June 1974, p. 29.
72 Briggs, *A history of Longmans*, pp. 441–83.

the twentieth century. In the 1950s many educational publishing houses were run by publisher-owners, such as the Longman or Macmillan families, but a wave of mergers and acquisitions from the early 1960s onwards meant that by the 1990s the publishing business as a whole was made up of a handful of large corporations, each an umbrella organisation for many imprints.[73] As Thompson describes, there were two phases of consolidation in educational publishing. Firstly, from the early 1960s to the early 1980s, educational publishers became attractive to large corporations with substantial stakes in industries such as information, education and computing because it was hoped that the content they owned might be 'repurposed', for example through new technology such as computers. In the second phase, educational publishers became attractive to corporations with an existing interest in publishing but based outside the UK and USA, for example in Australia or Europe.[74] These corporations needed to grow through the acquisition of other publishing houses. Thus, in 1962 the Scottish educational publisher Thomas Nelson & Sons merged into the North American Thomson Organisation in an effort to sustain its educational publishing interests on a global scale. The new management separated the editorial and printing operations, and the printing and binding division of the company, based in Edinburgh, was sold in 1968. In 1983 the colophon showing Thomas Nelson's shop in Edinburgh was dropped from the imprint, and in 2000 Thomas Nelson merged with Stanley Thornes to form Nelson Thornes, part of the Wolters Kluwer group, which has its head office in the Netherlands.

A new National Curriculum

The 1980s proved to be particularly testing for educational publishers as school budgets were squeezed throughout the UK. Report after report from organisations such as the Educational Publishers Council, the National Book League and the Book Trust found that schools were spending less on book provision. As the EPC pointed out in 1982, 'The practical test of many officially sponsored curriculum materials is not "Do they do what they aim to do?" but "Can they be produced at a price schools can afford?"'[75]

The Education Reform Act of 1988 introduced the National Curriculum, Ofsted (the Office for Standards in Education), national testing of pupils at the ages of seven, eleven and fourteen, and local management of school budgets.

---

73 Thompson, *Merchants of culture*, p. 102.   74 *Ibid.*, pp. 101–18.
75 Educational Publishers Council, *Publishing for schools*, second edition, p. 45.

Individual schools were given more responsibility for their own budgets away from local education authorities. This impacted negatively on book purchase as hard-pressed schools had to make decisions on which non-teaching costs to cut, making library and school books vulnerable. Schoolbooks exports, already suffering because of the strength of sterling, the continued growth of local publishing in developing countries and international competition, were also hit by the National Curriculum, making it more difficult to export books written specifically for English and Welsh schools (Scotland had its own 5–14 curriculum).

A response to concerns over a reported decline in educational standards and a reaction to the previous generation's child-centred approach, the 1988 National Curriculum was a subject-based and assessment-led curriculum that prescribed the content of what should be taught at all levels in schools. As a consequence, many backlist books became obsolete. For example, natural history books were suddenly no longer in demand because the subject had no official place in the curriculum.[76] The schools market thus became even more competitive, and some publishers, such as E. J. Arnold of Leeds (founded in 1863), found themselves forced out of business altogether.[77]

In response to criticism, the National Curriculum was slimmed down by the Dearing revisions in 1995, but such instability and recurrent changes caused further problems for publishers, as the *TES* reported in June of that year, because schools stopped spending money on books for the eighteen months prior to the changes until they knew what would be in the revised curriculum. Publishers were then given only a few months to incorporate all changes before the revised curriculum was put in place.[78]

Changing governments – changing priorities

A new Labour government was elected to power in 1997 with the promise that its priorities would be 'Education, Education, Education'. A massive increase in spending on books in schools followed to support its new National Literacy Strategy and the National Year of Reading (1998–99), which used schools and libraries to promote reading to both children and adults. In total, schools in the UK received grants amounting to £140 million between January 1998 and July 1999. According to the *Bookseller* publication *Book publishing in Britain*, sales to primary schools increased from £77 million

76 Diana Hinds, 'Pressed for time', *Times Educational Supplement Magazine* 1 March 2002.
77 Stevenson, *Book makers*, p. 74.
78 John Davies, 'Under the chariot's wheels', *Times Educational Supplement* 10 February 1995.

in 1997 to £90 million in 1998.[79] Publishers of reading schemes and children's books did well because the money was focussed on lifting reading attainment and reading for pleasure. However, industry observers suggested that other educational publishers suffered in comparison and, in particular, sales to secondary schools remained flat.

Educational publishers were also faced with the growing challenge of the digitisation of educational resources. Since 1981, when the Minister for Information Technology, Kenneth Baker, stated that his aim was to put a computer into every school, there had been political enthusiasm for the provision of computers and later internet access for all schools. A Department for Education and Employment survey in 1998 estimated that there were on average over one hundred computers per secondary school in England: one computer for every nine pupils.[80] Once schools had computers, there was a move towards the wider use of digital content in classrooms. In 2002 the Labour government introduced a funded initiative entitled Curriculum Online to create a framework for electronic schools publishing. Schools were given e-learning credits to spend through the Curriculum Online portal, which was launched to provide schools with a shop window on publishers' digital resources. The initiative spurred participating publishers to develop their digital content, although the system faced teething problems. In September 2003 the *Bookseller* reported that out of the first tranche of funding worth £30 million, only £25 to £27 million had been spent, with a further tranche of £100 million needing to be spent by August the following year.[81] The e-learning credit initiative was particularly welcome to educational publishers, however, because 2002–3 was a period of deep crisis for the sector. Drastic under-budgeting by local education authorities in the wake of a redistribution of funds and higher than expected salary, pensions and National Insurance costs led to a serious spending crisis. Faced with the need to cut their budgets or lose teachers, schools chose to slash their spending on schoolbooks. Approximately 10 per cent of the educational publishing industry's staff lost their jobs as a result.[82]

The e-learning credits initiative acted as a spur for publishers in a particularly dark time to digitise their resources, leading the EPC to state that the landscape of schools publishing had been dramatically altered by the

79 Mitchell, *Book publishing in Britain.*
80 Hayden, 'Subject discipline dimensions of ICT and learning'.
81 Tom Holman, 'Back to school with a bump', *Bookseller* 4 September 2003.
82 Tom Holman, 'Cuts cripple schools sector', *Bookseller* 9 September 2003.

initiative.[83] However, further complications were introduced in early 2003 when the government approved plans by the BBC to create its own digital curriculum to be offered in parallel to Curriculum Online. The materials would be funded by licence-fee money and be offered free, thus limiting opportunities for paid-for material. The BBC did promise to spend half of its £90 million budget for content with commercial suppliers, and the government imposed limitations on the amount of material the BBC could produce focussed on core subjects. Educational publishers joined forces with other publishers, the Booksellers Association, the British Educational Communication and Technology Agency and the British Educational Supplies Association to coordinate opposition to the BBC's plans. Publishers producing materials for Welsh and Scottish schools were particularly concerned because e-learning credits were not available there, leading to fears that the BBC's resources would dominate the digital education market. The BBC Digital Curriculum – later known as BBC Jam – was launched in January 2007 and soon attracted 170,000 registered users. In March 2007, however, the BBC Trust suspended the service in response to the news that the European Commission had received complaints from publishing companies in the commercial sector that it was damaging their interests by supplying so much free material. The following May the BBC announced that it was axing 200 jobs from its online education service. E-learning credits were scrapped in August 2008, leading the Publishers Association to call for schools to make proper allocations out of their own budgets to fund the purchase of e-learning resources,[84] although such budgets were also squeezed tightly by the economic conditions of the time. Other possibilities beginning to be explored included e-books, with the suggestion that an e-book reader would be much lighter to carry than a fully loaded school bag, although the *Bookseller* warned in 2012 that the UK was lagging behind other countries in this area, for example the Taiwanese government's 'e-schoolbags programme'.[85]

Recent years

By 2010 the EPC estimated that educational resources were worth at least £270 million per year, perhaps as much as £370 million, to the publishing industry, with textbooks making up around £150 million (just over half) of this

83 'The £280m windfall', *Bookseller* 17 January 2003.
84 Victoria Arnstein, 'Back to school', *Bookseller* 12 June 2008.
85 Sara Lloyd, 'Child benefits', *Bookseller* 5 March 2012.

amount and digital materials around £65 million (around one quarter). A Conservative–Liberal Democrat coalition government came into office in 2010, meaning new educational policies and – in particular – a commitment to spending cuts. In November 2010 new funding arrangements for schools were announced by the coalition government in which previously separate funding streams were grouped together in a single grant. One of the early cuts instigated by the new government was the removal of the quango Becta – the British Educational Communication and Technology Agency – which had worked with the EPC in its campaigns against BBC Jam. By 2011 the Publishers Association was warning that schoolbook purchases had been hit by recent cutbacks and that they anticipated further cuts in 2012. At the same time, the coalition government announced sweeping changes to the curriculum, with a return to 'conventional approaches to teaching'[86] and a refocussing on what was taught rather than how it was taught. The response of the EPC was to launch an advocacy campaign in autumn 2010 focussing on a study that showed that pupils in schools that spent more on professionally published resources, both printed and digital, improved faster than those in schools that spent less.

Conclusion

Over the course of the twentieth and early twenty-first centuries, the market for educational publishers has been very susceptible to political and socio-economic forces. Educational publishers have had to respond not only to alterations in political ideologies but also to shifts in educational theory and practice. Publishers have needed to respond quickly to changes in government policy, and the relationship of publishers with educational reformers such as Newbolt and Newsom, who both later moved into educational publishing to put their theories into practice, demonstrates a close, if not symbiotic, link. The curriculum development reforms of the 1950s and 1960s urged a more child-centred curriculum, while the 1980s brought in a more prescribed and assessment-led national curriculum. Both reforms impacted heavily on the products and the practices of educational publishers.

Over the century, educational publishers have had to adapt to supply schools not just with textbooks but also with classroom materials, audio-visual products, teachers' aids, software and related internet sites. While there remains an overseas market for educational publishers' products,

---

86 'Schools Bill boost for publishers', *Bookseller* 3 December 2010.

materials have to be very market specific, take into account local needs and local curricula, and be produced locally – all of which requires investment. Educational publishers therefore tend to be branches of larger multinationals. For these publishers, educational publishing can provide a solid and profitable list that can support more risky publishing. It is more difficult for new publishers to enter the market because of the requirement for investment and product development before large sales can be achieved, although some smaller publishers have survived by identifying a niche market. Nonetheless, in 2011 the EPC listed forty-four members publishing educational resources, representing over 80 per cent of market turnover, demonstrating that educational publishing was still a healthy industry in the second decade of the twenty-first century.

Popular science

PETER J. BOWLER

The production of popular literature devoted to science had flourished in the Victorian period and developed further in the early twentieth century.[1] Further media developments in the later twentieth century and into the twenty-first have affected the public's interaction with science, reinstating in some ways the more fluid situation that existed before the emergence of a professionalised scientific community towards the end of the nineteenth century. From the inclusion of science news in mass-market newspapers and magazines to the emergence of the internet, information on science and comment on its significance has flourished alongside technical scientific publication (although, as will be discussed later, there are formats that blur the latter distinction).

The study of popular science thus offers an excellent platform from which to view the effects of new media on the relationship between writers, publishers and readers, to say nothing of the growing input from other forms of communication. But the topic also raises specific problems of interest to scholars seeking to understand the relationship between those who actually produce scientific knowledge (and apply it) and the mass of the public affected by these developments. Should popular science be seen as a process in which knowledge produced by experts is disseminated in a simplified form to an essentially passive public which needs to know about discoveries of cultural or practical significance? This is the so-called 'dominant view' of science popularisation, favoured by some scientists in the mid-twentieth century. It assumes that the flow is one-way and top-down, and gives control to the scientists or to science writers who are trained in science and sympathetic to scientific progress. However, historians have shown that the 'dominant view' did not operate in the periods before the emergence of a professionalised scientific community at the very end of the

---

1 On the Victorian era, see Secord, 'Science, technology and mathematics'.

nineteenth century.[2] Experience in the modern world from the 1960s onwards also displays its weaknesses: much popular interest in science reflects public concerns about its impact that are ambivalent to, if not openly critical of, the scientists' ambitions. To understand what is going on we need a more fluid and interactive model, and the scientists themselves have learned that they must now accept the role of mass media which respond to the public's concerns rather than the scientific community's expectations. To have any hope of influencing the process, the scientists must get involved with the media, and the twentieth century is a period in which they have been forced to relearn skills once central to the careers of earlier figures such as Michael Faraday and Thomas Henry Huxley.[3]

The dominant view of science popularisation has sometimes been linked to the assumption that, once the scientific community became truly professionalised, it retreated into an ivory tower and lost interest in communicating with the public. With assured funding from government and industry, the scientists felt that they should concentrate on their research – writing for a wider audience was discouraged. A new generation of science writers would take over the job, but because they had scientific training they would continue to reflect the interests of the scientific community. This was the situation which went so badly wrong from the 1960s onwards when the public became concerned about the threats of nuclear weapons and pollution, and the science writers began to take those concerns into consideration. There had always been trivialised and sensationalised stories about science in the mass media, much distrusted by the scientists themselves, but now the whole process of interaction began to reflect the pressures that led to the over-simplification and manipulation of information about science. This chapter discusses how, like the dominant view itself, this image of a scientific community that temporarily abandoned its responsibility to communicate is something of a myth. There were always professional scientists willing to produce popular texts, although they certainly felt more comfortable with some modes of dissemination than others. The transition to the era of dedicated science writers and science correspondents was thus a slow and complex process. The first full-time science writers of the 1940s and 1950s were preceded by a generation of part-timers working from both within and without the professional scientific community.

2 See, for instance, Cooter and Pumphrey, 'Separate spheres and public places', and Morus, *Frankenstein's children*.
3 Critiques include Hilgartner, 'The dominant view of popularization', and Whitley, 'Knowledge producers and knowledge acquirers'.

It should be noted that the situation in Britain was significantly different from that existing in the United States. Like many European countries, Britain had a long tradition recognising the role of experts, and the experts had often addressed the general public directly. In America there was much distrust of experts, and the folk-hero for science and technology was the self-taught inventor Thomas Edison. It was assumed that ordinary people could make their own judgements about scientific progress. This attitude existed in Britain, especially for areas such as astronomy and new technologies such as radio, but the expert (now professional) scientist was also expected to play a more active role. Where the American scientific community had to struggle to gain a hearing, in Britain there were avenues readily available for the scientists to communicate.[4]

Promoting science: the scientists

In the Victorian era eminent scientists such as T. H. Huxley were public intellectuals who fought to gain a role for science in the national culture by writing and lecturing. They promoted science, and conducted their debates over its religious and ideological implications, in the widest possible arena. The professional scientists of the early twentieth century no longer needed to make their case in this way, and it has sometimes been assumed that they lost interest in, or even actively discouraged, popular writing.[5] This was not, in fact, the case: many still took seriously their perceived obligation to make the public better informed about science. Nor was this a simple effort to dis-seminate a scientific consensus, since non-specialist books and articles offered the only forum within which the scientists could debate the larger issues raised by their work. During the 1920s and 1930s the religious implications of new developments in physics and biology were commented on by scientists from both the rationalist and the more traditional perspectives, while the role of science in national culture still prompted exhortations from liberal thinkers and, increasingly, from the political Left.[6] In addition, though, there was a strong tradition of trying to inform ordinary people about knowledge on which consensus had been reached. The Marxists of the 1930s dismissed the efforts of the previous generation, but in fact a significant number of scientists were making serious efforts to ensure that ordinary people were made aware

4 On America see Burnham, *How superstition won and science lost*, LaFollette, *Making science our own*, and Tobey, *The American ideology of national science*.
5 See, for instance, Knight, 'Getting science across'.
6 Bowler, *Reconciling science and religion*.

of developments that might affect their everyday lives. That such efforts tended to assume that science played a role in the industrial developments sustaining the Empire should not detract from a recognition that they were serious and well meant. Many scientists felt that their field offered an important route for people seeking to improve themselves.[7]

Inevitably much of what was written in the first half of the twentieth century reflected a top-down model of disseminating knowledge, but there was a significant market for improving literature. It was the decline of this market later in the century that may have prompted many scientists to lose interest in popular writing, because they felt much less comfortable writing for a wider audience that needed greater stimulation before they would take an interest in such technical issues.

Nevertheless, books written by scientists could become best-sellers, especially when they expounded controversial opinions on the latest developments. Sir James Jeans and Sir Arthur Eddington conducted a friendly rivalry at Cambridge University Press in the production of commentaries on the religious implications of the latest developments in cosmology and atomic physics, and Jeans's *The mysterious universe* of 1930 sold well over 100,000 copies.[8] Even the more down-to-earth educational material could achieve big sales if well promoted: written from the political Left, Lancelot Hogben's *Mathematics for the million* (1936) and *Science for the citizen* (1938) reached a wider audience than most self-education material.[9] The biologists J. Arthur Thomson and Julian Huxley both achieved considerable publishing successes, especially in the format of works originally published in parts resembling magazines. Huxley's *The science of life* (written in conjunction with H. G. Wells), for instance, was issued in fortnightly parts before appearing as a single volume. As scientists were notoriously badly paid, especially at the start of their careers, the extra money to be made from writing would have seemed very attractive.

For the significant proportion of the scientific community that engaged in popular writing in the first half of the century, there was little evidence of disapproval from their peers so long as the activity did not interfere with research and had obvious educational value. However, the situation was different when it came to writing for popular magazines and the newspapers, where science news was often sensationalised by journalists with little knowledge of the field. There were exceptions, of course: the annual meetings of

7 The role of scientists in this period is explored in Bowler, *Science for all*.
8 Whitworth, 'The clothbound universe'.
9 Unwin, 'The advertising of books'; Unwin, *The truth about a publisher*, p. 228.

the British Association for the Advancement of Science were widely and usually seriously reported in the press, as were the Royal Institution's popular lectures (the latter usually translated into book form soon after delivery). Those scientists who did make the effort to reach a wider audience through the popular press risked being tarred with the brush of sensationalism, and Julian Huxley's election to the Royal Society was delayed because of fears that he was becoming a dilettante.[10]

When the market for serious self-education literature declined later in the century, fewer scientists were willing to take the risk of devoting serious time to the interaction with the mass media needed to reach a wide audience. This was especially true once television became the main medium (although the accompanying books sometimes took a more traditional approach). A few scientists such as Jacob Bronowski were able to take control of their own programmes, but all too often scientists were merely interviewed by presenters whose real aim was to maximise public impact. Bronowski's *Ascent of man* (1973) was a great success, but this can be contrasted with a series such as Nigel Calder's *Violent universe* of 1969 which expounded new developments in cosmology by focussing on the battle between supporters and opponents of the 'big bang' theory. Successful scientist-popularisers such as Carl Sagan and Stephen Jay Gould found their reputations tarnished because their colleagues thought they were wasting valuable research time.[11]

Only in the later twentieth century did the scientific community wake up to the fact that it needed to interact with the mass media if its voice was to be heard at all.[12] The claim that real scientists should concentrate on their research and leave communicating with the public to specialist writers and television presenters was based on the assumption that these communicators would always promote a positive image of science and present the information that the scientists themselves thought appropriate. But as public concerns about the potentially harmful consequences of some technologies mounted in the 1960s the communicators responded by producing much more critical accounts of the latest developments, some being openly hostile as in the case of Rachel Carson, whose 1962 book *Silent spring* became a bestseller by highlighting the environmental problems generated by pesticides. Other threats also became apparent, including the rise of the creationists' attack on evolutionism. By the later decades of the twentieth century, scientists had begun to recognise that to make their views heard they

10 Bowler, *Science for all*, pp. 221–7. 11 Goodell, *The visible scientists*.
12 Surveys of popular science over this wider period include Broks, *Understanding popular science*, Gregory and Miller, *Science in public*, and Knight, *Public understanding of science*.

would have to take a more active role in popularisation. The temporary phase of hostility to successful scientist-authors evaporated and soon scientific organisations such as the Royal Society were actively encouraging their members to get involved with the public. Some efforts were rather simple minded, as with the 'public understanding of science' movement which simply assumed that the public lacked accurate information about science. More recently it has been recognised that the scientific community needs to engage more actively with the public's genuine concerns about where new technologies are taking us.

Engaging with science: the science writers

Where the scientists themselves were not involved, who did write the books and articles read by the general public? At the most popular level – newspapers and weekly magazines – short articles were produced anonymously, presumably by hack writers who borrowed from trivial and sometimes out-of-date sources. To justify this, W. T. Stead, the editor of *Cassell's Magazine*, insisted that professional scientists couldn't write without using jargon incomprehensible to the public.[13] But to produce a substantial article, let alone a book, required some familiarity with technicalities, and there were numerous writers who produced texts at this level. Some wrote in their spare time, and were thus only semi-professional writers. The hugely prolific Charles R. Gibson was the manager of a carpet factory, but produced books on many aspects of physical science and technology, including the innovative *Autobiography of an electron* of 1911. This and many other of his books were published by Seely (later Seely, Service & Co.), a firm specialising in the well-produced books for teenagers sometimes referred to as 'reward books' (see below). Such authors had often had some exposure to applied science early in their careers (the Great War offered many opportunities in this respect) or had built up contacts with the local academic and industrial communities – Gibson, for instance, collaborated with teachers at a nearby technical college in Glasgow. Such contacts supplied advice and information, but also tended to ensure that writers from this background reflected the interests of the scientific community by promoting the image of science as the motor of technical and social progress.

There were also areas where the most enthusiastic amateur specialists rubbed shoulders with the professionals, but were in a better position to

13 Broks, *Media science before the Great War.*

write at the popular level. This was the case for astronomy and natural history, but also for new technologies such as radio and photography. The best of these amateur enthusiasts wrote for their less advanced brethren, and sometimes collaborated with professional scientists in this activity. The publisher Wireless Press issued books and magazines building on this collaboration and also published the popular science magazine *Conquest*. But sometimes there was tension between the professionals and the expert amateurs, since the latter had little time for the more abstruse theoretical aspects of their fields. 'Professor' A. M. Low was a prolific author of books and articles on technical matters, and became the science advisor of the magazine *Armchair Scientist* in 1929. But he had no academic qualifications and was suspicious of 'big science' done in universities and industry. Active into the 1950s, he was an inventor of the old school, and thought that technical developments should still come from amateurs working on their own. Although he promoted scientific progress, he was more in tune with the American vision of how this should be done. Not surprisingly, the academic experts were hostile to this rival vision, especially as Low did not hesitate to express himself in the popular press. His articles frequently hailed visionary technical possibilities. Some were serious, such as the mobile telephone, still a long way ahead in the 1920s (and he predicted that they would become a nuisance on trains). But many were simply ridiculous, such as an electric bed which tipped the occupant out when the alarm rang.[14]

The literature on technical progress was often more concerned with news of the latest developments, although there was also much self-educational material available. Getting the latest news out to the public was always a problem for the scientists, since they disliked writing at the level of the daily or weekly publications. At the beginning of the century, *The Times* was the only newspaper with a science correspondent. The biologist J. B. S. Haldane later tried to offer himself as a correspondent to the national newspapers, but ended up writing for the Communist *Daily Worker*. It was only in the middle decades of the century that the profession of science correspondent begin to emerge, J. D. Crowther and Ritchie Calder being early examples (and both also the authors of numerous books). In 1947 the Association of British Science Writers was formed, yet in the same year it was said that all the science correspondents in the country could fit into a single

---

14 On Low, see Bloom, *He lit the lamp*. On the science magazines generally, see Bowler, *Science for all*, chapter 9.

taxi-cab.[15] In the subsequent decades, however, their number would grow, and expand even further as new media came on stream. Although these writers built up good contacts with the scientific community, their interactions with editors and publishers made them well aware of the demands of the mass media, and increasingly they would become less willing slavishly to follow the line preferred by the scientists.[16]

Science and self-education

The scientists themselves felt most comfortable writing for the substantial market in what can be called 'self-education' literature. By the early twentieth century, secondary education was widely available but few had the opportunity to study at college or university. Many sought to improve themselves by studying at home or through an extramural scheme, and they required what were, in effect, sugar-coated textbooks – cheap, reasonably authoritative surveys written in an attractive manner. Publishers were anxious to reach this market and founded numerous series of self-education books. Typical was the Home University Library launched by Williams and Norgate in 1911 at the price of one shilling. The science editor was Professor J. Arthur Thomson and about a third of the titles were in this area. Authors were offered an advance of £50 and could expect sales in the tens of thousands. In 1926 Benn's Sixpenny Library introduced a series of short paperbacks, again including numerous science topics ranging from relativity to the age of the earth. For most of these series, the authors were almost all professional academics and scientists – the publishers knew that their readers expected the texts to be written by acknowledged authorities. Some series had a deeper agenda: the publisher C. A. Watts was linked to the Rationalist Press Association and published several series promoting the rationalist ideology, including its Thinker's Library, which specialised in reprints of classic texts by Darwin, among others.

In 1937 the Pelican series was launched as a spin-off from Penguin books, offering cheap paperbacks in a much more attractive format than the Sixpenny Library. There was a substantial science presence in the series, mostly reprints in the early years, but as the series became more popular during the Second World War it increasingly published up-to-date surveys written by working scientists. Pelicans were the last great success of the self-

---

15 Editorial in *Penguin Science News* 4 (1947), pp. 6–8. Presumably this meant only the full-time science writers.
16 Bowler, *Science for all*, chapter 10.

education series, surviving until the market itself began to decline in the latter decades of the century. Penguin also issued two series of works featuring semi-popular articles by scientists, *New Biology*, started in 1945, and *Science News* in 1946. Each volume had the format of a thin paperback and contained news items and a number of longer pieces. They appeared several times per year and both series continued through the 1950s.[17]

Even more successful in terms of sales – sometimes exceeding 100,000 – were the serial works issued in magazine format which accumulated to form an encyclopaedic text on a particular subject, which was then often subsequently reissued in book format. The great success of this genre was H. G. Wells's *The outline of history*. Issued by Newnes in 1920, it contained some science in the form of an introduction to the evolution of life on earth.[18] Even before the Great War, Newnes, along with Cassell, Harmsworth and Hutchinson, had issued numerous serial works of an educational nature, and in 1911 Harmsworth launched their *Popular Science*, edited by Arthur Mee (of the much-loved *Children's Encyclopaedia*), with a full-page advertisement in the *Daily Mail*. Unlike the book series, these serials were mostly written by experienced popular authors rather than academics, although the latter did get involved in some cases, as when Julian Huxley teamed up with Wells to write *The science of life* (1929–30), offered as a follow-up to *The outline of history*.

Much less successful were the popular science magazines, which tried to combine self-educational articles with news about the latest developments. *Discovery*, launched in 1920 by John Murray, was very much a vehicle for the scientific community, and it was run at a loss with sales of only a few thousand a month. *Conquest*, founded in the previous year by the Wireless Press, sought to combine articles written by popular authors and by experts, but it too struggled and closed down after six years. *Armchair Science*, founded in 1929, was even more aggressively populist and openly proclaimed its intention of not publishing contributions by professional scientists. Its science advisor was A. M. Low, and its focus resolutely on applied science of value to the ordinary citizen. The first magazine successfully to present news from the mainstream scientific community to the public was *New Scientist*, founded in 1956 and increasingly using material produced by the new breed of science correspondents. Although working scientists now contributed fewer articles to magazines, it became increasingly obvious that the scientific community could not afford to remain aloof from popular concerns and interests. In the

17 *Ibid.*, chapter 7.
18 Skelton, 'The paratext of everything'. On the science serials, see Bowler, *Science for all*, chapter 7.

1980s the formation of the Committee on the Public Understanding of Science (COPUS) by the Royal Society and other professional bodies began to encourage scientists to gain experience in how to deal with journalists, correspondents and television presenters anxious to interview them for news on the latest developments.

Hobbies and big issues

In addition to the texts aimed at self-improvement, there were books, serial works and magazines for those with more specific interests in topics with some science content. Natural history is perhaps the best example, although there was also a considerable body of amateur astronomers. Huge numbers of books aimed at all levels of interest and with a wide range of prices were produced for these readers. Many were written by amateur experts, but some professional scientists also addressed this market. The serial Hutchinson's *Animals of all countries* (1923–24), for instance, featured articles by both professional and expert amateur zoologists.

The same was true for hobbyists attracted to new technologies such as radio, photography and new methods of transport. The Wireless Press produced books and magazines aimed at the radio ham (in addition to the general magazine *Conquest*), and there was a strong market for books on aeroplanes, shipping and the new-fangled motor car – long before the latter came within reach of the ordinary person.

A characteristic product of the early decades of the century was the so-called reward books, well-printed and illustrated texts intended as school prizes or as presents for middle-class children. The publisher Seeley, Service specialised in these texts, many of which featured technical developments and had titles hailing the 'romance' or 'triumphs' of modern science and engineering. Some of the reward books were written by scientists but the majority were by expert amateurs, of whom Charles R. Gibson was probably the most prolific. Gibson stressed the progress of applied science and industry, although we have also noted A. M. Low's less enthusiastic attitude towards 'big science' – he was more in tune with the amateur hobbyist tinkering in his garden shed.

Because this literature focussed on practical interests, it tended to bypass the big theoretical developments in science, although Gibson wrote *The autobiography of an electron* (1911) to highlight the latest developments in atomic physics. The big theoretical issues were more usually addressed by the scientists who were directly involved – the theory of relativity, for instance, gained notoriety precisely because it was held that only a handful of specialists could understand it.[19] Some scientists, for example Sir James Jeans and Sir Arthur Eddington, gained considerable public profiles commenting on the apparently bizarre philosophical implications of nuclear physics. Other intellectuals also got involved – Bertrand Russell wrote introductions to the new developments in physics to make money at an early stage in his career.[20] The new physics seems to have replaced evolution as a topic of public concern (in Britain, but not in America), although books and articles on fossils were popular and were becoming increasingly better illustrated. Scientists such as Fred Hoyle and Jacob Bronowski continued the tradition of commenting on big issues into the age of radio and television, with figures such as Brian Cox representing its current manifestation. Like Bronowski's hugely successful BBC series *The ascent of man* of 1973, Cox's *Wonders of the universe* and *Wonders of the solar system* have been turned into copiously illustrated and best-selling books. Cox's sales have been boosted by his image being promoted as a former pop-star turned noted physicist.

Challenging technoscience

In addition to the tensions within the popular presentation of science between the supporters of the scientific community and those who preferred a more direct involvement by interested amateurs, a more systematic challenge to the increasingly strong link between science and big business came from the Marxists of the 1930s. The work of Lancelot Hogben and J. B. S. Haldane was typical of this effort to empower the general public so that it could understand the science and hence perhaps influence government policies.[21] Hogben's *Science for the citizen* of 1938 was intended to give ordinary people the background they needed to assess new developments, while Haldane wrote prolifically for magazines and popular newspapers – including, as noted, the Communist *Daily Worker*. There was also considerable suspicion of the scientific enterprise emanating from public intellectuals such as J. W. N. Sullivan, Aldous Huxley and Gerald Heard – the latter a prolific broadcaster on the BBC. The science fiction stories of H. G. Wells adopted an increasingly ambivalent tone towards technical innovation, as

---

19 Friedman and Donley, *Einstein as myth and muse.*
20 Monk, *Bertrand Russell*, pp. 22–4.   21 Werskey, *The visible college.*

in *The shape of things to come* (1933) and the blockbuster film based on it – a premonition perhaps of the attitudes displayed in later decades and today.[22] Tensions between the intellectual and scientific communities continued to hit the headlines later in the century, most notably in the controversy sparked by C. P. Snow's 'Two Cultures' lecture and the more recent 'science wars'. In the latter episode, scientists protested against what they perceive to be a dismissal of their claim to provide objective knowledge by sociologists and postmodernist scholars.[23]

Public concerns about the unpredictable or even dangerous manifestations of applied science increased from the 1950s onwards, coinciding with a growing reluctance of the scientific community to engage in public relations. Improved educational opportunities undermined the market for the more didactic kind of popular science, while television offered a far more challenging medium for a scientific community that preferred to control how its discoveries were presented. The scientists may have hoped that the increasingly numerous body of full-time science correspondents would present their case, but these writers – to say nothing of other media professionals – were necessarily responsive to public concerns. Meanwhile, the trivialisation of science in the mass media, always the bugbear of the scientists, continued unabated. Now the internet has transformed the public's ability to both access and comment on science news, allowing anyone with a critical perspective potentially to reach a huge audience. Anti-science movements flourish, including opposition to genetic engineering, the denial of global warming and the creationists' rejection of evolutionism. In despair, scientists called for better 'public understanding of science', but attempts to reinstate a top-down model of communication were doomed to fail in the age of television and the World Wide Web. Led by organisations such as the Royal Society and the British Science Association, the scientific community has begun to learn how to engage with public concerns and appreciates the value of individual scientists who become media-savvy.[24] Paradoxically, the internet has also opened new opportunities to enlist the public's help in certain kinds of research projects, such as gathering information on environmental changes. The internet also

---

22 On Wells, see, for instance, Mackenzie and Mackenzie, *The time traveler*. On science fiction generally, see Aldiss and Wingrove, *Trillion-year spree*.

23 Ortolano, *The two cultures controversy*. On the science wars, see Gross and Levitt, *Higher superstition*.

24 These concerns are articulated, for instance, in Gregory and Miller, *Science in public*.

allows ordinary people to help analyse masses of observational data unsuitable for computers, such as the classification of galaxies observed by the Hubble space telescope (www.galaxyzoo.org). So there may be an eventual synthesis of the top-down and the more interactive models of science communication.

12

Popular history

HELEN WILLIAMS

As Leslie Howsam has noted, most research into book culture has addressed 'the publishing histories of canonical or popular literature, or of science. The publishing history of history has been neglected.'[1] Twentieth-century social and cultural historians have examined the nature of historical writing alongside debates on the nature of history itself but have paid little attention to the economics of publishing history books for the general reader. Likewise, little research has been done in archives to illuminate the publishers' perspective and decision-making processes in relation to particular works. Given the paucity of existing work, this chapter can only serve as an introduction and general review of publishing practices and developments since 1914.

'Popular history' is a broad field, encompassing general histories of Britain and its constituent nations, of Europe and of the world; military history; historical biography; pictorial history; local history publications of many varieties; history-as-fiction; 'niche' histories; and genealogy. Related media are also a significant consideration: not only are books published as tie-ins to television series, but they can be accompanied by CD-Roms, DVDs and websites. Even before new media had an impact, improved and cheaper printing techniques, developed at an increasing pace over the last half-century, allowed the inclusion of more illustrated matter. It is difficult to be sure how many history titles were published, or were in print, over the period. Definitions of the genre are vague: historical biography may or may not be included; some statistics include academic publications, others only 'trade'. However, overall there has been an increase in popularity of history as a genre over the period, with occasional 'fast-sellers' and many more 'steady-sellers'. Publishers both seek new authors (including books for use in schools) and rely on republished 'long-selling' backlist titles.

1 Howsam, *Past into print*, p. x.

At the beginning of the twenty-first century there was, according to David Cannadine,

> an unprecedented interest in history: among publishers, in the newspapers, on radio and on film, and (especially) on television; and from the general public who, it seemed, could not get enough of it. Translated into the market-orientated language of our day, it looked as though more history was being produced and consumed than ever before.[2]

Comparable figures for the whole period are not available, but Cannadine's assertion is borne out, as far as print publication is concerned, in the statistics brought together on the *Making History* website. The figures given for five-year periods, beginning in 1971, show a steady growth initially, with a more rapid rise from the late 1980s onwards. Thirty-five years later, about two-and-a-half times as many historical publications are recorded for the five years from 2001 to 2005.[3] These figures do, of course, include 'academic' history, but the overall pattern of growth is clear, and is reflected elsewhere: Eric de Bellaigue cites statistics showing that twice as many history books were published in the early 1990s as in the early 1970s.[4]

Since 1914 the theoretical frameworks within which historians work have evolved, new resources and areas of interest to both academic and non-academic historians have become available, and publishing practices and educational frameworks have changed. Debates on the relative merits of analytical (or scientific) versus narrative (or popular) history, begun towards the end of the nineteenth century, have continued. E. H. Carr's George Macaulay Trevelyan lectures at the University of Cambridge, published under the title *What is history?* (Macmillan, 1961) were not written as a work of 'popular' history. The book remains in print fifty years later, reflecting the growth of student numbers in higher education rather than a general engagement with historiographical debate. General readers have consistently preferred narrative in preference to analysis, leaving the publications of professional / academic historians to be read by their peers. Jerome de Groot wrote of the 1990s, that 'While professional historians busied them-selves with theoretical argument, "History" as a leisure pursuit boomed.'[5] Academics whose books have sold in large numbers, however, have some-times experienced surprising consequences. Following the publication of

2 Cannadine (ed.), *History and the media*, p. 1.
3 www.history.ac.uk/makinghistory/resources/statistics.
4 De Bellaigue, *British book publishing*, p. 17. Norrie, *Mumby's publishing and bookselling*, pp. 221–2, notes that the number of titles defined as history trebled between 1937 and 1981.
5 De Groot, *Consuming history*, p. 2.

Europe: a history (1996), Norman Davies found that journalists 'appear[ed] on the phone or on the doorstep, full of the phoney bonhomie that is required to extract details of a "scholar's war" which no-one was actually fighting'.[6]

The authors of history books for the general reader have varying backgrounds: academic historians (Trevelyan, A. J. P. Taylor, Norman Davies, Simon Schama and others), novelists (John Buchan, H. G. Wells) and journalists (Andrew Marr). The lament that the general reader is poorly served by history books written by non-professionals is frequently repeated: 'If readers were a little more discriminating and demanding and sufficiently venturesome now and then to try a scholarly book, the payoff – a firmer sense of the past, and perhaps even a new insight or two into our own condition – might be considerable.'[7] In 2008, Alastair Harper complained that 'The kind of historical writing that sells at present is comfortable, unchallenging nostalgia fodder', though a 'generation ago things were very different. Eric Hobsbawm, A. J. P. Taylor, Richard Hofstadter or Arthur Schlesinger were all academic writers who crossed over into the mainstream ... their books were read as often in train carriages as they were in lecture theatres.'[8]

One author omitted from Harper's list, A. L. Rowse, successfully combined his role as an academic historian of the Tudor period (he was elected a Fellow of All Souls College, Oxford in 1925) with radio broadcasts, and a prolific writing career encompassing poetry, autobiography and popular history. His scholarly reputation was established with the Cape publications *Sir Richard Greville of the Renown* (1937) and *Tudor Cornwall* (1941). *The spirit of English history* (1943) was reprinted and distributed overseas by the British Council, and in 1944 *The English spirit* was published by Macmillan in an edition of 10,000.[9] In the 1950s, the Macmillan titles on Elizabethan England (*The England of Elizabeth*, 1950; *The expansion of Elizabethan England*, 1955) sold widely, partly through book clubs. Rowse was also the general editor of the *Teach Yourself History* series published by the English Universities Press (an imprint of Hodder & Stoughton) from the mid-1940s, and his biographies of the Churchill family (*The early Churchills*, 1956; *The later Churchills*, 1958) were also popular. Some of his later works were aimed squarely at the general reader, including *Bosworth Field and the Wars of the Roses* (1966) and *The Tower of London in the history of the nation* (1972).

6 Davies, *Europe east and west*, p. 75.
7 Paret, 'John Keegan's *The price of admiralty*', pp. 230–1.
8 Alastair Harper, 'A popular history of history', *Guardian* 26 August 2008, www .theguardian.com/commentisfree/200//aug/26/history.celebrity.
9 Ollard, *A man of contradictions*, pp. 174–9.

Rowse's focus on the English nation highlights the problem of terminology. Norman Davies has commented that 'Most British libraries and library catalogues are structured on the false assumption that English and British history form one single subject while Welsh history, Irish history and Scottish history belong to separate compartments.'[10] This usage is not unique to Britain, but throughout the twentieth century awareness has grown that 'British history' is actually a synthesis of the histories of the English regions, rural and urban, of Wales, Scotland and Ireland in all their diversity, as well as that of the metropolitan political and economic elites. In one of the most popular history books of the mid-twentieth century, *English social history*, first published in 1944, G. M. Trevelyan acknowledged that 'social life in England would have been a very different thing if it had not been the centre of a great maritime trade and moreover of an Empire'.[11] However, he implicitly includes Scotland, Ireland and Wales in 'England', although one chapter in the book is specifically devoted to Scotland. A. J. P. Taylor could still write in 1965 that 'When the Oxford History of England was launched a generation ago, "England" was still an all-embracing word.'[12] Latterly, T. C. Smout's *A century of the Scottish people 1830–1950*, originally published in 1986 by William Collins (republished Fontana, 2011), is described as 'one of Fontana Press's hardiest perennials'.[13]

A major sub-genre of popular history is the general survey of an extended period or broad area, not presenting new research but summarising 'accepted' knowledge of a period. According to Norman Davies such surveys are distinguished by a 'high degree of selectivity and compression, the unavoidable generalisations and the reliance on secondary sources' which means that one 'loses in precision but one gains in breadth of vision and comparison'.[14] Some remain in print for extended periods. H. G. Wells's *A short history of the world*, first published by Cassell in 1922, followed his *Outline of history*, published in twenty-four instalments over 1919–20 and thereafter in book form. New editions of the *Short history* were published with additions and revisions up to 1987 (Wells died in 1946), and the original edition was republished as a Penguin Classic in 2006. A. J. P. Taylor's volume of the Oxford History of England series was originally published in 1965 and numerous editions have followed, the most recent being that published by Read Books in 2007. More recently, the 'world history' by academic J. M. Roberts has appeared in a range of guises. It was first published as

10 Davies, *Europe east and west*, p. 87.   11 Trevelyan, *English social history*, p. 588.
12 Taylor, *English history*, Preface, p. x.   13 www.harpercollins.co.uk.
14 Davies, *Europe east and west*, p. 79.

The Hutchinson history of the world in 1976, and then reprinted with revisions in 1983. Revised editions were published as *The Pelican history of the world* (1980, reprinted and revised in 1983, 1987 and 1988) and *The Penguin history of the world* (1990, reprinted in 1992 and again, without illustrations, in 1995).

According to Stefan Collini, the impressive sales for Trevelyan's *English social history* (1944) – up to half a million in the first ten years – fed the wartime sense that by contemplating 'thatched hamlets nestling in the folds of grassy downs, hearing the drone of German bombers overhead, stirred to thoughts of Agincourt and Trafalgar as well as of 1688 and 1832, it was easy to feel that in staving off the Hun one was defending civilization, liberal principles, and Olde England all in one'.[15] This also highlights the 'inherent conservatism' of histories written for the popular market.[16] Arthur Bryant's books tapped the same vein, notably the trilogy published towards the end of his life. *Set in a silver sea*, published in 1984 as the first volume of *A history of Britain and the British people*, was partially based on material originally published in 1953 and 1963. Parts of volume 2, *Freedom's own island*, were originally published in 1942. In the introduction, Bryant writes: 'When I was a boy every educated Briton had a rough general knowledge of the country's history' but 'Today such popular awareness of the nation's history has largely been lost', a lament that has been heard since the days of Macaulay, who wrote about what 'every schoolboy knows' in the mid-nineteenth century. While Bryant wrote specifically for this market he understood the importance of the scholarly underpinning, and *King Charles I* (Longmans, 1931) was praised by academic reviewers for its research, though not necessarily for its conclusions. It was a Book Society choice and went through seven impressions in eighteen months.[17] His three volumes on Samuel Pepys – *The man in the making, The years of peril* and *The saviour of the Navy* (Cambridge University Press, 1933–38) – sold well though not spectacularly; his wartime social history publications for Collins – *English saga 1840–1940* (1940), *The years of endurance, 1793–1802* (1942) and *The years of victory, 1802–1812* (1944) – sold in large numbers, however. The latter two, and the later volume *The age of elegance, 1812–1822* (1950), explored Britain's role in the earlier pan-European conflict, and had combined sales of 800,000 copies over the next thirty years.[18]

Winston Churchill's *A history of the English-speaking peoples*, substantially prepared before the outbreak of the Second World War, was published in the 1950s. He was not a professional historian, but for much of his adult life

---

15 Collini, *Common reading*, p. 135. 16 Melman, *The culture of history*, p. 10.
17 Stapleton, *Sir Arthur Bryant*, p. 59. 18 *Ibid.*, p. 162.

derived his income from his writing, assisted by a team of research assistants.[19] His six-volume account of the First World War, during which he had been a member of the Cabinet, was published between 1923 and 1931, and outsold the contemporary *War memoirs* of former Prime Minister David Lloyd George.[20] A four-volume biography of his ancestor *Marlborough: his life and times*, was published in the 1930s. His research for both was enhanced by privileged access to government papers in the first case, and to family archives in the latter. It was inevitable that he should write a history of the Second World War, and he was able to negotiate access to documents that remained closed to other researchers for the next thirty years. *The history of the Second World War*, published in six volumes between 1948 and 1952, was a best-seller despite its scale, and Churchill was awarded the Nobel Prize for Literature in 1953 for 'mastery of historical and biographical description as well as for brilliant oratory'.[21] Churchill's work established an orthodox vision of the Second World War that obtains in Britain to this day, with Britain centre-stage. Bryant's books on the Second World War, however, based on the diaries of Field Marshall Alanbrooke – *The turn of the tide, 1939–43* (1957), *Triumph in the West, 1943–46* (1959) – and critical of Churchill's 'legend', also had impressive sales.

Churchill's assessments of the two wars are also examples of 'contemporary history': retrospectives written soon after the events described. Books on recent events, though not strictly history books, often sell well: John Sutherland notes that in the 1960s, 'New printing technology allowed books to respond with almost the speed of newspapers.' Clive Irving's 'instant book' in 1963 on the Profumo affair, *Scandal*, 'appeared, it seemed, barely hours after what it chronicled'.[22] This was not actually anything new: John Buchan's work on the First World War was published during the war from 1915 until 1919 by Thomas Nelson & Sons, of which he was a Director, in twenty-four parts, as *Nelson's history of the war*.[23] It was later republished in a revised four-volume edition in 1921–22. Because it was published as the fighting was going on, some details (for example, exactly which brigades and divisions were involved in the fighting on the Somme) had to be omitted, but were included in the second edition. Although Buchan's wartime role in the

19 Rose, *The literary Churchill*.
20 A. J. Balfour described it as 'Winston's brilliant Autobiography, disguised as a history of the universe'. Cited by Reynolds, *In command of history*, p. 5.
21 www.nobelprize.org/nobel_prizes/literature/laureates/1953.
22 Sutherland, *Reading the decades*, pp. 66–7.   23 Grieves, 'Nelson's history of the war'.

Ministry of Information gave him special insight, it also left him open to the charge of writing propaganda.

Churchill's and Buchan's works are also examples of a perennially popular sub-genre: war and military history. The military history section of any bookshop today is usually equal in size to that for general history, and displays works on a range of topics from the ancient world to the most recent conflicts in the early twenty-first century. Books on both World Wars and other conflicts have been popular sellers. Paul Brickhill's books on *The dambusters* (1951) and Douglas Bader – *Reach for the sky* (1954) – and *The Colditz story* (1952) by P. H. Reid not only were best-selling books but were made into films. Military memoirs were – and remain – popular steady sellers, from Robert Graves's *Goodbye to all that* (1929) to memoirs of more recent conflicts. The Falklands War in the 1980s gave rise to numerous publications, some by journalists, for example *The Battle for the Falklands* (1983, republished 2010) by Simon Jenkins and Max Hastings, and some by military figures such as Admiral Sandy Woodward – *One hundred days* (1992, updated 2012). Towards the end of the century, Anthony Beevor's *Stalingrad* (1998) was another best-seller.[24]

The relationship between historians and the mass media was established early. A. J. P. Taylor was one of the earliest 'media dons': he was involved in print journalism before the Second World War and radio broadcasting during it, and later gave a number of television lecture series, as well as appearing as a panellist on discussion programmes. Some of his television lectures were reproduced in print, for example six lectures 'given a more literary form' as essays in *Revolutions and revolutionaries* (1980). A series on the Crimean War, broadcast by Channel 4 in 1997, was accompanied by a generously illustrated book – *The Crimean War* (1997). David Starkey's best-selling book on Elizabeth I's early years, *Elizabeth: apprenticeship* (2000) which won the W. H. Smith prize, accompanied a four-part series on Channel 4, and the book accompanying Simon Schama's series on British history spent a number of weeks in the non-fiction best-seller lists in 2000.[25] Starkey and Schama are academics with a media profile. The political journalist Andrew Marr, who studied English literature rather than history, has made two television series with accompanying books on the *History of modern Britain* (2009) and *The making of modern Britain: from Queen Victoria to VE Day* (2010). Ancient history and archaeology have proved equally popular in this context: *In search of the Trojan War* (1985) presented by Michael Wood was both a popular

24 *Ibid.*, pp. 27–8, 162.   25 *Ibid.*, p. 164; Snowman (ed.), *Past masters*, p. 257.

television series and a best-selling book. The Time Team archaeological series, on Channel 4 from 1994, which epitomises John Sutherland's characterisation of television archaeology as 'Talking heads, shovels and the occasional reconstruction', has resulted in several spin-off books.[26]

Archaeology and ancient history were, in any case, steady sellers throughout the period. In the 1920s, Oxford University Press began publishing a series on ancient history. *The legacy of Greece* (1921) and *The legacy of Rome* (1923) were two of the earliest, and later titles covered Egypt, China, India, Islam, Israel and the Middle Ages, with new, updated editions throughout the century. Historical biography has also never lost its popularity. Those written in the nineteenth century were respectful, not to say hagiographical, but in 1918 Lytton Strachey's *Eminent Victorians* set a new tone. It has been republished throughout the century and in 2009 was canonised as an Oxford World's Classic. Antonia Fraser's biography of *Mary Queen of Scots* won the James Tait Black Prize for Biography in 1969, and her *Marie Antoinette* won the Franco-British Society Award in 2001. Although not an academic historian, she studied history at Oxford University and has also written novels. Before becoming a successful author, she had worked for Weidenfeld & Nicolson, a major publisher of history books. Her other award-winning works include *The weaker vessel* (1984 – Wolfson Award for History) and *The gunpowder plot* (1996 – Crime Writers' Association Golden Dagger Award). Her mother, Elizabeth Longford, wrote biographies of the Duke of Wellington (two volumes published 1969 and 1975) and of Queen Victoria (1971). Amanda Foreman's biography of an eighteenth-century aristocrat, *Georgiana Duchess of Devonshire*, won the Whitbread Prize in 1998. It successfully crossed the boundaries of scholarly and popular approval: it was 'rigorous, scholarly and extremely engaging'.[27] A film based on the book, *The Duchess*, was released in 2008.

Illustrations were used increasingly in history books during the second half of the twentieth century. A signpost for this trend was a new magazine which aimed to be both scholarly and popular: *History Today*, first published in January 1951, with numerous illustrations. However, it was 'fifteen years before the rest of the publishing industry began to catch up, and illustrated history books became two-a-penny'.[28] New historical periodicals catering to a general reader were established, for example the *BBC History Magazine* in 2000, coincidentally providing space outside national daily and Sunday

26 Sutherland, *Reading the decades*, p. 132.　27 De Groot, *Consuming history*, p. 38.
28 Snowman (ed.), *Past masters*, p. vi.

newspapers for reviews of history books. Trade publishers also exploited the magazine format: H. G. Wells's *An outline of history* was published as twenty-four fortnightly parts (1919–20).[29] Churchill's *History of the English-speaking peoples* was used as the basis of the 112 weekly parts with the same overall title published from 1969 by BPC Publishing. The format was also used for the history of technologies, such as the seventy-two weekly parts of a *History of aviation* (1970–71), and a *History of the motor car* (1970) in twenty-three parts, republished in book form in 1974. *Nelson's history of the war* has already been mentioned and part-publication continued to be used for histories of individual conflicts. Regional and local newspapers also produced historical material in supplementary parts, over several days or weeks, to mark particular events either in their own history (a centenary for example), nationally or locally. The re-establishment of the Scottish Parliament in Edinburgh in 1999 was marked by the publication of a six-part history, *The story of a nation: 300 years of Scottish history*, as a supplement to *Scotland on Sunday*.

Printing technologies facilitating the reproduction of illustrations also encouraged the exploitation of collections of photographs, some dating from the mid-nineteenth century, and illustrations from early postcards, particularly in local history books. These are often published by small concerns, including printers of the local newspapers: *Pride of the North: a fascinating look at the North's heritage* (1998), published by the *Newcastle Chronicle and Journal*, is an example of this. Alan Sutton Publishing, based in Gloucester (now an imprint of the History Press), has also successfully exploited this area of the market. Pitkin, publisher of pictorial guides for heritage tourists, is now part of the same company. The Scottish publisher Stenlake, established in 1987, developed this market in Scotland, with titles such as David Anderson's *Old East Lothian villages* (2000) as well as illustrated books on Scotland's mining industry, for example Guthrie Hutton's *Mining the Lothians* (1998), and books of historic railway photographs such as *Shropshire's lost railways*. Other local publishers include independent book-shops: Richard Milward's *Historic Wimbledon: Caesar's camp to centre court* (1989) was published jointly by the Windrush Press and the local bookshop Fielders of Wimbledon. David Lewis's *The illustrated history of Liverpool's suburbs* (2003) is a joint publication of Bredon Books and the City of Liverpool.

Local interest histories form a large sub-genre, and cannot be addressed in detail here, but the 'local studies' department of any public library service in the United Kingdom points to the scale of the market. Local antiquarian and

---

29 Skelton, 'The paratext of everything'.

historical societies led the way in the nineteenth century, and continue to publish local records and histories. For example, *The castle of Northampton* by Robert Meyricke Serjeantson was reprinted as a pamphlet in 1908, having first appeared in the journal of the Northamptonshire Natural History Society & Field Club. Books as diverse as *The story of Garston and its church* by J. M. Swift (Liverpool, 1937) and *An introduction to the archaeology of Wiltshire from the earliest times to the pagan Saxon* by M. E. Cunnington (Devizes, 1933) were published in great numbers. Library services and other local government bodies also became active in this area: examples include Katharine Jordan's *The folklore of ancient Wiltshire* (Wiltshire Library and Museum Service, 1990) and Liverpool's City Libraries' *Childwall: a brief history* (1985). These publishing programmes often fell victim to funding cuts. As noted in the previous paragraph, local newspapers also exploited their local knowledge and resources: by 1947 D. Croal's *Sketches of East Lothian*, first published in 1873 in Haddington by the family firm, printers of the *Haddingtonshire Courier*, had reached its fifth edition. Churches and other institutions published historical guides for visitors. In 1956, a revised edition of the booklet *St Gregory's Minster, Kirkdale* by the Reverend F. W. Powell, originally published in 1907, was produced in Helmsley at the Rydale Printing Works. Thirty years later, a revised edition of a newer guide, compiled by Arthur Penn, was published by the Kirkdale Parochial Church Council itself.

Guidebooks are outside the scope of this study, but mention should be made of the publications of heritage bodies such as the National Trust, the National Trust for Scotland and the official and quasi-official bodies responsible for heritage sites, now known as English Heritage, Cadw (for Wales) and Historic Scotland. Collectively their guidebooks constitute a major publishing programme in themselves, and in most cases the guide for each site has gone through several editions since its first publication. These bodies, together with institutions such as the British Museum, also produced more general historical guides which became more heavily illustrated as the twentieth century progressed. W. Douglas Simpson's *Scottish castles: an introduction to the castles of Scotland* (HMSO, 1959) is illustrated only with black and white plans. In contrast, the National Trust produced a full-colour volume by Christopher Rowell and John Martin Robinson, *Uppark restored* (1996), charting the history of the house before the disastrous fire of 1989, and the project to restore it.

In 1981, the novelist Peter Vansittart compiled *Voices from the Great War*, a personal anthology of quotations from poems, official documents, letters and diaries among other sources. The title has been echoed by others in the newly emerged sub-genre of oral history, which developed as an academic discipline in the second half of the twentieth century with the advent of improved recording machines.[30] Recordings made by the Imperial War Museum in the 1960s were transformed by Max Arthur into *Forgotten voices of the Great War: a new history of World War I in the words of the men and women who were there* (2002). Other titles include Joshua Levine's *Forgotten voices of the Blitz and the Battle for Britain* (2006), another television tie-in, and Ian MacDougall's *Voices from work and home* (2000). These titles indicate how, over the period, historical interests have shifted away from the activities of the 'great and the good' to the lives of 'people like us'. Examples include Liza Picard's books on 'everyday life' in London – *Restoration London* (1997) and *Elizabeth's London* (2003) – and Angus Calder's *The people's war: Britain 1939–1945* (1969, and still in print nearly fifty years later). The latter exploited, among a wide range of sources, the Mass-Observation Archive, compiled from the notes on 'everyday lives of ordinary people'.[31]

History books for a juvenile readership also came to focus more on the lives of 'ordinary citizens'. A detailed consideration of children's history publishing belongs more properly with a general survey of children's books, but some trends are clear. At the end of the twentieth century, history books for children took three main forms: textbooks (intended for use in schools by students preparing for examinations), general interest, and 'alternative' histories. The two latter market sectors were dominated by three publishers: Usborne, Dorling Kindersley and Scholastic. Titles used in schools were mainly published by firms active in the general educational/ academic market, and were often narrowly focussed on a topic or period, with added teaching materials and sample examination questions, and designed for students in the last two years of school. Examples for Advanced Level students include *The extension of the franchise 1832–1931* by Bob Whitfield (2010, Heinemann Advanced History), and *The American Civil War 1848–65*, third edition, by Alan Farmer (2006, Access to History series, Hodder Murray). Scottish students, following a different scheme of examinations, were also catered for with titles such as *Higher history: Britain and Scotland 1850s–1979* by Sydney Wood (Hodder & Stoughton Educational Scotland, 1999).

Children's history books outside the classroom are a mixture of the traditional and the new, alternative genre. The most successful of the latter,

---

30 www.history.ac.uk/makinghistory/resources/articles/oral_history.html.
31 www.massobs.org.uk/a_brief_history.htm.

Terry Deary's Horrible Histories series, are published by Scholastic: the first titles, *Awesome Egyptians* and *Terrible Tudors*, were published in 1993. By 2012, books in this series ranged from *Angry Aztecs* (2008) to *Woeful Second World War* (2003), covering all periods of British history from the *Cut-throat Celts* (2008) onwards, as well as *The horrible history of Britain and Ireland* (2012) and *The horrible history of the world* (2007).[32] The self-consciously subversive tone of these is in contrast to the traditional style of books such as *Britannia: 100 great stories from British history* by Geraldine McCaughrean (originally published in 1999) which retells the same historical tales (Alfred and the cakes, Arthur and the round table, Bruce and the spider) nearly 200 years on from the publication of the earliest history books for children, such as Mrs Markham's *History of England* (1823) and *Little Arthur's history of England* by Lady Callcott (1835). The modern version does, however, include text panels with some guidance to the accepted facts to give some context.[33] Other history books for children cover a range of topics, concentrating on those popular as part of the school curriculum (Romans, Egyptians, medieval castles and the Second World War). *The young Oxford history of Britain and Ireland* (1996) trades on the reputation of Oxford University Press for accuracy and thoroughness. Unlike the Horrible Histories, this category seems aimed more at the gift market, to be bought by adults as gifts to children rather than being purchased by the children themselves.

The volumes in the Dummies series, published by John Wiley, are the adult version of Terry Deary's approach to history. They range from *The Tudors for dummies* by David Loades and Mei Trow (2010) to *British History for dummies* by Seán Lang, which reached its third edition in 2011, and *World history for dummies*, second edition by Peter Haugen (2009). Other niche interests are reflected, for example, in *British military history for dummies*, by Bryan Perrett (2007). Sample chapter titles from the volume on British history include 'Saxon, drugs and rock 'n' roll', 'Have axe, will travel: The Vikings' and '1066 and all that followed'.[34] The last of these refers to the ancestor of this style of presentation: one of the most enduring 'popular history' books of the twentieth century, *1066 and all that* by W. C. Sellar and R. J. Yeatman, serialised in *Punch* and published in book form by Methuen in 1930. It covered nine centuries of British (mainly English) history, claiming in the 'compulsory' preface that 'History is not what you thought. It is what you

32 http://horrible-histories.co.uk/books. The site also links to other media and resources.
33 Howsam, *Past into print*, pp. 10–11. 34 http//:eu.wiley.com/WileyCDA.

can remember. All other history defeats itself.' It remains a best-selling title in 2012.

According to John Sutherland, in 1996 Dava Sobel's *Longitude: the true story of a lone genius who solved the greatest scientific problem of his time* 'created a genre, the "biography of a thing" ... books on cod, the potato and the lead pencil followed; most alas, were not bestsellers.'[35] Sobel wrote that, because it is 'intended as a popular account, not a scholarly study, I have avoided using footnotes or mentioning, in the body of the text, most of the names of the historians I have interviewed or the works I have read and relied on for my own writing'.[36] Mark Kurlansky's *Cod: a biography of the fish that changed the world* (1998) includes recipes as well as the history of a global fishing industry. An extension of this 'niche' approach to history is Judith Flanders's *The Victorian house: domestic life from childbirth to deathbed* (2003), which illuminates social history through a detailed examination of a particular group and its lifestyle. Similarly, Ian Mortimer has written *The time traveller's guide* to medieval England (2008) and to Elizabethan England (2012) in an attempt to make the business of day-to-day living and the beliefs that informed it from 500 years ago more comprehensible to today's readers. The interest in social history has grown alongside the expansion in genealogy, opening a new market in guides to personal genealogical research. Human interest is also served by the history retold in a fictionalised format: novelist Josephine Tey's *The daughter of time* (Peter Davies, 1951) discussed the historical evidence for the story of Richard III and the 'princes in the Tower'. There have been many editions, including one from Heinemann Educational in 1959, and most recently (2009) from Arrow.

In the twenty-first century, popular history books cover a range of histories: constitutional/political, social, and economic, but also sub-genres such as gender and race, and many others. Labour history and regional and local histories provide new perspectives on the development of the nations that make up the UK. Much has been written on the changing nature of historical enquiry, but less on the changes in the publishing of history for the general reader. Space has not allowed full exploration of the role of book clubs, including ones appealing to specialist interests such as military history, in the promotion and sale of books on history, although this was undoubtedly significant. A survey of publishing patterns of history based on publishers'

---

35 Sutherland, *Reading the decades*, p. 174.   36 Sobel, *Longitude*, p. 177.

archives and other sources remains to be done to provide a comprehensive survey of this area of book culture. All that remains to be said here is that 'Popular history is not bad history. When written with integrity and moral purpose, it is simply history written and communicated in a different way.'[37]

37 Champion, 'Seeing the past', p. 157.

13

Religion

MICHAEL LEDGER-LOMAS

How can the Gospel be preached to a post-literate society in which the image is the principal currency of communication? How will Protestants especially, who proudly claim the title of the People of the Book, fare when they encounter head-on the People of the Screen? What will be the fate of the Church as a community if the ultimate privatisation of society takes place around the domestic god with the square eye in the forehead?

The missionary turned television executive Colin Morris opened *God-in-a-box: Christian strategy in the television age* (1984) with these challenges.[1] If Christians such as Morris worried about declining church attendance and the book trade fretted that reading faced damaging competition from new media, especially television, then throughout the twentieth century religious publishers and booksellers faced both fears at once. From the late 1950s onwards, these fears assumed sophisticated, or at least theoretical, form as theologians turned to Marshall McLuhan and to reflection on communication.[2] If McLuhan was right that the 'Age of Writing' was ending, what use would 'post-literate man' have for dense theological print?[3] In *The gagging of God* (1969), Gavin Reid, a minister on a suburban housing estate, dismissed Christian publishing as 'In Talk' and urged the churches to follow advertisers in searching for the 'pre utterance' factor: the visual or emotional hook that snared an audience. The cover image of his book, a Hodder & Stoughton Christian paperback, envisaged religion's future: a television set dressed up as an altar.[4] If some felt that the Roman Catholic McLuhan had a vested interest in prophesying the demise of print-bound Protestantism, then the Vatican's publication of an encyclical on 'Pastoral

---

1 Morris, *God-in-a-box*, p. 10. 2 Dillistone, *Christianity and communication*.
3 Morris, *God-in-a-box*, p. 10, citing Harvey Cox. 4 Reid, *The gagging of God*, p. 24.

instruction in the mass media' (1971) showed that it too was worried about the arguments of this 'Canadian don'.[5]

This chapter, though, will not tell the story of religious publishing as simply a slide from complacent prosperity to near extinction. At the turn of the twenty-first century, religious books still supplied a respectable 2 per cent of hardback and 1 per cent of paperback best-sellers.[6] It begins by tracing the imaginative if sometimes defensive responses of religious publishers to interlocking religious, social and cultural change – 'religious' used here as an adjective never limited to but always heavily dominated by Christianity, and 'publishers' as a category extending from modest denominational outfits to major firms for whom religion was just one aspect of their operations. It traces the importance of several Christian strategies in the face of the expanding mass market, followed by the spectre of secularisation and a 'post-literate' age. The chapter then assesses how different kinds of text served these strategies. It begins with the Bible, showing that publishers successfully modernised it while inadvertently fragmenting and partially secularising Britain's strong, comparatively unified culture of Bible reading. Then it turns to the changing fortunes of theological publishing, arguing that it both prepared the way for and lost ground to a more expansive literature which prioritised a questing, eclectic 'spirituality' over the statement and inculcation of Christian doctrine. Finally, it makes the cautionary point that religious publishing cannot be neatly reduced to Britain's distinctive experience of dechristianisation. Some organised religions, notably Islam, have grown in numbers and confidence in later twentieth- and twenty-first-century Britain: their relationship with publishing is an interesting variation on the patterns traced here.

Religious publishers and publishing houses with strong religious interests had close links with Christian churches in the early twentieth century. They worked to ecclesiastical rhythms, focussing their promotional efforts on the seasons when most religious book reading, buying and giving happened – at Lent and, to a lesser extent, Christmas. Victorian missionary societies remained key players in publishing: the Society for the Promotion of Christian Knowledge (SPCK), the Religious Tract Society (RTS), the British and Foreign Bible Society (BFBS) and the National Sunday School Union (NSSU). Many were imperial and transnational rather than domestic in their focus. From the thirties, the SPCK's home profits subsidised

---

5 H. R. F. Keating, 'Media are important even to the Church', *Catholic Herald* 17 September 1971, p. 3.
6 Feather and Woodbridge, 'Bestsellers'.

a network of overseas bookshops, and after the Second World War it pressed ahead with new openings in the West Indies, Baghdad and Rangoon.[7] Some key publishing firms emerged from churches, denominations or movements: the Epworth Press (1918) from the Methodist Book Room, SCM Press from the Student Christian Movement.[8] High churchmen had Mowbray, whose catalogues also sold the Anglo-Catholic paraphernalia that one customer fondly remembered as 'ecclesiastical pornography'.[9] Even general publishers often reflected the religious zeal of their founders. If Hodder & Stoughton was a major commercial operator throughout our period, its editorial policy reflected an abiding sense of Christian mission. Founded by devout Congregationalists, it was by the Second World War closely aligned with the Church and especially its evangelical wing. The Dean of St Paul's, one of their authors, laid the foundation stone of its post-war headquarters with the biblical injunction: 'Except the Lord build the house their labour is but lost that build it.'[10] Similarly, Collins reflected the vision of its Scottish Presbyterian founder and prided itself on Bible publishing.

While the First World War exposed the flaws of Edwardian Christianity, it also stimulated much Christian publishing, not just Bibles and prayer books for soldiers but literature on everything from the need for national missions to the spiritualist pursuit of dialogue with the dead. Religious books remained a solid part of the market thereafter, constituting over 5 per cent of all titles published by the early thirties.[11] As in the United States, all denominations saw 'book culture' for the masses as a form of evangelism.[12] To take one example, the Australian Frank Sheed (1897–1981) had hurled himself into street corner proselytising for the Catholic Evidence Guild on his arrival in Britain in 1919.[13] In 1926, he married its chair Maisie Ward, before they founded their eponymous publishing house, which was designed to bust the 'plaster' sanctity of the Catholic market leaders, Burns, Oates & Washbourne.[14] Sheed believed Catholics must read voraciously and

---

7 '30 years of the SPCK', *Bookseller* 30 August 1947, pp. 524–5; 'Following the fortunes of the SPCK', *Church Times* 30 April 1954, p. iv.
8 Cumbers, *The book room.*   9 Williams, *Some day I'll find you*, pp. 63–4.
10 Attenborough, *A living memory*, pp. 192–3.   11 *Bookseller* 1 January 1932, p. 14.
12 Hedstrom, *The rise of liberal religion.*
13 J. Seymour Jonas, 'Ronald Flaxman and Maisie Ward remembered', *Catholic Herald* 28 February 1975, p. 10. See also 'What a glorious mourning to start the day', *Catholic Herald* 27 November 1981, p. 9.
14 Sheed, *The church and I*; Sheed, *Frank and Maisie*; Sheed, *Sidelights on the Catholic revival*, pp. 27–30.

systematically to survive in a secularised culture and suggested that his authors could offer them mental 'fumigation'.[15]

Several strategies created a mass Christian market. The first was the identification of religious readers neglected by the book trade. This strategy was identified with the Religious Book Club, which rivalled the Left Book Club in its reach. Although Sheed & Ward lacked the capital to make their Catholic club successful, they did well out of supplying an American equivalent.[16] By contrast, the book club launched by the SCM's director Hugh Martin lasted for forty years and had 20,000 members at its peak.[17] Religious bookshops, of which the SPCK had forty-seven at home and abroad by the early 1950s, represented another means of concentrating on niche consumers.[18] A second strategy exploited broadcast media to sell books. Lord Reith had given the churches a permanent seat in the BBC studio and made unlikely clerical stars out of 'Dick' Sheppard, the neurasthenic vicar of St Martin in the Fields whose *The impatience of a parson* (1927) quickly sold over 100,000 copies, and the brittle W. H. Elliott, who persuaded 'millions' that there was 'still some decency in the world' and published a string of books such as *The sunny side of life: addresses broadcast for London* (1927).[19] Radio rejuvenated sermons by recasting them as demotic 'talks'. Father C. C. Martindale's *What are saints?* (1932) sold out in two days.[20] A year later, a series of Adult Education talks given by church leaders demonstrated the new symbiosis between spoken and written word. This hesitant exercise in popularisation – F. R. Barry started his talk with the admission that 'there have been a good many complaints about this series on the ground that it has been too highbrow' – still made a successful two-volume book for the SCM Press, which published a second series as *The way to God* (1935).[21]

The Second World War confirmed radio's importance to national life, giving an unrivalled 'platform' to Christian authors, particularly Anglicans such as Elliott who had inherited the expectation that the Church had a unique call to negotiate national crises.[22] Radio was just as important in boosting lay authors such as C. S. Lewis, Dorothy L. Sayers and Herbert Butterfield. When published by Geoffrey Bles, the sale of the talks that made

15 Sheed, *Ground plan.*   16 Ward, *Unfinished business*, p. 155.
17 Bowden, 'SCM Press', p. 2,270. See also John Bowden, 'The writing on the publisher's wall?', *Church Times* 8 October 1976, p. 11.
18 'SPCK moving to new offices', *Church Times* 2 July 1954, p. 1.
19 Wolfe, *Churches and the British Broadcasting Corporation*; Roberts, *H. R. L. Sheppard*, pp. 171–2.
20 'Some books for Lent', *Bookseller* 24 February 1938, p. 237.
21 Barry, 'Can we imitate Christ?', p. 164.   22 Grimley, 'The religion of Englishness'.

up Lewis's *Mere Christianity* traded on the intense, although not uniformly positive, response they aroused in listeners.[23] Sayers was uncomfortable to find that the radio plays published as the best-selling *The man born to be king* (1943) had anointed her a Christian apologist. In October 1945, she declined Mowbray's proposal to publish some devotional readings from her works – 'I should go crimson in the face every time I saw the thing about.'[24] Sayers insisted that the vocation of believing artists like herself was to be not evangelists, but rather spokespeople for 'educated near-Christians or woolly Christians' who were 'the sheep of our pastures'.[25] These attempts to please the cultured despisers of Christianity were fraught with contradictions but were successful enough to annoy humanists such as Kathleen Nott, whose *The emperor's clothes* (1953) attacked 'lay theologians' for producing dogma without literature.[26]

Nott's was a minority voice. After the Second World War, religious publishing shared in the recovery of the trade. The 827 religious titles published in 1948 overhauled the pre-war total and constituted 5.6 per cent of all titles published.[27] Moreover, religious publishers organised to defend the spiritual gains of the war, founding the Religious Books Group of the Publishers Association, which with its twin in the Booksellers Association steeled itself for 'the necessity of combating an increasing tendency to disregard books on religious subjects'.[28] That required demonstrating that doctrinal differences between Christians mattered less than a joint commitment to propagate 'religion' and Western freedoms. Their 'Christianity in Books' exhibition, first held in 1950 and supplemented by an annual Christian Book Week, was designed 'to show to the British public, in contrast to the almost daily reports of religious suppression in other countries, the range and variety of books concerning every aspect of Christianity'.[29] Broadcasters gave talks and the Bishop of London observed that 'he was today selling ten times as many books of sermons as he sold before the war'. His confidence was underpinned by continued access to the BBC's invisible pulpit. The reprinting of radio talks paralleled other experiments with missionary print during the 1950s, a decade retrospectively associated with Billy Graham's crusade to Britain. The Bible translator J. B. Phillips thus produced twenty leaflets for the

23 Phillips, *C. S. Lewis at the BBC*, pp. 80, 138.
24 Reynolds (ed.), *The letters of Dorothy L. Sayers*, vol. 3, p. 165.
25 Reynolds (ed.), *The letters of Dorothy L. Sayers*, vol. 4, p. 145.
26 Nott, *The emperor's clothes*, pp. 2, 256. 27 *Bookseller* 1 January 1949, p. 3.
28 Cumbers, *The book room*, p. 40; *Bookseller* 18 February 1950, p. 223.
29 *Bookseller* 26 August 1950, p. 587; 'Christianity in books exhibition', *Church Times Supplement* 30 April 1954.

Lutterworth Press with titles like 'Are you a man or a mouse?' which had a circulation of over a million copies.[30]

Yet the 1950 exhibition also hinted at problems ahead: to the frustration of its organisers, it was overlooked by the press. By the 1960s, the Religious Books Group came to share the perception – informed by falling attendance at Protestant churches and aired in print and broadcast media – that organised Christianity was in crisis.[31] Robin Denniston (1926–2012), the savvy managing director of Hodder & Stoughton, feared that the churches had lost the public. An Anglo-Catholic lay reader who eventually quit publishing to become a parish priest, Denniston confessed that 'in times of depression' he imagined his life to be 'linked with two dying institutions – the Church of England and the British book trade'.[32] The problem went deeper than the rising price of books. Denniston called for 'new movements in the church' to focus on 'communication with the outside world' and to engage with the new view that human flourishing meant 'sexual prowess' and 'keeping up with the Joneses'.[33] Finding books that drew in unchurched readers might mean abandoning entire categories of religious literature. By 1967, one publisher advised the Group that religious books were 'no longer classed with general reading at all'. There were no longer buyers for the 'run-of-the-mill fairly good book ... [the] minor biblical study by a country parson, with one or two curious discoveries that nobody has made before'.[34] His gloom was reinforced by a sense that radio then television were becoming less a shop window than a pillory for Christianity. Television in particular appeared to vitiate the reading habit, while the controllers of both the BBC and commercial television now apparently privileged iconoclastic talking heads if they deigned to cover religion at all.[35] Lectures given at All Souls, Langham Place in 1977 by the Christian broadcaster Malcom Muggeridge – a 'man playing a piano in the brothel, who includes "Abide with me" in his repertoire in the hope of thereby edifying both clients and inmates' – presented television as an all-conquering menace to Christ.[36] This was an extreme position, not least because television welcomed a range of presenters

---

30 Phillips, *The price of success*, pp. 125–6.
31 Brewitt-Taylor, 'The invention of a "secular society"?', pp. 327–50.
32 Robin Denniston, 'The state of the trade', *Church Times* 22 November 1963, p. 1.
33 Robin Denniston, 'Protest of an orthodox rebel', *Church Times* 5 February 1960, p. 18; Denniston, 'Future of the Catholic Movement', *Church Times* 8 February 1963, p. 39. See also Denniston, *Partly living*, pp. 17, 25, 37 and *passim*.
34 'A future for religious booksellers?', *Bookseller* 16 April 1967, p. 1,839.
35 Brown, '"The unholy Mrs Knight" and the BBC'.
36 Muggeridge, *Christ and the media*, p. 14.

and authors, including many convinced Christians, but in 1984 Colin Morris echoed Muggeridge in identifying television's subversive 'Young Turks' as the 'most powerful preachers of our time'.[37]

The paperback briefly offered a means of fighting back. The market leader was Fontana, an imprint of Collins. Reflecting in 1980 on 'a quarter-century of religious publishing', its founder Priscilla Collins, the wife of the last William Collins to head the firm, noted that spotting St Augustine's *Confessions* alongside thrillers in an American drugstore had alerted her to the paperback's power to reach people ignorant of Christianity.[38] In British bookshops, she observed, religious literature meant Bibles 'with locked glass doors to protect them, and no one seemed to know where the key could be found'.[39] Collins created a strong religious list for Fontana. By the end of the sixties, Lewis's *Mere Christianity* (acquired along with its publisher Geoffrey Bles) had sold about 400,000 copies and J. B. Phillips's translation of Paul's Epistles about 675,000.[40] From 1977, religious Fontana books were branded 'Fount', and by 1980 total sales had reached 23 million.[41] Other publishers followed suit: Hodder & Stoughton's Christian Paperbacks sold up to a million copies a year by the early 1980s and venerable firms such as Mowbray, SPCK and the evangelical Marshall, Morgan & Scott also launched paperback divisions.[42]

The cheapness of paperbacks lent them to polemical and contemporary interventions. Yet on the whole religious paperbacks became synonymous with 'comforter books' of a kind once reserved for 'elderly ladies'. Basic to their 'unquestioning "I Believe" attitude' were narratives of endurance and conquest.[43] The genre was defined by David Wilkerson's *The cross and the switchblade* (1962), an account of how a homespun minister had reclaimed New York City gang members for Christ. Total sales worldwide reached the millions. Published in Britain by Hodder & Stoughton, the book inspired tame British imitations, such as Phyllis Thompson's *The midnight patrol* (1974), about the Salvation Army's crusade against Soho prostitution.[44] If criminals made good enemies for Christians, so did Nazis and Communists. Pastor Richard Wurmbrand's *Tortured for Christ*, which recounted his sufferings at

37 Morris, *God-in-a-box*, pp. 53–4. 38 John Trevitt, 'Collins family', *ODNB*.
39 Priscilla Collins, 'A quarter-century of religious publishing', *Bookseller* 26 January 1980, pp. 342–3.
40 'Fontana sales', *Bookseller* 4 January 1969, p. 11.
41 Collins, 'A quarter-century of religious publishing'.
42 John Todd, 'Religious books in general bookshops', *Bookseller* 31 March 1984, p. 1,383.
43 Darley Anderson, 'Religious publishing: inspiration and comfort for the "80s"', *Bookseller* 26 January 1980, pp. 332–5.
44 *Bookseller* 10 August 1974, p. 609.

the hands of the Romanian regime, sold 160,000 copies in eighteen months and eventually 2 million copies in twenty-three languages, encouraging Hodder to hire the Royal Festival Hall to promote its sequel.[45] The developing world also remained the field of witness it had long been for Protestant missionaries, occasioning such texts as Phyllis Thompson's *Minka and Margaret* (1976), the tale of a leprosy worker from the Rhondda gunned down by Thai bandits, which was designed to induce a 'thrill of pride' and redoubled commitment in the domestic reader.[46]

It did not take martyrs to write comforter literature: celebrities would do. Back in 1968, one commentator identified Cliff Richard as exemplary in reaching 'the person who reads the cartoon page of the *Daily Mirror*'.[47] Hodder & Stoughton published him, while Mowbray published Jimmy Savile's *God'll fix it* (1979) complete with a prefatory endorsement from the BBC's head of religious broadcasting. Yet cheap paperbacks did not secure Christianity's place in the mainstream. By the end of the 1970s, members of the Religious Book Group who belonged to major houses complained that most were not profitable enough, being ignored by mainstream reviewers and turned down by major retailers such as W. H. Smith.[48] Christian Book Week events became an exercise in circling the wagons.[49] Specialist publishers remained defiant. The newly formed Religious Book Foundation put what was now Christian Book Fortnight on a showier footing in 1979, while the evangelical Christian Booksellers Convention began in 1976.[50] Yet by the time a *Bookseller* reporter visited the 1986 Convention in Blackpool, religious bookselling could be introduced as 'specialised, even archaic, [and] of scant commercial interest'.[51]

Publishers accordingly needed Christian bookshops more than ever to sell religious books. In 1999, one survey found 577 of them in the United Kingdom – the category 'Christian bookshop' including everything from the SPCK bookshop in Cambridge, with 30,000 books, to the Cornerstone in Ashford, which had fourteen. Publishers often had little time for the smaller shops, alleging that they were uneconomic enterprises, while

---

45 'Points from publishers', *Bookseller* 8 March 1969, p. 1,666; Attenborough, *A living memory*, p. 208.
46 Thompson, *Minka and Margaret*, p. 188.
47 Guy Hitchings, 'Trends in religious bookselling', *Bookseller* 27 April 1968, p. 2,220.
48 'A controversy in religious circles', *Bookseller* 9 September 1978, p. 2,070.
49 'Good news on the bookshelf', *Church Times* 8 October 1976, p. 10. See also 'Are the books being read?', *Church Times* 14 October 1977, p. 10.
50 John Capon, 'The rising tide of religious publishing', *Bookseller* 25 March 1978, p. 2,008.
51 'CBC Blackpool', *Bookseller* 15 March, 1986, p. 1,056.

'publishers of catholic, radical and liberal theology' felt that they were dominated by evangelicals who screened out publications that did not fit their 'Christian' vision.[52] In recent times, Christian bookshops have struggled just as much as their secular equivalents, many owing their survival to gifts, stationery, multimedia products or coffee. The major Christian bookshops have been taken over or gone under. Wesley Owen, which absorbed the Scripture Union's bookshops, was in turn bought by Koorong, an evangelical Australian chain. The St Stephen the Great Charitable Trust (SSG), a Texan charity, acquired the SPCK's bookshops in 2006. Citing concerns over the SSG's hostile attitude to academic freedom, the SPCK withdrew the right to use its name for the bookshops in 2007. Soon after, the Charity Commission seized control of its operations, a move followed by the closure of the chain. Only the few SPCK shops that had struck out as independents continue to trade.[53] Perhaps the most resilient forms of distribution now run on zeal rather than profit. In 1970, Burns & Oates handed over their bookshops to the Daughters of St Paul, 'mass media nuns' who sell books alongside posters, calendars and 'interactive software for Christians of all denominations'.[54] The Protestant equivalent of the religious orders were church bookstalls, often run by volunteers. By the end of the 1970s, some bookstalls shifted up to 1,000 books a year and there were around 3,500 book agents in this lively but rather marginal field.[55]

Just as the retail of Christian books substantially depends on a resilient minority, so the most viable publishers now cater to sub-cultures dispersed both within and beyond a post-Christian nation. By the early eighties, evangelical publishers were expanding into a shrinking market, reflecting the shift in the larger American market towards evangelicalism.[56] The first convention of the evangelical Christian Booksellers Association took place in 1950, while the Evangelical Christian Publishers Association was founded in 1974. The latter represented powerful firms such as Zondervan, Baker Books and Moody, who acquired British publishers and vigorously promoted their own products here. Sam Moore bought the Bible specialists Thomas Nelson in 1969 and was in turn absorbed by Zondervan, while David C. Cook

---

52 Capon, 'The rising tide'. See also *Bookseller* 16 April 1967, p. 1,838.
53 See testimony of former SPCK employees at http://spckssg.wordpress.com. See also Christopher Howse, 'The bare and desolate SPCK bookshops', *Daily Telegraph* 21 June 2008.
54 'Mass media nuns open Liverpool Centre', *Catholic Herald* 4 April 1975, 2. See www .pauline-uk.org.
55 www.thegoodbookstall.org.uk.
56 Hollinger, *After cloven tongues of fire*; Hedstrom, *The rise of liberal religion*.

acquired Kingsway (1977), a publishing and distribution house which is now one of the largest distributors of Christian multimedia in the country.[57] Conglomeration advanced further when generalists bought specialists. HarperCollins, which had already absorbed Zondervan, bought Thomas Nelson in 2011 to create a Christian Publishing division, which quickly became the market leader.[58] At the same time, Britain still produces successful publishers. Founded in 1971, Lion became the largest independent Christian publisher in the UK after its merger with Angus Hudson in 2003, setting a new record with its 2012 turnover of £9,258,484. Specialising in children's books, Bible handbooks and testimony literature, it is as intent as any missionary society on projecting Christianity abroad, through the work of its 'Aslan Trust'.[59] As evangelical publishing expanded, other players suffered. The travails of Catholic publishing after Vatican II are surveyed below, but their outcome was that diminished versions of Burns & Oates and Sheed & Ward survived only as minor imprints for other presses.

While evangelical Protestantism thrives, its more sectarian forms survive through neo-Victorian forms of tract distribution. The jubilee edition of the *Christian yearbook* listed over a hundred such enterprises, such as the 'Bible text publicity mission', which displays 'Bible texts to the public on railway and Underground stations and in prisons throughout the UK'. Many not only looked but were Victorian, such as the Scripture Union (1868), Message on the Move (founded in 1883 as the Tramcar and Omnibus Scripture Text Mission) or the Protestant Truth Society (1889). Their work remains textual but favours scriptural cards, leaflets and posters over books, and they increasingly favour cyberspace over print, with the Scripture Union, for instance, backing *Wordlive*, a website that coaches users in Bible reading.

Unread best-seller

'Once an author was lamenting that he could get no money for his books, whereupon his small boy remarked, "Daddy, I wish you would write a Bible; Bibles I see everywhere."' W. R. Inge's joke to the Booksellers Provident Association hints at the importance of the Bible to religious publishing. Admittedly, Christians spent much of the twentieth century lamenting that no one read it. In *Unread best-seller: reflections on the Old Testament* (1967), Mary Stocks reflected that even though Bibles were everywhere in Britain, they

57 Fisher, 'Evangelical-Christian publishing'.
58 www.harpercollins.com/footer/release.aspx?id=1007&b=&year=2012.
59 'Lion Hudson annual report 2012', www.lionhudson.com/page/investors.

'don't look inviting'.[60] She was reiterating a mounting anxiety. Broadcasting on *The book for to-day* in 1949, Donald Coggan had told a West African audience that 'private and family Bible reading has declined pretty seriously recently' and blamed diminished tolerance for the archaic Authorized Version (AV).[61] A few years later, B. Seebohm Rowntree's *English life and leisure* (1951) provided sociological evidence to confirm the death of Bible reading.[62] The problem of an unappealing product was exacerbated by the fossilisation of the voluntary societies founded to distribute the Bible and encourage its study. The British and Foreign Bible Society (BFBS), the biggest customer for the privileged presses which had a monopoly in printing the AV, suffered when decolonisation snapped off its colonial branches, while its constitution obliged it to offer its public only either the AV without note or comment, or the rather stiff Revised Version (RV).[63] The Sunday School movement experienced relative then absolute decline, even if this was compensated for by the continued need for Bibles in both primary and secondary education, with the 1944 Education Act entrenching the role of collective Bible reading and Christian religious instruction in the latter. Cultural and legal changes eroded the 'British Sunday' when most Bible reading had happened.[64] Nonetheless, Bibles and other authoritative texts such as the Book of Common Prayer proved more life-jacket than albatross to sufficiently enterprising publishers.

Even if people did not read the AV, it remained a national totem. During the First World War, Bibles, notably Oxford's Penny Testament, sold enormously well.[65] The Second World War occasioned another surge, with Collins printing 2 million copies, bound in khaki for the army, dark blue for the Royal Navy and light blue for the RAF.[66] Alongside Khaki Bibles, there has been enduring demand for 'white Bibles': expensively bound volumes given to mark baptisms, weddings and funerals. Visitors to the 1954 Christianity in Books exhibition could marvel at one of only twenty-five copies of the *Oxford coronation lectern Bible*, an exact replica of the Bible presented to the Queen at her coronation, bound in scarlet and white morocco and stamped with 'ER' and the crown.[67] This was a princely example of efforts by the privileged presses to take back profitable control

---

60 Stocks, *Unread best-seller*, p. 9.   61 Coggan, *The book for to-day*, p. 76.
62 Green, 'A people beyond the book?'
63 Dean, 'London Bible House in the 1950s'; Steer, '"Without note or comment"'.
64 Green, *The passing of Protestant England*, chapters 4 and 6.
65 McKitterick, *A history*, p. 222.   66 Keir, *The house of Collins*, p. 273.
67 'Christianity in books', *Church Times Supplement* 30 April 1954.

over the binding and illustration of the AV and RV from religious societies.[68] By the early sixties, Cambridge University Press's executives conceded that its Bible trade was as much in fancy goods as in books.[69]

Excessive diversification did not make commercial sense, as it eroded the profit margins on any one format. A better tactic was to commission a new translation. The RV was followed by many new versions, particularly of the New Testament. The colloquial tone of James Moffatt's New Testament (1913) and of the whole Bible (1924) for Hodder & Stoughton struck a new and distinctively Scottish note, turning paradise into a 'park' and the ark into a 'barge'. Strict Presbyterians grumbled that the choice now lay between 'Moses or Moffatt', but sales were good.[70] Yet although Hodder & Stoughton issued Moffatt's translation in numerous formats, their determination to regard quotation from it as a breach of copyright denied it cultural supremacy.[71] If Moffatt's impact had been merely respectable, then J. B. Phillips's was meteoric. A depressive South London vicar who had got a third in classics at Cambridge, he was an unlikely translator of the New Testament. It was only the good offices of C. S. Lewis that persuaded Bles to take *Letters to young churches* (1947), his translation of Paul's epistles.[72] Once in print, though, first Phillips's *Letters* then his translation of the whole New Testament reached millions on both sides of the Atlantic. By 1972, Fontana sales in the UK had reached 1.75 million copies. Phillips's critics winced at his flat, theologically shaky language, as in his rendering of the opening to the Gospel of John: 'At the beginning God expressed himself.'[73] Yet his prose suited Austerity Britain, reflecting his belief that the war had brought Britain closer to the apostolic age. Phillips boasted that his 'close packed files', filled with grateful letters from readers, were 'evidence' to the truth of Scripture that 'our modern clever-clevers' could not match, while his *Ring of truth: a translator's testimony* (1967) sold 250,000 copies for Hodder & Stoughton.[74]

The most significant result of the war was the plan for a New English Bible (NEB). The publication of the New Testament on 14 March 1961 was a publishing sensation brought off by the combined efforts of the churches and the university presses. National dailies devoted 978 column inches to the events of 14 March, dwelling on whirring presses and eager crowds. The City Bookshop reported a queue at 9 a.m. and had sold 1,000 copies by teatime;

68 *Bookseller* 7 July 1933, p. 112.   69 McKitterick, *A history*, p. 333.
70 Bruce, *History of the Bible in English*, pp. 167–70.
71 Attenborough, *A living memory*, p. 127.   72 Phillips, *The price of success*, pp. 107–9.
73 Bruce, *History of the Bible in English*, p. 225.
74 Phillips, *The price of success*, pp. 149–50.

W. H. Smith put in the biggest pre-publication order in the firm's history; the total number of copies in print or on order by 14 March stood at 1.5 million copies and rising.[75] In due course, 6 million copies were sold in four years.[76] The NEB marked a change in the relationship of the privileged presses to the Bible. Rather than trading on their monopoly in printing the AV and RV, they had invested capital in producing a new copyright, a move that reflected their unease with privileged status.[77] Eyre & Spottiswoode received short shrift when they asserted that as Queen's Printer they could publish a version they had not paid to produce.[78] The trade rode on the coat-tails of NEB, working up 1961 into a 'Bible year' and encouraging the purchase of other versions. According to one bookseller, the 'trade can rejoice in the fact that it has had the opportunity of removing the taste left by the sale of "Lady C" [*Lady Chatterley's lover*] . . . practically every customer and 'phone call [has] brought another order for the "Book of Books", thereby proving that despite the pessimists the Bible remains the world's bestseller'.[79] Yet commentators soon noted 'growing disenchantment' with the NEB. Men of letters protested that the avowedly 'provisional' and contemporary translation had vandalised the AV's heritage. F. L. Lucas was tempted to echo William Morris's exclamation on strolling through an over-restored church: 'Beasts! Pigs! Damn their souls!'[80]

Rather than becoming *the* English Bible, the NEB authorised endless experiments in Englishing the Bible. In 1968, for instance, the Scottish Bible commentator William Barclay published a new translation of the Gospels and Acts for Collins. If their rationale for commissioning Barclay was his celebrity – he had sold around 466,000 Fontana paperbacks and was an unlikely star on television – then the justification was that the RSV and NEB were 'official' versions, which left room for a single translator's effort.[81] Proliferating translations also blurred the lines between Protestant and Catholic, opening the prospect of making the British genuinely a people of one book. Ronald Knox's authorised Bible (1944–49), translated from a Vulgate text that Protestants had long impugned, summed up a Catholic story of vigorous but segregated activity. Burns & Oates nonetheless launched an Oxford India paper edition in 'Bible Year', with the claim that

75 *Bookseller* 11 February 1961, p. 350.
76 Nineham (ed.), *The New English Bible reviewed*, p. ix.
77 McKitterick, *A history*, pp. 332–3.
78 *Bookseller* 1 July 1961, p. 2,406; 'The dispute', *Bookseller* 8 July 1961, p. 2.
79 'Letters: the New English Bible', *Bookseller* 18 March 1961, p. 1,362.
80 Nineham (ed.), *The New English Bible reviewed*, pp. 99, 133.
81 *Bookseller* 7 September 1968, p. 775.

it 'is not for Catholics only (as some booksellers might suppose), but for all lovers of the Bible'.[82] There was also movement in the other direction, in which Protestants supplied Catholics with their Bibles. Thomas Nelson's Catholic Revised Standard Version in 1966, used the Revised Standard Version – the AV revised by the American Standard Bible Committee (RSV, 1901). One of its promoters hoped it could be a revived Vulgate: the Bible not of any one faction, but of all Christians.[83] The Catholic Truth Society replaced the Douay Bible with Nelsons' RSV when it issued a new paperback Bible in 1966.[84]

A genuinely ecumenical Bible that might sell to Protestant and Catholic churches was therefore an appetising prospect. The founders of the new firm Darton, Longman & Todd (1958) were well placed to create one, being high-church Anglican, non-aligned and Catholic.[85] Michael Longman brought to the firm the plan for a 'Jerusalem Bible', an English translation of a version produced by the École Biblique of French Catholic scholars. Its publication in 1966 was a gamble. The book ran to over 2,000 pages, cost £100,000 to produce, and was nearly a disaster when a misprint in the first verse of Genesis caused the first run to be pulped.[86] Yet its later history bore out Todd's claim that 'no Bible has ever failed', as it went on to sell somewhere in the region of 2 to 3 million copies by 1980.[87] The virtue of new as of established translations of the Bible was that publishers could issue them in many different formats: Darton, Longman & Todd had twenty-nine editions for sale by 1980, ranging in price from £20 to £1.25.[88] By the time the *New Jerusalem Bible* was launched in 1986, the publishers could boast that congregations rated its 'clarity and dignity' over the NEB, even if some judges have criticised its rebarbative Franglais.[89]

The production of the Jerusalem Bible had been an act of faith: a missionary as well as a commercial venture. John Todd was on the executive committee of 'The Word', which in 1967 set up lecterns in London where members of the public and invited celebrities could read aloud from the Bible. A Victorian missionary would have recognised the

82 Burns & Oates, advertisement in *Bookseller* 17 June 1961, pp. 2,264–5.
83 *Bookseller* 12 February 1966, p. 352.   84 *Bookseller* 6 May 1966, p. 2,172.
85 Brown, *Darton, Longman and Todd*, pp. 7–8.
86 *Bookseller* 10 September 1966, pp. 1,594–5.
87 John M. Todd, 'Publishing Bibles . . . and other books', *Bookseller* 26 January 1980, p. 346; Brown, *Darton, Longman and Todd*, p. 1.
88 Brown, *Darton, Longman and Todd*, p. 346.
89 Hammond, 'The New Jerusalem Bible', p. 309; Todd, 'Religious books in general bookshops', *Bookseller* 3 August 1985, p. 25; Daniell, *The Bible in English*, p. 753.

stunt but not the Bibles: readers could choose between the NEB, Phillips, the RSV and a cloth-bound reader's edition of the Jerusalem Bible New Testament. An important development in this missionary understanding of Bible translation was the embrace by evangelicals of modern versions. Transatlantic fundamentalism had committed many evangelicals not just to plenary but to verbal inspiration as well. Though the originals of the Scriptures were supposed to be infallible rather than the translations, many nonetheless suspected all attempts to improve on the AV.[90] It did not help that translators were often mildly but openly liberal in their attitudes to inspiration. William Barclay once received a letter from one disgruntled reader that simply ran: 'Dear Dr Barclay, I know now why God killed your daughter; it was to save her from being corrupted by your heresies.'[91] Increasingly however, leading evangelicals found it convenient to renounce 'fundamentalism' and claim that the substance rather than the wording of the Bible was infallible. This opened the door to new, 'dynamic equivalence' translations.[92] The publication in the United States first by Tyndale House and then in Britain by Hodder & Stoughton of Kenneth Taylor's *The living Bible* (1967) was a breakthrough. The cover image for the Hodder paperback (1969) captured its modernising agenda: St Paul's Cathedral, sharing the London skyline with post-war office blocks. *The living Bible* was followed by the *New international version*, first published in Britain by Hodder & Stoughton (1974) and widely circulated once adopted by the national branch of the Gideons International.[93] The *Good news Bible: today's English version*, published by Collins with the Bible societies (1976), racked up sales of a million copies in three months and was the centrepiece of that year's Christian Book Week.[94] In 1981, the Bible Society even brought it out in a Royal Wedding edition, complete with a full-colour picture of Charles and Diana.

There is, then, no end to the making of Bibles, particularly because new versions have generally been first produced by and for the robust American evangelical market.[95] Nelson has produced such curios as *The new King James version* (1982) as well as unashamedly modern versions as the *New century version*, while a galaxy of evangelical seminaries worked on Tyndale's *New living translation* (1996; 2004), which claimed to be 'exegetically accurate and

90 Barr, *Fundamentalism*, p. 211.   91 Barclay, *Testament of faith*, p. 45.
92 See the indicative Packer, *Fundamentalism*, chapter 4.
93 Bruce, *History of the Bible in English*, p. 260.
94 '"Christian book week" begins on Sunday', *Church Times* 8 October 1976, p. 1.
95 Fisher, 'Evangelical-Christian publishing'.

idiomatically powerful', while enforcing that modern shibboleth, gender-neutral pronouns. When modernisation of language is combined with formal experimentation and heavy use of images, the result can be Bibles that look not just like any other book, but any other magazine. Nelson has led the way in consulting the marketing department alongside the seminaries, following the success of its 'Bible-zine' *Revolve* (NCV), which seeks to lure teenage girls by embedding the Scripture in articles on dating and fashion.[96] Nor is this just an American phenomenon. In 2009, Tyndale produced *WORD*, a 'Bible magazine' for 'today's visual generation' whose layout owed much to social media. Members of London's Hillsong church contributed the images and worked on their layout. The relationship between text and glossy photographs is playful rather than literal, with footballer Ryan Giggs illustrating 1 Corinthians 9:25 ('All athletes are disciplined in their training') and a tourist's snap of Venetian masqueraders Matthew 23:25 ('Hypocrites!').[97]

The publishing of the Bible had, then, complex effects on its place in British culture. The Authorised Version was dethroned but did not disappear. New versions sold but had little staying power. The words of the Bible became less sacred, because less familiar. Reviewing the revised Jerusalem version, Paul Hammond regretted that it was now not lepers but 'those suffering from virulent skin-diseases' who were 'cleansed' (Matthew 11:5), yet conceded that new translations could 'neither provide nor draw upon a national religious idiom'.[98] The ongoing work of translation chimed not just with the pluralisation of English but the radical historicism of leading theologians, which led them to insist that not just the Bible's language but also its thoughts were the 'expression, or at any rate the outcrop, of the meaning system of a relatively primitive cultural group'.[99] Yet less sophisticated readers, such as those targeted by evangelical paperbacks, remain loyal to an older conception of the Bible as a 'reservoir' of narratives able to convert hardened or desperate people.[100]

This fragmentation of readerships for Scriptures finds a parallel in the publication of liturgical texts. The Book of Common Prayer had resembled the AV in being the property of the church and the privileged presses, which had printed them for wholesalers like the SPCK. The refusal by a low church parliament to authorise the BCP's use (1927–28) created a chaotic situation in

96 Gutjahr, 'The Bible-zine *Revolve*'.
97 Thanks to Sarah Cardaun for alerting me to this text.
98 Hammond, 'The New Jerusalem Bible', pp. 309–10.
99 Nineham, *The use and abuse of the Bible*, p. 28.   100 Nash, *Christian ideals*, p. 65.

which it and the revised version were both employed in churches and opened up the way for further liturgical experiments.[101] The 1980 Alternative Service Book (ASB), intended to consolidate several new service booklets, was one product of that movement. Its critics condemned its bulk and its trendiness, wondering sardonically that it did not contain 'a form of prayer for the blessing of a nuclear shelter'.[102] Yet they also regarded it as a low commercial calculation. The sales jubilantly forecast by the hierarchy had to come from congregations, a mild form of extortion hardly softened by discounts on pew editions and bulk purchases.[103] Price and print quality became political issues, one *Church Times* correspondent grumbling that the ASB's small type reserved it for 'relatively young middle class intellectuals'.[104] These sensitivities meant that the hierarchy 'commended' rather than promoted the ASB as a successor to the BCP.[105] Shifting fashions in liturgy and speech limited its lifespan and it was replaced by *Common worship* (2000), a publication likewise preceded by wrangles over language, and which was deliberately designed as a liturgical smorgasbord, rather than a *prix fixe*.[106]

While the Bible and the prayer book were unique in their relationship to the Established Church in England and Wales, most religious bodies exploited their literary property in hymn books and liturgical texts. Church bureaucracies ranging from the Church Assembly to the Spiritualists' National Union authorised the use and arrogated profits from such publications, which reach institutional and thus captive audiences. The Canterbury Press (an imprint of Hymns Ancient and Modern Ltd) boasted that it had sold nearly a million copies of its *Hymns ancient and modern: new standard* (1983) and 400,000 of the *New English hymnal* (1986) in a decade.[107] Throughout the twentieth century, scholarly interest in accurate or modernised versions of such texts entailed constant pressure towards their revision. Yet the end result has often been to produce not consensus but fragmentation, as new books join without supplanting the old. By contrast, the Roman Catholic Church retains the central authority to substitute one version of its liturgy for another, with the Catholic Truth Society publishing a new English missal for

---

101 Maiden, *National religion*.
102 Roy Arnold, 'Grist to the ASB mill', *Church Times* 3 April, 1981, p. 5.
103 'Doubts about the ASB', *Church Times* 9 December 1983, p. 12; Shepherd, 'Swallowing the ASB', p. 83; Lawrence, 'Prayer and Mammon', pp. 179–82.
104 'For and against the ASB: the debate continues', *Church Times* 28 November 1980, p. 5.
105 'Primates' Pastoral commends the ASB', *Church Times* 21 November 1980, p. 1.
   'Diocesan discussions on Prayer Book', *Church Times* 3 July 1981, p. 1.
106 'Lord's Prayer to lose "trial"', *Church Times* 10 July 1998, p. 7.
107 Advertisements, *Church Times* 13 November 1992, p. 13; 1 October 1993, p. 11.

universal use in the church (2012), despite complaints about its literary quality.[108]

Jewish publishing presents a fascinating variant on attempts to modernise scriptural and liturgical texts without detracting from their authority. Given the equal weight accorded to the oral and written Torah, printing the Talmud had always been a key concern of Jews, but the growing Anglicisation of British Jewry prompted translations of it by the twentieth century. Isidore Epstein, librarian then Principal of Jews' College, super-intended a thirty-five-volume edition of the Babylonian Talmud with accom-panying translation for Soncino Press (1935–52) – a firm named for a fifteenth-century printer of the Talmud, Joshua Solomon Soncino. Writing in the appendix to Epstein's last volume and after the Holocaust, the Chief Rabbi Israel Brodie emphasised that 'English is now the vernacular of more than half the Jewish population of the world.'[109] Several times republished, the Soncino Talmud eventually gave way to the Schottenstein Talmud (1991–2005): 35,000 pages in seventy-three volumes, employing eighty rabbi-nic scholars.[110] Its publisher was ArtScroll, an American firm whose success in Britain reflected the shift from a diaglossic, polycentric Yiddish culture towards an Angloworld in which readers in London, Toronto or Melbourne looked to New York for their books.[111] ArtScroll's foundation in 1976 coincided with the rise of the evangelical Protestant conglomerates. Like them, it mastered the techniques of computerisation and just-in-time print-runs that allowed it to respond nimbly to ordinary worshippers, and devel-oped genres – from self-help manuals to cook books – that mimicked trends in secular culture. With 80 per cent of its sales in North America, ArtScroll nonetheless supplied up to 50 per cent of the stock in London's Judaica shops.[112] ArtScroll's Talmud printed the authoritative Vilna Shas (1886) ver-sion of the Aramaic and Hebrew texts, accompanied by an English transla-tion, commentary and a surprising amount (for an iconophobic religious tradition) of visual illustration.[113] Yet the authorisations (Haskamot) that ArtScroll obtained from halakhic authorities in Israel insisted that theirs was not a translation of the Talmud, merely an 'elucidation' or an 'explana-tion' of it. As Rabbi Yosef Sholom Eliashiv commented, 'Since we live in

---

108 Rupert Shortt, 'Tactical missal', *Times Literary Supplement* 12 December 2012, p. 2.
109 Mintz, 'The Talmud in translation', p. 127.   110 Stolow, *Orthodox by design*, p. 30.
111 A US directory from 1979 listed 179 North American Jewish publishers but only two British: Soncino Press and the *Jewish Chronicle*. See Berliant and Abit, *Jewish literary marketplace*.
112 Stolow, *Orthodox by design*, p. 78.
113 Stanislawksi, 'The "Vilna Shas" and Eastern European Jewry'.

a generation in which people are translating the Talmud irresponsibly in a way that lessens the sanctity of the Talmud, it is a great *mitzvah* to continue in this project.'[114] Nineteenth-century rabbis had often felt that English translations of the Talmud violated the prescription against teaching Torah to gentiles, who might exploit such knowledge to belittle Judaism. In the twentieth century, Orthodox rabbis came to fear the impact of English versions less on gentiles than on Jews, in case it encouraged them to neglect their Hebrew and to prefer modish interpretations of modern translators to the true meaning of the oral law. Rabbi Adin Steinsaltz's Hebrew and English translation of the Talmud (1965–2010) ran into fierce Orthodox criticism from the late 1980s because he had tampered with the traditional layout of the texts and allegedly intruded bad interpretations into his accompanying commentary.[115] ArtScroll's imposing, pleather-bound volumes answered such fears by suggesting that even largely monoglot readers who leaned on the English translation were using it as a stepladder to approach the Vilna Shas.[116] If the Haredi founders of ArtScroll professed a Scripturalism even more uncompromising than that of the Orthodox, it also enabled them to market their Talmud to Jews of all theological persuasions as a standard work whose modernity and beauty left the authority of the ancient Torah undisturbed.

The Bible as history

In another way, twentieth-century Bible publishing confounded the founding vision of the BFBS, which was to present a mass readership with the AV unadorned by note or comment. Throughout the nineteenth century, publishers had dodged the monopoly of the privileged presses by issuing paraphrased or annotated Bibles and multi-volume commentaries on Scripture. All these forms proved to be ungainly but buoyant vessels. New translations of the Scriptures demanded new commentaries, while old commentaries were revived by integrating them with new translations. Moffatt edited and contributed to an eighteen-volume commentary on the New Testament for Hodder & Stoughton (1920–50) with his new translation as its basis. Thomas Nelson, a leader in this field, had republished A. S. Peake's *Commentary on the Bible* (1919) and later commissioned a revised edition based upon the RSV (1962). Indeed, one sign of the NEB's failure with academics as well as literary

---

114 Mintz, 'The Talmud in translation', p. 139. 115 *Ibid.*, pp. 138–40.
116 Stolow, *Orthodox by design*, pp. 169–70.

types was that publishers generally preferred the RSV in commissioning new or revising old commentaries. Secondly, the sensibilities of different churches and their factions required different commentaries. The hesitant welcome to biblical criticism in the papal encyclical *Divino afflante spiritu* (1943) chartered Nelson to publish a progressive *Catholic commentary on Holy Scripture* (1953), while the crabwise engagement of evangelicals with higher criticism has resulted in major commentaries for Tyndale and Inter Varsity Press. Dedicated commentaries were just one way of rearranging and reinterpreting Scripture. At the beginning of the period, James Hastings's bulky dictionaries on biblical themes were popular, not least with the Oxford don who propped its volumes against the small of his back to stop him nodding off while studying.[117]

Printed images also formed a vital commentary on the Bible, either when reproduced in auxiliary works or given central billing in illustrated Bibles. The popularity of the latter grew in the nineteenth century with every advance in mechanical reproduction of visual images and continued into the twentieth. Oxford's *Illustrated Old Testament, with images by contemporary artists* (5 vols., 1968–69), featuring images from Peter Blake and David Hockney, was a princely example but many were humbler and cheaper productions, often pitched at children. A pioneer here was Harold Copping, Croydon's Tissot, who used his wife's tea towel as headgear for the models who appeared in his gently orientalised tableaux. The Religious Tract Society, which published Copping's illustrated Bible in 1910, issued numerous books for children illustrated with Copping plates. Works like these established a perennial genre, as evinced by the appearance of books such as *The Ladybird New Testament* (1981), with 140 illustrations for just 158 pages and a tie-in with the television series 'God's Story'.[118]

If images explained Scripture, they often rivalled it for the reader's attention. A similar observation holds for other kinds of aid. To pick out just one example, biblical archaeology attracted publishers throughout the twentieth century, doubtless because guides to this developing field permitted photographs of alluring Mediterranean destinations. Poring over books such as Alan Millard's *Treasures from Bible times* (1986) promised not just entertainment, but reassurance. For evangelicals in particular, the archaeological evidence lent itself to a scientific defence of the Bible's infallibility. Evangelical apologetics were increasingly insistent that the truth of

117 Wand, *Changeful page*, p. 34.
118 John M. Todd, 'Religious books in general bookshops: children's religious books', *Bookseller* 19 October 1985, p. 1,661.

Scripture lay in the correspondence between texts and external reality as reconstructed by historians, philologists and archaeologists.[119] That thesis was implicit in the title of such works as Werner Keller's *The Bible as history* (1956), the first edition of which sold 190,000 copies for Hodder & Stoughton.[120]

Yet such books were not only written against the growing insistence of archaeologists that theirs was an autonomous field which does not lend itself to the authentication of Scripture.[121] They also helped to secularise the Bible, establishing a market for writers who used history to unravel rather than buttress its claims. Hugh J. Schonfield was one early example. A publisher, newspaperman and Jew, Schonfield argued that he could see in the New Testament what Christians had overlooked: the human and Jewish Jesus. *The Passover plot* (1966) was a sensation, the cover of its Corgi paperback featuring a crucified Jesus on a puppeteer's strings.[122] Schonfield faded into obscurity, but was succeeded by still quirkier figures. John Marco Allegro, a philologist who had played a disputed role in the decipherment of the Dead Sea Scrolls, had shot to celebrity as author of a Pelican paperback (1956) on the discoveries, which sold a quarter of a million copies.[123] Additional, speculative publications on the Scrolls pitted Allegro against his academic colleagues. His frustrations exploded in 1970 when Hodder & Stoughton published, to their speedy mortification, his *The sacred mushroom and the cross*, which argued that the New Testament was just 'the "surface" tale of Jesus', in which 'Jesus' was merely the half-remembered code word for a psychoactive mushroom on which early Christians, members of a fertility cult, had feasted.[124] Christians alleged that he would allow 'the man in the traffic jam the opportunity of heightening his sexual pleasure with the approval of religion'.[125] Yet Allegro, who soon resigned his university position, thought of himself as the high-minded nemesis of a 'querulous clergy'. In *The end of a road* (1972), he argued that in confronting Christians with the fact that their God was 'originally conceived of as a mighty penis in the sky, ejaculating semen as rain', he was emancipating them from their Scriptures.[126]

If Allegro was too odd to last, then other authors also traded lucratively in biblical conspiracies. In 1972, Henry Lincoln made the first of the programmes

119 Harris, *Fundamentalism and evangelicals.*   120 Attenborough, *A living memory*, p. 257.
121 Davis, *Shifting sands.*
122 'The Passover plot', *Bookseller* 5 February 1966, p. 366; 'Declined with thanks', *Bookseller* 28 October 1967, p. 2,191.
123 Brown, *John Marco Allegro*, pp. 51–7.   124 Allegro, *The sacred mushroom*, p. 193.
125 King, *A Christian view*, p. 145.   126 Allegro, *The end of the road*, p. 12.

which generated *The holy blood and the holy grail* (1982). Co-authored with Michael Baigent and Richard Leigh, it sold 30,000 for Cape in hardback and 300,000 for Corgi in paperback. This gripping tale aped the Protestant quest for the historical Jesus but was innocent of its theological preoccupations and could be read against its grain: as pure entertainment. Lincoln, Baigent and Leigh inspired still wilder speculations, such as Richard Andrews and Paul Schellenberger's best-selling *The tomb of God* (1996) as well as fictional travesties like Dan Brown's *The Da Vinci code* (2003). When Baigent and Leigh sued Brown for plagiarism, the trial ruined them, but enriched Random House, which had inherited *The holy blood* from Cape as well as publishing Brown, and exemplified Robin Denniston's prescient observation of 1968 that the Bible now interested the public only insofar as it generated 'rows and money'.[127]

Such sensational books were the shadow side to the enduring appetite for books about Jesus and to a lesser extent Paul. If 'lives' of both had long been a popular genre, then developments in biblical criticism made it harder for academics to combine edification and scholarly certainty. Theologians did still publish best-selling 'lives', C. J. Cadoux's *The life of Jesus* (1948) selling almost 100,000 copies for Penguin.[128] Yet the most popular were often works of the devotional imagination rather than exercises in scholarship, particularly when written by Catholics. Protestant authors too followed flights of fancy, especially when it allowed them to dwell on their rambles around the Holy Land. The travel writer H. V. Morton sold hundreds of thousands of copies of his 'Palestine masterpieces', *In the steps of the master* (1934) and *In the steps of St Paul* (1936). There were also repeated attempts to capitalise on the buoyant market for fiction by retelling the New Testament as a novel. Popular post-Second World War works included Leslie Paul's *Son of man* (Hodder & Stoughton, 1961), one angry young man's portrait of another, and Gerald Kersh's novel of Paul, *The implacable hunter* (1961).[129] If these books were strong meat, others were milk for babes: the work of religious education relied on heavily illustrated retellings of the New Testament. Lutterworth claimed that by 1966 they had sold a million copies of *Picture stories of Jesus*, 1s 6d tales featuring Copping's illustrations. If such works once more deploy the lure of images, then so did 'lives' tied in with cinema

127 'Obituary: Michael Baigent', *Daily Telegraph* 21 June 2013.
128 Kaye, *C. J. Cadoux*, p. 193.
129 *Bookseller* 28 January 1950, p. 118; *Bookseller* 13 May 1961, pp. 1,910–11.

or television, such as William Barclay's *Jesus of Nazareth* (1977), a commentary on colour plates from Franco Zeffirelli's NBC mini-series.[130]

Wilderness voices

Writing in the 1980s, one commentator explained that it was easy to understand why theology made news in a 'small and fairly-well educated country, where journalism, TV and bookshops can communicate the thought of the universities to a fairly wide non-academic public'.[131] Of course the prestige of theology waned over time – a decline captured in Harold Wilson's remark that debates on Clause 4 were merely 'theology' – but even agnostics might be piqued by scholarly games whose rules they grasped only imperfectly.[132] How did publishers sell them? It was tempting but risky to concentrate on radical theologians who would tickle the public, because they had to guard against disgruntling church members. A 'wilderness voice' might capture the attention of book-buyers, but as Leslie Houlden complained in 1986, congregations insisted that theologians 'should not push novelties in our faces or provoke churchpeople to too much self-scrutiny'.[133] Leading publishers wobbled between backing iconoclastic books and blander fodder, which restated old truths for ageing as well as shrinking congregations. What gave a peculiar character to this tension in Protestant and Catholic communities was that controversial scholarship could often be dressed up as a foreign import: French Catholic modernism, Karl Barth's neo-orthodoxy or American 'death of God' theology. Yet just as significant was the popularity of quieter genres which catered to the growing numbers who wanted religious books which avoided theological jargon and instead defended theism by appropriating the languages of other disciplines, notably the human and biological sciences. The crisis of Christian theology thus became an opportunity for publishing on and defending 'religion'.

The responsibility for theological publishing in the early twentieth century was split between publishers such as T. & T. Clark, who were closely linked to the universities and committed to the translation of German theology,[134] and houses such as the Lindsey Press (Unitarian) and Carey Kingsgate Press (Baptist) which published the thinkers of their denominations. Publishers burnished their reputation by collecting such works into 'libraries' (such as the Lutterworth Library) and series such as Duckworth's Studies in

130 *Bookseller* 11 February 1961, p. 593.   131 Edwards, *Tradition and truth*, p. 10.
132 *Ibid.*, p. 11.   133 Houlden, 'A wilderness voice', p. 340.
134 Dempster, *The T. & T. Clark story*.

Theology. Catholic theological publishing emerged from its slumbers after the First World War. When Frank Sheed arrived, Burns & Oates's gloomy catalogues were as remarkable for hairshirts as for books.[135] The papal bull *Pascendi* (1907), a turbid condemnation of Catholic modernism, discouraged lively publishing, while guides to this market confessed that Catholics did not relish 'sheer theology'.[136] Sheed & Ward were determined to be more dynamic. In the words of their author Ronald Knox, 'Sheed and Ward / Offer sacrifice to the Lord / Not of the blood of bulls and goats / But of Burns and Oates.'[137] Sheed and his collaborators were gifted translators who made 'jawbreakers' by Karl Adam or Nicholas Berdyaev readable.[138] Clarity also meant aggression. The relish with which authors such as Knox or Arnold Lunn pitched into agnostic contemporaries challenged the idea that Catholics were intellectually stunted. Crucial to this perception was Sheed & Ward's determination to maintain operational independence from the church. In the firm's early, under-capitalised years, this pose was underwritten by money raised on Sheed's American lecture tours rather than by book sales.[139] Admittedly, no book of theirs ever featured on the Index and it was fairly easy to secure an imprimatur, not least because censors rarely read the books.[140] Yet their authors also fostered an illusion of boldness. The jaunty tone of Knox's *The Mass in slow motion* (1948) thus disguised its uncompromising defence of the Tridentine Mass.[141] Sales of this and other apologetic works accordingly took off in 'fat comfy America'.[142]

The inter-war years saw a broader emancipation of theological publishing. In the United States, this was synonymous with cross-cultural and trans-historical studies of 'mysticism' and psychological studies of religious experience by liberal Protestants.[143] The leading authors in this vein were popular in Britain and were complemented by home-grown authorities, particularly once Protestant churches and then the Catholic Church conquered misgivings that the 'new psychology' was synonymous with atheistic Freudianism.[144] Leslie Weatherhead, a nonconformist minister in Leeds

---

135 Sheed, *The church and I*, p. 107.
136 Ernest Oldmeadow, 'Some Catholic books for Lent', *Bookseller* 6 March 1935, p. 384.
137 Sheed, *Frank and Maisie*, p. 186.   138 *Ibid.*, p. 67.
139 Ward, *Unfinished business*, pp. 114–15, 201.
140 Hastings, 'Some reflexions on the English Catholicism of the late 1930s', pp. 114–16; Sheed, *The church and I*, pp. 184–7.
141 Sheed, *The church and I*, p. 160.
142 Ward, *Unfinished business*, p. 322; Sheed, *Frank and Maisie*, pp. 184–5.
143 Schmidt, 'The making of modern "mysticism"'.
144 Richards, 'Psychology and the churches'; Bowler, *Reconciling science and religion*, chapter 9; Kugelmann, *Psychology and Catholicism*.

and then at the City Temple, Holborn, emerged as one leader in this field. He began with imitations of the American liberal Protestant H. E. Fosdick, such as *The transforming friendship* (1928), which sold over 100,000 copies, and went on to produce a string of frank discussions of the relationship between religious belief, sex and psychology.[145] If the Epworth Press blanched at *The mastery of sex through psychology and religion* (1931), then SCM put out ten editions in as many years and nineteen by 1964.[146] Weatherhead's profile was boosted by wartime broadcasting, and after the war he became an authority on psychology and healing, complete with a PhD (1950). *Prescription for anxiety* (1956) sold 30,000 copies in six weeks after being excerpted on *Woman's hour* and in the *Daily Mail*, and 100,000 in all. Much to the chagrin of the Epworth Press, his main publisher, it was published by Hodder & Stoughton.[147] A Christian equivalent to Rabbi Joshua Liebman's American best-seller *Peace of mind* (1946), it touched similar chords, with both authors drawing not just on depth psychology and on Fosdick but on their own sufferings to comfort their readers.

This interest in psychology reflected the demand for books that reconciled religion and the sciences. Victorian conflicts between scientists and the churches rumbled on in the early twentieth century, sustained by the Rationalist Press Association's tracts and shilling reprints. The former supported Arnold Lunn in his teenage godlessness, while C. S. Lewis gratefully snapped up a reprint of Tylor's *Anthropology*, even though 'one [does not] like to read books in an edition called *The thinker's library* with a picture on the jacket of a male nude sitting thinking'.[148] There were fluent scientific and philosophical voices against theism, such as C. E. M. Joad, whose controversy with Lunn, *Is Christianity true?* (1932), was promoted by Eyre & Spottiswoode as 'the most sensational book on Christianity published in the last twenty years'.[149] Yet authors who promised to reconcile religion and science were increasingly popular. They might be scientists in search of Julian Huxley's *Religion without revelation* (1927) or modernist Anglicans such as Bishop Barnes. The optimism that evolution meant spiritual progress explains enthusiasm for the Jesuit palaeontologist Pierre Teilhard de Chardin, whose teleological burbling was championed by Priscilla Collins and Fontana. By 1968 one million copies of his books had been sold.[150] One

---

145 Travell, *Doctor of souls*, p. 56.   146 *Ibid.*, p. 63.   147 *Ibid.*, pp. 215, 219.
148 Lunn, *Now I see*, pp. 20–1; Hooper (ed.), *Letters*, pp. 75–6.
149 *Bookseller* 27 January 1933, p. 19.
150 *Bookseller*, Spring export issue, 12 February 1966, p. 523; 'Spring books: philosophy and religion', *Bookseller* 17 February 1968, p. 543.

notable bit of Teilhardiana was an admiring biography for Collins by Charles Raven, an Anglican clergyman and keen ornithologist whose most successful book, *Science and the Christian man* (1952), was that familiar thing: a republication by SCM Press of talks for the BBC.[151]

The palmiest years for theological publishing were the decade from the mid-fifties to the conclusion of the Second Vatican Council (1962–5). That went above all for publishers of Roman Catholic theology, who traded off interest in the continental theologians who were dismantling neo-scholasticism. Karl Rahner was popular with a wide readership, despite being as obscure as he was prolific, while new Catholic firms such as Darton, Longman & Todd and Geoffrey Chapman snapped up the French pioneers of *Ressourcement*. Like Francis Sheed, Geoffrey and Rosalind Chapman had stepped off the boat from Australia and into religious publishing. Their firm identified itself with dissident voices, such as Rosemary Haughton, a convert and confident media performer, an authority on the family who was Catholicism's first 'pregnant theologian'.[152] The emergence of the SCM Press as the herald of continental theology and radical liberalism complemented these innovations in Catholic publishing. Post-war Protestant theology had got stuck on such recondite questions as liturgical reform or the mechanics of ecumenicism, while the 'biblical theology' books published in this period had little to say to readers who did not have the Bible at their fingertips. SCM's growing adventurousness under its new associate editor Roland Gregor Smith thus filled a need. Smith, who had got to know Germany's theologians while doing his National Service there, replaced Martin as managing director and editor in 1950. He filled SCM's lists with books by Karl Barth, Dietrich Bonhoeffer, Martin Buber, Rudolf Bultmann and Ernst Kaesemann, who variously challenged theological complacency.[153] Smith's successor David Edwards continued this work, embracing paperbacks with alacrity, and commissioned John Robinson's *Honest to God* (1963), which sold quickly from the outset and a million copies in total. Reflecting on its appearance, Edwards said that the decision to publish it – only 10,000 copies at first – reflected not so much programmatic liberalism as 'healthy anarchy' in SCM's thinking. It was neither the only nor the most radical book they published, while the 'death of God' school with which it was (misleadingly) associated represented a small part of its output. It remains hard to explain why the book resonated with readers such as the leather-clad biker

151 Raven, *Teilhard de Chardin*.   152 *Bookseller*, Autumn export supplement, 1968, p. 444.
153 Bowden, 'SCM Press'.

Edwards saw wordlessly buying it in Mowbray's Cambridge shop.[154] Harold Macmillan's verdict – 'I have not read Bonhoeffer, but the Bishop of Woolwich seems to lean very heavily on him' – was echoed by the reviewers.[155] What mattered more was that Robinson was a bishop comfortable in making television news.[156] Once cried up in the media, *Honest to God* became an icon rather than a text, invoked by many thousands to voice their own intellectual enfranchisement.[157]

John Bowden, who succeeded Edwards, wondered whether *Honest to God* had done much for SCM or for theological liberalism: perhaps it had mainly confirmed many readers in thinking that 'religionless' Christianity was as abstruse as biblical theology.[158] The very production of masochistic ruminations on the intellectual failings of the churches could be attacked as a sign that the clergy were more interested in their navels than in social problems. In *Include me out! Confessions of an ecclesiastical coward* (1968), Colin Morris dismissed the 'word game[s]' which would not 'make much of a dent in the hard crust of modern society'.[159] One sign of the SCM's failure to capitalise on its coup was Bowden's preoccupation with the pigeonholing of its books in the 'devil's corner' of religious bookshops.[160] In 1978, he withdrew the SCM from the Religious Book Publishers Section of the Publishers Association, arguing that it threatened to become a 'ghetto' rather than a clearing house for beliefs of all kinds.[161] He had been bruised by the reception of *The myth of God incarnate* (1977), an essay collection edited by John Hick, a liberal Presbyterian professor of theology. Bowden had backed Hick to restage Robinson's revolution and to rescue religious publishing from its 'doldrums'.[162] Yet *The myth* garnered all the odium and few of the sales that greeted Robinson. The problem began with that 'German word' myth, which to non-theologians meant fib.[163] It continued with the press

---

154 *Bookseller* 20 April 1966, p. 1,838.   155 Stockwood, *Chactonbury Ring*, p. 149.

156 David Edwards, 'Twenty years after', *Church Times* 11 March, 1963, p. 11.

157 Towler, *The need for certainty*, which analyses Robinson's postbag.

158 Bowden, 'SCM Press'.

159 Morris, *Include me out!*, pp. 30–1. See also Nash, *Christian ideals*, chapter 8.

160 Bowden, 'SCM Press', p. 2,270.

161 'A controversy in religious circles', *Bookseller* 9 September 1978, p. 2,070.

162 Hick, *An autobiography*, p. 135; John Bowden, 'The writing on the publisher's wall?', *Church Times* 8 October 1976, p. 11.

163 J. G. Bates, 'Letters to the editor', *Church Times* 15 July 1977, p. 12; David Edwards, 'Seven against Christ?', *Church Times* 1 July 1977, p. 1. Michael Green's edited counterblast to the book, published by Hodder & Stoughton for eighty pence, was titled *The truth of God incarnate*, and Hick's chastened reworking of the same theme *The metaphor of God incarnate* (SCM Press, 1993).

launch.[164] Bowden had trailed the book in the *Observer* and drawn a swarm of journalists to the launch. But the result was incomprehension, with Hick parrying questions about his subversive intentions with the formula, 'It depends what you mean by.'[165] The book did sell 30,000 copies and was reprinted six times. Yet the *Church Times* groaned with letters from the likes of Mary Whitehead '(aged 93)' who attacked its authors for scorning the faith of 'untold millions'.[166]

By 1980, SCM was newly tame: as known now for its worthy Classics of Western Spirituality library as for 'prophetic spirituality'. When Hymns Ancient and Modern Ltd bought it in 1997, it was without too much incongruity. Prominent Anglicans with radical things to publish continued to be greeted with fitful publicity but ecclesiastical displeasure. Hugh Montefiore, then vicar of Great St Mary's church in Cambridge, endangered his career with an essay for an SCM collection, *Christ for us today* – a meditation on the marginality of Jesus, which included the suggestion that he may have been homosexual. The result was 2,000 splenetic letters, the pithiest a telegram from Northern Ireland: 'Bible Protestants of Ulster abhor your smear on Christ and charge you with diabolical blasphemy – Ian Paisley.'[167] Montefiore dodged that thunderbolt but the link between brief notoriety and a stymied career was evident in Don Cupitt's case. Cupitt was Dean of Emmanuel College, Cambridge when he emerged as that most familiar author, the Anglican doubter with friends in television. His most successful book, *The sea of faith* (1984), was the product of a television series and published by the BBC. *Taking leave of God* (1980) had sold 3,000 copies for SCM and was greeted by Bowden and Robinson as a renewal of their Christian radicalism.[168] His books stripped religion of metaphysics. But while Cupitt's tenure sheltered him from the church courts, he experienced clerical displeasure at *Taking leave of God* as a 'psychological setback', regarding himself as a 'fallen angel'. In due course, he gave up on the priesthood.[169]

The tension between the desire to reach a broad market and the need of churches for authoritative teaching also became marked for Roman Catholics after the Second Vatican Council. The controversies that followed its implementation certainly sold books. If the publication of *Humanae vitae* (1968) was

---

164 Hick, *An autobiography*, p. 229.   165 *Ibid.*, p. 230.
166 'Advice from primate', *Church Times* 15 July 1977, p. 1; 'Furore on book of the "myth"', *Church Times* 8 July 1977, p. 12.
167 Montefiore, *Oh God, what next?*, p. 145.
168 Alan Macfarlane, interview with Don Cupitt (16 February 2009), available at www.alanmacfarlane.com/ancestors/index.html.
169 *Ibid.* See also Don Cupitt, 'When doubt is desirable', *Guardian* 24 May 2003.

one harbinger of a revived authoritarianism, it also represented a windfall for the book trade. Customers of Howard Books' *Sex in marriage: thirty-eight questions posed by Pope Paul's encyclical* (1968) were said to 'queue for it at bookstalls'.[170] Yet the clouds gathering over the Vatican soon burst over publishers. Burns & Oates were sunk by the Council, which in modernising the liturgy and championing the vernacular rendered their costly missals obsolete at a stroke and imperilled a business model which depended on expensive but authoritative books for seminarians – now an endangered species in Britain.[171] The conversion of Burns & Oates to *Aggiornamento* had never been convincing because their holding company still sold devotional objects, 'so that Burns and Oates sad to say, meant plaster statues to much of its potential, and indeed actual, public'. Failing to make profits, the firm could not look to the Church for salvation because all Catholic publishers resented clerical involvement in their business. Burns & Oates went under in 1970. When Charlotte de la Bédoyère resurrected them in 1974 her 'streamlined' strategy rested on its backlist and unexceptionable reference works.[172] If Sheed & Ward briefly outlived Burns & Oates, they also struggled after hitching themselves to *Aggiornamento*. Under Sheed's son-in-law Neil Middleton, they published *Slant* (1964–70), the loss-making journal of Catholic radicalism, and storm petrels such as Hans Küng, Brian Wicker or Charles Davis.[173] Yet it was not the 'ecumenical, sociological, biff-bang New Churchy books' which sold, but the backlist. The 'jig was up with Catholic publishing' and Frank Sheed returned from retirement to sell off the firm.[174]

One lasting effect of Vatican II was that the papacy loomed ever larger in publishing by and about Catholicism, especially when aimed at non-Catholics. Rebels against the papacy, such as Küng, or theologians who aroused its displeasure, such as the meek Dominican Edward Schillebeeckx – whose translator was John Bowden – were assured of a welcome in what remained a viscerally if mildly anti-papal culture. Every rumble of displeasure was good for their publishers, selling as it did their books and generating a small literature of its own.[175] The papacy attracted a literature of conspiracy. Tom Maschler of Cape triggered a bidding war for

170 *Bookseller* 16 November 1968, p. 1,678.
171 Paul Burns, 'The final chapter of the Burns and Oates Story', *Bookseller* 4 July 1970, pp. 26–30.
172 'Publishing's bold success story', *Catholic Herald* 7 August 1981, p. 5.
173 '"Slant" magazine to close', *Catholic Herald* 27 March 1970, p. 1; Sharratt, 'Roman Catholicism in the 1960s'.
174 Sheed, *Frank and Maisie*, pp. 267–71.
175 Bowden, 'SCM Press'; 'Cleric arraigned', *Bookseller* 8 December 1979, p. 2,528.

foreign rights to David Yallop's *In God's name* (1978), which alleged that the death of John Paul I pointed not just to corruption but to murder in the Vatican. Corgi bought the paperback rights for the largest sum ever spent on a non-fiction work.[176] In a more benign way, celebrity and theology fused in lives of Popes, rushed out at their accession or following their deaths. Peter Hebblethwaite, who shot to notice with *The year of three Popes* (1978), a Fount paperback, became a leading figure in the Pope business, which was boosted by the accession in 1978 of the glamorous 'Pope from Poland'. With Paul Vallely's *Pope Francis* (2013) recently selling well for Bloomsbury, this genre continues to exploit public curiosity in these increasingly mediatised figures.

Halfway to faith

In 1999, 61 per cent of Britons said that they believed in God, but only 28 per cent in a personal God or in hell. Only about half claimed to belong to a Christian denomination.[177] The decay of organised Christianity in later twentieth-century Britain is indubitable, but such ambiguous figures cause historians and sociologists to debate whether it is really a prologue to total secularisation – defined as apathy in the face of transcendent questions – and thus to the extinction or curtailment of the publishing described in this chapter. The declining intellectual authority and social presence of churches has undoubtedly opened up the market in spiritual goods to new entrants and their publishers, even if it is still unclear how long they can count on a viable consumer base.[178] From the late Victorian period, increasing numbers of people have wished to publicise their 'private', 'invisible' or 'common' religion, which owed little to Christian clerics and everything to their own intellectual explorations.[179] Moreover, spiritualists, neo-pagans, theosophists and occult practitioners developed a rich literary culture, which presented their rituals as the revival of traditions suppressed by the churches. The aftermath of the war and anxieties about economic upheaval were a propitious environment for spiritualists and theosophists.[180] Witches were expected to read and to write books and 'Wicca' was the product of literary artifice before it was a lived religion.[181] They were served by firms such as

---

176 'Book news: murder in the Vatican?', *Bookseller* 16 June 1984, p. 2,210.
177 Lambert, 'A turning point'.
178 Bruce, 'Les limites du marché religieux', for a sceptical view.
179 For these terms, see Luckmann, *The invisible religion*; Towler, *The need for certainty*.
180 Sutcliffe, *Children of the New Age*, p. 36 and *passim*; Hazelgrove, *Spiritualism and British society*; Byrne, *Modern spiritualism*.
181 Hutton, *The triumph of the moon*.

Rider, Aquarian Press, Wildwood House and a host of cottage operators.[182] The proportion of religious books classifiable as occult has doubled since the 1930s: rising from around 7 per cent in 1930 to 17 per cent in 1990 and then subsiding to 15 per cent in 2000.[183] Spiritualism and occultism also penetrated the mainstream. The first horoscope appeared in the daily press in 1931, while major houses dabbled in spiritualist and occult thinking. The Sheldon Press, initially an SPCK imprint for children, published 10,000 copies of Barbara Cartland's *I seek the miraculous*, which related 'her lifelong search for the Inner World'.[184]

If spiritualism and occultism generated one kind of literature, the seekers drawn to mystical and psychologising exploration of truth beyond the churches were producers and market for another. The dust jacket of Lord Eccles's *Halfway to faith* (Geoffrey Bles, 1966), a spiritual autobiography by a government minister, featured a drawing of book spines labelled 'D. H. Lawrence', 'St Augustine', 'Teilhard de Chardin' and 'The Bishop of Woolwich' – the texts which had forged his inquisitive creed. Had Eccles's spiritual struggles begun rather than peaked in the 1960s, his bookshelf might have included 'Buddha' or 'Bhagwan Shree Rajneesh', for questing increasingly exploited literature about or by members of other, eastern religions and spiritual movements. The literature of this kind published by the missionary movement and presses attentive to its concerns had been driven by the concern to demonstrate that Christian revelation was compatible with or completed the insights of other religions. From the 1940s, non-Christian religions spoke more directly to readers thanks to scholarly publishers such as the East and West Library (specialising in Judaism) or Curzon Press. Some eastern leaders became celebrities. Rom Landau's *God is my adventure* (1935), which gathered a motley collection of roving stars, was reprinted seven times, hinting at a market that matured in the sixties. Its leaders would be people like the guru Bhagwan Shree Rajneesh, published by Sheldon Books. The journey of an ex-chaplain of Churchill College, Cambridge to his Poona ashram began with reading his *The mustard seed* (1978).[185] The early appearance of home-grown teachers, who tailored Zen, Yoga or Tai Chi to the West by relaxing their severities, was similarly important.[186] Changes in state religious education supported that shift, as it drifted in the interval between

---

182 Sutcliffe, *Children of the New Age*, p. 39.
183 Partridge, *The re-enchantment of the west*, pp. 666–7.   184 *Bookseller* 21 January 1978.
185 Thompson and Heelas, *The way of the heart*, p. 82.
186 Rawlinson, *The book of enlightened masters*; Van Hove, 'L'émergence d'un marché spirituel', p. 167.

the 1944 and 1988 Education Acts from vindicating the truth of Christianity to phenomenological exploration of plural religions.[187]

The New Age, which commentators identified as existing from the late 1960s onwards, is hard to characterise accurately. New Age centres such as Scotland's Findhorn Community (and its press) were founded on the principle that its seekers should not have to choose between traditions. Its leading authors were 'wandering stars' who roved across eastern traditions, or celebrities, such as the existentialist turned occult explorer Colin Wilson, or the actress Shirley MacLaine.[188] 'Alternative' and 'mind-body-spirit' bookshops made it possible to realise their injunctions to eclecticism. If the essence of the New Age is its 'cultic milieu', whose participants raid different religious traditions for inspiration, then bookshops and the towns such as Glastonbury which shelter them, are where such *bricolage* literally took place.[189] Here, scholarly works on Buddhism, theosophical classics and guides to channelling or shape-shifting rub up against one another. Like Christian bookshops, they are often run by enthusiasts, for meagre returns and depend for their survival on modest rents, gifts from enthusiasts or the sale of crystals or essential oils. The 'esoteric economy' to which they belong is a modest affair. Unit sales for mind-body-spirit books were between 1.6 and 1.8 million around the turn of the twenty-first century – one successful video game could outsell the whole sector.[190] Alternative bookshops matter though, because like occult bookshops they worked as clearing houses for information about or even venues for seminars and ritual events.[191]

The texts and genres generated in this milieu have escaped this now shrinking and ageing 'occulture'.[192] 'New Age' texts now pass under hazier descriptors such as 'mind-body-spirit', with one chain reporting that they sell four times the number of mind-body-spirit books as of theistic texts.[193] The restless innovation of authors such as Deepak Chopra and Louise Hay has made them robust best-sellers. For critics, such 'mainstreaming' shows New Age writing to be complicit in its own commodification – a symptom of, rather than an exception to, the vicissitudes of religious publishing.[194] The seriousness of these charges depends on whether the 'everyday

187 Parsons, 'There and back again?'   188 Sutcliffe, '"Wandering stars"', p. 19.
189 Mayer, 'Biens de salut et marché religieux'; Bowman, 'Understanding Glastonbury'.
190 Bartolini et al., 'Psychics, crystals, candles and cauldrons', p. 378.
191 Sutcliffe, Children of the New Age, p. 41.
192 Rose, 'An examination of the New Age movement'; Mears and Ellison, 'Who buys New Age materials?'; Heelas and Seel, 'An ageing New Age?'
193 Heelas, Spiritualities of life, p. 75.
194 Carrette and King, Selling spirituality; York, 'New Age commodification'.

spirituality' these texts outline is a meaningful alternative to the transcendent claims of historic religions: are its readers changed by what they consume?[195] This is as much an evidential as a conceptual question: further research might reveal how readers who haunt the 'mind-body-spirit' section of bookshops or online retailers use the texts they buy.[196]

The contrast between a 'spiritual market' and an ailing Christian sector is easily overstated. Many Christian publishers are increasingly attentive to mind, body and spirit. The charismatic and Pentecostal movements of the 1970s and 1980s both within and beyond existing churches generated a 'charismatic bookshelf' whose appeals to unmediated experience outsold 'radical theology'.[197] The Alpha Course, with its sociable Brompton bookshop and its Kingsway published books, such as Nicky Gumbel's *Challenging lifestyle* (1996), embodies these experiments in a mass movement.[198] The contemporary evangelical who reads Gumbel or Rick Warren's *The purpose-driven life* (1978) is as deeply engaged as any New Age dabbler in shaping the self. Secondly, an interest in healing has long united 'spiritual' and Christian publishers. If Pentecostalism and the charismatic movement were synonymous with the healing work of the Holy Spirit, then liberal Protestants who flinched at such claims found their balm in psychology, while evangelical literature is now as interested in health, diet and the endurance of terminal illness.[199] Prayer anthologies and manuals were another area in which Christian publishers embraced change, as evangelical readers begin to assess mental technologies less for their abstract truth than their positive effects on users.[200] One last symptom of the broadening of the religious marketplace has been the recent popularity of attacks upon religion. Amazon reported in 2007 that while recent growth in sales of 'religion' books outstripped the history book boom, the two best-selling books in the category were Richard Dawkins's *The God delusion* (2006) and Christopher Hitchens's *God is not great: how religion poisons everything* (2007). Between April and June 2007, *The God delusion* was the fourth-best-selling book in all categories, leaving Dawkins second only to Harry Potter and Gordon Ramsay. While Dawkins and Hitchens aped the ferocity of the early twentieth-century scientific naturalists, the New Atheism genre they helped to

---

195 For arguments for, see Mackian, *Everyday spirituality*, and against, Bruce, 'Good intentions and bad sociology'.
196 Heelas, *Spiritualities of life*, p. 15.
197 'The Church's growth point', *Economist* 19 January 1974, p. 16.
198 Hunt, *Anyone for Alpha?*, pp. 6, 14.
199 Gerard Noel, 'The charismatic bookshelf', *Catholic Herald* 10 November 1978, p. 8.
200 Luhrmann, *When God talks back*, chapters 6 and 7.

found did as much to revive interest in as to bury 'religion': Amazon reported, for instance, that sales of Bibles had risen by 120 per cent in tandem with Dawkins.[201]

World of Islam

If this chapter has stressed the anxieties and realities of dechristianisation, then publishers to other organised religions are experiencing growth rather than decline in the communities they serve. Since the 1960s, growth in Muslim numbers has been particularly marked, rising from around 50,000 in 1961 in England and Wales (0.11 per cent of population) to 1.6 million in 2001 (3.07 per cent), with registered places of worship rising from seven to 614.[202] Publishing by and for Muslims has grown in step with this development. It initially reflected a determination to defend Muslim identity. Organisations such as the Muslim Education Trust (1966) and the Islamic Foundation (1973) in Leicester sought to preserve immigrants from the 'flood of obscene publications' they might encounter in the West. They were unhappy about British schools, particularly their supposedly reticent or unfair portrayal of Islam in religious instruction, and were therefore intent on publishing rival materials for use in state schools as well as in madrasahs. The Islamic Foundation was connected from its inception with transnational Islamist movements. It published translations both of Maulana Abu al-A'la al-Mawdudi, the founder of Jamaat-e-Islami, and of Sayyid Qutb, the Egyptian leader of the Muslim Brotherhood, authors who demand the transformation of society along Sunni principles. The Foundation's vision would be most stridently articulated not in any book it published but in its campaign against Salman Rushdie's *The satanic verses*: on 3 October 1988 it issued a circular to Muslim organisations and mosques, inviting them to concerted protests against Penguin for publishing it.[203]

Muslim interest in publishing is not, though, always so strident, or political. The Foundation has hived off its publishing activities to the blandly named Kube Publishing (2006). Alongside dense works of Qur'an commentary and *hadith*, it prioritises digital publishing, lively illustrated books for children and even teen fiction. Works such as Rae Norridge's *Hilmy the hippo becomes a hero* (2003) or Fawzia Gilani's *Snow White: an Islamic tale* (2013) allow children to access Allah outside the difficult Arabic of the Qur'an. While most

201 David Smith, 'Believe it or not: the sceptics beat God in the bestseller battle', *Observer* 12 August 2007.
202 www.brin.ac.uk.   203 Keppel, *Allah in the West*, pp. 121–2, 131–3.

Muslim publishers are modest outfits, reliant on donations to fund their work and concentrating primarily on distributing the Qur'an and on cheap translations of works by religious scholars from across the centuries, often as e-books, there are signs that other publishers are following Kube in their willingness to innovate. Children's literature is a staple for firms such as Ta-Ha and al-Hidaayah, reflecting the fact that Muslim parents lay great emphasis on nurturing the faith in madrasahs – institutions which superficially resemble now vanishing Sunday schools – and within the home. If this process prioritises the recitation of Qur'an in Arabic it also makes extensive use of books, DVDs and websites in a 'multi-media experience' designed to 'nurture' Islamic identities.[204] Muslim publishers thus concentrate as much on helping British readers to live Islam as on defending or extending its frontiers. There is a growing self-help literature, such as Sayeda Habib's *Life coaching for Muslims* (2013), which complements the marketing of classic works by authors such as al-Ghazali in such terms. Another sign of incipient mainstreaming is the appearance of writers such as Ziauddin Sardar, whose work ranges from educational treatises for the Islamic Foundation to fluent works for mainstream presses such as Granta. Amal Press UK, whose core business is reprinting classical texts, sought to intervene in debates over the War on Terror by publishing such works as Abdal Hakim Murad's *Bombing without moonlight* (2008), Murad being a leading convert intellectual. From 2007, many of these publishers gathered together as part of the London Islamic Book Fair, which in 2013 took place in the decidedly secular setting of the Excel Centre.[205]

The distribution of books is just part of a broader attempt to nurture an Islamic material culture. Books are often just one commodity among many, even in Islamic bookshops. Customers of the Islamic Impressions chain (in Greater London and Birmingham) can consume halal confectionery alongside books, while the very name of Manchester's World of Islam reveals that it is a place to pick up not just a copy of the Qur'an but also scarves, ornaments and alcohol-free perfumes. Such examples illustrate that Colin Morris was only half right. Religious Britons are still People of the Book, but not all People of the Book are Protestants. God has not been confined to a box, but conversely neither He nor the religions that variously invoke Him are limited to the page, if indeed they ever were.

204 Scourfield *et al.*, *Muslim childhood*, pp. 81–2 and chapter 5.   205 http://libf.org.uk.

14

Publishing for leisure

SUSAN PICKFORD

In a sense, all publishing that is not strictly informational in content is publishing for leisure, as reading is itself one of the most popular leisure activities there is. This chapter cannot hope to encompass all the ways in which people have turned to books in their leisure time over the twentieth century and into the twenty-first, from the long-established practice of reading for pleasure to the emergence of audiobooks[1] (available as talking books for the visually impaired from the early decades of the century) that enabled people to combine 'reading' with other activities. Rather, it focusses on four areas in which books acted as adjuncts to other popular pastimes. In this, it follows the chapter on 'Publishing for leisure' in the preceding volume of the *Cambridge history of the book in Britain*, covering three of the categories explored in that chapter: cookery, gardening and sport (music is covered elsewhere in this volume). In addition, I have chosen to include a new category that blossomed later in the century – self-help or MBS (mind-body-spirit) – which is connected to issues of lifestyle choice that play into the conceptualisation of leisure as a consumer category.

The trends noted in the previous volume – a shorter working week, technological developments, and an expanding middle class with disposable income – continued in the twentieth century, leading to an ever greater range of, and engagement with, leisure activities in British society. Mid-century was an age of weekly cinema trips and vast crowds at football matches; later decades saw the rise of the cheap package holiday and a shift to private, home-based leisure activities such as TV viewing and video games. The increasing social and economic significance of the leisure sector has led leisure history itself to become a vibrant research area in recent years, leading to a more sophisticated understanding of the nature of leisure than the straightforward dichotomy between work and play. This traditional model

---

1 Rubery, *The untold story of the talking book.*

is particularly inadequate in responding to two major social forces that shaped the period under study – feminism (where does unpaid housework fit into the 'free time' model?) and unemployment (does being on the dole equate to unlimited leisure?). Consequently, it is important to acknowledge that cookery and gardening are not unproblematic leisure categories, as many books in both categories were aimed at readers who undertook the activity in question professionally and/or through necessity rather than choice. I shall be addressing how the publishing industry reflects the shifting perception of these activities from profession or duty to hobby in the course of the chapter.

Cookery books: from the servant problem to culinary superstars

Cookery books are fascinating social documents, offering rare glimpses into an aspect of daily life that is by its very nature ephemeral. The genre is, in the words of Janet Theophano, 'fluid and eclectic, embodying an array of knowledge',[2] not only on food preparation, but also on issues such as the changing social role of women, attitudes to consumption, and patterns of immigration. While the main focus in this section is on books, it should be borne in mind that women's-interest magazines were equally, if not more, significant as a means of disseminating culinary information in this period, with readerships regularly in the millions.

Nineteenth-century cookery writers such as Isabella Beeton tended to publish compendious books for readers for whom cooking (or overseeing others doing so) was a necessity of life rather than a creative outlet. Where Mrs Beeton's *Book of household management* (1859–61) weighed in at well over a thousand pages, covering every kitchen eventuality, the early twentieth century saw the emergence of more niche titles. Vegetarian and health food recipe books increased in number, for instance, thanks to the late Victorian domestic science movement which introduced nutritional value to cookery discourse: Jean Mill's 1909 *Reform cookery book: up-to-date health cookery for the twentieth century*, for example, includes advertisements for 'uric-acid-free' bread, 'the best brown bread for gouty subjects'.

Like every aspect of British life, cookery was thrown into upheaval by the First World War. The influential French tradition, typified by Escoffier's *Guide to modern cookery* (1907), lost ground as rationing led to a rise in titles

2 Theophano, *Eat my words*, p. 269. See also Humble, *Culinary pleasures*.

such as Florence George's *Economical dishes for wartime* (1916). The books themselves became thin, drab affairs, closely printed on cheap paper. The most significant change wrought by the war, however, was the change in employment patterns, as the servant class went into rapid decline; by 1951, just 1 per cent of households employed some form of live-in help. This meant that many middle-class women who had been brought up with the expectation of overseeing other women's work now needed books to teach them this new skill. Publications such as the 1925 Bride's Primer of Cookery series in *Good Housekeeping* and Hester Tuxford's *Cookery for the middle classes* (1929) catered for this new market; the latter's subtitle, *Useful hints on gas stove cooking including the new automatic control*, reflects the emergent preoccupation with labour-saving devices, since, as the magazine *Women's Life* noted in 1926, 'elaborate entertaining's always difficult for the servantless woman'.[3] As a result, there was a certain anxiety over the loss of traditional cooking skills. The food journalist Florence White set out to counter this threat, travelling round England to collect traditional recipes for her 1932 *Good things in England*, paving the way for an interest in the social history of food that is the hallmark of later writers such as Jane Grigson.

Food was fast becoming a feminist issue: the first issue of *Good Housekeeping* argued that 'There should be no drudgery in the house. There must be time ... to have leisure for one's own.'[4] However, cookery was to remain firmly within the female sphere. Men like Marcel Boulestin might *write* prestigious cookbooks devoted to *haute cuisine*, but their expected readership was predominantly female. The few books aimed at a male readership tended to adopt a rather jokey tone, as if to defuse any perceived threat to the reader's masculinity. Wilson Midgley's 1948 *Cookery for men only or I.Y.G.T.T.L.A.F* (the rather cryptic subtitle standing for 'if you go to the larder and find ...') is a case in point. As the *Publisher* noted in its review, 'Mr. Midgley assumes that the reader knows nothing of the subject, not even how to boil an egg.'[5] The book is illustrated with cartoon vignettes and includes suitably 'manly' tips such as how to skin a rabbit and what to do with whale meat. Its cover illustration, featuring a pair of scissors chopping up a carrot, also reflects another interesting social trend – the rise of the single-person bedsit household, as heralded in titles such as Ambrose Heath's *Cooking for one* (1942).

3 Quoted in Mennell, *All manners of food*, p. 242.   4 Quoted in *ibid.*, p. 245.
5 *Publisher* 162 (1948), p. 1,181.

One trend to have emerged in the inter-war period – earlier than might be expected – is the arrival of international cuisine in Britain. French cuisine had long been a presence, of course, while Indian food was enjoyed in the colonies; Mrs John Gilpin's cloth-bound octavo *Memsahib's guide to cookery in India*, printed in Bombay in 1914 by A. J. Combridge and selling for three shillings, was just one of many similar titles. However, British cookery books of the period also reflect a degree of engagement with other culinary traditions; one early example is Robert Christie's 1911 *Banquets of the nations: eighty-six dinners characteristic and typical each of its own country* – a lavishly produced octavo volume, cloth-bound and stamped, produced for the Edinburgh Cap and Gown Club, with a lengthy introduction on dining practices from Madagascar to Siam.

Christie's work can only have reached a very limited readership: it was to be several decades before works featuring international cuisine achieved mainstream distribution, though several such works by authors showcasing their own native culinary traditions were published with limited distribution in the intervening period. The great Indian author Mulk Raj Anand began his literary career in 1932 with *Curries and other Indian dishes*. Though described in one review as 'for the benefit of the English housewife',[6] it is doubtful whether this was indeed the main readership for a work with an avowedly anthropological bent, reviewed in the *Times Literary Supplement*; it was printed in London by Desmond Harmsworth, whose list included modernist writers such as James Joyce, Ezra Pound and Wyndham Lewis.

Another example is Shao-ching Cheng's 1936 *Chinese cookery book*, a self-published octavo volume bound in red cloth with a Chinese-style font for the title, price four shillings, by the proprietor of one of London's early Chinese restaurants in Greek Street. Since the preface notes that all ingredients were on sale in the Shanghai Emporium, next door to the restaurant, it can be presumed that the work's distribution circuit was geographically limited. One intriguing title that makes the political significance of this trend explicit is the 1944 *Cook's tour of the Soviet Union: eating with our ally*, a short illustrated pamphlet (twenty-four pages) published by the Russia Today Society, price one shilling. Other culinary traditions, most notably those from the Mediterranean basin, only gained widespread popularity after the Second World War, due both to immigration (especially from Italy) and to the hugely influential work of Elizabeth David.

6 *Calcutta Review* March 1933, p. 99.

The outbreak of the Second World War made food a national priority. The Ministry of Food became the principal source of culinary information, publishing pamphlets such as *Hedgerow harvest* (1943) and *Your baby's food in wartime* (1942). Food rationing was introduced early in 1940 and lasted until 1954; cookery became to a great extent a question of making do with scarce ingredients, while the authorities strove to minimise risks to public health by providing supplements for children and using additives such as calcium and iron in bread. Rationing arguably contributed to a broad improvement in cookery skills due to the need for ingenuity with limited ingredients, the pleasure of cooking with home-grown allotment produce, and the need to preserve seasonal or perishable produce by means of bottling, pickling and jam-making. The cookery books published in these years of austerity were surprisingly aspirational in tone and increasingly glossy in content. Philip Harben, who had hosted radio cookery programmes before and during the war, made the transition to television in 1946, publishing the *Television cooking book* in 1951. Television sets were still only owned by a minority of homes, though the Coronation saw the number of television licences pass 2 million in 1953. That same year, Harben anticipated another major cookery trend when he cooked frozen scampi, or 'nephrops tails', for his show. As home refrigerators, let alone freezers, were still a luxury item in the mid-1950s, this suggests Harben's audience consisted largely of the well-to-do middle classes.

As post-war austerity gave way to the economic boom, however, home refrigeration became more affordable. By the mid-1960s many housewives were doubtless pleased to discover the instant, chilled and frozen foods devised by nutritionists who moved into private industry when the Ministry of Food was merged with Agriculture and Fisheries in 1954. Cookery writer Nigel Slater's memoir of his 1960s childhood, *Toast* (2004), recalls in loving detail the place that foodstuffs like Angel Delight and Arctic Roll played on British dinner tables at the time. The reliance on convenience foods and white goods (41 per cent of homes had a freezer by 1978) was similarly driven by the increasing presence of women in the workplace, leading to titles such as Bee Nilson's *Career woman's cookbook* (1966), which placed a premium on time management.

Paradoxically, by taking much of the potential drudgery out of day-to-day cooking, convenience foods enabled cookery to gain ground as a creative outlet, as predicted by John Fuller in his 1944 *Wine and food* when he wrote that housewives would soon be able to 'pursue cookery as a fascinating hobby'.[7] The move towards cookery as a leisure pursuit in the post-war period arose in large part due to the influence of a new breed of food writers, first and foremost Elizabeth David, whose *Mediterranean cooking* (1950) introduced exotic new ingredients such as garlic and olive oil to the relatively small, but growing, sector of British society with the appropriate culinary capital and income. The increasing sophistication of attitudes to food is reflected in food photography, used in the 1930s to illustrate the stages of a recipe; by the 1970s such photographs commonly included wine glasses, suggesting a more cosmopolitan approach to dining. A further factor was the by now widespread presence of cookery programmes on television, with TV chefs like Fanny Cradock becoming popular media figures; tie-ins like Stuart Hall's 1972 *Cook the 'Look North' way*, published by John Sherratt & Son, paved the way for the cross-media synergies between TV and publishing that now dominate the sector.

The 1970s saw a rise in titles reflecting the green politics of the day, such as Richard Mabey's 1972 *Food for free*, a guide to foraging, while vegetarian and ethnic cookbooks joined the publishing mainstream thanks to authors such as Madhur Jaffrey and Kenneth Lo. The synergy between television and publishing developed apace. By the end of the century the cookery book market was dominated by TV chefs, many of whom have become publishing brands in their own right: Delia Smith's *How to cook book 2* sold 110,000 copies in just three days when it was launched in December 1999,[8] while 'a Delia' has now passed into common use, to the point that it has been included in the Collins English Dictionary. While many of the top TV chefs are men, no doubt helping to break down gender perceptions around cookery, it remains the case that there is a peak in cookery book sales around Mother's Day, suggesting that gender stereotyping is not yet fully a thing of the past. Books such as Nigella Lawson's *How to be a domestic goddess* (2003) – glossy hardbacks with high-end production values – are used as much to signify an aspirational lifestyle as they are for their recipes.

Like other publishing sectors with informational content, cookery book publishers have begun to develop e-content such as blogs and apps, particularly targeted at younger user categories such as students. However, there will doubtless always be room for print cookery books, which are less likely to be ruined by a spatter of cake mixture than a hand-held electronic device would be.

---

7 Quoted in Mennell, *All manners of food*, p. 281.
8 Ashley *et al., Food and cultural studies*, p. 154.

Gardening books: how big is a small garden?

Gardening is big business in Britain. A 1989 Mintel study reported that 20 million British people self-identified as gardeners, while the UK gardening magazine sector was worth $89.5 million (approximately £57 million) in 2009.[9] Like cookery books, gardening books are a rich, albeit often neglected, source for social historians: Gertrude Jekyll's suggestion in her 1908 *Children and gardens* that 'if any of you go to the Riviera in the winter, you would be sure to find this plant' is full of class assumptions, while Thomas Henslow's *Allotment gardens and management* (1942), which recommends using 'your wife's washing soda' for growing onions, is equally presumptive about the nature of its readership.

Nature pronounced in a 1903 review that 'gardening books are becoming noted for containing a small amount of gardening information largely diluted with something that has little or no relevance to horticultural pursuits'.[10] Horticultural musings certainly accounted for much of the gardening book market in the first half of the century, with books such as Marion Cran's *Joy of the ground* (1928) enjoying popular success. These existed alongside guides that gave practical advice, particularly to the growing numbers of middle-class home owners who found themselves with a patch of land for the first time. This new class of gardener grew rapidly after the First World War, which brought about a number of changes in gardening practice. First of all, many great estates lost staff, not to mention owners, in the war; there were 120,000 staff gardeners in 1911, but the post-war period saw a considerable shift towards casual jobbing. As a result, the Victorian practices of hothousing in coal-fired greenhouses and bedding out proved too labour- and energy-intensive and fell out of favour; fashionable hothoused plants such as anthurium gave way to flowering shrubs that largely looked after themselves – though amateurs no longer able to delegate to a professional head gardener might still require a book such as Stanley Johnson's *Flowering shrubs and how to know them* (1922) to identify non-native species imported by specialist nurseries.

Some 4 million new houses were built in England and Wales from 1919 to 1939, most of which had small gardens attached. One signifier of how hobby gardening spread down the social scale is the expectation of garden size. H. H. Thomas's *Little gardens and how to make the most of them* (1908) still assumes that the owner will have room for a tennis lawn and summer house,

9 Parker, *2009 report on gardening magazines*.
10 'A Gloucestershire wild garden', *Nature* 13 August 1903, p. 342.

while Gertrude Jekyll wrote the same year 'I have to be content with my little wood of ten acres.'[11] By 1940, Harry Roberts argued in *Keep fit in wartime* that every British citizen should have an eighth of an acre, gardening being excellent exercise; by the early 1990s, the average garden size was one-twentieth of an acre. This downsizing led to a rise in titles aimed at novices with limited time and space to garden: Phoebe Gaye's *Weekend garden* and Allen Wood's *Grow them indoors: window ledge and house gardening* (both 1939) reflect this tendency. Arthur Johnson's *Plant names simplified* (1931), which set out to demystify Latin botanical names, is a further interesting indication of how hobby gardening moved down the social scale.

Developing self-sufficiency in food became a theme of national importance between the wars, as it had been recognised that Germany's greater harvests of crops such as potatoes offered the country a significant advantage in case of conflict. As Geoffrey Henslow pointed out in *Garden development* (1923), this brought about a balance of payments issue: Britain imported £8 million worth of apples in 1931, while growing just £2.5 million. As war loomed, what had been a hobby became a necessity: flowerbeds were replaced with vegetable patches and 'digging for victory' became a national cause, encouraged by titles such as George Copley's 1939 *Vegetable growing in war-time.* The Garden Book Club (founded in the late 1930s along the lines of the Left Book Club and run by Foyles to the 1980s) reprinted books such as E. Graham's *Gardening in war-time* (1941) to the 'war economy standard', distributing them to its 10,000 members at 'only a fraction of the normal cost!' as an advertisement in a 1939 issue of *My Garden* put it.[12] A 1954 advertisement in *Gardening Illustrated* listed books published at 12s 6d on sale for 3s 6d.[13] Gardening also moved to the airwaves, with C. H. Middleton broadcasting popular talks on 'Your garden in wartime' in 1941, heralding a lasting symbiotic relationship between broadcast media and gardening books similar to that of cookery books.

Gardening regained its hobby status after the war: as J. E. B. Maunsell noted in *Natural gardening* in 1958, 'there are some 300,000 new houses (and gardens) being acquired every year by potential gardeners'.[14] Garden centres began to appear in the mid-1950s to meet the needs of these new car-owning suburban gardeners, replacing the specialist seed merchants once found in every town; they soon became destinations for weekend outings, reflecting

11 Quoted in Hoyles, *Bread and roses*, p. 141.
12 Advertisement, *My Garden* 17 (1939), p. 291.
13 Advertisement, *Gardening Illustrated* 71–73 (1954), p. 248.
14 Quoted in Hoyles, *Bread and roses*, p. 52.

the rise of gardening as a consumer and leisure experience. Garden centres and even DIY stores became significant outlets for gardening books; one 2007 study reported that 7 per cent of visitors bought books from garden centres. Alan Titchmarsh's series *How to garden* (Ebury, 2008) was the object of a marketing campaign targeted at garden centres, with the author making appearances for signings, while the DIY retailer B&Q signed a contract to promote the series at its 330 stores, dropping David Hessayon's *Experts* series despite having sold 500,000 copies in its stores over the previous decade.[15]

The shift towards gardening as a leisure pursuit is also related to the professionalisation of landscape design. The preoccupation with the aesthetic dimension of gardening, apparent from the start of the period in the works of writers such as Gertrude Jekyll, led to the foundation of the British Association of Garden Architects in 1929, followed by the creation of a degree course in landscape architecture at the University of Reading in 1949. Books such as Christopher Tunnard's *Gardens in the modern landscape* (1938) reflect this aesthetic approach. Appropriately enough, one of the earliest expressions of modern art in landscape form was the courtyard garden at the Penguin headquarters, based on a Mondrian abstract. The fashion for modernist garden design has now given way to a preference for more traditional cottage-style gardens, but coffee-table gardening books such as Tim Longville's *Gardens of the Lake District* (2007) are popular avatars of this trend. Such books rely on advanced colour printing technology, which has improved greatly since Vita Sackville-West wrote in frustration in *Some flowers* (1937), illustrated with black and white photographs, 'I am afraid that my illustration gives no idea at all of what this rose is really like.'[16]

In recent years, the gardening book sector has seen a number of trends emerge. Environmental concerns are reflected in the proliferation of titles on organic and urban gardening, while TV garden makeover programmes have led to a boom in garden design books. The gardening book sector reveals a similar, though less intense, crossover between print and television as was apparent in cookery publishing: the BBC held 26.6 per cent of the gardening books market in 2003.[17] Laetitia Maklouf's 2010 *Virgin gardener*, recording the experience of a first-time city gardener, applies a marketing concept that proved highly successful in the case of Jamie Oliver's *Naked chef*, while titles such as Matt James's TV tie-in *The city garden bible* (2005) act more as

15 Matthew Appleby, 'Hessayon books ditched by B&Q for Titchmarsh guides', *Horticulture Week* 30 April 2010, p. 13.
16 Sackville-West, *Some flowers*, p. 40.
17 Giles Elliot and Caroline Sanderson, 'Back to their roots', *Bookseller* 15 April 2005, p. 31.

aspirational lifestyle guides than the sort of book that can be 'thrown around the garden', as Nicola Williams, leisure and lifestyle manager at Waterstone's, put it in a 2005 interview.[18] In this sense, gardening, like cookery, is a category where print has a distinct advantage over e-content.

Sport: from gentleman amateurs to WAGs

The chapter on leisure in the preceding volume records the sort of socially elite sports that dominated nineteenth-century sports publishing: horse-racing, golf, cricket. Signs of democratisation began to creep in at the end of the period when football in its modern, codified form began to make an appearance in publishing; club handbooks, histories and rulebooks began to be printed in the early years of the twentieth century in an attempt to legitimise interest in a sport that was gaining ground, particularly in schools. *How to play association football: a short practical treatise on laws, principles and practice of the game* (1905) is one example of this trend. The author, P. Walker MA, insists on his academic credentials, while a review in the *Publisher's Circular* notes that he is 'an enthusiast and a scholar'.

The gradual diversification of the sports covered by publishers reflected two key developments in the social role of sport across the period. The first of these is the shortening of the working week from an average of fifty-four hours in 1900 to thirty-nine by the 1980s, leading to an increased interest and participation in sport by all sectors of society: one study noted an increase of 13 per cent for participation in outdoor sports and 60 per cent for indoor sports between 1977 and 1987. The second was the rise of professionalism in sport. Events such as the ending of the division between amateur and professional cricketers (the latter referred to by their surnames while addressing the former as 'Sir') in 1963 not only enabled formerly elite sports to extend their reach down the social scale, but also ended what Jeff Hill calls the ethos of 'distaste for trade and money-making'[19] that pervaded such sports, paving the way for their mass commercialisation and consumption. Interestingly, a similar class-based pattern is apparent in the way sports are represented in fiction: P. G. Wodehouse's golfing stories are typical of the first half of the period, while Alan Sillitoe's *The loneliness of the long-distance runner* (1959) and Barry Hines's *Kestrel for a knave* (1968), featuring a schoolboy football match, herald the way working-class engagement in sport, long confined to the margins of print culture in weekly papers such as

18 *Ibid.*, p. 32.   19 Hill, *Sport, leisure and culture*, p. 34.

The Football Favourite (1920–29), acceded to the cultural mainstream in later decades. While class has now lost ground as a factor in sports publishing, the market still remains strongly segmented along national lines; the best-selling sports in the USA in publishing terms – wrestling, baseball, basketball – have next to no foothold in the UK.

Reginald Moore, himself a sports publisher with decades of experience, noted in the mid-1970s that sports books in the earlier decades of the period tended to be the work of 'distinguished amateurs, usually university blues, reflecting on their sporting careers'. *My cricketing life* (1921) by the amateur batsman and Oxford blue Pelham 'Plum' Warner, son of Trinidad's Attorney General, is typical of such works. However, the rise of professionalism led to a new breed of sports book, written by 'the supreme young professional eager to augment what in the early 1950s was a fairly modest income from his football or county cricket club'.[20] Len Hutton's *Batting strokes* (1950), published the year after England's first professional cricket captain had his most successful batting season, is one such. Taking financial advantage of sporting success in this manner had been considered *infra dig* under the amateur model; Fred Perry, who co-authored *The P-M way to improve your lawn tennis* in 1948 (published by Perry's sponsor Slazenger), was virtually ostracised by the tennis establishment when he turned professional in the 1930s.

Though (auto)biography has been a constant of sports publishing across the period, one significant shift has been the move away from what Mary McElroy calls the 'elder statesman' model. As sport has become an increasingly significant consumer and media category, leading sportsmen and women have become celebrities, even brands; interest in them now reaches far beyond their sporting achievements to encompass not only their private lives, but those of their families, and the rights to their stories are negotiated for millions. While Chris Evert could refuse to write an autobiography in 1977 on the grounds that a book about a twenty-two-year-old tennis player seemed premature,[21] Wayne Rooney's *My story so far* – ghostwritten by Hunter Davies, itself a sign of the genre's increasing legitimacy – came out in 2006 when the footballer was just twenty-one; at the time of writing he has twelve biographies referenced in the British Library catalogue, his spouse one.

As sport reached wider and wider audiences, from the 120,000 people who attended the FA cup final in 1913 to the 10 million who watched the televised

20 Moore, 'The development of sports publishing', p. 157.
21 McElroy, 'Athletes displaying their lives', p. 170.

final of the same competition in 1953, so sports publishing developed and expanded. Interest in the topic was such in the post-war period that membership of the Sportsman's Book Club (part of the Readers Union stable) trebled between 1952 and 1957. Publishers, both non-specialist and specialist, recognised the market for sports titles and began either to include them in extant series (Frederick Warne's Observer series included titles on coarse fishing, motor sport, golf and football) or to create new series devoted solely to sport, such as the Know the Game series of rulebooks produced by EP Publishing in conjunction with each sport's governing body; by the mid-1970s, EP's list covered sports as diverse as table tennis, hockey, basketball, orienteering, netball and rock climbing. Reginald Moore in fact claimed that sports coaching titles were the biggest sector in 1970s sports publishing,[22] while improved printing techniques drove the production of expensive coffee-table books for elite sports like sailing.

The diversification of sports publishing in the post-war period was largely driven by media coverage: Moore reports that the 1970s boom in gymnastics, and therefore in gymnastics titles, was driven by 'much-televised Russian sylphs' (a rare moment in the spotlight for women's sport). Similarly, he suggests that the rise in martial arts titles drew on the popularity of TV series like *The man from UNCLE*. One interesting trend at this time was underground sports publishing, inspired by the counter-culture aesthetic. The football fanzine *Foul!*, started in 1972 by Cambridge graduates who eventually moved on to full-time sports journalism, is a case in point. This shift from underground, amateur to legitimate, professional sports writing reflects the increasing cultural legitimacy of sport as an area of interest: by the early 1990s, Bill Brewster, editor of the fanzine *When Saturday Comes* (launched in 1986), felt able to say that 'football writing in the quality press is not as condescending as it was'.[23]

The late twentieth century was a golden age for sports publishing, driven by the omnipresence of sport in other media and the assimilation of (football) fandom into middle-class mores. Sport entrenched its cultural, and indeed literary, legitimacy through books such as Nick Hornby's (semi-autobiographical) 1992 *Fever pitch*, now a Penguin Modern Classic, and publishers such as Yellow Jersey Press, a Random House imprint launched in 1998, which claims to offer 'a literary edge'. The William Hill Sports Book of the Year prize, launched in 1988, brought the sector publicity; sales rose to

22 Moore, 'The development of sports publishing', p. 160.
23 Brewster, 'When Saturday Comes', p. 17.

the point that the Sportspages specialist bookshop, founded in 1985 when 'it was difficult to find more than the odd smattering of titles'[24] in traditional bookshops, expanded its shelving by 50 per cent in 1998. Twenty-nine new football magazines were launched between 1994 and 1996 on the back of England's hosting of the new Euro '96 competition and Sky TV's live coverage of premiership matches; by 2004, *Four Four Two* had an average circulation of 100,000. However, although the British sports book market as a whole was more representative of the full range of sporting practices than it had been a century before, the omnipresence of football limited the visibility of other sports: Liam Doyle of Sportspages wrote in 2009 that 'it would be nice to see other sports promoted more actively to help reduce the stranglehold football has'.[25] This situation in fact reflected the economic significance of football overall, with TV rights and player transfers being the object of multimillion-pound deals. The commercial synergy between sport and publishing reached a new level in 2008 when Manchester United appointed Simon Trewin to represent its book publishing interests worldwide.

One rare challenge to football's dominant market share comes from *Wisden cricketers' almanack*, published annually since 1864 to provide detailed coverage of English and international cricket. *Wisden*, as it is familiarly known, was published by the Cricket Reporting Agency for much of the twentieth century; it joined Robert Maxwell's publishing conglomerate Macdonald in the 1970s before being acquired by Sir Paul Getty in the early 1990s. Since 2008, it has been brought out by A. & C. Black, a Bloomsbury company. The publication survived near-bankruptcy in 1937, undergoing a radical redesign in 1938 to make it easier to consult – the counties were listed in alphabetical order, for instance. The result was an increase in its print-run, from 8,500 in 1936 to 31,500 in 1949.[26] Successive editions of *Wisden* offer a fascinating glimpse into the social role of sport in British society: it began recording women's cricket in 1938, for example, and still devotes considerable coverage to public schools matches. The usefulness of the print volume as a source of statistics can now be questioned, given that most of its data are now instantaneously available online, not least on Wisden's own websites; however, sales remained in the tens of thousands in the early years of the twenty-first century, reaching 50,000 in 2006.[27] *Wisden* has become a highly collectible national treasure, suggesting that a print

24 www.wordofsport.com.
25 Liam Doyle, 'Winning books', *Bookseller* 15 May 2009, p. 32.
26 Gutteridge, 'A history of Wisden'.   27 Winder, *The little wonder*, pp. 362–3.

edition is likely to remain a fixture of the publishing calendar for years to come.

Unsurprisingly, the sports book market is largely shaped by, and responsive to, sporting events. The England football team's poor performance at the 1998 and 2006 World Cups limited sales of memoirs by players Ashley Cole and Rio Ferdinand; conversely, after England won the rugby world cup in 2003, pre-orders for captain Martin Johnson's autobiography reached 100,000 copies, leaving the editorial team and Johnson himself six days to update and finalise the book. Minority and women's sports struggle for visibility in this crowded market; Nicole Cooke, who won gold in cycling at the Beijing Olympics, sold just 5,000 copies of her *Race for life* in the four years after her win.[28]

Like every other book sector, sports have been affected by the move online. The Sportspages bookshop is now run as an online venture, while Olympic rower Greg Searle's memoir *If not now, when?* was launched as an e-book prior to its print publication in 2012. It remains to be seen whether football's stranglehold on the genre and the multimillion-pound advances for sports megastars typical of recent years will remain sustainable in this new publishing environment.

Self-help: Samuel Smiles's descendants

Self-help, now also referred to in the trade as MBS (mind-body-spirit) publishing, is defined by Christine Whelan as 'non-fiction books that offer advice for behaviour modification and make explicit promises for positive change'.[29] As such, its relevance to this chapter lies in the rise of leisure as a consumer category and the promotion of self-transformation as a means of forging personal identity.

Though we tend to think of it as a very modern genre, publishing on 'alternative' issues has in fact enjoyed a long tradition, albeit largely on the margins of mainstream book publishing and distribution. The roots of self-help publishing can be traced back at least to the nineteenth century, most notably in Samuel Smiles's best-selling *Self-help* (1859) – a work that, typically of the early history of the genre, was self-published. One early incarnation of the self-help sector to have found a foothold in the British market was

28 Charlotte Williams and Lisa Campbell, 'Big boost for sports books', *Bookseller* 10 August 2012, p. 4.
29 Christine Whelan, 'Self-help books and the quest for self-control in the United States, 1950–2000', unpublished doctoral thesis, University of Oxford (2004).

esoteric literature, with titles on mysticism, non-mainstream religions and the occult sold through specialist bookshops such as Watkins (founded 1893) and Atlantis (1922). As interest in such topics rose, the trend eventually began to spread to the mainstream: Swami Akhilananda's *Hindu psychology: its meaning for the West* (1948) was published by Routledge, for example.

Self-help underwent a considerable expansion as a genre in the latter decades of the period. Whelan documents that the genre accounted for 1.1 per cent of the US book market in 1973, rising to 2.4 per cent by 2000 – an expansion due in large part to widespread availability of desktop publishing, enabling the baby boomer generation to explore counter-cultural issues in print. The market has long been US-led, with classic titles such as Dale Carnegie's *How to win friends and influence people* (1936) and Susan Jeffers's *Feel the fear and do it anyway* (1987) being brought out in UK editions. However, a new generation of specialist publishers arose in Britain in the 1970s, such as Wildwood House (1972), Element (1975) and Piatkus (1979). Many such small independents were absorbed into multinationals in the 1980s as self-help became one of the fastest-growing mainstream publishing categories.

The term MBS – an expansive category covering everything from dieting and beauty to astrology – became a distinct category in the *Bookseller* buyer's guide in the early 1980s; it has now largely displaced 'self-help' in publishing terminology.[30] Bookshops soon recognised the category's marketing potential: Waterstone's became the first mainstream MBS stockist in 1982, while W. H. Smith set up 'personal development' sections in its shops in 1994. The increasing visibility afforded the genre by such initiatives led it to rise from 0.9 per cent of sales of UK-published books in 1998 to 5.8 per cent in 2002. There is still some stigma attached to the genre: Crown House's 2004 launch of books with removable cover stickers enabling readers to hide the titles may have been a marketing gimmick, but it is nonetheless indicative of the genre's struggle to overcome prejudice. However, there are signs that the genre is striving to achieve a degree of cultural legitimacy: Vermilion brought out a gift box of four self-help 'classics' in 2012, suggesting the emergence of a self-help canon, while the *Penguin book of New Age and holistic writing* (ed. W. Bloom, 2000) is another sign that the genre is gaining a degree of literary respectability.

Like the other sectors explored in this chapter, self-help publishing is increasingly driven by crossovers with other media, especially television: best-selling authors now include TV personalities Gillian McKeith and

---

30 Puttick, 'The rise of mind-body-spirit publishing'.

Carol Vorderman. Author and concept branding have become increasingly important as a means of standing out in a crowded market: Allen Carr's *Easy way to* ... and Paul McKenna's *I can make you* ... are both trademarked. The genre has become increasingly interactive, seeking to engage readers not only through book-based activities, but also in such things as workshop sessions, often held at MBS shows and festivals: as such, the sector is a natural fit for new online modes of dissemination, and indeed publishers such as Icon have experimented with subscription websites, text message services and apps. On current evidence, it seems likely that MBS will remain a significant sector of the book market for the foreseeable future.

15

Museum and art book publishing

SARAH ANNE HUGHES

The production of twentieth-century books on the visual arts shows the effects of two factors: one technical, particularly changes in colour printing, and the other cultural, a widening of the appeal of the visual arts. These factors influenced the numbers of titles published and the style of art-related publications produced by both commercial publishers and museums and galleries. This chapter explores the inter-relationships in the production of such books between producers and audience, as well as analysing improvements in the quality of production and design of books, the style of writing and the breadth of content. Changes in books produced by museums over the course of the century also reflect the increasing demand for a financial return on enterprise activities; yet, despite these pressures to democratise content, institutions continued to produce specialist literature for the arts. Supported in the later decades by sponsorship and to some extent by sale of commercially viable books, printed catalogues for permanent collections and catalogues raisonnés for individual artists continued to disseminate scholarship generated by gallery curators and art critics for a specialist audience.

The paucity of formal studies of museum and art book publishing leaves gaps in the understanding of the responses, particularly of commercial art publishing, to the social and technological changes which influenced other forms of publishing during this period. While further research is required before a definitive history of art and museum publishing can be presented, the information that is available for the twentieth century points to the impact of both collaboration and competition between commercial and institutional publishing in art book production.[1] Most museums and galleries, even those with small collections and budgets, produced printed books and other materials to support their public and research activities during this period, but the highest numbers of titles were published by national

1 Shone and Stonard, *The books that shaped art history*.

museums, whose activities are documented via their annual reports. Commercial companies and university presses also published in the sector, for example Oxford University Press, Penguin, and the London office of Yale University Press. Among other UK firms during this period, Phaidon and Thames & Hudson were prolific and influential specialist publishers of art books, producing reference books on art history and handbooks on single artists and art movements that both reflected and influenced developments in the field of art history.

Between 1900 and 1996, the Victoria and Albert Museum generated over 2,000 titles relating to its collections, and a consideration of these publications demonstrates the changing nature of UK museum publishing.[2] In the first decade, many of the ninety-nine titles (six in 1910 alone) addressed the institution's concerns with audience behaviour in the galleries by providing guidance for visitors while briefly presenting information on objects in the galleries. By 1996, of the twenty-four books published in that year, four catalogued permanent collections, three related to temporary exhibitions and fifteen addressed topics written, designed and titled to appeal to a general audience.[3] This change from directing the visitors' gaze to engaging and responding to the visitors' interests reflected transformations in public programming and in the design of permanent and temporary exhibitions.[4] Two additional and related trends became evident during this century. Concomitant with this appeal of books to a general readership was an increasing emphasis on the design and layout and on an accessible style of writing. As the appeal of the books broadened beyond a specialist audience, the commercial viability of the titles and their contribution to the income of the institution influenced the selection of titles and the decision to publish. By the end of the century, the requirement for publications to 'pay their way' and for publishing overall to generate funding for the museum was well established. Additional support for the production of high-quality books at accessible prices was provided by sponsorship by commercial companies seeking association with the cultural values of the institution.

Annual reports from UK national and regional collections build a picture of a cautious expansion of books for sale to the public, starting, in the early years of the century, with satisfying visitors' requirements for souvenirs through the sale of postcards of works from the collections. At the National Portrait Gallery, the trend started with a commercial company, Messrs Emery

2 James (ed.), *The Victoria and Albert Museum.* 3 *Ibid.*
4 Hooper-Greenhill, *Museums and the interpretation of visual culture,* pp. 142–4.

Walker, which sold larger format images of paintings from the collection for wall display.[5] By 1921, the Gallery had started producing postcards itself and offered thirteen sets of portraits (six to a set), which were also sold at the National Gallery.[6] Their sales increased in the following years, so that, by 1923, seventeen postcard sets were available, providing a total of 102 individual images. Sales of individual cards totalled 26,357 to over 182,000 annual visitors.[7] Two years later, an existing unillustrated publication that functioned as a very basic guide merely listing the paintings on display with an artist index was enhanced through the addition of 122 images.[8] Through the 1920s, sales of these lists and postcards increased and the types of publications expanded to include more illustrated editions and a closer focus on specific schools of art. These guides had the purpose, explained the introduction to one of them, of enabling visitors to 'make good use of their time, to pick out the things most worth seeing, to get some idea of the artistic qualities which have made these masterpieces famous, and to refresh their memories when the visit is over'.[9] By 1933, sales of postcards totalled 65,000 and the gallery offered a shorter guide to the collection for a general audience. It provided '20 pages of text, 33 illustrations and 3 plans for the price of two pence'.[10] By 1939, the sale of these illustrated guides (13,717) far exceeded that of the annotated list of images on display which were designated as catalogues (426). In that year, the gallery welcomed 146,847 annual visitors, indicating that approximately one in a hundred visitors bought a guide.[11]

The development of publications at other national museums demonstrated similar trends. Those at the Victoria and Albert Museum showed a widening range of publications with increased numbers of images, designed to appeal to art students and to a general readership. These booklets were published by Her (His) Majesty's Stationery Office (HMSO) and sat alongside the catalogues of exhibitions and art handbooks which had begun publication in 1872.[12] In 1925, a small-format Picture Book series intended for adults, with black and white illustrations, was launched with four titles. These publications would have been on sale to visitors in the museum's entrance at the Catalogue Stall.[13] By the following year, twelve of the sixteen publications

5 National Portrait Gallery Annual Report (1917), p. 7.
6 National Portrait Gallery Annual Report (1921), p. 10.
7 National Portrait Gallery Annual Report (1923), p. 11.
8 National Portrait Gallery Annual Report (1925), p. 10.
9 Holmes, *National Gallery*, p. 1.
10 National Portrait Gallery Annual Report (1933), p. 13.
11 National Portrait Gallery Annual Report (1939), p. 9.
12 James, *The Victoria and Albert Museum*, p. xxi. 13 *Ibid.*, p. 21.

issued by the V&A were part of this series. In 1947, these titles were relaunched as Small Picture Books in a series which eventually totalled over sixty publications. In 1972, with the increasing advent of more inexpensive colour reproduction, these themed publications featuring objects from the museum's collections grew to include the Small Colour Books.[14]

In the early decades of the century, then, museum-centred publishing consisted primarily of ephemeral publications which served the immediate interests of gallery visitors. The more elaborate art books, even though often relying on and interpreting museum collections, were produced by commercial publishers because of the financial risks and production resources demanded of illustrated art books at the time. While commercial companies produced these books, the organisation of content by national schools reflected the categories apparent in the art on display in the galleries and in consequence continued to tie the publications to the institutions. George Newnes Ltd, publisher of the illustrated periodical the *Strand*, produced a series of volumes on galleries in Europe, seven of which presented the collections of the National Gallery for a general audience. From the series, *The early British School* by Robert de la Sizeranne (1906) introduced aspects of the paintings that characterised the School and listed the paintings on view in chronological order by the artists' birth date. The brief commentary and list is augmented by over 100 black and white photographs of the paintings. The structure of the content (introduction, list, illustrations) reflects the production technology for images and text at the time, with the sections of the book combined at the point of binding subsequent to separate printing on different paper stocks. The size and weight of these early twentieth-century art books indicate that despite the direct reference to gallery paintings these publications were not intended to accompany a museum visit, but rather served as introductions to art history for consumption in the owner's home or in libraries, with publication in series encouraging further purchases.[15]

Books on historical paintings in public galleries account for the content of most commercial art book publishing until the 1930s. However, as the art movements of the preceding decades of the century became more widely known, commercial publishers recognised the need for publications that clarified the complex transnational influences apparent in contemporary European and American painting. *Art now: an introduction to the theory of modern painting and sculpture* (1933) by the critic Herbert Read, published by Faber & Faber, provided an interpretive background to modernism and was

14 *Ibid.*, pp. 749–51.   15 Holman, 'The art book', p. 70.

written for scholars, students and the general public. The audience for this and similar art publications of the period was 'people in general and not specifically for those people called artists or those called connoisseurs and collectors'.[16] These books provided the information necessary to understand and appreciate contemporary art. That they were widely read during the 1930s and 1940s may be gauged by the listing of Read's subsequent book, *Education through art* (1943), among the most popular titles borrowed from Bristol's libraries in 1944.[17] Subsequent titles – *A concise history of modern painting* (1959) and *A history of modern sculpture* (1964), both published by Thames & Hudson, were written alongside his work in support of contemporary artists – and continued his influence in the formation of an audience for art and for books on art into the late 1960s.

The Penguin Modern Painters series, established in 1944 under the editorship of Kenneth Clark, then Director of the National Gallery, both responded to and fuelled the public's interest in art at a time when access to the national collections was restricted. The series was conceived with the intention of 'introducing ... [artists'] work in a far wider field than has been attempted hitherto'.[18] Art printing paper and accurate colour reproduction resulted in a series of high-quality publications that benefited the careers of the British artists, including Henry Moore, Graham Sutherland, Duncan Grant and Paul Nash.[19]

The demand for art books from the general public is also apparent in the growing number of art titles published from the 1930s onwards. In 1937, the record year of publishing prior to the Second World War, 230 titles relating to art and architecture were published. This figure dropped to sixty-seven in 1943, the year of lowest art publishing during the war. By 1955 a recovery in publishing, with continued commercial success of books on art and architecture, was reflected in the figures of published titles (591) for this year, a rise which continued to 858 in 1965 and 1,730 in 1981.[20]

Alongside companies producing series books on art, the independent publisher Batsford stands out in its commitment to innovative and scholarly books on British architecture. The company's interest in this field and its use of photographic techniques dates to the late nineteenth century. William J. Anderson's 1896 *Architecture of the Renaissance in Italy* was one of the first books on architecture to be fully illustrated by photography, using both collotype and halftone processes. In the years to the Second World War,

16 Gill, *Art*, p. 7.   17 Holman, *Print for victory*, p. 236.   18 Hare, *Penguin portrait*, p. 34.
19 Baines, *Penguin by design*, p. 42.
20 Norrie, *Mumby's publishing and bookselling*, pp. 221–2.

the company produced books on historic buildings and the attendant crafts relating to interior and exterior design. By the 1940s this focus on architecture, crafts and ornamentation titles had expanded into the British Heritage series, which 'told the country about its landscape, castles, churches and houses'.[21] Published with the iconic dust-jacket designs by Brian Cook, the series celebrated the arts as central to British culture and helped re-establish their importance as the country experienced and then emerged from the austerity of war.

The 1930s saw the arrival of immigrants who would change the publishing landscape of the UK in the twentieth century.[22] Their knowledge, derived from working within the high production standards of German and East European publishers and printers, enabled these individuals to effect improvements in page design, typography, picture research and photographic reproduction, among other aspects of production and marketing, while offering the resulting books at affordable prices.[23] They either worked for or established publishing enterprises that specialised in illustrated books and had a profound influence in the publication of art books in Britain. The Phaidon Press, founded in Vienna by Béla Horovitz and Ludwig Goldscheider in 1923, initially thrived through high design standards that integrated images with text, and through links with the printing industries of central Europe in Leipzig and Vienna.[24] The Nazi persecution of Jewish-owned companies resulted in Phaidon's move to Britain in 1938. Assisted by Stanley Unwin, who purchased the book stock held in Vienna to protect it from confiscation, Horovitz and Goldscheider re-established their enterprise initially in Oxford, later in London, and continued to produce the innovative art books that invoked Kenneth Clark's description of them as 'the first exciting art books to appear'.[25] In the decades following the Second World War, Phaidon's output of art books included publications prepared with a number of private collections, such as Christ Church, Oxford, the Royal Collection and Wilton House.[26]

The founder of Thames & Hudson arrived in Britain in 1938, also as a refugee from Nazi persecution. Walter Neurath initially worked at the book production company Adprint, where he produced the King Penguin series (1939–59). In 1949, Neurath and Eva Feuchtwang, a colleague from Adprint who became his wife, established their own publishing company

21 Bolitho, *A Batsford century*, p. 66.   22 Abel and Graham (eds.), *Immigrant publishers*.
23 Nyburg, *Émigré*, p. 9.   24 Spivey, *Phaidon*.
25 Norrie, *Mumby's publishing and bookselling*, p. 134.
26 Miller, *Phaidon and the business of art book publishing*, p. 352.

named after the rivers of London and New York. Transatlantic links stabilised the early finances of Thames & Hudson which published and printed books in the UK for US art publishers such as Abrams. Thames & Hudson also acted as distributors for books produced by the Metropolitan Museum of Art and the Museum of Modern Art in New York. This pioneering association of a commercial publisher with art collections demonstrated the benefits of the reciprocal relationship which would develop later in the twentieth century. While all publishing was limited due to wartime paper rationing, the early 1940s witnessed the incubation of some of the most influential art books of the century. The first of these was published in 1950 by Phaidon. Over sixteen editions later, E. H. Gombrich's *The story of art* remains the book that frames art history for many non-specialists – promotional material on the jacket of the sixteenth edition claimed that the book had sold over 6 million copies. In creating this readable historical sweep through Western art, Gombrich understood the importance of photographs and limited his references to works that could be illustrated; he favoured painting over the other arts because 'less is lost in the illustration of a painting than in that of a round sculpture'.[27] This and his later books contributed to the author's award of the 1975 Erasmus prize for 'developing relations between the visual arts and the public'.[28]

As the availability of individual art titles increased, the major art book publishers also focussed their efforts on series titles which through their breadth nurtured the general public's access to and enthusiasm for Western art and architecture. The scholarship of Nikolaus Pevsner's English county architectural guides, the Buildings of England, published by Penguin starting in 1951 and completed by 1974, appealed to enthusiastic amateurs and scholars alike and was equally influential in developing an informed public. As with other Penguin publications, the use of inexpensive paperback bindings reduced the price of the books with the result that they were accessible to a wider audience. In contrast, the Pelican History of Art (1953), conceived at the same time and also edited by Pevsner, was published initially as a large-format hardback and only entered paperback format in 1970. The series was published by Yale University Press from 1992. The most recent title, *Art in Britain 1660–1815* by David Solkin (2015), brings the total in the series to thirty-nine. From their inception, these long-term publishing projects encouraged a wide audience for art by enabling collections of illustrated, well-written and

---

27 Gombrich, *The story of art*, p. 10.
28 'Erasmus prize awarded to Sir Ernst Gombrich', *The Times* 17 December 1974, p. 17.

scholarly texts to be acquired by the general public.[29] The books appealed also to students: the Thames & Hudson World of Art series launched in 1958 was credited with a 'powerful impact on international art education'.[30]

Updated and reissued in new editions, these series fuelled the market for a range of comprehensive reference books each of which offered distinct approaches to the fields of art and art history. The *Grove dictionary of art* was conceived in the late 1980s as an adjunct to the successful multi-volume dictionary on music. This comprehensive art publication sought to distinguish itself through approach and subject coverage. Published by Macmillan in 1996, it presented 'an entirely different approach from that of existing art reference books'.[31] With film as the only excluded art form, the 45,000 entries in these volumes treat the decorative arts 'as seriously as the traditional "fine arts" of painting, sculpture and architecture'. References include artists' biographies, art movements and techniques, performance art and multi-media installations. The range of books on art 'increased public interest in painting and further stimulated demand for art books'.[32]

The production of guidebooks for the Festival of Britain in 1951 initiated a collaboration of the publisher George Rainbird with event and museum publishing. Rainbird first made use of colour photography to illustrate objects from the tomb of Tutankhamen. These Egyptian treasures had not previously been photographed in colour in a studio setting, so the publication in 1963 of *Tutankhamen: life and death of a pharaoh* with photography by F. L. Kenett used 'four-back-two' printing in signatures that interspersed black and white and colour photographs throughout the book and consequently allowed illustrations to be 'printed on the same page or opposite the actual text'.[33] This edition went through four printings in its first two years and, in all, the book sold over a million copies in English and in translation. Its success both established the finances of Rainbird and pointed the way to the production processes (using Italian printers and binders) of other colour books that drew on the financial support of foreign rights sales, particularly to publishers in the United States.

The popularity of this title provided additional impetus to the plan for an exhibition of the Egyptian treasures in the UK; a plan which culminated in fifty objects, including Tutankhamen's gold mask, travelling to the British

29 Pevsner also authored *An outline of European architecture* (1942) which became a standard reference work for the subject.
30 Rosenthal, 'Walter and Eva Neurath', p. 16.
31 Turner (ed.), *The dictionary of art*, p. vii.   32 Holman, 'The art book', p. 73.
33 Rainbird, *The Rainbird archive*, p. xxx.

Museum in 1972. The catalogue for this exhibition included Rainbird's colour photographs. While designed by the Exhibition Office of the museum, it was produced by George Rainbird Ltd. Costs were kept to a minimum by confining the twenty-three colour photographs to a single signature of eight pages. The square format, left-aligned paragraphs, generous white space and cut-out black and white images alongside the text columns lent a modern look to the design of the book. Trade editions of the catalogue were published by Michael Joseph in the UK and Viking Press in the USA a year later. The newly created British Museum publishing enterprise, however, was unable to benefit from sales of the Tutankhamen catalogue due to the agreement with the Arab Republic of Egypt which required the proceeds of the exhibition, after deducting expenses, to be 'paid into the fund . . . for the preservation of the treasures of Philae'.[34] Nevertheless, the catalogue's sales figures – over a million copies had been sold by 1985[35] – demonstrated the potential profitability of well-designed illustrated books based on exhibitions attracting large visitor numbers. As a collaborator with one of the blockbuster museum exhibitions of the 1970s, Rainbird's association with the British Museum led to further publishing partnerships for temporary exhibitions, such as *The genius of China* (1973) for the Royal Academy exhibition and *Happy and glorious: 130 years of Royal photography* (1977) for the National Portrait Gallery.

Collaboration between art publishers and institutions enabled the relatively high production costs of illustrated art books to be offset by risk-averse museums, while the guaranteed purchase of part of the print-run by the institution offset some, or in some cases all, of the printing costs for the commercial publishers. It was this collaboration between art publishers and institutions that determined the need for commercially aware institutional publishing. British Museum Publications was created in 1973 as a limited company owned by the trustees but financially independent. Michael Hoare, previously at Collins and Longman, was its first managing director tasked to 'unlock the financial potential of the British Museum'.[36] The Victoria and Albert Museum appointed its first director of publishing in 1976, although HMSO continued to publish their books until the early 1980s. In 1979, the National Portrait Gallery offered visitors an inexpensive souvenir book illustrating over 200 of the gallery's portraits in colour which was produced

---

34 Lord Trevelyan, 'Foreword', in *Treasures of Tutankhamun* [Trustees of the British Museum] (1972), p. 9.
35 Rainbird, *The Rainbird archive*, p. xxvii.
36 'Michael Hoare', *The Times* 13 June 2003, p. 38.

with Cassell, an affiliate of Macmillan Publishing, and the publishers of the Studio Vista imprint.[37] Lund Humphries, renowned for its colour printing and the production of monographs on British painters, brought this expertise to co-edition publishing with art galleries in the 1980s.

In the 1960s, the visual properties of television were harnessed to entertain and further educate a general audience about the visual arts. By this time, the BBC, and in subsequent decades Channel 4, capitalised on the commercial and information potential of television productions with associated publications. One of the most successful early books produced jointly by BBC Publications and John Murray accompanied Kenneth Clark's television series *Civilisation*. The book of the series illustrated Clark's personal view of Europe's evolution through Western art and architecture and became the best-selling non-fiction title of 1969.[38] Its success established a precedent of celebrity art scholars' association with television programmes, for example *The shock of the new: art and the century of change* (1980) by the critic Robert Hughes, which supported his television series on new art. Buoyant sales figures of the hardback edition took this book through several printings and resulted, in 1991, in Thames & Hudson's paperback version. Sister Wendy Beckett continued the appeal of accessible art history books from celebrity presenters through the 1990s with several books derived from her popular television programmes, culminating in *Sister Wendy's Impressionist masterpieces* (2001).

As museums sought to gain greater financial return from their collections (in response to government requirements to diversify 'funding streams away from government'[39]) picture reproduction fees were viewed as an asset suitable for financial exploitation. Consequently, fees increased for images in books not directly associated with a museum's imprint.[40] This maintained pressure on commercial publishers to seek cooperative publishing projects. Art publishers provided a reciprocal benefit to museums through their links to the trade. Yale University Press, for example, distributed National Gallery books, and Thames & Hudson distributed for the British Museum. The professionalisation of museum publishing in national museums with the appointment of managers from trade publishing initiated a more commercial approach to the commissioning of titles based on collections. The requirement to contribute to the overall funding of museums and the

37 Ormond, *National Portrait Gallery in colour.*   38 Sutherland, *Reading the decades*, p. 65.
39 AEA Consulting, *National dimensions* [National Museums Directors' Conference report] (March 2004), p. 11.
40 Silver, 'The crisis in publishing and the problem of art history tenure'.

location of publishing within the enterprise area of the institution, rather than in the curatorial divisions, fuelled debate over writing styles appropriate for various audiences, and the possible loss of scholarship from exhibition catalogues.[41]

The changes in style and content of art books are associated with new channels for their sale to a wider public. Until the latter half of the century, specialist art bookshops and mail order catered to a limited public. With the ending of the Net Book Agreement in the 1990s, the rise of internet sales and the decline of independent bookshops in Britain, retail space within museums and galleries associated with the cultural integrity of the institution attracted the book-buying public. In some instances visitors eschewed the galleries themselves: a survey of visitors to the National Portrait Gallery found that 54 per cent of those visitors came to the bookshop but did not enter the gallery.[42] At that time, the requisite visit to the museum shop did not constitute an integral part of a museum visit, as the survey also recorded that 55 per cent of visitors left the gallery without diverting to the bookshop. By the end of the century, public art galleries were recognised as locations where curated collections of art books, published both by museums and by art publishers, were available for browsing and purchase. To cater for this demand, national museums developed specialist areas for the sale of art books.

In addition to museums and commercial publishers, the production of art books has been provided for by a range of enterprises in the period. The Walpole Society, for example, was founded in 1911 for the purpose of promoting the study of the history of British art. This purpose was to be achieved by publishing, in annual volumes, primary research by its members and by international scholars. These publications are available to members and non-members but are not sold commercially.[43] In contrast to this highly scholarly and exclusive style of publication, Public Catalogue Foundation (trading as Art UK), a charitable organisation founded in 2003, utilises technologies of the Web and print to disseminate its comprehensive documentation of the estimated 200,000 oil paintings in public ownership in the UK. Printed catalogues are published by county, and in 2012, in association with the BBC, the images were published online. Tags, added by the general public, enable the images and their graphic content to be searched.[44] This exemplifies the continuing support of publishing for printed art books while

41 Haskell, *The ephemeral museum*; Thorp, 'Publishing on art'.
42 Harvey, *Visiting the National Portrait Gallery*, p. 22.   43 www.walpolesociety.org.uk.
44 www.bbc.co.uk/arts/yourpaintings.

also demonstrating the uses of Web technologies such as metadata to provide greater public access to art scholarship. While commercial art galleries represent their artists' work through regular exhibitions, at international art fairs and online, they continue to publish printed catalogues as a means to promote the sale of work and to maintain a connection with collectors. Gagosian, for example, publishes scholarly exhibition catalogues, artist monographs and catalogues raisonnés.

In the first decade of the twenty-first century, sales of art books both from galleries and from art publishers remained buoyant. There are several possible reasons for this resilience: the reproduction of paintings on the printed page provides readers with more immediate access to the image and its relationship to the textual commentary; physical books provide tangible souvenirs of a museum visit that can be shared easily with other people as coffee-table books; and the primary audience purchasing museum and art books consists of older individuals who are more familiar, and therefore more comfortable, with physical books. Technical developments will continue to improve the rendering of images and text for electronic delivery. These innovations, combined with animation and other interactive media, have the potential to make electronic art books and apps attractive to even wider audiences. A recent catalogue (Clayton and Philo 2012) published by the Royal Collections to accompany an exhibition, *Leonardo da Vinci anatomist: inside his mind, inside the body*, was augmented by an app that reproduced the pages of da Vinci's notebooks in the collection and allowed users to compare his anatomical drawings with three-dimensional models that could be rotated. The phenomenal success in 2010 (over 10 million downloads) of the BBC radio programme *A history of the world in a hundred objects*, produced with the British Museum, and the sales (over 150,000) of the subsequent book, which was published by the Penguin Group, demonstrate the impact other media may have on the audience for art books. There remains, however, evidence of the continued resilience of physical books as a primary delivery medium for art scholarship and appreciation in the twenty-first century. In 2010, Yale University Press published the first volume of a two-volume set comprising a catalogue raisonné of the artist Ford Madox Brown at £125.[45] A year later, a three-volume set describing the history and evolution of illuminated manuscripts was published at £250 by the Victoria and Albert Museum.[46] Purchasers of these publications are likely to agree with the director's statement that 'a book's scope is immediately comprehended; it

---

45 Bennett, *Ford Madox Brown*.   46 Watson, *Western illuminated manuscripts*.

is clear and readable; above all the book is a portable object and its format is permanent. In itself it becomes an historic document of the state of knowledge and angle of interest at the time of publication.'[47] Art book publishing by both commercial and non-commercial enterprises at the start of the twentieth century offered books written and designed for an audience of knowledgeable specialists. In the first decade of the twenty-first century it appeared that the general audience may embrace digital platforms and the audience for printed books would comprise, once again, art specialists. However, while digital platforms offer searchable and immediate access to images and information, the haptic and visual experience of art books retains its attraction for readers and scholars.

47 Borg, 'Director's Foreword', p. ix.

16

Music

JOHN WAGSTAFF

This chapter will look at music books and sheet music in terms of their varied audiences, and – in the case of sheet music – will also take some account of developments in the production and printing of musical material intended for performance.[1] Music has always been expensive to produce, whether in manuscript or in print using movable type, engraving or more modern techniques, so sheet music origination and production has tended to be concentrated among a small number of specialist publishing and printing houses. At the beginning of the twentieth century, origination of sheet music publications was still the predominant activity undertaken by a music publisher; by its end, especially in the field of popular music, origination of print copies had become subsidiary to product promotion and placement, and to the exploitation, by such promotion and placement, of performance and other rights. As Helen Gammons noted in 2011, 'Today, music publishers are concerned with administering copyrights, licensing songs to record companies and others, and collecting royalties on behalf of the songwriter', an observation that applied to the situation at the end of the twentieth century too.[2]

At the beginning of the century the market for sheet music was still divided between material for the professional (meaning the performer and teacher, hardly yet the musicologist) and the amateur, whose needs, chiefly in the areas of solo song and piano music designed for performance in the home, were catered to by a large number of publishers. Many of these amateurs were also members of choral societies, a market that generated a great demand for scores of both sacred and secular music. Cyril Ehrlich notes that 'There was an enormous demand for sheet music in Britain. By the end of the nineteenth century annual sales were estimated to be some

---

1 'Sheet music' is used here as a catch-all term for any type of printed music product, from single-sheet songs to large-format printed volumes.
2 Gammons, *The art of music publishing*, p. 57.

twenty million pieces with 40,000 new titles, each printed in runs of at least 200. Popular hits often sold 200,000 copies.'[3] In such an environment, a music publisher needed only to have a few sure-fire hits to stay in business. Chamber music, although practised by groups of enthusiasts in Britain, was not an attractive publishing proposition when sales could be measured in the hundreds (at best) rather than thousands, but where origination costs, due to the requirement for a separately engraved score and parts, were high. The rise during the twentieth century of classical music of great complexity that often also demanded large performing forces brought music origination full circle back from printing to manuscript, with publishers prepared to provide copies of a composer's fair-copy manuscript to customers on an 'on demand' basis, sometimes for purchase, more often on a 'hire-only' basis. Faber Music's Faber Print series was an early example of this from the 1990s, and included Peter Sculthorpe's *From Nourlangie* and *The stars turn*, plus Jonathan Dove's *Figures in the garden*. This avoided print origination costs for the publisher (and also the cost of warehouse storage of unsold copies, which could take years to sell), but could bring problems of legibility and accuracy, since publishers were unlikely to commit expensive editorial resources to editing and proofreading a composer's manuscript. By the end of the century, 'scorewriter' notation software such as Score, Finale and Sibelius enabled composers to originate printed copies of their scores themselves, and gave them the option either to submit their works directly to a publisher as a digital file or to self-publish. Working from digital copy made economic sense from a publishing point of view, but some outside the publishing industry – scholars, notably – have expressed concern that the previous 'paper trail' of classical compositions – i.e. (i) a composer's working manuscript and perhaps sketches, (ii) the composer's (or a copyist's) fair copy for the engraver, (iii) the engraver's proof copy and (iv) the printed copy made available for sale – has been broken, with composers now simply writing to the computer and deleting earlier versions of their work in favour of the final version.[4] This means that it is no longer possible to track the different stages of the creative process in the same way as in previous centuries. Furthermore, although self-publication allows composers to reap all the benefits of copyright protection for their work, and to keep all the copyright, sales and performing royalties earned from it rather than having to share these with a publisher, the ability of established publishers to market

3 Ehrlich, *Harmonious alliance*, p. 5.
4 See, for example, Mosch, 'Musikverlage, Komponisten-Institute und das zeitgenössische Schaffen'.

and, especially, to exploit new works effectively is not to be underestimated. In the classical music world in particular, having a real contract with a known publisher remained – and remains, even in the early twenty-first century – a desirable step in the building of a reputation. It is important to remember that relationships between composers and publishers have often been more than simply economic in nature, and the two parties have frequently enjoyed good creative relations – in Britain the case of Edward Elgar and the firm of Novello is probably the best known, but there are other examples too, including Boosey & Hawkes's support for Benjamin Britten in the early part of his career.[5]

Two other phenomena that must be taken into account in this chapter are the effect on composers, publishers and audiences of broadcasting; and music's increasing role as an object of academic discourse, in universities and other academic institutions such as conservatoires. In the first three-quarters of the century this primarily meant classical music, though by the final two decades popular music was also gaining ground as a legitimate area of study. The Institute of Popular Music at the University of Liverpool, founded in 1988, was an important milestone in bringing respectability to the study of popular music, and a masters course in popular music studies was available there from 1990.[6] An academic title, *Popular Music*, published by Cambridge University Press (1981–), was the first British journal for this market. The development of musicology in all its forms, including music theory and ethnomusicology (the study of the music of non-Western cultures), led to the creation of books for the specialist, often using a *Fachsprache*, or technical language, that was somewhat impenetrable to those outside the discipline; and also to the rise of textbooks specifically intended for use in university and college courses. It also encouraged the production of authoritative, detailed and expensive scholarly editions of the musical works of individual composers and repertoires of the Western musical canon, usually issued on subscription and mostly acquired by libraries rather than by private individuals. While Germany has dominated in the publication of these specialist editions, there have also been some notable British examples. Academic (chiefly university) presses such as Oxford and Cambridge gained dominance in publishing musicological books in Britain, with Ashgate Publishing arriving on the scene late in the century; but the market for musicological material also relied heavily on the output of American

---

5 Moore, *Elgar and his publishers*; on Delius, see Montgomery and Threlfall, *Music and copyright*.
6 A further organisation, the International Association for the Study of Popular Music (IASPM), was founded in 1981.

university presses (Yale, Harvard, California and Princeton, among others) and on publishers such as W. W. Norton.

At the same time, non-specialists with an interest in music were catered to by a large music education and music appreciation market. Thousands of children and adults purchased examination pieces published by the Associated Board of the Royal Schools of Music. 'How to' books for instruments or voice, particularly piano, were issued, sometimes accompanied by a television series and more recently by a DVD. Examples included John Pearse's guitar course *Hold down a chord*, a BBC2 series from the mid-1960s, with a book and LP available for purchase; Ulf Goran's *Play guitar* (Yorkshire Television, 1974), which had started life earlier in the decade on Swedish television; and Harry Junkin and Cyril Ornadel's *The piano can be fun* (ATV, 1970s). Finally, non-scholarly autobiographies by stars of popular or light music, by opera singers and – in a couple of cases – by music publishers and music critics supplied what might be termed a 'middlebrow' market.

The production of music journals of various types developed strongly during the century, catering for a wide variety of tastes. One of the oldest titles on the market was Novello's *Musical Times*, first issued in the 1840s and still published. Oxford University Press's authoritative and respected *Music & Letters* commenced publication in 1920, and still appears quarterly. *Gramophone* magazine (monthly, 1923–) has the distinction of being the oldest magazine of its type in the world; and *Classical Music* magazine is a newsy publication founded in the late 1970s. *Tempo* (Boosey & Hawkes, 1939–) concentrated on covering modern music. By the end of the twentieth century, fanzines devoted to particular pop performers or ensembles, if previously published in print at all, had almost entirely migrated to the internet.[7] A feature of the 1980s and 1990s was the arrival of glossy, coffee-table musical magazines. *Opera Now* was the quintessential example of this (1989–), along with others such as *Goldberg: The Early Music Magazine* (from 1997) and the *BBC Music Magazine* (from 1992; issued monthly with an accompanying CD). The upwardly mobile but not necessarily music-savvy audience was also catered to by the arrival in 1992 of radio station ClassicFM (with an associated magazine from 1995), originally seen as a 'dumbed-down' alternative to the BBC's Radio 3 but subsequently accepted as a part of the classical music landscape. Finally, the music industry also had its own 'trade'

---

7 The terms 'pop' and 'popular music' are used here, non-pejoratively, to refer to any genre – including rap, hip-hop, rock – of pop music. Clearly pop music is at least as multi-layered and multi-faceted in genre as classical music.

journals, firstly *Musical Opinion (and Music Trades Review)* (from 1877), and later *Music Week* (from 1983).

Editions for the specialist

Musicology – the 'scientific' study of music – developed during the nineteenth century in large part as a branch of positivistic antiquarianism. A 'Musical Antiquarian Society' was founded in England as early as 1840, and published large and worthy volumes of English music of the sixteenth and seventeenth centuries. Later, those interested in musical research and musical antiquarianism could become members of the Musical Association, founded in London in 1874 and given royal patronage some seventy years later. Members communicated with each other either through attendance at the Association's meetings, or in the pages of its annual *Proceedings*. Their efforts led to the resurrection of much music of previous centuries. Significant in the British context were the commencement of a complete edition of the works of Henry Purcell, probably England's first composer of international renown, in 1878 and still under revision; and the series Musica Britannica, founded in 1951 in conjunction with the Festival of Britain that same year. Publishing Britain's (not only England's) music from earlier times has been just one among Musica Britannica's several significant achievements.

A significant figure in terms of the scholarly revival of national musical heritage was cleric Edmund H. Fellowes, who was responsible almost single-handedly for the production of a thirty-six-volume series, the English Madrigal School, between 1912 and 1924.[8] The series can justifiably claim to be the first successful British attempt at a large-scale, 'monumental' edition, and like similar projects was first offered for sale by subscription.[9] This method, whereby a potential publisher issues a prospectus inviting subscriptions to what is likely to be a drawn-out, risky and expensive enterprise, dates back several centuries, and its survival as a way of publishing music into the twentieth (and twenty-first) centuries is another reminder of how expensive and financially precarious music origination can be. Fellowes later followed up his efforts in the madrigalian, secular music field with a ten-volume edition of *Tudor church music* (1922–29).

8 Fellowes, *Memoirs of an amateur musician.*
9 The use of the word 'monument' to describe these large editions derives from early German examples, which were published under the title 'Denkmäler', the German word for monuments.

British editions devoted to a single composer have included the Elgar Edition (from 1981; originally published by Novello, and later by the Elgar Society), and that devoted to the works of William Walton (Oxford University Press, 1998–2014). Of books produced for the academic and professional market, the most celebrated examples are probably George Grove's *A dictionary of music and musicians* (first edition published by Macmillan in fascicles between 1879 and 1889) and from Oxford University Press the *Oxford history of music* (1901–5, revised edition 1929–38, superseded by the *New Oxford history of music* from the 1950s). The *New Oxford history* was unique for its time in that records accompanied each print volume. The recordings, issued under the title *The history of music in sound*, were accompanied by printed booklets describing the music on the discs. For those interested in researching popular music, Colin Larkin's four-volume *Guinness encyclopedia of popular music* arrived in 1992.

'Music appreciation' and the 'amateur' market

At the beginning of the century, domestic music-making in British homes was, by all accounts, alive and well. Songs and piano pieces were issued in the thousands, and pianos purchased in enormous quantities.[10] As for reading matter, those who were interested in educating themselves further on musical topics were catered to by self-help books such as Sir John Stainer's *Dictionary of musical terms* (1889), and a large number of 'primers' from the house of Novello.[11] Music publisher Augener issued similar books, on counterpoint, harmony and fugue by Ebenezer Prout; and John Curwen published material on the 'sol fa' method of teaching singing. Interested parties could also learn about music by turning to newspapers, many of which employed regular music critics of standing during the century, including Robin Legge (*The Times*), Neville Cardus (*The Manchester Guardian*), Michael Kennedy (*The Daily Telegraph*) and Andrew Porter (*The Financial Times* and *The Observer*). Musicians both professional (occasionally) and amateur (frequently) seem to enjoy reading about those who create music, and a market developed for musicians' biographies and autobiographies. In the classical field this had begun late in the nineteenth century with Charles Hallé's autobiography from 1896, and continued with contributions from conductors such as Thomas Beecham (*A mingled chime*, 1944), Henry Wood (*My life of*

---

10 Ehrlich, *The piano*, p. 222 notes that 75,000 pianos were manufactured in England in 1910.
11 [Novello], *A century and a half in Soho*.

music, 1938) and Adrian Boult (*My own trumpet*, 1973). Singers included stars of both the classical recital and opera, including light opera – some better-known examples are Ian Wallace's *Promise me you'll sing 'Mud'* (1975), Sir Geraint Evans's *A knight at the opera* (1984), Robert Tear's *Tear here* (1990) and Janet Baker's *Full circle* (1982). From the 1960s a market developed for books about the lives of pop stars, such as Adam Faith (*Poor me*, 1961) and Cliff Richard (*It's great to be young: my teenage story and life in show business*, 1960) either written by the stars themselves or ghostwriters, or by others, as with John Janson's *Helen Shapiro, pop princess* (1963).

Aside from biographies of this sort, the market in music books also included J. M. Dent's highly successful Master Musicians books, a series that in general kept to the safe waters of canonic composers from Bach to Elgar. The first series of the Master Musicians, under the editorship of Frederick Crowest, commenced in 1899 with a volume on Wagner. A new series began in 1931, and continued to be published by Dent until Oxford University Press took over publishing responsibility towards the end of the century. Further milestones were Donald Tovey's seven volumes of *Essays in musical analysis* (Oxford University Press, 1935–45), Percy Scholes's *Oxford companion to music* (1938, with several later editions) and A. L. Bacharach's *The musical companion* (Gollancz, 1934). A large, multi-authored volume produced at a cheap price (six shillings, compared with a guinea for Scholes' *Oxford companion*), *The musical companion* continued to sell well for Gollancz over a long period, with an American edition, under the title *A musical companion*, published by Alfred Knopf in 1935.[12] By the time the *Oxford companion* was published, Scholes had already firmly established himself in the field of music appreciation, and was probably the first writer on music to have his name – and, consequently, his influence – disseminated through the medium of broadcasting when the BBC appointed him to the position of BBC Music Critic in 1923. Scholes's *First book of the gramophone record* (1924) was an early attempt at evaluative discography. In 1928 he left the BBC and moved to Switzerland, where he produced his popular and enduring *Oxford companion to music* after what he termed 'five or six years of very unremitting labour' (preface, p. x).

Broadcasting and the availability of gramophone records were clearly likely to have an effect on music appreciation and on music-making by the

---

12 Hodges, *Gollancz*, p. 85, reports that Gollancz sold 170,000 copies of the *Musical companion* between 1934 and 1957.

British population.[13] Ernst Roth's opinion was that 'Broadcasting, which left the book trade unharmed, struck the music trade a heavy blow. The still imperfect but much improved gramophone record was another contributory factor.'[14] The influence of the new technological media in these matters remained a contentious issue, such that, over January and February 1938, the *Listener* (a journal founded by the BBC in 1929, mainly as a vehicle for reprinting the texts of broadcast talks) published a series of four articles under the title 'Broadcasting and private music-making', by Francis Toye, Edmund Rubbra, F. H. Shera and Cedric Glover. Toye, while admitting that the answer to the question about any influence, good or bad, exerted by broadcasting and recordings was that 'nobody knows', amplified this somewhat laconic and reductive response by suggesting that 'on the whole the more serious-minded music lover relies to a greater extent on the gramophone than on the radio', in part because recordings enabled listeners to purchase what they liked rather than having to accept what they were given, and to enjoy repeated hearings. Shera's opinion was that broadcasting had stimulated a liking for instrumental rather than vocal music, and was making recruitment to local music societies more difficult. Given the forum in which they were published, none of these talks was ever likely to attribute a pernicious effect to the BBC's activities, and of course the Corporation needed to attract and maintain the widest possible audience for its musical broadcasts at a time when radio licences were an important source of revenue. It may also be appropriate here to note the foundation of the UK Federation of Gramophone Societies in 1936. Such societies met in public spaces such as libraries as the audio equivalent of a book club or reading circle.

Music appreciation for the 'ordinary listener' as exemplified by Scholes was continued from 1954 by Anthony Hopkins, in his long-running series Talking about Music. Hopkins, like Scholes, produced several books for the musical amateur, including *Talking about symphonies* (1961) and *Talking about concertos* (1964), published by Heinemann and providing a more lightweight alternative to the formal analyses of these genres set forward in Tovey's *Essays in musical analysis*. With his *Understanding music* (1979) Hopkins began publishing instead with J. M. Dent, a firm that continued to play an important role in

---

13 Nott, *Music for the people*, is the most comprehensive study of the influence of the gramophone and radio on British musical life.
14 Roth, *The business of music*, p. 85. Roth's memoir was originally published in Zurich as *Musik als Kunst und Ware* (Atlantis, 1966). References in this chapter are to the English-language edition.

publishing for a middlebrow market, as did Penguin, publishers of Otto Karolyi's *Introducing music* (1965), of Alec Robertson's *Chamber music* (1957), and of recommendation guides such as the *Penguin stereo record guide* (first published 1975, preceded by *The stereo record guide* (LP Record Library, 1960–74)). In the 1960s the BBC began publishing a new series of books for the interested amateur and student, the BBC Music Guides, short books of approximately sixty-four pages mostly devoted, like Dent's Master Musicians series, to composers of the eighteenth to early twentieth centuries. The guides typically confined themselves to one aspect of a composer's output, as with the first titles, on Haydn's symphonies by H. C. Robbins Landon and on Bach's cantatas by Jack Westrup. Radio and television series resulted in spin-off books such as *My music* (1979) by Steve Race and Frank Muir, based on a popular BBC Radio 4 music quiz, and *Robin Ray's music quiz* (1978) by a well-known contestant on the BBC2 television programme *Face the music* in the 1970s. Such programmes were a mixture of information and entertainment that no longer assumed a high degree of musical literacy on the part of their audience.

Sheet music printing, publication and economics

Reference has already been made to the massive market for popular sheet music in the first half of the century, and the few 'serious' music publishing outlets founded by Oxford University Press, Stainer & Bell and Faber Music during the century were rare examples of new classical enterprises.[15] This section will look more closely at the output and publishing methods of sheet music publishers. Information on actual print-runs of music publications, as on the real-life, day-to-day operations of publishers, is scattered widely among multiple sources.

Christian Baierle makes a helpful and valid distinction from around 1900 between publishers of 'serious' music, whose business remained a paper-based one, and those of 'popular' music, which, while also being initially paper-based, increasingly adopted technological means to distribute their products.[16] In 1900, popular music publication in Britain was dominated by a small number of publishers such as Francis, Day & Hunter, Ascherberg,

---

15 Wright, *Faber music*. A useful history of Stainer & Bell, founded in 1907, is available at www.stainer.co.uk/100years1.html. Oxford University Press's music department was founded in 1923 by Hubert Foss. Hinnells, *An extraordinary performance* and *Oxford music: the first fifty years*.

16 Baierle, *Der Musikverlag*, p. 92.

Hopwood & Crew, and Chappell, all three of which were eventually taken over by, or amalgamated with, record companies.[17] Francis, Day & Hunter held rights to such popular hits as 'If you want to know the time, ask a policeman' and 'Lily of Laguna'; Chappell to 'Roses of Picardy' and to musicals and operettas including works by Gilbert and Sullivan.[18] Ascherberg's catalogue included a large number of music hall songs.

The economics of music production also tended to vary between the two different types of publisher. Songs would likely appear in a standard form of an engraved or (more likely) lithographed front page announcing the song within; then would come two central pages that contained the song itself, in the form of a vocal line with piano accompaniment, and an advertisement for other available publications on the back wrapper would complete the item. This basic format survived right into the pop and rock era, now often with a photograph of the artist associated with the song on the front cover, and with guitar chords added. Songs were also issued by 'serious' music publishers, of course, but in addition they also had to originate, often by engraving, large full scores of choral and orchestral works. H. W. Heinsheimer (who first worked for Universal Edition in Vienna, and subsequently in New York for G. Schirmer) noted in his memoirs that 'Music engraving and love-making seem, so far as I can ascertain, the only human endeavors that have not made any progress since the time of Bach.'[19] Ernst Roth (of Boosey & Hawkes)[20] claimed that 'A good engraver needs four working hours for a quarto page of piano music of medium difficulty, and the best engraver cannot complete more than three pages of a difficult orchestral score in a working week', a comment closely echoed by Heinsheimer: 'It will take a skilled man two to three hours of intensive and concentrated work to finish one plate of normal difficulty and size. He can do three to four plates a day and will do less if it is a difficult and complicated work.'[21] Small wonder that Roth claimed that 'A thirty two page volume of music costs more than a book of a hundred and twenty pages.'[22] Helen Wallace notes that Boosey & Hawkes was still using engravers into the 1980s; and in his 1981 book on Novello, Michael Hurd reported that, 'From the days when they could employ a dozen engravers working long hours, Novello's are now reduced to two. Indeed, there are

17 Abbott, *The story of Francis, Day & Hunter*; Mair, *The Chappell story*.
18 Chappell also had strong connections to Broadway theatre because of the Dreyfus brothers, Max and Louis. Max owned the Harms publishing house in the USA, and Louis owned Chappell's in London from 1929. I am indebted to Donald Krummel for this information, and for comments on an earlier version of this chapter.
19 Heinsheimer, *Menagerie in F sharp*, p. 71.   20 Roth, *The business of music*, p. 71.
21 Heinsheimer, *Menagerie in F sharp*, p. 178.   22 Roth, *The business of music*, p. 71.

only half a dozen such men in the country.'[23] (For comparison, Heinsheimer wrote in 1947 that there were only about fifty music engravers left in the USA.) Novello was an interesting case: it set up its own printing division in the late 1840s, on which occasion the company issued a small pamphlet that discussed engraving and music printing from movable type.

Roth also has some useful information about print-runs of classical works, noting that orchestral scores 'by prominent composers are printed in quantities of 200 or 250 copies, and this is usually sufficient for many years'.[24] Lesser-known composers might have only fifty copies printed. This shows just how much classical music publishing was on a financial knife edge, and it has continued to be so.

Up until the 1980s the UK classical music publishing market had continued to operate in a traditional way, with many firms, including many foreign-owned ones, having a foothold in the marketplace. Since sheet music is an international commodity, catering for a British public that wanted Stravinsky as well as Stanford, and Poulenc as well as Purcell, involved importing music from abroad. Under a system that went back at least to the early nineteenth century, music publishers based in Britain – which almost invariably meant in London – became official distribution agents for the products of overseas firms; or occasionally a foreign publisher would establish additional premises in London. An example of the former arrangement was J. & W. Chester, which as the British agent of Wilhelm Hansen of Copenhagen distributed the works of many Scandinavian composers including Carl Nielsen and Jean Sibelius; while the latter is illustrated by the German company Schott, founded in Mainz in 1770. Schott has a long-established music shop in London.

UK music publishers' incomes were made up of a complex mixture of sheet music sales, of revenue derived from hiring out music for performances, and of income from public performance and/or recording royalties shared by composer and publisher. John Abbott, of Francis, Day & Hunter, tells of the important role that music publishers such as his firm, along with those of Hawkes and Chappell, played in the representation of publishers' interests, both in the framing of the Copyright Act of 1911 and by the creation of the British Performing Right Society in 1914.[25] It is impossible to go into the subject of musical copyright in any depth here. Suffice to say, copyright of printed music operates in a similar fashion to that for printed books, and the

---

23 Wallace, *Boosey and Hawkes*, p. 139; Hurd, *Vincent Novello*, p. 142. On Novello see also Cooper, *The house of Novello*.
24 Roth, *The business of music*, p. 94.   25 Ehrlich, *Harmonious alliance*.

length of the copyright term is the same. However, music publishers and composers also earn royalties from performance rights; these are usually collected on their behalf by either the Performing Right Society, which is responsible for collecting fees from performances in public venues ranging from church hall to concert hall and opera house, or by the Mechanical Copyright Protection Society, established in 1911, which collects fees arising from recordings and broadcasts. Hire fees, which are not part of copyright legislation, are charged by publishers when an ensemble wishes to perform a work such as a musical, an opera or an orchestral piece. While it is often possible to purchase a printed full score of a work that will be perfectly satisfactory for musical study, a performance requires a large number of other materials that are often issued on 'hire only', and not made available for sale. The publisher charges a hire fee for these materials based on such factors as the quantity of materials required, the size of the performance venue, and the duration of the work. In addition, of course, a performance fee will be due to the Performing Right Society if the work is still in copyright.[26]

Thanks to copyright, hire fees and performing rights income, some publishers were in the twentieth century able to make a good living from the continuing revenues earned by the works of composers who were long dead, such as Elgar and Ralph Vaughan Williams. The income derived from all these sources could be used to promote younger composers, with companies such as Boosey & Hawkes, Novello, Chester Music, Faber Music, Universal Edition (London) and Oxford University Press's music department issuing respectable lists of new publications on a regular basis. However, in a world of harsh economic realities this slightly quaint way of operating by firms that had often begun as family concerns began to look rather outdated when set against the large sums being made by new companies, which had a keener interest in exploiting their copyrights and performing rights income, and promoting their composers and artists, than they had in publishing new music. American entrepreneur Bob Wise, creator of the London arm of the Music Sales Group in 1970, is often credited with bringing this way of thinking to the British classical music market. In 1988 Music Sales Group purchased classical publisher Chester Music, then in 1993 paid £2.5 million to acquire Novello, making Music Sales Group a very significant player in the British music publishing market. Unsurprisingly, this amount of market concentration caused alarm in some quarters as former household names were

---

26 For a useful overview of hire libraries, see Wright, 'Music hire libraries'. The early chapters of Montgomery and Threlfall, *Music and copyright*, give a clear history and explanation of music copyright issues.

swallowed up into what was seen as an American conglomerate determined to derive maximum income from rights exploitation (for example, by placing its music into films or into television advertisements) and without any obligation to promote new composers of classical music.[27] A feature of the popular music publishing industry was the establishment of companies with the specific purpose of promoting a particular artist or band – Baierle gives the examples of Essex Music, founded in London in 1975 to publish David Bowie, and Hit and Run Publishing, set up in 1977 to promote Genesis. Another example is Northern Songs, formed in 1963 to publish The Beatles.[28]

Conclusion

Christian Baierle calls the period 1900–90 the 'period of electronic media' in music publishing, and assigns four main characteristics to it: (i) the rise of publishers of popular music; (ii) new distribution and reproductive possibilities brought about by electronic media; (iii) a growing trend towards internationalisation and takeovers; and (iv) tie-ins between music publishers and film or record companies. The final decade of the twentieth century he characterises by a globalised and digital music market. In the case of Britain these propositions held broadly true, as reflected elsewhere in this chapter. Industry takeovers and increasing globalisation of the market, of course, closely reflected developments in the book market in the same period, and specialist music book publishers became scarcer over the course of the century. This is not the place to attempt to second-guess what a 'music' chapter of a subsequent volume of this history might look like, but the market for books in general seems likely to move increasingly towards an electronic, 'e-book' model. The model for sheet music will remain more complex because of the performing/recording rights aspects, and of licensing. Ernst Roth stated in 1969 that 'the future development of musical copyright will have to revoke some of the rights granted by an over-zealous legislation under the impact of technical change. In the meantime, music will have to tread the hard road of money and commerce.'[29] In some respects he might have been writing about the early twenty-first century. The production of sheet music surrogates of popular music created in the

---

27 The problems besetting British classical music were well surveyed and summarised in Anne Inglis, 'Music publishing: a catalogue of woes', *Independent* 7 September 1991. Similar alarm is expressed in Stoianova, 'Der Untergang der Casa Ricordi'.
28 Baierle, *Der Musikverlag*, p. 114. See also Southall, *Northern songs*.
29 Roth, *The business of music*, p. 38.

recording studio is likely to continue to shrink, and perhaps disappear altogether; and at the time of writing a massive amount of the world's music publishing – both popular and classical – is controlled by just a handful of firms, all of which have connections to the recording industry and often to film studios. More music is being originated on the computer, and the publisher has become a marketing outlet for creators rather than an originator of a print or electronic edition, with quality control not always overseen by editors, typesetters, engravers and others as in the past. Bricks-and-mortar music publisher outlets have all but disappeared in favour of online shops – Music Sales Group again took the lead here during the mid-1990s, and by the turn of the century others, such as Boosey & Hawkes, had followed suit. Fortunately, the public's appetite for music seems undiminished, especially in the online marketplace. It is no exaggeration to say that music production, publishing and consumption in the twentieth century probably saw more change than in any prior one. Perhaps even that level of change will be eclipsed in the twenty-first.

17

University presses and academic publishing

SAMANTHA J. RAYNER

Academic publishing, as John Thompson claimed in 2005, 'has become one of the terrains on which the logics of two different worlds – the world of publishing and the world of the academy – come together and clash, leading on occasion to tension, misunderstanding and mutual recriminations'.[1] As this implies, however, there hasn't always been such a tension between the two sides, and this chapter maps out the history of academic publishing in the hundred years between 1914 and 2015, looking at the changing research landscape and the ways university presses and commercial academic publishers have engaged with it. Academic publishing is a rapidly developing and changing area: this chapter comes with the caveat that anyone interested in learning about the most up-to-date news should consult sources such as *The scholarly kitchen*.[2]

In the period following the First World War, the number of universities in Britain began to grow rapidly. In 1918 there were just over twenty universities and university colleges in the UK.[3] By the end of the 1960s this figure had more than doubled, the result of the Robbins Report of 1963 which recommended a major expansion of the British university system.[4] By the end of the 1990s the Further and Higher Education Acts of 1992 had given polytechnics university status, and the number rose sharply again; today there are well over one hundred.[5]

At the start of the period under consideration universities could be described as serving 'a small social elite', and attendance, even until the

---

1 Thompson, *Books in the digital age*, p. 175.   2 https://scholarlykitchen.sspnet.org.
3 Made up of the so-called 'ancient' universities of Oxford, Cambridge, St Andrews, Aberdeen, Glasgow and Edinburgh, and the initial wave of 'red-brick', civic universities – the University of London, Durham, Birmingham, Liverpool, Manchester, Leeds, Sheffield, Bristol and the University of Wales.
4 Universities formed during this time are often referred to as 'plate glass', after a phrase coined by Michael Beloff. Beloff, *The plateglass universities*.
5 www.universitiesuk.ac.uk/aboutus/members/Pages/default.aspx.

1950s, was still only about one in twenty-five of each generation. At the beginning of the twenty-first century it was one in two.[6] This expansion fuelled a corresponding rise in the demands made on academic publishers to disseminate research, a demand that intensified after the introduction of the Research Assessment Exercise in 1986. The range of subjects being taught and studied increased dramatically as disciplines such as psychology, management, media studies and education became part of the curriculum. Publishers had to respond to all this, and master the new digital production workflows that began to impact on business models and dissemination of scholarly communication in the latter half of the twentieth century.

The dominant university presses in the UK throughout the period 1914–2015 are Oxford and Cambridge: Oxford University Press is by far the larger of the two, turning over more than three times what its rival does.[7] Arguably these are also the most stable presences over the decades, as other presses fold, are bought out, or are born. In the first half of the century, these two kept company with university presses such as Liverpool (1899), Manchester (1904) and the University of Wales (1922), along with Edinburgh (1940s), Leicester (1952) and Athlone, for the University of London (1948). Competition for content is widening as new open access initiatives enter the market.[8] However, commercial academic publishers, operating alongside the university presses, have often demonstrated that they can be as successful (and in many instances more so) than their university-based counterparts.

At the time of the First World War, Oxford University Press was an institution that managed its own paper mill, printing house and publishing business, this last being split between the Oxford site in Walton Street and the London Office in Amen Corner. It was run 'less like a single company and more like a feudal state'[9] with continuous tensions between the Printer, the Secretary and the Publisher. Decisions on what scholarly texts were to be published were approved by the Delegates, but on the basis of summaries and recommendations prepared by senior editors.[10] While the Oxford side concentrated on the scholarly outputs, the London office was free to publish more commercial, general interest books, and, under the aegis of the publisher Humphrey Milford,[11] expanded to include children's books, poetry and

---

6 Anderson, *British universities past and present*, p. 1.
7 Clark and Phillips, *Inside book publishing*, fifth edition, p. 67.
8 For example Ubiquity Press, founded in 2012, and Open Book Publishers, begun in 2008.
9 Whyte, 'Oxford University Press, 1896–1945', p. 72.
10 Louis, 'The Waldock Inquiry', p. 767.
11 Milford held the job of Publisher from 1913 to 1945.

music, as well as an Overseas Education Department.[12] At Cambridge University Press, which also had an office in London, the management was very different, with the Syndics responsible for financial matters as well as choosing the books to be published.[13] This was still a time when scholarship, as well as publishing, was considered a genteel calling: at Oxford, just before the First World War, two men who were to become key players in publishing of this period, Basil Blackwell and Geoffrey Faber, joined the University Press. Blackwell is quoted as saying that his time at the Press gave him a lasting impression 'of reverence for scholarship and enthusiasm for any books which might advance its cause'.[14] Faber's experience was less happy, and he did not stay very long at the Press. One of his memories of working for OUP was that, on requesting whether he might learn something about book production, he was told by Humphrey Milford, then Assistant Publisher in the London Office, that 'a first-class man is a Greek among the barbarians'.[15] The implication was that such direct interaction was frowned upon: practical knowledge of production was not what gentlemen publishers in the early twentieth century needed to know about, as it was still so distinct from the rest of the business.

These attitudes were beginning to change, however. In contrast, publishers like Macmillan, Allen & Unwin, Methuen or Blackie & Sons were less hampered by these attitudes and working practices. They developed their own lists in different academic areas: Blackie, for instance, from 1920 'embarked on a world-class list of scientific books at the cutting edge of research that eventually became the strongest British publishing list in the area from a commercial publisher'.[16] When Stanley Unwin took over George Allen & Sons in 1914, he began to cultivate new authors, and philosophy books in particular emerged as a key focus: Bertrand Russell's works helped build this list. In the field of literary studies, Chatto & Windus's impact was so strong after 1930 that it has been claimed 'there can rarely have been such a close and sustained association between a publisher and an individual discipline'.[17] Meanwhile, the Macmillans were busy: 'in the midst of the 1914 war, even the large scale books came out as they always had'.[18] The Macmillan firm adapted, and this period 'was remarkable not only for the number and weight and authority of the books, political or economic, which expressed the thoughts of the times, but for the area of diverse opinion

12 See Chapter 31 for information on OUP overseas.   13 McKitterick, *A history*.
14 Sutcliffe, *The Oxford University Press*, p. 163.   15 *Ibid.*, p. 168.
16 Stevenson, *Book makers*, p. 78.   17 Collini, 'The Chatto List', p. 636.
18 Morgan, *The house of Macmillan*, p. 218.

covered by those books'.[19] The Macmillan family were well connected, and could still compete with the university presses for academic works: Herbert Gladstone, J. M. Keynes and A. C. Benson were just a few of their authors in the early part of the twentieth century. Sir Frederick Macmillan had passed on the running of the company to younger family members, and this helped propel it through the uncertain inter-war years. The other major trade publishers who produced academic titles, Longmans and John Murray, were also seeing moves at the top of their companies, so the period was characterised by changes in management, and in some cases commissioning direction, throughout the industry.

Academic publishing grew via new companies, too: Geoffrey Faber, having left OUP, founded Faber & Gwyer in 1925, followed by Faber & Faber in 1929. In a speech to booksellers in 1931 he made clear that he believed that the bad times people were facing would force them to 'ask themselves all kinds of questions that only books can answer'.[20] He predicted 'a revival of seriousness'[21] and to meet this demand concentrated on developing a literary and non-fiction list that, with the help of T. S. Eliot and Richard de la Mare, built the firm's reputation for marrying 'commercial and literary judgement in an unique and highly original mixture'.[22] The poetry list, for instance, was a successful part of Faber's broader academic publishing contexts: as Stevenson has noted, 'much of what we would today describe as academic publishing was in the 1930s and earlier classified as "general" on the lists of trade publishers'.[23] Firms like Blackwell's also emerged in the early twentieth century, with Basil Blackwell building on an annual series of poetry books that published work by W. H. Auden, Stephen Spender and Louis MacNeice, then through ventures like an Oxford University magazine called *Oxford Outlook* (which ran for nearly twenty years), and on to scholarly reprints of works such as the plays of George Etherege. Soon academics brought new work to be published, and Virgilian studies became a specialism.[24] Other new publishers, like Gollancz and Cape, were to produce high-quality books that crossed over into academic areas: this was, despite the complex economic climate, a strong era for publishing in general, and for academic books in particular.

Publishers such as Nelson Thornes took advantage of the growing demand for educational books, and, as the Second World War receded, even more mainstream general publishers like Penguin followed suit with cheap but

---

19 *Ibid.*, p. 225. 20 Faber, *A publisher speaking*, p. 56. 21 *Ibid.*, p. 57.
22 Stevenson, *Book makers*, p. 71. 23 *Ibid.*, p. 77. 24 Norrington, *Blackwell's*, p. 66.

well-edited classic texts, ideal for students, via series such as their Pelican and Penguin Classics lists. 'These high class Pelicans are a real nuisance', complained Arthur Norrington in 1952, when he was Senior Administrative Officer of Oxford University Press,[25] and it is not hard to sympathise with his concerns: in 1952 Allen Lane's assets were valued at nearly £215,000.[26] It has been argued that 'university presses ought to have been in a privileged position to exploit the hectic development on their doorsteps, but the commercial publishers were quicker off the mark'.[27] Pelicans and the Penguin Classics lists were edited by experts, looked fresh and appealing, and were cheap. Penguin both reprinted books in paperback, like E. M. W. Tillyard's *The Elizabethan world picture* (1942) which had been formerly published in hardback by Chatto, and published new titles, such as E. V. Rieu's translation of Homer's *Odyssey*, which went on to sell over 3 million copies and 'form the foundation stone of the Penguin Classics'.[28] University presses, whose production values were different, could not immediately compete with such an adversary, but series such as the Oxford World Classics and J. M. Dent's Everyman's Library, published originally in hardback, would eventually move to the cheaper paperback format to compete more effectively.[29] In 1957 Cambridge University Press published Brian Pippard's *Elements of classical thermodynamics* simultaneously in paper and hardback, believed to be the first example of this in the academic market.[30]

However, this took time. The university presses moved within their own traditional working practices, and although they were expanding internationally, and evolving with the new demands these additional territories were giving them, by the mid-twentieth century things were still dominated by earlier patterns. When Michael Black joined Cambridge University Press in 1951, he commented: 'I had joined not just a business, or a university department, but a class – indeed a caste.'[31] The men (for they were largely male) he worked alongside,

> were mentally and spiritually at one with other groups which were running the country, the services and the colonies. They had a common ethos as well as common habits. One most striking thing about them is that although to their enemies they seemed class-ridden, they were in fact open to new talent,

25 *Ibid.*, p. 273.   26 Lewis, *Penguin special*, p. 268.
27 Sutcliffe, *The Oxford University Press*, p. 272.   28 Lewis, *Penguin special*, p. 251.
29 Twenty-four Oxford Paperbacks appeared in 1960, including *A preface to 'Paradise Lost'* by C. S. Lewis, *The Roman revolution* by Ronald Syme, and E. J. Dent's *Mozart's operas*. Flanders, 'The Press in London', p. 174–5. Everyman paperbacks first appeared in 1960. Rose, 'J. M. Dent and Sons'.
30 McKitterick, *A history*, p. 324.   31 Black, *Learning to be a publisher*, p. 6.

knew that they depended for success and continued life on getting it – or the cleverest of them did.[32]

For academic publishing this was key, for as the spread of other universities continued to rise in the 1950s and 1960s, so too did the prevalence of the non-Oxbridge scholars, and the pool of available research material and platforms to publish that came with them. Not only were there more scholars, there was more awareness of the need to accommodate the demands of the modern age, where technology and convenience were replacing the slower, more traditional production methods of earlier in the century. This openness to new ideas helped to move both the Oxford and Cambridge presses to the next phase in their development. Production methods, for example, were updated, replacing Monotype with litho methods: by 1978 letterpress had practically disappeared from OUP altogether.[33] The Delegates and the Syndics were aided by an expanded and increasingly female staff, who oversaw the growth of the businesses through the post-Second World War expansions of the university and publishing sectors.[34]

The 1960s saw the publication of the Robbins Report, which called for more university places for able students. The result was an increase in universities across the UK, and an optimism about the future of scholarship: this 'exuberant innocence'[35] was not to last, but while it did significant developments occurred, not just in the way university education was configured but also in the ways academic books were produced and consumed. This Report impacted directly on academic publishing: Robbins was critical of both Oxford and Cambridge for failing to meet the economic and social needs of post-war Britain. Oxford's response was twofold, via the Franks Report (begun in 1964), which examined the University itself, and the Waldock Inquiry, which looked specifically at Oxford University Press. The Waldock Inquiry concluded in 1970, and advised that the Press should continue to expand and diversify. Although the conclusions were not severely damaging to the Press, this did have far-reaching consequences: the abolition of Perpetual Delegates, and increase in the number of Delegates from ten to fifteen, and full financial disclosure. But perhaps its greatest significance is 'that the work of the committee reflected the rationale for

---

32 Ibid., pp. 6–7. 33 Maw, 'Printing technology, binding, readers, and social life', p. 289.
34 See copies of The Clarendonian, OUP's in-house staff magazine, for a glimpse into how the gender balance (and hence working and social activities) changed at the Press after the Second World War.
35 Halsey, Decline of donnish dominion, p. 1.

reforms already under way and modernization at a particular time, May 1970'.[36]

In the USA and other territories, as in the UK, universities were on the rise, and the UK Presses were keen to have stakes in these markets. By the 1960s, so significant was this wave of new institutions and potential markets that it was claimed that a major academic library was opening every week in the USA, and that 'future economic historians of the book trade will be able to demonstrate that never since Gutenberg had edition-sizes of learned and academic books been so large, or the market so receptive'.[37] This was a decade of abundance, and in the world of academic publishing in the UK, as elsewhere, the 1960s seemed to promise prosperity for all:

> In scholarly publishing, the expansion of higher education throughout the world, the increasing dominance of English as a world language, new investment in the sciences and the re-examination of educational practices more generally brought demand on a scale and at a pace the was simultaneously welcome and perilous.[38]

These were the times for universities to grow, and other university presses along with them. It is no coincidence that during this period enterprises such as the University of Exeter Press and Edinburgh University Press were launched: in 1962 there were 119,000 full-time undergraduates in the UK, and by 1969, 219,000.[39]

Academic publishers also became far more export-focussed during this period, as the US and Asian markets opened up, and as these territories became an increasing source for sales and content. John Thompson has undertaken a detailed and thorough analysis of the history of academic publishing during this period, and although his focus is as much on US as on UK publishers, this is helpful in a climate where both markets are increasingly linked by international expansions by the major UK presses. He makes the point that during the 1960s and 1970s the two countries underwent similar changes. Both benefited from the baby boom and the relatively high domestic economic growth rates of the times, and this phenomenal increase, coupled with the fact that in the 1960s more new members of faculty were taken on than in the entire 325-year history of American higher education up to that point, caused the university presses

---

36 Louis, 'The Waldock Inquiry', p. 789.   37 Black, *Cambridge University Press*, p. 227.
38 McKitterick, *A history*, pp. 375–6.
39 Halsey, *Decline of donnish dominion*, p. 93. The number of US undergraduates increased by 500 per cent between 1945 and 1975, making this the golden age of higher education. Thompson, *Books in the digital age*, p. 181.

to hold a justifiably optimistic outlook. The period of growth was even honoured by President Jimmy Carter: in the summer of 1978, he proclaimed a University Press Week 'in recognition of the impact, both here and abroad, of American University Presses on culture and scholarship'.[40] The presses fulfilled a vital scholarly function: as the number of scholars increased, so too did the need to publish. However, this was not paralleled in the UK. Here, the 1970s saw the post-war prosperity fail, as traditional industries like engineering, shipbuilding, textiles and motor manufacturing could no longer compete with other countries. Unemployment rates climbed under Edward Heath's Conservative government, and inflation – and industrial unrest – rose. Britain joined the European Economic Community in 1973, which had implications for business management, and Irish Republican Army bombing attacks brought the fear of war back into people's minds. As Stevenson points out, this all contributed to an environment where, for only the second time since records were kept, fewer new books were published in 1975 than in 1974.[41]

For academic publishing, as with publishing more generally, this decade saw the map shift as London became too expensive as a main base, so companies like Longman, Macmillan, Allen & Unwin and Butterworth had all moved out of the city by 1973. This strategy enabled them to continue to grow, but was not an option so easily available to the two main university presses. Cambridge University Press suffered the most, as it differed from its Oxford counterpart in having all parts of the business integrated together: 'Whether in commissioning, printing, publishing or in the balance-sheet, the Press's success or failure was ultimately judged not by any one of its activities, but by the whole.'[42] Bentley House, the Press's London base, was shut in 1978. Oxford University Press, in the wake of the Waldock Inquiry, reorganised too: it moved all London activity to Oxford in 1976, and streamlined the business into new divisions.[43] It was a mark of how great the challenge to the university presses from their trade opposites had become that the first contracts for publishing for the newly established Open University went to Macmillan in 1970.[44]

---

40 Quoted on the website of the Association of American University Presses, www.aaup net.org/about-aaup/aaup-history.
41 Stevenson, *Book makers*, p. 205.
42 McKitterick, *A history*, p. 375. See the rest of this chapter, 'A developing crisis', for a full description of what happened.
43 The International Division, the UK Publishing Services Division, the Academic Division, the Education Division and the General Division. Sutcliffe, *The Oxford University Press*, p. 288.
44 McKitterick, 'Looking further', p. 812.

However, other significant developments show this period reflecting a growing sense of academic publishers as a set of organisations with a distinctive set of common challenges. The University of Toronto Press's establishment in 1969 of the journal *Scholarly Publishing* is one such indicator. In the first editorial, Marsh Jeanneret highlighted the tendency of institutions to ignore university presses when installing new information systems, and the implications in terms of profit loss and operation.[45] It is worth noting that this is very much a concern of academic presses in the twenty-first century, too, as open access publishing initiatives complicate the business models of established presses. In addition, the Association for Learned and Professional Society Publishers was set up in 1972, and the Society for Scholarly Publishing in 1978: clearly responding to the need for academic publishers to have professional bodies to represent them.

As the 1980s began, economic recession in the UK and withdrawal of levels of government funding to higher education meant that the presses were going to have to adapt again in order to survive. While libraries were well resourced, and there was a market for the specialist monograph, the system worked, but as economic pressures began to be felt the university presses turned to more lucrative textbook publishing to bring in additional revenue, and the monograph market began to wane. Thompson explains this situation by pointing to the financial pressures faced by research libraries as university budgets were cut, coupled with the growing proportion of the remaining budget for periodicals and content in electronic formats.[46] By the 1990s, the Society of College, National and University Libraries (SCONUL) reported that between the academic years of 1991/92 and 1999/2000 the percentage of books bought had dropped from 40.2 per cent to 32.6 per cent, while electronic texts rose from 2.3 per cent to 11.5 per cent.[47]

The future of scholarly publishing, a report produced by the Modern Languages Association of America in 2002, explored this past and continuing tension between the university presses and the institutions with which they worked, emphasising that while these budget cuts were being made tenure standards had risen, which created an impossible situation long-term.[48] In the UK, the introduction of the first Research Assessment Exercise (RAE) in 1986 meant that conditions quickly mirrored those of the USA: the publication of academic research was made a key performance indicator for universities, and this has inevitably continued to build with each successive round of

---

45 Jeanneret, 'Universities as publishers', p. 3.
46 Thompson, *Books in the digital age*, p. 99. 47 *Ibid.*, p. 104.
48 *The future of scholarly publishing*, p. 172, https://apps.mla.org/pdf/schlrlypblshng.pdf.

assessment. As will be seen below, as the open access debates escalated in 2015, publishing and academia in the UK were facing a major challenge, as new mandates from bodies such as the Higher Education Funding Council for England (HEFCE) started to impact on the whole ecosystem that makes up the production and consumption of academic books.

In the 1990s, bookselling changes affected the publishing marketplace, too.[49] With the abolition of the Net Book Agreement in 1997 and the growing strength of a few large bookselling companies, it was a time of strong sales for academic books, as more titles were sold through shops like Blackwell's and James Thin where stock could be bought centrally and then held on shelves throughout the chains. However, these chains would soon be under threat from the rise of the online bookshop. In 1995, Amazon opened for business in the USA, and by 1998 it had arrived in the UK. It was the beginning of the online shopping age, and 'the university presses and many smaller publishers found that Amazon would quickly become one of their most important accounts'.[50] Amazon's impact went beyond *how* academic publishers could sell books via their platform, however: it also helped transform *what* the publishers could sell. The powerful search facility it offered, alongside increased efficiencies of short-run printing, meant that titles were more discoverable and accessible than ever before. But, as Thompson also points out, Amazon and other 'e-tailers' soon started extending the used book market too, which impacted in negative ways on sales of new books.

This was also a period of mergers and acquisitions in academic publishing: the Macmillan Group was bought by the German group Holtzbrinck in 1995, Routledge was bought by Taylor & Francis in 1998, and Pearson acquired Simon & Schuster in the same year. These mergers meant that by the end of the twentieth century academic publishing business models were changing, not just from the need to restructure internally, but in response to higher education developments and to the rapid rise of computers and electronic technologies. The Dearing Report of 1997, the first review of higher education in the UK since Robbins, made eight key suggestions: full-time under-graduates should contribute £1,000 per year of study after graduation on an income-contingent basis; there should be a return to the expansion of student numbers; the world-class reputation of UK degrees must be protected; higher education should make greater use of technology; the government should increase funding for research; there should be more professionalism in university teaching; there should be a stronger regional and community

49 See also Chapter 6.   50 Thompson, *Books in the digital age*, p. 73.

role for universities; and there should be a review of pay and working practices of all staff.[51]

At the time, universities were underfunded and, as Dearing himself said, 'The crisis in 1996 was the result of a period of very fast growth in student numbers, financed in very substantial part by severe reductions in the unit of resource [the amount a university spends on each student] for teaching, and massive decay in research infrastructure.'[52] As a result, library resources were cut, and students bought fewer textbooks and supplementary texts. Photocopying, and more judicious textbook buying habits by students, meant sales dropped, along with the increased modularisation of courses which meant books were useful more transiently than previously, when core texts would be used substantially as part of degree courses.[53]

In 2011 the Association of American University Presses (AAUP) produced a report, *Sustaining scholarly publishing: new business models for university presses*. This document, which represented the outcomes of discussions by university presses from all around the world, including those from Cambridge and Oxford, attempted to explain what had passed, what was happening in the present, and what could and should happen in the future. 'Publishers were essential to the scholarly ecosystem of the pre-web age', the report says, because 'for scholars to see their work disseminated within their scholarly community, it had to be published by a publisher'.[54] But now, in an age of information 'hyperabundance', publishing is within everyone's reach: 'Raw dissemination is now so easy that anything, and everything, can be "published" online – made available to Google, and Bing, and that moment's Twitter feed.' Rather than see this as a threat, however, the Report asserts that:

> The scholarly enterprise is in it for the long haul, not the next viral hit. As such, the scholarly ecosystem – libraries, universities, scholarly publishers, scholars – needs to ensure that the entire ecosystem remains strong over time, and that scholarship is well served by the systems we construct.[55]

Partly in response to this context, new initiatives were created, among them the *Journal of Scholarly Publishing* (a relaunch in 1994 of *Scholarly Publishing*),

---

51 John Crace and Jessica Shepherd, 'The right prescription?', *Guardian* 24 July 2007, www .theguardian.com/education/2007/jul/24/highereducation.tuitionfees.
52 Quoted in *ibid*.
53 Thompson, *Books in the digital age*, pp. 272–5, for a discussion of this shift.
54 *Sustaining scholarly publishing*, p. 6, available at www.aaupnet.org/policy-areas/future-of-scholarly-communications/task-force-on-economic-models-report.
55 *Ibid*.

the Scholarly Kitchen, the blog of the Society for Scholarly Publishing, in 2008,[56] and the Association of European University Presses (AEUP), founded in 2010.[57]

In Britain, the Working Group on Expanding Access to Published Research Findings, chaired by Dame Janet Finch, delivered their Report, *Accessibility, sustainability, excellence: how to expand access to research publications*, in 2012.[58] In this, so-called 'gold' open access publishing was recommended for academic journal articles: that is, where the funding for the article is paid up front to the publisher by the author, or author's institution, and then the work is made available via an online platform. The Finch Report has accelerated efforts to try and create robust new models for scholarly publishing via open access, for example by working more closely with libraries to make free online access to books, with a print on demand service attached, so that books can be bought if required; by aggregating content via online platforms; and by creating new university presses. Initiatives such as JSTOR (started in 1995 and short for Journal Storage) now offer monograph access as part of their services, while Project MUSE (started in 1993 by the Johns Hopkins University Press and the Milton S. Eisenhower Library at the Johns Hopkins University) has offered e-books as well as journals since 2010. Oxford University Press released University Press Scholarship Online in September 2011, and Cambridge University Press launched University Publishing Online one month later.[59]

There were casualties: Middlesex University Press closed in 2009, and Northumbria University Press had a management buy-out – all titles are now owned by McNidder & Grace. But there are signs that there is a growing place for new university presses too, including some from the newer universities: in 2001 the University of Chester Press began; Liverpool University Press was relaunched as a limited company in 2004; and in 2009 Kingston University Press announced it was open.[60] Others, like Liverpool University Press and Nottingham University Press, have found success and built reputation in niche areas such as gypsy studies and science fiction. In addition, the trade companies diversified, with publishers such as Bloomsbury starting a Bloomsbury Academic arm in 2008, under the leadership of Frances Pinter.

---

56 http://scholarlykitchen.sspnet.org/about.   57 www.aeup.eu.
58 www.researchinfonet.org/wp-content/uploads/2012/06/Finch-Group-report-FINAL-VERSION.pdf.
59 www.universitypressscholarship.com and http://universitypublishingonline.org.
60 'Kingston University launches press', *Bookseller* 6 November 2009, www.thebookseller.com/news/kingston-university-launches-press.html.

Bloomsbury Academic pulled in lists from elsewhere, such as the Arden Shakespeare and Methuen Drama, to create an imprint that regularly wins awards.[61] New forms like the short monograph are appearing via initiatives like Palgrave Pivot, and new organisations such as Open Humanities Press, Open Book Publishers, Open Edition, Open Library of the Humanities, Ubiquity Press and Knowledge Unlatched are showing how open access can work successfully via different business models, in addition to other new university presses, from UCL, Goldsmith's and the White Rose consortium, who are focussing on open access publications.[62]

Political moves continue to drive academic publishing debates on both sides of the Atlantic: in December 2012 the US Research Works Act was introduced, and supported by the AAUP.[63] This argued for the protection of copyright and access to material: a stance which angered many, and which caused dramatic headlines such as 'Academic publishers have become the enemies of science.'[64] In the UK, the government report *Innovation and research strategy for growth* anticipated the Finch Report and stated that publicly funded research should be available free of charge.[65] These diametrically opposed stances mean that the next chapter in the story of scholarly publishing is set to be a complex one. This is acknowledged by research funders and councils: in the USA, the Mellon Foundation is supporting several projects under their Scholarly Communications strand, and in the UK, the Arts and Humanities Research Council, in partnership with the British Library, has funded the Academic Book of the Future Project.[66] This latter built on work of previous initiatives, particularly work done by OAPEN-UK and HEFCE's 2015 Report on Monographs and Open Access.[67]

Open access publishing challenges scholarly publishing from every context: as Geoffrey Crossick, author of the HEFCE report, said, 'from licensing

61 Bloomsbury Academic won Independent Publisher of the Year and Academic & Professional Publisher of the Year awards in the Independent Publishers Guild Awards 2013, and in the Bookseller Industry Awards 2014: Academic, Educational & Professional Publisher of the Year.

62 See also Chapter 18.

63 www.congress.gov/bill/112th-congress/house-bill/3699/text.

64 *Guardian* 16 January 2012, www.theguardian.com/science/2012/jan/16/academic-publishers-enemies-science.

65 *Innovation and research strategy for growth*, p. 3. Available at www.gov.uk/government/uploads/system/uploads/attachment_data/file/32450/11-1387-innovation-and-research-strategy-for-growth.pdf.

66 https://mellon.org/programs/scholarly-communications and http://academicbookfuture.org.

67 Particularly OAPEN's 2014 Researcher Survey: see http://oapen-uk.jiscebooks.org. For the HEFCE Report on Monographs and Open Access, see www.hefce.ac.uk/pubs/rereports/year/2015/monographs.

and copyright to business models and quality, the issues that must be tackled are thorny and numerous'.[68] Richard Brown, past President of the Association for American University Presses and Director of the Georgetown University Press, proposed a metaphor for the current state of university presses as they move forwards 'towards a brave new world of knowledge': he claimed that the future lies in 'communities of practice'.[69] By this he meant working collaboratively with scholars and librarians, 'the thought leaders and gatekeepers and teachers and students and stakeholders in a variety of disciplines'.[70] This is essentially, and perhaps reassuringly, a more joined up way of defining what has always been at the heart of the academic publishing world. As Brown admitted, 'communities of practice are not simply about individual and social relationships and information sharing. They also lie at the heart of scholarly communication and serve as the lifeblood of any business model.' These relationships are, he believes, 'utterly essential for the survival and flourishing of university presses'.[71] This is a view underlined by Crossick, who concluded his report by reflecting on the willingness of the academic community to engage with his work: 'It is important that this engagement continues, because there is much to gain by working with the grain, and much to be lost by not doing so.'[72] This, and John Thompson's contrasting comment at the start of this chapter, neatly bookend the changes of the past hundred years or so in academic publishing history: today there is a much broader range of participants in the field, and a greater awareness of the need for all partners, whether academics, librarians, policy makers, booksellers or publishers, to work together to ensure academic research continues to be disseminated widely, to acknowledge the value-added contribution each makes to the system of scholarly communication, and to innovate collaboratively to protect the future sustainability and availability of that research.

---

68 Crossick, *Monographs and open access*, p. 4.
69 Brown, 'University press forum 2011', p. 9.   70 *Ibid.*, p. 13.   71 *Ibid*, p. 9.
72 Crossick, *Monographs and open access*, p. 70.

18

Journals (STM and humanities)

MICHAEL MABE AND ANTHONY WATKINSON

Learned journals, which are different from books and magazines, form one segment of the wider group of periodicals and the even wider group of what librarians call serials.[1] These are journals primarily concerned with communication between scholars. They are owned sometimes by learned and professional societies and associations and sometimes by commercial companies, but most of the former are actually published by partners who may be for-profit or not-for-profit. There are a few important hybrids between journals and magazines, some such as *Nature* covering key scientific advances, others found in the professional sphere, particularly in medicine, such as the *British Medical Journal* and the *Lancet*. During the twentieth century, publications intended both as a vehicle for scholarship and as a source of enlightenment for the educated lay public gradually disappeared. Professional publications, which sometimes contain peer reviewed articles, have never quite slipped away, but in many disciplines societies have split their main publication so that the learned journal is separate from the professional magazine.

The origin of the main features of the modern learned journal lies in the seventeenth century when Henry Oldenburg (1619–77) created the world's first research journal (*Philosophical Transactions* from 1665) as first Joint Secretary of the newly founded Royal Society of London. The four functions of Oldenburg's journal – registration of new research, dissemination, peer review and archival record – are so fundamental to empirical scholarship that during the period under consideration journals, even those published electronically in the twenty-first century, have conformed to Oldenburg's model.[2]

The structure of the scholarly paper established in the sciences eventually became the norm in almost all disciplines.[3] The format of an introduction,

---

1 Meadows, *Communicating research*, pp. 6–8.   2 Mabe, 'Scholarly publishing', pp. 4–6.
3 Gross *et al.*, *Communicating science*, p. 230.

methods and materials, results, discussion and references, all preceded by an abstract, has become standard. In this chapter science is taken to cover engineering and medicine and the quantitative social sciences; journals in the humanities are not mentioned specifically except when there are distinct differences to note. As a 2015 report emphasised, monographs were and have remained 'a vitally important and distinctive vehicle for research communication' in the humanities.[4]

The way in which journals have been paid for and distributed has become significantly different from the book supply chain during the course of the twentieth century. Subscriptions diverged from other forms of prepayment. By the start of the period a subscription, at least in the publishing world, came to mean something that happened annually and most often for a defined number of issues. By the 1960s specialist subscription agents became central to library purchasing of journals, and bookshop share of the market declined.[5] The shift from print to online as the basic form for publishing journals has, since the late 1990s, led to a decline in business for these intermediaries and a new relationship between publishers and librarians.

Most journal publishers in the first half of the twentieth century were also printers, and for many, such as Taylor & Francis, journals sustained the printing business as a reliable source of copy.[6] Journals did have higher production costs, partly because of the need to maintain efficient schedules, and in the last quarter of the last century this led to a move offshore first with composition and then with manufacture. Blackwell Science took the lead in the UK in the 1990s following the Dutch giant Elsevier. The trick lay in maximising cost savings from rationalised work-flows integrated with suppliers and automated and standardised processes, which, as well as saving money, enabled greater efficiency, accuracy and speed in delivery online.

During the period covered in this chapter the importance of journals to publishers and libraries, as well as researchers, increased first gradually, and then much faster after the 1950s. Reciprocally, books became less important in the sciences. In 2010 it was claimed that UK journal publishers employed 10,000 people, 10 per cent of the world total.[7] Publishers Association statistics for 2014 showed revenue from journals up to over one billion pounds.[8]

---

4 Crossick, *Monographs and open access*.
5 Frederikkson, *A century of science publishing*, chapter 23.
6 Brock and Meadows, *The lamp of learning*, p. 196.
7 Richardson and Taylor, *PA guide*, pp. 32, 34.   8 *PA statistics yearbook 2014*, pp. 81–3.

1914–1945

In the first half of the twentieth century, Cambridge University Press and Macmillan continued to be the two main publishers of journals, with Longman, Taylor & Francis and Oxford University Press also important players. For many publishers, however, journal publishing was conducted only as a support for book publishing. (Longman had cut back on journal publishing by 1980; the *English Historical Review* remained until 1997 when it was transferred to OUP. In 2014 only the two university presses remained in British ownership.[9]) Most British journals continued to be owned by learned societies or other non-profit organisations such as trusts and foundations. They usually partnered with publishers, mainly for printing services. During this period these journals, with a few exceptions, were essentially a vehicle for the publications of society members and were dependent on their financial support. Institutional subscriptions were often charged at the same rate as non-member subscriptions, with appropriate postage added if overseas.

There was an unsurprising drop-off in the number of articles being submitted to journals during the First World War, as there was to be in the Second World War.[10] Cambridge University Press, however, saw a rapid increase in the number of pages accepted by their journals from 1918.[11] There is no reason to suppose other journals had a significantly different experience. There were no major innovations during the following three decades and no leap forward in the number of new titles. New twentieth-century journals emerged mainly as a result of increasing specialisation and the creation of new research groups. Entrepreneurial scholars got together to start a new journal, rather than a society making a decision to do so as had been the case before 1914. Such 'private journals', as McKitterick describes them,[12] seem to have been more agile during the twentieth century, whether they constitutionally became an association (*Mind*), a limited company (*British Journal of Surgery*) or a trust (*New Phytologist*). Examples of major medical journals started in the first half of the twentieth century, as clinical specialties became more important, were the *British Journal of Anaesthesia* (1929) and the *British Journal of Urology* – now *BJUI* (1929).

The two major British self-publishing learned bodies of today, the Institute of Physics (IOP) and the Royal Society of Chemistry (RSC), did not immediately emerge as major publishers in this period. The IOP was founded in 1921, partly as a response to the emergence of physicists as a recognised

9 Briggs, *A history of Longmans*, p. 436.   10 McKitterick, *A history*, p. 289.
11 *Ibid.*, p. 214.   12 *Ibid.*, p. 509.

professional group during the First World War, and slowly started publishing journals from 1922. The RSC in its present form only came into being in 1980 and is the heir to four organisations all founded before 1914. Another emerging discipline was economics, with the *Economic Journal* founded in 1902. The leading mathematical society (London Mathematical Society) added only one journal in this period, in 1926, to supplement the *Proceedings*, an example of the continued move away from the idea of journal papers reflecting presentations at meetings. The Royal Statistical Society started a 'supplemental journal' in 1934, almost a century after their first journal venture. Some society journals such as the *Journal of Physiology* (a subject in which, over our period, British research was unusually fruitful) did move towards a position of international importance, but on the whole 'membership' journals did not attain the global importance that American journals achieved.

1945–1995

During this period the landscape of journal publishing changed dramatically with the gradual replacement of German by English as the language of scholarship and also the increasing internationalism of scholarship.

A government initiative to take advantage of the weakness of German science as a result of the war, and policies under the Nazis leading up to the war, did not succeed.[13] In any case, by 1950 German publishers began to revive.[14] In science, it became recognised that journals founded in accordance with the German model of journal publishing, with international editorial boards and interest in submissions from throughout the world, were likely to become the journals of choice for the best papers. Most of the new commercial British companies absorbed this lesson quicker than the older-established publishers.

The model was introduced into Britain after the war by immigrants originally from Germany, mainly of Jewish origin, either indirectly through the arrival of Academic Press and Wiley Interscience from the USA, or directly with the creation of Pergamon Press by Robert Maxwell. Elsevier had a related but different trajectory of growth. The other two big European players, Wolters Kluwer and Springer, had only small publishing presences in Britain until the twenty-first century. Kluwer, using the imprint of Lippincott,

---

13 Jones, *Butterworths*, chapter 28.
14 Frederikkson, *A century of science publishing*, chapter 3.

Williams & Wilkins, remained small but respected. Springer became important in the UK in the next century.

These were the decades of growth for some journal publishers, and during the 1960s and 1970s in particular it seemed to them that every new journal had a market. Cox describes how during the earlier decade he was able to grow institutional subscriptions by 5–10 per cent per year in his role as subscription manager for Pergamon Press.[15] Fredriksson, who worked for Elsevier/North-Holland during this period, concurs.[16]

The massive investment in research throughout the developed world both during the war and in the following Cold War led to a demand for more outlets for articles recording this research. The early growth was in the 'big science' directly related to defence, particularly in physics.[17] However, Maxwell foresaw the growth in biology in the 1970s and started new journals accordingly. New communities were growing up as disciplines sub-divided, but the big learned societies organised around the undivided disciplines usually failed to cater for the new groups of researchers. In sciences and medicine, in particular, new commercial publishers often filled the gap.

The most important British journals publisher founded in Britain after the war was indeed Pergamon Press.[18] Robert Maxwell, it has been argued, brought 'Springer know-how and techniques of aggressive publishing in science' to British publishing.[19] Iain Stevenson rightly points out that he adopted the practices of German publishing, including blind peer review and the structure of editorial board and regional editors.[20] Such practices were also and independently being brought into English-language journal publishing by Academic Press and John Wiley (though less enthusiastically), and particularly and even more vigorously by Elsevier-North Holland (see below). When Pergamon Press was sold to Elsevier in 1991 (six months before Maxwell's death), 418 journal titles were transferred.[21] It is not possible to determine how many of these titles were published from Britain.

The influence of the two major US scholarly publishers – Academic Press (AP) and John Wiley & Sons – is less obvious than that of Pergamon. They both started publishing in Britain around 1960. AP quickly established three major journals in new fields with highly visible editors-in-chief, all of which became large and profitable: *Journal of Molecular Biology* (Kendrew), *Journal of*

15 Cox, *The Pergamon phenomenon*, p. 275.
16 Frederikkson, *A century of science publishing*, p. 62.
17 Mabe and Amin, 'Growth dynamics'.   18 Cahn, 'The origins of the Pergamon Press'.
19 Haines, *Maxwell*.   20 Stevenson, *Book makers*, p. 142.
21 Cox, *The Pergamon phenomenon*, p. 278.

Sound and Vibration (Doak) and *Journal of Theoretical Biology* (Danielli).[22] Charles Hutt, the first managing director of AP London, and his successor Roger Farrand, also partnered with leading learned societies such as the Linnean Society of London and the Zoological Society of London, both with well-established journals. Such was the nature of publishing accountancy in these years that it was not realised by the AP board until after 1980 that its journals represented profits while its books did little more than break even. By that stage there were over fifty journal titles based in London but growth slowed. In 2001 the company, by then fully integrated into what had become Harcourt General, was bought by Elsevier.

Wiley, founded in 1807, acquired Interscience in 1961 – a company founded by Maurits Dekker and Eric Proskauer, who were also refugees from the Nazis.[23] Until exposed to the influence of Proskauer, Wiley does not appear to have considered the possibility of setting up new journals. The official history suggests 'Wiley seemed to think that the seven years it took a journal to be profitable was a bit long to wait.'[24] The merger bought ten significant titles, but Wiley did not get seriously into journals publishing from its Chichester office until the appointment of John Jarvis (from Elsevier) in 1979, after which it issued several new journals a year.[25]

In 2015 Elsevier was in a different category from all other journal publishers in terms of sheer number of titles, even though its first international journal was only founded in 1947.[26] The merger with North-Holland led to a combined list of eighty-eight titles, some of them very large, and from then the start-up of new journals and (in those days) the developments of partnerships with international learned societies were vigorously and efficiently addressed.[27] Elsevier became the model for other publishing houses to follow or react against. Elsevier Applied Science in Barking was set up under Leslie Rayner in 1961 and there were small offices in Oxford and Cambridge, but before 1991 the company did not regard Britain as a publishing centre. After 1991 the combination of the lists of Elsevier and Pergamon Press made it the largest British company in the sector.

Older-established British publishers were not much interested in journals. Norman Franklin, who joined Routledge in 1949 and almost immediately launched the *British Journal of Sociology*, recorded: 'I was keen on journals but the editorial staff looked down on them as uncreative.'[28] (Routledge as

---

22 Brown, 'The move of US publishers overseas'. 23 Beschler, 'The immigrants', p. 153.
24 Jacobson, *Knowledge for generations*, p. 220. 25 *Ibid.*, p. 295.
26 *A short history of Elsevier*. 27 Andriesse, *Dutch messengers*, p. 183.
28 Personal communication with Norman Franklin, 2012.

a journal publisher now flourishes as part of Taylor & Francis.) Noel Hughes became managing director of Chapman & Hall in 1966 and, in spite of internal opposition, founded the immensely successful *Journal of Materials Science*[29] and a small number of other titles, including the monthly *Applied Economics* – an early example of the application of models drawn from science publishing to the social sciences and humanities, a process which continued throughout the rest of the century and beyond. Both Routledge (from 1985) and Chapman & Hall were part of Associated Book Publishers, bought and subsequently energised by the Canadian-owned Thomson Corporation in 1987.

Some journals started before the 1970s did become extremely profitable later in the century and came to underpin whole publishing programmes. Examples include the *Journal of Materials Science* and the *Journal of Molecular Biology*, already mentioned, and the *Biochemical Journal* published by the Biochemical Society. Success depended on increasing the number of pages to absorb the continued increase in research, having the mechanism for building up institutional subscriptions worldwide by cooperation with sub-scription agents, and increasing the prices pro rata. Most humanities journals remain smaller (quarterlies) and less profitable.

During this period, the two main university presses failed to invest in journals, and although in 1947 Cambridge published thirty-six titles,[30] and gradually increased the number, it also gradually lost its once predominant position in the UK. During this period, however, Cambridge did publish their wholly owned *Journal of Fluid Mechanics* from 1956, which became the leading title in its field. In 1967 it was already clear that journals were a good business for the Press[31] but somehow, until much later in the period, Cambridge did not compete well with the commercial publishers. Oxford, whose first journal (the *Quarterly Journal of Medicine*) was not started until 1907, was publishing forty-five titles in 1971, but during the following decade numbers of titles declined, and there was a draconian control on budgets to avoid increases in prices. Under the leadership of Robin Denniston and Richard Charkin, however, there was significant growth in the late 1980s. In two years alone (1986 and 1987) thirty journals, either as take-overs or as new starts, were added. The big step forward, nonetheless, came in 1988 with the purchase of IRL Press, and by the end of the decade the OUP journal list had grown to over a hundred titles.[32]

29 Personal communication with Professor William Bonfield, 2011.
30 McKitterick, *A history*, p. 312.   31 *Ibid.*, p. 409.
32 Martin Richardson, 'Growth of journal publishing', unpublished paper.

Butterworth, seen by other UK scholarly publishers as the firm that 'did' journals,[33] established a total of about eighty UK titles during this period, many of them representing the growing demand for academic research in technical subjects. Macmillan's post-war experience, in contrast, was not one of growth. Some key journals such as *Brain* and the *Economic Journal* were, indeed, lost to other publishers. There was a significant development in 1971 when Dr John Maddox, editor 1966–73 and 1980–95, began the 'leveraging of the brand' by starting *Nature New Biology* and *Nature Physical Science*.[34] This prefigured much more important developments after 1995. The growth, mainly by acquisition from a relatively small base, of Taylor & Francis is also a matter for discussion in the next section: its number of journal titles rose from thirty-eight in 1984 to 130 in 1996 and 150 in 1998.[35]

More important were the two Blackwell publishing companies.[36] Both were founded before the Second World War. Blackwell Scientific Publications published its first journal (the *British Journal of Haematology*) in 1955, but even twenty-five years later had fewer than fifty-five on its list. The explosion came in the 1980s under Bob Campbell, who identifies 1987 as the moment when Blackwell Science really embraced journals.[37] Blackwell Publishers, publishing in the social sciences and the humanities, showed a similar trajectory, reaching one hundred titles before its sister. Its success in achieving acceptable profitability, while actively seeking partnership with small learned society publishers, was partly due to careful spending and the use of automated production processes wherever possible. By 1995 Blackwell Publishers had over 200 journal titles and Blackwell Science had over 150 and continued to take on more journals.[38] Both companies specialised in working as partners for learned societies, and their systems were organised to cater for the needs of such bodies and their publication committees. Whereas in the nineteenth century and the first half of the twentieth century publishers usually provided services to learned societies on a commission basis, the Blackwell companies and other commercial partners tended to publish for society owners on the basis of a royalty on revenue or a share of profits.

33 Personal communication with Noel Hughes, former Managing Director of Chapman & Hall, 1991.
34 Information provided by Alysoun Sanders, archivist at Macmillan Publishers.
35 Brock and Meadows, *The lamp of learning*, p. vii.
36 Norrington, *Blackwell's 1879–1979*.
37 Personal communication with Bob Campbell, former Managing Director of Blackwell Science, 2012.
38 Lafaye, *Blackwell Publishing*, p. 9.

These sorts of partnerships led to both parties having a stake in the development of the journals.

Another publisher founded on medicine but, unlike Blackwell Science, remaining purely in that discipline was Churchill Livingstone, a merger of two existing companies in 1971. By 1995 they had about fifty British journals, many of which had been created in the previous decade.[39] Other medical publishers, for example the *British Medical Journal*, were much less significant, although the *BMJ* became a serious innovator later in the century.

British learned societies gradually added journals and new societies started with journals. Most partnered with commercial publishers or one of the university presses. An exception was the Geological Society which, having worked with a number of partners from 1811, formed its own publishing house in 1988.

'Electronic' publishing was much discussed before the 1990s and there were several experiments with journals in the 1980s.[40] By 1992 the potential of the Web as a vehicle for putting journal articles online was recognised. British publishers led transformative developments in this area. Deborah Kahn at Chapman & Hall worked with nascent Adobe software (PDF) and had PDF full text and SGML headers journals online during 1993 as part of the CAJUN project.[41] David Pullinger at the Institute of Physics Publishing put the first journal articles on the Web in HTML at about the same time.

Post-1995

The period from 1995 has one main theme: that of the digital revolution and its impact on journals publishing. Changes affected librarians and researchers as well as publishers. Since 1995 it can be argued that British journals gradually became less important in the scholarly world as a whole. *Nature* and the *Lancet* held their ground against mainly US competition but they are in their different ways unrepresentative. Nevertheless many of the developments in the period were pioneered by British companies and organisations.

The big companies quickly discovered that bundles of discrete articles lent themselves to easy digitisation and hence monetisation.[42] In 1995 Academic Press prompted the Higher Education Funding Council for England and Wales (HEFCE), which worked out the Pilot Site License Initiative (PSLI).

39 Personal communication from Sally Morris, former Journals Director, 2011.
40 Pullinger, 'Journals published on the net', and Shackel and Pullinger, *Blend 1*.
41 Smith *et al.*, 'Journal publishing with Acrobat'.
42 Thompson, *Books in the digital age*, p. 322.

The idea was to use the opportunities created by online publishing to achieve a lower unit price per article and break out of the spiral of ever increasing costs.[43] AP, Institute of Physics Publishing and the two Blackwell companies contributed 457 electronic versions in PDF from (in some cases) a standing start.[44] One direct result of PSLI was that British journal publishers became more used to working together in pre-competitive activities. The incoming publishers like Academic Press and Wiley with experience of US anti-trust legislation had been resistant to most forms of collaboration.

The project was successful and led on to the National Electronic Site Licensing Initiative (NESLI) in 1998 under the control of the Joint Information Services Committee (Jisc), itself a subset of HEFCE.[45] NESLI acted as a huge national consortium offering deals to the academic library community, and between 1996 and 1968 Jisc offered twenty-one companies an opportunity of collaborating on the Super Journal project.[46] Research from the project concluded that scholars wanted more e-journals and 'the ability to browse, search, and print'. Most publishers had entered the project expecting that the authors wanted to use multimedia, but desktop access proved more desirable.

An initiative from AP led to the first commercial 'Big Deal' starting in 1998. Under its terms, AP sold a package or 'bundle' containing all their research journals to a consortium of libraries (OhioLINK), which then gave online access to all a publisher's journals for a surcharge on the price of print subscriptions.[47] For AP and OhioLINK the signing of the contract was a win/win for both parties and academic users, and subsequently Big Deals became the main way in which larger and medium-sized publishers sold journals to libraries.[48] The casualties of the new arrangement were monograph purchasers and the journals of smaller publishers. Academics became used to the hugely increased access. However, squeezed budgets in the twenty-first century led to librarians seeking changes to the model, especially a freeze on pricing and more flexibility.[49] The push towards open access, discussed below, also stemmed from concerns with pricing. New procedures and infrastructures were developed to enable electronic bundles, for example giving access to individual library users first by passwords but soon through

43 Follett, *Joint Funding Council's libraries review group report*.
44 Hitchcock *et al.*, 'Web journals publishing', p. 288.   45 White, 'From PSLO to NESLI'.
46 Pullinger and Baldwin, *Electronic journals and user behaviour*.
47 Velterop, 'Keeping the minutes', pp. 16–17.
48 Ware and Mabe, 'The STM report', pp. 20–2.
49 See www.stm-publishing.com/wiley-announces-new-agreement-with-jisc-collections and www.jisc.ac.uk/news/springer-and-jisc-reach-agreement-31-mar-2015.

IP addresses. These transitions were expensive, but a fully formed platform was provided by Elsevier's Science Direct in 1997, the first and biggest of many.

As earlier sections have detailed, many learned societies had traditionally worked with publishing partners, but others self-published. For this latter group the costs of going online were often prohibitive. The creation of Stanford University's HighWire Press in 1995 proved a natural home.[50] By 1998 British society publishers joined, beginning with the *British Medical Journal* and the *Society for the Study of Reproduction*. Most important was the finalisation in that year of a continuing relationship with Oxford University Press and subsequently the commercial company Sage in 2004.[51] Most commercial publishers either developed their own platforms or worked with commercial hosting companies.[52] Smaller companies building substantial journal lists during the 1990s were Emerald and Sage, with 300 and 400 UK-based journals respectively, mainly in the social sciences.[53]

During the twenty-first century, the biggest journal publishers have got bigger. The years 1995–2005 were a period of 'accelerated growth for Sage'. The acquisition of Technomic in 2001, bringing more than twenty engineering journals, and of Hodder's Arnold Journals in 2006 'established Sage firmly in STM publishing'.[54] Further acquisitions meant that by 2016 Sage published over one thousand journals, more than 400 on behalf of learned societies and institutions.[55] After its 1998 flotation, Taylor & Francis more than doubled in size with the acquisition of companies including the Routledge Group and, with 220 journals, Carfax. Since 2004, they have been owned by the US group Informa. In 2002 AP and Churchill Livingstone journals (as part of Harcourt General) came into Elsevier hands and hence into Science Direct, making it an even bigger bundle. The competition commission report which gave the go-ahead for the deal indicated that Elsevier was over twice as big in terms of revenue as its nearest competitor.[56] The acquisition of Blackwell Publishing by John Wiley & Sons was completed in 2006, to create the other very large UK-based journals publisher.[57] At the time of the merger, a significant

50 Keller, 'Science, scholarship and internet publishing'.
51 http://.highwire.stanford.edu/announce/details.dtl?journalcode=sagepub.
52 Jacobson *et al.*, *Knowledge for generations*, pp. 370–2.
53 *The Sage story*, available at http://connection.sagepub.com/wp-content/uploads/2013/08/SAGE-STORY.pdf.
54 *Ibid.*   55 https://us.sagepub.com/en-us/nam/Journals.
56 Competition Commission, *Reed Elsevier plc and Harcourt General Inc: a report on the proposed merger* (2001).
57 Jacobson *et al.*, *Knowledge for generations*, pp. 432–9.

proportion of the 1,200 journals were published from the UK, with half the total journal programme owned by learned societies, professional associations and other not-for-profit entities.

In 2015 there was a merger of Springer Science and Business Media (the owner of BioMed Central since 2008) with Macmillan Science and Education to create Springer Nature. The Macmillan Group, the owners of *Nature*, had been particularly innovative both in embracing the digital opportunities and in adapting their structures for profitable growth. There was an increase to nearly forty *Nature*-branded journals, and a range of experiments in reaching out and providing for the needs of the research community were continued in the separate company Digital Science, which remains outside the merger arrangements. These mergers and takeovers have on the whole strengthened the British component of international companies, in terms of both staff numbers and journals published.

The biggest contribution of the publishing community to making digital journals was the foundation of CrossRef.[58] CrossRef, which soon after its start became Oxford-based, was based on the Digital Object Identifier (DOI) which 'held the key to a broad-based and efficient journal reference linking system'.[59] CrossRef also presented a model for other collaborations, such as COUNTER initiative, which enabled standardised usage statistics from 2002.[60]

Cooperation among publishers has become customary. The International Association of Science, Technical and Medical Publishers (STM), founded in 1968 in Amsterdam and now headquartered in Oxford, is the international representative of both not-for-profit and commercial journal publishing.[61] STM works closely on national and European concerns with the UK Publishers Association (PA), which has its own dedicated committee, and the Association of Learned and Professional Society Publishers, which since 1972 represents self-publishing society publishers.

Since the turn of the century the digital form of the journal has become normative. Print versions continue to be in demand for traditional journals from some libraries and society members, but they are perceived as 'legacy', and eventually due to die away. It has become standard to produce both PDF

---

58 *Formation of CrossRef,* http://www.crossref.org/08downloads/CrossRef10Years.pdf, p. 11.
59 www.crossref.org.
60 www.projectcounter.org/about.html. For what it means for librarians, see Morris *et al.,* *The handbook,* pp. 164–5.
61 Andriesse, *Dutch messengers,* pp. 244–7.

and HTML formats.[62] Some users still print out but want to link online. Since the late 1990s publishers have gradually adopted electronic online systems (EOS) to enable quicker and more efficient ways of receiving submitted 'manuscripts', peer reviewing them, and (more recently) passing accepted manuscripts through to the production system.[63] XML enables semantic enrichment which aids discovery of the individual article or part of it. The form of the article did not change for many years, but by the 2010s, the enhanced 'article of the future' had begun to be taken up.[64]

Open access is the most important development taking advantage of a digital-only model. The principle that information should be free is widely supported by librarians and researchers, and those wishing to access academic research outside the academy.[65] Some in the academic community believe that the business model for scholarly communication is broken and needs to be transformed, as costs of journal bundles have grown exponentially, leading to protests among the academic community.[66] The first important open access initiative in the UK, however, and the first commercial open access company in the world, was BioMed Central (BMC), founded in 2000 by the visionary Vitek Tracz in London. BMC published its first journal in 2001. Another landmark was the conversion of the major scientific journal *Nucleic Acid Research* (owned by OUP) to complete open access in 2005.[67] More recently, the majority of British companies and organisations have started open access journals programmes, and also enabled open access articles in all their journals (the 'hybrid' model).

The increase in the number of open access journals (the 'Gold' route to open access) has been consistent but slower than many expected, as the Directory of Open Access Journals (DOAJ) demonstrates.[68] Researchers making their articles available via open access by placing them in a subject or institutional repository – the 'Green' route – has also been slow.[69] However, strict mandates from both private research funders such as the Wellcome Trust[70] and, under government encouragement, the UK Research

62 Boeing, 'Editorial and production workflows'.
63 Ware, 'Online submission and peer review systems'.
64 www.articleofthefuture.com and Aalbersberg, 'Bringing digital science deep inside the scientific article'.
65 Suber, *Open access*; Eve, *Open access and the humanities*.
66 Ryam Crow, 'The case for institutional repositories: a SPARC position paper', *ARL Bimonthly Report* 223 (2002), http://sparcopen.org/wp-content/uploads/2016/01/instr epo.pdf.
67 Bird, 'Oxford Journals' adventures'.   68 www.doaj.org.
69 Ware and Mabe, *The STM report*, pp. 88–131.
70 www.wellcome.ac.uk/about-us/policy/spotlight-issues/Open-access/index.htm.

Councils are changing the UK picture.[71] At present, revenue from subscription income is holding up, judging by the recent financial results from the larger publishers, and open access is (not yet) the default position. The gold route is funded by author publishing charges (APCs) paid to publishers via funders. UK Funders have emphasised that open access is not just about access but is also concerned with enabling reuse. They are mandating a CC BY licence for APC-funded publications, which has caused some concern among humanities researchers who fear loss of control over their content.[72]

Peer review has been a sine qua non of journal publishing throughout the period covered by this chapter, and open access journals which use peer review are trusted.[73] One open access publisher has introduced a new model of peer review (PLOS One) whereby the article is judged on its methodology rather than its importance. The model proved so successful that in 2014 the journal was the largest in terms of articles published, and other publishers had started competitors.[74] Other new models have been less successful so far. Scholarly communication in the twenty-first century has developed to incorporate social media such as blogs and Twitter, and tools such as Altmetrics have been developed to quantify the dissemination of research. In addition the digital environment has enabled sharing on an unprecedented scale through sites such as ResearchGate and Academia.edu. The emphasis on demonstrating the broader 'impact' of scholarly research in society, as well as the desire to communicate research findings rapidly, has been enabled by digital technologies. It might have been expected that the journal would suffer as a means of communication in the digital world but this has proved not to be the case. Researchers (and audit mechanisms such as the Research Excellence Framework) put journals in a category quite separate from social media. Publishers and libraries have worried that researchers would cease to go to the collection that libraries had paid for or to the site of the publisher because Google (the main means of discovery) would show them other places where the article is located. However, research has shown that, when citing, scholars use the publisher's site to check the record.[75] Like many areas of publishing in the twenty-first century, journals publishers find themselves, their business models, their platforms and their modes of

---

71 www.researchinfonet.org/finch; and www.rcuk.ac.uk/documents/documents/rcuko penaccesspolicy-pdf.
72 Vincent and Wickham, *Debating open access.* 73 Nicholas *et al.*, 'Peer review'.
74 Bo-Christer Bjork, 'Have the "mega-journals" reached the limits to growth?', *PeerJ* 26 May 2015, https://peerj.com/articles/981, table 2.
75 Morris *et al.*, *The handbook*, pp. 123–6.

dissemination and discovery under a period of significant pressure and change. Given the numerous stakeholders and significant business interests within journals publishing, it is likely that these changes will continue for some time yet.[76]

76 Cope and Phillips (eds.), *The future of the academic journal*. Given the rapidly evolving nature of the scholarly publishing environment, further changes have already occurred in the market sector since delivery of this chapter. The 2018 STM report by the present authors provides an outline of some of these changes at the time of going to press. See https://www.stm-assoc.org/2018_10_04_STM_Report_2018.pdf.

19

Information, reference and government publishing

SUSAN PICKFORD

Information and reference

Information and reference publishing is something of a Cinderella topic in book history, often overlooked for more 'glamorous' sectors. Yet a 2009 US market survey noted that reference publishing (dictionaries and encyclopaedias) was a significant export market worth an annual $28 million to the British economy,[1] while the information publishing sector (represented in the present chapter by 'how-to' books and travel guidebooks) boasts some of the global publishing industry's most identifiable brands. As a 1948 Library Association guide to reference material noted, however, 'One of the difficulties facing the student of this subject is that there are an enormous number of reference books in existence', from dictionaries and bibliographies to atlases and yearbooks.[2] Another challenge is that time-dependent information publishing is logically issued largely in little-studied ephemeral or periodical formats, such as the *Radio Times*. This makes full coverage of what is a very large and diverse field of publishing a challenging task. The present chapter does not seek to cover the entire field in comprehensive detail, but attempts to tease out some of the key developments over the period, focussing on specific sub-genres which are held to be representative of the trends and issues that have arisen over the course of the twentieth century and beyond.

Some of today's most respected works of reference have their roots in Victorian mass literacy and attitudes to self-improvement,[3] not to mention the can-do approach to large-scale projects – the *Oxford English dictionary*

---

1 Parker, *The 2009 import and export market*, p. 11.
2 Roberts, *Introduction to reference books*, p. vi.
3 Older titles include the *Encyclopaedia Britannica*, launched in 1768, and *Burke's peerage*, first published in 1826. *Who's who* dates from 1849.

(OED), commissioned in 1879 and completed in 1928, was an achievement to rival a nation-wide rail network. Familiar titles such as *Whitaker's almanac* (1868), *Brewer's dictionary of phrase and fable* (1870), *Grove's dictionary of music* (1879–89) and *Fowler's dictionary of modern English usage* (1926, based on the 1906 *The King's English*) all sprang from individual attempts to document one particular area of expertise. Such works were regularly updated in new editions over the course of the twentieth century.

Successive editions of reference works shed light on changing attitudes to language and to wider social issues. Dictionaries are an interesting case in point. Britain long had its own lexicographical heritage, distinct from the more encyclopaedic American tradition, though the two have merged in recent decades. One example of these changing attitudes is the way British dictionaries have broadly shifted from prescriptive (deeming what was standard or acceptable language) to descriptive (describing language as it was actually used) over the course of the period. Where Daniel Jones's *English pronouncing dictionary* (first edition 1917) held up 'public school pronunciation' as the standard as late as 1937, the less socially connoted 'standard southern British'[4] is now preferred, recording, rather than stipulating, how words are pronounced (though typically northern English pronunciations of words such as 'bath' were only given official phonetic recognition in 2001, in the *Oxford dictionary of pronunciation*). Evolving dictionary definitions are similarly of interest to social historians, from the 1921 *Chambers's twentieth-century dictionary* definition of 'Woman' as 'The female of man' and the 1948 *Learner's dictionary of current English* definition of 'Imperialism' as 'the policy of maintaining the safety and protecting the welfare of the various parts of an empire', to the 1965 *Penguin English dictionary*'s decision to include a lemma for 'Fuck'.

A similar trend is apparent in encyclopaedic works. In the first edition of George Grove's *A dictionary of music and musicians* (1878–89), the classical tradition reigned supreme; by its fifth edition in 1954, the canon had expanded to include jazz, folk and non-Western music. The liberalisation of post-war social attitudes is likewise reflected in the place of women in works of bibliographical reference. The first edition of the *Dictionary of national biography* (*DNB*, 1885) featured 34,533 men and 1,518 women (or 4 per cent), often included as spouses or mothers rather than in their own right; the publication of a 'Missing Persons' volume in 1994 included a further 130 women in 1,086 new entries (though this still only represents 12 per cent). The editors of the

---

4 Cowie (ed.), *Oxford history of English lexicography*, p. 188.

2004 *Oxford dictionary of national biography*, recognising that women were still under-represented, made a concerted effort to include typically female spheres of endeavour such as nursing and charity work in their purview: the final dictionary included entries on 5,627 women.

Reliability of content was – and is – the stock in trade of both reference and information publishing. If compiling a dictionary is an endeavour comparable to building a rail network, then ensuring its ongoing relevance is comparable to the need for constant track maintenance. Fittingly, perhaps, one high-profile Victorian publication to fall victim to the twentieth century's capacity for improving the flow of information was Bradshaw's railway timetable. As the number of individual rail companies fell from well over one hundred at the turn of the century to four in 1923 and then one following nationalisation in 1948, timetabling issues became far less complex and rail companies were able to produce their own comprehensive, reliable tables, leading Bradshaw to close in 1961.

Some works had to achieve annual updates to stay relevant, notably travel guides such as Thomas Cook's *Continental timetable* and the biographical compendium *Who's Who*. Being up-to-date was less of an issue elsewhere, perhaps most notably in the *DNB*, which recorded lives past – fortunately so, since a second edition was a daunting prospect: the process of revision, launched in 1992, was completed in 2004. Responsiveness to current events was a considerable challenge for encyclopaedias, however, and one that could undermine the reputation for reliability that was the essence of their brand: the *Encyclopaedia Britannica* (which, though American-owned since 1901, maintained a London presence and put out a yearbook for British readers for part of the period) still put the Jewish population of Tarnow, Poland, at 40 per cent as late as 1958.[5] This was due in part to the decision to adopt a policy of ongoing revision in the early 1940s. The strategy proved unsatisfactory, as conflicting information was given in updated and non-updated entries. *Chambers's encyclopaedia* chose the alternative strategy for its fourth edition in 1967, evenly revising all entries – though a contemporary study of one hundred articles selected at random found that only fifteen had been substantially altered, and events as significant as the deaths of John F. Kennedy and Winston Churchill and decolonisation across Africa were barely touched on, if at all.[6]

By the mid-1960s, the expectation was that works of reference would be no more than a year or two out of date: one review of American librarian

---

5 Einbinder, *The myth of the Britannica*.   6 Walford, *Guide to reference material*, p. 90.

Constance Winchell's *Guide to reference books* states that 'the most disappoint-ing feature of this new edition is the closing date for entries of 1964, which is extraordinary for a reference work published in mid-1967'.[7] It took two years to produce a 600-page encyclopaedia in the early 1970s: by 1976, it took less than half the time to produce a 3,000-page, three-volume set.[8] By the late 1980s it was becoming possible for reference works to record events within weeks: David Crystal has written amusingly of how he took Mrs Thatcher's resignation, two days before the deadline for an encyclopaedia he was editing, as a personal affront.[9] Nowadays, online resources are updated within minutes.

The speed with which reference works were able to update their material reflects two significant developments: the advent of computing and the concomitant rise of the age of information. Information had long been growing in importance as a commodity, providing reference and information publishing with its raw material and creating a market for the finished product. Specialist information provision was becoming big business. By 1963, there were 1,855 independent abstracting and indexing companies worldwide, such as the American giant H. W. Wilson (founded 1898).[10] These joined numerous similar services run by and for professional bodies: the Bureau of Chemical Abstracts, founded by the Chemical Society in 1926, is one British example. One work whose roots lie firmly in the commodification of information is the *Guinness book of records*, first published in 1955, which grew out of the business founded by twin brothers Norris and Ross McWhirter in 1951 to supply to publishers and advertisers facts and figures on everything, from the fastest tennis serve to the longest fur on a cat. The brothers' father was a newspaper editor; they attributed their passion for trivia to the numerous reference books he kept at home. The partnership with Guinness was the brainchild of the brewing company's managing director, Sir Hugh Beaver, who realised that pubs and trivia were a natural fit: the first edition was advertised as a 'tool for settling arguments'. The concept proved an immediate success, with sales of 187,000 within four months, eventually giving rise to spin-off television programmes and publications based on subsets of record categories such as sports.[11]

The advent of computing enabled vast quantities of raw data to be handled, leading to the professionalisation of information treatment, as indicated by the launch of the journal *Information Manager* in 1978: the

---

7 *Ibid.*, p. 86.   8 Tobin, 'The book that built Gale Research', p. 94.
9 Crystal, *Just a phrase*, p. 223.   10 Kovecci, 'Solution to information problems', p. 217.
11 Whittington, 'Unbeatable', p. 139.

cover tagline for the first issue, 'Coping with the information explosion', hints at contemporary anxieties about the proliferation of information and the need for professional expertise in controlling it.[12] The computer age revolutionised reference and information publishing alike, not only radically reducing publication schedules, but also vastly increasing the ready availability of data, and changing the way books were produced. The creation of central databases enabled publishers to tailor their products to specific market niches: the *Oxford dictionary* range has gone from under a dozen English language titles in the 1970s to three or four times that in the new century, as it has become easy to extract information concerning, for example, New Zealand or Australian English.

Traditional monolingual and bilingual dictionaries were joined in the 1930s by monolingual dictionaries for English learners, such as Michael West's *New method English dictionary* (Longmans, Green, 1935). This and other works, such as the *Advanced learner's dictionary* (OUP, 1948), were compiled by English teachers working abroad, reflecting the rise of English as a Foreign Language (EFL) as a significant economic asset for Britain. As English came to be studied increasingly in language schools overseas, dictionaries began to record not the language of literature, but that of everyday communication. The way previous dictionaries were compiled had led to an over-emphasis on high culture: it has been shown that Shakespeare is significantly overstated as the first documented source for words in the *OED*.[13] The shift from 'literary' to 'everyday' English was not always welcomed: one learners' dictionary was criticised by reviewers as recently as the late 1980s for excluding the term 'mizzenmast' on the grounds that readers would encounter it in *Moby Dick*.[14]

This new style of dictionary reflected burgeoning research in the post-war period into the links between lexicography, language pedagogy and linguistics, that led to the most significant development in post-war lexicography: the emergence of corpus-based dictionaries. These aimed to reflect a descriptive, rather than prescriptive, use of language. The 1978 *Longman dictionary of contemporary English*, the first large-scale computerised dictionary, was innovative in incorporating valency into definitions. It was followed in 1987 by the first truly corpus-based dictionary, the *Collins cobuild*, which drew on the Bank of English, a joint project set up by Collins and the University of Birmingham (home to the Dictionary Research Centre) in 1980 to build up a corpus of everyday English.

12 Crickman, 'The emerging information professional'.
13 Schäfer, *Documentation in the O.E.D.*, p. 61.
14 Krishnamurthy, 'The corpus revolution in EFL dictionaries'.

The creation of reference databases has likewise had a profound impact on how works are produced. The market was traditionally dominated by a few long-standing players – Collins, Chambers, OUP – as high development costs proved a barrier to new entrants. Though reference works were a reliable backlist source of revenue, it took deep pockets to start up a reference division: one of the few to do so successfully in the latter decades of the century was Cambridge University Press, in 1990. The exception to this general rule is professional reference, often selling through direct mail order, which remains accessible to mid-sized independents such as Oxford-based Atlas Medical, publishers of the Atlas of Investigation and Diagnosis series. However, by the late twentieth century, much in-house work consisted of project management, rather than the creation of new content, while a market has emerged for packagers and freelance lexicographers to provide content to reference publishers who prefer to focus on financing and distribution rather than product development. A related development facilitated by the existence of databases has been the ease with which publishers can now easily extract reference subsets for specific areas of interest, so that Grove encyclopaedias have been published for aficionados of jazz, opera and American music, for example. This has enabled publishers to match their products closely to social and research trends: as Women's Studies grew in universities from the 1970s, so did the number of bibliographical reference guides to women. Reliance on databases has, however, caused problems on occasion: when a joint reference publishing venture between Chambers and Cambridge University Press collapsed in 1989, the fact that the now competing companies shared the same source material meant they risked publishing almost identical products and had no choice but to invest in developing their own version of the initial database.[15]

The late 1980s and early 1990s were a golden age for reference publishers: Mintel put the UK market share for reference at 16 per cent in 1991, while according to Business Monitor it was the fastest-growing hardback sector.[16] The boom was to prove short-lived, however, as new technologies affected the market. A 1997 book trade survey revealed that the reference sector was in the vanguard of the shift to multimedia.[17] The first step, from print to CD Rom, gave publishers a useful new tool: a definition of reggae could be enriched with a sound clip, for example. However, CD Rom technology proved a dead end, as it was costly to publishers – one study calculated that

---

15 Crystal, 'Some indexing decisions'. 16 Attwooll, 'Reference publishing', p. 298.
17 Book Marketing Ltd, *Multimedia and the internet*, p. 7.

up to 30 per cent of buyers required some form of customer support[18] – and it was supplanted within a few years by online sources. However, it was significant for two reasons: first, it marked the arrival of computer companies in reference publishing – Bloomsbury's *Encarta world English dictionary* (1999) was produced on behalf of Microsoft (who also bought a share of Dorling Kindersley) – heralding the shift in consultation from page to screen. Second, reference CD Roms were commonly bundled with purchases of home computers, helping create an expectation of free access to online information.

The traditional print reference and information markets were severely challenged in the closing years of the century by the expansion of the World Wide Web. As Charles Levine noted in 2001, 'printed, multi-volume general English encyclopaedias for all intents and purposes have gone extinct – from somewhere in the range of 500,000–750,000 sets sold worldwide in 1990, to significantly less than 100,000 today'.[19] This market shift led to some high-profile casualties: Chambers Harrap was forced to close its Edinburgh office in 2009, for instance, moving publication of its *Dictionary* to London after 200 years. However, publishers recognised that the Web was in many ways a natural fit for reference publishing, due to the 'bitty' way users consulted works, typified by the 2008 Dorling Kindersley children's reference title *Pick me up, put me down*. Alison Jones, reference publisher at Palgrave Macmillan, detailed the advantages of online reference in 2007: 'no sprained wrists lifting heavyweight volumes, no eyestrain reading pages of closely argued prose on screen, the ability to update as necessary'.[20] The key issue was how to charge for content in a Wikipedia world. Though the online encyclopaedia has struggled to achieve credibility due to a reputation for amateurism, with critics pointing to factual errors and deliberate hoaxes such as a page on fictitious pirate George Colby which survived undetected for nearly seven years,[21] the Wikipedia model of user-generated, crowd-funded, freely available, constantly updated information has proved to have a surprisingly well-developed capacity to detect and correct errors, hoaxes and bias: a widely reported study in *Nature* in 2005 revealed that Wikipedia rivalled the *Britannica* for reliability.[22] The Wikipedia crowd-sourcing model was also innovative in opening up the handling of information to scrutiny via its 'view history' function, which enabled users to track the editorial changes made to material.

18 Cowie, *The Oxford history of English lexicography*, p. 472.
19 Levine, 'The coming boom'.   20 Interview, *Publishers Weekly* 21 September 2007.
21 http://en.wikipedia.org/wiki/Wikipedia:List_of_hoaxes_on_Wikipedia.
22 Giles, 'Internet encyclopaedias'.

Traditional reference publishers responded to the Wikipedia model in four ways: first, by creating added value for online customers, offering services such as click-through links to a classical music library on the OUP Grove Music website, for example. Second, they repositioned themselves as guides, helping consumers hack through the jungle of information. Miriam Farbey of Dorling Kindersley summed up the problem as 'A million entries on Google – who can tell what to read first or what's true?'[23] A product like Oxford Bibliographies Online, available on subscription, targets this problem. Third was a shift from one-off sales to subscriptions, although this was not always a successful tactic: Microsoft closed its digital multimedia encyclopaedia *Encarta* in 2009 in the face of competition from Wikipedia. Fourth, as Casper Grathwohl of OUP noted, the future for reference and information lay in 'academically validating the growing world of available information rather than adding to it'.[24] The new 'Britannica checked' stamp, marking publisher-led rather than user-generated content, is one such initiative. Reference and information publishers are now moving onto tablets and e-readers via apps, including agreements with technology companies to pre-install material on devices: Amazon, for instance, has teamed up with the *Oxford dictionary*, which is pre-loaded onto all Kindle e-readers. Such partnerships give publishers real-time feedback about what people are looking up, enabling them to tailor their products to users' expectations. Reciprocally, reference has begun experimenting with crowd-sourcing: Collins Online, for instance, invites readers to suggest new words for inclusion.

One further significant change wrought by the shift online has been a change in the way information is presented, answering the key issue raised by Herbert Spencer's 1969 investigation in *The visible word* of how traditional print layouts hinder the presentation and distribution of information. While print reference works had already made strides in legibility in comparison with the 1911 *Concise Oxford*'s use of three close-set columns to define the lemma 'set', online sources can abandon linearity altogether: thesauruses can depict relations between synonyms visually in word webs, for example. Not all reference publishing has gone online, however: there is still a place for print in children's reference, for example, particularly for the school and library markets. Likewise, the top print reference sellers in 2011 were from the Collins Gem (bilingual) and Oxford Mini (monolingual) series, suggesting the portability of paper is still an advantage in the classroom and for travellers.

---

23 Interview, *Publishers Weekly* 21 September 2007.
24 Kuzyk, 'Reference into the future', p. 8.

How-to titles, defined for the purposes of this chapter as a broad category of practical manuals representing a significant subset within the information publishing sector, have undergone a similar trajectory to reference publishing in many ways. They have precursors reaching back centuries; they were similarly boosted by mass literacy and the Victorian drive for self-improvement, continued in the twentieth century by initiatives like the Workers' Educational Association; and they have been profoundly affected by the advent of multimedia and the digital realm.

Joseph O'Connor's description of a typical bookshelf holding 'trashy airport thrillers and battered teach-yourself manuals, a couple of pornographic paperbacks and glitzy-jacketed bodice-rippers'[25] reflects the how-to book's occasional status as a poor relation even to reference publishing, but likewise hints at its cultural ubiquity from the early years of the twentieth century: the *Bookman* noted in 1902 that 'If Mr. Grant Richards goes on with his series of How To books, the next generation will have less excuse than we have had for any want of success.'[26] Richards's series lasted until the early 1920s: covering such topics as *How to dress well on a small allowance* (1901), *How to appreciate prints* (1915) and *How to use a player-piano* (1922), it seemed to address anxieties about how best to emulate the accomplishments of middle-class life.

One intriguing early experiment in multimedia for the purposes of self-improvement was the Hugophone series of language learning manuals and gramophone records (1929–33), launched by Charles Hugo, who ran language schools in London for several decades from the 1890s on. One of the longest-running how-to collections was founded slightly later: the Teach Yourself series, now one of the best-known brand names in the sector, was launched in 1938 by English Universities Press, and from 1974 was published by Hodder.

The importance of how-to books to society was highlighted when titles such as Penguin's *Aircraft recognition* and the *St John's nursing manual* were deemed 'essential' books and granted additional paper rations during the Second World War. A few years later, servicemen were reintroduced to civilian life with the help of vocational training programmes, for which Penguin reprinted a series of thirty Specials covering everything from health to trades to arts and crafts. The sector sold well in the post-war period, as austerity created a market for series such as Burke's 1950s Help Yourself, offering titles like *Soft fruit growing for profit and pleasure*. A Havant bookseller noted in 1962 that technical car manuals, gardening, Teach Yourself manuals and so on were quick sellers, particularly when the consumer had the choice

25 O'Connor, *Inishowen*, p. 258.   26 Pett Ridge, 'Guide to Fleet Street', p. 53.

between several titles in the same field.[27] The sector continued to reflect social trends: rising rates of car ownership created a market for Haynes Manuals, a series of step-by-step car repair manuals founded in 1960, while the emergence of home computing was the driver for the market-leading For Dummies series, published by John Wiley & Sons. The *Bookseller* reported in 2004 that top sellers in the sector included titles such as *How to make money from property* and *Going to live in Spain*.[28]

Unlike reference publishing, where entrance costs are prohibitive, the information sector is relatively open to new entrants and mid-sized independents, as it requires less up-front investment. The Bluffer's Guides launched by Ravette in 1985 are a case in point. However, major information series with significant brand recognition such as Teach Yourself and For Dummies now cover everything from languages and computing to complementary therapies and professional development, meaning that independent publishers struggle for visibility. The Oxford-based independent How To Books reported in the *Bookseller* in 2002 that it had survived only by evolving away from series publishing to offer stand-alone titles of varying formats and prices. Much how-to content is now available online, with sites such as dummies.com and YouTube featuring step-by-step video instructions on a host of topics. How-to books on niche subjects are now commonly self-published as e-books by authors looking to profit from their expertise on a peer-to-peer basis: John T. Reed's *How to write, publish and sell your own how-to book* (2005) is one typical example.

Another representative form of information publishing, in the broad sense of providing consumers with practical information in readily accessible format, is the travel guidebook. Travel guides in the early decades of the twentieth century were very much the heirs to the nineteenth-century tradition – literally so, in the case of the Blue Guides, which were the successors to John Murray's Handbook series. The first title in the series was *London and its environs*, launched in 1918 by James and Findlay Muirhead, Baedeker's English editors. The brothers had acquired the rights to Murray's series from the map-seller Edward Stanford, who had purchased them at the turn of the century. The guides were co-published with Hachette in French and English until 1933: international co-editions have long been a feature of reference and information publishing alike.

---

27 Barker and Davies, *Books are different*, pp. 264, 282.
28 'How To Books helps itself grow', *Bookseller* 2 June 2004, p. 8.

Travel guides shed fascinating light on the social and political history of travel. The *Anglo-South American handbook*, initially produced in the early 1920s by the Federation of British Industry, advises readers on how to dress for dinner on board ship. The guide, updated for the backpacking generation, became the independent Footprint Travel Guides' flagship title when it launched its new Footprint imprint in 1997 (the company was acquired by the US-based Morris Communications in 2007). The 'Baedeker raids', carried out by the Luftwaffe in 1942 in retaliation for the British bombing of Lübeck in northern Germany, targeted picturesque cities of limited strategic interest, such as Exeter, Bath and Norwich, said to have been selected by Nazi propagandist Baron Gustav Braun von Sturm on the basis of their star-rating in the Baedeker guide to Britain. Conversely, Jay Garner, US administrator in Iraq in 2003, was said to have used the Lonely Planet guide to draw up a list of historical sites that should be spared bombing and protected against looting.[29]

Guidebooks changed little in terms of content and visual format from the nineteenth century to the 1970s. One early marketing innovation in the field was the decision by Thomas Cook to offer monthly subscriptions to its *Continental timetable* as Bradshaw began to lose its dominant position in the timetable market. Another unique post-war product was Alfred Wainwright's much-loved seven-volume *Pictorial guide to the Lakeland fells*. The first of the series was printed by Henry Marshall in 1955, reproducing Wainwright's painstakingly drawn and lettered manuscript: the editions feature no typeset material. The rights were acquired in 2003 by the then independent Frances Lincoln, whose new editions feature handwritten updates carefully imitating Wainwright's original manuscripts. To date, the series has sold over 2 million copies.[30]

The principal development in the post-1945 period came with social change in the 1960s and 1970s, as backpacking became a rite of passage for young people. The Interrail travel pass was launched in 1972, allowing young people to journey round Europe on a controlled and limited budget. The first American backpacking travel series (Let's Go, 1960) was followed in Britain by Bradt travel guides (1974) and the Rough Guides (1982). Lonely Planet was launched in 1973 in Australia with a hand-collated and stapled brochure, ninety-six pages in length, entitled *Across Asia on the cheap*. The company eventually expanded into Asia in the 1980s and Europe and America in the

---

29 Friend, 'The parachute artist', p. 78.
30 'Wainwright guides saved', http://news.bbc.co.uk/2/hi/uk_news/england/2761445 .stm.

1990s. The typically iconoclastic founding ethos of such guides, launched in an era which saw the rise of the hippie trail across south-east Asia, makes social responsibility a particular marketing point. The Rough Guides series, part of the Penguin stable since 2002, includes a 'health warning' in every guide about the environmental impact of travel. Similarly, the reliance of such guides on reader feedback for regular updates makes them sensitive to consumer pressure: 2008 saw calls to boycott Lonely Planet over its guide to Myanmar, which was seen to lend legitimacy to the country's military dictatorship. The sector relies heavily on being seen to offer disinterested expertise; statements to the effect that guides will not accept advertisements of the sort found in company directories, or discounts in exchange for coverage, are common practice, as any perception that a guide is unduly influenced by the interests of the travel industry would undermine its credibility as an independent source of information for travellers. The sector was thus challenged by revelations by the 'whistle-blowing' travel guide author Thomas Kohnstamm, whose 2008 title *Do travel writers go to hell?* alleged that budget restrictions led authors to fabricate research,[31] and Bob Andrews wrote of how the pressure of a tight deadline on a guide to Germany for an unnamed publisher led him to overlook Stuttgart entirely.[32] The travel guide market inevitably reflects, and is dependent upon, the global context: global financial crisis from 2007 led to the rise of titles for the 'staycation' market (i.e. holidaying at home) by 2012, while a guide to Syria, described in an early 2011 industry round-up as 'a very fashionable destination',[33] proved ill-timed as the country sank into civil war within weeks of its publication.

By 2008, the travel guide market was dominated by three main players who held 66 per cent of the market between them: Lonely Planet, Penguin with Dorling Kindersley Eyewitness and Rough Guides, and the Automobile Association.[34] However, the sector is still home to a number of independent publishers such as Crimson and Trailblazer. As the main tourist destinations are comprehensively covered by the larger brands, which have largely left behind their 'alternative' roots and shifted their sights to mainstream travel, independents tend to specialise in unusual destinations such as Liberia and Azerbaijan, or in niche sectors such as gap-year travel or coastal walks. One such publisher is Cicerone, founded in 1967 in the Lake District, which specialises in trekking and mountaineering guides.

31 Kohnstamm, *Do travel writers go to hell?*, p. 4.   32 Andrews, *The fixer*, p. 132.
33 Alex Stewart, 'Expertise repackaged', *Bookseller* 21 January 2011, p. 10.
34 Clark and Phillips, *Inside book publishing*, fourth edition, p. 176.

As in all fields of reference and information publishing, the travel sector has developed web-based and app-based guides – a logical development in that such guides can be updated with immediate effect, posting updates on local events, for instance. However, travel guides are one form of information publishing where the print medium still offers a distinct advantage: as Tony Wheeler, the founder of Lonely Planet, said in 2008, 'It may be on your computer but it is going to take three minutes to boot up and then the battery is going to go flat.' However, he then acknowledges that the future of the sector may be electronic, at least for less exotic destinations: 'I think for a long time we will be researching guidebooks, the only thing I don't know is whether what we write will appear on paper.'[35] This raises a similar set of issues to those faced by reference works. The BBC's disastrous 2007 purchase of Lonely Planet, which it sold in 2013 for less than half of what it had paid, and the decision of new owners NC2 Media to move away from in-house content creation to drawing on material from community and social media,[36] symbolises the challenges facing the sector in an age in which consumers no longer automatically expect to pay for information commonly freely available online in the form of peer recommendations on websites such as TripAdvisor. If the twentieth century was the era of the democratisation of *access* to information, the major issue facing the sector in the twenty-first century would appear to be how to generate profit within the new economic model brought about by the advent of the digital era and the concomitant rise of user-generated information that is free at the point of use.

Government publishing

While the history of government information in Britain can be traced back at least as far as the Domesday Book, the modern era has witnessed a massive expansion in the amount of government-issued information available for public consultation. The nineteenth century paved the way, as the spread of literacy, improvements in communication technologies and the rise of sociological enquiries such as Henry Mayhew's *London labour and the London poor* (1851) increased awareness of the importance of public access to information in a participatory democracy.

---

35 Victoria Arnstein, 'Wheeler dealer: controversy still surrounds Lonely Planet's majority buy-out by the BBC a year ago', *Bookseller* 26 September 2008, p. 26.
36 Helen Davidson, 'Lonely Planet staff face job losses', *Guardian* 19 July 2013, www .theguardian.com/world/2013/jul/19/lonely-planet-staff-job-losses.

Defining the object of study is fraught with complication: what counts as government, and what counts as publishing? Jack Cherns's definition is broad: 'state publishing is ... a process of communication by various means, but mainly in print, at all levels between government and governed'.[37] Much research in the field to date has focussed on the role of His (or Her) Majesty's Stationery Office, as its output is relatively identifiable and accessible.[38] However, as Eve Johansson noted in 1976, HMSO publications accounted at that point for at most 30 per cent of material catalogued by the British Library's Official Publications division.[39] The remaining 70 per cent hints at a vast grey area of official publications issued by government departments, nationalised industries, quangos and the like, shading off into photocopied handouts, maps, and Christmas cards sold to support national museums.

What follows focusses on central government's core publishing activity through HMSO, while bearing in mind that for much of the period there have been three tiers of official publishing, with increasing amounts of information coming from Europe and local authorities from the 1970s. EEC information was available from HMSO bookshops and a network of information centres following Britain's accession to the European Economic Community in 1973: Britain boasted forty-eight such centres by 1977, though managers lamented that 95 per cent of them were under-used.[40] The reform of local government in 1974 led many local authorities to set up their own information departments (many later closed on cost grounds). The Greater London Council ran not only a research library from 1969, but also a bookshop in the 1970s and early 1980s. Local authority reports on topics such as racial equality are valuable resources for social history, though such material can be hard to find: of an estimated 50,000 local authority publications issued in 1980, the British National Bibliography lists just 250.[41] The production, printing and distribution of local authority material such as town guides, street plans and newsletters is now commonly subcontracted to the private sector, though much content is still produced in-house and increasingly delivered online. Local authority publishing has occasionally led to friction with the commercial local information sector, as in the 2011 debate over proposals to limit the frequency and scope of local council newspapers,

37 Cherns, *Official publishing*, p. 3.
38 Butcher, *Official publications in Britain*; Smith, 'British official publications'.
39 Johansson, 'The reference work', p. 273.
40 Jeffries, 'European document centres', pp. 127–8.
41 Nuttall, 'Local government information', p. 473.

described by the Conservative Minister Eric Pickles as 'town hall Pravdas' that 'swallow[ed] much-needed advertising revenue from local papers'.[42]

The issue of access to government-held information shaped official information policy for much of the twentieth century. The overall trend was towards increasing access to information and therefore government accountability, culminating in the Freedom of Information Act of 2000, enshrining a public right of access to information held by public authorities (albeit within certain parameters). The reporting of parliamentary proceedings is a case in point. While parliamentary debates began being reported in the late eighteenth century, eventually taking the name Hansard from the printer who produced them from 1809, their publication remained a commercial venture for much of the nineteenth century.[43] Only in 1889 did Hansard become an official record, when it began receiving a government subsidy. An early indicator of the twentieth century's trend towards transparency came in 1909, when parliament took over publishing Hansard and moved from condensed to daily verbatim uncorrected reports of Commons debates; these are now posted online by 6 a.m. the day after proceedings. Similarly, 1967 saw Britain become the first country to formalise public consultation by issuing green papers. A constant feature of the debate over access has been whether government information should be treated as a commodity or be freely (or cheaply) available to taxpayers. The debate was summed up in 1932 by a government committee which dryly noted that while, in the Treasury's view, 'if the world wants to know, the world should buy', the departments themselves held that 'if the world will not buy copies it must be given copies'.[44] This debate has particularly shaped the extent to which the private sector has been involved in government publishing.

The beginning of our period saw a clear shift away from private involvement in public information. In the nineteenth century, government documents were printed and distributed by a number of private entrepreneurs, of whom Thomas Hansard is the best known. The early years of the twentieth century saw increasing dissatisfaction with this arrangement, which saw officials selling knowledge gained in the course of their duties for private gain, while parliamentarians were offered the opportunity to amend their statements to the House in print, thereby impacting the authenticity of the resulting document as an official record of government business. At the same time, having become a printer in addition to its role as stationer in 1882,

---

42 www.communities.gov.uk/publications/localgovernment/publicitycode2011.
43 Trewin and King, *Printer to the House*.
44 Quoted in Cherns, *Official publishing*, p. 259.

HMSO expanded to take on the bulk of government publishing as private companies proved unequal to the task of issuing vast numbers of documents. These included the standardised forms required by the National Insurance Act of 1911, which had to be distributed nationwide. HMSO acquired its own printworks in 1917, enabling it to handle large-scale, sometimes confidential projects. By the end of the First World War, HMSO employed 1,355 men and 1,287 women.[45]

In the early years of the twentieth century, then, HMSO became responsible for both parliamentary publications (the definition of which has narrowed over time, largely on cost grounds, the annual reports of nationalised industries being reclassified as non-parliamentary in 1972, for instance) and non-parliamentary publications. The latter category was extremely broad, consisting of whatever government departments chose to entrust to the service. Some departments had tied arrangements to print all their material with HMSO, a system that ended in 1982. Others had more freedom to call on external suppliers, though in practice HMSO enjoyed a near-monopoly over government printing at least for part of the century, from 1920 to 1945. Initially, projects had to be individually approved by the Treasury – a highly inefficient management method that came to an end with the introduction of standing instructions in the 1930s. Though departments and other bodies such as the Forestry Commission were increasingly printing their own material from the 1960s on, HMSO was long among the largest publishers by volume in the UK; it has remained so following the 1996 privatisation of its publishing role as The Stationery Office (TSO), issuing some 9,000 titles a year.[46]

HMSO's budget was voted annually by parliament until 1980. Operations were for a long time conducted on a not-for-profit basis: consequently, professional practices such as cataloguing and promotion were sporadic in the early years. However, the sheer scale of projects such as printing and distributing telephone directories forced HMSO to professionalise and adopt, to a certain degree, commercial publishing strategies: a Typefaces Committee was set up in 1922, reflecting awareness of the importance of production values, and an HMSO stand was present at the Frankfurt Book Fair beginning in 1956. Similarly, the government publishing sector was so large that it drove technical innovation: warehousing was mechanised as early as 1912, while computerised typesetting was developed for telephone directories by 1964.[47]

---

45 Barty-King, *Her Majesty's Stationery Office*, p. 60.   46 www.tso.co.uk/about-tso.
47 Barty-King, *Her Majesty's Stationery Office*, pp. 144, 92.

One aspect of HMSO's activity that sets it apart from commercial publishers has been its lack of choice over material to be published, however unprofitable the result. This has given HMSO a bewilderingly diverse catalogue, covering everything from the *Highway code* to *Tsetse flies in British West Africa* (Thomas Manly Nash, 1948, printed for the Bureau of Hygiene and Tropical Diseases). These were distributed through a regional network of HMSO bookshops, the first of which was established in Edinburgh in 1912, replacing the previous unsatisfactory system of private sales agents. This move was made on the grounds that setting up bookshops to sell material on a non-profit basis (though at somewhat more than cost to cover discounts for libraries) would prove far less wasteful in getting information into the hands of those that needed it. As a Select Committee report stated in 1915, 'the sum at stake is trivial compared with the hundreds of thousands of pounds spent in the preparation and printing of State papers the full return for which is not now received'.[48] Publications were eventually made available through mail order, British Information Service offices (in India, Australia and New Zealand, for instance), and authorised sales agents in Britain and overseas. This network made sources such as the *British manual of firemanship* available worldwide: to this day, countries like Australia, India, Abu Dhabi and Zimbabwe base their fire crew training on this manual.

HMSO's relationship with the private sector was often prickly, as commercial publishers resented the competition from quasi-commercial branches of HMSO such as the British Museum Press and from HMSO bookshops, which, though members of the Net Book Agreement, long excluded commercially printed material such as tourist guides, while heavily subsidising their own publications. Competition from advertising in subsidised HMSO publications that had no obligation to pay royalties or show a profit was a particular bone of contention. However, collaborations with commercial publishers were not unheard of: one such was the Penguin Hansard series of 1940–42, an attempt to make significant political debates of the day available to a popular readership in digest format. The pendulum eventually swung back towards private sector involvement in the latter decades of the period: by the 1950s, two-thirds of printing was being tendered out to approved contractors. Government-held information came to be seen as a saleable commodity rather than the property of the taxpayer, as indicated by a 1983 HMSO report entitled *Making a business of information: a survey of new*

---

48 Quoted in Cherns, *Official publishing*, p. 253.

opportunities.[49] HMSO (which had moved from London to Norwich in the mid-1960s) had been under pressure to emulate the private sector for years. Prime Minister Edward Heath told the House in 1972 that HMSO needed 'systems appropriate to a trading organisation'.[50] When HMSO was required to produce an operating surplus of 5 per cent in the early 1980s, prices rose steeply as subsidies for parliamentary printing were removed. Staff numbers fell from 6,000 in 1981 to 3,500 in 1985, and tasks such as supplying reprints and microforms were outsourced to the commercial sector.[51] HMSO's successor TSO approaches the publication and sale of official and regulatory information as a commercial venture, framing its role as the provision of expertise in public sector information management.[52] Those functions of HMSO to have escaped privatisation, administering Crown copyright and regulating contracts for printing and publishing legislation, were brought under the umbrella of the Office of Public Sector Information in 2005, merging with the National Archives in 2006.

The situation in government publishing in the twenty-first century is somewhat paradoxical as regards access. Privatisation has restricted access in some ways, challenging the principle that government-held information paid for by taxpayers should not be a source of private profit. The HMSO bookshops have been replaced by ordering through TSO's online shop or through authorised high street booksellers (though legislative documents are available free online). Yet, at the same time, the advent of the digital age has placed an abundance of material just a click of the mouse away. In this sense, Jack Cherns's 1979 statement that 'freedom of access to a single document might be held tantamount to publication' is prophetic.[53] While PDF copies of government legislation are theoretically available to all, they do raise two potentially problematic issues in terms of long-term accessibility. Firstly, readers must be able to find what they need among the sheer quantities of information available – not always an easy task. Secondly, and perhaps more importantly, print copies of government documents are a vital democratic tool, providing a tangible, unalterable record of government activity on library shelves. Their disembodied electronic counterparts surely must not be allowed to vanish into the ether.

49 Picton, 'Electronic official publishing', p. 36. 50 Hansard, 5 May 1972, online version.
51 Barty-King, *Her Majesty's Stationery Office*, p. 125. 52 www.tso.co.uk/about-tso.
53 Cherns, *Official publishing*, p. 5.

Maps, cartography and geographical publishing

IAIN STEVENSON

The compilation, publishing and to a great extent retailing of maps and related geographical products had long been the purview of specialist organisations. Although these were very much part of the book trade (most cartographic publishers retained membership of the Publishers Association), their output was distinct in format, pricing structure, market and ultimately, at the end of the period covered by this volume, response to the challenge of digital alternatives. Even when maps were presented gathered in book form as atlases they were unlike other reference products in their markets. This chapter reviews the history of cartographic publishing over the period, but in the space available can only give a selective overview of this field made complex by a multiplicity of formats, scales and editions.

Definitions

Maps fall into numerous categories.[1] The most basic and familiar is the flat topographic sheet which depicts an area at a specific scale (normally quoted as a representative fraction, e.g. 1:25,000, i.e. one unit on the map represents 25,000 units on the ground). (Maps on the scale of 1:2,500 or less are conventionally referred to as 'plans'.) In the earlier part of the period, scale was often quoted in the form of, for example, 'one inch to the mile', but after metrication in the early 1970s this convention was dropped. These maps were often printed in as many as eight colours to show topography or cultural features, and the style of gradated layer colouring related to precise contour lines, invented by John G. Bartholomew (1860–1920) in the 1880s, was the standard form of presentation. Although always available unfolded, flat sheets were often sold folded in card or cloth covers and premium issues were dissected and mounted on linen for durability. From about 1960, maps

---

1 Keates, *Understanding maps*.

were laminated by plastic sheets to enable their use outdoors in inclement weather. Some sheets, usually smaller scale, were also presented mounted on rollers and varnished for use in education and for wall display. Most topographical maps published in the United Kingdom were local, but other national series like those of the United States Geological Survey (USGS) or the French Institut Géographique Nationale (IGN) were widely retailed by specialist booksellers like Stanfords. Thematic maps show the distribution of specific phenomena like population, land use or rainfall, usually overprinted on a simplified base map, showing outlines of physical features, settlements and communications. Perhaps the most well known of these are the geological maps showing rocks and superficial features which are striking in their colouration. They often include cross-sections to show superposition of strata. Special-purpose maps are devised for specific commercial use, like the Fire Insurance plans published by the Charles Goad Company, now part of the credit rating agency Experian.

Charts are specific maps of the sea and inland coastal waters used for navigation and show underwater hazards, detailed soundings and other vital information for mariners; they are compiled and issued by the UK Hydrographic Office (UKHO), a Trading Fund of the Ministry of Defence. Decorative and commemorative maps are issued to mark key national events like the British Empire Exhibition (1924–25), the Festival of Britain (1951) or the 2012 Olympic Games and serve a dual purpose of practical wayfinding and providing souvenirs. Although often commissioned by a sponsoring organisation, they are generally compiled and published by commercial publishers. A subset of these are propaganda maps which aim to make social, economic or political points by exaggerating or distorting geography; a recent notorious example was the World Map produced by the German historian Arno Peters, which used a selective projection to 'redress' the representation between northern and southern nations. Allied to these are cartograms, which are abstract simplified representations of geographical reality to avoid confusion among users; the most famous example is the diagrammatic representation of the London Underground network designed in 1932 by H. S. Beck and still used today.[2]

Atlases are collections of maps bound in book form and can be national, global or thematic. A specific twentieth-century addition to the genre is the road atlas, which first appeared in the 1920s with the rise of widespread private motoring, and until the recent arrival of digital satnav systems was

2 Garland, *Mr Beck's Underground map*.

ubiquitous in British motor vehicles (and accounted for a large proportion of map sales). Similar in concept were A–Z guides which were indexed town plans to show large-scale representations of streets. Developed by Phyllis Pearsall of the Geographers' A–Z Map Company (see below), they were enormously popular and lucrative but have been more or less completely superseded by online mapping systems offered free of charge by Google and other internet providers. A highly specialised yet significant form of map publication was the globe, essentially a model of the earth. Globes were manufactured by cartographic publishers who designed and produced printed gores that depicted the earth's surface and were precision-shaped with deep dissections which, when mounted on a sphere of wood or later plastic, fitted together exactly to show the land masses and oceans of the earth in almost exact geographical relationship. Large detailed globes have always been expensive items but smaller directly printed plastic models have become cheap and commonplace. Virtually all globes are now manufactured overseas. Their near relative the topomodel, a flat map printed on plastic with the topography embossed out to represent elevation at an exaggerated scale, has never been widely available from British map publishers but in countries like France and Switzerland has been popular.

The Ordnance Survey

The Ordnance Survey (OS), founded in 1791, is the British National mapping agency, and for much of its history was essentially a military organisation charged with providing accurate and detailed topographic maps of the entire British Isles for defence purposes.[3] It created the primary triangulation of the country and surveyed the entire nation, originally at the scale of one inch to the mile, but by the end of the nineteenth century many areas were mapped at larger scales of up to twenty-five inches to the mile (some city centres were at even larger scales). Although it printed and sold its County Series of one inch maps to the public, at the beginning of the twentieth century it did not see map publishing as a major part of its activity, with its main efforts directed to surveying and recording landscape features. Its maps were monochrome, and, while regularly updated with new features, the modifications were made on the original plates so they looked very old-fashioned, even retaining the obsolete relief representation technique of hachuring, which used a series of parallel lines to indicate slope steepness well into the twentieth century.

3 Seymour, *A history of the Ordnance Survey*.

The First World War transformed OS's perspective with an enormous demand for maps of European battle zones. Its first post-war Director-General (until 1992 the OS was always directed by military officers) Colonel Charles Close sought to extend the market and appeal of OS Maps radically, by widening the range, modernising the style of presentation, and positively marketing its products by advertising and particularly attractive packaging. OS Maps appeared folded in full-colour card covers with illustrations of high artistic merit.[4] Special maps of archaeological sites were published, and the growing leisure market for motoring and hiking in the 1930s was targeted with specially designed presentations like the one inch maps of the Norfolk Broads and the Lake District. These were competitively priced and commercial map publishers complained of unfair competition by a government agency.

In 1935 the Davidson Committee recommended that the OS complete a new triangulation, and the National Grid system of coordinates was introduced to enable the precise location of features by a six-figure numerical reference. A new one inch series was launched, despite the grid system being based on metric measures, and it was not until 1975 that the one inch maps were superseded by a metric 1:50,000 series (the larger scales had already been metricated).

The range of maps continued to widen after the Second World War. Recreational and tourist maps were produced, often with vibrant and striking design to show relief added to the basic topography using relief shading and an extended colour palette. The *Lake District National Park one inch map* of 1970 is a particularly dramatic and successful example. A network of sales agencies, mainly booksellers, was established to commercialise OS maps, and a new manufacturing facility in Southampton was opened in 1969 to draft, print and warehouse its products.

Until 1995, paper maps dominated the OS output, and for many users its Explorer (1:25,000) and Landranger (1:50,000) series, with the option of 'Active' format protected by rainproof plastic lamination, are still its most familiar products. However, the major part of the OS output is now digital in the form of Geographical Information Systems (GIS) technology. This uses the MasterMap system which produces customised mapping at a wide range of scales for mainly business and commercial users. This enormous database includes almost 450 million unique geographical references and can produce customised mapping to suit most purposes. In 2010, OS ceased printing its

4 Browne, *Map cover art*.

own maps and closed its factory and warehouse, moving to a new digitally orientated campus nearby in Southampton. Its enormous investment in the creation of digital geographical data has led it to pursue an active policy in protecting its intellectual property, often criticised as unfairly restricting the use of data created by public funding. Nevertheless, the OS successfully pursued a major copyright infringement case against the Automobile Association (AA) in 1999, which had been shown to have used OS data on its branded road atlases without permission. The OS received damages of £20 million and guaranteed royalties. At the time of writing, the success of OS, currently an arm's length trading agency of government, has caused it to be a potential privatisation candidate.

The OS only publishes maps of Great Britain. A much smaller organisation provides maps of Northern Ireland and a separate state body publishes maps of the Irish Republic. Neither Irish publisher has the resources to develop significant digital mapping. A sister organisation, the Directorate of Overseas Surveys (DOS), was created in 1946 to provide accurate and up-to-date mapping originally in the British colonies, and later, as these countries achieved independence, as contributions to their economic development.[5] It worked closely with the OS and pioneered survey techniques like the photomap which used photogrammetic measurements from remotely sensed satellite and aerial data. The 1:50,000 map of the Kingdom of Tonga produced in 1971 is a notable example. Despite producing emergency mapping of the Falkland Islands in 1982 to aid the recapture of the islands from the Argentine invaders, the DOS received unfriendly government scrutiny and it was closed down in 1985, with its few remaining staff transferring to the OS. At its peak it employed over 300 people and had mapped over 2 million square miles covering over eighty countries from Bolivia to Yemen, for whom the DOS-published maps still remain the only accurate geographical coverage available.

Commercial map publishers

Despite the wide availability and relative cheapness of OS maps, commercial map publishers have flourished (at least until recently) by creating cartographic products that the national mapping agency neglected. Foremost among these was the Edinburgh-based publisher John Bartholomew and Sons.[6] Bartholomew was originally a family-run

---

5 Macdonald, *Mapping the world.*   6 Gardiner, *Bartholomew.*

engraving business but by 1914, under the visionary guidance of its principal J. G. Bartholomew, it had developed a substantial business in the compilation, design and printing of a wide range of cartographic publications. Until 1919 it operated in a loose partnership with the publisher and printer Thomas Nelson & Sons with whom it shared manufacturing facilities, but the relationship was uneasy and it was dissolved. By that time, Bartholomew had built its own extensive offices and plant (The Edinburgh Geographical Institute) which included the largest and most modern colour lithographic presses in Europe.

Bartholomew's flagship and most successful product was the 'half inch' contoured maps of Great Britain which covered the country in sixty-two sheets. Printed in eight colours, these adopted the system of layer contour colouring which combined the precise rendering of topography by using 100 foot contour intervals, to which the impression of height was presented by using gradated colours in gradually deepening shades of green (to 400 foot elevation) and brown (above 400 feet). This system produced a particularly attractive impression, and since OS maps were not available in this scale they were a convenient format for motoring and cycling. In fact, the first series was produced in a special edition for the Cyclists' Touring Club and showed steep hills and other hazards. The maps were based (with permission) on OS one inch maps, but Bartholomew compilers were often ahead of the national agency in the details they included. When Ministry of Transport road classification and numbering was introduced in the 1930s, Bartholomew maps were the first to include these, as they were the location of aerodromes, electrical transmission lines, youth hostels, golf courses and National Trust properties. While the OS, true to its military heritage, tended to omit details of sensitive government installations like army camps, naval harbours and airfields, these were generally included on Bartholomew maps, occasionally to the chagrin of security conscious administrators.

From the 1920s Bartholomew devoted an increasing proportion of its resources to atlas production which will be discussed in the next section. Nevertheless, its business was always dominated by 'flat sheet maps'. As well as the half inch maps available in three formats – paper, cloth and 'dissected' – a wide range of touring maps, town plans, 'continental' maps and illustrated maps was published. The last type became popular in the 1930s and were drawn by notable artists like Macdonald Gill (the brother of the eminent sculptor and typographer). A significant source of revenue was the customisation and printing of coloured 'in text' maps for other publishers' reference works, like Macmillan's annual *Statesman's year book*.

Bartholomew was bought by the Reader's Digest Association in 1980 after many years of informal association, although it continued to be managed by family members. This was not a successful merger. The company embarked on an unproductive policy of diversification away from its core cartographic business and produced a rather incoherent list of books on crafts, pets, cookery and popular history, and tourist guides, generally inferior to those produced by other publishers, which sapped its vitality and prosperity. An attempt to revitalise in 1975 by the publication of a metric 1:100,000 series to compete with the new OS 1:50,000 maps had been unsuccessful, probably due to poor marketing. The business was sold in 1985 to News International. Shortly afterwards the Edinburgh works was closed and it became part of the HarperCollins Atlas and Reference division in Glasgow.

Remarkably, two of the UK's other leading map publishers were also based in Edinburgh.[7] W. & A. K. Johnston specialised in atlases and wall maps, particularly for educational use, and was a major exporter to British imperial territories.[8] It too owned a modern printing plant and diversified its business into security printing, producing currency notes for Scottish banks. It too produced a half inch topographic series notable for its patented folding system that allowed easy opening and manipulation when driving. A much smaller enterprise was Gall & Inglis which originally had been a publisher of ready reckoners and commercial guides but, probably at the behest of one of its early members who had invented an innovative map projection, soon added map publishing to its repertoire. This initially took the form of monochrome 'road contour books' aimed at motorists, but following its construction of a new printing works in 1924 Gall & Inglis also launched a half inch coloured map series which remained available until the Second World War. It also produced a series of astronomical charts.

After Edinburgh, London, unsurprisingly, was the next largest centre of map publishing. Historically the map and globe trade has been concentrated in Fleet Street and up until 1960 a number of cartographic firms were located there. The oldest was G. W. Bacon, which had inherited the business of G. Cruchley, the leading nineteenth-century producer of county maps. Bacon produced a large range of town plans and guide maps (including the famous *Ten miles round London*), and was a noted globe maker. Among its innovations was the Tape Map, which incorporated a graduated linen measure in its maps to facilitate calculation of distance. Bacon unsuccessfully tried to compete

---

7 On the history of cartographic publishing in Scotland, see Stevenson, 'Cartographic publishing'.
8 Johnston, *An Edinburgh centenary*.

with Geographers' A–Z by producing a series of indexed town plan guides. It was taken over by W. & A. K. Johnston in 1956 although the imprint remained in London.

The Geographers' (A–Z) Map Company was established in 1936 by Phyllis Pearsall, a redoubtable self-taught map maker whose A–Z guides, as noted above, dominated the market for urban street plans.[9] Pearsall claimed that she walked the streets of London herself to establish the accuracy of her guides, but it seems more likely that she used large-scale OS plans as her base. Nevertheless, her business prospered and the series expanded to include street atlases of most major British cities and a range of small-scale touring maps. Pearsall remained in charge of the company until she died in 1996 at the age of eighty-nine. Just before her death she transferred ownership of the company to an employee trust and today it claims to be Britain's largest independent map publisher.[10] It sold its London base and showroom in 2004 and now operates from modern premises in Borough Green, Kent. It continues to publish street maps on paper but is increasingly concentrating on digital cartography, including apps for mobile telephones and tablets.

The firm of George Philip, founded by another Scottish map maker in Liverpool in 1848, soon moved to London where it produced county maps in competition with Bacon. By 1914 most of the business was educational maps and atlases (including the famous *University atlas*) but it also produced sheet maps. In 1987 it was sold to Reed International, but after a short unhappy period a management buy-out occurred which in turn led to its acquisition by Octopus Publishing. In 2001 it was acquired by Hachette and it continues to publish atlases under the Philip imprint.

Perhaps the best-known map specialist in London is Edward Stanford whose Geographical Establishment was set up in Charing Cross Road in 1862 and moved soon afterwards to its present location in Long Acre, Covent Garden. Both a map retailer and a publisher, it maintained a drawing office above its shop until the mid-1960s. Although it had been bought by George Philip in 1947, it operated independently and was demerged in 2001. After a chaotic period (it was managed for some time as a workers' cooperative) it successfully emerged as the UK's leading map retailer with several branches and a significant part of the OS Mastermap business.

There are numerous examples of small map publishers, usually for highly specialised purposes like mountaineering or orienteering, but they have

9 Pearsall, *A–Z maps.*   10 www.az.co.uk.

tended to base their products on OS maps. One particularly interesting example is Geographical Publications, which was set up in 1934 by Sir Lawrence Dudley Stamp, Professor of Geography at King's College London and the London School of Economics. Stamp was concerned that British agriculture in the 1930s was in serious decline and that food security was threatened. He reasoned that an inventory of how land was used was necessary, and with great energy and vision engaged an army of volunteers (mainly geography teachers and students) to map every field in the country as to its land use on 1:25,000 OS maps, which were later collated and published on one inch sheets. This monumental task was completed by the outbreak of the Second World War and Stamp wrote up the conclusions in *The land of Britain* (1946), which was very influential in the form of post-war planning rules and procedures. An attempt to replicate the survey in the *Second land use survey of Great Britain* was initiated by Stamp's disciple, Professor Alice Coleman of King's College, in the 1950s and 1960s, but although several maps were completed and published its impetus ran out and it remains unfinished.

Atlases

Most of the commercial map publishers produced atlases. The concept of a collection of maps brought together in a volume was long established, dating back to the sixteenth century in the Netherlands, but atlases remained expensive until modern printing and publishing techniques, particularly the introduction of chromolithography and machine-driven presses, made it possible to make them more widely available in the twentieth century. Bartholomew produced the *Citizen's atlas* in 1898 which passed through several editions until 1952, as well as the *Survey atlas of Scotland* (1898 and 1912) based on his half inch sheets. This was republished by Birlinn in a centenary reproduction in 2012. Bartholomew produced the first edition of the *Times atlas* in 1922, and has continued to produce it in various formats to the present, most recently under the imprint Collins Bartholomew. In 1961 it produced the *Reader's Digest great world atlas*. This increasingly began to take up most of Bartholomew's activity until the company was bought by the Reader's Digest Association in 1980. Bartholomew also produced the first full-colour road atlas in 1944 and a number of specialist volumes like the *Atlas of the moon* (1969) and *China* (1974).

Johnston also produced a series of Library Atlases like the *Royal handy atlas of modern geography*, which despite its title was a large-folio format containing, in the 1914 edition, over sixty double-page full-colour maps and over eighty pages of Gazetteer. Educational atlases from the elementary to the advanced were also produced for classroom use, and special editions were tailored to the needs of schools in Australia, Canada and India. Several other publishers like Philip, Oxford University Press and a joint venture of Collins and Longman, produced school atlases. Although now largely superseded by digital and multimedia mapping, at least in education, the atlas format continues to produce interesting and important publications. Daniel Dorling's *New social atlas of Britain* (1997) used advanced computer techniques to create striking cartograms of social phenomena at a highly granular scale, which revealed patterns that would have been invisible on conventional maps. This was the first major mapping project where the printing plates were created directly from the author's data files without intermediate photography.

One of the puzzles of British map publishing is why there has never been an officially sponsored National Atlas such as the major state-funded carto-graphic projects in countries like Sweden or Canada. Such a prestigious and useful scheme was investigated by the Royal Geographical Society in the 1930s but, despite a positive recommendation, funds were not forthcoming, and the outbreak of the Second World War effectively killed any further development for security and financial reasons.

Mapping the future

Digital publishing has transformed cartography perhaps more than any other source of reference information. The invention of the geospecific postcode as an aid to mail sorting and delivery in 1959 has enabled the unexpected bonus of an easily understood search mechanism for online digital mapping pro-vided by companies like Google to the resolution of a few metres, supple-mented by photographic images of Streetview. Google maps are accessible and flexible but their conventions are not clear and scales are not clearly indicated. Particularly in urban areas, and for the location of businesses, they are not systematically revised and their up-to-dateness is questionable. Streetview, which captures images by special car-mounted cameras, has been criticised as a breach of privacy and, of course, is limited to areas with vehicular access.

Postcodes are also widely used in satellite navigation devices to locate destinations in vehicles. Google also provides global mapping free of charge. Accuracy and efficiency of digital mapping, especially when accessed on the move via mobile devices, is generally satisfactory – although there have been some spectacular mis-allocations recorded, like the identification of Dublin airport in a small residential street in the city centre, and the appearance of an entirely fictitious city in the north-west of England. While some predict that map publishing will migrate entirely to digital formats in the near future, map users remain quite stubbornly attached to printed cartography, not least because paper maps tend to be durable in inclement weather which, at present, defeats the delicate electronics of digital devices.

Magazines and periodicals

ANTHONY QUINN

Commercial magazines today can be classified in sectors: general consumer; consumer specialist/hobby; trade and technical; part works; and contract magazines. Within these sectors, magazines focus on a particular type of reader, identified by age, occupation, attitude and social class. General consumer would include women's magazines, television listings and illustrated weeklies. The dominant distribution method for consumer magazines is through newsagents. More specialist consumer titles covering hobbies, e.g. cycling and motoring, are, again, usually sold in newsagents but with more emphasis on subscriptions. Business, professional/trade and technical publications sell to a specific industry or specialism. They are mainly delivered on subscription or through controlled circulation, whereby recipients who meet certain criteria receive free copies. The term business-to-business (B2B) has gained popularity since the 1990s. Broadly, print circulations are slowly declining as more media move online.

Part works are published for a fixed number of issues to address a specific topic in an encyclopaedic way. Historical examples include Hutchinson's *Edward the peacemaker* in 1902 and Purnell's *History of the 20th century* (1965) edited by A. J. P. Taylor. The sector became more specialised in the 1970s with the formation of Marshall Cavendish, Eaglemoss and Orbis. The 1990s saw part works grow to depend on a gift alongside the publication, such as a video, part of a model or a figurine. The emphasis is on television marketing in January and February to achieve large initial sales and persuade buyers to order the series through a newsagent. Starting sales of the order of 200,000 copies will have been whittled down to 20,000 collectors of the last issue for most releases. Eaglemoss has worked with publishers to create series such as Best Food Fast! with *Best* magazine and a World War Two collection for the *Daily Telegraph*.

Contract/customer magazines are developed by a publisher to meet the marketing demands of a company or organisation. The 1980s saw the formalisation of the sector as it adopted a business model akin to advertising agencies, with free circulations in the millions exceeding even the best-selling consumer magazines. Some titles carry third party advertising to offset their costs, but most are financed by the marketing budgets of large companies. Some publishers are independent, while others are part of marketing agencies or mainstream publishers. Contract publishers marketed themselves as publishing agencies in the 1990s, rebranded themselves as customer publishers and then, since 2012, as content marketers that are 'channel neutral'. They use digital distribution, such as smartphone apps and tablet computers, websites, video and branded TV, as well as customer magazines to promote their clients.[1]

Publishing companies tend to specialise, although the bigger ones have divisions that might together address all the sectors, and the biggest have interests in other media. Some trade publishers have large consumer readerships. A few large publishers are responsible for the bulk of sales, with the number of trade titles exceeding consumer titles by about 5,000 to 2,800. The Periodical Publishers Association (PPA) has about 200 members, of which the top four account for about 60 per cent of consumer sales.[2] The UK market is well developed, with only the USA, with a far larger population making more focussed niches viable, having more titles.

The magazine industry is characterised by continual renewal as magazines are launched – typically about 500 a year in the twenty-first century – and closed to reflect changing trends. Alongside professional publishers are individuals and organisations that use the magazine format to publicise their agendas, campaign for a cause or run a fan club. Most of these titles fade away but some expand, such as *Viz*, which was started by three teenagers from a bedroom in Newcastle and was selling a million copies an issue at its peak.

Advertising revenue accounts for about 60 per cent of revenue across all magazines. However, this average disguises great variation: many business titles, contract magazines and free weeklies rely totally on such revenue, whereas the weekly *Loot* is full of free classified advertising and relies on copy sales revenue. The Audit Bureau of Circulations (ABC) verifies print and digital sales (or number of free copies distributed) and the National Readership Survey (NRS) measured readerships until 2018 (now done by PAMCo).[3] The price a magazine can charge for a page depends on the quantity and spending power of its audience.

1 See the-cma.com. 2 www.ppa.co.uk. 3 www.abc.org.uk and www.nrs.co.uk.

Magazines in 1914

By 1914 a mass media had been created through national distribution of magazines selling between half a million and a million copies an issue alongside popular daily papers with sales figures of the same order.[4] Claims made for sales were often dubious because there was no independent auditing.[5] Key to maintaining sales were marketing techniques established in the 1880s and 1890s. These included prize competitions and free life insurance against railway accidents. *John Bull* claimed to have paid out £620,000 in prizes to its weekly Bullets competitions in 1912–35.[6] Among the general interest magazines were cheaply produced weeklies that sold in large numbers (such as *Tit-Bits, Answers* and *John Bull*) and expensive weeklies and monthlies aimed at the middle and upper classes (such as *Illustrated London News, Tatler,* the *Strand* and *Queen*). The poor-quality paper used for the cheap weeklies and the cost of reproduction precluded much use of photography and anything but line illustration.

The biggest publishers were Amalgamated, Newnes and Pearson.[7] All three are linked through George Newnes and his founding of *Tit-Bits* in 1881 as a pioneer of 'New Journalism'.[8] Although Newnes died in 1910, the company had carried on. Amalgamated was founded by Alfred Harmsworth (later Lord Northcliffe) who, after becoming editor of Iliffe's *Bicycling News* and contributing to *Tit-Bits*, went on to establish *Answers*. Harmsworth had then turned to newspapers, bringing the pithy writing and entertainment found in magazines to newspaper journalism with the *Daily Mail* and *Daily Mirror*, before winning control of the *Sunday Dispatch, The Times* and the *Sunday Times* newspapers. Cyril Arthur Pearson had become manager of *Tit-Bits* and *Review of Reviews* at Newnes before leaving to establish *Pearson's Weekly* (1890) and *Pearson's Magazine* (1896), winning control of *London Opinion* and launching the *Daily Express*.

The House of Cassell was a diminished force since its heyday in the 1880s, but *Cassell's Magazine of Fiction*, a monthly, still sold well and the *Story-Teller* (1907–37) and the *New Magazine* (1909–30) focussed on the publisher's strength in fiction. Fiction was vital to magazines, but older monthlies such as *Cornhill, Temple Bar* and *Blackwood's* were outbid for popular writers by the big weeklies and monthlies. Demand had switched to short story series from serials, as exemplified by Conan Doyle's Sherlock Holmes over almost thirty years in

---

4 Law and Patten, 'The serial revolution'.   5 Reed, *The popular magazine*, pp. 171–2.
6 *Dictionary of 'Bullets'* published by the magazine in 1935.
7 Simonis, *Street of ink*; Reed, *The popular magazine*.   8 Jackson, *George Newnes*.

the *Strand* (1891–1950).[9] Among the leading cheap women's weeklies were Pearson's *Home Notes* (1894–1957), Amalgamated's *Home Chat* (1895–1960) and Newnes' *Woman's Life* (1895–1934).

The technical press appealed to the hobbyist as well as the professional. Iliffe Press, a Coventry printer, started with *Bicycling News* and the *Cyclist* and produced nine magazines by 1920, including *Autocar* (1865) and *Motor Cycle* (1903–83), *Amateur Photographer* (1884) and engineering and agricultural titles.

The Great War: opportunities and threats

For some publishers, the war provided an opportunity. At *London Opinion* it sparked one of the world's iconic images – the portrait by Alfred Leete of a pointing Lord Kitchener with the words: 'Your country needs you.' The image was taken for the government's recruitment campaign and continues to be repeated or imitated.[10] However, war with Germany did not seem an opportunity, unlike the Boer wars, which had generated demand for news and illustration and spurred the launch of the *Sphere*. 'Circulation slumped horribly in the first few weeks of the war, and advertising dropped alarmingly', said Lincoln Springfield, proprietor of *London Opinion*, in 1917, 'but things gradually mended, and then improved, and then boomed, until to-day circulation and advertising, revenue and turnover are all at record heights'.[11]

As the war progressed, paper and ink became scarce. *Vogue*, which had been imported from the USA, could no longer rely on shipping, so Condé Nast set up a full publishing operation in Britain. This cemented the model of a fashion magazine with a small, affluent readership that would commission the best contributors to appeal to companies and shops wanting to advertise luxury goods. Yet, there were opportunities. Amalgamated launched the weekly *War Illustrated*, with John Hammerton as editor. Another launch, 'in the service of the nation', was *Blighty* with patrons such as Lord Jellicoe and Sir Douglas Haig. This was sent free to the troops and funded by advertising and the public buying seasonal specials. *Tit-Bits* did its bit for morale, publishing the words and music to songs such as 'Keep the home fires burning' by Ivor Novello. It also introduced war insurance for civilians killed or injured while carrying the latest issue.

9 Ashley, *The age of the storytellers*; Baldwin, *Art and commerce*.
10 Thatcher and Quinn, *Kitchener*.   11 Simonis, *Street of ink*, p. 272.

Illustrated magazines showed events to a world yet to hear a radio broadcast, never mind watch television. The *Graphic* carried editorial notices that it 'paid liberally' for sketches or photographs of striking episodes in the field. Paintings from the front were popular, such as Fortunino Matania's 'Good bye old man' in the *Sphere* (24 June 1916), which was taken up as a poster by American Red Star Animal Relief to raise funds for stricken animals. Among the cartoonists were Captain Bruce Bairnsfather with his Old Bill character in the *Bystander*, and William Heath Robinson in the *Sketch* and the *Tatler*; both inspiring phrases that entered the common language.

Domestic help was scarce, so weeklies such as *Woman's Own* (W. B. Horner) stepped in with advice. The 24 April 1915 issue carried a laundry supplement. Inside, a rose-framed editorial, 'Honour for the Housewife', read: 'What task can there be so wonderful and beautiful as to make our household feel nested in the home, safe and cosy?' Pages carried slogans across the top, some making use of social marketing: 'Let your neighbours know that we are giving another free knitting supplement next week.'

Pearson's eyesight failed in 1912 and he sold his magazine and newspapers to devote his wealth to supporting the National Institute for the Blind and the St Dunstan's homes for ex-servicemen. The *Express* fell under the control of the Canadian-born Sir Max Aitken (later Lord Beaverbrook). Newnes took over the magazines. Pearson had backed Baden-Powell in setting up the Scout movement and published Baden-Powell's magazine, *Scouting for Boys* – as a book, it became one of the best-sellers of the twentieth century. In turn, scouts raised money for Pearson's scheme to publish books in Braille for the blind. While most magazines took a patriotic line, the greatest publishing success of the war was a thorn in the government's side, *John Bull*. It entered the war selling about half a million copies a week and ended it selling probably three times as many. Its editor, Horatio Bottomley, was the founding chairman of the *Financial Times* in the 1880s and, when he brought his idea to Odhams in 1906, was a Liberal MP. *John Bull* not only looked different from *Tit-Bits* – its cover was dominated by a drawing of John Bull with his bulldog rather than by advertising – but covered social issues and campaigned on behalf of the troops. This gave Bottomley a platform to return as an independent MP in 1918, but he was sentenced to seven years of hard labour for fraud in 1922.

Most magazines were printed letterpress in or around London's Fleet Street, with the better titles using gravure. Twenty-five miles north in Watford, Hertfordshire, however, what was to become one of the world's largest printers, Sun Engraving, printed its first periodical in 1919, the *Draper's Organizer*, a letterpress weekly with four-colour illustrations.[12]

1920s: post-war boom

The end of the war brought with it an economic recession, but there were new ventures in domestic subjects. In 1919, Newnes launched *Homes & Gardens*, which was followed by *Ideal Home* from Odhams and a British edition of US publisher Hearst's *Good Housekeeping* (1922). The shortage of domestic staff and the government's promises to build more houses combined to create a boom for such magazines. *Woman & Home* would follow in 1926 and *Woman's Journal* a year later, both from Amalgamated. *The Times* relaunched its *Woman's Supplement*, which had been suspended during the war, though it was merged into *Eve* in March 1921. *Time & Tide*, a left-leaning review, was founded by Viscountess Rhondda. Her aim, stated in later issues, was to put 'the woman's point of view in what was then a man-ruled world'. *Woman's Weekly*, which had launched in 1911 with a focus on crochet and fiction, by the 1920s had switched to knitting and fiction. An editorial bemoaned the fashionable shape for women: 'How long the present slim-line silhouette will continue, it is hard to say. I think a new shape would be a pleasant change don't you?' (28 May 1927).

There was consolidation within the industry. The death of Harmsworth (Lord Northcliffe) in 1922 saw Amalgamated fall into the hands of William and Gomer Berry, who combined the company with Cassell along with the interests of Sir Edward Iliffe.[13] For the cheap weeklies, it was a sad time. With Bottomley in prison, *John Bull* lost its edge and sales halved. The production values of *Tit-Bits, Answers* and *Pearson's Weekly* stayed at wartime levels and the three looked almost identical, distinguished only by the colour of their covers.[14] The wireless was triggering new technical and hobby titles and *Popular Wireless* (1922, Amalgamated) claimed 'half a million readers monthly' (6 December 1924). In 1923, the BBC's *Radio Times* appeared, with production and printing handled by Newnes. Cheap paper dictated the use of line illustration by pen, scraperboard, lino or wood cut and engravings, rather than halftone photographs. However, the use of artists such as Edward Ardizzone, Eric Fraser, Robin Jacques and Lynton Lamb created a classic illustration heritage.[15] The first issue of the *Melody Maker* (1926) noted the

12 www.sunprintershistory.com/timeline.html.
13 Dilnot, *The romance of the Amalgamated Press.*   14 Quinn, *A history*, p. 84.
15 Baker, *Artists of Radio Times*; Driver (ed.), *The art of Radio Times.*

danger of the new media to an older tradition: 'Broadcasting is having disastrous effect on the sales of sheet music.' It focussed on a new style of music – jazz.

This was also the era of the 'bright young things', an upper-crust circle to which the aspiring photographer Cecil Beaton attached himself. His images in *Tatler* and *Vogue* promoted the Sitwells and the people that surrounded Stephen Tennant. To such society contacts he would add the stars of stage and screen on both sides of the Atlantic, and the royal family. His work runs like a thread into the sixties, with photographs of Mick Jagger and David Hockney, and he inspired younger photographers such as David Bailey.

1930s: a colourful era

Cheap weeklies stayed with letterpress and its poor halftones, but the quality magazines mixed letterpress for its clarity of text with gravure for the subtlety it could bring to large reproductions of photographs – and the ability to 'bleed' images off the page. In 1929 the country's biggest printing company, Sun, produced the first all-gravure weekly, *Picturegoer*. On the opposite side of Watford, Odhams Press set up its own factory, where the first issue of *Woman* was produced (11 September 1937). Odhams distinguished its offering by using illustration for its covers and a larger format (265 × 360 mm). On a smaller scale, in an alleyway off Fleet Street, *London Life* (fig. 21.2) was printed (1922–60). It was a men's weekly with a colour cover and as well as being a primer in inventive typography – its title design changed every week – encouraged fetishism, with letters about cross-dressing, high-heeled shoes, boots, corsets, rubber clothing and amputated limbs.

The women's weeklies illustrate the changes in technology. Newnes launched *Woman's Own* (fig. 21.3) in 1932 with a cover-mounted gift (three skeins of wool); a reader offer for a domestic encyclopaedia based on collecting coupons; and better production. 'Turn right away to our unique pictorial supplement produced by the new photo-tone process', said the editorial. 'These beautifully printed pages help us to give you week by week many new and attractive features never before possible in a women's weekly.' The covers marked a departure in that they were photographs, and used spot colour. The following year, Newnes relaunched the weekly with a full-colour illustrated cover, larger format (258 × 320 mm) and greater extent (sixty-four pages). The 'editress' gushed: 'our big new *Woman's Own* makes me feel all "new" . . . stepping on to this gay page is rather like pulling up the blind to let in the sunlight'. Extensive use was made of a single spot

Figure 21.1 *Blighty* (Summer 1917). (Photograph: Max J. Quinn)

colour on editorial and advertising with full colour on the centre spread – to promote a dressmaking pattern costing one shilling, making it a lucrative business for the publisher.[16]

Another trend was seen in February 1936, when two weeklies, *News Review* and *Cavalcade*, tried their hand, even though *Everyman* 'the world news

16 Beetham, *A magazine of her own?*; Braithwaite and Barrell, *The business of women's magazines.*

Figure 21.2 *London Life* (2 February 1935). (Photograph: Max J. Quinn)

weekly' under editor Viscountess Dunedin had not lasted a year after its 1933 launch. Both survived into the 1950s. Two new sectors were also under development. There were already men's magazines, such as *London Life* and the monthly *Razzle* (1933–57), but *Men Only* was a departure from accepted practice in using a pocket format (115 × 165 mm) to attract commuters. It was published by Pearson/Newnes. The editorial noted: 'We don't want women readers. We won't have women readers.'

Figure 21.3 *Woman's Own* (21 May 1938). (Photograph: Max J. Quinn)

In 1937, another pocket monthly appeared. *Lilliput* claimed a circulation of 300,000, the largest of any monthly, by 1940. It covered humour, short stories, photographs and the arts, led by a Hungarian photojournalist who had fled Germany, Stefan Lorant. The covers always showed a man, a woman and a dog drawn by Walter Trier, another émigré from Germany.[17] One feature was its 'juxtapositions': full-page bleed photographs with a short caption on facing pages that created a visual pun. It also featured full-page nudes.[18]

17 Webb, *Lilliput goes to war*; Grove, *So much to tell*.
18 Lorant, *101 best picture comparisons*.

Photojournalism was another front.[19] Émigrés from continental Europe had bought with them 35 mm Leica cameras as well as layout skills honed on image-led publications such as *Berliner Illustrirte Zeitung* and *Arbeiter-Illustrierte Zeitung (AIZ)* in Germany and the French *Vu*. Amalgamated's *Pictorial Weekly* was using dynamic layouts with pictures printed across gutters, montages, cut-outs and tint boxes in 1933. Stefan Lorant developed such techniques on *Weekly Illustrated* for Odhams in 1934 before leaving to publish his book, *I was Hitler's prisoner*, and establish *Lilliput*. The success of the pocket monthly brought Lorant to the attention of Sir Edward Hulton, who bought up *Lilliput* and gave Lorant the resources to launch *Picture Post* (1938–57).[20] Again, he brought in émigrés, including John Heartfield with his surrealist photomontages. Lorant used images by Heartfield that had appeared in *AIZ*, first in *Lilliput* and then in *Picture Post* to warn against Hitler. A Heartfield photomontage from *AIZ* of Hitler as the Kaiser was reused as a *Picture Post* cover (9 September 1939).

As the decade progressed, more magazines adopted gravure, among them the large-format colour launches *Wild West Weekly*, *Modern Wonder* and *Flying* (which carried the Biggles stories of editor W. E. Johns).[21] However, growth was about to come to a shuddering halt.

The war years

The Second World War, along with the rationing that continued until 1954 and austerity measures that followed, cast a long pall over the magazine industry. In 1939, Odhams merged *Passing Show* into *Illustrated*. Newnes shrunk its weekly *London Opinion* to a monthly pocket format and merged the *Humorist* into it in 1940. One result of this was a collapse in demand for illustrators. *Vogue* had run a colour photographic cover in July 1932 but reverted to its illustrators, and it was only in the monochrome weekly photomagazines that the camera established itself over the pen for covers.

Picture Post took a stance against government censorship – printing blacked-out photographs to highlight the problem – while *John Bull* started a Voice of the Troops column. The free services magazine *Blighty* (fig. 21.1) was relaunched and other familiar faces from the Great War were revived. Bairnsfather's Old Bill ran as a cartoon strip in *Tit-Bits*. Amalgamated resurrected *War Illustrated* in a format and with production values that could have been mistaken for the 1914 original. In 1939 Hutchinson published

19 Owen, *Magazine design*.   20 Hopkinson, *Picture Post*; Kee, *The Picture Post album*.
21 Crowley, *Magazine covers*.

a translation of Hitler's *Mein Kampf* in eighteen parts. The covers declared that the royalties would go to the Red Cross and St John Fund.

Under rationing, publishers could only consume paper at a rate of 19.5 per cent of their pre-war usage; advertisements were restricted to the same proportion of space as before the war and launches were prohibited. The results were clear. *Picture Post* cut its extent from more than a hundred pages to twenty-eight. *Good Housekeeping* kept its pagination but reduced its format three times, eventually becoming pocket-sized. The May 1941 issue of *Men Only* complained: 'We have worked hard for success, and now that it has come we are robbed of it by this paper shortage. Believe us, we are properly browned off.'[22]

Mary Grieve replaced John Gammie as editor of *Woman* – a job she would hold until 1962 – when he went into the RAF in 1940. During the war, she helped advise the government on how women could help the war effort. Articles switched from high fashion to how to repair clothes or adapt them. Cookery features were based on recipes approved by the Ministry of Food.[23] The *Woman's Own* editorial of 12 July 1941 ran: 'Things have been grim, raids and crises aren't over but ... nothing is so fearful as being afraid.' Covers portrayed the unfamiliar jobs women had taken on: 'There may be snags and drawbacks in the job we hesitate to plunge into – almost certainly there will. But one thing is certain about it – we'll be putting one more nail in Hitler's coffin ... even if it's going to take a little time to hammer it down.'

In a House of Commons debate on 20 May 1942 the government was attacked for allowing *Vogue* to be published. Why, an MP asked, was 'a useless paper of this kind' allowed to circulate when 'there is a very widespread feeling in the country that luxuries of this kind, and advertisements of luxuries of this kind, are completely out of tune with the appeals which come from the government?' Even worse, 'large numbers of each issue' were bought by the Ministry of Information and the British Council for distribution in neutral countries. However, from 1943, the subject matter lightened. The women on the covers of the weeklies were no longer in uniform; instead, they looked off the page into a brighter future.

When the war ended, *John Bull* was first to react, doing away with its advertising-dominated covers to introduce 'this new age of colour' (2 March 1946) with an illustration by Clixby Watson. But Odhams was the only publisher with the resources to make such a leap. The following winter, snow storms caused electricity shortages because coal could not reach power stations. The government decreed that magazines must stop publishing for two

22 Quinn, *A history*, p. 106.
23 Waller and Vaughan-Rees, *Women in wartime*; Dancyger, *World of women*.

issues. The *Economist* appeared as a page in the *Financial Times*.[24] At *Woman*, Grieve wrote: 'Those power shortages achieved what Hitler could not.'

1950s: the shackles come off

Rationing of paper ended in 1950, so *Woman's Own* (2 March) ran a forty-eight-page issue, up twelve pages. On the cover was a photograph, rather than one of the Aubrey Rix illustrations that had led the magazine for several years. The issue also introduced former royal governess Marion Crawford. 'The little princesses' by 'Crawfie' heralded an approach that would see such coverage dominate women's weeklies for a decade.

In response to *John Bull*, *Tit-Bits* dropped its advertising covers in favour of photographs of sports and film stars and in 1950 adopted a tabloid format with pin-up covers and newspaper-style layouts. It seemed a reverse of the 'magazinisation' that had seen *Tit-Bits* inspire the New Journalism of Harmsworth, but in fact these issues were the forerunner of an approach that was to make the tabloid *Sun* such a success for Rupert Murdoch in the 1970s.[25] Techniques and styles developed by magazines in America, where there was no rationing or austerity measures, influenced British publishers, and syndicated copy was cheap to buy.[26] Imports also promoted American films, goods and ideas directly to the public.

In 1950, the *Strand* was merged into *Men Only*. MacDonald Hastings had taken over as editor on the pocket-format magazine in 1944 and complained: 'Where are the Conan Doyles today, and where are the readers who want them anyway? What people want today is imaginative reporting; the day of fiction has gone.'[27] In 1954, *Men Only* took over *London Opinion* and relaunched itself. Out went cover caricatures of the great and the good for racier cartoons of leggy women. Inside, colour plates by pin-up artists were labelled 'Let's Join the Ladies.' *Men Only* ran issues of nearly 200 pages in 1955, but it faded from then on. Yet, this racier look paled in comparison with a 1957 launch in London's Soho district. There, the art-school-trained model Pamela Green and photographer George Harrison Marks provided the seed for the modern-day pornography industry with the glossy *Kamera*.[28] This was a large-format colour title from the start but alongside it grew numerous black and white pocket titles with names like *Spick*, *Span* and *Carnival*.

Lilliput was forced to react to segmentation. In 1954 it adopted a larger format, and in 1955 its covers declared: '*Lilliput* is a man's magazine.'[29] However, in 1960, it folded into *Men Only*. For the illustrated weeklies, things

24 Dudley Edwards, *The pursuit of reason*, pp. 879–84. 25 Engel, *Tickle the public*.
26 Owen, *Magazine design*. 27 'Death of a tradition', *Time* 2 January 1950.
28 Hanson, *The history of girly magazines*. 29 Quinn, *A history*, p. 129.

happened more quickly. Falling sales saw *Picture Post* succumb in 1957 and *Illustrated* and *Everybody's* merged into *John Bull*.

Amalgamated Press led the industry at this time, publishing seventy-three magazines by 1951, with a total circulation of 14 million copies. Newnes had fifty-five magazines, with *Woman's Own* selling about 1.5 million copies each week. The women's weeklies trailed only the overall sales leader, *Radio Times*. Magazines had to 'sell' themselves, with colourful covers and arresting cover lines, bigger pictures and better paper in the face of new competition from television. *Punch* dropped the Dicky Doyle cover it had used for a century in favour of colour cartoons. In 1955, in the week that ITV launched, *Radio Times* claimed world record sales of 8,832,579 copies – an astounding figure for a total population of about 50 million.[30] The rise in television brought a decline in cinema, and people turned away from film magazines. Amalgamated's *Picture Show* and Odhams' *Picturegoer* had both closed by 1961.

Printing strikes hit the industry in 1950, 1956 and 1959. The 1956 dispute saw the *Radio Times* reduced to a four-page broadsheet printed in France; the *Economist* had one issue produced in a Swiss convent. Many weeklies simply failed to come out. Throughout the turmoil, though, there was growth. John Taylor, editor of the trade magazine *Tailor & Cutter* – 'the most quoted trade paper in the world'[31] – launched a quarterly, *Man About Town* (fig. 21.4), which was distributed through tailors' shops.[32] It was still a tough market, however, with a UK edition of *Esquire* failing to establish itself. For women's magazines, new product advertising created a boom time, and as the magazines grew in size, so did their print-runs. Both *Woman* and *Woman's Own* were approaching sales of 3 million copies, so to take the strain off their presses their owners launched new titles. *Woman's Realm* (Odhams) and *Woman's Day* (Newnes) appeared in 1958, and *Woman's Mirror* (Amalgamated) in 1960. However, even bigger changes were afoot.

The birth of IPC

The magazine and newspaper industries responded to the advent of television by restructuring. In 1958, the Mirror Group had bought Amalgamated and its technical and trade arm Associated-Iliffe, renaming it Fleetway. In turn, Odhams bought Hulton Press, giving it control of titles such as *Farmers Weekly*, *Housewife* and *Lilliput*. It then proceeded to close *Lilliput*. These moves led to takeovers that would see Odhams, Newnes and Fleetway

---

30 Advert in the *Economist* 10 September 1955, p. 821.
31 John Taylor Obituary, *The Times* 6 January 2004, p. 26.
32 Taylor, *From Ovaltiney to angry old man*.

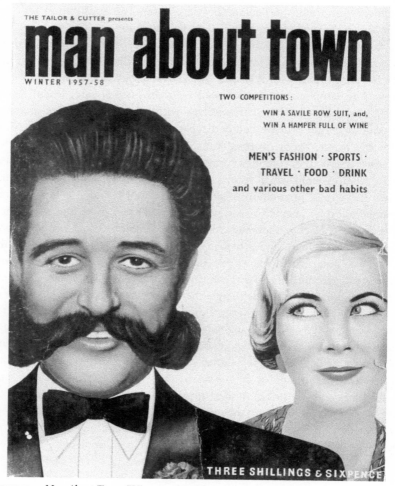

Figure 21.4 *Man About Town* (Winter 1957). (Photograph: Max J. Quinn)

merge into the behemoth International Publishing Corporation (IPC) in 1963.[33] One company now owned the 'big four' women's weeklies – *Woman, Woman's Own, Woman's Realm* and *Woman's Weekly* – but their sales had peaked and they together entered a gentle decline with the first to close, in 2001, being the relative newcomer, *Woman's Realm*.

The decline of other general interest weeklies continued. *Tit-Bits* was subject to numerous relaunches, first losing the green that had marked out

33 Cox and Mowatt, *Revolutions from Grub Street*.

its covers since the 1880s, then reverting to a magazine size and structure. IPC sold the magazine and it was merged into Associated Newspapers' *Weekend* in 1974. The company partly blamed the way papers such as the *Sun* had adopted the *Tit-Bits* formula for the magazine's demise. The name was sold on to become a top-shelf men's magazine. *John Bull* saw a similar fate. It was relaunched as *Today*, with photographic covers and more of a focus on topical articles than fiction, but IPC sold it in 1964 to *Weekend*.

However, some more specialised weeklies were more in tune with the times. The *New Musical Express*, which had been renamed in 1952 from *Accordion Times and Musical Express*, published the first singles chart (14 November 1952) and aligned itself with Beatlemania and bands such as the Rolling Stones, until sales peaked at 300,000 a week in the early 1970s. Alongside it were other 'inkies', *Melody Maker*, *Disc*, *Record Mirror* and *Sounds*. Many titles such as *Pop*, *Pop Ten*, *Beat* and *Rave* in a small or standard format built on the music boom and there were magazines for dedicated fans such as *Beatles Monthly*.

Younger readers took on a greater significance. Fleetway's *Honey* (1960–86) was for 'the teens and twenties' or the 'Young, gay and get-ahead'. The look of magazines changed too, as the influence of the international design movement made itself felt.[34] Jocelyn Stevens bought *Queen* and employed Mark Boxer to redesign the society magazine started by Samuel Beeton in 1861.[35] Two other young entrepreneurs, Michael Heseltine and Clive Labovitch, took over *Man About Town* in 1959, shortening its name to *Town*. These magazines personified the Swinging Sixties, but although influential, neither survived; *Queen* was subsumed into *Harper's Bazaar* in 1970 and *Town* closed in 1967. Heseltine has described *Town* as being 'too expensive to survive'[36] but his lasting success was in bringing a quality approach to trade magazines, in the form of advertising weekly *Campaign*, which formed the backbone of Haymarket.

As the decade advanced, David Bailey, Terence Donovan, Brian Duffy and Don McCullin made a visual splash, whether it was photographing models or portraying war. Bailey created the supermodel Jean Shrimpton, and Barry Lategan sold Twiggy to the nation as 'The face of 1966' in the *Daily Express*. John Parsons redesigned *Vogue* with a larger format in 1963 and stepped down as art director a year later after sixteen years in the job.

Offset lithography was replacing letterpress and gravure. Photocomposition replaced letterpress for magazines within twenty years. Letraset handed out

---

34 McLean, *Magazine design*; Owen, *Magazine design*; Hollis, *Graphic design*; Hollis, *Swiss graphic design*.
35 Crewe, *Frontiers of privilege*; Spain, *Mrs Beeton and her husband*.
36 Michael Heseltine, 'My 30 years in advertising', *Campaign* 18 September 1998, p. 19.

a similar fate to hand-drawn lettering. Offset litho, golfball typewriters and Letraset together lowered the barriers for new magazines, enabling the foundation of *Private Eye* and many fanzines and underground magazines.[37] The inability to reproduce colour advertising had frustrated newspapers and in 1962 the *Sunday Times* addressed the problem by bringing in Boxer to launch a colour supplement. The Thomson group had bought *Illustrated London News*, the *Sphere* and *Tatler* the year before. The paper's sales rose within six months to exceed a million copies a week.[38] The *Observer* and the *Telegraph* followed suit, again taking big advertising campaigns from weekly magazines.

The women's sector was stirred by Newnes/IPC launching *Nova* (1965–75).[39] Harry Fieldhouse was the launch editor, but it took off under Dennis Hackett (who came from *Queen*) to become a groundbreaking magazine with challenging articles and a design to match by Harri Peccinotti and David Hillman. However, as with *Town* and *Queen*, profits were thin and the magazine adopted smaller formats until it closed as a shadow of its original self.

The success of *Playboy* in the USA in the 1950s led to its distribution in the UK. Paul Raymond, owner of Raymond's Revue Bar in Soho, backed the launch of a similar title, *King*, in 1965. He pulled out within months, leaving the other investors to continue. However, Bob Guccione's *Penthouse* (1965) and then *Mayfair* (a Paul Raymond launch in 1966) overwhelmed *King*. IPC's *Club* tried with a similar formula in 1970 but folded after twenty-one issues, essentially shutting the men's lifestyle magazine.[40]

In the late 1960s a thriving underground press produced such titles as *International Times* (1966–72), *Oz* (1967–73), *Time Out* (1968) and *Friends* (1969–72).[41] The designer Pearce Marchbank worked on both *Time Out* and *Oz*. One of the latter's editors was Felix Dennis, who would go on to found Dennis publishing. Germaine Greer also worked on *Oz* and featured on the covers of at least two issues. On safer ground, International Thomson Publishing negotiated an exclusive deal for *Family Circle* (1964–2006) to be sold at check-outs in supermarkets. The result was a best-selling monthly selling 625,000 copies an issue by 1988, when ITP sold the title to IPC. However, publishers had started to sell their magazines through supermarkets in 1984 and *Family Circle* lost ground to launches, particularly *Prima*, from 1986.

37 Miles, *London calling*; Triggs, *Fanzines*; MacQueen, *Private Eye*.
38 Hobson et al., *The pearl of days*.   39 Hillman et al., *Nova*.
40 Brian Braithwaite, 'The evolution of men's magazines', *Campaign* 11 April 1997, p. 3.
41 King, '*Time Out* cover design'.

1970s: the new woman

The early 1970s saw the general interest weeklies wilt as readers preferred glossier monthly magazines. It was also a time of recession with the 1972 miners' strike leading to a three-day week. Problems were reinforced with an oil crisis the following year and inflation becoming a household word. Most publishers were cautious about launching magazines. Reed, a paper and building materials group, bought IPC in 1970 to form a global conglomerate, Reed International. *Woman* and *New Scientist* found themselves controlled by a group that made wallpaper and paint, but had links to the industry going back to 1904, when it provided the smoother newsprint that enabled better reproduction of photographs for the relaunched *Daily Mirror*.

Women's liberation was gaining momentum. *Woman's Own* editor Jane Reid rejected an advert for bras that showed a woman wearing no knickers (1 April 1971). The magazine's art department painted knickers on to the advert. NatMags followed the trend by bringing *Cosmopolitan* to Britain. It was the first international version of a title that had been recast for 'liberated' women by Helen Gurley Brown (author of *Sex and the single girl*). The UK launch editor was Joyce Hopkirk, former women's editor at the *Sun*. A TV campaign by Saatchi & Saatchi helped the print-run of 350,000 sell out. The second issue featured a male nude (Paul de Feu, Greer's husband). *Cosmo*'s arrival led to the sale of NatMags' *Vanity Fair* to IPC and killed off IPC's *Nova*. *Cosmopolitan* would become the best-selling monthly and hold the title until 2002. Another boost for women's lib was *Spare Rib* (1972–93), despite W. H. Smith refusing to stock it at first (see Chapter 27). One of its editors, Rosie Boycott, would later edit the *Independent* newspaper, men's monthly *Esquire* and the *Daily Express*.

Emap made a challenge to IPC when it launched *Smash Hits* (1978–2006). The company – originally East Midlands Allied Press – ran regional newspapers but had launched *Angling Times* in 1953 and expanded through acquisitions, such as *Motor Cycle News* in 1956. Although sales of the inkies rose and fell with musical trends – *NME* reinvented itself with the 'hip young gunslingers' Julie Burchill and Tony Parsons to thrive on the Punk scene – they began to lose out to more focussed music magazines such as *Kerrang!* (1981) and *Metal Hammer* (1994).

In November 1978, *The Times* and the *Sunday Times* shut down in a labour dispute that lasted for a year. Sir James Goldsmith, nicknamed 'Goldenballs' in his legal disputes with *Private Eye*, stepped in to launch a news weekly, *Now!* (1979–81). Sales were reported at 410,000 for the first issue, but, like many attempts before and since, the title failed to make headway against US weeklies *Time* and *Newsweek* and the strong Sunday papers.

1980s: style bibles and computers

Angelo Zgorelec had launched *Personal Computer World* in 1978 but it was the advent of home computers that created a big market. A June 1984 survey in *Campaign* identified forty-six titles from fifteen publishers. The best-seller was IPC's *Your Computer*, with a circulation of 122,642. But computers did not just create a market for magazines; they reduced production costs and made it easier to set up companies. In 1982, *Acorn User*, produced by US book publisher Addison-Wesley under licence from BBC Micro maker Acorn, began using a subscription-based email system to communicate with authors. When the magazine moved to contract publisher Redwood, it introduced a network based on BBC Micros to replace the company's typewriters. This grew to about eighty terminals. Emap, which published several computing magazines, established a home bulletin board and email system, Micronet, using Prestel computers for micro users with modems. It peaked with about 90,000 subscribers.

Another wave of computerisation was set off by desktop publishing on the Apple Macintosh in 1985 and would become the standard production method for magazines within a decade.[42] By 1989, Adobe Illustrator was used for creating line graphics, Quark Xpress for page layout and Adobe PhotoShop for sizing and editing digitised photographs.[43] Desktop publishing (DTP) destroyed typesetting companies: magazine editors made up pages on screen and sent the files on disc so printers could output film directly. *Car* was a rare example of bypassing paper-based typesetting by switching from letterpress straight to DTP in 1991. It would be another decade before in-house scanners, digital cameras and massive online image libraries such as Getty Images would do away with the need for colour repro suppliers at many publishers.

Three magazines launched by independent publishers in 1980 revolutionised graphic design and influenced the fashion and music industries: the *Face* (1980–2004), *Blitz* (1980–91) and *i-D* (1980).[44] Nick Logan had edited music weekly *NME* for IPC and invented *Smash Hits* for Emap. His *Face* provided the platform for designer Neville Brody and would lead to a resurgence of men's magazines with the follow-up *Arena* (1986–2009).[45] It also nurtured Corrine Day, publishing her photographs of a sixteen-year-old Kate Moss on its cover (July 1990). These magazines encouraged the use of stylists, Ray Petri and the 'Buffalo' look being influential internationally.

---

42 Pipes, *Production for graphic designers.*   43 Sanders *et al.* (eds.), *The impossible image.*
44 Jones and Enninful, *i-D covers*; Morgan and Lorenz, *Buffalo.*
45 Taylor and Brody, *100 Years of magazine covers*; Wozencroft, *Brody.*

Over the decade, celebrities began to replace models, who were not usually credited, on magazine covers, a trend accelerated by Spanish import *Hello!* (1988), which paid for interviews and let subjects vet words and pictures. Also, publishers began to look for more brand extensions, for example in television, and Emap began to build up radio assets that could exploit its music titles.[46] Contract magazines became a recognisable sector under the influence of Redwood Publishing from 1982. Although such magazines had long existed, British Airways' *High Life* being one example, Redwood launched magazines for American Express, InterCity, Marks & Spencer and Unisys that raised the profile of the sector. The company was taken over by BBC Magazines in 1988. Redwood split from the BBC in 1993, retaining the contract titles such as the *Sky TV Guide*, then the UK's biggest-circulation magazine. Redwood drove the formation of the Association of Publishing Agencies, encouraging companies to behave like advertising agencies. By 2012, the APA had sixty-eight member companies. In 1994, Redwood became part of advertising agency Abbot Mead Vickers.

IPC was the dominant publisher, but was shaken by German group Gruner & Jahr launching *Prima* (1986). This overtook *Family Circle* as the UK's best-selling women's monthly. Two weeklies followed: *Best* (Gruner & Jahr) and *Bella* (Bauer) in 1987. Then, Bauer launched *Take a Break* (1990), which would become the best-selling weekly. Gruner & Jahr sold its magazines to Natmags in 2000. It was an IPC magazine, *Woman's Own*, that sparked one of the controversies of the decade, with an interview in which Prime Minister Margaret Thatcher used the phrase 'There is no such thing as society.'[47]

Alongside challenges in the women's market, IPC faced decline in its music titles, *NME* and *Melody Maker*, as did *Record Mirror* and *Sounds* owned by *Daily Express* group United Newspapers. These were losing sales to more focussed magazines such as clubbing title *Mixmag*. IPC responded by relaunching *NME* and *Melody Maker* in a magazine format. United's titles closed. Another threat to IPC would emerge in 1986, when BBC Enterprises took a controlling stake in Redwood. The BBC wanted to reduce its dependence on *Radio Times* because, with the advent of satellite and cable broadcasting, the government had decided to deregulate the TV listings market. This meant the BBC would have to sell its programme listings to any publisher. The same change would affect ITV and *TV Times*. The BBC immediately put its name on Redwood's two non-contract titles to become *BBC Acorn User* and *BBC Educational Computing*. BBC/Redwood's big launch was *Good Food* (1989), which included

---

46 Gough-Yates, *Understanding women's magazines*, p. 49.
47 Keay, 'Aids, education and the year 2000!'

every recipe on a BBC television or radio programme in the current month. IPC complained to the Office of Fair Trading about the free on-screen promotion these received. BBC/Redwood would become a much bigger force in the industry; first, though, it had to weather a storm for *Radio Times*.

As soon as TV listings became available, they were taken up by newspaper supplements and magazines. By 2011 there were seven listings titles from three publishers, two of them, Bauer's *TV Choice* and IPC's *What's on TV*, being the country's best-sellers. Sales of *Radio Times* fell from about 3 million in the 1980s to under a million, though, at £1.20, its cover price was almost three times that of the two best-sellers.

1990s: supermodels, men and the Web

Vogue showed five models – Naomi Campbell, Cindy Crawford, Christy Turlington, Linda Evangelista and Tatjana Patitz – photographed by Peter Lindbergh on its January 1990 cover.[48] George Michael then cast the same quintet in his music video for single 'Freedom! '90'. It was the era of the supermodel. Style magazines continued to expand, with *Dazed & Confused* (1991) started by John Rankin Waddell and Jefferson Hack establishing links with the fashion industry and the Young British Artists. Givenchy creative director Alexander McQueen was guest editor for the September 1998 issue. Its stylists, Katy England and Katie Grand, and later Nicola Formichetti, set fashion trends.[49] Its upmarket readers were international and attracted global advertisers. Tyler Brûlé used the strategy for interiors title *Wallpaper* (1996), which was bought by Time Warner in 1997.

Stand-up comedians, television show *Men Behaving Badly* and *Viz* – which sold a million copies an issue in 1990 – inspired the 'lads' mag', James Brown's *Loaded* (1994) at IPC. It passed 100,000 sales within six months[50] and attracted young men in a way that *Arena* (1986), Condé Nast's *GQ* (1989) and Natmags' *Esquire* (1991) had been unable to do.[51] However, whereas *Loaded* ran covers showing comedians, sportsmen and musicians with the occasional model, *FHM* from Emap started with Madonna and then went almost exclusively with models and actresses. Its circulation peaked at 775,000 in 1998 – outselling even *Cosmopolitan*. Emap launched or licensed several overseas versions of *FHM* and the concept was copied in many other territories, but the biggest success internationally was Dennis's *Maxim* (1995–2009). Although it

48 Derrick and Muir, *Vogue covers.*   49 Hack and Furniss, *Dazed and confused.*
50 Southwell, *Getting away with it.*   51 Tungate, *Branded male*, p. 118.

never rivalled *Loaded* and *FHM* in the UK, *Maxim* became the world's biggest-selling men's magazine.[52]

The new humour was to claim a victim though, *Punch*. The 150-year-old magazine was closed by United Newspapers after sales had fallen from 175,000 in the 1940s to 33,000 in 1992. The company blamed advertisers shifting to colour supplements. Harrods owner Mohamed Fayed resurrected the magazine in 1996 with a 'New Punch, new danger' cover aping advertising by the Conservatives attacking Tony Blair. However, it failed to attract readers and closed in 2001. A website survives selling cartoons.[53]

BBC/Redwood repeated the success of *Good Food* with *Gardeners' World* and *Top Gear* (1993) both becoming the leaders in their markets. *Gardeners' World* made extensive use of cover gifts, including a plastic trug that was far larger than the magazine. Garden gnomes – reading the magazine – were sent to subscribers. The strategy encouraged a spate of gifts.

Concern about contract magazines and 'advertorials' – advertising pages produced by publishers to look like editorial – prompted the PPA and the British Society of Magazine Editors to release guidelines covering 'special advertising opportunities'. Another worry for the industry was public concern over the sexualisation of teen magazines: this led to the formation of the Teen Magazine Arbitration Panel under the auspices of the PPA.[54]

The middle of the decade marked the start of the digital era. Specialist magazines set up online first, such as Futurenet (1994), and Planet Science, IPC's *New Scientist* website (1995). Some publishers tried interactive magazines on CD-Rom, such as IPC's *Unzip* (1995),[55] but these failed. Mainstream magazines began also to move online. IPC launched NME.com (1996) and *Yachting and Boating World* (1997), which acted as a 'portal' to content from four magazines. *Computer & Video Games* (1981) was closed in 2004, though the website lived on until 2015. The final few years of the decade saw a shake-up when Reed – which had merged with Dutch academic publisher Elsevier to form Reed Elsevier plc in 1993 – sold IPC Magazines to Cinven, a private equity company, for £860 million in 1998. Reed focussed on its fifty business magazines, which included *New Scientist* and *Farmers Weekly*, and academic journals, which could be distributed online, and conferences and exhibitions.

As well as BBC/Redwood, Emap, Gruner & Jahr and Bauer snapping at IPC's heels, there was now Bath-based Future, founded in his garage by

52 'The 10 most-read consumer magazines in Europe', *Campaign* 17 December 2001, p. 17.
53 Walasek, *Best of Punch cartoons*.
54 www.ppa.co.uk/tmap/guidelines/~/media/PPANew/TMAP/tmap_guidelines.ashx.
55 www.magforum.com/digital_history.htm#unz.

computer journalist Chris Anderson with *Amstrad Action* (1985). Anderson used computers to cut costs. The company expanded into other hobby subjects, such as *Cross Stitch* and *Good Woodworking* – 'anorak' publishing. In 1999, the group – which had built up subsidiaries in the USA, France, Italy and Germany – was floated on the stock exchange as Future Network. Meanwhile, Emap sought a boost overseas in 1988 by buying US group Petersen for $1.5 billion.

2000s: digital turmoil and the fall of the British publishing company

The millennium announced the 'dotcom' boom and launches reflected the trend. In May, Future bought new economy magazine *Business 2.0* to Britain from the USA. However, the boom came to an abrupt halt at the end of the year and Future sold the title to AOL Time Warner – a US company predicated on the imagined potential from merging a dotcom star, AOL, with a print media giant, Time Warner. IPC Magazines renamed itself IPC Media and in 2001 was bought from Cinven by US media group AOL Time Warner for £1.15 billion, the strategy being to develop broadcast and online brands from the magazines. Emap was turning magazine brands such as *Kerrang!* and *Smash Hits* into TV shows and radio stations. However, it was in debt. The purchase of Petersen in the US was a disaster and it sold the company at a £600 million loss.

A buzzword of 2000 for publishers was 'middle youth' – women aged thirty-five and over. A spate of launches arrived, including IPC trying to rekindle *Nova*, but only two lasted more than eighteen months and those both closed by 2008. Condé Nast launched *Glamour* in 2001. This brought back the small 'handbag' format that had been popular until the 1970s and set a £1.50 cover price, to outsell NatMags' *Cosmopolitan* within a year.

Newspaper supplements had been recognised as affecting weekly magazine sales and advertising revenues since the launch of the *Sunday Times Magazine* in 1962. The *Mail on Sunday* was seen to have a similar effect when it launched its female-focussed supplement *You* in 1982.[56] In 2007, it tried to sell *You* on the newsstands each Tuesday with a £1 cover price and target sales of 50,000, but it was withdrawn within a year. *You* was the first app the *Daily Mail* launched for the iPad in 2011.

ABC figures for the first half of 2001 showed celebrity coverage driving sales. Emap had repositioned entertainment weekly *Heat* (1999) as a gossip magazine

---

56 Fountain, 'A splash of colour'.

and sales doubled to 235,450. Phil Hall, a former *News of the World* editor, was appointed editor of *Hello!* The weeklies *OK!* and *Hello!* vied for exclusives of celebrity weddings and ended up in the High Court over *Hello!* printing 'spoiler' photographs of the wedding of Catherine Zeta-Jones and Michael Douglas, for which *OK!* had paid £1 million to secure exclusive access. The Douglases sued *Hello!*, which was forced to pay damages. As the decade wore on, legal battles were fought between the press and celebrities over rights to privacy.

Changes in shopping patterns began to drive launch strategies. Supermarkets had only begun selling magazines in 1984, but by 2005 their share of total magazine sales was 31 per cent. However, supermarkets preferred the higher turnover from weekly magazines and this encouraged publishers to invest more in weeklies. IPC went up against Emap to create a weekly lads' mag market with, respectively, *Nuts* and *Zoo* in 2004. The weeklies, along with the growth of pin-up websites, resulted in plummeting sales for the monthlies *Maxim* (closed 2009), *Loaded* and *FHM* (both closed 2015). However, readers were going online, and *Nuts* and then *Zoo* soon also closed.[57] The beneficiary was *Men's Health*, with sales of about 216,000 in 2012.

IPC then produced several women's and TV weeklies. Emap created a glossy weekly sector with Italian import *Grazia* (2005). IPC developed more portals and bought websites such as TrustedReviews (2007) and Mousebreaker (2008). Although Emap could hail success with *Grazia*, investor pressure led it to sell its French arm in 2006 and two years later to dismember itself. The consumer division was sold to Bauer, making the German company the largest magazine publisher in Britain. The trade division, which retained the Emap name, was sold to a joint venture between private equity investor Apax and Guardian Media Group, which added its weekly car sales title Trader Group to the mix. The shake-up meant the biggest consumer magazine publishers by newsagent sales revenue were: Bauer 26 per cent; IPC (Time Warner) 20 per cent; BBC Magazines 8 per cent; and National Magazines (Hearst) 7 per cent.

International expansion was working for other groups. *Time Out* had twenty-eight editions worldwide by the end of the decade. *Wallpaper* launched in Moscow, as did *NME*, and Tyler Brûlé, who had left the magazine after AOL-Time Warner put it under IPC's control, launched *Monocle* with offices around the world and a subscription strategy akin to access to an exclusive club. The *Economist* achieved sales of a million copies. The ability to market

---

57 Henry Mance, 'Lads' mags consigned to the dustbin of history', *Financial Times* 20 November 2015.

a consistent brand drove the decision at NatMags to drop the 144-year-old *Queen* name from *Harper's & Queen* in favour of US brand *Harper's Bazaar*.

NME's sales had slid steadily since 1980. Owner IPC treated it as a brand – described in marketing material as a 'truly unique multi-platform media proposition' with TV and radio channels, live events and awards – but closed long-time rival *Melody Maker* in 2000. The other music weeklies, and fort-nightly *Smash Hits*, went the same way as the number of teenagers fell and they turned to digital media. As a brand, in late 2012 *NME* could claim to reach 'over one million music fans every week', and although the magazine could still be marketed as 'the longest published and most respected music weekly in the world' and the website 'the world's biggest standalone music site', print sales were less than 24,000 copies a week.

The international model with magazines able to sell themselves to upmar-ket buyers in specialised shops and airports enabled the growth of indepen-dent magazines, such as *i-D*, *Sleazenation* and *Dazed & Confused*. More niche titles, often quarterly or biannual, followed in their wake, such as *Wonderland* (2005), which won funding on the BBC's *Dragon's Den* series; *Bad Idea* (2006), a 'magazine of modern storytelling'; and men's quarterly *Port* (2011). *Sublime* (2007) was founded on ethical values.

The Church of London, a design agency, launched *Huck*, a lifestyle maga-zine for surfers, skaters and snowboarders that was published in English, German and French and distributed worldwide. *Fire & Knives* publishes 'new writing for food lovers'; *Karen* (2005) is about finding the extraordinary in the ordinary in Wiltshire; the short-lived *Rotten Apples* (2010) was about 'the extremes of food culture' – the first cover showed a Chihuahua standing on a beefburger. Stack Magazines was set up to sell subscriptions, but with a different independent magazine arriving each month.

The BBC was again forced to review its commercial activities after accusa-tions of being an 'out-of-control juggernaut'.[58] The result was that it sold or licensed its magazines to Exponent, a private equity firm that owned website specialist Magicalia, for £121 million in 2011. These were bundled into a single company, Immediate Media. Magazines continued to expand online through digital facsimile magazines at news-stand websites such as Exact Editions; and on YouTube and Facebook. Dennis launched *Monkey*, a free digital weekly lads' magazine sent as an email to PCs and mobile phones in 2006. The ABC began to audit digital-only distribution in 2007.

---

58 Amanda Andrews, 'BBC Worldwide faces restraint', *Daily Telegraph* 19 November 2008, p. 4.

In 2007, former *FHM* editor Mike Soutar launched men's free weekly *Shortlist*. This followed a free London weekly, *Sport*, based on a French model, and, with Soutar's next launch, *Stylist* for women, established a 'freemium' sector with about 500,000 copies distributed each week in British cities. Listings veteran *Time Out* switched to free distribution in 2012, as did *NME* three years later. Emap's celebrity weekly *Heat*, which had kept up sales by criticising celebrities, over-stepped the mark when it printed stickers showing the disabled son of Katie Price (aka Jordan). The magazine apologised and made a donation to charity. The incident was brought up at the Leveson inquiry into press standards in 2012, where evidence was called from magazine editors, including *Heat*, *Hello!* and *OK!*[59]

In January 2010, IPC Media restructured around three audiences: men, mass-market women and up-market women. This was followed by a cull – which included *Loaded*, *Cage & Aviary Bird* and *Aeroplane* – and saw the number of titles published drop to sixty in 2012 – a fall of about a third since 1980. The growth had been in websites, and in 2010 IPC launched *Goodtoknow Recipes*, a print spin-off from the Goodtoknow web portal. The 2011 royal wedding saw sales of both *Hello!* and *OK!* more than double for a week to a million copies each. The year also reinforced the importance of magazine supplements to newspapers. When Rupert Murdoch closed the *News of the World*, over the phone-hacking scandal, its supplement *Fabulous* was retained and published with the Saturday *Sun*, and then taken on by the *Sun on Sunday* at its launch in February 2012.

The magazine industry in 2016

In 2016 four of the top five consumer publishers were controlled from overseas. German-based Bauer was the largest publisher in the UK; IPC Media, owned by US group Time Inc., had changed its name to Time Inc. UK in 2014; Condé Nast and Hearst UK (formerly National Magazines) were offshoots of US companies. The largest British-owned companies were Immediate (formerly BBC Magazines), Future and Dennis. Bauer and Time Inc. had moved some con-sumer specialist titles out of London, to Peterborough and Farnborough respec-tively. Also, Time Inc. had sold its headquarters building in London (2015) to become a tenant. Since the death of founder Felix Dennis in 2014, Dennis Publishing had been run 'for the benefit of the Heart of England Forest Charity'.

The largest trade groups were Reed Business Information (controlled by RELX Group, formerly known as Reed Elsevier), Emap and Haymarket. Reed

Elsevier tried to sell RBI in 2008 but was unable to find a buyer. In 2015, Emap announced the closure of its print editions as it focussed on digital delivery. It described itself as a 'content, subscription and networking business' with a 'leading portfolio of brands'. There was no mention of the word 'magazine'.

Of the top consumer magazines, many were versions of overseas magazines, particularly the women's monthlies, with *Glamour, Vogue, Cosmopolitan* and *Good Housekeeping* being US offshoots. Both *Marie Claire* and *Elle* were licensed by their French owners. The biggest-selling women's weekly, *Take a Break*, was German-owned. The extent of the decline in women's weekly sales is shown by the fact that *Take a Break* would not have been in the top seven in 1959: its 589,495 figure at the end of 2015 pales against *Woman's* 3,173,000 at that time.[60] Other big US titles included the biggest-selling men's monthly Rodale's *Men's Health, Reader's Digest* and *National Geographic.*

The consolidation continued as readers and advertising revenue moved online. Even Immediate – and hence the BBC magazines – fell into the hands of German group Hubert Burda; IPC became Time Inc. UK and was sold to Epiris, a private equity group. Emap rebranded itself as Ascential and disposed of its magazines as 'heritage brands' in favour of exhibitions. A raft of closures, including *NME and Glamour*, prompted hand-wringing about the future of magazines.[61] Amid the turmoil, magazines have become 'content neutral' brands for which print is just one 'channel' among website, mobile edition, exhibition, TV programme and radio station. Yet, alongside the mainstream print decline, independent magazines have thrived.[62] Ultimately, individuals drive innovation, and although the likes of Heseltine, Logan, Anderson, Brown, Hack and Brûlé can no longer dominate such a mature industry in the way Newnes, Harmsworth and Pearson did, the future of that industry still lies with such entrepreneurs.

---

60 www.magforum.com/glossies/womens_magazine_sales.htm.
61 Jasper Jackson, 'As Glamour goes "digital first", what does the future hold for magazines?', *New Statesman* 19 October 2017; Matt Moore, '"Magazines will be around for many years yet – the world needs editing"', *The Times* 8 December 2018; Laura Snapes, '"Its soul was lost somewhere": inside the demise of NME', *The Guardian* 15 March 2018.
62 Leslie, *Issues*; Losowsky (ed.), *We love magazines.*

Comics – the telling of stories by means of a sequence of pictures and, usually, words – were born in Britain in the late nineteenth century, at least since *Ally Sloper's half-holiday* (Gilbert Dalziel, 1884) and subsequent imitators, although new scholarship has sought to push back the 'birth' of comics to ever earlier publications.[1] These publications were a few pages long, unbound and cheap – and intended for working-class adult readers. During the twentieth century, bound books of picture stories developed in Europe and North America, and grew to become a significant factor in British publishing and popular culture.

At the beginning of the twentieth century, the market was dominated by Harmsworth, whose *Comic Cuts* and *Illustrated Chips* (both 1890) provided the template for the industry: eight-page, tabloid-sized publications with a mixture of one-panel cartoons, picture strips and text stories, selling at a halfpenny. In 1898 Harmsworth had introduced strips aimed at children in *Funny Wonder*, and in 1904 launched *Puck* with a children's pull-out section, *Puck Junior*. *Playbox* (1905) cemented the move towards a children's comic market, and by the First World War the adult comics market had all but disappeared, with Harmsworth's Associated Press (AP) offering picture-papers for pre-teens and story-papers for those aged ten and over.

In the 1920s, D. C. Thomson (DCT) entered the story-paper market with *Adventure* (1921), and then challenged AP's near-monopoly in picture-papers with *Dandy* (1937) and *Beano* (1938). These two titles created a new template in both content and style, with mischievous characters in irreverent stories told by means of speech bubbles rather than captions (a style borrowed from the newspaper strips which also provided much of the creative talent for the new comics). This was evident in AP's direct challenge to DCT's funnies, *Knockout* (1939). During the Second World War, paper rationing caused those titles which did survive to cut their number of pages, but the period also saw the

---

1 Grove and Black, 'The invention of comics'.

appearance of new entrepreneurs such as Gerald Swan, whose titles including *Thrill Comics* and *Topical Funnies* (both 1940) were based on US formats which had begun to be imported into Britain. Whereas British comics were anthologies, presenting a number of different, continuing stories, American comics relied on a stand-alone main story and one or two supporting short stories. Although usually more expensive than anthology comics, US-modelled comics did not require a commitment to ongoing purchase and tended to sell by way of cheap book stalls rather than newsagents. In the late 1940s, new titles were introduced by independents, such as J. B. Allen's *Comet* (1946) and *Sun* (1947), and more American stories appeared either by import or reprint, such as Arnold Book Company's reprints of EC Comics' *Tales of the Crypt* and *The Haunt of Fear* in shilling editions, alongside original British comics in the US mould, such as Boardman's *Buffalo Bill, Swift Morgan* and *Roy Carson* (all 1948). The new independents often offered 'on delivery' payment to writers and artists, rather than 'on publication', attracting many creators. Most of these independent publications, however, appeared in only small print-runs and did not threaten the market dominance of AP and DCT; indeed, in 1949 AP bought J. B. Allen's titles, relaunching both *Comet* and *Sun* under their own imprint.

In 1950, Revd. Marcus Morris convinced Hulton Press, publishers of *Picture Post*, to launch *Eagle*, a mixture of adventure, true-life stories and features, printed on high-quality, glossy paper (rather than rough pulp) at threepence (AP's and DCT's anthology comics typically sold for twopence). Backed by a major marketing campaign, *Eagle* was an immediate success, with sales of around one million. As well as creating a fashion for science fiction in response to its cover story 'Dan Dare', culminating in the first solely-SF British comic *Rocket* (Express Newspapers, 1956), the success of *Eagle* inaugurated the period of the dominance of adventure comics in Britain. AP's response to *Eagle* included the war- and adventure-dominated *Lion* (1952) and the sports-dominated *Tiger* (1954), while DCT at first sought to hold on to the story-paper format for its adventure titles until relaunching *Adventure* in 1958 as a picture-paper. In tandem with the hugely successful relaunch in 1950 by AP of girls' story-paper *The Schoolfriend* as a picture-paper, these titles also created a gendered market; AP's and DCT's story-papers had been aimed at either boys or girls, but their picture-papers had always been seen as being for both. In 1951, Hulton launched a sister paper for *Eagle* aimed at girls, called simply *Girl*, again offering better paper and print quality at a higher price (4½d compared to *Schoolfriend*'s threepence).

The girls' market in the early 1950s is one of the great success stories of British comics; *Schoolfriend* outsold *Eagle*, and a 1953 study demonstrated that 94 per cent of girls aged fourteen to fifteen read one or more of the three leading titles.[2] As a result, the 1950s saw many new girls' titles, most notably in the new romance comics such as AP's *Marilyn* (1955) and *Valentine* (1957), Pearson's *Mirabelle* (1956) and DCT's *Romeo* (1957), as well as the launch in 1958 of DCT's *Bunty*, the first girls' comic explicitly marketed to working-class readers, which quickly established itself as the market leader. Further markets were developed with the 1950 launch of AP's version of the American single- or main-story format, the 'picture library' with *Cowboy Comics Library*, leading to the series *War Picture Library* (1958), *Air Ace Picture Library* (1960) and *Battle Picture Library* (1961), each marketed at an older audience than their anthology titles; DCT belatedly entered this market with *Commando* in 1961.

The late 1950s saw two further significant developments. The impetus behind *Eagle* had been Morris's worries about the corrupting influence of US horror, crime and western comics on Britain's children. While he had sought to counter these comics with his own title, others actively campaigned against the importation or reprinting of American titles. In 1953 the Comics Campaign Council was founded, and in 1955, following the publication that year of a British edition of Fredric Wertham's *Seduction of the innocent*, the Children and Young Persons Harmful Publications Act effectively banned the importation or printing of US comics.[3] British independents who had specialised in this material, such as Len Miller, suddenly had to find original (or reprint old) British stories to fill their publications and many went to the wall, a development exacerbated once American comics resumed official importation in 1959, now under the jurisdiction of the Comics Code Authority. Principally with original material such as *Marvelman* (1954), Miller survived until becoming subject in 1970 to the first prosecution under the 1955 Act. These effects contributed to the other significant development of the late 1950s, the consolidation of the AP-DCT duopoly, the former dominating the adventure comics market, the latter the 'funnies' (by this time *Topper* and *Beezer* had joined its stable), with the two sharing much of the girls' comic market. Only Hulton, with the declining *Eagle* stable, offered significant resistance to the duopoly. By 1961, further major consolidation and rationalisation had taken place. In 1959, Mirror Group purchased AP, renaming the company Fleetway, and two years later purchased Odhams (which had itself acquired Hulton in 1959) to form IPC, a major periodicals publisher with over 200 children's and adult titles on the newsstands.

As the 1960s began, then, two publishers – DCT and IPC – dominated the British comics market, although the reintroduction of American comics brought new competition for sales from superhero comics, in particular those of Marvel

---

2 Cited in Chapman, *British comics*, p. 108.   3 Barker, *A haunt of fears*.

Comics. Both Fleetway/IPC, with *Princess* (1960), *June* (1961) and *Sally* (1969) and DCT with *Judy* (1960), *Diana* (1963) and *Mandy* (1967) continued to launch new girls' comics.[4] The most significant new title was *Jackie* (DCT, 1964), with its development of magazine-style features alongside the more traditional picture-stories of the romance comics; during the mid-1970s, *Jackie* sold in excess of 500,000 copies a week.[5] Boys' comics also saw new titles: in addition to new adventure comics from IPC, such as *Valiant* (1962) and *Hurricane* (1964), DCT aimed to catch up in the field it had finally entered with the relaunched *Adventure* with new titles including *Victor* (1961) and *Hornet* (1963). Continuing to operate the Odhams imprint, IPC sought to compete with DCT in the funnies market, principally through *Wham!* (1964) and *Smash!* (1966), later using those titles and their sister papers in the Power Comics line as the carriers of the Marvel reprints it had licensed.[6] IPC's comics usually appeared in slightly larger formats on higher-quality paper and thus tended to have higher cover prices (e.g. *Valiant*'s sevenpence compared to *Hotspur*'s fivepence in 1967).

The 1960s saw the first serious problems for British comics publishers. A number of the new titles, including *Hurricane*, lasted only a short while despite high-profile launches and large marketing budgets, and the decade saw the beginnings of what was to become termed the 'hatch, match & dispatch' method of publication, with the mergers of unsuccessful new titles or failing old titles. The first major example was the merger of *Princess* with *Girl* in 1964, although perhaps the most noteworthy was the merger of *Eagle* with its former rival *Lion*, in 1969. The only major new growth area in the 1960s was the TV comic. Modelled on AP's *Film Fun* (1920) and *Radio Fun* (1938), as early as 1951 the first television-inspired title, *TV Comic* (News of the World), had been published, followed by *TV Fun* (AP, 1953). However, the field did not seriously develop until television ownership became more widespread: *TV Express*, an offshoot of the *Daily Express* newspaper, appeared in 1962, followed by *TV Century 21* (City, 1965), based on the characters of Gerry Anderson. The genre proved popular, although the 1970s saw the end of this brief boom with the collapse of the re-titled *TV21* in 1971 following on from the failed launch of *Joe 90* (City, 1969) and the failure of new titles *Countdown* (Polystyle, 1971) and *Target* (Polystyle, 1978). Only *Look-In* (IPC, 1971), a children's sister paper to *TV Times*, achieved any degree of longevity.

The 1950s and 1960s also saw the early stages of the development of comics in book form in Britain. In the late 1940s, DCT had launched its Famous Books in

---

4 Brewer, *The history of girls' comics.* 5 McRobbie, *Feminism and youth culture*, p. 81.
6 *Wham!* and *Smash!* were rebranded as part of the Power Comics line in 1967; they were joined in the new line by *Pow!, Fantastic* and *Terrific* (all 1967).

Pictures series, comprising adaptations of British classic novels with four panels per page accompanied by abridged versions of the original texts. Each ran to around 120 pages and they were published in the shape and style of hardback children's books. Although not comics in any sense accepted by most scholars – for instance lacking the by-now almost ubiquitous speech bubbles – they can lay claim to part of the evolution of what have come to be known as 'graphic novels'. In the 1950s, the first English translations of the *Tintin* stories were published in collected albums – as books – and the 1960s and 1970s saw the appearance of other continental European comics in this format, including *Asterix* (1969) and *Lucky Luke* (1972), both by Brockhampton Press. A few British comic books had appeared as early as these European translations, such as Clifford Makins and Frank Bellamy's *The happy warrior* (Hulton, 1958), their biography of Winston Churchill which had first appeared in serialised form in *Eagle*. Bound in picture boards, running to a little over sixty pages, and selling at sixpence, *The happy warrior* is an extended comics narrative published in a book format – a 'graphic novel' by most contemporary definitions of the form. Nevertheless, the books of this period represent only a beginning, with no significant growth in market or form; further development, particularly in books for adults, only followed the growing sophistication of comics in the 1970s and 1980s, and crucially the (re)appearance of comics for adults.

During the late 1960s, weaknesses had become apparent in the children's comics market, with falling sales and failing titles. During the 1970s, these trends became more apparent. In 1977, the Royal Commission on the Press reported that weekly sales of *Bunty* had dropped from 466,000 to 199,000 and *Victor* from 340,000 to 195,000 in the five years from 1971.[7] However, the decade did see crucial developments in non-mainstream comics which were to shape the future of British comics. At the beginning of the decade, the alternative magazine press gave birth to alternative comics, reprinting some US 'comix' alongside original British material, starting with *Cyclops* (1970) and *Nasty Tales* (1971), both deriving from *IT*, and *Cozmic Comics* (1972), part of the *Oz* stable. In 1975, *Brainstorm Comix* was launched, the first all-British alternative comic. Although aided by the introduction of cheaper offset lithography printing, which ended reliance on large printing presses for production, these comics were relatively expensive, reflecting both the intended market and smaller print-runs: the first issue of *Cyclops* sold for three shillings at a time when the more expensive children's comics were selling for around sevenpence, and Issue Four of *Street Comix* sold for 60p (the equivalent of twelve shillings) in the same year, 1977, that *2000AD*

---

7 Chapman, *British comics*, p. 125.

launched at 8p (less than 1s 6d). As well as introducing new creators, these comics created new patterns of working (such as cooperative production), new markets and new distribution methods (including record shops and 'head' shops).

During the 1970s, weekly anthology comics were launched, merged or discontinued with bewildering rapidity. Two new trends were apparent. Thematic comics, particularly in the boys' market, dominated the new launches. IPC began with *Scorcher* (1970), a football comic, and in 1974 DCT followed with *Warlord*, which was immediately successful, selling well in excess of 200,000 copies by 1977.[8] Many of these comics also displayed the other notable trend of the 1970s, a growing social realism and/or psychological sophistication, albeit often within bizarre storylines, which had first become an important feature in girls' comics. In 1971, IPC had launched *Tammy*, a title replete with stories of terror and suffering, often within a class-conscious setting. Although stories of girls struggling against insurmountable odds (often disability), cruel families and bullies had long been a staple of more conservative titles such as *Judy*, the new stories were of a different order, and for many followers of British comics *Tammy* heralded the classic period of girls' comics, with *Jinty* (IPC, 1974), *Spellbound* (DCT, 1976) and *Misty* (IPC, 1978) following, and even the more traditional *Mandy* (DCT, 1967) shifting its style to fit the new concerns. In boys' comics, the more explicit violence of *Warlord* was reflected in the even grittier *Battle* (IPC, 1975)[9] as well as adventure comics including *Bullet* (DCT, 1976) and *The Crunch* (DCT, 1979). This trend reached its zenith with *Action* (IPC, 1976), launched by much the same freelance editorial team as had been responsible for *Tammy*. Among man-eating sharks and violent futuristic sports inspired by Hollywood cinema, the stories of *Action* featured teenage gangs in an anarchic near-future Britain and a World War Two Panzer commander as (anti-)hero. It soon drew tabloid backlash and a reported boycott threat from the largest newsagent chains.[10] It was pulled from the listings and relaunched later in the year in a significantly toned-down form which failed to attract the size, and older profile, of the original's readership. From the ashes, however, came *2000AD* (IPC, 1977), with editorial and creative staff drawn from the offices of *Action* alongside some of the new creators who began to cross over to the mainstream from alternative comics. These editors and writers, who had worked with comics for adults and were immersed in the culture of international, especially US, comics, delivered

---

8 *Ibid.*, p. 129.
9 Although generally known to scholars and readers by the shorter title *Battle*, this title launched as *Battle Picture Library*, before becoming *Battle*, *Battle Action* and then *Battle Action Force*.
10 Sabin, *Adult comics*, p. 53.

a readership to *2000AD* that was older, broader and more sophisticated than the ostensible target audience of boys aged eleven to fourteen; by 1982, it was selling around 120,000 copies a week, the one great success of the period.[11]

The creation of new distribution networks by alternative comics had taken place at the same time as a change that was to have perhaps a more important role for the long-term development of comics in Britain. In 1969 Dark They Were and Golden Eyed, the UK's first specialist comics shop, opened in London, inaugurating a small but growing retail market not focussed on the wider sectoral interests of general bookshops or newsagents. It was subsequently joined by Forever People (Bristol, 1973), Nostalgia and Comics (Birmingham, 1977), Forbidden Planet (London, 1978) and others. In the USA, where there was a much larger number of specialist shops, direct sales marketing came in the late 1970s. Bypassing traditional distribution through newsstands, these techniques utilised the market knowledge of the comics while relying on the willingness of such shops to hold back issues for subsequent sale; formerly, unsold issues were pulped when the new issue came out. In 1977 Titan Distributors was founded, bringing direct sales techniques to Britain, and in the late 1970s Marvel UK sought to apply this specialist-sales basis to British markets. In the USA, direct sales saw the birth of new independent publishers which did not require or seek wholesale distribution through the big retail chains, a pattern which came to Britain in the 1980s with Harrier, Trident, Quality and other independents, while DCT and IPC continued to distribute through newsagents.

At the end of the 1970s, self-published, often photocopied comics began to appear in Britain, not coincidently alongside the advent of punk and fanzine culture. At first sold almost exclusively at comics marts and through small ads, these cheaply produced comics, often produced by only one or two individuals rather than the cooperatives of the alternative comics scene, reflected the social realism of mainstream comics while drawing upon the adult audiences of alternative comics. In 1980, Paul Gravett started the Fast Fiction stall at the Westminster Comics Mart, later developing a mail order service and an anthology comic with the same name, which was also the name by which these kinds of comics became known. Independent British creators of this period were at least as likely to draw on European influences as they were North American influences. In 1982, the short-lived *Pssst!* was launched, clearly modelled on the French anthology comic *Métal Hurlant*, and in 1983 Gravett joined with Peter Stanbury in launching *Escape*, with a first editorial calling for a 'UKBD', that is a British *bande dessinée*. Many of these titles and their publishers also supported the publications

---

11 Newsinger, *The Dredd phenomenon*.

of 'one-shots', standalone stories which wedded higher production values to the narratives and formats favoured by the Fast Fiction writers, as in Eddie Campbell's 'Alec' trilogy (Escape, 1984–86). Less seriously, perhaps, but also based on adult markets, the photocopying revolution also saw the birth of Viz (1979), a deeply irreverent and scatological comic that drew upon certain stylistic elements of the classic British funnies and grew during the 1980s into one of the biggest titles in British periodical publishing.

Very few mainstream titles first published in the 1980s lasted to the end of the decade, and none lasted to the end of the century, disappearing along with long-established titles such as *Tiger* (last issue 1985), *Look-In* (1994) and *Victor* (1994). After nearly forty years of publication, the last issue of AP/IPC/Fleetway's leading funny paper, *Buster*, ended with the dateline 4 January 2000, and *Bunty*, the most successful of all the girls' comics, ceased publication in 2001. By 2010, the only weekly British comics still in print were *Beano*, *Dandy* and *2000AD*. Leaving aside these three titles, two things marked both the more commercially successful and the most critically lauded titles of the 1980s: adult readerships and a shift to irregular or monthly publication. With longer lead-in times for publication, and prices reflecting adult purchasing power, print quality could be much higher than with the weeklies, often featuring full-colour painted 'splash' pages. A key title was *Warrior* (Quality, 1982), which featured many of the notable creators to be found in mainstream comics, especially *2000AD*, attracted by the offer of ownership rights and royalties; although IPC and DCT had introduced creator bylines during the 1970s, with almost all stories fully credited by the 1980s, the retention of ownership and the denial of royalties to creators by the big publishers had caused resentment. Nevertheless, monthly anthology publications also ran aground during the early 1990s, despite the entry of some major, heavily trailed titles such as *Crisis* (Fleetway, 1988), *Deadline* (Cardrest/Deadline, 1989), *Revolver* (Fleetway, 1990) and *Toxic!* (Apocalypse, 1991).

The monthly periodicals had been inspired by the attention generated by the publication of three books during 1986 and 1987: Frank Miller's *Batman: the dark knight returns*, Alan Moore and Dave Gibbons's *Watchmen* (both Titan) and Art Spiegelman's *Maus: a survivor's tale* (Penguin). For a time, the British press was full of stories of comics having 'grown up', of a renaissance that was taking the publishing world by storm. A major shift in the cultural position of comics was posited, with first bookshops and then public libraries starting to feature 'graphic novel' shelves. There was a flurry of new publications, including the reprinting of US comics (particularly through Titan Books) and both European and Asian comics. The decision of Penguin Books to become involved in the burgeoning field was a crucial factor, making available traditional book marketing resources and outlets to *Maus* and Keiji Nakazawa's *Barefoot Gen* (1987); Penguin also bought the rights to the US avant-garde anthology comic *Raw*, relaunching it in the format of a standard paperback book. Another early entrant in the market from the ranks of traditional book publishers was Gollancz, who published Alan Moore and Oscar Zarate's *A small killing* (1987).

The British origins of some of this material and the prehistory of comic books in the UK helped cement the apparent importance of these new books in the British press. For example, Alan Moore, a graduate of the alternative comics scene and then of *2000AD* and other IPC titles, had come to the attention of the US publisher DC with *V for vendetta* (art by David Lloyd), a story begun in *Warrior* and completed with DC.[12] In 1982, Bryan Talbot had published the first volume of *The adventures of Luther Arkwright*, arguably the first British 'graphic novel' for adults, and Raymond Briggs had published *When the wind blows*, in which he brought his children's book style to adults. By 1992, however, there had been a crash in the market, perhaps as a result of saturation or perhaps because many of the new books attracted only an 'art house' audience rather than the general readership of the key books of 1986–87. Graphic novel sections disappeared from bookshops and a number of publishers withdrew from publishing comics.

A more positive impact of this period of excitement was an enormous growth in the number of specialist comics shops in Britain: in the mid-1980s there had been around fifty across the UK, but by 1992 there were about 300, including chains such as Forbidden Planet.[13] Although many failed to survive to the end of the century, a large-scale specialist retail sector was now established, and provided a supportive outlet for continuing (and growing) US imports, newly translated volumes of European and (especially) Japanese and other Asian comics, and those companies – most notably Titan – who continued to publish comics in Britain.

During the first decade of the twenty-first century, however, comic books began to receive greater attention outside of specialist markets once more. Alongside the continued success of established publishers (such as Titan's reprints of British and US comics) and established creators (such as Alan Moore's *From hell*), new publishers have entered the market: North American comics and books continue to be imported, as do US-produced translations of Asian comics, and more European comics are available in translation, as well as a few south Asian and African comics. Topics continue to widen, including the growth of non-

12 Di Liddo, *Alan Moore*. 13 Sabin, *Adult comics*, p. 96.

fiction comics such as journalism, memoir and travelogue. At the time of writing, graphic novel sections in both bookshops and public libraries have become almost ubiquitous, and comic books feature regularly in the reviews sections of the mainstream press. There continues to be a small but creatively exciting periodical comics market, and although an attempt to launch a new (subscription-only) anthology title for children in the tradition of the British comics of the mid-twentieth century, *The DFC* (Random House, 2008), failed after only forty-three issues, a successor, *The Phoenix* (David Fickling Books), was launched in 2012 and remains in print at the time of writing. British authors such as Posy Simmonds have appeared on best-seller lists, with sales coming mainly through general bookshops. Large publishers are releasing comic books, led by Random House imprint Jonathan Cape which has in recent years published new British books by stalwarts of British comics such as Bryan Talbot (including Mary & Brian Talbot's *Dotter of my father's eyes* (2012), the first comics winner of the Costa Biography Prize). These are appearing alongside new British comics and UK editions of key comic books from elsewhere such as Chris Ware's *Jimmy Corrigan: the smartest kid in the world* (2001), which in winning the *Guardian* First Book Award became the first comic to win a major literary prize in the UK.

A notable feature of recent comics publishing from a British perspective has been the reprinting of stories from the history of comics, such as Pat Mills and Joe Colquhoun's *Charley's war* (from *Battle*), and the revival of some characters in new stories. Perhaps most interesting of these are Paul Grist's *Jack Staff* series (Image, 2003–6) and Leah Moore and John Reppion's *Albion* (Titan, 2006), both inspired by classic British adventure comics of the 1960s and 1970s. In 2007 *Crikey!*, a magazine dedicated to British comics, was launched, although it only lasted for sixteen issues. Several museums and other institutions have hosted exhibitions about comics, such as 'Comics Unmasked' (British Library, 2014). This new popular interest in British comics may give urgency to future scholarship. The entire British comics field is under-researched (certain areas, such as girls' comics, funnies other than *Dandy* and *Beano*, and the inter-war period, are even less well served than others), although recent work in reader studies from Mel Gibson and others has opened up new avenues of interest.[14] Comics have become a significant factor in British publishing, and have had major impact across popular culture: the present and perhaps also the future for comics in Britain looks healthy, and our attention to their past should reflect it.

14 See, for example, Gibson, *Remembered reading*.

PART IV

★

23

The book in wartime

JANE POTTER

The nineteenth century had seen British publishing 'become a modern industry in every way',[1] so that by the first decade of the twentieth century, the book trade was, on the whole, stable and prosperous. Technical innovations, marketing and advertising strategies, and distribution networks based around an efficient railway system, were firmly in place. The Net Book Agreement regulated, though not without challenges, the prices of new books, while a public library system and cheap reprints as well as a lively periodical press meant that 'common readers' were not short of printed material to educate and amuse them. An export market for educational books, especially in the colonies, provided economic prosperity for firms such as Longmans, Macmillan, Nelson and Oxford University Press. Established firms such as these were in their heyday, while newer, entrepreneurial businesses found the economic and social climate at the turn of the century conducive to their enterprise. Perhaps most significantly for the book trade – and for the literature of war that was to follow in the twentieth century – literacy levels were higher than they had ever been, thanks to the Education Acts that had continually improved school provision since the 1870s. British publishing was thus in its golden age when the cataclysm of the First World War descended in 1914.

1914–1918

'The age without pity had begun', declared Frederic Warburg,[2] and although Iain Stevenson has shown that 'the initial impact of the outbreak of [war] in August 1914 on British publishing was rather muted', with publishers recognising new markets for 'patriotic tracts and accounts of German

1 Feather, *A history of British publishing*, second edition, p. 95.
2 Warburg, *An occupation for gentlemen*, p. 7.

brutality' and facing 'the emergency with stoicism rather than panic',[3] there was genuine concern in the trade that the demand for books would plummet under the harsh conditions of war. The rise in the cost of materials and production as well as loss of staff to the Forces added further burdens. The seemingly gilded world of publishing was, like everything else in British society, faced with enormous professional and personal challenges. Stanley Unwin, who formally took over the ownership of George Allen (to form George Allen & Unwin Ltd) on 4 August 1914, the very day Britain declared war on Germany, found that the value of the assets he had just acquired dropped by a third, and turnover, 'which even during receivership, when nothing was being published, had always remained at over £1,000 a month, dropped to a few hundred'.[4] As a new firm, George Allen & Unwin had no paper ration and had to purchase paper on the open market at vastly inflated and fluctuating prices: 'as much as 1s 7d a pound for paper greatly inferior to what we could have bought at 2¼d before the war'.[5] Established firms, too, struggled: 'Dividends fell at Hodder and many other publishers saw their profits decline [and some] faltered or collapsed, among them Smith, Elder which was merged with John Murray'.[6] The Great War tested the business acumen, if not the patriotism, of all in the book trade.

The pages of the trade periodicals in the latter months of 1914, including the *Bookseller*, the *Bookman* and the *Times Literary Supplement*, featured editorials and articles expressing the fears of publishers and booksellers, yet it soon became clear that, with little competition from other media, reading was an important source of distraction from the hardships of war: 'What is wanted ... is the friendly companionship of a good and kindly book to take the mind away from the contemplation of the terrible environment', declared the *War Illustrated* in 1915. And as Edmund King has observed, 'The First World War was a highly *textual* conflict',[7] with fiction and non-fiction, poetry and educational texts, political tracts and light-hearted comic sketches feeding a reading public's desire for amusement and information. For civilians on the home front, medical and military memoirs, such as *A VAD in France*, *A regimental surgeon in war and prison*, *Twenty-two months under fire* (all published in 1917) and *The soul of war* (1915), provided first-hand accounts that complemented newspaper reports. Fiction, whether in the form of detective stories, spy thrillers or romantic yarns, sold extremely well. Hodder & Stoughton, one of the most successful purveyors of popular

3 Stevenson, *Book makers*, p. 37.   4 Unwin, *The truth about a publisher*, p. 131.
5 *Ibid.*, p. 141.   6 Stevenson, *Book makers*, p. 43.   7 King, 'Reading and World War I'.

fiction, counted amongst its stable of best-selling authors Ruby M. Ayres, John Buchan, Ian Hay, Joseph Hocking and Herman Cyril McNeile (better known as 'Sapper'). Books with titles such as *Richard Chatterton, V.C.* (1915), *All for a scrap of paper* (1915) and *Men, women and guns* (1916) used war as a backdrop for thrilling adventure and love entanglements. Nelson, renowned as an educational and religious publisher, made its mark on the wartime market for books with its twenty-nine-volume *Nelson's history of the war* (1915–19) by John Buchan, who had been key in revamping and extending the firm's brand image in the years before the conflict.[8] Nelsons' main rival in the children's literature market, Blackie, transformed its Edwardian school boys and girls into young patriots for the consumption of an adolescent readership: Angela Brazil, Captain Brereton and Bessie Marchant spun yarns including *A girl munition worker* (1917) and *With French at the front* (1914).[9]

Poetry, too, flourished in the Great War. Sidgwick & Jackson were the preeminent poetry publishers of their day, a reputation that survived the death of R. C. Jackson who was killed in action in 1915. Katherine Tynan proclaimed that 'Sidgwick & Jackson's name on a volume of poetry is nearly always a guarantee of its quality.'[10] The firm published Rupert Brooke's *1914 and other poems* (1915) and Ivor Gurney's *Severn and Somme* (1917) among volumes by other poets. William Heinemann, who bore the opprobrium of some members of the public for his German surname (which he refused to change), published the collections of Robert Graves and Siegfried Sassoon. Galloway Kyle on the other hand, under the guise of Erskine Macdonald, can be said to have 'cashed in' both on the new market for war poetry and on the grief of parents and loved ones. Kyle 'was able to perfect an ingenious racket' of publishing volumes of verse at the author's (or the author's family's) expense and at being elusive when it came to royalties: 'Kyle well knew that his authors, if still alive, would be more interested in getting into print than in being paid.'[11]

Various charities set up schemes to collect and distribute books to the wounded and prisoners of war (POWs), both truly captive audiences. The Camps Library, the Red Cross, the YMCA and the British War Library among others were instrumental in keeping the troops supplied with reading material. Educational books were especially popular among POWs and many organised their own prison-camp lending libraries.[12] National Book Fortnight

8 Macdonald, 'The symbiotic relationship', p. 160.   9 Potter, *Boys in khaki*, chapter 3.
10 Tynan, 'War books and others'.
11 Hibberd and Onions (eds.), *The winter of the world*, p. xxii. See also Hibberd, 'A publisher of First World War poetry'; and Hibberd, *Harold Monro*, pp. 270–3.
12 King, 'A captive audience?'

was inaugurated in 1915 by British publishers in order to 'quicken public interest in the use of books for reading solace and instruction as well as to encourage people at home to keep the fighting men well supplied in this respect on all fronts'.[13] In addition to Bibles for men in the services, publishers tailored their lists to suit the war climate, with everything from issuing books that explained the political and military dimensions to rebranding novels as 'action series'.[14]

Books played their part in propaganda, official and unofficial. As evidenced by many of their titles, fiction and non-fiction books were carriers of patriotic messages and reinforced ideas that Britain was the righteous defender of liberty against the evil aggression of the Hun, the German foe. Despite efforts to quell anti-war messages, from Mrs Henry Hobhouse's defence of the conscientious objector in 'I appeal unto Caesar' – published in 1915 by Stanley Unwin who felt that 'Conscientious Objectors were most stupidly handled' during the war[15] – to Siegfried Sassoon's public protest published in *The Times* in June 1917 and for which he was committed to Craiglockhart War Hospital for shell-shocked officers, there was an ongoing debate about the aims of the war, especially as casualties mounted year on year. Yet the waves of protest and pacifism struggled against the current of a seemingly all-encompassing national voice of unity.

The government propaganda bureau at Wellington House was initially set up soon after the outbreak of war to counter German propaganda abroad, especially in the United States where a large immigrant population might find itself torn between loyalties. Under the leadership of Charles Masterman and with the declared support of numerous well-known authors and public figures, from Mrs Humphry Ward and Arthur Conan Doyle to May Sinclair and H. G. Wells, all of whom signed the Authors' Manifesto pledging support for the British war effort published in the *New York Times* on 18 October 1914, Wellington House also enlisted the cooperation of British publishers. With the '5/5 arrangement', commercial publishing houses disseminated books and pamphlets for the government. Publishers received £5 for the cost of production and distribution and £5 for the use of their imprint on texts either commissioned or selected from existing lists by Masterman and his colleagues. It was felt that reading material with no outward connection to the government would appeal more widely to the

---

13 Mumby, *Publishing and bookselling*, p. 374. Potter, 'For country, conscience and commerce', p. 16.
14 Stevenson, *Book makers*, p. 43. 15 Unwin, *The truth about a publisher*, p. 154.

target audience. Virtually all established publishing firms participated in the scheme, with Hodder & Stoughton producing the most material.[16] Despite Stanley Unwin's avowed pacifism, George Allen & Unwin were also among those supplying a number of tracts. Masterman's desire to avoid rampant propaganda and to maintain secrecy worked against him, however. Many in the government did not even know of the true purpose of Wellington House and thus questioned the amount of money being spent on an agency that appeared to do little to further the British cause. As casualties mounted, the propaganda machine was reorganised and intensified under successive leaderships of John Buchan, Lord Beaverbrook and Lord Northcliffe. Renamed the Ministry of Information (MoI) in 1918, it was the precursor of a far more complex and controlled propaganda machine in the Second World War.

1939–1945

On the outbreak of war in 1939, books were not the unchallenged media for entertainment and information that they had been in 1914, with radio and cinema having become ever more popular and affordable. But nevertheless books were again marshalled for the war effort. As in the First World War, it was believed that 'Propaganda was most effective when least visible.'[17] The MoI believed that 'books had cultural and symbolic value' and 'that they were an effective means of boosting morale and discreetly spreading propaganda'.[18] Elizabeth Bowen, Graham Greene, Cecil Day-Lewis, Louis MacNeice and Evelyn Waugh were just a few of the leading authors, poets and intellectuals marshalled in the propaganda effort. The MoI began work on 4 September 1939, with three divisions: the Censorship Bureau, Home Publicity, and Foreign Publicity (which covered allied and neutral countries). At its height it employed a staff of 2,950 in the UK and 3,600 overseas.[19] As Valerie Holman records, in August 1940, a Literary Section was established, headed by a 'Mrs Hamilton', with sections run by J. M. Parrish (publishers), Graham Greene (editorial, authors and cartoons) and John Hampden (books and periodicals in neutral countries).[20] In May 1941, further divisions were added: a Publications Division (feature articles, books and pamphlets) led by Robert Fraser and Parrish, and a Books and Pamphlets Committee, itself carved into three sections: Editorial (Day-Lewis); Publishing (R. J. Mitchell); Selection and Distribution (David Fullerton).

16 See Potter, *Boys in khaki*, pp. 227–8.   17 Holman, *Print for victory*, p. 102.
18 *Ibid.*, p. 105.   19 *Ibid.*, pp. 90, 91.   20 *Ibid.*, p. 100.

In *Put out more flags* (1942) Evelyn Waugh characterised the MoI as a labyrinthine organisation run by eccentrics and housed in the imposing 'vast bulk of London University', a 'great hive' later portrayed with much less benign satire as the Ministry of Truth by George Orwell in *Nineteen eighty-four* (1949). A publisher in Waugh's novel, Mr Geoffrey Bentley, 'working there at the head of some newly-formed department', tells the author Ambrose Silk, who resists recruitment: 'You might do worse, you know. We all abuse the old M. of I., but there are a number of quite human people here already, and we are gradually pushing more in every day. You might do much worse.'[21]

Publishers were certainly quick to recognise a commercial opportunity when they saw one and pushed the idea that books were as much a part of the war effort as any other material item. An advertisement from Harrap, for instance, declared 'Carry On! – Always carry your gas mask! Always carry a book!', whilst Hutchinson advised 'Keep a Novel by your Gas-Mask', and Hodder & Stoughton 'announced their own *Blackout book*, "the wartime friend in every home"'; as Holman notes, 'it was not unusual for book promotions to share the metaphorical language and sharply-drawn polarities of official propaganda'.[22]

Yet despite F. A. Mumby's assertion that 'under wartime conditions the book trade grew to know itself better',[23] publishers struggled with hardships that were greater than any experienced between 1914 and 1918. The demand and market for books was never a problem: supplying that demand and market was. All manner of trade restrictions on currency and imports, the loss of staff to the Forces, a surge in production costs, the severe rationing of paper, and destruction of material in aerial bombardment meant that 'embattled publishers found themselves fighting not only to continue their professional activities as individuals, but to ensure that book publishing itself survived the War'.[24]

In practical terms, paper shortage was the chief difficulty. Rationing became effective from March 1940. Allocations were fixed at 60 per cent of the individual publisher's consumption in the twelve months prior to August 1939. During the next two years it was reduced by as much as 30 per cent for a time. Frederic Warburg found himself 'crippled by an exiguous paper quota' and was 'feeling the symptoms of slow strangulation'.[25] For Jonathan Cape, paper supply 'had become so meagre, and all production processes so slow through lack of manpower' that the firm

---

21 Waugh, *Put out more flags*, pp. 61, 63.   22 Holman, *Print for victory*, pp. 25, 26.
23 Mumby, *Publishing and bookselling*, p. 85.   24 Holman, *Print for victory*, p. 61.
25 Warburg, *All authors are equal*, p. 25.

managed to publish 'barely fifty new books a year' and reprints all but ceased, with many books in the Cape catalogue marked 'Discontinued for the duration of the War'.[26] And Stanley Unwin recalled how 'A large proportion of my time during the war was occupied by a prolonged fight for paper for books.'[27] The Moberly Pool was set up to supply paper for essential books, though what constituted 'essential' was often a source of contention: 'criteria could never be absolute, and they changed with the progress of the War and shifts in Government priorities'.[28] Partly as a consequence of rationing, large quantities of books were recycled during the Second World War.[29] Paper rationing did not end until 1949.

While other publishers struggled, Allen Lane and Penguin Books could be said to have been 'made' by the Second World War. Lane, who was 'just too young for active service in the First World War and too important to join in the more obviously military activities of the Second',[30] put his Penguins at the service of the nation. Blessed by an especially generous paper ration due to the phenomenal success of Penguins in the year preceding the outbreak, Lane was able to 'make the most of every accident that might present opportunities to his creation'. Yet as Morpurgo points out, much of the firm's wartime success seemed 'incidental and even coincidental': the books continued to appeal to the men and women readers Penguins already catered to; W. E. Williams, Lane's principal advisor, had an influential role in the directorate of Army Education; and the uniform physical size of Penguin books made them 'inexpensive to buy and inexpensive to post'.[31] Moreover, they 'fitted as precisely as if it had been tailored for the purpose' in service gas-mask haversacks and above-the-knee pockets in battledress.[32] The Prisoners of War Department of the British Red Cross had its own 'Book Section', and through an arrangement with Penguin Books prisoners' relatives were able to order through any bookseller 'for a selection of ten Penguins a month, chosen by the publisher, to be sent to prisoners in Germany and Italy for an annual subscription of three guineas, payable in quarterly instalments'.[33] So popular and sought after were Penguins that the Red Cross used volunteer workers to rebind second-hand ones using wallpaper and the backs of older books. In all, 111,208 were recycled. The Armed Forces Book Club produced ten titles per month in runs of 75,000 each. For this Lane received an extra paper allocation of sixty tons a month.

26 Howard, *Jonathan Cape*, p. 195.   27 Unwin, *The truth about a publisher*, p. 257.
28 Holman, *Print for victory*, p. 90.   29 Thorsheim, 'Salvage and destruction'.
30 Morpurgo, *Allen Lane*, p. 156.   31 *Ibid.*, p. 158.   32 *Ibid.*, p. 157.
33 Holman, *Print for victory*, p. 159.

Such advantages meant that, as other publishers were contracting their output, Lane was expanding his, most notably in the areas of literature and children's books. *Penguin New Writing* was launched under the editorship of John Lehmann in November 1940, followed by Puffin Picture Books and, in 1941, Puffin Story Books. As Stevenson judges, Lane thus 'transformed his already robust fledgling into a cultural institution by clever promotion, excellent publishing, cunning manipulation of paper-rationing and all-round charm when making use of his influential contacts. He was both brave in trying out new ideas ... and enjoyed more than his fair share of luck.'[34]

Luck was not always with the book trade during the war, however, particularly so on the night of 29–30 December 1940. Paternoster Row, the traditional publishing area, was bombed and seventeen firms lost everything. Payouts from the required War Risks Insurance that was initially a great source of debate amongst publishers did little to soften the blow of the losses.[35] While characterising the destruction of Simpkin, Marshall, the book wholesaler, as 'a disaster from which the trade never completely recovered', Stevenson also asserts that this was a 'blessing in disguise' as it broke the monopoly on supply held by Simpkin's and 'provided a clean slate that enabled the book business successfully to reinvent itself yet again'.[36] Nevertheless, the event provided yet another vision of the 'unreal city', so taken up by fiction writers such as Elizabeth Bowen in her novel *The heat of the day* (1948). Hubert Wilson's article in the *Bookseller* of 2 January 1941 is one of the most often quoted depictions of this infamous night for British publishing: 'the crematories of the City's book world', where 'the hub of the English book trade lies in smoking ruins' and where, in the basements of the 'gutted shells' of firms such as Longmans, Nelson, Hutchinson and Collins, 'glowed and shuddered the remnants of a million books'.[37]

Despite the chaos, publishers, with the assistance of various aid organisations, struggled to supply demand, particularly from the wounded and POWs, who, as in the First World War, were especially captive audiences. The Red Cross and the Order of St John of Jerusalem 'provided books for patients and specialist training for a thousand hospital librarians when the "hospital library" might well be a tent in the featureless desert terrain of North Africa'.[38] Detective stories, westerns, thrillers and romance were

34 Stevenson, *Book makers*, p. 127.
35 For a discussion of the varied fortunes of the publishers affected, see Holman, *Print for victory*, pp. 30–3.
36 Stevenson, *Book makers*, p. 107.   37 Quoted in Morpurgo, *Allen Lane*, p. 87.
38 Holman, *Print for victory*, p. 154.

hugely popular, and the Red Cross collected and distributed overseas 1.75 million second-hand books. POW camps received 263,000 books between October 1940 and February 1945, thanks to the Red Cross and Order of St John of Jerusalem. Those prisoners who expressed a wish to study for an examination through Oxford University could borrow books from the Bodleian Library. C. S. Lewis and J. R. R. Tolkien 'compiled an honours-level degree course in English and volunteered to mark examination scripts sent from German prisoner-of-war camps.'[39]

Thus the book defied all manner of destructive or potentially fatal forces to retain its role as an essential part of the British war effort. A typically defiant Stanley Unwin issued a 'counterblast to the Nazi suggestion that [the British book trade] had been completely put out of business', saying that, 'unlike Wren churches, books could easily be replaced, and that, given paper, modern printing machinery could reproduce books faster than any Hitler or Goering could destroy them'.[40] But just as the war against fascism had ended, another had begun in which the book would again play a defining role in shaping ideology and enshrining history.

The Cold War

First used by Orwell in his 1945 article 'You and the atom bomb', the label 'The Cold War' denotes not a single conflict but a forty-year series of skirmishes, uprisings and stand-offs between East and West, between the two great superpowers of the USSR and the USA, both possessors of nuclear weapons, and their attendant political ideologies.[41] As Alex Goody has observed, 'unlike the technologies used every day, nuclear weapons are only experienced as symbolic or imaginative artefacts',[42] for a 'first-strike' by one superpower would inevitably mean mutually assured destruction. The Cold War witnessed the deaths of thousands in conflicts that took place in Korea, Vietnam, Afghanistan, South America and elsewhere, but as Adam Piette points out, this was also an ideological war, one that 'was waged as a form of words as well, with its own systems of propaganda and persuasion'.[43]

The way that books played a role in this nebulous, drawn-out war of action and ideology echoes its role in earlier wars, with the British government

39 *Ibid.*, p. 156.   40 Unwin, *The truth about a publisher*, p. 260.
41 Hammond, *Cold War literature*, p. 1.
42 Goody, *Technology, literature and culture*, p. 78.
43 Piette, 'Pointing to East and West', p. 644.

opting for the covert influencing of public opinion and the employment of commercial publishers and well-known writers. While much Cold War rhetoric was orchestrated by and in the United States, Britain had played its part in an effort to challenge the predominance of American culture. In 1948, the British government set up the Information Research Department (IRD). Not unlike Charles Masterman and others in the First World War, British print Cold Warriors believed propaganda would be more readily accepted if not linked to any government. But its initially 'benign' intentions of 'highlighting the benefits of British social democracy compared with American capitalism or Soviet Communism' was soon supplemented by 'the production of a range of aggressively anti-Communist material' by covertly subsidised publishing ventures.'[44] Penguin Books, Allen & Unwin and the Bodley Head were among the commercial firms that took part in the 'see-safe' agreement with the IRD, through its front company Ampersand. A publisher would be financially 'safe' because the IRD would guarantee sales that would at least break even.[45] Both a subsidy and a 'laundering exercise', the arrangement allowed for IRD material to seem independent of any government influence, particularly important when attempting to influence opinion abroad.[46] The IRD's series Background Books, which ran to over 100 titles, was launched in 1951. Authors included many of the leading lights in philosophy, politics and Sovietology, among them Bertrand Russell. With such titles as *What is peace?*, *What is freedom?*, *What is NATO?* and *How did the satellites happen?* (all published in 1952), the series was issued by three publishers in succession: Batchworth Press, Phoenix House and the Bodley Head. Allen & Unwin distributed a series of fifteen publications under the imprint Allen & Unwin Ampersand Books by 1966. Prices ranged from three shillings up to thirty shillings for the 'substantial editions of academic bibliographies'.[47]

It was hoped that 'people of influence' would read the books, and filter down the ideas into their own work and into public discussion within academic journals and other media. Thus the IRD 'did not seek to saturate the market', but to 'steer paradigms of debate'.[48] It did not censor books so much as not use material or approach authors who were not sympathetic to the cause or sufficiently 'on message'.[49] The influence of the United States in Britain's Cold War print culture has been documented by scholars such as

44 Smith, 'The British Information Research Department', pp. 112–13.   45 *Ibid.*, p. 116.
46 *Ibid.*, p. 119.   47 *Ibid.*, p. 120.   48 *Ibid.*   49 Piette, 'Pointing to East and West', p. 644.

Greg Barnhisel, James B. Smith and Frances Stonor Saunders.[50] Outrage followed the discovery in the early 1960s that the CIA – operating under the cover of the Congress for Cultural Freedom – was funding the journal *Encounter* co-edited by Stephen Spender and American Irving Kristol, both of whom claimed to have been 'hoodwinked as to the financing of the journal'.[51]

The CIA also took particular interest in Orwell's *Animal farm* (1944) when it arranged for translations to be smuggled into the Ukraine in the early 1950s and funded a cartoon based on the novel in 1955. This was a turnaround from the initial reaction of a number of publishers who, in 1943, rejected Orwell's novel at a time when the USSR was an ally of the West. It was published in the face of much opposition by Frederic Warburg and went on to sell out its first print-run of 4,500 copies almost immediately. By the time Warburg published his second memoir *All authors are equal* in 1973, *Animal farm* had sold over 9 million copies. Intended 'primarily as a satire of the Russian Revolution', Orwell 'did mean it to have a wider application in so much as I meant that *that* kind of revolution (violent conspiratorial revolution, led by unconsciously power-hungry people) can only lead to a change of master'.[52] Like Orwell's next novel *Nineteen eighty-four* (1949), a Swiftean satire of totalitarianism, *Animal farm* transcended the Cold War, as evidenced by continued sales and rebranding in series such as Penguin Classics.

For the popular reading public, the Cold War was also fought in the books of such novelists as Graham Greene, Ian Fleming and John Le Carré. Their differing brands of spy fiction 'became increasingly popular and tended to affirm readers' beliefs in a secret world existing beneath ordinary reality'.[53] Here was 'the human individual facing vast, faceless bureaucratic and military systems and avoiding technological annihilation'.[54] While Fleming's James Bond 'evinced the triumph of the West and of commodity over numerous totalitarian demagogues representing such well-concealed but pervasive enemy organizations as SPECTRE and SMERSH',[55] Greene delved into the 'moral complexity' of espionage in novels like *The quiet American* (1955) and the screenplay of *The third man* (1949).[56] In his novels *The spy who came in from the cold* (1963), *The looking-glass war* (1965), *A small town in Germany* (1968) and *Tinker, tailor, soldier, spy* (1974), Le Carré explores 'the elaborate

50 Barnhisel, *Cold War modernists*; Smith, 'The British Information Resesarch Department'; Barnhisel and Turner (eds.), *Pressing the fight*; Saunders, *Who paid the piper?*
51 John Sutherland, 'Spender, Sir Stephen Harold (1909–1995)', *ODNB*.
52 Davison (ed.), *George Orwell*, p. 334.   53 Diemert, 'The anti-American', p. 214.
54 Goody, *Technology, literature and culture*, p. 90.
55 Diemert, 'The anti-American', p. 214.
56 Goody, *Technology, literature and culture*, p. 90.

machinery of Intelligence and present[s] the dispassionate power of institutions that dehumanize or crush individuals on both sides of the East–West divide'.[57] The mass-market paperback, which by the 1960s 'had become respectable' and 'was increasingly the format in which most book buyers bought their books',[58] seemed the ideal vehicle for such stories in a world that was constantly in flux. And there is no doubt that the cross-media success of these authors has ensured the ongoing popularity of their books, from the Bond movie franchise and continuation novels by John Gardner and Sebastian Faulks among others to the television and film adaptations featuring Le Carré's protagonist George Smiley.

Coda

As rapprochement between the USSR and the West marked the end of the Cold War in the 1980s, such books may have been expected to be of less interest to the reading public. But as the Cold War gave way to the War on Terror, the themes of totalitarianism and repression continued to have resonance – and, with some, nostalgia for a perceived cosier age of gentleman spies and easily identifiable and ultimately defeatable villains. Along with other conflicts such as the Falklands War, the War on Terror, played out not only in the Middle East but globally, has spawned its own book culture in Britain. Hundreds of historical non-fiction, military and journalist memoirs and first-hand accounts have been issued by both trade and specialist publishers from HarperCollins and Random House to Osprey and Pen & Sword Books.[59] By contrast, fiction lags behind. As Bryan Appleyard commented in the *Sunday Times* on 8 July 2012, despite Britain being 'the constant ally of the United States in these wars', and having 'produced some of the best reporting . . . the big new British war novels have not yet appeared, assuming you discount indirect treatments . . . Perhaps it is simply that we are bit players in these new wars, and this is echoed in our fiction: adjuncts to the imperial power, rather than makers of our own warrior narrative.' The aggressive marketing techniques and appetite for thrills so characteristic of the late twentieth and early twenty-first centuries are obvious in titles such as: *Scram! The gripping first-hand account of the helicopter war in the Falklands* (2012) by Harry Benson; *Task force black: the explosive true story of the SAS and the secret war in Iraq* (2011) by Mark Urban; and *Sniper one: the blistering true*

57 *Ibid.*, p. 93.   58 Feather, *A history of British publishing*, second edition, p. 209.
59 Brian Appleyard, 'Incoming: fiction from the front line', *Sunday Times* 8 July 2012.

story of a British battle group under siege (2008) by Sgt. Dan Mills. Covers of books about the Falklands War originally published in the 1980s and 1990s have been rebranded to fall in line with the iconography of the more recent conflicts in the Middle East. This is to do not just with the changing tastes of a reading public used to visual, cinematic representations of war, but with the fact that books now compete with more interactive media, with a 'militainment' industry.

Militainment is 'the alliance between the entertainment industry and the military to promote war as a consumable product rather than a distracting spectacle'.[60] Many books about the wars in Iraq and Afghanistan started as blogs and other forms of social media. This can, according to Ian Campsall, present 'both a potential goldmine and major headache' for it is 'vital' that 'publishers rely on their reputations as purveyors of quality books ... they must ensure that the writing is of a sufficient standard to carry their logo. While the Web offers powerful systems and tools to make content more findable, the sheer volume of content being produced makes this difficult.'[61]

Is the book destined to become a less central force in times of war? Will this once powerful tool of propaganda and persuasion, amusement and historical chronicling be relegated to a mere artefact of culture in the face of more immediate and interactive forms of communication? Such questions dog the printed, physical book in general, but they are perhaps particularly acute for the book in wartime. Yet the quantity of 'war books' published each year illustrates that the form is not dead yet. Combatants in and witnesses to war still appear to find the book an important medium for making sense of and communicating the individual experiences of war. And the reading public still seems to desire this more permanent, considered record of conflict.

60 Campsall, 'From the front line of war', p. 9.   61 *Ibid.*, p. 21.

24

Books, intellectual property and copyright

CATHERINE SEVILLE[1]

Copyright remains a crucial part of the author's and publisher's armour. Since the 1880s there have been significant changes in the law, in response to growing pressure to harmonise copyright internationally. The book trade has had to adapt to an increasingly global marketplace, in which territorial rights continue to be vital. In addition, the digital environment has rendered both the exploitation and the infringement of copyright works far easier than in previous centuries. As other chapters in this volume demonstrate, copyright holders have learned to put their copyrights to an ever-increasing and imaginative range of uses.

This chapter outlines the law of copyright during the twentieth and twenty-first centuries. It explains the international context and the influence of the European Union, summarises the British responses to the important international instruments which now set the framework for UK copyright law, and offers illustrative examples of the interaction between copyright law and the practices of the book trade.

International copyright – 1914 to the twenty-first century

The importance of international copyright protection had been obvious to publishers since the late 1830s. National copyright laws differed significantly, and bilateral treaties had offered only a very partial solution, since substantial publishing markets remained outside these agreements. The pressure for international copyright grew increasingly formal, and led to the signing of the Berne Convention.[2] Britain's adhesion to the Convention, with her colonies,

---

1 This chapter was completed before the author's untimely death in 2016.
2 Ten states signed the Convention in September 1886, and it came into force the following year. For the history of the negotiations and further details see Seville, 'Copyright'.

brought 300 million people within the Union – more than double the combined populations of the other original signatories. Given the differences in the legal systems and outlook of the states involved, the level of accord achieved was astonishing.

The 1886 Berne Convention created a 'Union for the protection of the rights of authors over their literary and artistic works'.[3] The Convention was based on the principle of national treatment, requiring signatories to treat foreign nationals no less well than their own nationals. Formalities such as registration and deposit were not prohibited initially, being very common in national laws at the time.[4] The 1908 Berlin conference resulted in substantial revision. The enjoyment and exercise of rights under the Convention were no longer to be subject to any formality. A minimum term of the author's life plus fifty years was agreed in principle, even by countries (such as the United Kingdom) which had shorter periods. Translation rights became coterminous with the reproduction right, and a number of previously controversial indirect appropriations (such as dramatisations and novelisations) were now also brought under the author's control.[5]

Significant though the Berlin revision was, the pattern of international copyright protection was still patchy. The refusal of America to acknowledge Berne's norms was problematic, particularly because of the size of its publishing market. Until 1891 the only protection afforded to foreign copyright works in America was informal and ad hoc. A change of heart among the American publishing and printing trades, who had previously resisted international copyright, led to the Chace Act of 1891.[6] A protectionist 'manufacturing clause' in the Act provided that foreign authors could obtain US copyright only if their work was printed and typeset in the United States. British authors had to publish in both countries simultaneously if they were not to lose their British copyright, which required considerable coordination by their publishers.[7] Authors whose works were already published remained unprotected. J. M. Barrie was one of several British authors

---

3 Berne Convention 1886, Article 1. Text available at *Primary Sources on Copyright (1450–1900)*, www.copyrighthistory.org.
4 Seville, *The internationalisation of copyright law*, pp. 63–5.
5 Berlin Act, 1908: Revised Berne Convention for the Protection of Literary and Artistic Works, text available in Ricketson and Ginsburg, *International copyright*, appendix 17.
6 International Copyright Act (The Chace Act), Washington, DC (1891), *Primary Sources on Copyright (1450–1900)*. For the history of the Chace Act see Seville, *The internationalisation of copyright law*, especially chapter 5.
7 West, 'The Chace Act and Anglo-American literary relations'.

to issue revised American editions of their works, in an attempt to take advantage of the new law.[8]

Berne Convention countries were unwilling to compromise their standards of copyright protection, and America remained outside the Berne Union until 1989. Eventually UNESCO took the initiative in drafting a less onerous treaty – the Universal Copyright Convention (UCC), signed in 1952.[9] Signatory states which required formalities were permitted to retain them for their own nationals. However, for non-nationals publishing outside that state's territory, the UCC provides that any formalities shall be regarded as satisfied if all the copies of the work bear the now-famous copyright symbol ©, accompanied by the name of the copyright proprietor and the year of first publication.[10] The duration of copyright protection under the UCC is far shorter than that under the Berne Convention, the standard term being the author's life plus twenty-five years.[11] The UCC was useful as a stepping-stone to genuine international copyright relations for many countries – most notably the USA and the USSR. Nevertheless, its importance has decreased significantly, as more and more states have chosen to join the Berne Union in preference.

The Berne Convention remains fundamental to international copyright law, setting minimum standards for protection which members of the Berne Union must meet. Authors and copyright owners enjoy a number of exclusive rights: to make reproductions of the work 'in any manner or form'; to perform/recite it in public; to translate it; to make adaptations and arrangements of the work; and the broadcasting right, or right of communication to the public.[12] The Convention acknowledges that there is a need for limited exceptions to these rights in certain special cases.[13] The general rule is that protection must last for the author's life and fifty years thereafter.[14]

The Convention also provides for certain 'moral rights' – the right of attribution and the right of integrity. Moral rights protect an author's non-pecuniary interests. These rights are given to the author alone, and may not be transferred with economic rights. They were developed in civil law

---

8 Seville, *The internationalisation of copyright law*, p. 303.
9 Universal Copyright Convention (UCC) as revised at Paris on 24 July 1971, with Appendix Declaration relating to Article XVII and Resolution concerning Article XI 1971. Available at http://portal.unesco.org.
10 UCC Article III.   11 UCC Article IV.
12 Berne Convention Articles 9, 11, 8, 12, 11*bis*. Text available at www.wipo.int/treaties/en/ip/berne/trtdocs_wo001.html.
13 Berne Convention, Articles 9, 10, 10*bis*. Copyright, Designs and Patents Act 1988, Chapter III (Acts Permitted in relation to Copyright Works).
14 Berne Convention, Article 7.

countries, and fit less easily with common law systems. Examples include the right to divulge a work, the right to be named as a work's author and the right of integrity in the work. Only the last two are explicitly protected by the Berne Convention (Article 6bis).

The World Trade Organization's 1994 TRIPS agreement (Agreement on Trade-Related Intellectual Property Rights) has also had an important impact on international copyright law. Before TRIPS, the extent of protection and enforcement of copyright (and other intellectual property rights) varied widely around the world. The Berne Convention contains no mechanism for ensuring that a signatory meets its obligations. Intellectual property's increasing economic importance resulted in pressure for internationally agreed trade rules covering intellectual property rights. The TRIPS agreement brings intellectual property enforcement under common international rules, establishing minimum levels of protection.[15] TRIPS has a number of specific provisions which affect copyright. The point of departure is the existing level of protection under the Berne Convention, although there is an exception for moral rights.

Throughout its history copyright law has been strongly influenced by developments in technology. Users of copyright works have been quick to take advantage of the latest digital copying technologies, and would like more freedom to do so. Copyright holders often argue in response that stronger protection is necessary. This can be seen clearly in the submissions to the Hargreaves Review, an independent review of the UK's intellectual property framework, and how it supports growth and innovation, which reported to government in May 2011.[16] Excessive protection, though, has the potential to harm the public domain and to restrict the creativity which copyright law seeks to foster. Legislators face a difficult challenge in balancing the needs of copyright holders for protection against the needs of the public for access to creative works.

Some of these challenges have been addressed by the WIPO Copyright Treaty (WCT), which demands higher standards of protection than TRIPS, in particular in areas affected by technological change.[17] The WCT addresses

---

15 Agreement on Trade-Related Aspects of Intellectual Property Rights (1994). Text available from www.wto.org.
16 Compare, for example, the submissions of Google, the National Centre for Text Mining, and the Pirate Party UK, with those of the Alliance of Managers, Artists and Performers, the BPI (British Recorded Music Industry), and the Creator's Rights Alliance. See Ian Hargreaves, *Digital opportunity: review of intellectual property and growth* (2011). Available at www.gov.uk/government/publications/digital-opportunity-review-of-intellectual-property-and-growth.
17 WIPO Copyright Treaty 1996. Available at www.wipo.int/treaties.

three important authors' rights: the right of distribution, rental right and the right of communication to the public.[18] The distribution right is somewhat extended beyond the terms of both the Berne Convention and TRIPS. Perhaps most significant is the grant of an exclusive right of communication to the public, by wire or wireless means. Although there were elements of this right in the Berne Convention, the coverage of the newly defined right is more coherent, and includes new methods of distribution through the internet.

The European Union's influence on copyright law has been substantial. Copyright, like other forms of intellectual property, creates problems and raises issues for the EU. National rights can act as barriers to the free movement of goods. There are important dissimilarities in the approach taken by the various member states, some of which stem from different understandings of the role that copyright should play. The European Commission's priority has been the functioning of the internal market. A host of directives concerning copyright are in force; these cover computer programs, rental and lending rights, neighbouring rights, cable and satellite broadcasting, copyright term, databases, the royalty on resale of an artist's work, copyright in the 'information society' and, most recently, the licensing of so-called 'orphan works' (copyright works whose authors are not known or cannot be traced).[19] The Orphan Works Directive permits the digitisation of orphan works by certain cultural organisations (such as libraries and archives) for non-commercial use throughout the EU. The intention is to promote access to the EU's cultural heritage.

In achieving EU-wide harmonisation, where national approaches have differed, the tendency has been to adopt the highest level of protection. The Term Directive, which came into force on 1 July 1995 and was implemented in the UK on 1 July 1996, offers a good example, whereby the standard term of copyright was raised to the author's life plus seventy years (the then term in Germany), in preference to adopting the fifty-year term laid down in

---

18 WCT Articles 6–8.
19 Directive 2009/24/EC on the legal protection of computer programs; Directive 2006/115/EC on rental right and lending right (codified version); Directive 93/83/EEC on copyright and neighbouring rights relating to satellite broadcasting and cable retransmission; Directive 2006/116/EC on the term of protection of copyright (codified version); Directive 96/9/EC on the legal protection of databases; Directive 2001/29/EC on copyright and related rights in the information society; Directive 2001/84/EC on the resale right for the benefit of the author of an original work of art; Directive 2012/28/EU on certain permitted uses of orphan works. For texts see http://ec.europa.eu/internal_market/copyright/index_en.htm.

the Berne Convention, and in use in many member states at that time.[20] The Information Society Directive harmonises the rights of reproduction, communication to the public/making available, and distribution. Balancing these rights is a system of exceptions.[21]

The Commission continues its efforts to harmonise aspects of EU copyright law, and remains committed to its modernisation. The proper functioning of the 'Digital Single Market' is a priority, but a challenging one. The aim is to encourage investment in a diverse range of cultural content, and to promote access to it, whilst acknowledging the changing technological environment and its impact on the market. At the time of writing, proposals regarding EU-wide licensing for online rights, and levies on recording equipment and media, are being considered.[22]

UK copyright law – 1914 to the present day

Despite its significant limitations, Talfourd's 1842 Copyright Act formed the backbone of UK copyright law until 1911. The original Berne Convention requirements were implemented by the 1886 International and Colonial Copyright Act, which simply made the minimum alterations needed to enable the UK to give the required protection to foreign authors. However, for the UK to ratify the important 1908 Berlin revision of the Berne Convention, significant modifications to domestic law were required. The Berlin Act required signatory states to provide a copyright term of at least the author's life plus fifty years, and also specified that protection should be granted without the need for any formality such as registration or deposit. These requirements did not in themselves present a major policy difficulty for the British government. Far more sensitive was the position of Britain's colonies. Canada, in particular, was acutely resentful of the prevailing constitutional situation, and the fact that she could not legislate for herself on copyright matters.[23]

The 1911 Copyright Act came into force on 1 July 1912. It abolished the registration requirement entirely, and extended the basic term of protection

---

20 Transitional provisions had the effect of reviving copyright for authors who died on or after 1 January 1925 and before 1 January 1945, if copyright in the work subsisted in an EEA state on 1 January 1995. See Garnett et al., *Copinger and Skone James on copyright*, pp. 6–15.
21 Information Society Directive, Articles 2–5.
22 http://ec.europa.eu/internal_market/copyright/levy_reform/index_en.htm.
23 An Imperial Copyright Conference resolved many of the outstanding problems, though not all. For further details see Seville, *The internationalisation of copyright law*, pp. 136–45.

to the author's life plus fifty years.[24] Authors of literary dramatic and musical works were given a new right 'to make a record, perforated roll, cinematographic film, or other contrivance by means of which the copyright work may be mechanically performed or delivered'.[25] Copyright was to subsist in these for fifty years from making. The author of a copyright work was also given dramatisation and translation rights.[26] The 1911 Act set Britain firmly within the new international context which had been forged for copyright law. However, the hesitancy of the self-governing dominions was a concern which continued for a number of years.[27]

There were further revisions of the Berne Convention, in Rome (1928) and Brussels (1948). The Copyright Act 1956 repealed the compulsory licence provisions of the 1911 Act, which were no longer permitted under the Brussels Act of Berne. Additionally, the 1956 Act introduced reforms to deal with the technical advances which had affected copyright since the 1911 Act. For the first time, specific protection for fifty years from publication for films (cinematographic works), sound and television broadcasts, and published editions of works was introduced.[28] The Act also established the Performing Right Tribunal.[29]

The next major legislative change was the Copyright, Designs and Patents Act 1988 (CDPA). This was a comprehensive restatement of the law. One notable amendment was the creation of moral rights for authors and film directors, as required by the Paris Act of the Berne Convention (1971). The Performing Right Tribunal was replaced with a Copyright Tribunal. The CDPA is currently the UK's governing Act, as amended to comply with EU and international obligations. As noted above, copyright term has been harmonised within the EU; the basic term is now the author's life plus seventy years. One extraordinary anomaly relating to this term was introduced by the CDPA, thanks to the outgoing Prime Minister, James Callaghan. J. M. Barrie died in 1937, and under the law as it stood prior to the CDPA the copyright in all his works would have expired on 1 December 1987. But the House of Lords introduced a unique exception to the standard copyright term, especially for the play *Peter Pan*. The CDPA grants the trustees of the Hospital for Sick Children, Great Ormond Street, London, a 'right to a royalty in respect of the public performance,

---

24 Copyright Act 1911, s. 3.   25 Copyright Act 1911, s. 1(2)(d).
26 Copyright Act 1911, s. 1(2)(a)–(c).
27 For example, it was not until 1924 that the United Kingdom was in a position to give notice of Canada's accession to the Berne Union.
28 Copyright Act 1956, ss. 12–15.   29 Copyright Act 1956, s. 23.

commercial publication, broadcasting or inclusion in a cable programme service of the play "Peter Pan" by Sir James Matthew Barrie, or of any adaptation of that work', in perpetuity.[30]

A rental and lending right has been in place since 1996, again as a result of EU legislation. Copyright defences are also now subject to EU rules, which limit member states to a closed list of possible exceptions, although member states may choose which of these they wish to implement.[31] Defences offer a mechanism for balancing a copyright owner's right to protection with the more general needs of the public. The Hargreaves Review recommended that the UK should make wider use of the exceptions permitted under EU law, and the defences were amended as a result. Currently, in the UK, limited access to copyright works is permitted for purposes such as news reporting, criticism and review, and research and private study. These 'fair dealing' defences have recently been augmented to include a specific quotation exception, and one which covers parody, caricature and pastiche. There is now also a very limited private copying exception, which allows individuals to copy content which they own and acquired lawfully, onto another device for their own private and non-commercial use.

Themes and examples

The global book market and technological changes

From the mid-nineteenth century onwards, book markets became progressively more international. Works would be issued in several different countries, in numerous formats, translated into many languages, and adapted for stage and later film. Merchandising became lucrative, and writers achieved celebrity status on a scale not previously imagined. Although the Second World War disrupted publishing severely, the end of the war saw further remarkable growth in demand, and a corresponding response from publishers. Book markets became increasingly global.

International copyright law underpinned the necessary contractual arrangements to support this expansion, and gave authors and publishers the rights needed to exploit their texts in a variety of ways. The literary profession became better organised, and more aware of the importance of intellectual property rights. The rise of the literary agent from the 1880s testifies to the need for a specialised negotiator, familiar with the diverse

---

30 CDPA s. 301. See Seville, 'Peter Pan's rights', p. 4.
31 Information Society Directive, Article 5.

range of opportunities for an author interested in maximising earnings, and with the legal framework for such deals. The book market became increasingly democratic, with a much wider range of cheap books, including paperback books, available from a wider range of sources. Of course, not all of these reprints were copyright works, and there were many series of 'classics' of one sort or another. But Allen Lane was one of the first to see a market for good-quality reprints of contemporary fiction, and he began buying reprint rights for this purpose, and with this created the hugely successful Penguin paperbacks. The model was soon copied, and the paperback 'revolution' has never stopped. This trend of increasingly ready access to texts has accelerated as digital technology has become ubiquitous.

The ease with which digital copies of works can be distributed across national boundaries challenges copyright law. It has responded with increased harmonisation in the international and regional spheres, including attempts to keep pace with technological changes. Copyright holders have struggled to control copyright infringement, as access to copying technologies has become widespread. In terms of book production, there has been a positive side to these developments, in that those addressing a minority or niche audience are able to publish far more readily than before. But technology such as the photocopier seemed to pose a serious threat to the book trade, particularly scholarly publishing and textbooks. Attempts to strike at copying technology itself have been unsuccessful. The argument that the act of selling or providing a photocopier (for example) amounts to legal authorisation of copyright infringement has not been accepted, except in the most extreme circumstances.[32] However, an Internet Service Provider (ISP) which actively sanctions copying of copyright works by its users will be liable for the authorisation of copyright infringement, and may be restrained by injunction.[33] Furthermore, an ISP with actual knowledge that their service is being used to infringe copyright works, such as allowing access to a site which encourages illegal copying, may be subject to a blocking order requiring it to prevent its users from accessing a named site.[34]

Digital technology has been embraced by users, and is available at a price which makes it accessible to almost everyone in the UK. The enjoyment

---

32 *CBS* v. *Amstrad* [1988] RPC 567.
33 *Twentieth Century Fox* v. *Newzbin Ltd* [2010] EWHC 608 (Ch).
34 *Twentieth Century Fox* v. *British Telecommunications* [2011] EWHC 1981 (Ch), where BT was required to block access to the peer-to-peer sharing site known as Newzbin2. Likewise, *EMI & Others* v. *BSkyB & Others* [2013] EWHC 379 (Ch); *1967 Ltd & 6 Ors* v. *British Sky Broadcasting Ltd & Ors* [2014] EWHC 3444 (Ch).

which follows from the accessibility of copyright works, apparently 'for free', has led to tensions between owners and users. The infamous peer-to-peer copying site The Pirate Bay openly ridiculed those who threatened legal action against it, and stated defiantly, 'zero torrents has been removed, and zero torrents will ever be removed.' Nevertheless, within the UK at least, the major ISPs have consented to legal orders requiring them to block this and similar sites.[35]

The scale of copyright infringement is enormous, particularly online. Different responses are advocated. The Pirate Party, a political party which has had some success in national and European elections, campaigns on a manifesto which includes a promise to reduce the normal copyright term to ten years, renewable for five years. Creative Commons, a non-profit organisation, takes a practical and positive approach. It offers free copyright licences and other tools to help authors who want actively to share their work.[36] Lawrence Lessig's *Free culture* has been both influential and controversial. There he argues not for anarchy, but for balance, and resistance to what he sees as 'the increasing extremism' within intellectual property.[37] He, too, proposes shorter renewable periods of copyright and a limitation on derivative rights. Fundamental reform of copyright law seems unlikely, however, given the entrenched international norms. Most responses focus on attempting to control or influence the user. Some countries have adopted a graduated approach to the pursuit of infringers on the internet; beginning with several warning letters, the termination of internet connections is a last resort. Education of users is another option. Technological locks of various sorts are also being tried. Offering consumers legitimate products at an attractive price has proved somewhat effective in certain markets.

The low cost of desktop publishing equipment has enabled sellers to offer out-of-print titles 'on demand'. Often this is done by scanning a copy of the published work. In 2002, Google began digitising books in libraries on a very large scale. It later launched Book Search, which allowed users to search its database of digitised books, to view snippets of books in copyright, and to download entire copies of works in the public domain. The Authors Guild, and later the Association of American Publishers, filed a class action lawsuit,

---

35 *Dramatico Entertainment* v. *British Sky Broadcasting & 5 Ors* [2012] EWHC 1152 (Ch).

36 www.creativecommons.org.uk. See also the 'Copyleft' approach, which, again, rather than using copyright law to prevent distribution, uses it to promote it. Copyleft licences commonly give the right to distribute copies and modified versions of a work, embedding a requirement that the same rights be preserved in modified versions of the work.

37 Lessig, *Free culture*, p. 270. For responses see Keen, *The cult of the amateur* and Lanier, *You are not a gadget*.

arguing that Google's activities amounted to massive copyright infringement, because in creating the database it necessarily created digital copies of entire copyright works. However, the Google Books project was held to be 'fair use' under US copyright law, the judge describing it as delivering 'significant public benefits'.[38]

Sales of e-books are now considerable. But although there was a huge surge in e-book sales following the launch of the Kindle in 2007, e-book gains seem to have stabilised. Decline of print sales has slowed, and hardcover and paperback books are still comfortably dominant in the market. Co-existence seems likely for the foreseeable future. The digital format of an e-book allows the seller to restrict what may be done with it, using technological protection measures (TPMs) and Digital Rights Management (DRM).[39] The WIPO Copyright Treaty requires signatories 'to offer adequate legal protection and effective remedies against the circumvention of effective technological measures' used by authors to protect their rights under the Treaty or the Berne Convention. TPMs may do more than prevent copying and further distribution of the work, perhaps restricting the user's ability to 'cut and paste' from the text, or to print the work, or to transfer it from one device to another. There are concerns that the restrictions imposed by TPMs prevent or inhibit the use of defences permitted under copyright law, thus tipping the balance previously determined by the legislature further towards the right holder.

The complications of global mass-market publishing success – the Harry Potter phenomenon

The British author J. K. Rowling's Harry Potter books have achieved a penetration in world culture which is unique and unprecedented. The first of her seven fantasy novels, *Harry Potter and the philosopher's stone*, was published in 1997. The series has sold over 400 million copies, making it the best-selling book series in history.[40] The phenomenon displays many of the characteristics discussed in this chapter. The books are sold in hard and soft covers, with different covers for adults and children, and have been translated into sixty-seven languages. There are film versions, computer

---

38 *Authors Guild, Inc.* v. *Google Inc.*, 954 F. Supp. 2d 282 – Dist. Court, SD New York 2013.
39 WCT Article 11. It also requires signatories to offer the same protection and remedies against those who knowingly remove or alter rights management information without authority: WCT Article 12.
40 http://news.bbc.co.uk/1/hi/entertainment/7649962.stm. See also Gunelius, *Harry Potter*; Patterson (ed.), *Harry Potter's world wide influence*; Whited (ed.), *The ivory tower*.

games based on the characters, and merchandising. Many websites are dedicated to the books, their characters and their world. The characters are analysed and discussed in chatrooms across the internet, and developed in new settings in fan fiction. As a result of this saturation, fans feel a type of ownership of the Harry Potter universe which does not always sit easily with the intellectual property rights that arise in these products. Consumers can be uncomprehending when told that they have strayed beyond the limits of what is legally permitted.

Twelve-year-old Owen Rickards, from North Wales, paid £100 to buy a Harry Potter domain name (harry-potterfanclub.com) so that he could set up his own fan website. In 2001 Warner Bros. insisted it be closed down. The BBC publicised the story, quoting Owen as saying: 'Warner Bros. is a big company, what harm is a website fan club going to do to them, if not boost their income from the film and the books?'[41] An intellectual property right gives its holder a choice as to whether and how to exploit it, and that is its aim. While some right holders insist on their strict legal rights, others choose to embrace this sort of non-commercial use, perceiving benefit to themselves in doing so. Some fan websites offer an extraordinary range of material. The Harry Potter Lexicon, created by school librarian Steve Vander Ark, describes itself as 'The most compleat and amazing reference to the wonderful world of Harry Potter!'[42] The Lexicon is a past winner of Rowling's own Fan Site Award, and she has admitted to using it herself for checking facts. Nevertheless, in 2008 Rowling and Warner Bros. sought to prevent the publication of a companion *book* of the same title, based on the website. A New York court held that the book version of the Lexicon contained more extracts from the original books than could be justified as 'fair use' under US copyright law.[43]

Fans impatient for the 'next' Harry Potter story have been known to create entirely new books based on the characters, or have produced unauthorised translations. Rowling is supportive of non-commercial fan fiction which is not published in a traditional sense, as long as authorship is not attributed to her.[44] But Rowling prevented the publication in the Netherlands of a children's book called *Tanya Grotter and the magic double bass* (a Dutch

41 http://news.bbc.co.uk/1/hi/wales/1709758.stm.   42 www.hp-lexicon.org.

43 *Warner Bros. Entertainment Inc. & J. K. Rowling* v. *RDR Books & Does 1–10* US District Court (Southern District of New York) 8 September 2008. Vander Ark later revised his work and published *The lexicon, an unauthorized guide to the Harry Potter novels and related materials* (2009).

44 http://news.bbc.co.uk/1/hi/entertainment/arts/3753001.stm.

translation of a Russian work), which was found to be a colourable imitation of *Harry Potter and the philosopher's stone*, and thus a breach of copyright.[45] Notwithstanding, Tanya Grotter still thrives in Russia, in novels which allude to Russian folklore and culture, and which their author Dimitri Yemets terms a 'cultural reply' to the Harry Potter books. There is a growing body of academic commentary defending at least non-competitive activities by fans.[46]

Embedded in these skirmishes lie potentially serious challenges to current cultural and legal assumptions. Copyright law must continue to adapt to these fluid and changing cultural boundaries if it is to remain serviceable to all those who currently rely on it, whether creators, publishers or users of copyright works.

---

45 *Uitgeverij Byblos BV* v. *Joanne Kathleen Rowling* (District Court of Amsterdam) [2003] ECDR 23.
46 For example, Noda, 'Copyrights retold'.

25

Books and the mass market: class, democracy and value

RONAN MCDONALD

In his 1910 novel *Howard's End*, E. M. Forster kills off the lower-middle-class Leonard Bast by having a bookcase collapse upon him. Like many real working men and autodidacts of the Edwardian period, the hapless Bast craved books and culture. In *The intellectual life of the British working classes* Jonathan Rose reads Bast as representative of a whole reading class at the beginning of the twentieth century, one that saw reading books as a path to knowledge and education and a clear opportunity for elevation, social mobility and freedom. His death, then, seems a bitterly ironic image of the relationship between books and class power. Books and high culture are a means for individual self-realisation and self-advancement within existing social structures. They are also, however, constitutive of class difference and hierarchy, a sign of privileged knowledge, social status and standing.

So great books have been seen by some as a ladder out of ignorance and deprivation. But who is to say what is great? How could such claims exist outside of existing, exclusionary social structures? Are claims to literary value that seek an objective status not inevitably compromised and contaminated by class hierarchies, even as they purport to provide social mobility? The answers to these questions, and the relationship of cultural value to social standing and cultural identity, is inextricable from wider social and technological changes, not just to the publishing and book retail industries, but also to education, working life and leisure.

As examined elsewhere in this volume, over the last 150 years the numbers of readers, books and reading opportunities have expanded beyond the wildest imagining of Victorian educationalists. The early twentieth century began with a rising tide of literacy as more people benefited from the free and later compulsory education introduced by Acts from 1870 onwards (see Chapter 10). Subsequent educational reforms in the twentieth century culminated in the 1944 Butler Education Act, which made secondary education free. The paperback revolution, new communications and transport technologies made books and distribution cheaper, quicker and more mobile. Public libraries, book clubs and working men's educational initiatives all contributed to reading opportunity, as did labour reform which expanded leisure time for middle- and working-class readers. So the surge in educational and literacy levels greatly increased the cultural power of the middle and lower classes, with all the ideological perils and possibilities this entailed. The arrival of the internet in the late twentieth century heralded a whole new phase to this revolution. By the end of the century, anyone with a laptop or a smartphone could access almost any book ever published, from the latest best-seller to Shakespeare's first folio.

The cardinal trope in twentieth-century reading history, then, is an unprecedented, even unthinkable, increase in access. A rapidly expanding potential readership had a rising tide of books and information from which to select, whatever the motivations for reading: entertainment, edification or education. The challenges for people of all classes became not how to read or how to obtain reading material but, rather, how to *select* from the overwhelming abundance of reading possibilities. Selection demands evaluation, which in turn demands criteria, but as access expanded in the final decades of the twentieth century so too the idea of a canon of timelessly great literature was queried and challenged on various fronts. Moreover, the culture of Reithianism (the vision of public sector broadcasting propounded by Lord Reith, Director General of the BBC) and its attempts in the mid-twentieth century to resynthesise the public sphere, to bring a wide, enlightened population together under a shared culture, lost its momentum in the closing decades. The idea of a shared literary culture dilated into reading communities – our 'individual libraries' and 'inner books', as Pierre Bayard calls them – becoming more and more divergent.[1] In the twenty-first century, there is far more pressing on our reading attention than we can ever hope to read. Ironically, the vertiginous possibilities can lead to attenuated selections, as we follow our social groups or the algorithmic marketing of Amazon, Facebook and Google.

In the nineteenth century, the fear of increased access to books often took on a patrician cast. It was important that people read the 'right books'. Matthew Arnold had in 1869 famously urged 'culture' as a solution to the alienating effects of modernity, the coarsening of mechanised habit and routine:

---

1 Bayard, *How to talk about books you haven't read*, pp. 71–4.

culture being a pursuit of our total perfection by means of getting to know, on all the matters which most concern us, the best which has been thought and said in the world, and, through this knowledge, turning a stream of fresh and free thought upon our stock notions and habits, which we now follow staunchly but mechanically.[2]

The Arnoldian belief in the value of books as edifying and improving was greatly influential in the ideology of reading in the twentieth century, in both a positive and a negative sense. High-quality culture could elevate national life, low-quality debase and threaten it. The masses should be steered away from vulgar or subversive books and magazines towards morally uplifting and enriching culture. The rapid expansion of literacy at the end of the nineteenth century threatened to be a vehicle of social and political instability: widespread reading could lead to the spread of radical socialism or suffragism, fuelling disquiet and the demand for reform. Outside the directly subversive, books had the power to unleash dangerous feelings and inappropriate desires, to debase and debauch, or at the very least to lead to a distracted and wayward attention.[3] Long-standing fears of the excessive stimulation that 'novel' reading could induce, especially in young women, endured into the twentieth century.[4] It mutated into a wider concern with bad reading habits, evident for example in Q. D. Leavis's *Fiction and the reading public* (1932), with its lament at 'the supremacy of fiction, and the neglect of serious reading which characterize the age'.[5] The danger of novels, their capacity to deprave or to lead to superfluous sensibility, is a venerable topic for the novel itself, for example in Jane Austen's *Northanger Abbey* (1817) and Gustave Flaubert's *Madame Bovary* (1856). The same attitude appeared as late as 1960 in the obscenity case against Penguin for publishing an unexpurgated edition of D. H. Lawrence's 1928 novel *Lady Chatterley's lover*. Mervyn Griffith-Jones, the chief prosecutor, notoriously asked the jury if this were the kind of book 'you would wish your wife or servants to read'.[6]

It seemed that too many working-class readers at the end of the nineteenth century preferred the mass-circulation penny papers *Tit-Bits* and *Pearson's Weekly* to classical literature, philosophy or the great British authors. The nation's reading habits should, therefore, be uplifted by the active promotion of edifying, high-quality material. This project began to take on

2 Arnold, *Culture and anarchy*, p. viii.
3 See the various attitudes discussed in Bradshaw and Potter (eds.), *Prudes on the prowl*.
4 Humble, *The feminine middlebrow novel*, chapter 1.
5 Leavis, *Fiction and the reading public*, p. 4.
6 Rolph (ed.), *The trial of Lady Chatterley*, p. 17. See also Chapters 5 and 8 in this volume.

nationalist overtones at the turn of the twentieth century. While Arnold's 'best which has been thought and said' came ostensibly from the 'world', the instrumental value of books and reading could also be aligned with what Stefan Collini has called the 'Whig interpretation of English literature', the 'enduring spirit' of a specifically English literary tradition.[7] If literature could increase the sense of a unified national culture, a distinctly British literary heritage in which all citizens could take pleasure and pride, then it would perform a valuable ideological function, especially when class distinctions were under threat. Literacy then could be rechannelled from a force of social disruption to one of cultural cohesion. The state therefore promoted the national culture and the education of the citizenry through funded public libraries and educational reforms that promoted reading in schools (see Chapters 7 and 10). The National Home Reading Union had been formed in 1889, as an attempt to guide uneducated people in what to read. The English Association, dedicated to furthering the study of English language and literature, was formed in 1906. When modern literature entered the universities as a discipline in the late nineteenth century, it became known as 'English'. The Board of Education commissioned the 1921 Newbolt Report: The Teaching of English in England, which articulated the ideology behind the institutional teaching of English in the educational systems. It presented English as a mechanism for cross-class national unity, reinforcing a common culture:

> the common discipline and enjoyment of it, the common possession of the tastes and associations connected with it, would form a new element of national unity, linking together the mental life of all classes by experiences which have hitherto been the privilege of a limited section.[8]

Arnold's 'best' culture, by which he meant Greek epic poetry and European philosophy, had shifted into a more island-based state culture that would, it was hoped, unify classes and internal divisions into an imagined community. The strain in this attempt to find cultural unity as a compensation for political division would become apparent in the second half of the century. Not only did it occlude class and gender inequality, it also tended to marginalise the non-English dimensions of 'British' literary culture. It would certainly be ill-equipped to include the widening diversity of British society as the century progressed. Nonetheless, the idea of national literary culture, a Britain of Shakespeare, Austen and Dickens, routinely re-enters public debate in

---

7 Collini, *Public moralists*, p. 359.   8 Newbolt, *The Newbolt Report*, p. 15.

Britain, by pundits and politicians wary of 'dumbing down' or by a heritage industry keen to associate British culture with the aura of literary prestige.

According to Stefan Collini, the terms 'highbrow', 'middlebrow' and 'low-brow' took hold in the 1920s.[9] The concepts presumed an alliance between class and cultural taste, which arguably did not pertain, since then (as now) there were plenty of lowbrows in the upper classes and plenty of opera goers in the traditional working classes. But the term highbrow could function as a pejorative handle of the *ressentiment* against toffs, while 'middlebrow' showed the disdain of those defending minority culture against the incursion of middle-class and mediocre tastes, which were often seen as stemming from America. The resistance from those established in the educated class to the expansions of reading – a sense that the rise of this new bourgeois, news-paper-reading public might debase the quality of the best of the culture – has been the topic of much discussion among literary historians.[10] To what extent this reactionary impulse motivated the experimental and obscurantist works of high modernist fiction is a moot point. Did modernist writers respond to increased literacy by deliberately making books less accessible to the mob?[11] The urge to experiment and challenge realist practices was felt across the arts, in painting and music as well as literature, and came from both right and left. Whatever the outré elitism of the Bloomsbury set, other modernist writers embraced and celebrated demotic culture. James Joyce's *Ulysses* (1922), for example, a book of unrivalled prestige, has a reputation for difficulty and inaccessibility. Yet its politics are arguably democratic and expansive.[12]

The increased access to books and other cultural forms opened the way for interminable debates during the twentieth century: is it really art or just entertainment? Many intellectuals felt that popular magazines, cinema and later television were a threat to the great literary inheritance of the nation and that firm vertical line had to be preserved. F. R. Leavis carried the spirit of Arnold into a zealous mission of cultural elevation in the face of coarse populism. Against this force must be placed a minority culture, a bulwark against the incursions of banal uniformity. 'In any period', Leavis wrote in *Mass civilisation and minority culture* (1930), 'it is upon a very small minority that the discerning appreciation of art and literature depends.'[13] The gatekeepers of culture are few, argued Leavis, and so too are the great works allowed for admission into the canon. The role of the gatekeepers was

---

9 Collini, *Absent minds*, pp. 110–12.   10 See, for example, Hilliard, *To exercise our talents*.
11 This case is argued in John Carey's polemic *The intellectuals and the masses* and in Harrison, *The reactionaries*. For a counter-argument, see Collini, *English pasts*, chapter 15.
12 Kiberd, *Ulysses and us*.   13 Leavis, *Mass civilisation*, pp. 4–5.

above all to evaluate and discriminate, to form judgements that find their validation in immanence and intuition rather than abstract theories or set criteria. At a time when the public were being flooded with entertainments and distractions – Lord Northcliffe's press, mass advertising, Hollywood gangster films – it was seen by Leavis as all the more vital that literary quality was asserted with force and authority.

Importantly for Leavis, while the guardians of culture certainly partook of an elite, this did not align with social class. Like Arnold, Leavis was an advocate of education and dissemination. Minority culture would never translate into mass civilisation, but it must connect with a wider public sphere in order to keep up its work of elevation, sensibility and social cohesion. He found the phrase highbrow 'an ominous addition to the English language' and was dismayed that the 'finest creative talents' were directed towards high modernist literature, like *The waste land, Hugh Selwyn Mauberley, Ulysses* or *To the lighthouse*, which 'are read only by a very small specialized public and are beyond the reach of the vast majority of those who consider themselves educated'.[14] Leavis sought to reconcile the horns of a recalcitrant dilemma: the quality literature he championed was exclusive and minority (if not as mandarin and obscurantist as high modernism). But the edification and moral uplift that such literature provided was as broadly significant and popularly impactful as a religious movement. There is a paradox at the heart of Leavis's evangelical elitism: it needed to be both exclusive and widely disseminated.[15]

As the century proceeded, increasingly, figures chafed against the idea that literary quality belonged only to a rarefied and restricted number of authors, an exclusive high table policed by a stringent and elite caste of discriminating arbiters of taste. A key figure in the opening up of the vertical categories was George Orwell, who, just as he sought to become class-less himself, also attempted to uncouple literary quality from social hierarchy. His attitude to culture was marked by a political ideology that advocated a deep connection to everyday life and an insistence on the emotional depths and value of demotic culture, a culture which often remains invisible and overlooked by dominant beliefs and practices. Simon During argues that Orwell, working outside traditional academic institutions, sets out 'to demonstrate that the commercial popular culture produced for the working class expresses a basic will to survival and, beyond that, a stoic yet boisterous defiance'.[16] Orwell did

---

14 *Ibid.*, p. 25.
15 For a taxonomy of reasons as to why Leavisism 'failed' see During, 'When literary criticism mattered'.
16 During, *Cultural studies*, p. 35.

not go to university himself and often styled himself as a left-wing gadfly of donnish stratifications. Having spent time in the Indian police force in Burma and as a down-and-out in London, he saw the brutalities of empire and the squalor of the British urban poor from the inside, and developed an affection for the working class and a belief in the validity and value of their modes of expression. In works such as *The road to Wigan pier* (1937), and in essays on topics like detective fiction and the sea-side postcards of Donald McGill, Orwell turned a critical light on the middlebrow and lowbrow, areas hitherto deemed unworthy of intellectual analysis. Yet it was not just in his subject matter that Orwell countered elitist ideas of quality – it was in his own style. His refusal of cant, pretension and obscurantism tapped into a deep English ethos that prized honesty, decency and clarity, epithets often applied to Orwell's own writing, even if his bluff persona sometimes veers towards anti-intellectualism. His observational, autobiographical style also exposed the class pretensions lurking behind purported literary taste, as in the essay 'Bookshop memories' (1936):

> In a lending library you see people's real tastes, not their pretended ones, and one thing that strikes you is how completely the 'classical' English novelists have dropped out of favour. It is simply useless to put Dickens, Thackeray, Jane Austen, Trollope, etc. into the ordinary lending library; nobody takes them out. At the mere sight of a nineteenth-century novel people say, 'Oh, but that's *old!*' and shy away immediately. Yet it is always fairly easy to *sell* Dickens, just as it is always easy to sell Shakespeare. Dickens is one of those authors whom people are 'always meaning to' read, and, like the Bible, he is widely known at second hand.[17]

The distance between what someone purchased and what was borrowed bespeaks a fiscal investment in cultural capital. The aspirant reader planned to read the canonical novel, or perhaps to display the prestigious 'literary' book for public view. But the real reading, for pleasure or distraction, was often performed more furtively, outside the authorised literary hierarchy. It was just the sort of social quirk or pretension that Orwell's no-nonsense approach sought to expose.

In taking popular modes of writing and culture seriously, Orwell antici-pated the major intellectual revolution around books and mass culture that marked the second half of the twentieth century in Britain, namely the rise in cultural studies, led by academic figures including Richard Hoggart,

17 Orwell, 'Bookshop memories', pp. 275–6.

Raymond Williams and Stuart Hall.[18] Hoggart and Williams studied with Leavis in Cambridge and their work demonstrates a complex Oedipal reaction to him.[19] The former's *The uses of literacy* (1957) made a decisive move, as Hoggart took popular culture seriously. English people were reading the wrong things, Hoggart argued, but the solution was not to give them more of the edifying 'classics', but rather for them to embrace the local and rooted, not the 'shiny barbarism' of homogenised global culture. Hoggart, from a working-class Leeds background himself, deplored shallow entertainment and formulaic dross. He lamented the loss of the close-knit communities and their replacement by pulp fiction, popular magazines, advertising and Hollywood, all of which for him deprived local culture of its distinctive features. Hoggart's attack was not on *popular* culture; rather it was on *mass* culture, imposed not from above by patrician educationalists, but created by the rapacious marketing and machinations of the international entertainment business.

Leavis's agenda for the importance of culture was maintained in Hoggart's thinking, as was his emphasis on discriminating between good and bad books. However, the vertical hierarchy was no longer an abstracted concept of the 'best'. Hoggart brought the anthropological concept of culture – an expression of a group identity – to bear on the Arnoldian idea of 'culture' as the mark of quality. The impact of this combination on how we perceive the relationship of literary value to social class was immense. Outside his influence on cultural criticism, Hoggart afforded local, working-class and demotic traditions and customs a 'literary' aura. The Yorkshire-born writer Alan Bennett said as much, identifying *The uses of literacy* as a crucial inspiration to him as a young man: 'it was reading Hoggart forty years ago that made me feel that my life, dull though it was, might be made the stuff of literature'.[20]

However dated Hoggart's paean to gendered working-class culture might now appear (he has little to say about race or immigration), it was strikingly proleptic. He attacked the condescension and ingratiation of tabloid newspapers, stressing that these organs were big business, owned by magnates and tycoons with scarce knowledge of or interest in working communities.[21] He targeted celebrities who exaggerated their working-class credentials as 'ordinary' working people in order to maximise their mass appeal, a tactic that has become familiar among politicians in our era.[22]

---

18 Roberts, 'How are George Orwell's writings a precursor to studies of popular culture?'
19 Hilliard, *English as a vocation*.　20 Bennett, 'Preface', p. xxii.
21 Hoggart, *The uses of literacy*, pp. 272–4.　22 *Ibid.*, pp. 151–2.

The sense that books come from a particular place and time, that working-class and minority communities might have their own valuable cultural expression, gained traction as the British Empire collapsed and new waves of immigrants arrived in the 1960s. The Birmingham Centre for Cultural Studies, founded by Hoggart in 1964, became the world's first institutional home of cultural studies. The Jamaican-born cultural theorist Stuart Hall, who directed the school from 1968 to 1979, expanded the scope of cultural studies to deal with race and gender.

The third founding figure of British cultural studies was a working-class Welsh Marxist, Raymond Williams. Williams argued that the notion of the mob, or of 'mass culture', is itself a construct, a way of seeing other people shot through with prejudice. 'I do not think of my relatives, friends, neighbours, colleagues, acquaintances as masses', Williams insisted, 'we none of us can or do. The masses are always the others who we don't know, and can't know . . . There are in fact no masses. Only ways of seeing the masses.'[23] In its very title, Raymond Williams's *Culture and society* (1958) evoked Arnold's *Culture and anarchy*, but he brought a sociological perspective to assessing culture that would reinforce the seriousness about popular and regional modes that Hoggart had begun the year before. The face-off between minority culture and mass civilisation was no longer a straightforward clash between a rarefied elite and the semi-educated hordes. The anthropological perspective seeped into the aesthetic/evaluative hierarchy so that the value of books was not simply a vertical, divided across high, middle and low, but rather incommensurate expressions of cultural identity. The sense that society was made up of different cultures, genders, races and classes, each with its own integrity and validity, gained traction, especially in the anti-authoritarian 1960s.

The waning of absolutist and rigid cultural hierarchy has democratised elective choices around books, opened the canon up to women's writing and minority voices, removed much of the stigma around 'low' culture and pushed home the reality that yesterday's popular entertainment is today's classic. Parents now urge novel-reading, once regarded as a trivial pastime for overly imaginative ladies, on screen-hypnotised teenagers. The idea that certain sorts of books – detective fiction, romance or fantasy – are intrinsically inferior and unworthy of attention underestimates the literary qualities that some 'genre' fiction has achieved. The Arnoldian idea of an abstractable 'best' seems much less identifiable and uncontroversial.

23 Williams, *Culture and society*, p. 299.

Do we thereby live in a literary republic, where reader-citizens choose their books with democratic autonomy? There are, obviously, other forces impacting on readerly choices, which if not directly graphed onto social class are nonetheless closely wedded to different senses of the aspirational. People read what comes before them, what friends, peers and the marketplace present to them, what is hyped and of-the-moment. The cultural studies pioneers advanced the value of demotic culture and everyday practices against those fusty gatekeepers and snobbish guardians of the highbrow. But anti-elitism could also play into the hands of an entertainment industry, eager to give the public just what they wanted, which sometimes could amount to the sort of homogeneous pap and depthless gratification decried by Hoggart. In any case, the figure of the tweedy critic and privileged 'literary intellectual', who acted as an arbiter of artistic value in the mid-twentieth century, began to go the way of the rag-and-bone man and the chimney sweep.[24] What one should read came to seem more a question of taste and individual opinion, rather than 'expert' judgement. Even before the internet afforded platforms for reader reviews and literary blogs of various sorts, the culture of literary hierarchy and the hierarchy of literary culture were devolved and disseminated. In practice, and paradoxically, this often meant that celebrity and marketing hype gained ever more leverage on readerly choices: powerful publishing enterprises and big-name authors were pro-moted through canny media profiling, book festivals and the rise of literary prize culture. Aspirational reading did not disappear, but the 'literary' itself became branded as a sort of genre, the type of book that might be shortlisted for the Booker, read in a reading group or reviewed in a broadsheet.

What institutions or venues now have the leverage to direct the national conversation around books? Print journalism hardly seems likely to play that role, threatened as it is by rolling and online news media. Equally, in the university, literary academics who loomed so large as public intellectuals in earlier decades now usually write for small audiences of their peers and have an increasingly embattled air about the role of the humanities in an instru-mentalist and globalised economy. There is much book reviewing on the internet and blogosphere, gifted and expert critical commentary on every literary form from young adult fiction to experimental poetry. However, it is hard to imagine the multiple corners of the internet buttressing a 'common culture', where people of diverse identities and backgrounds could find a shared civil space. Just as the idea of a public sphere has fragmented, so

24 McDonald, *The death of the critic*.

too has a venue for a common conversation, voices which might help us select the 'best' (however contested it might be) from the ocean of literary options. So the removal of critical authority, of a canon, has not always led to emancipation and enablement of readers. If access has opened, the mechanisms of *selection* have loosened. And even if the 'best' is available at a click of a mouse, how will readers find it amongst the tidal alternatives? If we only listen to those who already share our proclivities and interests, the supposed critical democracy will lead to a dangerous attenuation of taste and conservatism of judgement.

Fixed ideas of high culture, of the Arnoldian 'best', however elitist and suffocating, did at least encourage aspiration and self-improvement. They fuelled the autodidactic traditions of British society in the nineteenth and early twentieth centuries. Jonathan Rose's *The intellectual life of the British working classes* uses voluminous evidence – library records, educations archives, oral histories, as well as an exhaustive compilation of working-class memoirs and diaries – in order to explode the idea that working-class readers were unthinking consumers of 'low' culture. Like Leonard Bast, working-class people before the First World War often displayed a deep desire to consume the culture of those who were highly educated, seeking out the 'classics', Shakespeare, Dickens, the Brontës, the works that would furnish the cultivated mind (though not, notably, their high modernist contemporaries). The ethos that some books were good, good for individuals and good for society, fuelled early education reform, revolutions in printing, working men's clubs, the settlement movement, the Workers' Educational Association and the Open University. In the days before television, Welsh miners and Lancashire cotton spinners sought to climb the vertical, which – for all its exclusivity and partiality – could function as a ladder as well as a pyramid. Whatever the social divisions reinforced by cultural capital and the aura around high culture, however narrow the canon could sometimes be in terms of gender, class and race, it encouraged readers to search for reading material that might offer more substantial fare than immediate gratification and amusement.

However emancipating it has been to demolish that vertical axis and tear down the presumptions of high culture, it may be that social mobility is enhanced by cultural aspiration. The internet promises a golden age for autodidacticism, but it is no longer so clear what one should read to become educated and cultivated. Cultural choices are often influenced by our cadres, in-groups, social media circles or simply the advertising of online retailers. In short, it may be that the removing of the vertical barriers has contributed to the introduction of more horizontal ones. This is the paradox of the twenty-first century. The abundance of mass media offers a greater choice than ever. We are adrift in a sea of information, written and visual. But how do we navigate? From the 1930s to the 1950s, driven by the Leavisites in university departments and a general Reithian ethos of edification, it looked as if literature had a vital social and civilising mission, however etiolated and puritanical some of its proponents. The rise of cultural studies and the anti-authoritarianism of the 1960s democratised public taste, but arguably at the price of some of the aura and power around the category of the 'literary'. In the twenty-first, we have many voices in the literary world, a voracious publishing industry, designated star writers cleverly marketed and hyped, the rise of the literary festival. Every reader can be a writer and a critic: we have Goodreads, Amazon reader reviews, a literary blogosphere, a burgeoning creative writing sector. For a reader with interests in anime or avant-garde poetry, there are many with whom to share tastes online, as well as excellent critical commentary. Venues for printed criticism in Britain still remain, including the venerable *London Review of Books* and the *Times Literary Supplement* as well as the criticism that survives in the serious newspapers and weeklies. Shakespeare, Austen and Dickens maintain an aura of greatness and are still read and widely loved, though they have also been caught up in various forms of mass commodification, tourist kitsch and heritage merchandising. But the sense of a clearly identifiable canon which every educated person should read seems hard to re-imagine, because a unified national culture does not exist. That unity has gone not just because the class privilege has been challenged by alternative voices and diverse communities but also, more invidiously, because book buying and reading has become so caught up in the swirls of aura and allure strategically generated by a savvy book industry. Quite often, tastes in books are already anticipated by our demographic and social position, often laced through with more local or boutique forms of snobbery than the old highbrow distinctions – the idea of 'cool' defined by our friends, peers, social class and generation, the choices which Amazon, Facebook and Google will steer us towards with the algorithms that often define our selection horizons. When there is neither a clear public to address, nor a recognised authority with a right to speak above the din of voices, the divisions of our reading groups are no longer vertical but – like the bookshelf that fell on Leonard Bast – horizontal.

26

The book and civil society

KATE LONGWORTH

Throughout this and the period covered by the previous volume of the *Cambridge history of the book in Britain*, the various conditions that make 'the book' a matter for consideration in terms of state and society are evident. Developments in education and in print technology and distribution had by 1914 made the book, in theory, an object of almost universal consumption. Who was reading what was a matter of public interest.

Definitions of 'state' and 'society' have been and remain areas of intense contestation, both scholarly and political.[1] To acknowledge that fact is not to leave matters unproductively vague or open-ended, but rather to point to the equally contested positioning of the book in such debates. A working definition put forward by the Centre for Civil Society at the London School of Economics conceives its subject as:

> The arena of uncoerced collective action around shared interests, purposes and values. In theory, its institutional forms are distinct from those of the state, family and market, though in practice, the boundaries between state, civil society, family and market are often complex, blurred and negotiated.[2]

It is equally illuminating in this case to draw another project into the frame of reference, that of the *Cambridge social history of Britain*. In volume 3 of that series, *Social agencies and institutions*, José Harris reflects that 'in the immensely complex and continually changing relationship' between British state and society in the twentieth century, 'the exact nature of [that] changing relationship . . . remains obscure'.[3] It is frequently over the book – or the idea of the book – that battle lines are drawn. 'The book' has an existence throughout the period in question not only in its material manifestations

---

1 For a summary of range and chronology see Pierson, *The modern state*.
2 Centre for Civil Society, *Report on activities*. Available at http://eprints.lse.ac.uk/29398/1/CCSReport05_06.pdf.
3 Harris, 'Society and the state', pp. 63–5.

and the web of practice and institutional structure described in detail throughout this volume: there is an *idea* of 'the book', sets of associations and emblematic qualities that amount to a public reification of 'the book', as variously understood in relation to the interests of the *res publica*. Ideas of 'the book' are engaged and deployed in such a way as to illuminate the 'complex, blurred and negotiated' boundaries between state, market and civil society.[4] 'The book' is necessary, educating and civilising, but also dangerous in its capacity to influence.

Civil society: agencies for the book

One of the book trade's most enduring representative institutions of the twentieth century provides an apposite example of those blurred boundaries described above by the Centre for Civil Society. The National Book Council (later National Book League and now Booktrust) was initially a trade organisation, albeit a non-profit one framed not simply in terms of potential advantage to the trade, but, as an early mission statement suggested, 'with the object of rendering good service to the community'.[5] It emerged from the Society of Bookmen, which had been established in 1921 by Hugh Walpole at his home in Regent's Park, London, with the collective aim of 'the advancement of literature by cooperation of the various branches of the book trade'.[6] As precedents for 'co-operative publicity', where publishers and booksellers might 'pay a certain percentage of their total turnover into a common fund to be used for co-operative advertising', the cases of the British Commercial Gas Association and the Safety First Council were put forward. Each had employed 'mass suggestion . . . to awaken in the consciousness of the general public a desire for an abstraction (warmth, light, security)' by 'emphasising the concrete personal implications of that abstraction'. It was suggested that '*The habit of reading* is now the abstraction. The joys, the advantages, the economies of buying books are now the concrete implications of that abstraction.'[7]

It was 'with no desire to trespass on the preserves of the trade associations to whom [the] appeal is made' that the Bookmen summoned two representatives each from the Society of Authors, the Associated Booksellers, the Publishers Association and the Publishers' Circle to meet and discuss the question. The memorandum prepared by the Bookmen for the trade

---

4 Centre for Civil Society, *Report on activities.*
5 Sanders, *British book trade organisation,* p. 101. See also Norrie, *Sixty precarious years.*
6 *Ibid.,* pp. 100, 106. 7 *Ibid.,* p. 123.

associations opened with the claim that Britain 'lags behind some of the other great national communities of the day' in that 'books – whether they be works of philosophy, poetry, history, sociology, fiction, science or technology – are not yet accepted ... as *necessities*'. The scheme represented nothing less than a 'joint assault' on 'the public consciousness of the millions of potential readers inhabiting the United Kingdom'.[8] Rather than directly promoting the sale of books, it would 'create the taste and habit of reading' by means of 'propaganda' and 'appeals to national pride'. Of particular concern would be 'young people of school, university and early adult age', and thus the 'active sympathy' of educational bodies, teachers, parents and public librarians would be of crucial importance in reaching these 'impressionable' and 'idealistic' readers of the future.[9] The proposed campaign would 'endeavour to mobilise the educated members of the community' and secure 'really distinguished backing' by 'appealing to them for the support of an ideal, namely, the extension to others of the pleasure and profit which they have themselves found in books'.[10]

It was largely by means of the determination of Stanley Unwin that a qualified and hard-fought consensus was reached. By 1925 the newly formed NBC 'was no longer in the hands of the [Bookmen] alone, but became the concern of the trade as a whole'.[11] Its website currently states with some justification that it has 'been promoting books, reading and writing for more than eighty years'.[12] Though by no means the only organisation concerned with holding British government or society accountable on the basis of the perceived advantages of the promotion of reading, it has never been far from any related debate or controversy, and has been instrumental in many.

The 'propaganda' efforts of the NBC in its early years were aimed at publicity and increased membership, as well as increasing 'skilled use of books as essentials in modern civilisation': films and BBC broadcasts; a campaign of letter writing to the press; syndication of articles without charge 'aimed at relating subjects of all kinds to the use of books'; lectures from 'personalities of the moment'; exhibitions; book lists on specific subjects; and an 'enquiries bureau' and reference library of 'books about books'.[13] Two days after the outbreak of the Blitz, in 1940, it opened a 'Books and Freedom' exhibition in association with the Ministry of Information, and

8 *Ibid.*, p. 122.   9 *Ibid.*, pp. 128–9.
10 National Book Council, *Report of a special committee*, pp. 2–3.
11 Sanders, *British book trade organisation*, p. 103.
12 *The story of Booktrust*. Available at www.booktrust.org.uk/about-us/story-of-booktrust.
13 Marston, *National Book Council*, p. 4.

a decade later the renamed National Book League was appointed as one of four constituent bodies on the administrative council of the Festival of Britain. The Arts Council was another, and the NBL has worked closely with that body on several subsequent exhibitions and research projects, first securing funding in 1969.

The nature of civic participation has transformed since 1945, with the 'transfer of formerly political subjects' to the realm of 'experts and professionals'.[14] Successive directors at the NBL and Booktrust (the name was changed again in the mid-1980s) have been much consulted by the government up to ministerial level. As the following sections will demonstrate, rhetoric concerning the value of books and of reading was increasingly displaced over the course of the century by the assumption of that value, demonstrated in coordinated action. It acted as a mark of the increasingly important role played by the 'third sector' in both society and the economy when the government created the Office of the Third Sector in 2006, with a view to leading and coordinating funding for charities, social enterprises and voluntary organisations in the Cabinet Office. It has not been without controversy: there are those who feel that 'when government control these contracts, it can detract from the vitality of the civic organisation'.[15] It does, however, offer an indicator of the perceived value of such organisations, not as an alternative to state provision, but as a crucial complement. Ideas of the book, and increasingly of literacy and the value of reading, remain potent drivers for change into the twenty-first century.

Defining purpose: education and literacy

It is, broadly speaking, in the name of literacy and education that much campaigning in the name of the book has taken place.[16] As the Hadow Report on Books in Public Elementary Schools suggested in 1928, the question of the supply and use of books in education had proved so central an issue that 'a good account of the progress of primary education during the nineteenth century might be built up from a detailed study of the various types of schoolbook in use at successive periods'.[17] 'The need for a more adequate supply' of books to schools, the report suggested, had now begun 'to be acutely felt'.[18] For Henry Newbolt, however, in the 1921 report of the

---

14 Matthew Hilton *et al.*, '"The big society": civic participation and the state in modern Britain', *History and Policy Papers* (June 2010), www.historyandpolicy.org/papers/policy-paper-103.html#S8.
15 *Ibid.*   16 See also Chapter 11.   17 Hadow, *Report*, p. 1.   18 *Ibid.*, p. 17.

Departmental Committee appointed by the Board of Education, it was not simply a question of supply and demand but equally a matter of the proper use of books. He advocated (via Wordsworth) 'the transmission, not of book learning, but of the influence of personality and the experience of human life'.[19]

> The distinction here made between book learning and true education is of the first importance. Books are not things in themselves; they are merely the instruments through which we hear the voices of those who have known life better than ourselves.[20]

Rhetoric such as this, which characterised a vigorous debate on the proper ends of education at that time, was somewhat eclipsed during the Second World War, when paper, as well as machinery, binding materials and skilled labour, was in short supply. Much of the NBC's energies during the war years were spent gathering support and lobbying the government for a more sympathetic handling of the 'arrangements and "priorities" for the production of books to educational institutions', and the proposed imposition of purchase tax on books inspired some particularly powerful pro-book polemics (more on which to follow).[21] If the nation was winning the struggle for social progress, suggested a representative of the National Committee for the Defence of Books, it was 'very largely because of the work of the schools, and the main instrument of success in the schools is the book', not the teacher.[22]

What is perhaps most notable about the period during and after the war is an adjustment of what was by then felt to be an elitist attitude towards educational reform. For Dr Jimmy Mallon, Warden of Toynbee Hall, the question was not simply one of the supply of books to schools, but equally of their availability to those 80,000 or more people that the Workers' Educational Association (founded at Toynbee Hall in 1903) attracted to its courses annually. In addition, the Youth Hostels Association, the British Association of Residential Settlements and the Association of Educational Settlements 'represent something that is invaluable in our national life'.[23] Governments, he claimed, had 'never declared wholeheartedly for education'. The term 'Elementary Education' itself demonstrated that fact, 'elementary' having 'no connection with the language of education', but rather suggesting the view that 'we had to teach the child of the working man

---

19 Newbolt, The Newbolt Report, pp. 16–17.   20 Ibid., p. 17.
21 Hopkins, The battle of the books, p. 37.   22 McAllister et al., The book crisis, p. 40.
23 Ibid., p. 38.

something', and 'if we taught him too much or too little he would be a nuisance to employers'.[24] In 1962 the NBL's Work and Leisure exhibition toured cities in collaboration with the Trades Union Congress; the League, it suggested, 'was no ivory-towered organisation, holed up in London, supping fine wines'.[25]

In accordance with its early mission statements, much of the NBL's activity was focussed upon the quality of textbook provision for schools. From the 1950s it started to collate and publish data on spending in this area.[26] It joined forces with the School Libraries Association to issue guidance on the stocking and operation of libraries in schools, published annotated book lists for education professionals in all areas, and toured exhibitions that promoted education at home and in the Commonwealth.[27] More recently, Booktrust's efforts have mainly been concentrated on expanding literacy and encouraging the reading habit in children. In planning Bookstart, the first free books programme in the world, it worked in partnership with libraries and health visitors; since then it has given away nearly 30 million books to babies, and is establishing similar programmes for older children. In the new century it successfully bid to the Department for Children, Schools and Families to establish the Letterbox Club, supplying parcels of books to children in care with a view to improving their educational outlook. By 2011, 113 local authorities were signed up to the scheme, with 4,499 children enrolled.[28]

In the context of post-2010 'austerity' measures, however, funding for Booktrust has been under continual threat, and the idea of the book is increasingly conceptualised along party-political lines. In December 2010 Booktrust was told that in the next financial year it would lose the £13 million it received from the Department of Education towards the programmes outlined above. Children's author Michael Rosen held this up as 'an indication of where the government's priorities lie'. The new government was 'not prepared to acknowledge the power of reading for pleasure, even though research shows how much it helps children to achieve at school'.[29] After a campaign of outcry from writers and a rapid government U-turn, journalist Samira Ahmed noted 'how the programme epitomises the

24 *Ibid.*, p. 41.   25 *The story of Booktrust.*
26 National Book League, *Enquiry into expenditure*; National Book League, *Books for schools.*
27 See for example National Book League, *Education: a touring exhibition* (1965); Healy and Marland, *Language across the curriculum*; Moyle and Ainslie, *Teaching reading.*
28 *The story of Booktrust.*
29 Benedicte Page, 'Government withdraws all funding for book-gifting programmes', *Guardian* 21 December 2010, www.theguardian.com/books/2010/dec/21/government-withdraws-funding-book-gifting.

difficulty in measuring value rather than cost'. As a mother whose children had benefited from Booktrust's book gifting scheme, Ahmed suggested that the incident had served to demonstrate the need for government to gain 'a more instinctive sense of civic values, and the input of the people who know what they are for'.[30]

In the promotion of literacy, Booktrust was joined in 1992 by another notable institution, the National Literacy Trust (NLT). Inspired by his work as a trustee for the British Dyslexia Association, Sir Simon Hornby commissioned a research report from the public relations department at W. H. Smith, of which he was a former Chairman. With input from educational and literacy professionals and government officials, the study concluded that 'no agency existed whose specific remit was to promote the issue of literacy, in its many social, political and cultural dimensions, to stimulate new literacy initiatives, and to promote public awareness of the significance of the issue and of practical means to improve literacy standards in all age groups'.[31] Since its official launch in 1993, the Trust has aimed 'to raise awareness of the vital importance of literacy and ensure the Government takes action'.[32] It has, it claims, 'leveraged over £3 million from the business sector and £2.7 million from trusts and foundations to support its work, which has potentially reached well in excess of 18 million children and adults'.[33]

In 1997 the government made available a budget of £4 million for a 1998 National Year of Reading, to form a key part of the National Literacy Strategy and its policy for lifelong learning. It is a mark of the increased importance of the 'third sector' that the government contracted the NLT to deliver the project. Its partners in the project included Booktrust, the Reading Agency (launched in 2002, promoting reading via libraries), the Centre for Literacy in Primary Education (founded in 1972, becoming an independent charitable trust in 2002, offering training and consultancy for educational professionals) and Volunteer Reading Help (1973, training and supporting volunteers to provide one-to-one support to children who have fallen behind with their reading). With the stated aim of 'engaging the whole community in reading,

---

30 Samira Ahmed, 'Government backtracks on funding for Book Trust', Channel 4 News, 27 December 2010. Available at www.channel4.com/news/government-backtracks-on-funding-for-book-trust.
31 The quote is taken from the NLT's entry on Wikipedia, where its own website directs its visitors and with which it is in partnership. The latter hosts 'Wikireadia', an interactive good-practice guide for those involved in supporting literacy development. See http://en.wikipedia.org/wiki/National_Literacy_Trust#cite_note-0.
32 www.literacytrust.org.uk/about.   33 'National Literacy Trust', Wikipedia.

for pleasure and for purpose, in order to build a nation of readers', there followed a major media publicity campaign with the message 'a little reading goes a long way'. 'The logo', the Department for Education and Employment and NLT joint-authored review boasted, 'was used widely on everything from council correspondence and vehicles, to balloons and booklets.'[34] Financial support totalling £800,000 was awarded for eighty-six projects in libraries, schools and communities, and a grant was made of £100,000 to the Arts Council, who matched it and worked with its own ten Regional Arts Boards and with local education authorities on library promotion and school writing projects. Further funding of £50,000 was granted to the Commission for Racial Equality to run its Global Words project. The Year of Reading was repeated in 2008.

These details are offered not to suggest that an ideal has been realised. Literacy and the resourcing of education remain an ongoing struggle and a regular focus for post-2010 anti-austerity campaigners. In 2014 the British Youth Council, National Union of Teachers and charities Child Poverty Action Group and Kids Company demonstrated the 'uncoerced collective action around shared interests, purposes and values' that forms the focus of study at the Centre for Civil Society. It collaborated with social policy analyst Rys Farthing, using its collective network of beneficiaries, to gather young people's thoughts about the impact of family income on their ability to do well at school, using both online surveys and focus groups. Participants were asked about the extent to which their ability to pay for uniform, equipment and extra-curricular activity like school trips affected their choice of subject and academic engagement. Results were presented in *The costs of going to school, from young people's perspectives*, which reported as a key finding that 'most young people reported not having all the books and equipment needed for their studies . . . A lack of books, revision guides and stationery meant that their ability to study was reduced.'[35] 'School doesn't provide them', a young person is quoted as saying, 'and it's expensive to buy everything I need, even second-hand'.[36] This and other campaigning in relation to public policy makes clear the extent to which a value that inspired significant theorising and propaganda in the early twentieth century was 'taken as read' long before that century was out, and remains a significant weapon in the endeavour to realise many further national and global ideals.

34 *Building a nation of readers: a review of the National Year of Reading (1998–1999)*. DfEE & National Literacy Trust. Available at www.literacytrust.org.uk/resources/practical_re sources_info/749_national_year_of_reading_1998_1999.
35 Farthing, *The cost*, p. 5.   36 *Ibid.*, p. 23.

Government intervention: 'the book crisis'

The book trade's engagement with government certainly does not represent a line of happy progress. It was not lost on the NBC in its early years that 'a close relation [with] outside bodies is often made difficult by the suspicion that we represent solely the interests of the trade'.[37] This sense of disparity lingered without resolution, until the outbreak of war in 1939 forced into clearer focus for all its members the object for which it had been founded, and in particular its aim of 'influencing public policy'.[38]

Further details on the trade's response to both paper rationing and the proposed imposition of purchase tax are covered elsewhere in this volume.[39] Worthy of note here, however, is an extraordinary outpouring of polemics in support of the book during and after the Second World War, from the Publishers Association, the NBC, individual publishers and more: *The book crisis* (1940); *Britain needs books* (1942); *Battle of the books* (1947); *How governments treat books* (1950); *Books are essential* (1951); and so on. As the Labour politician and future MP John McAllister suggested, the Chancellor had, by effectively 'threatening to abolish books for the duration of the war', possibly 'done the cause of books more good than any of his predecessors'.

> This threat has given the cause of books – and the cause of books is the cause of civilisation, human worth and human dignity – such an advertisement as might tempt the National Book Council to invite the Chancellor to become its Honorary President.[40]

And 'what champions he has mobilised!' The issue brought forward the sort of support for the book for which the NBC had aimed from the start. It was a 'distinguished deputation' that carried the case for books to the Chancellor, led by the Archbishop of Canterbury, and including prominent academics Sir Arthur Eddington, Sir Charles Grant Robertson and Professor R. H. Tawney, as well as MPs A. P. Herbert and Professor A. V. Hill. 'In parliament itself, a hundred Members rose to protest.'[41] McAllister collected quotations from *The Times*, the *TLS* and the *Manchester Guardian*, amongst others. 'The three great English weeklies, despite their differences of Left, Right and Centre' (the *Spectator*, *New Statesman* and *Time and Tide*) 'were united in their defence of books.'[42] 'It is only when we are threatened with the loss of something that we appreciate its true worth', McAllister suggested, and the book trade seized the opportunity to cement its position as a trade, yes, but equally as

37 Marston, *National Book Council*, p. 12.   38 *Ibid.*, p. 7.   39 See Chapters 5 and 23.
40 McAllister *et al.*, *The book crisis*, p. 10.   41 *Ibid.*, p. 14.   42 *Ibid.*

a mainstay of education, civilisation and public morale.[43] 'Questions of mere trade and business and questions relating to man's immortal soul somehow don't seem to blend', said then-President of the NBL Norman Birkett, just a few years after having served as the alternate British judge at the Nuremberg trials. 'Yet the truth would appear to be that all these things are inextricably intertwined.'[44]

Indeed, as John Brophy went to great lengths to explain in *Britain needs books*, as well as professionals representing the book trade from every conceivable angle in *Books are essential*, 'no one makes a fortune out of the book trade. No one at all.'[45] Publishers issue books they expect to make a loss to support new writing of quality, booksellers stock them for the same reason, and librarians dedicate their evenings and weekends to reading that they might assist their borrowers to their best ability. Books were as vital as ever in the years following the war. Without them 'you couldn't heal the sick, develop industry, teach the young, or repair the complicated machinery of economics and politics'.[46] More than this, though, the recent memory of global conflict was fuel for a less utilitarian view of their value and purpose. 'A Goering may speak with contempt of culture', said Stanley Unwin, 'but not civilised human beings proud of the intellectual and moral status of the countries to which they belong.'[47] The question of the 'necessity' of books, he suggested, was a vital one that the government – and the public – must face.[48] 'The invention of printing revolutionised man's way of life', insisted Birkett, and has 'remained the most powerful and significant thing in our history'. If it was not, then 'dictators and evil men' would not attempt to repress it. 'They know its overwhelming power, and that is why enlightened and free men everywhere fight for full and unrestricted expression.'[49]

McAllister was right in suggesting that 'the defenders of a free literature dare no more relax their vigilance against this danger from within, than the defenders of Britain can relax their vigilance against the invader from without'.[50] Repeated hints that the Treasury was considering the imposition of VAT on publishing in the early 1990s drew vehement opposition once again. The Hands Off Reading campaign was mounted to persuade the Chancellor against such a measure, with Lords Skidelsky and Beloff as its Chair and Deputy Chair. Lord Beloff suggested that 'unequivocal demands from both the Prime Minister and Secretary of State for Education for an

---

43 *Ibid.*, p. 20.   44 Birkett, *Books are essential*, p. 9.   45 Brophy, *Britain needs books*, p. 4.
46 Hopkins, *The battle of the books*, p. 7.   47 Unwin, *How governments treat books*, p. 8.
48 Hopkins, *The battle of the books*, p. 11.   49 Birkett, *Books are essential*, p. 17.
50 McAllister *et al.*, *The book crisis*, p. 10.

expansion of education and a raising of standards' would surely 'bind the Chancellor's hands'.[51] Although printed (not e-) books and newspapers remain exempt from VAT, the very fact that the 1997 Labour manifesto made a virtue of their intention to maintain that status to some extent highlights the fact that it remains an active threat.

Conclusion

John Feather has suggested that the book 'is no longer the uniquely prestigious symbol of Western culture and civilisation. Neither it nor the industry which produces it can continue to expect the political and economic privileges that they enjoyed for so long.'[52] Those individuals who pooled resources in order to press the merits of that symbolic quality upon successive governments expended much energy and print in doing so. The sum of their efforts is undoubtedly evident in the durability of institutions such as Booktrust or the NLT, in the relative freedom of expression enjoyed by the book trade, or in the maintenance of purchase tax exemption. It remains to be seen how future challenges will be faced, in the context of the precedence of multinational conglomerates.

51 Hansard HL Deb 03 March 1993 vol. 543 cc663–5.
52 Feather, *A history of British publishing*, second edition, p. 228.

27

Sex, race and class: the radical, alternative and minority book trade in Britain

GAIL CHESTER

What is radical and minority publishing?

Dissenting publications have a long history, but until the dawn of the Industrial Revolution and the Enlightenment the bulk of oppositional litera-ture tended to focus on questions of morals and religion. It could be argued that the publication of Tom Paine's *Rights of man* (1791) and Mary Wollstonecraft's *A vindication of the rights of woman* (1792) heralded the arrival of oppositional literature concerned with issues of sex, race and class. Such publications evolved through the nineteenth century and gained momentum in the twentieth, particularly from the late 1950s/early 1960s with the more or less simultaneous arrival of the Affluent Society, the Permissive Society, the New Left and the small offset litho machine.

Since the 1990s there has been a stream of academic books addressing the topic of 'alternative media'. Though they have addressed media practices of the Left, they have all refrained from calling them 'radical', and while they have considered magazines and newspapers within their remit, like most titles within Media Studies, they have paid virtually no attention to the Book. Yet the production of books, pamphlets and other non-periodical print media is a crucial component of the media industries, and nowhere is this more evident than in the field of radical and alternative media. Arguably, it is in the history of the radical book that definitions of 'the Book' are most elastic, and the intersections between media forms particularly obvious.

This chapter will concentrate on Left oppositional material since 1914, using the broadest definition of the term, covering not just the publications of the various segments of the organised and 'disorganised' Left – the Anarchists, Situationists, Marxists, and the parliamentary Left of all varieties – but the peaceniks, beatniks, feminists and greens, LGBTQI (Lesbian, Gay, Bisexual, Trans, Queer, Intersex), BAME (Black, Asian, and Minority Ethnic),

Disability, and every other kind of activist aiming to reconstruct society into a less oppressive structure. This literature may be called dissenting, oppositional, radical, alternative, counter-cultural, underground, outsider, subaltern or minority interest, depending on the era and the orientation of the material and the labeller – all have validity and they are often used interchangeably.[1] All the publications under discussion here present ideas antithetical to, or at least challenging, societal norms from a broadly left-wing point of view, and so this chapter unashamedly uses the term 'radical' to cover this multitude.

In discussions of the term, scholars have argued that to be 'alternative' a media source advocates radical social change, is produced by a 'democratic/collectivist process of production', is aimed at audiences ignored by mainstream media, and may utilise innovative and experimental formats.[2] The rise of the counter-culture in the 1960s spread the idea that the transmission/production of publications could be as politically significant as their content, while incorporating a critique of conventional means of production into one's definition of 'radical' can help to distinguish between those advocating radical social change from the Right and the Left. Media which have pursued an explicitly right-wing agenda have included the Right Book Club, co-founded by popular historian Arthur Bryant in the 1930s, which in 1939, as part of the National Book Club, published a new English edition of *Mein Kampf*;[3] the Bow Group, whose pamphlets between 1953 and 1972 are collected in the British Library; and Elliot Right Way Books, founded in 1946, which concentrated on 'How To' titles such as *The technique of freshwater fishing and tackle tinkering* (1952), but also, through its Paperfront imprint, became the house publisher for Enoch Powell in the 1960s and 1970s. Most recently, in 2013, Melanie Phillips (whose political and journalistic trajectory has taken her from the *Guardian* to the *Daily Mail* and the *Spectator*) launched Electric Media Books, which specialises in her right-wing agenda.

The radical book trade has always been an intersecting network of activists and enterprises – publishers and distributors, printers and bookshops, writers and readers – and enjoys a more direct relationship with its audiences than the mainstream industry. This is a major factor in enabling most producers of radical literature to manage with a restricted budget, and can also influence the form that a publication takes and the methods of its production, promotion and distribution. This symbiosis is perhaps most obvious in the case of voluntary organisations, pressure groups and political parties, but it is also

1 For a specific account of 'counter-cultural' and 'underground' publishing from the 1960s, see Chapter 28.
2 Waltz, *Alternative and activist media*, p. 4. 3 Green, *Ideologies of conservatism*.

evident among non-aligned radical book publishers, bookshops and printers, who have relied upon their readers to suggest titles and commit to buying their books. Like the mainstream book trade, the radical book trade must break even or it perishes, though making money is not its main motivation. Nevertheless, in most important respects, it is merely an example of a niche publishing market. Essentially, radical publications are in the business of communicating their ideas to their intended audience, and ingenuity is required to achieve this, as the mainstream is generally unenthusiastic about supporting material which could help bring on its own collapse.

Not everybody who produces a radical publication would think of them-selves as a publisher – they are simply using the means at their disposal to convey their message. If the publisher is primarily an organisation which views its main function as changing public opinion, then its publications will be seen as an adjunct of this task, and whether it publishes an internal newsletter primarily directed to issues of current concern to its supporters, or a newspaper or pamphlets to disseminate its views to a wider audience, it is unlikely to publish beyond its self-defined remit. For example, many voluntary organisations and pressure groups put out information documents and practical handbooks to assist their members and the wider public in dealing with systems whose workings seem designed to disempower people. These have included the collectively written and produced series of short pamphlets from the 1970s Women's Rights Group in Manchester, on such topics as housing rights, social security and marital breakdown; the Child Poverty Action Group's *Welfare benefits and tax credits handbook*, whose sixteenth edition was published in 2014 (now a hefty professional guide, it has been updated annually since its first appearance as *The national welfare benefits handbook*, a seventy-two page pamphlet, in 1972); and the Directory of Social Change, which publishes a range of quite expensive books with high production values to assist small groups and charities navigate the minefields of fundraising and self-organisation. A mainstream publisher would be most unlikely to take on publication of such material. By producing it themselves, organisations are able to reach their target audience effectively, and in some cases generate income.

Book publishing

Some mainstream publishers have always been more receptive to publishing radical material than others, through political conviction or an astute eye to the market, and the business acumen to cross-subsidise their political output with more mainstream (and income-generating) publications. The extent of the crossover between material produced by mainstream and radical publishers has varied quite considerably depending on many factors, including the political and cultural climate of the time, the definition of what constitutes a radical publisher, the capacity of individual authors to choose their publisher, and the publisher's tastes and proclivities. However, prior to the 1960s, with the exception of a few specialists such as the Women's Social and Political Union (WSPU)'s Woman's Press,[4] and the Labour Press,[5] there were hardly any publishers dedicated entirely to radical books. Thus many key titles have been published by mainstream publishers, for example Trotsky's *The revolution betrayed* (Faber & Faber, 1937), E. P. Thompson's *The making of the English working class* (Victor Gollancz, 1963), Rachel Carson's *Silent spring* (Hamish Hamilton, 1963) and E. F. Schumacher's *Small is beautiful* (Blond & Briggs, 1973).

It would be wrong to suggest that no radical publications before the 1960s were concerned with what might now be called lifestyle or identity politics, or that all earlier material was restricted only to a conventional left-wing analysis, though clearly very little of it was consciously counter-cultural in the 1960s sense. All the important early radical firms, such as T. Fisher Unwin, George Allen, Swan Sonnenschein (which both became part of Allen & Unwin), Grant Richards, C. W. Daniel[6] and A. C. Fifield (the latter two having started their careers with the Free Age Press, which was mostly established to publish the works of Leo Tolstoy), published titles on a wide range of political topics.

Allen & Unwin, founded in 1914, was probably the early twentieth-century's most prominent and certainly Britain's longest-lasting radical publisher – a startling claim if one thinks only of the firm in the 1970s and 1980s, with its academic, education and trade divisions, and mainstream best-sellers like *The Kon-Tiki expedition* and *The lord of the rings*. However, the firm had its roots in the firms of George Allen, publisher of John Ruskin, and Swan Sonnenschein, publishers of Marx, Engels and Edward Carpenter.[7] Allen & Unwin's willingness to continue supporting Carpenter, whose sexuality and lifestyle were the exact opposite of Stanley Unwin's own very conventional marriage and Methodist outlook, epitomises the firm's commitment to resisting censorship and publishing books across the widest spectrum of beliefs. Carpenter devotes a chapter of his autobiography to the practical

---

4 Chester, 'The anthology', p. 196.   5 Carpenter, *My days and dreams*, p. 195.
6 Gassert, 'C. W. Daniel'.   7 Gallagher and Donovan, *A hundred years*.

and political vicissitudes of publishing his books.[8] As befitted his politics, his relationship with publishers was never simply commercial, but he wanted to earn money from his writing when he could. Thus, he was well matched with Unwin, who realised that Carpenter had to be promoted as a total package, declaring, 'Thanks to our handling all his books and thus being able to make one sell another, we were able to build up his income most agreeably.'[9] One of Carpenter's most popular books was *Love's coming of age: a series of papers on the relationships between the sexes*, first published by the Labour Press in Manchester in 1896. Rejected by T. Fisher Unwin, who cancelled Carpenter's contract in the wake of the Oscar Wilde trial, and then by Swan Sonnenschein and several other publishers, the book sold mainly by word of mouth and through the socialist movement.[10] By 1916 it had sold 100,000 copies worldwide. Its wide appeal was that it 'opened up an acceptable middle-ground between convention and the free lovers',[11] though it apparently divided the International Women's Suffrage Alliance's conference in Berlin in 1904.[12]

Allen & Unwin originated many radical titles, as well as reissuing reliable sellers such as Carpenter and, later, Engels and Marx. Often the publishing costs were underwritten by the individuals and organisations which produced them. For example, in 1917 the firm published *I appeal unto Caesar*, an impassioned plea to improve the prison conditions of conscientious objectors, written by Mrs Henry Hobhouse, whose son Stephen was then enduring those very conditions. In 1916, the firm issued *Nationalisation of the coal supply*, published for the Fabian Society, and *Poland's case for independence*, one of many titles printed over the years for governments in exile and émigré groups based in Britain – a small but obviously dedicated market.

Allen & Unwin enjoyed an ongoing relationship with trade unions. In 1917 it published *Trade unionism on the railways: its history and problems*, by G. D. H. Cole and Robert Page Arnot, again in cooperation with the Fabian Society, and in the 1950s and 1960s issued a series of books on the history of the miners and their trade unions in various parts of the country. Several of these Miners' Histories were written by Robert Page Arnot, who, in the period leading up to the General Strike, was one of twelve Communists jailed for six months for 'seditious libel' and a breach of the Incitement to Mutiny Act of 1797.[13] Alongside landmark Left books such as Clifford Allen's

---

8 Carpenter, *My days and dreams*, chapter 9.
9 Rowbotham, *Edward Carpenter*, pp. 342–3.
10 Carpenter, *My days and dreams*, pp. 195–8.   11 Rowbotham, *Edward Carpenter*, p. 219.
12 *Ibid.*, p. 345.   13 Arnot et al., *Forging the weapon*.

Labour's future at stake (1932) and Fenner Brockway's *Inside the Left: thirty years of platform, press, prison and parliament* (1942), the firm demonstrated a continuing commitment to publishing a range of radical books, including Colin Ward's *Anarchy in action* (1973), and works that responded to changes in the social and cultural make-up of the nation such as Ruth Glass's *Newcomers: West Indians in London* (1960).

Penguin is an interesting case of a mainstream company which published important radical literature. Producing good-quality books cheaply for a much wider audience than had previously had access to them was, in itself, a radical act. Even Allen Lane was surprised by the immediate success of Penguin's non-fiction imprint, Pelican, launched in 1937, with George Bernard Shaw's *The intelligent woman's guide to socialism, capitalism, Sovietism and fascism* as its first title, and V. K. Krishna Menon, socialist politician, as its founding co-editor with Lane. Not all of the 3,000 titles issued by Pelican were radical, but there was a general impulse of social radicalism in the list, associated with the popularising of social sciences and cultural studies, whose founding text *The uses of literacy* by Richard Hoggart was published by Pelican in 1958.[14]

In the 1960s and early 1970s, many of Pelican's titles emerged from the prevailing conjunction of counter-culture and radical politics. Among its 1968 titles were E. P. Thompson's *The making of the English working class* and *The dialectics of liberation*, selections from the 1967 Congress of the Dialectics of Liberation held in London, which aimed to promote, as the blurb recorded, 'a genuine revolutionary consciousness by fusing ideology and action on the levels of the individual and of mass society'. Racial discrimination in its national and international contexts was represented by *Racial discrimination in England* by W. W. Daniel (1968) and *Black power: the politics of liberation in America* by Stokely Carmichael and Charles V. Hamilton (1969). The 1970s saw landmark Women's Liberation titles such as *Woman's estate* by Juliet Mitchell (1971) and *Words and women* by Casey Miller and Kate Swift (1976).

Unsurprisingly, the inter-war years produced a number of other publishers with radical titles on their lists. Victor Gollancz founded his publishing company in 1927 and the Left Book Club in 1936 (see Chapters 5 and 6). Another radical publisher founded in the 1930s, and still in independent existence today, is Lawrence & Wishart, publisher to the British Communist Party until its dissolution in 1991, since when it has published

---

14 Paul Laity, 'Pelican books take flight again', *Guardian* 25 April 2014.

more wide-ranging radical titles with an emphasis on cultural politics. The company was formed in 1936 from a merger between Martin Lawrence and Wishart Books (founded 1925), its most notable volume being Nancy Cunard's *Negro* (1934). Merlin Press was founded in 1956 by Martin Eve. Originally intended as a cultural supplement to Lawrence & Wishart, it has always been independently Marxist rather than attached to any party, publishing the annual *Socialist Register* (whose fiftieth edition appeared in 2014), and the work of many independent socialists, including Eve's lifelong friend E. P. Thompson, as well as socialist feminists such as Sheila Rowbotham.[15] Merlin Press continues along similar lines today in the hands of Tony Zurbrugg, previously of Third World Publications and the Africa Book Centre.

Black book publishing

An example of the crossover between mainstream publishing and radical ideas is in Black publishing, perhaps because there has always been a significant element of cultural identity bound up with the overt politics. Several Black periodicals were published from the beginning of the twentieth century, and by the 1930s and 1940s books by a number of notable Black and Asian authors living in Britain, such as C. L. R. James, Una Marson and G. V. Desani, were published by Secker & Warburg, Aldor Publishing and the Fortune Press.[16] Marcus Garvey's volume of poems *The tragedy of white injustice* was published in 1935; George Padmore's *History of the Pan-African Congress* appeared in 1947, while his *Pan-Africanism or communism?* was published by Dennis Dobson in 1956. However, such publishing was sporadic until between 1948 and 1958, when mainstream publishers brought out some fifty books by writers from the British Caribbean, and then a similar number from West African writers in the succeeding decade. According to Gail Low, the unprecedented interest of the literary establishment during the period of decolonisation 'can be rationalised as a complex of responses, including curiosity, concern, exoticism and opportunism'.[17] The same could be said for any mainstream publisher publishing any radical book ever.

As mainstream interest began to tail off (with the notable exception of Heinemann Educational Books' African Writers Series, which continued until its extinction in 2003), the first two independent Black book publishers in Britain were starting up: New Beacon Books in North London in 1966 and

15 Kemsley, *Martin Eve remembered.*   16 Ireland, 'Laying the foundations', para. 18.
17 Low, *Publishing the postcolonial*, p. xiv.

Bogle-L'Ouverture in West London in 1968. Both also ran bookshops, and published significant works of fiction and non-fiction. Unlike the mainstream publishers, however, this was always done in the context of intense commitment to Black radical politics. They wanted, in the words of John La Rose, one of New Beacon's founders, to provide 'an independent validation of one's own culture, history, and politics – a sense of self – a break with discontinuity'.[18] Thus New Beacon's publishing programme started with a collection of La Rose's poems, followed by two books of criticism of Caribbean literature written by people from the Caribbean, and two reprints of nineteenth-century classics, again written by a native Caribbean. In 1971, New Beacon published the groundbreaking *How the West Indian child is made educationally sub-normal in the British school system* by Bernard Coard, a book that was not only intensely political but rooted in Black people's experience of Britain.[19]

A similar philosophy was evident in Bogle-L'Ouverture publications. They started publishing almost accidentally, with a single pamphlet of Walter Rodney's speeches, but went on to develop a significant list of books including Rodney's revolutionary *How Europe underdeveloped Africa* in 1972. As Jessica Huntley, one of Bogle-L'Ouverture's founders, wrote, '[its] founding was based on a corporate decision to make a total break with the usual tradition of publishing: that of Black people passively providing the human material to be written up and published by other people'.[20]

The race riots of the early 1980s increased the demand for books about the Black people who had settled permanently in Britain and been born here. The period has been described as a bonanza for minority publishing, not just by publishers and booksellers, but also by librarians, who were among the first to identify the demand. Major names to have emerged from that period and since include Hansib, Karnak House, Xpress, BlackAmber Books and Fahamu Books. In their very different ways they are fulfilling Jessica Huntley's early aspirations, so it is appropriate that when in 2013 Fahamu published the fortieth-anniversary edition of *How Europe underdeveloped Africa*, 40,000 copies sold without a mainstream publisher or media coverage.

These developments reflect general trends in the history of radical and alternative book publishing. The late 1960s and 1970s saw the rise of a range of publishers encouraged by the political climate, rising standards of living, increasing numbers of university students, and the decreasing unit cost of

18 Ireland, 'Laying the foundations', para. 4. 19 Alleyne, *Radicals against race.*
20 Ireland, 'Laying the foundations', para. 25.

book production arising from the widespread adoption of processes such as perfect binding and offset litho. The most prominent were New Left Books (which subsequently changed its name to Verso), Allison & Busby, Writers' & Readers' Publishing Co-op, Prism Press, Journeyman Press, Pluto Press, Zed Books, The Women's Press, Onlywomen Press, Gay Men's Press, Stage 1 and Brilliance. Of these, several remain in business as independent radical book publishers, and since that prolific period, others have emerged, but not in such numbers. Notable names from the 1980s include Peepal Tree Press, Green Books, Five Leaves, New Internationalist Books (initially a minor adjunct to the magazine) and Al Saqi Books, which have been joined in the new century by Minor Compositions, Zero Books, Ayebia Publishing and HopeRoad Publishing, all of which embrace varying levels of electronic publication as well as paper books.

Virago

Virago started in 1973 as an associate company of Quartet Books but went independent in 1976.[21] In 1982 it became a wholly owned subsidiary of the Chatto, Virago, Bodley Head and Cape Group (CVBC), but in 1987 the directors went for a management buyout, only to become part of the British arm of the American multinational Little, Brown in 1995. In its latest incarnation, it has lost its radical politics. It still publishes good women's writing, but rarely takes risks to promote untested authors. Even in its early days it consciously presented itself as part of mainstream publishing (albeit a dissident part), as opposed, for example, to Onlywomen Press, started around the same time, which has remained resolutely independent until today, publishing only a few books a year, which must conform to its ethos of radical lesbian feminism.

When Virago launched its Modern Classics series in 1978, making available to a new generation lost works with a feminist or proto-feminist message, they arguably moved classics towards the centre of mainstream publishing. The Classics series that already existed, notably Penguin Classics and OUP's World Classics, languished somewhat in a genteel backwater, whereas the Virago Classics were launched with Carmen Callil's customary flair for promotion. Their striking uniform green covers, which looked like very expensive design, were actually another example of radical publishing's capacity for turning a paucity of resources into an asset. The famous tagline, 'This novel changes lives', which was attached to Marilyn French's 1978 novel

21 Murray, *Mixed media*, chapter 1.

The women's room (included in Virago Classics in 1997), could equally be applied to many other works of fiction, both feminist and not, published with political intent, many by mainstream publishers, even though their political significance may only have been bestowed on them retrospectively. The importance of fiction and poetry to both second-wave feminism and the earlier women's movements is undeniable, as shown by Elizabeth Crawford's list of 155 novels with women's suffrage as their theme in her comprehensive reference work on the subject.[22]

Academic publishing

There are many in radical circles who regard academic publishing as a kind of cultural imperialism, as studying activism is not the same as doing it, and corralling radical thought within the academy has only served to de-radicalise it. Academic publishing has been a significant mechanism in this process, and its publishing houses have been subject to more conglomeratisation than other parts of the industry.[23] This, combined with the trend towards neo-liberal policies and the target culture in higher education, has led to the books that many on the Left want to read – mid-list titles for the interested general reader – being largely squeezed out. An indication that this trend might be slightly in reverse is the relaunch of Pelican Books (now an imprint of Penguin Random House) in May 2014, after a gap of twenty-five years.

Routledge is the premier example of these trends. For thirty years it has been the leading publisher in postcolonial studies, gender studies and other left-leaning areas of the Humanities. The firm has strongly influenced academic discourse in these areas, not least by acquiring committed editors who had developed radical lists while working for autonomous imprints. At the same time, Taylor & Francis, Routledge's parent company, has developed a substantial influence over academic journals, especially in the Humanities. In 2013–14, it actively suppressed an issue of *Prometheus: Critical Studies in Innovation*, because it contained articles debating the practices and profits of academic publishing generally, and extended the discussion of the offshore tax evasion practices of Informa, the overall owner of Routledge and Taylor & Francis.[24] Steffen Boehm, a professor at Essex University who contributed to the *Prometheus* debate, and who is on the editorial collective of the open access *Interface: A Journal for and about Social Movements*, pointed out that academics 'can only keep our freedom to publish what we like if we control

22 Crawford, *The women's suffrage movement*, pp. 467–71.
23 Parker, 'Becoming editor', p. 465.
24 Harvie *et al.*, 'What are we to do with feral publishers?'

the publishing process'.[25] This, of course, is true in all areas of the radical book trade, but becomes particularly difficult to navigate when your professional status and income become tied up with your politics.[26]

The effect of American cultural imperialism

In 1951, Jack Lindsay contributed an article on publishing to a special issue of *Arena* (a Communist Party journal), 'The USA threat to British culture', which explained how British book publishing was being overwhelmed by the capitalist methods and cultural domination of the USA.[27] Even though the article pre-dated the first major conglomeratisation of the British book trade by a generation, in many respects it accurately described what was to come. But it did not predict how the mainstream US publishing industry would be the first major source of counter-cultural and feminist books to reach Britain. Mainstream US publishers, especially paperback houses, were perhaps able to take more risks than British publishers because the US population is large and there was a vigorous underground scene with its own publications to provide a significant source of material and a market to exploit. This larger US industry was publishing mainly in English, so when resources were tight it was much more convenient for commercial publishers in Britain to issue a book from the USA rather than originate a similar title here. This has posed a significant problem for the radical movements in Britain, at least since the Second World War, and probably earlier, since such publishing can trick the unwary reader into believing that our cultural and political situations are more similar than they are, while our knowledge of political developments in Europe has too often been mediated by translations and authors being re-imported from the USA. Having been published in French in 1949, the first English-language edition of Simone de Beauvoir's *The second sex* was issued in 1953 in Britain by Jonathan Cape and in the USA by Knopf, who held the translation rights, in what was widely considered a poor translation which omitted 15 per cent of the original text. This US edition remained in print and was published as a cheap paperback by Bantam in 1961. Knopf consistently refused to have a new translation done, not relenting until 2009.[28]

---

25 Paul Jump, 'Resignations threat over Taylor & Francis "censorship"', *Times Higher Education* 5 June 2014, www.timeshighereducation.com/news/resignations-threat-over-taylor-and-francis-censorship/2013752.article.
26 Parker, 'Becoming editor'; Chester, 'Book publishing'; Chester, 'The anthology as a medium'.
27 Lindsay, 'Publishing'.   28 Bogic, 'Why philosophy went missing'.

Similarly, many texts perceived as pioneers of the modern Women's Liberation Movement emanated from outside Britain. Titles such as Betty Friedan's *The feminine mystique* (1963), Kate Millett's *Sexual politics* (1971) and Shulamith Firestone's *The dialectic of sex* (1971) came from the USA and were thoroughly publicised here, though *The female eunuch* by the Australian Germaine Greer (1970) was first published in Britain. Home-grown feminist books such as Hannah Gavron's *The captive wife* (1966), Eva Figes's *Patriarchal attitudes* (1970) or May Hobbs's *Born to struggle* (1973) fared less well, perhaps because they espoused a socialist feminist perspective. Micheline Wandor, editor of *The body politic* (1972), the first anthology from the British Women's Liberation Movement, failed to raise interest in the volume among commercial publishers who judged Women's Liberation as 'not hot' and didn't think interest in women would last.[29] *The body politic* was eventually published by Stage 1, a very small radical publisher (also responsible for *The little red school book* and works by Che Guevara and Fidel Castro) with a modest print-run, using cheap typesetting, paper and binding. Contrast this with the publication of *Sisterhood is powerful*, the first Women's Liberation anthology in the USA, edited by Robin Morgan and published by Random House / Vintage Books in 1970. Although Morgan describes vividly in her introduction the many problems she encountered with sexism and interference by male editors at Random House, they did publish a mass-market paperback of 600 pages with photographs, which also sold well in Britain.

Intersections and intersectionality

An important feature of the whole radical book trade is that printed objects are not produced in a vacuum, separate from other radical cultural activities. Moreover, people participating in radical movements rarely fit into neat boxes, either of personal identity or political affiliation. Thus, what we call the radical book trade has consisted of a range of intersecting activities and personnel: William Morris and the Arts and Crafts movement; Edward Carpenter, Havelock Ellis and their circles of sexual radicals; Sylvia Pankhurst and the East London Federation of Suffragettes; Claudia Jones, founder of the *West Indian Gazette*; and peace activists of all kinds. All have always engaged with organising and publishing about more than one political issue. However, until Black Consciousness and Women's Liberation pointed out that the personal is political, such intersections were not widely

29 Chester, 'The anthology as a medium', p. 198.

incorporated into radical activity, including its book trade. When they were, it was mainly among Black people and women. An outstanding example is Glenn Thompson, whose experiences of being an impoverished Black child in New York who only learnt to read at the age of twelve informed all his later activity. He came to London in 1968 where he was a youth worker in Hackney and helped to start Centerprise bookshop and its local publishing project, before moving on to co-found Writers' and Readers' Publishing Cooperative and its influential For Beginners series, graphic books introducing 'complicated' intellectual topics to general readers. But while undertaking these ventures with people from all backgrounds, his commitment to community and Black issues never wavered.[30]

The very act of cultural celebration is often, in itself, political, particularly when previously silenced members of an excluded group, such as Irish people or survivors of the mental health system, make their presence felt. With the rise of Women's and Gay Liberation, lesbians and gay men began to achieve some visibility, but combatting the fear induced by prosecutions of gay literature for obscene libel, such as *The well of loneliness* in 1928 (see Chapter 5), The Fortune Press in 1934,[31] and *Gay News* in 1976,[32] took courage, especially as male homosexual acts were illegal in Britain until 1967. Despite the launching of Gay Men's Press in 1979 and Brilliance Books in 1982, both of which published a wide range of fiction and non-fiction titles over the next two decades, and a growing list of established gay authors being published by the mainstream press, the BBC's Big Read in 2003 (a poll of the nation's favourite books) barely featured any gay books (or books from any other part of the radical book trade). Partly in response, the Queer Up North Festival in 2006 incorporated the Big Gay Read to celebrate and make gay literature visible.[33]

The most public manifestation of intersecting interests in the radical book trade has been its bookfairs. Foundational were the Socialist Bookfairs, run from 1978 by Bookmarks, the Socialist Workers Party bookshop. Their great innovation was to present together radical titles from all publishers, mainstream and radical. They attracted criticism for being entirely commercial, but helped inspire the Anarchist bookfairs, the International Feminist bookfairs, the International Radical Black and Third World bookfairs, and, since 2013, the Radical bookfairs, each with their own philosophies, though with

30 Margaret Busby, 'Glenn Thompson' obituary, *Guardian* 12 September 2001.
31 D'Arch Smith, *D. A. Caton and the Fortune Press*.
32 Sutherland, *Offensive literature*, pp. 148–59.
33 Rupert Smith, 'Swimming against the tide', *Guardian* 29 April 2006.

the shared aim of engaging a wide readership with radical ideas. The Anarchist bookfairs, started modestly in London in 1983 by a small group of anarchist distributors and bookshop workers disaffected by the lack of political discussion at the Socialist bookfairs, have grown steadily. In 2014 the London Anarchist Bookfair attracted well over 3,000 people, and there are now nearly fifty held in Britain and worldwide, some being cultural festivals lasting several days.[34] International Radical Black and Third World bookfairs were organised between 1982 and 1995 in London, with smaller offshoots in Bradford and Manchester. They were instigated and run by New Beacon Books, Bogle-L'Ouverture Books and the Race Today collective, as an extension of the work of the Caribbean Artists Movement, and of the principles of publishing books and providing culture for an audience ignored by the literary establishment. From the outset they deliberately combined cultural and political analysis. It was noticeable how many working-class people attended these bookfairs, and that tiny publishers came from around the world at their own expense.[35]

The First International Feminist Bookfair, held in London in 1984, with a Regional Book Week held simultaneously in twenty-seven towns and cities in Britain and Ireland, was also aware of its community, organising many book-related events. It nevertheless alienated many within the radical book trade by striking a deal with W. H. Smith for their stores to carry promotional material, even where there was a local radical bookshop organising events. Feminist Book Fortnight continued annually round Britain as a commercial promotion until the early 1990s, and subsequent International Feminist bookfairs were held bi-annually in Norway, Canada, Spain, the Netherlands and Australia.

By the mid-1990s, all the radical bookfairs, apart from the ever-expanding Anarchist Bookfair, had died, and the radical book trade generally appeared to be in serious decline. In an attempt at revival, however, the Alliance of Radical Booksellers organised the first London Radical Bookfair in 2013, and in 2014 teamed up with Alternative Press, a group dedicated to showcasing the depth and breadth of the UK small press scene.[36] Thus the Radical Bookfair now brings together not just books and pamphlets, but also self-published comics, zines, art books and prints, whether from photocopier or printing house, to show the full diversity of radical publications today. Not all the Alternative Press publishers would see themselves as overtly political, but

34 www.anarchistbookfair.org.uk.   35 Alleyne, *Radicals against race*, pp. 57–65.
36 www.alternativepress.org.uk.

each would identify as part of a self-publishing movement alternative to the mainstream.

Design and production

Radical publications have been produced in every format, from the ephemeral handbill to the multi-volume reference work, employing every available technology from the duplicator to newsprint to blogs and websites. Because of their financial constraints, radical publishers have become adept at utilising economic technologies such as the risograph, screen printing and small offset litho. An example of transition between technologies was the journal *Anarchy*, edited by Colin Ward from 1961 to 1971. Originally set in metal type and printed letterpress, it was printed by offset litho and pasted up in-house when the new series started in 1971.[37] Before the spread of more accessible technologies in the 1960s, and the concomitant rise of radical and community printshops,[38] radical publishers would mainly have been serviced by commercial printers who were politically sympathetic to the material but earned their main money doing jobbing work. An example from the early twentieth century was Workers' Friend Printing, who, as well as producing their own Yiddish anarchist paper, *Arbeyter Frynd*, published many books and pamphlets in translation and in their original language, as well as flyers in many languages for organisations such as Le Group d'Études Sociales de Londres, the London Section of the Anarchist International, the Russian Atrocities Protest Conference, and the Marylebone Anarchist Communist Group.[39]

By the 1980s, personal computing and desktop publishing meant that more production processes could be handled in-house by small publishers, and though this kept costs down, it could lead to ever more self-exploitation. Most recently, the increasing availability and affordability of digital print technology has enabled small presses and self-publishers generally to produce modest print-runs of books economically. However, this capacity has not yet been properly exploited by the newer radical publishers; where it has been, it is generally among the more academic lists, such as Minor Compositions. Among the few exceptions is *One of My Kind* (*OOMK*), which is described as 'a highly visual, handcrafted small-press publication whose content largely pivots upon the imaginations, creativity and spirituality of women . . . and

---

37 Poyner, *Autonomy*, pp. 279–80.   38 Kenna *et al.*, *Printing is easy . . .?*
39 Slienger, *Radical footnotes*.

is especially keen to be inclusive of Muslim women'. Sample pages are available free online, but full issues only in print.

In today's image-saturated and therefore design-conscious environment, even radicals worry about how to present themselves. Design is often a political as well as an aesthetic issue. The editorial collective of the *Occupied Times*, the newspaper which emerged from Occupy London, and is committed to offering 'a high-quality alternative to corporate media', believes that design is really important for catching people's attention. They distribute 4,000 free paper copies of each issue, as well as making it available digitally. Meanwhile, those zines that have grown out of the punk DIY ethic (such as most feminist zines) emphasise passion and creativity over a production that would be acceptable within mainstream publishing.[40] Concerns with design are not new – the redesign of the *Communist* newspaper in 1921 helped increase circulation fivefold.[41] When the first paperback edition of *Fat is a feminist issue* was published in 1979, Hamlyn promoted it as a diet book with an almost naked woman on the cover, contradicting the book's central message. Susie Orbach, the author, was denied any control over cover design in her contract. With her support, however, Women in Booktrades designed and printed a counter-cover, which bookshops were encouraged to place over the publisher's cover.[42]

The underground press of the 1960s did not have its own printing presses and continually ran into difficulties finding printers,[43] as did the WSPU, for example.[44] See Red's image (fig. 27.1) beautifully sums up the motivation behind the many alternative printshops established from the 1960s to serve radical and community publishers constrained by limited funds and unwilling commercial printers. But the very simplicity of screen printing and small offset litho, which were politically and practically attractive to radical printers and their customers, as they offered access to previously excluded groups, led to conflict between them and Trade Union printshops.[45]

Pamphlets

Pamphlets, magazines, journals, newsletters and newspapers are all vital parts of the radical book trade's synergistic ecosystem, far surpassing books in the number of titles produced. The astonishing surge of commercial

40 Freedman, 'Grrrl Zines in the Library', p. 53.
41 Meynell, *My lives*, p. 127. See also Chapter 9.   42 Cadman *et al.*, *Rolling our own*, p. 25.
43 Baines, 'The freedom of the press', p. 3.
44 Crawford, *The women's suffrage movement*.   45 Marshall, *Changing the word*.

the freedom of the press
belongs to those who
control the press.

WOMEN IN PRINT

Figure 27.1 'The freedom of the press belongs to those who control the press.' This image of two women using printing machines started as a screen-printed page in a See Red Women's Poster Collective's calendar. It was reproduced by Leeds Postcards as one in a fundraising set made for the Campaign for Press and Broadcasting Freedom, which has worked since 1979 for a more accountable and diverse media, and to challenge the myth that press freedom is best served by current forms of ownership and control, and by 'self-regulation', www .cpbf.org.uk. The slogan is an adaptation of A. J. Liebling's famous remark in the New Yorker in 1960: 'Freedom of the press is guaranteed only to those who own one.'

self-publishing, in both print and electronic books, from about 2011, is essentially a different phenomenon from the self-publishing which has always been part of radical politics.

Most radical self-publishing was done by political parties and formal organisations until the 1960s–1970s, since when the growth of radical print-shops has enabled the massive expansion of self-publishing by small auton-omous political groups and individuals. The contents of pamphlets have covered everything from the most analytically political to the most perso-nal, including life experiences and poetry. Pamphlets tend to be no more than eighty pages and without a spine, and until the advent of digital printing one needed to print several hundred to keep their unit price down. Even before the small offset litho machine came into widespread use in the late 1960s and 1970s, pamphlet publishing had been attractive for radical organisations, such as the Campaign for Nuclear Disarmament and the Movement for Colonial Freedom, and for individuals, because issues of content, format and price remained much more under their control, while such publications would have been most unlikely to find even a radical commercial publisher. For example, *Labour Monthly* published more than forty pamphlets between 1921 and 1950, 'many being expanded reprints of particularly striking articles'. These included from the 1920s *Problems of the labour movement* by P. Braun and *The burning questions of international unity* by A. A. Purcell, and from the 1930s, the Marxism Today series. The British Library catalogue gives 352 hits under 'Miscellaneous pamphlets and leaf-lets', the bulk of which are publications of organisations devoted to either politics, religion or advertising.

The Women's Liberation Movement was notable for the number of self-published pamphlets it produced.[46] The Feminist Library collection – the most comprehensive in Britain and now conserved in the Bishopsgate Institute Library in London – holds well over 3,000 titles. It could be said that feminist pamphlets were the foremothers of the feminist zines which arose with the advent of Riot Grrrls from the late 1980s on, while the football and punk fanzines from the late 1970s were their forefathers. As the organised women's movement declined, emphasis tended to be more personal and individual. This is not to say that the output was not feminist or informed by political fury, but zines at this period were less geared towards activism.[47]

46 Cadman *et al.*, *Rolling our own*, chapter 4.   47 Zobl, 'Cultural production'.

Newspapers, journals and magazines

Periodicals are key to all radical groups' capacity to communicate, though their sales and distribution methods often bypass completely the mainstream book trade (for example, the hand-selling of Left party papers outside political meetings and at demos) as they try to reach their audience with material that would not normally be found, or sought, in bookshops. The longevity of radical periodicals has varied from a single issue to many years – little worse than for the mainstream industry, and noteworthy, as almost all radical periodicals are produced by volunteers working in their spare time.

Periodicals of the organised Left

Each part of the Left has produced its own newspapers, journals and magazines, of which the Chartist newspaper the *Poor Man's Guardian* (commenced 1831) was one of the earliest. Prominent periodicals which have followed include the *New Statesmen*, launched by the Fabians in 1913 and published as a weekly magazine under slightly different names ever since; the *Labour Leader*, likewise under a variety of names and formats, published by the Independent Labour Party between 1889 and 1992; *Tribune*, issued by the Left in the Labour Party since 1937; and the *Socialist Worker* newspaper and *International Socialist* journal from the Socialist Workers Party. The New Left launched itself in 1957 with the rather staid *Universities and Left Review*. This morphed into *New Left Review*, which, as a self-published academic journal, is still going strong in 2016. The short-lived underground paper *Black Dwarf* was launched in 1968 from *New Left Review*'s offices (its title came from a satirical Chartist magazine of that name),[48] followed by *Red Mole* and *Red Weekly* (known by its critics as Read Weakly). From its inception, the Communist Party viewed the dissemination of its literature as extremely important.[49] In the Party's early decades, Central Books distributed many periodicals from the socialist countries and home-grown Communist journals, including dozens of different special interest papers, such as *Women Today*, *Architect and Allied Technicians Group Bulletin*, the *Esperanto Group Bulletin* and *Jewish Clarion*, plus papers from other Left groups such as *Young Socialist*, *Irish Democrat* and *Labour Research*.[50]

---

48 Fountain, *Underground*, p. 64.
49 Emile Burns, 'Twenty years of communist propaganda', *International Press Correspondence* 20:31 (3 August 1940), www.marxists.org/archive/burns-emile/1940/08/twenty-years.htm.
50 Cope, *Central Books*, p. 27; Arnot et al., 'Forging the weapon'.

Non-aligned periodicals

Many radical special interest magazines and newspapers have been produced in Britain over the last hundred years, at first coming mainly from the Left parties, the Anarchists and the peace movement. The No Conscription Fellowship produced a weekly newspaper, the *Tribunal*, during the First World War, as well as many leaflets and pamphlets, while the anarchist *War Commentary* was produced during the Second World War. The editors of both were jailed for their efforts. The longest-lasting and perhaps most influential peace movement paper has been *Peace News*, started in 1936 in the run up to the Second World War, as 'the only weekly newspaper serving all who are working for Peace'. It has gone through many manifestations since,[51] including, in the 1960s and 1970s, epitomising the coalescence between the political and the underground newspapers.[52] Alternative community newspapers flourished across Britain between the early 1970s and the mid-1990s. Of the eighty-plus titles, mostly run voluntarily by libertarian socialists, few printed more than 1,000 copies per issue. Yet they provided a vital link between local industrial struggles and feminist and anti-racist activities, and often took up campaigns that the local commercial press would not cover.[53] Since the 1960s, special interest periodicals of all sorts have proliferated, notably in the green/environmental area and those with internationalist concerns. A few have migrated entirely online, but there are countless paper magazines and bulletins remaining, often with a significant web presence, ranging from the four-page *Haiti Support Group Briefing* and *GM Freeze* bulletin, to magazines with glossy covers, like *Resurgence*, *Red Pepper*, *New Internationalist* and *Ethical Consumer*.

Feminist periodicals

Elizabeth Crawford lists fifty-two women's suffrage newspapers and journals, of which the *Voice of Women*, published by the WSPU between 1907 and 1918, was probably the most famous.[54] A few started publication in the mid-nineteenth century, but most were active between the 1890s and 1920s, although *Common Cause*, the newspaper of the constitutional suffragists, continued until 1932 as the *Woman's Leader*.[55] Following the passing of the first Franchise Bill in 1918, suffragist publications such as *Common Cause* broadened their interests, but with feminist activity subdued until the rise

---

51 Housmans Diary Group, 'Peace News'.   52 Fountain, *Underground*, p. 25.
53 Harcup, *A northern star*.   54 Crawford, *The women's suffrage movement*, pp. 456–62.
55 Di Cenzo et al., *Feminist media history*.

of the Women's Liberation Movement, feminist publishing was largely in abeyance. The only notable periodical at this period was *Time and Tide*, founded in 1920 as a left-wing feminist magazine supporting the Six Point Group, which campaigned for women's equal rights before moving to the Right by the 1960s. A few campaigning groups, such as the Abortion Law Reform Association, produced newsletters, and from 1963 to 1972 the Minorities Research Group produced *Arena Three*, the first British monthly for lesbians. By 1981 there was an outpouring of Women's Liberation periodicals, numbering eighty-eight: twenty-three local newsletters designed to be read by women only and sixty-five national newsletters and magazines covering particular areas of concern, of which the most public was *Spare Rib*, which covered the full spectrum of feminist concerns.[56] Begun in 1972, its founders wanted 'to put women's liberation on the newsstands', having worked on such underground papers as *Oz* and *Ink*, and having become disgruntled with the sexism of their male co-workers.[57] Despite a resurgence of the feminist movement from about 2008, there have been few periodicals published, though quite a few zines have appeared, many surviving only a couple of issues. Paper publication may seem to have been replaced by online blogs, yet many women yearn for paper communication. A failed attempt was made to launch a general feminist magazine, *Feminist Times*, in 2013, while in 2015 *Screaming Violets*, a socialist feminist magazine, publishing both on paper and online, was successfully launched.

Black periodicals

The first recorded 'Black' publications in Britain were edited by Celestine Edwards in the 1880s and 1890s: the weekly journal *Lux* and the monthly magazine *Fraternity*, an organ of the Society for the Recognition of the Brotherhood of Man. Following the first Pan-African Congress in London in 1900, the committee published one issue of the journal *Pan-African*, then in 1912 the *Africa Times and Orient Review* appeared and continued irregular publication until the 1920s. In the late 1920s the *International Negro Workers' Review* appeared, and in 1931 turned into a monthly, the *Negro Worker*. In the 1930s the League of Coloured Peoples started publishing the *Keys*, Marcus Garvey edited the *Black Man*, and the International African Service Bureau (IASB) published *International African Opinion*, as well as one-off publications.[58] Black periodicals (like other radical and small press

---

56 Cadman *et al.*, *Rolling our own*, pp. 71–87, 109–13.   57 *Ibid.*, p. 75.
58 Johnson, 'I think of my mother', pp. 74–5.

publications) suffered during the Second World War and had died out altogether until *Caribbean News*, published by the London Branch of the Caribbean Congress, started in November 1952 as the only Black newspaper until its demise in 1956. It was the first publication to raise the problems in the Caribbean – and Britain's role in them – to an audience in Britain.[59]

Black publishing, and community organising generally, took a big step forward in 1955 when Claudia Jones arrived in Britain, having been deported from the USA for her political activities. An experienced journalist and member of the British Communist Party, she was instrumental in setting up the Notting Hill carnival and managed and edited the *West Indian Gazette and Afro-Asian Caribbean News* from 1958 until her death in December 1964. Jones saw the need for a newspaper which could help cultivate a sense of identity among Black people in Britain, and the *West Indian Gazette* was aimed primarily, but not exclusively, at this readership. It achieved its goal by combining high and low culture – mixing international politics, workers' rights and British immigration policy with art reviews, recipes and gossip.[60] Jones laid the foundations for the radical Black publishers which followed: New Beacon Books, Bogle-L'Ouverture and *Race Today* magazine (founded following a split from the group which produced *Race and Class*). A 2010 list of English-language newspapers and periodicals of the African diaspora, mostly produced in the United Kingdom and Ireland, contained over 400 titles, and while many could hardly be described as radical, it is clear that a Black British identity had definitely been established.

Sales and distribution

In all periods, ingenuity has been needed to bring radical publications and ideas to their public: the Reformers Bookstall, a wholesale and retail business based in Glasgow, published around 1910 a series of socialist songs including 'The banner of freedom' by Keir Hardie; the suffragettes toured the country-side with their wares in caravans and on bicycles; and the Clarion vans traversed the country circulating their newspaper while literally providing a platform for radical speakers – the side or back of the van would be let down to provide an impromptu stage for public meetings.

The difficulty of distribution is particularly acute for the periodicals and self-published pamphlets in which the radical book trade specialises. Organising timely distribution is particularly costly, as was illuminated by

59 *Ibid.*, pp. 76–7. 60 *Ibid.*, pp. 90–1; Low, *Publishing the postcolonial*, pp. 170–1.

the rise and fall of the Publications Distribution Cooperative (PDC). Set up in 1976 in a spirit of great optimism to take on the arduous task of distributing radical magazines, journals and pamphlets, it succumbed to liquidators in 1984. The initiative to start PDC came largely from the group launching the *Leveller*, a non-aligned Left news magazine. They recognised the need for an alternative means of distribution for the growing number of radical publications whose content and format were unacceptable to commercial distributors on both political and financial grounds. They hoped to circumvent W. H. Smith's stranglehold on the retail newstrade by establishing a distribution network under radical control which could supply mainstream bookshops and newsagents, as well as radical outlets. Smith's had consistently refused to sell radical literature and in spring 1941, despite protests from retailers, stopped selling *Labour Research*, which had managed to evade Smith's ban during its first twenty years. The magazine survived because thousands of readers helped to get it into shops.[61] In its self-appointed role of defending 'family values', Smith's also refused to handle not only *Gay News* but also *Private Eye*, which did not sit well with its insistence on distributing 'girlie mags', which small newsagents have been forced to handle by the terms of their contract.[62]

PDC's initial concern was with distributing magazines and pamphlets, but to increase profit margins it soon started wholesaling books from small radical publishers, starting with Allison & Busby. PDC was a powerful catalyst for growth in the radical book trade, as radical bookshops, stalls, and groups running occasional events, could easily obtain a range of stock from one source, while publishers knew there would be a reliable market for their output. But its attempt to be all things to all radical publications was always likely to require ongoing external support, the lack of which was probably the main cause of its eventual collapse. This is clear from comparing PDC with Inpress, started in 2002 to provide marketing services for independent publishers (including radicals Smokestack Books, Five Leaves Publications and Peepal Tree Press) which specialise in literary titles. Inpress succeeds in selling its many small print-run titles, using Central Books for its bookshop distribution, but it would be hard for it to continue without support from Arts Council England.

The mid-1970s, when PDC was being set up, was the heyday of the Women's Liberation Movement, and the growing network of radical bookshops was a boon to the spread of feminist ideas. Interestingly, in Britain

---

61 Arnot et al., *Forging the weapon.*   62 Berry et al., *Where is the other news?*

there were only ever two or three specifically feminist bookshops and two gay ones, while most radical shops maintained a substantial section on sexual politics. This differed from the USA, where general radical bookstores were far outnumbered by feminist bookstores, of which there were over a hundred. Black bookshops were often also publishers and distributors of their own material, and derived much of their income from fulfilling mail order, so did not use PDC's services a great deal.

When PDC went bankrupt in 1984, there was much discord in the radical book trade. Many small publications lost money, uncertain for both financial and political reasons if and when to jump ship. Most of the more commercially viable publications were picked up by the other radical distributors – Central Books, Airlift, Third World Publications and Turnaround (the successor organisation to PDC, which began as a workers' cooperative, but in later years transformed itself into a conventional business). Turnaround decided not to accept any periodicals, and was highly selective about which pamphlets it accepted (rumours at the time suggested that such policies were a condition of its being given a start-up grant by the Greater London Enterprise Board).

Some of the more mainstream journals found other homes, notably with Central Books, but distributing radical publications widely, especially periodicals, has remained a significant problem. Central Books, founded in 1939, still survives as a distributor, and demonstrates how a radical business has adapted its practices to political and economic circumstances. Until the mid-1970s, it distributed almost exclusively Communist Party literature and material imported from the Soviet Union. From the late 1970s it started wholesaling general books, at first only to radical shops, but later to general London bookshops. This was a prescient move. Well before the collapse of Communism, Thatcherism was making life increasingly difficult for radical enterprises. Central Books got used to delivering small quantities of literature to many outlets, which helped it develop into a more general Left and small press distributor.[63]

In addition to new distributors AK and Counter Productions (see Chapter 28), dozens of small 'distros' of DIY material have come and gone since the 1990s, including several devoted to zines on sexual politics and Black politics. One founded in 2005 and still going strong is Dead Trees and Dye whose stated aim is to 'sell rad zines and meet like-minded DIY folk'.[64] The rise of feminist zines out of the Riot Grrrl movement, and the recent

63 Cope, *Central Books*, pp. 54–5. 64 www.deadtreesanddye.com.

renaissance of radical feminism, has seen the development of many informal distros, designed to get these most ephemeral (and often free) publications to their intended audience, often in return for sending some stamped addressed envelopes – even in these days of the internet and social media.[65]

Bookshops

There are records of radical bookshops going back to the nineteenth century; for example, a 'freethought' bookshop in Nottingham in 1826, and Freedom Books, the anarchist shop and publisher which still exists in Whitechapel. The Workers' Bookshop, the Communist Party's first retail outlet, opened in 1921, and many more followed from the 1930s, including Housmans Peace Bookshop (which also survives) founded in the 1950s.[66] The 1960s saw the opening of the first alternative bookshops, such as the Paperback Shop in Edinburgh in 1959, and, in London, Indica in 1966 and Compendium in 1968.[67] All were individually owned, unlike many of the alternative bookshops which followed in the 1970s and 1980s, such as First of May in Edinburgh and Sisterwrite (feminist bookshop) in London, which, from their inception, were run by collectives. The Federation of Alternative Booksellers was set up in 1975 for 'non-aligned/collective, non-hierarchical, non-profit shops/projects' with some fifteen members, none of which had existed before 1971. In 1980 it became the Federation of Radical Booksellers. The number of shops increased to around fifty in 1982, with a peak of over a hundred in the late 1980s.[68] After this, numbers started to decline fairly rapidly, reaching a nadir of eight in the early 2000s, but the renaissance of the radical book trade was marked in 2011 with the launch of the Alliance of Radical Booksellers (ARB) with seventeen members, including some distributors and online businesses. In May 2014, the ARB had thirty members, including Hydra Books which opened in Bristol in 2011, and Five Leaves bookshop in Nottingham in 2013. These trends are encouraging when so many independent shops have been forced to close following the demise of the Net Book Agreement and the rise of Amazon.[69]

Bookshops run by both political parties and autonomous groups have functioned as a resource for their local radical community, providing easy access not only to radical publications but to the means of political

---

65 Chidgey, 'Free, trade'.   66 Bradshaw, 'A huge comrade called Boris'.
67 Haynes, *Thanks for coming!*; Fountain, *Underground*. See also Chapter 28 in this volume.
68 Andrew Bibby and John Goodman. Unpublished presentation to Co-operative History Conference, New Lanark, 2008.
69 www.radicalbooksellers.co.uk.

networking, through facilities such as post boxes, notice boards, and meeting space for comradely groups and organisations. But being among the most visible parts of the radical community has also caused bookshops many difficulties, as their enemies have recognised their importance for encouraging genuine community cohesion. In London, the International Suffrage Shop in Covent Garden suffered a number of attacks in the 1910s, as did other radical shops through the century. In 1977 Bookshop Joint Action was founded to respond to a significant increase in racist attacks on Black and radical shops round the country – Walter Rodney Bookshop in Ealing alone experienced eleven attacks between 1977 and 1983,[70] while Housmans Peace Bookshop has experienced a number of Special Branch raids and a letter bomb attack, as well as facing, together with Bookmarks (the Socialist Workers bookshop), expensive libel actions for stocking anti-fascist magazines.[71] In 1984, Customs and Excise officers raided London's Gay's the Word bookshop and its shop directors' homes, seizing all their imported books and retaining thousands of others at their ports of entry. Customs and Excise decreed any book imported by the shop to be obscene, including works by Tennessee Williams, Kate Millett and Jean-Paul Sartre. The raids were a massive assault on the shop – a third of its stock was removed, and a further £12,000-worth seized in transit. Subsequently, seizure notices were issued on more titles, including standard academic texts, and the shop's eight volunteer directors and one member of staff were charged with 'conspiracy to import indecent or obscene material'.[72] Such attacks were not just on individual businesses, but on civil liberties generally. As the firebomb attack on Freedom Bookshop in 2013 showed, the need for support against fascist, racist and homophobic attacks still continues. Gay's the Word and Freedom Bookshop survived these assaults and continue to thrive. But the effect of online book-buying, and rising rents and business rates, especially in London, all pose an ongoing threat to radical and independent bookshops.

Some projects founded in the idealistic 1970s were more ambitious in their conception than being solely bookshops. The Union Place Resource Centre in South London, for example, not only ran a bookshop as part of its building, but housed a print shop, a food co-op, and communal living space. Centerprise in Hackney was another pioneer – in 1971 it started a community centre based on a general bookshop, with a coffee bar and

---

70 Ireland, 'Laying the foundations', p. 32.
71 Housmans Diary Group, '50 years at Caledonian Road'.
72 Colin Clews, '1984. The trials of Gay's the Word', www.gayinthe80s.com/2012/10/19
    84-the-trials-of-gays-the-word.

two meeting rooms. The *Bookseller* said it would close within six months, even though it was the only bookshop in the borough.[73] It actually thrived and moved to larger premises which also housed other organisations, such as Hackney Under Fives (which campaigned for nursery provision), as well as its own welfare rights and advice project and Hackney Writers' Workshop. After many attempts to kill it off, Centerprise's landlords, Hackney Council, finally succeeded in 2013, symptomatic of the way that spiralling rents and the marketisation of local authorities has led to the disappearance of the vast majority of radical spaces, especially in London.[74] A proud fighter against these trends has been the 56A Infoshop at the Elephant and Castle. Founded in 1991, it houses a food co-op, a bicycle workshop, a small printing press, a bookstall and book exchange, a meeting space and a large archive of radical material. It traces its antecedents not just to the radical projects of the 1970s and 1980s, but to the Walworth Working Men's Lecture and Reading Rooms, active in the nineteenth and early twentieth centuries.[75]

Centerprise's decision in 1973 to make local publishing an integral part of its work had a significant impact on the whole radical book trade. From its first publications it collaborated with other community writing projects and this led to the 1976 formation of the Federation of Worker Writers and Community Publishers (FWWCP),[76] whose influence on the development of working-class writers and literature cannot be over-estimated. Between them, FWWCP groups published thousands of titles written by people who were generally spurned by the mainstream industry (though an FWWCP group in Liverpool produced Jimmy McGovern, who has gone on to become a prolific and well-respected screenwriter). Between March 1976 and February 1977, Centerprise sold 6,922 copies of its local history titles in Hackney alone, partly by selling them through twenty local newsagents.[77] These and similar achievements demonstrate how the radical book trade serves as the soil in which to cultivate the ideas which are essential for radical communities to thrive. Particularly in bookshops, there is a cross-fertilisation of ideas when the publications and the people who write and read them come together in fruitful conversation. Indeed, one of the earliest radical bookshops, founded in Manchester in 1971, was called Grassroots.

---

73 [Worpole], *Local publishing and local culture.*
74 For a celebration and archive of the history of Centerprise, see http://justanotherbookshop.wordpress.com.
75 'Local tradition, local trajectories and us: 56a Infoshop, Black Frog and more in South London', https://socialcentrestories.wordpress.com/2008/04/24.
76 Known today as TheFED. See www.thefed.btck.co.uk.
77 [Worpole], *Local publishing and local culture.*

Libraries

Radical libraries and archives are usually started by people who want to enable radical and minority groups to retain a sense of their history and identity by making accessible material not typically considered worth preserving through mainstream libraries.[78] As the Director of the Black Cultural Archives said at its opening: 'When you know we've always been here, it gives you a different sense of belonging.'[79] Such collections come into being in a number of ways: the Working Class Movement Library was assembled by Ruth and Eddie Frow over their life together, and it gradually took over their house. It is now housed in a dedicated building in Salford.[80] The George Padmore Institute is a collection of documents recording the history of Black activism, mainly arising out of political organisations connected with New Beacon Books. Housed in rooms above the shop, it has grown organically into a major educational resource.[81] Although all the radical archives and libraries have developed from the political passion of a group or individual, frequently they have ended up as special collections in an institutional library. This generally works well in terms of access and conservation, as with Feminist Archives North in Leeds University Library, the Commonweal Library in Bradford University Library, and Bogle-L'Ouverture's archives, which were donated to the London Metropolitan Archive. There is some inevitable loss of autonomy, which may limit their use for political education and events, but when the Women's Library in London, which had previously been in its own purpose-built library, was absorbed into the London School of Economics' main library in 2013, there was a grievous loss of dedicated expertise, community engagement, and easy access to material for those outside academia. Wherever the libraries and archives are housed, they have similar problems of trying to sustain themselves, so in an attempt to support each other and share knowledge about issues of common concern, two networks have been set up: NORLA (Network of Radical Libraries and Archives) and FLA (Feminist and Women's Libraries and Archives Network).

---

78 Freedman, 'Grrrl zines in the library', p. 52; Andrew Flinn, 'Archival activism: independent and community-led archives, radical public history and the heritage professions', *InterActions: UCLA Journal of Education and Information Studies* 7:2 (2011), http://escholar ship.org/uc/item/9pt2490x.
79 Paul Reid, 'At last, a home for black history', *Guardian* 23 July 2014.
80 www.wcml.org.uk.   81 Alleyne, *Radicals against race*, pp. 100–5.

Conclusion

The strength of the radical book trade lies in its being able to control its own means of communication. Its relative quiescence over the last twenty-five to thirty years can be partly accounted for by the absence of an infrastructure of supporting organisations. It is not just the closure of radical bookshops and community print shops, but the absence of organisations like those that flourished in the 1970s and 1980s, such as the Radical Publications Group, Librarians for Social Change, Women in Libraries, and most radical and alternative bookfairs.

The rise of the internet in the 1990s and, even more so, of social media in the 2000s, has proved a mixed blessing for radicals, and the long-term effects are far from clear. Even studies which are highly positive about the influence of social media on the grassroots movements of 2011 nevertheless acknowledge that such activism is only possible when real human relations also exist.[82] More recent publications have expressed even more ambivalence about the benefits of the internet.[83] Some radical publications have followed the trend to publish online only; others have remained with or returned to print production, as they have realised the benefits of maintaining a human relationship with readers who do not find it congenial to read large quantities of text on screen and wish to hold a finished artefact. Many radical periodicals with a print edition, for example *Red Pepper*, supplement this with an active blog which can be updated regularly, whilst others, such as *Ethical Consumer*, provide more in-depth material online than would be feasible to fit on paper. Many radical book publishers now also offer e-books, some free and some paid for, as the controversy about the pricing of e-books is no more settled here than in other parts of the book trade.

Publishers are now beginning to recognise that discoverability on the internet is very poor. Although radical publications have a clearly defined niche market, radical publishers lack substantial marketing budgets to attract potential readers who do not know where to look, or even what they are looking for. Although print publications come and go, there is an instability to digital media which can make even fairly recent material irretrievable. For example, a study undertaken just a year after the Egyptian Revolution found that 10 per cent of the social media documentation had already vanished.[84]

---

82 Gerbaudo, *Tweets and the streets*.   83 Hill, *Not so fast*; McChesney, *Digital disconnect*.
84 Hany SalahEldeen Khalil, 'Losing my revolution: a year after the Egyptian Revolution, 10% of the social media documentation is gone', *Web Science and Digital Libraries Research Group Blog*, ws-dl.blogspot.co.uk.

Meanwhile, the closure of reliable online information sources, such as Indymedia London in 2012, can lead to fragmentation and isolation among the radical community who have no other easy access to such information.

Recent studies have confirmed that print media – from fliers to periodicals and books – are still an essential component of radical communication in the digital era,[85] while the notion that feminist zinesters have migrated entirely to the internet and become bloggers is far from the whole story. The production of paper zines is still strong, as most producers are still attracted by the material satisfaction of literally cutting and pasting their zines. And the DIY ethos flourishes, even though many are published as PDFs for free download, with the authors printing relatively few paper copies for their own circulation. Throughout the radical book trade, groups will no doubt continue to confront the difficulties of reconciling economic survival and political ambition. Dealing with these problems is perhaps exacerbated in the digital age, and, as with the rest of the book trade, a big element of these issues is the dominance of Amazon. Calls to boycott Amazon have been led by the radical book trade and are growing, not just because of their tax-dodging and poor treatment of their staff, serious though they are, but because their influence on the whole book trade is the total antithesis of radicalism.[86] Amazon seeks to remove control of the press from as many people as possible in its own individual interest. Many beyond the radical book trade are finally coming to realise this as well.

85 Barassi, 'When materiality counts'; Pimlott, '"Eternal ephemera"'.
86 'Buying books without Amazon', *Ethical Consumer*, special supplement (May/June 2013).

28

Counter-culture and underground

CHRIS ATTON

The history of counter-cultural and underground publishing in Britain is less a history of the book and more a history of periodicals and pamphlets. Nonetheless, as shown in Chapter 27 in this volume, independent and radical publishers, distributors and retailers have played a significant part in the shaping of a variety of organisations and movements for social, cultural and political change since 1900.

The British counter-culture tends to be located within a period spanning the 1960s and the early 1970s, and beginning as early as 1961.[1] This period will be the major focus of the chapter. However, the roots of counter-cultural publishing may be found much earlier in the century, amongst political dissenting movements such as the suffragists, anarchists and peace activists, who all published and distributed their own newspapers and pamphlets. Despite the differing sociopolitical and cultural contexts of these publications, they can offer valuable insights into a type of publishing that, for all its differing political and social locations throughout the period, can broadly be considered as focussing on social change. For example, these early practices offer early models for working with communities on an 'anti-mass' level by privileging local groups that are connected informally through international networks of solidarity and resource sharing. The chapter will therefore take account of the significance of such practices to manifestations of counter-cultural publishing in the latter part of the century. It will also explore developments beyond the 1960s, examining the changing nature of counter-cultural publishing into the twenty-first century.

Anarchism: an ideological model
for counter-cultural publishing

It can be argued that anarchism offers a paradigm of counter-cultural publishing. Not in its populist equation with chaos, but as social relationships based

1 Green, *Days in the life.*

on voluntary cooperation. Notions of individual freedom, unfettered by commercial or governmental interference; enterprises run on collective lines; the importance of diversity of opinion in publications: these are all anarchist ideals. In his history of British anarchism, Quail describes Benjamin Tucker's paper *Liberty* (founded in 1881) as 'the first systematic propaganda defining itself as Anarchist that had any effect within the Socialist movement'.[2] It was *Liberty* that in part prompted the editors of the British anarchist fortnightly *Freedom* to begin publishing in 1886 and by so doing to remain one of the longest-running anarchist periodicals in the world, still publishing today. Both *Freedom* and its precursor the *Anarchist* (which pre-dated *Freedom* by one year) offer historians of counter-cultural publishing an important perspective on early anarchist media. The *Anarchist* counted among its early contributors and supporters intellectuals from the Fabian Society. The intellectual base of the paper was strong: George Bernard Shaw was one of its contributors, as was Peter Kropotkin. Kropotkin was also a significant contributor to *Freedom*. *Freedom* was established not as a newspaper for the anarchist movement, but as the organ of the London-based Freedom Group. As such, its membership was limited and closed: there was no attempt to build a popular movement. Instead, the paper used the prestige of Kropotkin to distribute the paper through more established groups such as the Socialist League.

As has been shown, similar models were at work in the suffragist and early feminist presses of the first decades of the twentieth century. The suffragist movement is best known as highly organised, and focussed on the single aim of votes for women through publications such as the *Englishwoman* (founded in 1909) and the *Vote* (also founded in 1909), the periodical of the Women's Freedom League. However, as has been shown, it was often more independent publications that were able to address broader feminist and other constituencies.[3] The interests of the *Freewoman* (founded in 1911), for instance, included the psychology of sex, male homosexuality and the promotion of free love. Perhaps less controversially, and following the passing of the first Franchise Bill in 1918, suffragist publications such as *Common Cause* (under the new title of the *Women's Leader*) and the *Vote* broadened their interests to include issues of child welfare and violence towards women. Suffragist publishing might be thought of as paving the way for the focus on sexual liberation in much of the underground press of the 1960s and for the further

---

2 Quail, *The slow burning fuse*, p. 19.   3 DiCenzo et al., *Feminist media history*.

political and cultural demands in the feminist presses of the 1970s (see Chapter 27).

Underground press

The 'underground press' typically refers to those newspapers and magazines produced by the counter-culture that emerged in the mid-1960s and continued until the early 1970s. The counter-culture was concerned with establishing an alternative society in direct opposition to mainstream society, and the underground press became a vehicle for the elaboration of this ideal, along with social factors such as women's rights, ecology and racial equality. The underground press became politicised primarily by the US involvement in the Vietnam War; it sought to build a society where 'culture and society were regarded as one',[4] to propose norms and values that broke with 'straight' society absolutely. Interventions by the state were of particular concern, especially in areas of sexual freedom, drugs and press censorship.

Whilst we have seen how anarchism and suffragism might be seen as ideological precursors of the underground press, the most proximate influences were three American titles that began the underground press of the 1960s (the *Los Angeles Free Press*, the *Berkeley Barb* and the *East Village Other*). The first underground paper in the UK was *International Times* (founded in 1966 and known as *IT* after the threat of legal action by the London *Times*), followed by *Oz* (1967–73) and *Friends* (subsequently *Frendz*) in 1969 (until 1972). The counter-culture's most significant publications were based in London, predominantly a periodical press that presented discussions of politics, art, music and sexuality, often through experimental approaches to design and layout.

At this time there was relatively little book publishing activity in this field – what existed was sporadic and there is little documentation through which to examine it in any detail. The bookshop, however, plays an important role in the counter-culture, as an organising centre both for the counter-culture and for the distribution of the underground press. The Indica bookshop, founded in London in 1966, provides a vivid example of this double role, as well as highlighting the relationship between commerce, wealth and the avowedly anti-materialist hippie culture. Indica was set up by Barry Miles, but funded by a loan from Peter Asher, the brother of the actress Jane Asher. Paul

4 Nelson, *The British counter-culture*, p. 49.

McCartney of the Beatles was Jane Asher's boyfriend at the time, through which connection he became involved in the bookshop, assisting with the furnishing of the shop and even designing its first wrapping paper. Similarly, the radical socialist paper *Black Dwarf* (founded in 1968 and first edited by Tariq Ali) was funded by actor and literary agent Clive Goodwin; even the feminist magazine *Spare Rib* (1972–93) enjoyed the patronage of businessmen.

Indica (and its predecessor, Better Books) played host to lectures, readings, performances and political meetings. Distribution was effected through similar sympathetic outlets, as well as through 'head' shops, street sales and concert venues. The underground press had little or no presence in high street shops; its appearance and content made it almost impossible to find commercial distribution. Though limited largely to independent retailers and university campuses, circulation for the more established titles was healthy. There are no independent audits of circulation, but claims from the papers themselves suggest significant peaks: it has been estimated that *IT* and *Oz* each had a circulation in the region of 40,000 in 1971.[5]

It was also at this time that the British peace movement flourished, though its flagship publication *Peace News* was founded in 1936. The founding of the Campaign for Nuclear Disarmament and the Aldermaston March (both in 1958) gave new impetus to the paper. The amateur activism that was at the heart of the peace movement has resonances in the counter-culture of the 1960s, though again we should remember the role of the intelligentsia, public figures such as Bertrand Russell, J. B. Priestley and John Berger. Expertise was shared between the peace movement and the underground press: Tom McGrath, for instance, edited *Peace News* before moving on to edit *IT*. Again, a London bookshop (Housmans Peace Bookshop, opened in 1945 and still in business) formed a focus for distribution, publicity and activism associated with the paper and the wider peace movement.

The limits and longevity of the underground press

The underground press was typified by its metropolitan locations. Its primary method of finance was through voluntary, 'self-exploited' labour (though, as we have seen, this is not to discount occasional instances of patronage). Its writers came from the counter-culture itself; they were resolutely anti-professional, autodidacts of journalism. Production and skills such as type-setting and layout were often learned through experimentation, accounting

5 Green, *Days in the life*, p. 366.

in part for the visual innovations found in many titles (particularly in the colour pages of *Oz*). Perhaps the most significant innovation in the underground press was the use of offset litho printing. A paper could be laid out and pasted up by amateurs; typesetting could be done on a typewriter. It would be many years before the mass newspaper industry moved from hot metal to offset; for the underground press this new method gave it the freedom to experiment creatively and to be independent from at least one part of the printing industry.

The independence and innovation of the underground press also manifested itself in experiments with internal organisation. Richard Neville, founding editor of *Oz*, emphasised the individualism of its contributors: 'each reporter is, in a sense, his own editorialist'.[6] The absence of editorial direction led to democratic participation in the organisation of the underground press: many established workers' cooperatives; some experimented with collective organisation and with anarchist decision-making. Organisational experimentation did not necessarily result in equality of opportunity. Fountain notes that many papers divided their work according to gender divisions dominant in 'straight' society, with women given subservient roles as secretaries, typists and tea-makers.[7]

Most counter-cultural and underground publishing ventures were relatively short-lived, due to a combination of economic hardship, problems of distribution and the limited resources of largely unpaid labour. However, small print-runs and low circulation did not inevitably result in marginality or obscurity. Despite their narrow reach, counter-cultural publications have also been at the centre of moral controversy, as during the obscenity trials of the *Little red schoolbook* (1971) and *Gay News* (1976).[8] Controversy continues beyond this period: in the 1990s, anarchist and animal liberation publishers were successfully prosecuted for publishing and distributing seditious material.

The legacy of the underground press

As the counter-culture waned in the early 1970s, it left some lasting legacies. Seeking to attract what had become a lucrative counter-cultural audience, the British commercial music press hired writers from *IT* and *OZ*. Mainstream music papers such as *New Musical Express* and *Sounds*, now populated by

6 Quoted in Nelson, *The British counter-culture*, p. 47. 7 Fountain, *Underground*.
8 Sutherland, *Offensive literature*.

writers from the underground press, became places for experimentation in music journalism, where professional rock journalism was established. *Time Out*, founded in 1968 during the heyday of the underground press, took advantage of its metropolitan focus to provide cultural information and, in so doing, became the first British listings magazine.

The limits of metropolitanism were challenged by a resurgence of a localised radical politics that saw radical community newspapers emerging across the UK during the 1970s, in competition with the local commercial press.[9] Titles such as *Aberdeen People's Press*, *Brighton Voice* and *Liverpool Free Press* brought investigative journalism and the involvement of readers (largely drawn from the working class) to the fore. From such roots, a few national left-wing papers briefly flourished; chief among these was the *Leveller*. Experiments with collective organisation, consensus decision-making and the rotation of duties and responsibilities applied the social experiments of the underground press to local news reporting. Ultimately, though, these publications were short-lived, a combination of problems with finance and distribution, which have been abiding problems for all radical forms of publishing – Fountain has called them 'those two great rocks of the underground'.[10]

Whilst local communities may not have been sufficient to sustain radical publishing, broader communities of interest (feminism, anarchism, Marxism, environmentalism and the peace movement) were enough to enable a modest network of radical bookshops throughout Britain. As in the heyday of the counter-culture, these were often venues for political organising, art exhibitions and musical performances; such was the health of the network that a small-scale rival to the trade magazine the *Bookseller* appeared in 1980, titled the *Radical Bookseller* (a pilot issue had been printed in 1979). By 1992, in what appears to be its first and last directory, the organisation listed over 100 bookshops and mail order services.

Publishing, protest and postmodernism

The last quarter of the twentieth century saw a significant increase in anarchist publishing. In the UK, according to the 1996 edition of the *Anarchist Year Book*, there were over twenty newspapers and journals currently being published, and more than a dozen explicitly anarchist publishers. The reasons for this upsurge of publications lay primarily in the development

---

9 Dickinson, *Imprinting the sticks*.   10 Fountain, *Underground*, p. 198.

of grassroots political activism in the 1960s that took place outside the established political parties. Methods of organising media production were further enhanced during the 1970s by what has come to be known as the 'DIY culture' of political organisation that had developed from the Punk movement of the 1970s.[11] DIY culture emphasises small-scale, anti-party and anti-hierarchical methods of production that rely less on the established political ideologies of anarchism found in the anarchist press of the early twentieth century and more on independent, anti-elitist understandings of anarchism in contemporary society. These media developed out of what has become known as the New Protest, a plethora of diverse groups and movements in the 1990s that espoused direct action to further their causes.

The 1980s and 1990s saw an emphasis on printed zines and pamphlets by individual authors (often anonymous or pseudonymous). These occasional and one-off publications used anarchism as the basis for critiques of contemporary society and employed irony, humour and satire to argue for social change. They tended to use techniques familiar from the Situationist literature of the 1960s, critiquing commodity culture through cartoons and self-consciously overblown rhetoric. The anti-authoritarian philosophy of anarchism was melded with a postmodern fascination with the contingent and the playful to produce texts from fictitious groups such as the Fare Dodgers' Liberation Front and the Institute of Social Disengineering. Publications like these were not interested in using media in the longstanding tradition of establishing anarchism as a serious alternative to dominant currents of political thought, nor did they seek to promote and establish communication within the more recent activism of autonomous and collective protest groups. Instead, as suggested in the names of publishers such as Play Time For Ever Press, these were the media of a symbolic protest that 'disrupts and subverts everyday life and challenges taken-for-granted issues'.[12]

More broadly, the 1990s saw a resurgence of book publishing and radical distribution networks that might be generally considered counter-cultural. Anarchist publishers are very visible at this period, with a major distributor (AK) emerging. Counter Productions was founded as a distributor of less easily classifiable publishers, including Aporia (reprinting tracts and pamphlets from the English Revolution) and Atlas Press (a publisher of Dada, surrealist and other twentieth-century literary experiments). The 1990s also saw the flourishing of the National Small Press Centre, which acted as a clearing-house, repository and educational resource for small presses.

11 McKay, *DIY culture*. 12 Goaman and Dodson, 'A subversive current?', p. 90.

In the present day, radical print publishing and distribution have almost disappeared, along with the bookshops that so often sustained them. In an echo of the *Radical Bookseller*, however, 2011 saw the launch of the Alliance of Radical Booksellers. The Alliance began with only seventeen members, an indication of the increased marginality of the radical bookshop in Britain. As noted in Chapter 27, by 2014 membership totalled thirty. This modest resurgence, coming as it did in an environment dominated by online book-selling (primarily through Amazon), demonstrates that the ideological dimension of the radical bookshop has not entirely disappeared. Nevertheless, problems of publicity, visibility and competition remain – just as they remain for those counter-cultural publishers who have attempted online publishing as a cheaper and more effective method of dissemination. In an increasingly commercialised online culture, the voices of the under-ground still seem to find it difficult to make themselves heard beyond an already-committed readership.

29

Books and other media

ALEXIS WEEDON

It is difficult to overstate the impact of the rise of media industries on the book in the twentieth century. The book lost its status as the primary medium for the communication of stories, ideas and knowledge as film, radio, television, the personal computer, the mobile phone and the game console all created new forms of entertainment and provided faster ways of accessing information. Over the century electronic forms of communication became so ubiquitous within society that in the 1990s some commentators believed they were seeing the death of the book.[1] This chapter explores the significant effects of the revolutionary technological change in media and communications which characterise the twentieth and twenty-first centuries. It explores the dependence of the new industries of film, radio and television on books and magazine stories as source material, and on book publishing for the core values of education, information and entertainment. It examines the most radical change in the institutional structure of the book trade since the decline of the Stationers' Company: how family-owned limited publishing companies became absorbed into transnational media organisations. It also explores the social factors behind this change, asking to what extent the publishing and media industries benefited from the changing patterns of work, leisure and education in the twentieth century. The chapter also shows how technological development of the internet and the challenge of time-based and audio-visual media made the industry look again at the strengths and limitations of the codex at the end of the twentieth and beginning of the twenty-first centuries.

Electricity began to be installed more widely in homes from the end of the First World War, meaning not only a strong and reliable source of light, but also an opening of the way for domestic appliances from the fridge to the telephone, television and the personal computer.[2] By the end of the

1 Negroponte, *Being digital*; Gomez, *Print is dead.*
2 De Grazia and Furlough, *The sex of things.*

nineteenth century photomechanical inventions, from photolithography to the projection of powerful electric light through translucent film to create the illusion of moving images had given rise to a more visual culture, a trend which would intensify through the century.[3] In parallel, telecommunications supplanted older, slower modes of communication. Wired telecoms such as the telegraph which had been the first with the news since 1844 were challenged by the gradual adoption of the telephone in businesses and in homes.[4] But it was wireless telecommunications, beginning with Marconi's first transatlantic radio broadcast in 1901, which really heralded a change. In 1922 radio became the first media to broadcast news and information to the British population, and 79 per cent of households had a radio licence by 1937. After a further seventy years of innovation in media technology 97 per cent of households had a colour television licence, 22 per cent had a satellite dish, 34 per cent had a personal computer, 67 per cent had a compact disc player, 89 per cent had a video recorder and 95 per cent had a telephone.[5] Such electronic media challenged the book by providing alternative systems for validating and communicating new knowledge and formulating national culture.

Historians have observed that when a new media technology is introduced, the existing dominant mass media is not driven out entirely; rather it adapts to the new ecology by finding a specific market which it continues to serve.[6] For example, radio was the dominant medium of news in the Second World War, and 70 per cent of families gathered round the wireless to listen to three of the Prime Minister Winston Churchill's broadcasts in 1941–42. The wireless radio set's central position in the domestic household, however, was overtaken by television. By 1954, 3.2 million television licences had been sold, and approximately 20 per cent of households had a set.[7] This grew substantially after 1955 as the BBC vied with commercial television to provide entertainment for the masses, and led in part to a decrease in cinema-going.[8] Radio continued to co-exist with television in a gradual decline. Seeking new listeners amongst a youth audience, pirate radio stations led a revolution in radio programming and content which again increased its popularity and found radio its niche.[9]

3 Rampley, *Exploring visual culture.*   4 Parry, *The ascent of media.*
5 Gershuny and Fisher, 'Leisure in the UK', p. 25. See also Gershuny, *Changing times.*
6 Tabbi and Wutz, *Reading matters*, pp. 1–25.   7 Tunstall, *The media in Britain*, p. 33.
8 Holmes argues that there was a wider growth in leisure activities which also contributed to the decline in cinema audiences. See *British television and film culture, passim.*
9 Street, *The A to Z of British radio.*

Similarly, broadcast media usurped newspapers' primary position as disseminator of the news. Newspaper circulation fell in the quarter of a century after the arrival of commercial television in 1955, from a total daily sale of 30 million to 23 million.[10] In stating that 'not even the most powerful Press lord can keep his readers in ignorance', the Royal Commission on the Press in 1938 emphasised the virtues of the plurality of news sources and coverage for the reader which radio and television news brought.[11] With the growth in the acquisition of sets after the war, TV news bulletins in particular caused a decline of mid-range popular dailies and a parallel development in the indepth coverage of news in the broadsheets. Newspaper companies sought to find new markets, with bigger Sunday papers offering a commentary on the week's news, and Saturday papers with supplements, competing for the weekend trade. Competition between papers increased and ownership changed as many newspaper companies invested in commercial television. However the post-war boom in the consumer magazine market was worst hit by the competition for advertising revenue: in 1954 the sector attracted 32 per cent of advertising, but by 1960 this had fallen to 20 per cent, and by 1982 it was 15 per cent.[12] To capture specialist advertising, the magazine trade launched titles for niche markets in television lifestyle genres and hobbyist fields, and the big firms diversified into events, conferences and travel, and by the end of the century made successful moves into online publication.

Yet it was to the book industry that the film, radio, television and later media industries turned for stories, scripts, ideas, formats and all forms of creative content. By 2006 British publishers sold 787 million books, many of them for the export market.[13] The greatest increase in titles per population was between 1975 and 2013 when the British population rose from 55 million to 63 million and the number of titles from 35,526 to 184,000.[14] However, it is likely that there was a decrease in the length of the print-runs.[15] This increase in diversity, if not equalled by a parallel increase in volume, provided content for other industries. The book trade was helped by a change in the law in 1911 which extended the duration of copyright from seven to fifty years after the author's death. Publisher-owned copyrights became valuable assets. One early example is that of Chatto & Windus, who had bought the copyright

10 Tunstall, *The media in Britain*, p. 69 and fig. 3 p. 70.

11 *Report on the British press* (1938), p. 207.   12 Tunstall, *The media in Britain*, p. 84.

13 Clark and Phillips, *Inside book publishing*, fourth edition.

14 Miha Kovač, 'On fallen prophets and real problems: the death of the book and the growth of book industries', unpublished paper delivered to the By the Book2 Conference, Florence, Italy, 18–19 June 2015.

15 Thompson, *Merchants of culture*.

of eleven of Maria Louise Ramé (Ouida)'s novels from Chapman & Hall in 1889 for £3,219 and received in 1924 $8,000 (about £1,800) from Inspiration Pictures Corp., for seven-year options on just two of her novels. Her popular tale of heroism and divided loyalties *Under two flags* (1867) was made into five separate film versions between 1912 and 1936, culminating in Frank Lloyd's spectacular film in 1936.[16]

The visual culture which arose in the nineteenth century became the inspiration for the new industries. Graphic magazines with their lithographs and etchings were the first visualisations of characters and storyline, and sometimes formed the source material for the mise-en-scène of the silent movies. British filmmaker Oswald Stoll made this link explicit in his 'Strand Magazine series' of films (1921–23). Other film studios also sought to raise the quality of their films by associating them with the high status of authorship. In 1919 Samuel Goldwyn organised an Eminent Authors division within his company, specifically to attract American authors to adapt their own work; in return they would be given top billing in the resulting film. For a few, like Anzia Yezierska, Elinor Glyn and Mary Roberts Rinehart, it would become, at least for a time, more profitable than publishing.[17] However, the communal writing factories of the Hollywood studios were antithetical to many literary authors who were used to having control over their plots and characters, and the idea nearly bankrupted the studio. Even so, the potential reward was great, and the idea was adopted and adapted by others. Famous Players Lasky invited British authors such as Somerset Maugham, Hugh Walpole and Elinor Glyn to their Hollywood studios to write for the company, and in Britain Oswald Stoll ran his Eminent British Authors series from 1920 with adaptations from the works of H. G. Wells, Edgar Wallace, E. M. Dell and others. It was the beginning of the book–media tie-in and led to the creation of a new genre, the novelisation, or retelling of stories first told in other media.[18]

Radio and the later development of television took old genres and transformed them. The lecture and the public debate, formerly limited in audience numbers by location, could be broadcast to an increasing proportion of the population. With the inception of the Christmas transmission of the British Broadcasting Company in 1922, radio also demonstrated its potential as a creative medium by airing a new play. In 1926 the Company was given a royal charter and became the British Broadcasting Corporation,

16 Barnett and Weedon, *Elinor Glyn as novelist.*   17 *Ibid.*
18 Weedon, 'Textual production and dissemination'. Murray, *The adaptation industry.*

independent of government and overseen by a Board of Governors. John Reith, the first Director General, established a set of principles by which the BBC was to be run. Reith's famous formulation was that the BBC should 'inform, educate and entertain', and in its early days radio sought out spokes-people on art, culture, books.[19] Hugh Walpole, famously broadcasting in the interval of the opera, was an early commentator on the arts and literature in the 1920s. Authors appeared in front of the microphone, and actors and music hall stars performed plays, both adapted for or commissioned especially for the radio. This was a new form of mediated performance, travelling over distance, and later, through recording technology, over time. Radio broad-casters could, as the *Radio Times* supplement proudly announced on 11 January 1937, take the performance to the listener.

These developments opened up larger audiences for authors and added to their potential revenue streams, so many writers, poets, artists and perfor-mers were drawn towards the BBC. The broadcaster had a monopoly of the airwaves which made individual negotiation difficult, so the Society of Authors and the Publishers Association sought to negotiate terms for their members, including a scale for reading from authors' published works, and a standard contract for performance.[20] They viewed this as minimum remu-neration, and the BBC as a standard. Literary agents, following in their wake to protect individual authors' interests, took exception to the all-encompassing clauses some contracts contained, and became increasingly adept at reserving subsidiary rights so that they could re-license the property as new recording technologies were developed.

As subsidiary rights proliferated through the growth of new media for-mats, authors set up companies to control and exploit their intellectual properties. Thomas Hall Caine and his son set up a book publishing com-pany; similarly, Elinor Glyn Ltd was established to manage her literary property.[21] These initiatives led to independent companies whose purpose in business was to acquire and manage literary estates. For example, by 2011 Chorion managed the estates of Agatha Christie, Georges Simenon, Margery Allingham and Raymond Chandler amongst others, while other estates such

---

19 It continues to do so, quoting the first Royal Charter. See *The Review of the BBC's Royal Charter: 1st Report of Session 2005–06*. Great Britain: Parliament: House of Lords: Select Committee on the BBC Charter Review, paragraph 157.

20 Weedon, '"Behind the screen"'.

21 Greycaine Book Manufacturing Company, Watford: http://sfcwebserve.com/History Web/Docs/GREYCAINE_BOOK_MANUFACTURING_COMPANY.pdf. See also Weedon, 'Elinor Glyn's system of writing'.

as those of T. S. Eliot, Virginia Woolf and Freeman Wills Crofts used the services of the Society of Authors.

While many authors and public intellectuals engaged with the new opportunities, the BBC sought to avoid direct competition with the book trade, as Briggs argues: 'The BBC's general policy was never to issue any book which could be produced by an outside publisher.'[22] However, as the national broadcaster the BBC took a lead in the communication of culture and ideas and by doing so established new formats and new modes of writing. For example, with each of its landmark series, the BBC worked with publishers on a synonymous book rather than publishing it themselves. Perhaps the most best-known of these was art historian and public intellectual Kenneth Clark, with his series *Civilisation: a personal view* (1969). Clark authored the accompanying book, which was published by the BBC and John Murray. It set a trend both as a TV series and in publishing. The response to Clark's work, *Ways of seeing* (1972), was published with Penguin. Clark's format was copied by Jacob Bronowski in *The ascent of man: a personal view* (1973). Only David Attenborough broke away from the format by placing innovative wildlife filming techniques at the centre of his series. The book of the series *Life on earth: a natural history* (1979) was written for the layperson, and was originally published by Collins, with an augmented and enlarged edition, which reflected the visual richness of the series better, published with Reader's Digest.

One effect of the influence of television was that the broad categories of fiction, non-fiction and children's books, subdivided in libraries using Dewey's nineteenth-century decimal system, gave way in the bookshops and best-seller charts to categories and genres taken from the media: celebrity biographies, the seasonal cycle of sports coverage, lifestyle programme tie-ins, DIY, 'the making of' books, and fiction tie-ins with stars from the film or TV series featured on the cover. The Reithian presenters, public intellectuals or men of science from Desmond Morris to Stephen Hawking, who wrote their own books, gave way to professional presenters, although since the millennium we have seen a return to the academic as presenter. For the BBC the book was increasingly peripheral to the broadcast series, and in the debates prior to its charter renewal in 2007 the BBC refocussed on their broadcasting genres, moving away from general non-fiction. BBC Worldwide, the commercial subsidiary of the BBC, sold BBC Books to the Ebury Publishing division of Random House. Attenborough's subsequent

---

22 Briggs, *The history of broadcasting*, vol. 2, p. 282.

Life titles were published by Ebury. Ebury's BBC Books list includes works by TV personalities from Delia Smith on cooking to Alan Titchmarsh on gardening, and books based on BBC programmes such as the long-running radio soap *The Archers* to the science fiction TV series *Dr Who*.

A similar fate befell the BBC magazines – a staple of BBC finances between the wars. A short boycott of BBC programme listings by the newspapers in 1923, who feared their circulation would decline if their readership listened to the radio,[23] led to the launch of *Radio Times* published under an agreement with George Newnes. Instantly popular, by 1928 the circulation had passed a million. *Radio Times* continued publication throughout the century, surviving the deregulation of TV listings in 1991 and consequent competition in the listings magazine market. In 2011 BBC Worldwide sold its thirty-three magazines to Exponent, a private equity company, including *Radio Times*, *Olive* and *Gardens Illustrated*, but retained editorial interest in BBC programme-branded titles, such as *Gardeners' World* and *BBC Wildlife*.[24] Charter renewal and the growth of BBC online services focussed the broadcaster on its core business content.

Media institutions and the book trade

The twentieth century saw the most radical change in the institutional structures of the book trade since the Stationers' Company's loss of control of the trade in the eighteenth century. Publishing firms were bought out by media companies: vertical then diagonal integration in the first half of the century led to conglomeration and to specialist transnational multimedia companies in the second. Initially, the press barons such as Alfred Harmsworth (Lord Northcliffe) and Max Aitkin (Lord Beaverbrook) built news empires, acquiring presses and newspapers, and establishing regional chains. Transatlantic trade led to chains acquiring interests in other entertainment and publishing activities, building large multimedia companies such as that of William Randolph Hearst. A turning point was the Broadcasting Act (1954), which permitted commercial television and ended the BBC's monopoly. It established the Independent Television Authority, which awarded franchises to broadcast in a specified region and complemented the existing chains by enabling them to separate their audiences geographically.

---

23 www.bbc.co.uk/historyofthebbc/resources/factsheets/1920s.pdf.
24 Mark Sweney, 'BBC Worldwide agrees £121m magazine sell-off'. *Guardian* 16 August 2011, www.guardian.co.uk/media/2011/aug/16/bbc-completes-magazines-sell-off.

Granada was one of the initial franchisees in 1954. The fortunes of the company are a good illustration of the changes which affected the industry in the twentieth century, and how competition led to giganticism. In the 1930s the brothers Sidney and Cecil Bernstein, impresarios of the theatre and travelling shows, established the Granada Theatre chain along the south coast. They expanded into cinema and then, with the advent of commercial television, successfully pitched for the North of England franchise. The only original company to survive into the twenty-first century, they had an enormous impact on TV programming, from factual programmes such as *World in Action* (1963–89) to the soap opera *Coronation Street* (1960–). They won the 1991 franchise competition, beating other higher bidders by meeting the quality threshold set by the regulators. They were renowned for their TV adaptations of novels and stories, including Evelyn Waugh's *Brideshead revisited* (1981), Paul Scott's *The jewel in the crown* (1984) and Conan Doyle's *Adventures of Sherlock Holmes* (1984). As the century progressed, competition led to conglomeration as businesses sought to be bigger to stay in the market. In the 1990s, Granada followed this pattern, taking over smaller television companies: London Weekend Television (LWT), Yorkshire and Tyne Tees Television, Anglia Television and Meridian Broadcasting and some parts of HTV.[25] By 2002 Granada and Carlton had a duopoly of English television. However, digital television changed the market irrevocably and both companies lost heavily when ITV Digital failed in 2002. Granada and Carlton merged in 2004 to form ITV plc.[26]

Following the trend in media companies through the century, the Granada Group sought through acquisition to exploit its content across media. The group included Granada Studio Tours (an entertainment theme park at the Granada studios in Manchester), Granada Film and Granada Publishing.[27] The latter published the fiction of Robert Ludlum and Norman Mailer, and tie-ins including *The making of* The jewel in the crown (1983) as well as non-fiction, notably Halliwell's film guide, and educational books such as the *How things work* encyclopaedia. In the 1960s, 1970s and 1980s it acquired the imprints of Panther Books, MacGibbon & Kee, Rupert Hart-Davis, Arco Publications, Staples Press, Mayflower Books and later Paul Elek. In 1983 Granada sold its publishing business to William Collins Sons & Co.,

---

25 Briggs and Burke, *A social history of the media*; Briggs, *The history of broadcasting*, vol. 5.
26 'Granada and Carlton agree merger', *BBC News online* 16 October 2002, http://news
.bbc.co.uk/1/hi/business/2332149.stm.
27 Cox, *Granada Television*; Forman, *Persona Granada*.

who after merging with Harper & Row formed HarperCollins, one of the largest publishing firms in Britain at the end of the century.

The late twentieth century saw the growth of several transnational media companies with interests in many countries sustained by a decentralised management. As broadcast companies looked to export their audio-visual franchises to international markets, the British combination of education and publishing grew specialist publishing and media firms to a global pre-eminence. In the gap created when conglomerates such as Lonhro, which mixed mining with an increasing interest in media in the 1980s, refocussed on their core business in the 1990s, specialist media companies such as Pearson plc seized the opportunity to develop as multinationals, trading on the economies of scale they could provide. Pearson had started out as a publisher in 1921, but the firm's policy – to focus on educational publishing – became only gradually evident through their acquisitions. In 1968 Pearson plc bought Longman plc, whose pedigree in the education sector dates back to the eighteenth century, and which had extensive experience in English language markets in colonial and postcolonial Africa. Two years later the company acquired Penguin Books, and in 1972 the early-years education publisher Ladybird Books, later adding Frederick Warne & Co. in 1983 to form the Penguin Group. Looking to the American textbook markets, it acquired Simon & Schuster's educational division in 1998 and the innovative British book and CD-ROM publishing company Dorling Kindersley. In the twenty-first century Pearson developed their business, adding Harcourt Education (containing Heinemann's educational list) to their portfolio and extended from publishing into educational assessments, acquiring Edexcel examination board company in Britain and similar companies in the USA. In 1986 Pearson plc invested in the British Satellite Broadcasting (BSB) consortium and in the 1990s it acquired Thames Television and other television production companies. In 2000 it merged Pearson TV with the RTL group, a world-leader in game shows and soaps. Yet while Pearson plc has interests in other media the company's main focus remains on the perennial educational sector.

In his book *The business of books: how the international conglomerates took over publishing and changed the way we read*, André Schiffrin criticised the financial conservatism of the big companies, accusing them of restricting the editor's freedom to publish serious books. Business interests have certainly restricted when a book is published, and by whom, and even if it eventually appears: for example, HarperCollins refused to publish *East and West: China, power and the future of Asia*, the memoirs of the last British Governor of Hong Kong

Christopher Patten, allegedly because of his unfavourable description of the Chinese leadership.[28] Rupert Murdoch, CEO of the parent company, needed the leadership on his side to support his plans to broadcast in China. It was subsequently published by Pan Macmillan on 7 September and Crown on 14 September 1998. Business interests have, however, led to greater fluidity and exchange in media management personnel between organisations, as Sir Carlton Greene, Director General of the BBC, showed when he moved to Bodley Head, and Greg Dyke when he moved from journalism to London Weekend Television where he eventually became CEO.[29]

Changing patterns of work and leisure

Behind the growth in media industries lies a change in patterns of work, leisure, and expectations of education. At the end of the nineteenth century, literacy was very nearly universal in Britain, working hours were regulated by statute and free state-funded libraries were open to the public. Yet the working week was long, leisure time was devoted to chores, and for most people schooling finished at adolescence. Social scientists Jonathan I. Gershuny and Kimberly Fisher have calculated that the British worker gained 'seven extra weekly hours of leisure' over the century through shorter working weeks, time-saving domestic appliances and paid holiday.[30] To understand how people were spending their time, Charles Madge, Tom Harrisson and Humphrey Jennings undertook a Mass-Observation survey which collected data from volunteers on their everyday life and habits from 1937 to 1950. Amongst other activities, it asked questions about library use, cinema going and listening to the radio. To cater for this demand, the leisure industries have grown, and the percentage of the workforce employed in them increased from 3.5 per cent to 8 per cent from 1930 to 1990.[31] Even with the growth of leisure options, the time devoted to radio and television appears to have remained unchanged between 1961 and 1995, and the average seventy-four minutes given over to games, hobbies and reading each day has only marginally been reduced.[32] At the turn of the century, the home PC had led to increased use of information technology. This has had a larger impact on time devoted to radio and television, although it has taken some time

---

28 Schiffrin, *The business of books* and Dover, *Rupert's adventures in China*.
29 Other media executives who have moved between print, broadcast media and arts management include Baron Patrick Gibson, David Ure, Andrew Neil and Craig Oliver.
30 Gershuny and Fisher, 'Leisure in the UK', p. 33.   31 *Ibid.*   32 *Ibid.*

away from reading.[33] According to Hamill's data, between 2000 and 2005 time devoted to reading declined by four minutes, while the time devoted to hobbies and games increased by nine minutes.[34]

Over the course of the century the length of children's compulsory schooling increased, the school-leaving age rose from twelve years in 1899 to sixteen in 1972 and more young adults continued in education, achieving higher levels of literacy. Reading campaigns, such as the National Year of Reading in 1998 and the Bookstart programme, linked government, schools and philanthropic organisations who sought to raise literacy standards by working with publishers to commission and distribute books (see Chapter 26). In the earliest days of BBC radio, the corporation monitored its impact through measuring library borrowing in the areas it broadcast, commenting favourably in its Yearbooks when specific programmes led to loans.[35] Later, in 1971, the Open University started, with over 300 programmes broadcast by the BBC in the first teaching year. The BBC also supported the National Literacy 'Right to Read' Campaign, which targeted the 2 million adults who had a reading age of seven years or less, with its literacy series On the Move (1976), and BBC Education and BBC online still continue to make programmes, publish educational books and provide online study aids for the National Curriculum in schools. This has caused concern for educational publishers uneasy at a free service undercutting the potential market for online products.

Radio and the gramophone record industry enabled recordings of books, poems and plays to be broadcast to a wide audience. However, the consumer market for audio books only emerged in the 1980s following the BBC's launch of its Radio Collection, with selected works from its archive. Publishers Penguin, Hodder, HarperCollins, Random House and Orion followed suit. Tape and then compact disc players in cars created a new social space for audio books, and sales from 1995 to 2000 grew by about 20 per cent a year. In 2006 audio book sales were 2.8 per cent of the UK consumer book market.[36] Technological development facilitated downloading of digital audio files for listening on personal MP3 players, so that by 2010 the Publishers Association review of the year reported that 'consumer digital sales (including consumer e-books, downloads and audiobooks) showed the

---

33 Gershuny, 'Mass media, leisure and home IT'.   34 Hamill, 'Changing times', table 3.2.
35 Weedon, '"Behind the screen"'.
36 Liz Murray, 'The Publishers Association reveals accelerated growth in the 2010 digital book market', ljinteractive.com.

most rapid growth, having increased by 318 per cent since 2009 from £4m to £16m'.[37]

Social networking and online communities have foregrounded book reading as a shared activity. Reading circles and book groups have long existed, but the Web has added other means of recommendation, handing-on and swapping books through such sites as goodreads.com, librarything.com and bookcrossing.com. On the internet, real-time chat features enable readers to interview authors and vice versa. The Web has facilitated discussion boards on fan fiction sites, and readers have become interchangeable as co-creators or audiences of cultural products from books to films. Interactive services for online newspapers in 1996 were initially e-mailed comments or simple voting systems, and digital TV-i or interactive 'red button' services replaced the analogue closed captioning teletext system in 1999. In 2003 the People's Network, a government- and lottery-funded initiative to roll out network personal computers in public libraries, enabled the public to participate in the BBC's vote for Britain's favourite reads in the Big Read. Readers became active participants, as their voting choices formed the basis of the content of BBC discussion programmes. The People's Network also set up online interviews in libraries with authors, including J. K. Rowling, to celebrate the UNESCO World Book and Copyright Day in 2004. However, as households in the UK adopted the home PC, the importance of the library network declined.

The availability of book texts online, pioneered by the Gutenberg Project (started 1971), became a commercial reality following the Google Book Search agreement in 2008. Few authors who experimented with early forms of online writing gained remuneration for their publications, and commercial experiments to sell interactive books on CD-ROMs proved short-lived.[38] Reading online on cathode ray tube (CRT) screens was not comfortable for any period of time, but the development of e-readers with liquid ink technology screens led to new products designed specifically for reading e-books, e.g. Sony's e-reader (2006), Amazon's Kindle (2007), Nook (2009) and Kobo (2010), though customers could also read them on tablets such as Panasonics Raboo and the Apple iPad (see Chapter 3). Developed by the successful online bookseller Amazon, the Kindle secured the supply chain from the company's wide inventory of books via a patented online retailing and checkout system, through whispernet wifi delivery to a proprietary e-book format. Other companies, such as the publisher HarperCollins, used

---

37 Ibid. 38 Weedon, 'The book trade and internet publishing'.

a standard 'e-pub' format for e-books which can be read on a variety of e-reader devices and tablets. According to the Publishers Association, the value of digital content including e-books, audio downloads and subscriptions rose from 5 per cent of the total value of book sales in 2010 to 8 per cent in 2012, a growth that had a hiatus in 2015.[39]

Technological developments and the challenge of time-based and audio-visual media have made the book trade look again at the strengths and limitations of the codex. Michael Joyce's *afternoon, a story* (1987) was written in a HyperCard-style system, allowing readers to navigate their own way through the story. The format was similar to maze or puzzle books, but the HyperCard software surpassed the physical limitations of looking up the next page reference and allowed for multiple routes through the text. Such experiments tested the non-linear features of the digital text. Other experiments are kept in the trAce Online Writing Community archive from 1995 to 2005. Digital stories exist online – such as Geoff Ryman's underground train fiction *253* (1996 online, 1998 print) and Kate Pullinger's transmedia story *Inanimate Alice* (2005–), which is 'a story that unfolds over time and on multiple platforms'[40] – and illustrate the convergence of styles and techniques within media writing. Visual time-based media such as film and television, which required the audience to watch the narrative as it unfolded from the beginning and at the director's pace, have influenced novels and short stories, but arguably have had greatest effect on transmedia storytelling. Cinematic techniques and genres have crossed over: flashbacks, zooms, jump cuts, interior monologues, and attention to setting and pace have changed storytelling from its nineteenth-century print-led tradition. Similarly, elements of the book form have been taken into non-linear audio-visual media and other means of storytelling such as video gaming. Online or on DVD, the reader/player can 'open' the text at any point, facilitated by tables of content and menus, chapterisation, indices, saves/bookmarks and other peritextual elements. References and bibliographies link to other texts, which through online hyperlinks can be made active.

While the electronic media created new forms of entertainment and provided faster ways of accessing information, the book did not lose its status as the highest form for the communication of new knowledge and ideas. Major academic works appeared in print first, though this included the publication of scientific and other discoveries through online publication in journal form. Film, radio and television, which at their origin drew heavily on

39 Darren Allan, 'ebook sales more than quadrupled in 2011', IT PRoPortal, 2 May 2012, www.itproportal.com/2012/05/02/e-book-sales-more-than-quadrupled-in-2011/.
40 Kate Pullinger, *Inanimate Alice*, inanimatealice.com/about.html.

the earlier print forms for stories which could be adapted or appropriated, created their own audio-visual languages as they developed through the century. However, their dependence on the creative content which authors produced remained, albeit increasingly through the new form of authorship for the media: scriptwriting.

The challenge of time-based and audio-visual media made the industry look again at the role of the book at the end of the twentieth century and the beginning of the twenty-first. The electronic media appropriated the book's core values, taking access to education, information and entertainment beyond the walls of the library or schoolroom into the living room as the television set, and then the personal computer, entered the home. As leisure time increased through the twentieth century, and patterns of work changed, the amount of time spent on reading or watching TV and listening to the radio overall increased. In the Euromonitor survey 2013, 80 per cent of respondents had read a book in the previous year, down 2 per cent on six years previously; by comparison 77 per cent had watched a cultural programme on TV or the radio, a percentage which had remained the same.[41] Competition for time between the book and media was less than the competition within the media between television, radio and computer games.

Book publishing in Britain remained an essential part of an interconnected communications system for the commodification of ideas and cultural expressions. Yet, from Ted Nelson's original concept of a worldwide interlinking of texts in one great library in Project Xanadu (1960), to its current realisation in the twenty-first century e-books and online storytelling, digitalisation has challenged our notion of the book as a separate physical codex.[42] Even so the essential components of book publishing remain. Safeguarding creative property, the right to purchase a copy of a text, packaging and selling it with a retail system, creating new markets and means of distribution, augmenting the book and adding value through the technologies at hand – all are an enduring part of the book's dynamic system of cultural production.

---

41 Euromonitor Cultural access and participation 399 survey 2013, question Q B1.8 response of 1,012 people. The previous comparative survey of European Cultural Values 278 was in 2007 based on a response of 1008, http://ec.europa.eu/COMMFrontOffice/PublicOpinion.
42 Cope and Philips, *The future of the book in the digital age.*

30

Book events, book environments

DAVID FINKELSTEIN AND CLAIRE SQUIRES

Since the Second World War, a common conception has been that the literary festival has become one of the key sites for the promotion of books and literary culture in the UK. As currently conceived by the myriad festivals worldwide dedicated to celebrating literary culture and the book, the literary festival conjoins the commercial aspects found in trade bookfairs around the world (selling books, exhibiting new titles, offering space for trade representatives to meet) with the promotion of new and established writers through public readings, book signings and encounters with readers. The literary festival has become a major fixture on the publishing circuit, utilised to showcase new works by established authors and provide high visibility and marketing opportunities for publishers. The first multi-sessional literary festival of this sort in Britain was launched in Cheltenham in 1949.[1] In the post-war period, and particularly after 1970, the development of the literary festival continued, to the extent that, by 2015, the number of literary and literature-related festivals in England, Northern Ireland, Scotland and Wales had risen exponentially to over 217.[2] This growth, which is explored later in this chapter, attests to the values (social, cultural and financial) of such events to local economies and communities. The work of literary festivals in terms of shaping writing, publishing and reading communities has continued to grow in the era of digital media. The opportunity to meet authors and fellow readers face-to-face, to buy books and other merchandise, and to align a liking for literature with travel and tourism, is being taken up by hundreds of thousands of readers every year. In the twenty-first century, an event- and location-based literary culture has also expanded opportunities for face-to-face encounters with virtual participation via social media interactions, live streaming and podcasting.

1 Driscoll, *The new literary middlebrow*, p. 154.
2 'Festivals directory', http://literature.britishcouncil.org/festivals.

The exponential rise of literary festivals needs to be contextualised within a broader set of book events and environments which have shaped the cultural environment of Britain over the course of the twentieth and into the twenty-first century. The study of such events and environments might encompass a range of activities and spaces. These include literary festivals and other live literature events, but also the spaces of the bookshop, book and literacy promotional activity, literary awards ceremonies, mediatised book spaces, and sites of literary tourism. Such spaces are productive in examining the confluence of public sector funding and commercial operations, and the varying intents behind, and effects of, the making public of books and the literature they contain. It puts a particular spotlight on the author as the promoter of his or her books, the marketing of those books, and the ways in which readers have encountered both books and authors.

In the nineteenth century, there were already examples of literary events centred round the celebration of particular authors or texts that continue in renewed form to this day, such as the annual Robert Burns suppers organised worldwide on or near his birthday on 25 January to commemorate his contributions to Scottish literary culture, and extant in one form or another since 1805.[3] The book promotion tour, now so much a feature of authors for promoting their works, has its antecedents in nineteenth-century public lecture tours of celebrity authors such as Charles Dickens, who galvanised audiences in public performances across the UK and North America in the 1850s and 1860s, and Oscar Wilde, who lectured across the length of the USA in 1882 and 1883.[4]

Equally significant has been the incorporation of literary events within wider cultural contexts, as exemplified in the distinctive and vibrant annual Welsh, Scottish and Irish Gaelic language celebrations of literature, song, arts and culture, whose beginnings can be traced back to the National Eisteddfod, founded in Wales in 1861, the Royal National Mòd, begun in Scotland in 1892, and the Irish Oireachtas na Gaeilge (National Festival of Irish Language and Culture), founded by the Gaelic League in Dublin in 1897.[5] All include recitations of poetry and prose, alongside essay competitions within a full

---

3 Pittock (ed.), *Robert Burns in global culture*; and Watson, *The literary tourist*.
4 John, *Dickens and mass culture*; John Cooper, 'Oscar Wilde in America', www
.oscarwildeinamerica.org/index.html.
5 www.eisteddfod.org.uk/english/about-us/our-history/celebrate-150/early-eisteddfo
dau; www.ancomunn.co.uk/about/history. Records of the Irish Gaelic League, Collection List No. 14, MSS G 1,318 /1–MS G 1,416 /9, National Library of Ireland.

programme of cultural events, with the purpose of encouraging appreciation of literary texts within respective language contexts.

Aside from such specialised cultural events, in the first third of the twentieth century UK book culture initiatives tended to focus on the promotion of reading and literary appreciation through library events, educational lectures and book reading schemes. It was a period marked by public, charitable or educationally supported and focussed promotion of book culture. Generally non-commercialised in nature, it involved supporting activities such as talks and readings in library settings, lectures, book events and general book reading promotions run by and in Women's Institutes, Workers' Institutes, schools and bookshops.

During the First World War significant time and effort was invested in 'soft power' promotion by government agencies for particular propaganda or cultural purposes (see Chapter 23). A secret War Propaganda Bureau was set up in September 1914 (and led from 1917 by the author John Buchan), with the aim of steering book publishing and cultural promotion efforts towards the fulfilment of wartime aims. Books, pamphlets, photographs and films were commissioned, advertised and promoted with government funding, and authors were sent to friendly countries on extended promotional tours aimed at reinforcing support for Allied war efforts.[6] A typical example was Ian Hay (John Beith), author of the best-selling pro-war novel *The first hundred thousand*, which within two years of publication in December 1915 had sold 115,000 copies in Britain and its colonies and 350,000 copies in the United States. On the back of this success, as Beith jokingly remarked from New York prior to embarking on a nineteen-month lecture tour of North America, 'I was yanked off to this country a few weeks ago, and here I am, lecturing on the war and interviewing reporters, and generally countermining Boche propaganda.'[7] He would go on to speak in over 330 venues across Canada and the United States between October 1916 and May 1918.

Following the end of the war, the British newspapers began taking notice of various attempts on the continent to establish national book events. In 1922 Florence hosted the first of an intermittent series of international book festivals, the Foire Internationale du Livre, repeated in 1925, 1928 and 1932. The Instituto Italiano del Libro, created specifically to support book culture across the region, managed the 1928 event, to which seventeen

6 Buitenhuis, *The Great War of words*, p. 16.
7 Quoted in Finkelstein, 'Literature, propaganda and the First World War', p. 104.

European countries contributed representative material and participants.[8] Spain followed suit in 1926 with the establishment of an annual Fiesta del Libro (or Book Day) timed in October to coincide with the anniversary of Miguel de Cervantes's birth. Towns and cities across Spain were encouraged to put on events linked to reading and book promotion: publishers and booksellers offered 10 per cent discounts on purchases made or books ordered on the day, libraries and public institutions in Ceuta, Salamanca, Seville and Valencia (among others) featured lectures and exhibitions on book-related topics, and in Barcelona authors conducted readings and autographed books in local bookshops.[9] Correspondents commented on the way in which such locally based events were stimulating cultural interaction and reading, and recommended adoption of similar opportunities in Britain.

British publishers and national organisations considered ways in which such initiatives could be imported in manageable form. A few locally based groups began to run coordinated book events in which bookshops, libraries and local authorities joined together to promote books and reading. Early experiments in this direction included an annual book week begun in 1926 in Cheltenham, in which the latest works from fifty-three publishers were displayed in the Municipal Arts Gallery, accompanied by lectures and other book displays. By 1931 the number of publishers represented had risen to over one hundred.[10] Bath inaugurated a Book Week in 1928, the launch of which featured lectures by Michael Sadleir and Basil Blackwell and an exhibition on the history of the book from Egyptian to modern times.[11] Cardiff followed suit in 1929 with a Welsh Book Festival, run annually through to 1939. Such efforts exemplified a fixed model of literary engagement, involving static displays of new books, exhibitions in public libraries on historical themes, and public lectures by learned authorities on the value of books and reading.

In 1925 the National Book Council was formed by members of the book trade with the aim of promoting books and encouraging leisure reading (see Chapter 26). Seeing the potential of centrally organising an annual series of national book weeks, it launched a trial event in October 1931 focussed on

---

8 Williams and Noble, *Conference on international cultural, educational and scientific exchanges*, p. 125.
9 'From a correspondent', *The Times* 20 October 1927, p. 17.
10 'Mayor opens Cheltenham book festival', *Cheltenham Chronicle and Gloucestershire Graphic* 29 October 1932, p. 3.
11 '"Book Week" at Bath', *The Times* 22 May 1928, p. 10.

religious books, presided over by the Archbishop of York, Dr William Temple.[12] An annual Boys' and Girls' Book Week began the following year, featuring book-related items on BBC radio, an illustrated children's literature exhibition at the Victoria and Albert Museum in London, and public events and exhibitions in Birmingham, Glasgow, Liverpool and Oxford.[13] In 1933 Harrods experimented with a Book Week featuring author appearances and signings from popular novelists such as Gilbert Frankau, A. G. Street and A. J. Cronin. The high number of sales recorded during the promotion led one of its directors to conclude not only that people were reading more but that 'the public is hungry for books'.[14]

While such schemes involved general promotion of books in public spaces, the inter-war years also saw the rise of bookselling and book promotion schemes developed by commercial agents for private spaces, in particular the mail order book club, a US importation (see Chapter 6). Exportation of book schemes was not always a one-way flow between the USA and the UK. In 1943, at the height of the Second World War, a concerted effort was made to promote British cultural values to its US allies via a North American British Book Week, coordinated by the American Library Association, the British Information Services and the US Office of War Information. Information packs were prepared that included advice on themes for exhibitions at local libraries and schools, pamphlets on British values written by J. B. Priestley and others, posters, maps and book lists, and bibliographies on British civilisation and British contributions to civil democracy.[15] Books Across the Sea, a private, benefactor-supported initiative with branches in Boston, Edinburgh, New York and London (the latter led by T. S. Eliot), funded guest speakers for these events, including May Lamberton Becker, journalist for the *New York Herald Tribune*, and her daughter, the well-known typographic expert Beatrice Warde.[16] In the post-war period, books were again brought into play in the international environment in the exercise of soft power, alongside the growth of the global dominance of the English language. In 1970, for example, the British Council provided support for publishers and their products with an exhibition of 'Paperbacks for Universities' including more than 1,000 books from fifty publishers, which was shown in the Lebanon, Peru, Chile and Venezuela in 1970. By 1978, ten 'senior British

---

12 'Religious book week', *Devon and Exeter Daily Gazette* 22 August 1931, p. 5.
13 'A children's book week', *Tamworth Herald* 20 August 1932, p. 6.
14 'Harrods has a book week', *New York Times* 26 March 1933, E2.
15 Peterson, 'So you're celebrating British book week!', pp. 283–6.
16 T. S. Eliot, 'Books Across the Sea', *The Times* 9 November 1943, p. 5.

publishers' were invited by the Chinese government to visit the People's Republic of China, with a major exhibition of British books held in Peking the following year.[17]

The 1970s saw the development of the publishing trade fair SPEX (the Specialist Publishers' Exhibition for Librarians), which by 1975 'felt sufficiently established to carry the sub-title The London Book Fair'. The one-day event attracted around 140 exhibitors and over 1,000 visitors, among whom were counted 'more than 50 overseas publishers on their way to Frankfurt'.[18] (The Frankfurt Book Fair, a centuries-old institution, was resurrected after the Second World War, and over the coming decades established itself as the pre-eminent international rights fair.) In subsequent decades, the London Book Fair (LBF) would cement its place as one of the key events in the international publishing calendar, taking the decision by the 1980s to move its event to the spring, to avoid being overshadowed by Frankfurt. Establishing itself fully as an international rights fair, LBF's focus has been on trade interaction rather than with readers, unlike the continental European model of a bookfair, which caters to both.[19]

Despite the trade orientation of LBF, the post-war period was characterised by the internationalisation and commercialisation of book events and book culture, with an increasingly reader-orientated focus. The Cheltenham Literary Festival, established in 1949, had swiftly followed the foundation of the town's Music Festival in 1945. The Edinburgh International Festival (of Music and Drama) was first held in 1949, and would eventually lead to the Scottish capital hosting twelve major annual festivals, including, from 1983, the Book Festival.[20] This festivalisation process as an aid to, and symbol of, post-war recovery reached its zenith in 1951's Festival of Britain. This was allied to renewed efforts by the National Book League (NBL; formerly the National Book Council) to promote books through national exhibitions and events, such as the 1951 exhibition on contemporary book production.[21]

The literary version of the festival, in the initial guise of Cheltenham, was described by the *Times Literary Supplement* in 1962 as offering an alternative to a traditional literary society, 'with the additional and by no means negligible advantage that it is an "event"; interest is stirred, attention focused and the

17 'Paperback exhibition', *Bookseller* 4 April 1970, p. 1,904; 'The book trade in 1978 January–June', *Bookseller* 6 January 1979, p. 39; 'The book trade in 1979 July to December', *Bookseller* 12 January 1980, p. 153.
18 'The book trade in 1975 (II) July–December', *Bookseller* 17 January 1976, p. 163.
19 'Trade events', *Bookseller* 10 January 1981, p. 97. 20 Bartie, *The Edinburgh festivals.*
21 National Book League, *Exhibition of books.*

whole thing touches a much wider public than a literary society could ever do'.[22] The precursor of the Edinburgh International Book Festival had a similarly event-based imperative. In 1962, as part of the Edinburgh International Festival, an International Writers' Conference took place, organised by the publishers John Calder and Sonia Brownell and by Edinburgh's Paperback Bookshop's Jim Haynes, as an 'experiment', as Calder wrote in the programme, 'in bringing writers to the public and the public into direct contact with ideas in collision'.[23] Approximately seventy writers from Britain, Western Europe, America, Israel, Ceylon and India attended the five-day event, attracting large audiences (around 2,000) to hear, and participate in, their debates in the University's McEwan Hall.

Other reader-facing initiatives were trialled. In 1971, an experimental open-air book event took place in central London for two weeks in late May and early June, with tents hired from a circus.[24] Martyn Goff, the new Director of the National Book League (latterly renamed as Booktrust, and accruing increasing levels of public funding), with Tom Maschler of Jonathan Cape and the Publishers Association, ran the 'Bedford Square Book Bang'. The Book Bang was a space for events and a bookshop, modelled on the generic promotion – and a message of wellbeing – of agencies such as the Milk Marketing Board, as Goff explained to the Publishers Publicity Circle prior to the event.[25]

The Bedford Square Book Bang went hand-in-hand with NBL's broader activities to promote reading and literacy which are explored in Chapter 26. The NBL also became involved with the Booker Prize soon after its establishment in 1968 by Maschler in his role at the Publishers Association, and the food business Booker McConnell. From the beginning, Maschler was keen that the prize become an event in the literary calendar similar to that of the literary prize season in France. For the first ceremony in 1969 the organisers attempted to secure the Queen to make the inaugural award.[26] The ambition for the head of state to be present failed, but subsequently – particularly once Martyn Goff and the NBL had become involved – the Booker Prize would go on to achieve Maschler's intention of bringing worldwide attention to books, as an annual fixture in the bookish calendar.

22 Quoted in Driscoll, *The new literary middlebrow*, p. 155.
23 Calder, 'The first literary festival'. Original programme of the 1962 International Writers' Conference, cited in Bartie and Bell, *The International Writers' Conference revisited*, p. 5.
24 Report on meeting about the Book Bang, *Bookseller* 16 January 1971, p. 128.
25 'The shape of things to come in Bedford Square', *Bookseller* 28 November 1970, pp. 2,464–6.
26 Squires, 'Literary prizes and awards'.

Away from urban centres, the concept and creation of the 'book town' was born. Richard Booth, a bookshop owner in Hay-on-Wye in the Welsh Borders, saw an opportunity for targeted rural tourism by encouraging further second-hand and antiquarian bookshops to open. The designation of the book town was self-declared in 1961, and was followed in subsequent years by Wigtown in Scotland (1998) and Sedbergh in England (2003). Hay's designation initially owed more to an entrepreneurial local individual than to regional funding or tourism policy, but Wigtown's naming was the result of a competition adjudged by Scottish Enterprise in 1997. By the 1990s, Hay's success in quantitative terms was evident: tourist numbers were estimated at half a million a year, with one in twenty tourists to Wales visiting the small town. Both Hay (1987) and Wigtown (1999) would go on also to host large literary festivals, with Hay subsequently making international festival partnerships around the world in Columbia, Ireland, Mexico, Peru and Spain, as well as inspiring book towns from Australia to Finland, Malaysia and Switzerland.[27]

Other regional areas developed book events, with Ilkley setting up a Literature Festival in 1973. Inspired by Cheltenham, it was opened by poet W. H. Auden. From August 1983, the Edinburgh International Book Festival became the first regular event in Scotland to be dedicated solely to books and their creators. Unlike Cheltenham's use of its spa town infrastructure, Edinburgh featured events in outdoor, tented spaces circling Charlotte Square Gardens. Its first Director, Jenny Brown, cites the Bedford Square Book Bang as Edinburgh's inspiration, and indeed Martyn Goff acted as an early board member. Before the festival's arrival, Brown commented, 'There was no out-of-hours culture, no demonstrated thirst for books and hearing authors talk. Author book readings were just not around so much. It wasn't something that people did, or something that publishers demanded their authors do.'[28] The idea of an outdoor literary festival, akin in feeling to the music festivals that had sprung up throughout Britain in the previous two decades, was adopted by other UK literary festivals that followed, such as Hay (1988), the Bath Literature Festival (1993) and the Swindon Festival of Literature (1994). Such events operate via a mix of funding sources, ranging from local authorities, central and regional arts funding bodies, and commercial sponsorship, including newspapers. Tickets sales have rarely fully funded

27 Seaton, 'Hay on Wye'; Seaton, 'Book towns'; Murray, *The adaptation industry*, pp. 100–1. See also www.booktown.net.
28 'The little festival that grew', *Scotsman* 13 August 2004, www.scotsman.com/lifestyle/the-little-festival-that-grew-1-543467.

book festivals, and some, with controversy, have operated by expecting authors to perform without a fee.[29]

In the final decades of the twentieth century, and the early years of the twenty-first, the effects of globalisation, the rise of transnational circuits of book promotional events, and the international development of annual, reader-focussed cultural initiatives became central to the narrative of book events and environments. In 1995, UNESCO instituted World Book and Copyright Day (WBCD) on 23 April (the death day of Shakespeare, Cervantes – thereby moving the date of the traditional Spanish festival – and de la Vega) in order to foster a focus around the world for the promotion and dissemination of books.[30] In the UK, however, as the primary focus was on schools, 'World' Book Day came to be celebrated on an itinerant weekday in March or April and has, since 1998, delivered £1 book tokens to school-children, as well as inspiring events in which pupils (and teachers) dress as characters from books. By 2011, an 'adult' version of the event began in the UK as 'World Book Night' (WBN) under the instigation of Canongate publisher Jamie Byng. On WBN, which eventually settled on 23 April in line with the UNESCO WBCD, thousands of free books are given away by volunteers, and events take place around the country to celebrate books and reading.[31]

The events-based nature of the World Book Day and Night followed patterns of promotional activity around books at the turn of the twentieth and twenty-first centuries. It encouraged mass participation in which reading and literacy functioned in parallel with commercial imperatives. The apogee of such promotional activities were the launches for each of the successive books in J. K. Rowling's *Harry Potter* series. These events included the midnight opening of bookshops, with booksellers and buyers dressing up as witches and wizards, and for the fourth book in the series, in 2000, a promotional tour for the author in a steam-train replica of Hogwarts Express.[32] In *The late age of print*, Ted Striphas explains this activity as a consequence of an agreement by the English-language publishers of the

29 Benedicte Page, 'Authors call for boycott on non-paying festivals', *Bookseller* 15 January 2016, www.thebookseller.com/news/authors-call-boycott-non-paying-festivals-320338.
30 Larrea and Weedon, 'Celebrating book culture'. See also Brouillette, 'UNESCO and the book in the developing world' for further information on UNESCO's interactions with literature.
31 http://worldbooknight.org/about.
32 '2000: New Harry Potter most magical yet', http://news.bbc.co.uk/onthisday/hi/dates/stories/july/8/newsid_2496000/2496367.stm.

books for a 'global lay-down date' which, through a desire to regulate territorial rights, heavily embargoed press coverage and controlled sales start points.[33] By 2012, a simulacrum of the Harry Potter 'experience' found a permanent home in the Warner Bros. Studio Tour, using many of the sets, props and costumes from the film adaptations; and King's Cross station manufactured a 'Platform 9¾', the departure point for the Hogwarts Express, featuring a luggage trolley seemingly entering into a solid brick wall at which fans queue to take photos.[34]

Elsewhere in the UK, the opportunities for combining literature and locational tourism gave birth to UNESCO's first 'City of Literature', in Edinburgh. UNESCO already had from 2001 an annual 'World Book Capital' scheme, but a small group of individuals (including former Directors of the Edinburgh International Book Festival and Publishing Scotland, and the Chair of the Scottish Arts Council) made in 2004 a proposal for a longer-lasting designation of City of Literature.[35] Once awarded, the designation then spread among a network to include Melbourne, Dublin, Warsaw and Iowa City, as well as Norwich and Nottingham in England, and a greater Creative Cities network (encompassing gastronomy, music, film and crafts, among others).[36] The links to cultural tourism were evident in the bid and continuing activities of Edinburgh City of Literature, with the website promoting a range of literature-related visitor activities and attractions. It also offers a Literary Toolkit for Businesses, which emphasises that businesses might be 'sitting on a literary goldmine'.[37] The potential link between literature, tourism and business is clearly encapsulated in this statement.

Alongside such positive assertions surrounding the rise of book towns, Cities of Literature and literary festivals, and their contributions to the promotion of books and local economies, has also come critique. Such events and environments are broadly inhabited by a limited demographic: the middle class, predominantly female, and promoting books and authors which privilege a 'middlebrow' form of literature.[38] For others, the

---

33 Striphas, *The late age of print*, p. 146.
34 www.wbstudiotour.co.uk; and www.kingscross.co.uk/harry-potters-platform-9-34.
35 www.cityofliterature.com; and *Chapter and verse*.
36 http://en.unesco.org/creative-cities/home.
37 www.cityofliterature.com/the-literary-city/visit. See also Sarah Brouillette, 'UNESCO and the world-literary system in crisis', *Amodern* December 2015, http://amodern.net/article/unesco-brouillette.
38 Seaton, 'Book towns', p. 391; Murray, *The adaptation industry*, pp. 98–101; Driscoll, *The new literary middlebrow*, pp. 152–93; Fuller and Rehberg Sedo, *Reading beyond the book*, pp. 6–7.

festivalisation of literature, with its concomitant harnessing of literature to local and regional economies in the service of urban redevelopment and rural sustainability, links book events and environments to a reading of literature within a creative economy.[39] Book festivals have clear links to regional economies, and are heavily used in the promotion of tourist destinations, as testified by the strategic partnerships and sponsorship arrangements with a variety of agencies. Concepts of cultural identity are thereby forged and commodified, conjoining literature to cultural heritage, the creative industries and political ideology. As such, their manifestations – albeit covered with some brevity here – are worth adding to the overall understanding and analysis of the history of the book, and its wider contexts, in Britain during the period.

39 Brouillette, *Literature and the creative economy.*

31

The book, British imperialism and post-imperialism

CAROLINE DAVIS

By 1914, British book publishers had established a global distribution network – a 'cultural empire' – that stretched from Australia, New Zealand, India and South Africa to Canada.[1] At this time, Britain's possessions throughout the world amounted to one quarter of the globe's surface, and the country's economic success depended on its colonies and dominions. Yet, in the decades after the Second World War, rapid and widespread decolonisation left only traces of the British Empire remaining. This chapter assesses the role of the book in the British colonial and postcolonial enterprise in the context of this turbulent imperial history.

Harish Trivedi writes of the abiding piety 'that imperial rule offered the colonies ... the book'.[2] His assertion raises two key questions: what part did the book actually play in Britain's civilising mission to the Empire? And how was the association between the British book and British imperialism disrupted or modified by political decolonisation? This discussion draws on diverse and often competing accounts: archival, autobiographical and anecdotal accounts by publishers; case studies by book historians; critiques written by publishers and commentators in postcolonial countries; and recent trade and industry reports. Within the confines of this necessarily brief survey, the intention is to make some observations about both the commercial and the psychological impact of British imperialism on the metropolitan publisher, and also to consider some of the responses to this contentious book trade.

British books and the colonies

The British Empire has been described variously as an 'open market' and a 'captive market' for British publishers.[3] The colonial book trade enjoyed the

---

1 Barnes *et al.*, 'A place in the world', p. 595.   2 Trivedi, 'The "book" in India', p. 12.
3 Feather, *A history of British publishing*, p. 204; Lee, 'Exploiting the imprint', p. 26.

protection of copyright legislation: the 1842 and 1911 Copyright Acts applied throughout the colonies, with the result that any book published in Britain was automatically entitled to be published in the Empire. In the first half of the twentieth century, India was at the heart of British imperial strategy, and was a major export market for British commodities, including books. While the commercial imperatives behind the book trade to India and the other British colonies are self-evident, the cultural, educational and ideological dimensions to this trade are less immediately obvious.

English literature was exported to the colonies mainly in the form of colonial editions. These series of mainly new British novels were published in conjunction with UK editions and were sold by British publishers to exporters throughout the British Empire and dominions at 50 per cent less than they were sold to retailers in Britain, with an extended credit period.[4] Commercially, they were a great achievement: by 1919 there were 339 British publishers involved in their production, and in India from the late nineteenth century they were a 'resounding success', in Priya Joshi's view.[5] The cultural impact of these literary exports has been the subject of debate: Gauri Viswanathan considers that English literature served as a 'mask of conquest', a vehicle of colonial control and cultural assimilation in India, whereas Joshi's study of the production and consumption of the English novel in India attests that it 'emerged in India as one of the most effective vehicles for voicing anticolonial and nationalist claims'.[6]

The most commercially significant book trade to India, however, was in schoolbooks, and Longmans, Oxford University Press and Macmillan cornered this lucrative market. Longmans was the first to launch a strategy of expansion in the country, setting up new branches in Bombay (1895), Calcutta (1906) and later Madras. Macmillan established branches in Bombay (1901), Calcutta (1907) and Madras (1913) and OUP followed suit, with branches in Bombay (1912), Madras (1915) and Calcutta (1915). The business was developed by means of symbiotic relationships between the large British publishers, colonial education departments and British examination boards. Rimi Chatterjee has shed light on the means by which Macmillan and OUP were awarded long-term contracts by the colonial government for the supply of educational books.[7] The rewards of this business were high. At Macmillan in 1901, a remarkable 80 per cent of foreign book sales came from the Indian market, and by 1943 Macmillan was the largest educational publisher in India

---

4 Johanson, *Colonial editions in Australia*, p. 2.
5 *Ibid.* p. 83; Joshi, *In another country*, p. 94.
6 Viswanathan, *Masks of conquest*; Joshi, *In another country*, p. xvii.
7 Chatterjee, 'Macmillan in India', p. 159 and *Empires of the mind*, p. 114.

with an annual turnover of nearly £250,000.[8] At Oxford University Press, according to Chatterjee and Padmini Ray Murray, 'the Indian branch had a much higher profit margin than most other parts of the Press's enterprise', with India branch sales totalling £26,000 in 1919.[9] Likewise, approximately one-quarter of Longmans' profits were by 1923 derived from the Indian textbook market: of the total gross profit of £44,986, £12,029 was from its Indian branches.[10] British publishers were later criticised for these arrangements: the Indian publisher Shyam Lal Gupta accused them of collusion in the colonial government's educational and cultural agenda to create 'a class of brainwashed mediocrity' which impoverished readers: 'British books were marketed in India through the Indian branches of some British publishing houses and there was neither any competition nor any choice in adopting other books.'[11]

Drawing on their financial success in India, British publishers pursued similar links with the colonial education department in Africa, with Macmillan, Longmans, OUP, Thomas Nelson and Evans Brothers at the fore. They were encouraged by the colonial government to get a foothold in the African colonies by producing books for 'Native Education', and worked closely with the colonial office to support their educational agenda. This included the implementation of the highly controversial Phelps-Stokes policy of manual and vocational education for the British African colonies, which was introduced by the Colonial Office in the 1920s.[12] The role of schoolbooks in supporting the colonial ideology was made explicit; for example, OUP was instructed by the Chief Examiner in Science to the Board of Education in 1932 'to make science (as opposed to the classics, or literature) the vehicle for enlightening the native about Western civilisation, that is, as much of it as could beneficially be superimposed on his tribal life and traditions'.[13]

Teaching in the English language was an integral aspect of the Colonial Education Department's strategy, and publishers played a fundamental role in this process. Longmans was the market leader in English-language teaching books from the 1920s due to the success of Michael West's New Method Readers. The company's infiltration into Africa was the work of its dynamic and entrepreneurial Education Manager, C. S. S. Higham, who undertook

8 Joshi, *In another country*, p. 102; Chatterjee, 'Macmillan in India', p. 165.
9 Chatterjee and Ray Murray, 'India', pp. 652, 653.
10 Davis, 'Creating a book empire', p. 132.
11 Gupta, 'Educational publishing in India', pp. 71–2.
12 Davis, 'Postcolonial literary publishing', pp. 29–33. 13 *Ibid.*, p. 33.

a series of whistle-stop journeys across the continent between 1933 and 1948. He promoted the New Method series along with other textbooks to the colonial education departments, to mission-run and government-run schools and colleges, and to bookshops. West's successful series was in time customised for different markets, creating for example Longmans' Readers for Burma and Longmans' English Reading Books for Indian Students. OUP attempted to emulate Longmans' success by commissioning Laurence Faucett's *Oxford English Course*, which became the foundation of its publishing strategy throughout the Empire. During the 1940s and 1950s the course was tailored for various international markets of the Press, for example, the *Oxford English Course for Mauritius* (1948), the *New Oxford English Course for Southern Africa* (1952) and the *Oxford English Course for Bantu Schools* (1959).[14] Macmillan and Nelson also had a hand in this business, and these very profitable textbooks became the mainstay of British educational publishers' programmes throughout the British colonies, forming the foundation for the most profitable sector of the British book trade: ELT publishing. Philip Altbach considers that the spread of English constituted the most enduring impact of the British publishing industry in its former Empire: 'The dominance of the colonial language continued after independence, and in almost every former colonial area, the issue of language remains controversial and of primary importance to publishing, education and the nation's intellectual life.'[15]

The colonised world also had a major impact on the metropolitan book trade in the first half of the twentieth century, as British publishers continued to play a part in what Edward Said terms the 'codification of difference' about the Empire.[16] Scholars and publishers – the 'professional contributors to Oriental knowledge' – categorised the Empire through amassing empirical knowledge: ethnographic, economic, scientific, geographic, linguistic and historical.[17] Oxford University Press was at the forefront of this scholarly endeavour; Chatterjee's detailed study of OUP's publications for and about India notes that 'the Press made its money interpreting other civilisations for the West'.[18] However, what Chatterjee terms the 'saleability of the other' was also a significant feature of trade publishing in the first half of the twentieth century.

---

14 Davis, *Creating postcolonial literature*, p. 25.
15 Altbach, *Publishing and development in the third world*, p. 5.
16 Said, *Culture and imperialism*, p. 130.   17 Said, *Orientalism*, p. 205.
18 Chatterjee, *Empires of the mind*, pp. 10, 376.

The 'bard of empire', Rudyard Kipling, became one of Macmillan's most prolific and successful authors in the early twentieth century.[19] Macmillan published dozens of his works: *Land and sea, The jungle book, Just so stories* and *Kim*, along with many works of non-fiction, verse, essays, travel letters, etchings, illustrations, anthologies and treasuries. Methuen and Hodder & Stoughton also held the rights for Kipling's verse and short stories. Joseph Conrad's tales of maritime and imperial adventure were the valuable property of J. M. Dent and, to a lesser extent, of Methuen and T. Fischer Unwin. Books and journals depicting imperial exploration and the exotic Empire formed the staple of many smaller publishers' lists, including Seeley, Service & Co., Andrew Melrose and Herbert Jenkins.

Most profitable in this period were boys' imperial adventure stories, which had a remarkably enduring appeal. Blackie and Son benefited for decades from G. A. Henty's boys' tales of adventure and conquest in the British Empire: in 1915, they still had in their catalogue eighty of his stories, including *The young colonists* (first published 1884), *With Roberts to Pretoria* (1902), *With Kitchener in the Soudan* (1903) and *With the Allies to Pekin* (1904).[20] The total sales figures for Henty's adventure fiction have been estimated at 25 million copies.[21] Such imperial adventure stories were also a feature of the *Boy's Own Paper* (*BOP*) and the *Girl's Own Paper*, journals which in Joseph Bristow's words brought together 'different classes of reader under the influence of unifying ideology: imperialism'.[22] The Religious Tract Society (RTS) published the *BOP* from 1879 to 1967, first as a weekly paper and then as a monthly after 1914, and its sister paper from 1880 to 1956; the circulation figures for *BOP* have been estimated at 250,000 per issue.[23] Inspired by their success with these periodicals, the RTS also published the *Empire annual for girls* (1909–30) and the *Empire annual for boys* (1909–33). Thus, the Empire continued to haunt the imagination of authors, publishers and readers during the early decades of the century.

British books in the dominions

The prosperity of British publishers hinged in particular on the special commercial relationships with Britain's 'free empire': the self-governing dominions of Australia, Canada, South Africa and New Zealand. Australia

---

19 For an analysis of Kipling's earlier relationships with the publishers Thacker, Spink & Co. in Calcutta and A. H. Wheeler & Co. in Allahabad, see Towheed. 'Two paradigms'.
20 See back matter advertisements in *Tales from the work of G. A. Henty* (1905).
21 Bristow, *Empire boys*, p. 147.   22 *Ibid.*, p. 37.   23 *Ibid.*

was the largest market for British book exports in the first half of the twentieth century, with a trade based largely on colonial editions. In 1901, after self-government, British publishers moved in to ensure a continued commercial advantage: Macmillan led the way, opening a branch in Melbourne in 1905, followed swiftly by OUP in 1908.

According to Graeme Johanson, the colonial edition was the 'cornerstone of British-Australian control over production, distribution and sale of all books in Australia' from the nineteenth until the mid-twentieth century.[24] Australia imported more books than any other part of the Empire in the early twentieth century and it was the largest market for British book exports from at least 1889–1953.[25] Indeed he considers that the trade in colonial editions to Australia was crucial to the success of British book exports in the early decades of the century: 'When the British Empire went into decline in the early twentieth century, the structural remnants of the British publishing and booktrade empire could rely on colonial editions to prop it up.'[26]

Publishers sought to implement the same commercial arrangements in the other newly established British dominions, but soon discovered that they were vulnerable to domestic and international competition and had to adopt new tactics to survive. Canada, for example, proved to be a much less secure market for British books due to its proximity to America. Immediately following self-government in Canada in 1906, Macmillan opened a branch in Toronto, but the branch manager, Frank Wise, found that the firm's colonial editions could not compete with the cheap and widely available American paperbacks. Wise reported back to London in 1906:

> The more I go into the 'Colonial Library' matter the more hopeless it seems to revive any market for them. This is true not only of your 'Colonial Library' but of Longmans and every other one. The American market, for one thing, seems to have upset it.[27]

Wise turned instead to the educational market, and commissioned titles specifically for Canadian school children. He was cautioned against this by Frederick Macmillan, who advised him from London in October 1910 that he should stick to the branch's main purpose – to sell books:

> we should be more than a little surprised and displeased if you embarked on any 'publishing venture' of importance without first consulting us. The primary business of the Macmillan Company of Canada is to sell the

24 Johanson, *Colonial editions in Australia*, p. 1.   25 *Ibid.*, pp. 6, 15.   26 *Ibid.*, p. 33.
27 F. Wise to G. J. Heath, 6 February 1906. Macmillan archive, Vol. XI. Correspondence with the Macmillan Company of Canada, Ltd. 1905–1930. BL Add. MS. 54796.

publications of the New York and London Houses, and the only kind of publishing which ought to originate in Canada is the production of school-books authorised by one or other of the provincial governments.[28]

Nevertheless, according to Ruth Panofsky's case study of the firm's history in Toronto, Wise persevered in these new publishing endeavours, was finan-cially successful and was able to grow in autonomy as a result. Hugh Eayrs, who succeeded Wise in 1921, published indigenous titles to support 'a burgeoning Canadian nationalism',[29] and after his death in 1940 the same strategy was continued by his successor, Ellen Elliot, 'an ardent nationalist who upheld the role of publisher as arbiter of cultural taste and education'.[30] Panofsky concludes that Macmillan was successful in its attempts to 'establish a national cultural identity for Canada'.[31] Competition from US publishers was also a problem for other British publishers in Canada, and they realised that they could not simply transfer publishing strategies from other post-colonial markets but had to adapt to local conditions. Robert Fraser's study of Thomas Nelson & Sons in the 1920s, for example, examines how they were compelled to 'regionalise their provision' in Canada: working closely in collaboration with directors of education in the various Canadian provinces and tailoring their textbooks to the needs of pupils in specific regions, namely Quebec, Saskatchewan and Ontario.[32]

The unification of South Africa in 1910 promised to offer opportunities for British publishers to become established in the new country's educational system, but it proved to be a particularly challenging environment, and Macmillan, OUP, Blackie and Longmans all competed for a share in the book market. The English and Afrikaans educational market was occupied by South African publisher-booksellers Juta & Co., Maskew Miller, Nasionale Pers and Darter Bros., while African education was mainly in the hands of church groups and Christian missions, which frequently had their own printing presses.

OUP's early history in Cape Town demonstrates some of the problems facing British publishers in South Africa in this period. The branch opened in 1914, but it soon became clear that the Afrikaans schoolbook market was saturated and that their main market was the white English-speaking minor-ity. By 1928, the Secretary of OUP, Kenneth Sisam, expressed his pessimism about the future of the branch: 'I have the impression that South Africa is not a very favourable educational market . . . A small country with two languages

28 Panofsky, 'One series after the other', p. 186. 29 Ibid., pp. 188, 192. 30 Ibid., p. 192.
31 Ibid., p. 197. 32 Fraser, 'School readers in the empire', p. 92.

and plenty of local publishers is not likely to find us much money.'[33] In the 1930s, the branch depended on the sale of Oxford English dictionaries, New Clarendon Shakespeare editions and other out-of-copyright reprint editions, as well as on its agency work for other British publishers.[34] Meanwhile, Longmans was thwarted in its many attempts to get books prescribed for the Transvaal and Cape Province school syllabuses during the 1930s and 1940s.[35] Indeed, in 1940, the Cape Town Book Committee issued a memorandum which explained 'the present practice of the Department [of Public Education] whereby preference is given to South African publications over overseas publications wherever quality and price are equal'.[36] Thus, in the face of local competition and entrenched anti-British sentiment, British publishers struggled for a place in the English and Afrikaans schoolbook market in South Africa.

Post-war trade agreements

The Second World War presented a major threat to Britain's privileged imperial book trade, as publishers lacked both the resources and the means of transport to supply their foreign markets. This was the result of the cumulative effects of rationing, difficulties of transportation, the loss of shipping and freight space, and the bombing of publishers' stock both in warehouses and in transit. The resulting incursions of American books into Australia, New Zealand, South Africa and Canada caused great consternation in Britain. As John Hench observes, 'Exporting books ... was of the greatest importance for British publishers both economically and psychologically', and the British book trade rallied to repel the challenge of the USA and to reassert Britain's traditional prerogatives.[37]

Stanley Unwin, Chairman of the Publishers Association, organised several delegations of publishers to the USA from 1942 to 1945. The result was the formation of two trade agreements: the British Commonwealth Market Agreement of 1946 and the Traditional Market Agreement of 1947, the latter of which had the tacit agreement of American publishers. In effect, these led to the creation of two national cartels which carved up world rights: under the terms of this agreement, British publishers acquiring rights to a book

---

33 Kenneth Sisam to Eric Parnwell, 30 May 1928. Oxford University Press archive. 'South African branch' OxPkt 165 (1) May 1928–July 1975.
34 Humphrey Milford to Kenneth Sisam, 11 July 1940. Oxford University Press archive. 'South African branch' OxPkt 165 (1) May 1928–July 1975.
35 Davis, 'Creating a book empire', p. 133.   36 Ibid.
37 Hench, Books as weapons, p. 198.

automatically acquired rights to its publication in the fifty-six British colonies and former colonies, and US publishers were in return entitled to expand into other English-speaking countries. The only exception to this agreement was Canada, which in practice was a market frequently conceded to American publishers after the Second World War.[38]

The chief concern of the British book trade was to protect its vital market in Australia, and for three further decades these trade agreements successfully served to achieve this. British publishers set up subsidiaries in Melbourne in the 1940s and 1950s; for example, Penguin established a branch in 1946 and Heinemann in 1948. The continued British domination of Australian publishing became a subject of concern to the federal government, which held a commission of inquiry into Australian publishing in 1945, in which Harold White, the Commonwealth Librarian, bemoaned the fact that Australia had no national publishing industry.[39] Australian readers were considered to be particularly disadvantaged by the fact that British copyright holders held the right to control the importation of the copyright work into the country, which led to delays in getting books imported, and meant that Australian readers had to pay more for British books than they might have for American editions.[40] In Richard Flanagan's view, the Australian book market from the mid-1940s to the mid-1960s remained 'a milch cow of British publishing'.[41]

Publishing and decolonisation

When India achieved independence in 1947, the loss of this crucial book market was lamented in the British book trade: Michael Joseph wrote in 1949 that 'the partial disintegration of the British empire has deprived English publishers of some hitherto exclusive markets'.[42] All foreign firms at this time were required to reduce their equity in Indian subsidiaries, leading Macmillan and Longmans to undergo 'cataclysmic restructuring', according to Chatterjee, although she attests that OUP, as a department of Oxford University, 'sailed serenely on'.[43] British books were not immediately restricted in India, as the British education system remained in place for

---

38 *Ibid.*, p. 212.   39 Flanagan, 'Colonies of the mind', p. 134.
40 Wiseman, 'Copyright and the regulations of the Australian publishing industry', p. 189.
41 Flanagan, 'Colonies of the mind', p. 134.
42 Joseph, *The adventure of publishing*, pp. 123–4.
43 Chatterjee, *Empires of the mind*, p. 11. For a discussion of OUP in India in the immediate post-war period, see Fraser, 'War and the colonial booktrade', pp. 144–9; for details of OUP's 'consistent growth in sales' in India in the 1950s and 1960s, see Chatterjee and Ray Murray, 'India', p. 668.

some time and there was a continued need to import books to support the curriculum.[44] The Indian government then oscillated between protectionism and liberalism: until 1957, books were imported into India on the Open General Licence, but from 1957 to 1977 the importing of books was regulated to conserve foreign exchange and protect the Indian book industry. Other measures were also introduced to stimulate the national Indian publishing industry, including the National Book Trust in the mid-1950s, a textbook subsidy scheme and special tax concessions for Indian publishers. Despite these protectionist measures, the balance of the Indian book trade continued to show a deficit until 1980, and the rate of book imports was almost five times in value that of book exports.[45]

Faced with the end of their book empire in India and the damaging effects of the Second World War, British publishers turned attention to Africa. Several publishers capitalised on the limited programme of educational and cultural investment implemented by the colonial office in the post-war period, and in particular on the establishment of colonial literature bureaux across the continent in the late-1940s and 1950s.

The East African Literature Bureau was instituted in November 1948 by the British colonial government, with a grant of £99,000. Charles Richards, formerly Literature Secretary to the Church Missionary Society, was appointed Director of the Bureau from 1949 to 1963. The headquarters of the Bureau were established in Nairobi, with branch offices set up in Uganda and Tanganyika, and its main aim was to 'stimulate the production of cheap books in bulk in Kiswahili . . . and to promote the creation of an indigenous literature written by Africans and with an African background'.[46] The scheme was extended to Central and Southern Africa, with the foundation of the Joint Publications Bureau of Northern Rhodesia and Nyasaland in 1948–49 as a separate government department. A memorandum issued by the bureau in 1949 explained that its main aim was to control reading matter in the colonies, in the context of miners' strikes and growing anti-colonial movements in the region:

> the demand for reading matter is far ahead of the supply of sound literature. There is thus opened a wide field for exploitation by purveyors of morally and politically pernicious literature, and there is ample evidence that this

44 Gupta, 'Educational publishing in India', p. 72.
45 Malhoutra and Kumar, *Indian publishing since independence*, p. 163.
46 The Colonial Office, 'The East African literature bureau', March 1949, Native Education Commission, Eiselen Commission, 1952, BC282. B1.1. University of Cape Town.

field is in fact being exploited. This problem will best be met by supplying sound and interesting books.[47]

The 'sound' literature produced by the bureaux was wide ranging, encompassing school textbooks, 'tribal histories', pro-British propaganda pamphlets, and African literature. It was decided that neither bureau should have its own printing press or carry out its own printing. Instead, they should each enter into partnerships with 'representatives of British firms of the highest standing', which they identified as Oxford University Press, Longmans, Macmillan and Pitman.[48] The publishers were keen to take on the larger editions, with their guaranteed profits, but needed some persuasion to take on the shorter editions of books in African languages. A publishing fund was therefore set up to subsidise the titles that could not be published at a profit by commercial firms; nearly £500 of government money was set aside for funding this scheme.[49] Ostensibly a means of developing a commercially viable book trade in these countries, this strategy also provided support for Britain's ailing post-war book trade.

What then was the main effect of these literature bureaux on the development of African print culture? Robert Fraser considers that the colonial literature bureaux were an important local means of nurturing African writers, 'a proactive and influential feature of the post-war and post-independence scene', which 'played a major role in the nurturing of new literatures, both in the vernacular and in English'.[50] By contrast, Ngũgĩ wa Thiong'o considers that they had an adverse effect on the development of an autonomous African literary tradition:

> The African novel and its development, since its inception early this century, have been adversely affected by two factors. The printing press, the publishing houses and the educational context of the novel's birth were controlled by the missionaries and the colonial administration ... In Rhodesia the Literature Bureau would not publish an African novel which had any but religious themes and sociological themes, which were free from politics. Retelling old fables and tales, yes. Reconstructions of precolonial magical and ritual practices, yes. Stories of characters who move from the darkness of the pre-colonial past to the light of the Christian present, yes. But any discussion of or any sign of dissatisfaction with colonialism. No![51]

---

47 'Memorandum on reasons, objects, functions and organisation' [c. 1949], Nyasaland and Northern Rhodesia Joint Publications Bureau, Native Education Commission, 1952, Eiselen Commission, BC282. B1.1. University of Cape Town.
48 *Ibid.* 49 *Ibid.* 50 Fraser, *Book history through postcolonial eyes*, p. 97.
51 wa Thiong'o, *Decolonising the mind*, p. 69.

Further criticism of the literature bureaux came from the Kenyan publisher Henry Chakava, who argued that the partnership between the East African Literature Bureau and British publishers was 'preparing the ground for the entrenchment of foreign publishers, particularly Longman, Oxford University Press, Macmillan and Nelson', and claimed that, despite good intentions, Richards unleashed 'a multinational ogre that was to dominate the post-independence publishing scene for many years'.[52]

The real entrenchment of British publishers in Africa occurred after political decolonisation in the late 1950s and early 1960s, when they rushed in to seize opportunities arising from the newly elected governments' commitments to school expansion. By 1968 in Kenya, nearly eighty British publishers were present in some form or other: Longmans, OUP and Heinemann had publishing branches, while others including Nelson, Evans, Pitman and Cambridge University Press had representatives in place or agency arrangements.[53] In Nigeria, OUP, Longmans, Macmillan, Heinemann Educational Books, Evans Brothers, Thomas Nelson, Cambridge University Press and the University of London Press all had offices in either Ibadan or Lagos.

British publishers faced the challenge of reconciling two major imperatives: on the one hand, the need to reposition themselves ideologically as publishers of African nationalism, and on the other hand, the concern to protect their export markets and to benefit from the new nations' investment in educational books. One effective strategy was to cultivate new alliances with the new African leaders in order to perpetuate their influence in the post-imperial world. Thus, OUP published the works of Julius Nyerere (first Prime Minister of Tanganyka 1960–64 and first President of Tanzania 1964–85), Jomo Kenyatta (first President of Kenya 1964–78) and Léopold Sédar Senghor (first President of Senegal 1960–80), but it was surpassed by its main rival, Macmillan. Immediately after resigning office as Prime Minister in 1963, Harold Macmillan took up chairmanship of the family's publishing firm from 1964 until 1974; he used his influence to set up semi-state publishing partnerships with governments across Africa for the publication of primary and secondary schoolbooks, including Ghana (1965), Uganda and Tanzania (1966), Zambia (1967) and Northern Nigeria (1972). The arrangements were widely criticised: Hans Zell for example, described them as 'lopsided ... "partnerships", in which Macmillan had everything to gain and virtually nothing to lose'. He argues that it was this 'commercial

52 Chakava, *Kenyan publishing*, pp. 119.   53 *Ibid.*, pp. 122–3.

opportunism, coupled with an attitude of indifference towards serving local needs, that brought the multinationals into general disrepute'.[54]

During the 1960s and 1970s, the African market for books – and particularly the Nigerian market – was crucial to British publishers. In 1971, 80 per cent of books and pamphlets imported to Nigeria came from Britain and £13 million in foreign exchange was spent on book imports.[55] Longmans alone had an annual turnover in Nigeria of nearly $4 million in 1972.[56] By 1981, the UK book market to Africa was worth £85 million, £36 million of which was to Nigeria alone.[57] Accusations of neo-colonialism were levelled, culminating in the conference 'Publishing in Africa in the 70s' at the University of Ife in Nigeria in 1973. The conference verdict was that 'the time has now arrived for the book industry to become primarily indigenised'.[58] A Nigerian publisher, G. O. Onibonoje, decreed that: 'The form of cultural revolution we demand must ensure that publishing in Africa is by Africans to disseminate and inculcate African culture and heritage and make the voice of Africa heard, clear and loud.'[59]

Several British publishers also registered concern about neo-imperialism in the British book trade in Africa, and embarked on African literary publishing, either as a counter-strategy or as a form of compensation. Alan Hill, for example, as managing director of Heinemann Educational Books, described the foundation of the African Writers Series as 'a momentous event in the cultural development of black Africa', which was set up in opposition to other British publishers who 'were taking their profits out of West Africa and putting nothing back in the way of investment in local publishing and encouragement of local authors'.[60] Launched in 1962 with the paperback edition of *Things Fall Apart* by Chinua Achebe, this series went on to become the major vehicle for African literary publishing in English, releasing 360 titles in total by authors including Cyprian Ekwensi, Ngũgĩ wa Thiong'o, Peter Abrahams, Elechi Amadi, Ayi Kwei Armah, Tayeb Salih, Mbella Sonne Dipoko, Buchi Emecheta, Bessie Head, Okot p'Bitek, Charles Mungoshi and Nadine Gordimer.[61] In the same year of 1962, at Oxford University Press, Rex Collings, editor in the Overseas Education department, successfully campaigned for the publication of original African writing in the

54 Zell, 'Publishing in Africa', p. 368.
55 McLean Rathgeber, 'Nigerian university presses', p. 14.
56 Dodson and Dodson, 'Publishing progress in Nigeria', p. 68.
57 *The Book Trade Yearbook 1988*, p. 33.
58 Oluwasanmi *et al.* (eds.), *Publishing in Africa in the seventies*, p. 4.
59 Onibonoje, 'Wanted! A cultural revolution', p. 275.
60 Hill, *In pursuit of publishing*, p. 120. 61 Currey, *Africa writes back*, pp. 301–10.

London-based Three Crowns series. He argued, 'I am convinced also that there is still a place for us in African publishing if we can plainly show that we are not in fact only interested in selling enormous quantities of primary school books by expatriate authors.'[62] The focus of the Three Crowns series was African drama, short stories and poetry, including the work of Wole Soyinka, Lewis Nkosi, John Pepper Clark, Obi Egbuna, Oswald Mtshali, Joe de Graft, Léopold Sédar Senghor and Athol Fugard, amongst others. Meanwhile, in the Nairobi branch of OUP, the branch manager Charles Lewis established three new literary series, New Drama from Africa, New Fiction from Africa and Poetry in English, pronouncing that 'the OUP has a responsibility in developing countries to plough back some of its profits into local development'.[63]

During the 1960s, the publication of African literature was a growing trend among London publishers, including Allen & Unwin, Cape, Collins, Gollancz, Hutchinson, John Murray, Methuen, Michael Joseph, Nelson, Penguin, Thames & Hudson and the University of London Press. André Deutsch set up a London-based African literature list and founded the East Africa Publishing House in Nairobi, which published for the Kenyan market through its Modern African Library. Longmans was slower to establish an African literary publishing programme than its competitors. During the 1960s and 1970s, the company published only a few novels by Mbella Dipoko, Ama Ata Aidoo, Efua Sutherland and Raymond Sarif Easmon, usually following the selection of the text for secondary school examinations. However, in 1977, Drumbeat was established as a series of African and Caribbean literature, with the first title Ama Ata Aidoo's *Our sister Killjoy*, and the series developed rapidly thereafter, building up to thirty titles by 1981. While many were reprints of previously published titles, new work was also published, including works by Zaynab Alkali, Festus Iyayi, Ben Okri, Isidore Okpewho and Miriam Tlali. Acquisition rates slowed down thereafter, and the series closed in 1985 with the final title John Pepper Clark's *State of the Union*. OUP's Three Crowns series had closed in 1976 and the African Writers Series rate of acquisitions contracted dramatically to only four new titles a year after 1981, finally closing in 2003.[64] These British series of African literature were established in the context of a seemingly unlimited demand for educational books in Africa, and although they served to provide African novelists, poets and dramatists with an international readership, the books were destined

---

62 Davis, 'The politics of postcolonial publishing', p. 227.
63 Davis, *Creating postcolonial literature*, pp. 57, 50.
64 Currey, *Africa writes back*, pp. 301–10.

predominantly for African schools, particularly in Nigeria. However, this was a market that proved to be very fragile.

Collapse of book empires

The East African economy suffered a wide-scale crisis in the early 1970s that precipitated a rapid retreat of British publishers from the region. Collins, Pitman, Cambridge University Press, Nelsons and Evans either closed their businesses or left them in the hands of local agents. OUP closed its office in Uganda and cut down on Nairobi office staff, while Longmans, Heinemann and Macmillan introduced local equity in the early 1970s. By the 1990s, publishing in East Africa was mainly in the hands of local publishers or of largely localised British multinationals. Then the book market in Nigeria folded as indigenisation decrees brought about local ownership of publishing companies in 1978. There was a drop in the price of petroleum, education spending was cut, and the dramatic economic crisis that ensued led to the closure of the foreign exchange in 1982. UK book exports to Nigeria fell dramatically from 16 per cent of all exports in 1981 to only 1 per cent in 1987, and the total African book market dropped from £85 million in 1981 to only £45 million in 1987. The *Book Trade Yearbook* of 1988 concluded that the African book market was 'an exceptionally volatile one'.[65]

As the African book markets dissolved, so did the Traditional Market Agreement. American publishers sought its abolition, and in 1976 it was deemed to be both an agreement that favoured UK book exports and one that was in breach of American anti-trust laws in the Supreme Court.[66] British publishers were badly hit by the loss of sales to the 'traditional territories', in particular to Australia. Trade reports noted that in the 1980s British publishers were exporting only about one-third of output, whereas in the early 1970s they had exported about 40 per cent of output.[67] This appeared to signify the end of Britain's book empires, yet publishers were swift to adapt rapidly and seek out new global opportunities.

One former colonial market that British publishers re-cultivated was that of South Africa. Trade with South Africa in the era of 'high apartheid' was extremely controversial, but faced with the loss of other traditional markets, British publishers increasingly came to depend on it. The imposition of Bantu Education after 1957 had led to the closure of mission schools and mission

65 *Book Trade Yearbook 1988*, p. 33.   66 Johanson, *Colonial editions in Australia*, p. 223.
67 *Book publishing keynote report 1988*, p. 31.

publishers, and British publishers had immediately seized the new opportunities, despite widespread protests about the apartheid education system. Longmans and OUP in particular benefited considerably from the Bantu education market in the 1970s and 1980s.[68] The majority of British books sold in South Africa were mass-market paperbacks, and all had to be submitted to government censorship boards before importation. Peter D. McDonald notes the widespread cooperation of British publishers with the South African censors at this time, in particular of Penguin, Gollancz, Faber, Heinemann and OUP.[69] By 1980, South Africa became the third largest export market for British books after the USA and Australia and was worth £13.4 million.[70] This increased to £26 million in 1987, and the *Book Trade Yearbook* of 1988 wrote of the 'consistency of the market of South Africa' which at the time was responsible for half of UK book exports to the African continent.[71]

Legacies of imperialism

Several commentators and critics have drawn attention to long-lasting legacies of imperialism in the international publishing industry. Altbach's extensive studies of the international book trade concern the enduring 'center and peripheries in the knowledge system'.[72] He highlights the global divide in book production and distribution, and argues that 'aspects of the international publishing situation are also dominated by the industrialised nations and, generally, serve the interests of these nations'.[73] In relation to literary studies, Pascale Casanova's *The world republic of letters* defines a nation's position in the international cultural hierarchy according to its levels of cultural autonomy: former colonial powers are characterised as autonomous literary spaces, 'most endowed in literary resources' which also exercise linguistic dominance,[74] whereas nations subjected to or emerging from colonisation are described as dominated spaces, marked by dependence on other literary capitals and weak publishing networks.[75] Her model of the 'literature-world' proposes a division between 'consecrated' nations and

---

68 Davis, *Histories of publishing under apartheid*, pp. 85–90.
69 McDonald, *The literature police*, pp. 105–6. See also Davis, *Histories of publishing under apartheid*, pp. 88–9.
70 *Book Facts 1995*, p. 97.   71 *The Book Trade Yearbook 1988*, p. 33.
72 Altbach and Teferra, *Publishing and development*, p. 4.
73 Altbach and Rathgeber, *Publishing in the Third World*, p. 13.
74 Altbach and Teferra, *Publishing and development*, pp. 108, 133, 109.
75 Casanova, *The world republic of letters*, pp. 111, 109.

'literarily dominated nations', which include 'colonised or otherwise dominated regions'. Yet, how aptly do these generalisations apply to all postcolonial publishing contexts?

India and Canada are countries that appear to complicate Casanova's analysis. Reports of publishing in India claim that government protectionist policies have been successful in developing a national publishing industry that is able to withstand dominance by multinational corporations. The UK Publishers Association report on Indian publishing in 2008 concluded that 'The market is not yet dominated by a few players, as is the case in so many countries. There are hundreds, probably thousands, of local publishers, publishing in all the local languages, including English.'[76] This view was confirmed by Suman Gupta, who in 2009 referred to 'the happy cooexistence of growing numbers of independents and multinationals' in twenty-first-century India.[77] Similarly, in Canada, a history of legislating against foreign ownership of publishing house, coupled with government subsidisation of Canadian-controlled publishing houses, strengthened the national industry. According to the UK Publishers Association and British Council report of 2004, Canada had a 'strong and viable indigenous book industry'.[78]

In Australia, the effects of colonialism on the book trade have evidently been longer lasting. The rise of publishing conglomerates in Australia in the 1990s provoked anxiety, and several legal measures were implemented to restrict the dominance of foreign publishers, including the 1991 Copyright Act, which restricted the rights of copyright owners to control the import of books into Australia, and the 2001 Parallel Importation Bill, which sought to prevent international price discrimination. Yet, the Australian publishing industry in 2007 was still found to be largely foreign-owned: the top twenty publishers in Australia produced three-quarters of the total book output, but only one of them, Allen & Unwin, was an Australian independent publisher.[79] According to David Carter, literary publishing in 2007 was still dominated by multinationals:

> The overall pattern of literary fiction publishing is clear: a handful of large publishers, mostly multinationals, produce the bulk of Australian literary fiction, followed by a somewhat larger mid-range comprising medium-sized independents or larger publishers with small fiction lists.[80]

76 Francis, *Publishing market profile: India*, p. 33.
77 Gupta, *Globalization and literature*, p. 163.
78 Heasman, *Publishing market profile: Canada*, p. 9.
79 Carter and Galligan (eds.), *Making books*, p. 6.
80 Carter, 'Literary fiction publishing', p. 242.

Indeed, Anne Galligan and David Carter conclude that Australia has remained primarily a 'book export destination' for foreign books, rather than an originating source, and that 'publishing has been dominated by British companies established to distribute British products'.[81]

The most damaging impact of British colonial and postcolonial publishing evidently occurred in sub-Saharan Africa. African publishers repeatedly argued that British publishers, together with the state publishers, had served to undermine the development of an indigenous publishing industry by winning educational book contracts in preference to local publishers and thereby monopolising the textbook market, which was the economic basis of the entire publishing industry in developing countries. Furthermore, Altbach and Rathgeber argued in 1980 that British government schemes to promote British books overseas also had a damaging effect on publishing in Africa:

> The British government, through the British Council and the English Language Book Scheme, has exported many millions of copies of books aimed at text use at the university level. These books, while no doubt serving some educational needs in the Third World, have also affected local publishing negatively by supplying books at subsidized prices and thereby driving local competing books from the market.[82]

UNESCO called for a coordinated programme of book development in Africa and other developing countries with the high-minded objective to rectify international 'book hunger' in an 'unevenly developed global communications environment', in Sarah Brouillette's words.[83] A series of seminars on the African book trade took place from the late 1960s to the early 1990s, funded by UNESCO and the Dag Hammarskjöld Foundation, for example the 'UNESCO Book Development Meeting' in Accra in 1968, the 'Ife Conference on Publishing and Book Development in Africa' in 1973, and the 'Publishing in the Third World' conference, Bellagio, Italy, in 1991. Yet, decades later, British educational publishing in Africa continues to be contentious, as illustrated by two recent judgements by the UK Serious Fraud Office. In July 2011, Macmillan was found guilty of 'unlawful conduct' relating to bribery over the supply of educational materials in Sudan, and allegations of corruption in Rwanda, Uganda and Zambia; it was made to pay out £11.3 million in a civil settlement.[84] The following year in July 2012, Oxford

81 Galligan, 'The culture of the publishing house', pp. 44, 36.
82 Altbach and Rathgeber, *Publishing in the third world*, p. 12.
83 Brouillette, 'UNESCO and the book in the developing world', p. 34.
84 Benedicte Page, 'Macmillan Education to move out of Africa', *Bookseller* 29 July 2011, www.thebookseller.com/news/macmillan-education-move-out-africa.

University Press was brought to the high court by the director of the Serious Fraud Office and was ordered to pay £1.9 million after two subsidiary companies based in Kenya and Tanzania were found to have bribed government officials for contracts to supply school textbooks in East Africa.[85]

What, finally, has been the legacy of imperialism on the UK book trade in general? Undoubtedly, book exports to the Commonwealth continued to be crucial in the late twentieth century. The *Book publishing keynote report* of 1992 concluded that the UK publishers had built their sales in the century largely on the back of exports: 'the industry has always exported a good deal which is largely based around the Commonwealth'.[86] The trend continued to the end of the century with an average of 22 per cent of British books exported to Commonwealth countries from 1993 to 2001.[87] However, the years 2009–14 saw a 5 per cent overall decline in British export revenue for printed and digital books, to £1,444 million annually.[88] Most pronounced was the decline in UK book sales to Africa, which dropped by 33 per cent to £79 million,[89] while sales to Australasia declined by 13.5 per cent in the same period to £118 million.[90] Despite this, the notion of Britain as an international benefactor of books still resonates: the UK Publishers Association announced in 2013 that with 41 per cent of its book sales coming from exports, 'the UK is the largest exporter of books in the world'.[91]

The relationship between the British book trade and British imperialism was, therefore, reciprocal and mutually advantageous: the British book played a significant role in the cultural and educational mission of the colonial enterprise in the first half of the twentieth century, and the Empire was vital to the prosperity of British publishers. What is perhaps more striking is that, after decolonisation, British publishers continued to regard the book markets in former colonies as their prerogative. While local conditions in various colonial and postcolonial contexts led to markedly different outcomes, it is evident that highly asymmetrical relationships were established between the book industry in the metropole and in many of the dependencies. In the book trade – both in Britain and in many of its former colonies – the structures and hierarchies of imperialism long survived the demise of colonial rule itself.

85 Jeevan Vasagar, 'Oxford University Press fined £1.9m over bribery by African subsidiary firms', *Guardian* 3 July 2012.
86 *Book publishing keynote report 1992*, p. 2.
87 Calculated from statistics of book exports to the Commonwealth in *Book Facts 1996–2001*.
88 *PA Statistics Yearbook 2014*, p. 21.   89 *Ibid.*, p. 22.   90 *Ibid.*, p. 27.
91 Publishers Association, *Publishing and the economy*.

Bibliography

All books are published in London unless otherwise indicated.

A short history of Elsevier in celebration of the 125th anniversary of Elsevier and the 425th anniversary of the House of Elzevir (Amsterdam, 2005)

Aalbersberg, Ijsbrand Jan *et al.* 'Bringing digital science deep inside the scientific article: the Elsevier article of the future project', *Liber Quarterly* 23 (2014), pp. 274–99

Abbott, John *The story of Francis, Day & Hunter* (1952)

Abel, Richard 'Introduction', in Richard Abel and Gordon Graham (eds.), *Immigrant publishers: the impact of expatriate publishers in Britain and America in the 20th century* (2009), pp. 1–7

Abel, Richard and Gordon Graham (eds.) *Immigrant publishers: the impact of expatriate publishers in Britain and America in the 20th century* (2009)

Adamson, Judith *Charlotte Haldane: woman writer in a man's world* (1998)

Alderson, Brian 'Some notes on children's book illustration 1915–1985', in Alan Horne (ed.), *The dictionary of 20th century British book illustrators* (Woodbridge, 1994), pp. 45–63

Aldiss, Brian *Bury my heart at W. H. Smith's* (2013)

Aldiss, Brian and David Wingrove *Trillion year spree: the true history of science fiction* (1986)

Allegro, John *The end of the road* (1972)

　The sacred mushroom and the cross: a study of the nature and origins of Christianity within the fertility cults of the Ancient Near East (1970)

Allen, Walter *As I walked down New Grub Street: memories of a writing life* (1981)

　'Authorship', in John Hampden (ed.), *The book world today: a new survey of the making and distribution of books in Britain* (1957), pp. 17–29

Alleyne, Brian *Radicals against race: black activism and cultural politics* (Oxford, 2002)

Altbach, Philip G. (ed.) *Publishing and development in the third world* (1992)

Altbach, Philip G. and Eva-Maria Rathgeber *Publishing in the third world: trend report and bibliography* (New York, 1980)

Altbach, Philip G. and Damtew Teferra *Publishing and development: a book of readings* (Chestnut Hill, MA, 1998)

Anderson, Robert *British universities past and present* (2006)

Andrews, Bob *The fixer* (Bangkok, 2012)

Andriesse, Cornelius D. *Dutch messengers: a history of science publishing, 1930–1980* (Leiden, 2008)

Arnold, Matthew *Culture and anarchy* (1869)

Arnot, Robert Page *et al. Forging the weapon: the struggle of the* Labour Monthly, *1921–1941* (1941)

Ashley, Bob, Joanne Hollows, Steve Jones and Ben Taylor (eds.) *Food and cultural studies* (2004)

Ashley, Mike *The age of the storytellers: British popular fiction magazines, 1880–1950* (2006)

Ashton, Rosemary *146 Strand: a radical address in Victorian London* (2006)

Atkin, Jonathan *A war of individuals: Bloomsbury attitudes to the Great War* (Manchester, 2002)

Attenborough, John *A living memory: Hodder and Stoughton Publishers, 1868–1975* (1975)

Attwooll, David 'Reference publishing', in Philip Altbach and Edith S. Hoshino (eds.), *International book publishing: an encyclopedia* (1995), pp. 295–302

Avery, Gillian 'Popular education and big money: Mee, Hammerton and Northcliffe', in Julia Briggs, Dennis Butts and M. O. Grenby (eds.), *Popular children's literature in Britain* (Aldershot, 2008), pp. 229–43

Baggs, Chris 'How well read was my valley? Reading, popular fiction, and the miners of South Wales, 1875–1939', *Book History* 4 (2001), pp. 277–301

Baierle, Christian *Der Musikverlag* (Munich, 2009)

Baines, Jess 'The freedom of the press belongs to those who control the press: the emergence of radical and community printshops in 1970s London', in Nico Carpentier (ed.), *Communicative approaches to politics and ethics in Europe* (Tartu, 2009), pp. 113–27

Baines, Phil *Penguin by design: a cover story 1935–2005* (2005)

Baker, John 'Book clubs', in John Hampden (ed.), *The book world: a new survey* (1957), pp. 120–7

Low cost of bookloving: an account of the first twenty-one years of the Readers Union (1958)

Baker, Martin *Artists of* Radio Times: *a golden age of British illustration* (Oxford, 2002)

Baker, William and John C. Ross *Harold Pinter: a bibliographical history* (2005)

Baldick, Chris *The Oxford English literary history. 10. 1910–1940: the modern movement* (Oxford, 2005)

Baldwin, Dean *Art and commerce in the British short story, 1880–1950* (2013)

Ballard, J. G. *Miracles of life: Shanghai to Shepperton, an autobiography* (2013)

Bann, David *The all new print production handbook* (Hove, 2006)

Barassi, Veronica 'When materiality counts: the social and political importance of activist magazines in Europe', *Global Media and Communication* 9 (2013), pp. 135–51

Barclay, William *Testament of faith: a spiritual autobiography* (1975)

Barker, Martin *A haunt of fears: the strange history of the British horror comics campaign* (1984)

Barker, R. E. and G. R. Davies (eds.) *Books are different: an account of the defence of the Net Book Agreement before the restrictive practices court in 1962* (1966)

Barlow, Peppy 'Educational publishers: enquiry 2', *Education + Training* 11:7 (1969), pp. 270–1

Barnes, John, Bill Bell, Rimi B. Chatterjee, Wallace Kirsop and Michael Winship 'A place in the world', in David McKitterick (ed.), *The Cambridge history of the book in Britain. 6. 1830–1914* (Cambridge, 2009), pp. 595–634

Barnet, Belinda 'The technical evolution of Vannevar Bush's Memex', *Digital Humanities Quarterly* 2:1 (2008). www.digitalhumanities.org/dhq/vol/2/1/000015/000015.html

Barnett, Vincent L. and Alexis Weedon *Elinor Glyn as novelist, moviemaker, glamour icon and businesswoman* (Abingdon, 2014)

Barnhisel, Greg *Cold War modernists: art, literature and American cultural diplomacy* (New York, 2015)

Barnhisel Greg and Catherine Turner (eds.) *Pressing the fight: print, propaganda and the Cold War* (Amherst, MA, 2010)

Barr, James *Fundamentalism* (1977)

Barrie, J. M. *Sentimental Tommy* (1896)

Barry, F. C. 'Can we imitate Christ?', in Leonard Hodgson (ed.), *God and the world through Christian eyes*, 2 vols. (1933)

Bartie, Angela *The Edinburgh Festivals: culture and society in post-war Britain* (Edinburgh, 2013)

Bartie, Angela and Eleanor Bell *The International Writers' Conference revisited: Edinburgh, 1962* (Glasgow, 2012)

Bartlett, Sir Basil Hardington *Writing for television* (1955)

Bartolini, Nadia *et al.* 'Psychics, crystals, candles and cauldrons: alternative spiritualities and the question of their esoteric economies', *Social and Cultural Geography* 14 (2013), pp. 367–88

Bartram, Colin *Publishing in wartime: the survival & success of the book, 1939–1945* (Oxford, 1973)

Barty-King, Hugh *Her Majesty's Stationery Office: the story of the first two hundred years* (1986)

Batty, Ronald F. *How to run a twopenny library* (1938)

Bayard, Pierre *How to talk about books you haven't read*, trans. Jeffrey Mehlman (New York, 2009)

Beard, Roger 'Educational publishers: enquiry 1', *Education + Training* 11:7 (1969), pp. 268–9

Beauman, Nicola *A very great profession: the woman's novel, 1914–1939* (1983)

Becher, Tom and Brian Young 'Planning for change', in Asa Briggs (ed.), *Essays in the history of publishing* (1974), pp. 389–418

Bedford, Sybille *Aldous Huxley: a biography. 1. 1894–1939* (1973)

Beetham, Margaret *A magazine of her own? Domesticity and desire in the women's magazine, 1800–1914* (1996)

Bell, John 'Publishing for young readers', in John Hampden (ed.), *The book world today: a new survey of the making and distribution of books in Britain* (1957), pp. 90–5

Bell, Robert E., Gerald Fowler and Ken Little *Education in Great Britain and Ireland: a source book* (1973)

Beloff, Michael *The plateglass universities* (1968)

Bennett, Alan 'Preface', in *The history boys* (New York, 2004)

Bennett, Arnold *Arnold Bennett: the Evening Standard years*, ed. Andrew Mylett (Hamden, CT, 1974)

    Letters of Arnold Bennett. 3. 1916–1931, ed. James Hepburn (Oxford, 1970)

Bennett, Bryan and Anthony Hamilton 'Edwin Arnold', in Jonathan Rose and Patricia J. Anderson (eds.), *Dictionary of literary biography. 112. British literary publishing houses, 1881–1965* (Detroit, 1991), pp. 19–25

Bennett, Mary *Ford Madox Brown: a catalogue raisonné*, vol. 1 (2010)

Berliant, Howard M. and Bruce Abit *Jewish literary marketplace: a directory of the press, periodicals, publishers, and booksellers* (Milwaukee, 1979)

Berry, Dave, Liz Cooper and Charles Landry *Where is the other news? The newstrade & the radical press* (1980)

Beschler, Edwin F. 'The immigrants: Academic Press: Walter J. Johnson and Kurt Jacoby', *Logos* 18 (2007), pp. 153–66

Bird, Claire 'Oxford Journals' adventures in open access', *Learned Publishing* 21 (2008), pp. 200–8

Birkett, Jennifer *Margaret Storm Jameson: a life* (Oxford, 2009)

Birkett, Norman *Books are essential* (1951)

Black, Alistair 'The past public library observed: user perceptions and recollections of the twentieth-century British public library recorded in the Mass-Observation archive', *Library Quarterly* 76:4 (2006), pp. 438–55

   The public library in Britain, 1914–2000 (2000)

Black, Alistair and Peter Hoare (eds.) *The Cambridge history of libraries in Britain and Ireland.* 3. *1850–2000* (Cambridge, 2008)

Black, Michael *Cambridge University Press, 1584–1984* (Cambridge, 1984)

   Learning to be a publisher: Cambridge University Press 1951–1987, personal reminiscences (Cambridge, 2011)

Blackie, Agnes *A. C. Blackie & Son 1809–1959: a short history of the firm* (Glasgow and London, 1959)

Blond, Anthony *The publishing game* (1971)

Bloom, Ursula *He lit the lamp: a biography of Professor A. M. Low* (1959)

Bloomfield, Barry *Philip Larkin: a bibliography, 1933–1994* (2002)

Bloomfield, Barry and Edward Mendelson *W. H. Auden: a bibliography, 1934–1969*, second edition (Charlottesville, VA, 1972)

Blumberg, Rae Lesser *Gender bias in textbooks: a hidden obstacle on the road to gender equality in education* (2007)

Boeing, Volker 'Editorial and production workflows', in Sally Morris, Ed Barnas, Douglas LaFrenier and Margaret Reich (eds.), *The handbook of journal publishing* (Cambridge 2013), pp. 195–223

Bogic, Anna 'Why philosophy went missing: understanding the English version of Simone de Beauvoir's *Le deuxième sexe*', in Luise von Flotow (ed.), *Translating women* (Ottawa, 2011), pp. 151–66

Bolitho, Hector *A Batsford century: the record of a hundred years of publishing and bookselling, 1843–1943* (1943)

Bonham-Carter, Victor *Authors by profession.* 1. *From the introduction of printing to the Copyright Act of 1911* (1978)

   Authors by profession. 2. *From the Copyright Act 1911 until the end of 1981* (1984)

Book Marketing Ltd *Multimedia and the Internet: a survey of book trade activity* (1997)

Book publishing keynote report 1988 (Hampton, Middlesex, 1988)

Book publishing keynote report 1992 (Hampton, Middlesex, 1992)

Borg, Alan 'Director's Foreword', in Elizabeth James (ed.), *The Victoria and Albert Museum: a bibliography and exhibition chronology, 1852–1996* (1998)

Bowden, John 'SCM Press: fifty years of prophetic publishing', *Bookseller* 17 (November 1979), pp. 2,270–2

Bowen, Phil *A gallery to play to* (Liverpool, 2008)

Bowler, Peter J. *Reconciling science and religion: the debate in twentieth-century Britain* (Chicago, 2001)

    Science for all: the popularization of science in early twentieth-century Britain (Chicago, 2009)

Bowman, Marion 'Understanding Glastonbury as a site of consumption', in Jordan Lynch, Jolyon Mitchell and Anna Strhan (eds.), *Religion, media and culture: a reader* (2011), pp. 11–22

Boyce, David *This writing business* (1946)

Bradbury, Malcolm 'The bridgeable gap', *Times Literary Supplement* 17 January 1992, pp. 7–9

Bradford, Richard *The life of a long-distance writer: a biography of Alan Sillitoe* (2008)

Bradley, Sue (ed.) *The British book trade: an oral history* (2008)

Bradshaw, David and Rachel Potter (eds.) *Prudes on the prowl: fiction and obscenity in England, 1850 to the present day* (Oxford, 2013)

Bradshaw, Ross 'A huge comrade called Boris, or a short history of radical bookselling', *Federation Magazine* 22 (Summer 2001), pp. 8–11

Braithwaite, Brian and Joan Barrell *The business of women's magazines* (1988)

Brewer, Susan *The history of girls' comics* (Barnsley, 2010)

Brewitt-Taylor, Sam 'The invention of a "secular society"? Christianity and the sudden appearance of secularization discourses in the British national media, 1961–4', *Twentieth-Century British History* 24 (2013), pp. 327–50

Brewster, Bill '*When Saturday Comes* and other football fanzines', *Sports Historian* 13 (1993), pp. 11–21

Briggs, Asa *A history of Longmans and their books 1724–1990: longevity in publishing* (2008)

    The history of broadcasting in the United Kingdom. 2. The golden age of the wireless (Oxford, 1965)

    The history of broadcasting in the United Kingdom. 5. Competition, 1955–1974 (Oxford, 1995)

Briggs, Asa and Peter Burke *A social history of the media: from Gutenberg to the Internet* (2002)

Bristow, Joseph *Empire boys: adventures in a man's world* (1991)

Brock, William H. and Edgar W. Jenkins 'Frederick W. Westaway and science education: an endless quest', in Michael R. Matthews (ed.), *International handbook of research in history, philosophy and science teaching* (Dordrecht, 2014), pp. 2,359–82

Brock, W. H. and A. J. Meadows *The lamp of learning: two centuries of publishing at Taylor & Francis*, second edition (1998)

Brogan, Hugh *The life of Arthur Ransome* (1984)

Broks, Peter *Media science before the Great War* (1996)

    Understanding popular science (Maidenhead, 2006)

Brome, Vincent *J. B. Priestley* (Looe, 2001)

Brophy, John *Britain needs books* (1942)

Brouillette, Sarah *Literature and the creative economy* (Stanford, 2014)

    'UNESCO and the book in the developing world', *Representations* 127 (Summer 2014), pp. 33–54

Brown, Callum '"The unholy Mrs Knight" and the BBC: secular humanism and the threat to the Christian nation, c.1945–1960' *English Historical Review* 127 (2012), pp. 345–76

Brown, Douglas *Darton, Longman and Todd: a short history* (1980)

Brown, Judith *John Marco Allegro: the maverick of the Dead Sea Scrolls* (2005)

Brown, Peter 'The move of US publishers overseas', in Einar H. Fredriksson (ed.), *A century of science publishing: a collection of essays* (Amsterdam, 2001), pp. 139–45

Brown, Richard 'University press forum 2011' *Journal of Scholarly Publishing* 43:1 (2011), pp. 1–13

Browne, John Paddy *Map cover art: a pictorial history of Ordnance Survey colour illustrations* (Southampton, 1991)

Bruce, F. F. *History of the Bible in English* (1961; Guildford, 1979)

Bruce, Steve 'Good intentions and bad sociology: New Age authenticity and social roles', *Journal of Contemporary Religion* 13 (1998), pp. 23–35

'Les limites du marché religieux', *Social Compass* 53 (2006), pp. 33–48

Bryant, Mary Nell 'English language publication and the British traditional market agreement', *Library Quarterly* 49 (1979), pp. 371–98

Buchan, John *Memory hold-the-door* (1940)

Buford, Brian 'Introduction', *Granta* 3 (1980), pp. 7–16

Buitenhuis, Peter *The Great War of words: literature as propaganda, 1914–1918 and after* (1989)

Burke, Christopher 'The early years', in Andrew Boag and Lawrence W. Wallis (eds.), *One hundred years of type making, 1897–1997*, Monotype Recorder Centenary Issue, new series, No. 10 (Redhill, 1997), pp. 4–13

Burnham, John C. *How superstition won and science lost: popularizing science and health in the United States* (New Brunswick, NJ, 1987)

Butcher, David *Official publications in Britain*, second edition (1991)

Butts, Denis *Children's literature and social change: some case studies from Barbara Hoffman to Philip Pullman* (Cambridge, 2010)

Byrne, Georgina *Modern spiritualism and the Church of England, 1850–1939* (Woodbridge, 2010)

Cadman, Eileen, Gail Chester and Agnes Pivot, *Rolling our own: women as printers, publishers and distributors* (1981)

Cadogan, Mary and Patricia Craig *You're a brick, Angela! The girls' story 1839–1985* (1985)

Caesar, Adrian *Dividing lines: poetry, class and ideology in the 1930s* (Manchester, 1991)

Cahn, Robert W. 'The origins of the Pergamon Press: Rosbaud and Maxwell', *European Review* 2:1 (1994), pp. 37–42

Campsall, Ian 'From the front line of war to the front line of publishing: digital memory, milblogging, and the war memoir', unpublished MA dissertation (Oxford Brookes University, 2011)

Cannadine, David (ed.) *History and the media* (Basingstoke, 2004)

Carey, John *The intellectuals and the masses: pride and prejudice amongst the literary intelligentsia, 1880–1939* (1992)

William Golding: the man who wrote Lord of the Flies (2012)

Carnell, E. J. *County libraries: retrospect and forecast* (1938)

Carpenter, Edward *My days and dreams* (1916)

Carpenter, Humphrey *The seven lives of John Murray: the story of a publishing dynasty* (2009)

Carrette, Jeremy and Richard King *Selling spirituality: the silent takeover of religion* (2004)

Carter, David 'Literary fiction publishing', in David Carter and Anne Galligan (eds.), *Making books: contemporary Australian publishing* (Queensland, 2007), pp. 230–46

Carter, David and Anne Galligan (eds.), *Making books: contemporary Australian publishing* (St Lucia, Queensland, 2007)

Carter, John *Taste & technique in book collecting: a study of recent developments in Great Britain and the United States* (Cambridge, 1948)

(ed.) *New paths in book collecting* (1934)

Carter, Sebastian 'Printing and the mind of man', *Matrix* 20 (2000), pp. 172–80

'Typeface design for the Monotype Corporation', in Judith Slinn, Sebastian Carter and Richard Southall, *History of the Monotype Corporation* (2014), pp. 177–302

Casanova, Pascale *The world republic of letters* (Cambridge, MA, 2004)

Cauveren, Sydney *A. L. Rowse: a bibliophile's extensive bibliography* (Lanham, MD, 2000)

Cecil, Mirabel *Sebastian Walker 1942–91: a kind of Prospero* (1996)

Chakava, Henry 'Kenyan publishing: independence and dependence', in Philip G. Altbach (ed.), *Publishing and development in the third world* (1992), pp. 119–50

Chambers, Aidan *The reluctant reader* (1969)

Champion, Justin 'Seeing the past: Simon Schama's "A history of Britain" and public history', *History Workshop Journal* 56 (2003), pp. 153–77

Chapman, Ian 'Paperback publishing', in Peter Owen (ed.), *Publishing now* (1993), pp. 48–57

Chapman, James *British comics: a cultural history* (2011)

Chapter and verse: Edinburgh, a world City of Literature (Edinburgh, 2004)

Chatterjee, Rimi B. *Empires of the mind: a history of the Oxford University Press in India under the Raj* (New Delhi, 2006)

'Macmillan in India: a short account of the company's trade with the sub-continent', in Elizabeth James (ed.), *Macmillan: a publishing tradition* (Basingstoke, 2002), pp. 153–69

Chatterjee, Rimi B. and Padmini Ray Murray 'India', in Wm Roger Louis (ed.), *History of Oxford University Press. 3. 1896 to 1970* (Oxford, 2013), pp. 649–72

Cherns, J. J. *Official publishing: an overview* (Oxford, 1979)

Chester, Gail, 'Book publishing – the gentleperson's profession?', in Sarah Richardson (ed.), *Writing on the line: twentieth century working-class women writers* (1996)

'The anthology as a medium for feminist debate in the UK', *Women's Studies International Forum* 25:2 (2002), pp. 193–207

Chidgey, Red 'Free, trade: distribution economics in feminist zine networks', *Signs: Journal of Women in Culture and Society* 35:1 (2009), pp. 28–37

Child, John *Industrial relations in the British printing industry* (1967)

Church, Michael 'Survival of the fattest?' *Times Educational Supplement* 14 June 1974, pp. 34–5

Cinamon, Gerald (ed.) *Hans Schmoller: his life and work* (1987)

Clair, Colin *A chronology of printing* (1969)

Clark, Alan and Laurel Clark *Comics: an illustrated history* (1991)

Clark, Charles *Publishing agreements: a book of precedents* (1980)

Clark, Christina and Lizzie Poulton *Book ownership and its relation to reading enjoyment, attitudes, behaviour and attainment* (2011)

Clark, Giles and Angus Phillips *Inside book publishing*, fourth edition (2008)

Inside book publishing, fifth edition (2014)

Cockburn, Cynthia *Brothers: male dominance and technological change* (1983)

Coggan, Donald *The book for to-day: broadcasts on the bible* (1949)

Colclough, Stephen 'Distribution', in David McKitterick (ed.), *The Cambridge history of the book in Britain. 6. 1830–1914* (Cambridge, 2009), pp. 238–80

'"No such bookselling has ever before taken place in this country": propaganda and the wartime distribution practices of W. H. Smith & Son', in Mary Hammond and Shafquat Towheed (eds.), *Publishing in the First World War: essays in book history* (Basingstoke, 2007), pp. 27–45

Cole, Margaret *Books and the people* (1938)

Collini, Stefan *Absent minds: intellectuals in Britain* (Oxford, 2006)

Common reading: critics, historians, publics (Oxford, 2008)

English pasts: essays in history and culture (Oxford, 1999)

Public moralists: political thought and intellectual life in Britain 1850–1930 (Oxford, 1991)

'Richard Hoggart, literary criticism and cultural decline in twentieth-century Britain', in Sue Owen (ed.), *Richard Hoggart and cultural studies* (Basingstoke, 2008), pp. 33–56

'"The Chatto List": publishing literary criticism in mid-twentieth century Britain', *Review of English Studies* 63:261 (2012), pp. 634–63

Connon, Bryan *Beverley Nichols: a life* (1991)

Cooper, Victoria L. *The house of Novello: practice and policy of a Victorian music publisher, 1829–1866* (Aldershot, 2003)

Cooter, Roger and Stephen Pumphrey 'Separate spheres and public places: reflections on the history of science popularization and on science in popular culture', *History of Science* 32 (1994), pp. 232–67

Cope, Bill and Angus Phillips (eds.) *The future of the academic journal*, second edition (Amsterdam, 2014)

(eds.) *The future of the book in the digital age* (Amsterdam, 2006)

Cope, Dave *Central Books: a brief history, 1939 to 1999* (1999)

Cowie, A. P. (ed.) *Oxford history of English lexicography*, vols. 1 and 2 (Oxford, 2009)

Cox, Brian 'The Pergamon phenomenon 1951–1991: Robert Maxwell and scientific publishing', *Learned Publishing* 15:4 (2002), 273–8

Cox, Howard and Simon Mowatt *Revolutions from Grub Street: a history of magazine publishing in Britain* (Oxford, 2014)

Cox, Michael *Granada Television: the first generation* (Manchester, 2003)

Crandall, Nadia 'Children's authors', *New Review of Children's Literature and Librarianship* 12 (2006), pp. 117–25

'Children's book publishing in the United Kingdom: new models for a new marketplace', *New Review of Children's Literature and Librarianship* 12 (2006), pp. 215–29

'The UK children's book business 1995–2004: a strategic analysis', *New Review of Children's Literature and Librarianship* 12 (2006), pp. 1–18

Crawford, Elizabeth *The women's suffrage movement: a reference guide 1866–1928* (1999)

Crawford, Robert *The modern poet: poetry, academia, and knowledge since the 1750s* (Oxford, 2001)

Crewe, Quentin *The frontiers of privilege: a century of social conflict as reflected in the Queen* (1961)

Crickman, Robin 'The emerging information professional', *Library Trends* 28.2 (1979), pp. 311–27

Crisp, N. J. 'The short story scandal', *Author* (Winter 1965), pp. 14–16

Croome, Lesley 'A million a month', *TLS Children's Books* (15 June 1973), pp. 1–2

Crossick, Geoffrey *Monographs and open access: a report to HEFCE* (2015). www.hefce.ac.uk/pubs/rereports/year/2015/monographs

Crouch, Marcus *The Nesbit tradition: the children's novel 1945–1970* (1972)

Treasure seekers and borrowers (1962)

Crowley, David *Magazine covers* (2003)

Crutchley, Brooke *A printer's Christmas books 1930–58* (Cambridge, 1959)

Crystal, David *Just a phrase I'm going through* (2009)

'Some indexing decisions in the Cambridge encyclopaedia family', *The Indexer* 19:3 (1995), pp. 177–83

Cumbers, Frank *The book room: the story of the Methodist Publishing House and Epworth Press* (1956)

Currey, James *Africa writes back: the African Writers Series and the launch of African literature* (Oxford, 2008)

Currey, R. N. *Poets of the war of 1939–1945* (1960)

Currie, Tony *The Radio Times story* (Tiverton, 2001)

D'Arch Smith, Timothy *R. A. Caton and the Fortune Press: a memoir and a hand list* (1983)

Dancyger, Irene *World of women: an illustrated history of women's magazines 1700–1970* (Dublin, 1978)

Daniell, David *The Bible in English: its history and influence* (2003)

Darlow, Michael and Gillian Hodson *Terence Rattigan: the man and his work* (1979)

Davies, Alan *A. J. Cronin: the man who created Dr Finlay* (2011)

Davies, Florence *Books in the school curriculum: a compilation and review of research relating to voluntary and intensive reading* (1986)

Davies, Norman *Europe east and west* (2007)

Davis, Caroline 'Creating a book empire: Longmans in Africa 1900–1994', in Caroline Davis and David Johnson (eds.), *The book in Africa: critical debates* (Basingstoke, 2015), pp. 128–52

  Creating postcolonial literature: African writers and British publishers (Basingstoke, 2013)

  'Histories of publishing under apartheid: Oxford University Press in South Africa', *Journal of Southern African Studies* 37 (2011), pp. 79–98

  'Postcolonial literary publishing: Oxford University Press in Africa and the Three Crowns series', unpublished doctoral dissertation, Open University (2010)

  'The politics of postcolonial publishing: Oxford University Press's Three Crowns series 1962–1976', *Book History* 8 (2005), pp. 227–44

Davis, Thomas *Shifting sands: the rise and fall of biblical archaeology* (Oxford, 2004)

Davison, Peter (ed.) *George Orwell: a life in letters* (2010)

  (ed.) *Literary taste, culture and mass communication. 10: Authorship* (Cambridge, 1978)

Dawson, Paul *Creative writing and the new humanities* (2005)

Dawson, Michael 'S. Louis Giraud and the development of pop-up books', *Antiquarian Book Monthly Review* 18 (1991), pp. 218–22

De Beer, Marietjie, Marieta van der Merwe, Liezl Ball and Ina Fourie 'Legal deposit of electronic books – a review of challenges faced by national libraries', *Library Hi Tech* 34:1 (2016), pp. 87–103

de Bellaigue, Eric *British book publishing as a business since the 1960s: selected essays* (2004)

de Grazia, Victoria and Ellen Furlough *The sex of things: gender and consumption in historical perspective* (Berkeley and Los Angeles, 1996)

de Groot, Jerome *Consuming history: historians and heritage in contemporary popular culture* (2009)

de la Mare, Richard *A publisher on book production* (1936)

Dean, John 'London Bible House in the 1950s: an illustrated reminiscence', in Stephen Batalden, Kathleen Cann and John Dean (eds.), *Sowing the word: the British and Foreign Bible Society* (Sheffield, 2004), pp. 81–97

Deller, Ruth A., Sarah Harman and Bethan Jones 'Introduction to the special issue: reading the *Fifty Shades* phenomenon', *Sexualities* 16:8 (2013), pp. 859–63

Dempster, John *The T. & T. Clark story: a Victorian publisher and the new theology, with an epilogue covering the twentieth-century history of the firm* (Edinburgh, 1992)

Denham, Debbie 'Public library services for children', in Alistair Black and Peter Hoare (eds.), *The Cambridge history of libraries in Britain and Ireland. 3. 1850–2000* (Cambridge, 2006), pp. 92–109

Denniston, Robin *Partly living: some understanding of experience* (1967)

Derrick, Robin and Robin Muir *Vogue covers: on fashion's front page* (2008)

Di Liddo, Annalisa *Alan Moore: comics as performance, fiction as scalpel* (Raleigh, NC, 2008)

DiCenzo, Maria, Lucy Delap and Lelia Ryan *Feminist media history: suffrage, periodicals and the public sphere* (Basingstoke, 2010)

Dickinson, Robert *Imprinting the sticks: the alternative press outside London* (Aldershot, 1997)

Diemert, Brian 'The anti-American: Graham Greene and the Cold War in the 1950s', in Andrew Hammond (ed.), *Cold War literature: writing the global conflict* (2006), pp. 212–25

Dillistone, F. W. *Christianity and communication* (1956)

Dilnot, George *The romance of the Amalgamated Press* (1925)

Dodson, Don and Barbara Dodson, 'Publishing progress in Nigeria', *Scholarly Publishing* 4 (1972), pp. 61–72

Donahaye, Jasmine *Three percent? Publishing data and statistics on translated literature in the UK and Ireland* (Aberystwyth, 2012). www.lit-across-frontiers.org/wp-content/uplo ads/2013/03/Publishing-Data-and-Statistics-on-Translated-Literature-in-the-United-Kingdom-and-Ireland-A-LAF-research-report-March-2013-final.pdf

Donaldson, George 'Penguin English Library: a really good start for the general reader', in William Wootten and George Donaldson (eds.), *Reading Penguin: a critical anthology* (Newcastle upon Tyne, 2013), pp. 117–24

Douglas, Keith, 'Poets in this war', in *The Letters*, ed. Desmond Graham (Manchester, 2000), pp. 350–3

Dover, Bruce *Rupert's adventures in China: how Murdoch lost a fortune and found a wife* (Edinburgh, 2008)

Dowson Jane *Women's poetry of the 1930s: a critical anthology* (1996)

Dreyfus, John *A history of the Nonesuch Press* (1981)

Driscoll, Beth *The new literary middlebrow: tastemakers and reading in the twenty-first century* (Basingstoke, 2014)

Driver, David (ed.) *The art of Radio Times: the first sixty years* (2001)

Duffy, Maureen *A thousand capricious chances: a history of the Methuen list 1889–1989* (1989)

During, Simon *Cultural studies: A critical introduction* (2005)
　　'When literary criticism mattered', in Ronan McDonald (ed.), *The values of literary studies: critical institutions, scholarly agendas* (Cambridge, 2015), pp. 120–36

Eads, Peter *H. E. Bates: a bibliographical study* (1990)

Eccleshare, Julia 'Introduction', in *Children's Books of the Year 1990* (1990)

The Edinburgh history of the book in Scotland, gen. ed. Bill Bell, 4 vols. (Edinburgh, 2007–)

Educational Publishers Council *Publishing for a multicultural society* (1983)
　　Publishing for schools: a short guide to educational publishing (1977)
　　Publishing for schools: a short guide to educational publishing, second edition (1982)

Sex stereotyping in school and children's books (1981)

Edwards, David *Tradition and truth: the challenge of England's radical theologians 1962–1989* (1989)

Edwards, Owen Dudley *British children's fiction in the Second World War* (Edinburgh, 2007)

Edwards, Ruth Dudley *The pursuit of reason: The Economist 1943–1993* (1993)

Victor Gollancz: a biography (1987)

Ehrlich, Cyril *Harmonious alliance: a history of the Performing Right Society* (Oxford, 1989)

The piano: a history (Oxford, 1990)

Einbinder, Harvey *The myth of the Britannica* (New York, 1964)

Eliot, Simon *Some patterns and trends in British publishing, 1800–1919* (1994)

Eliot, Simon and Andrew Nash 'Mass markets: literature', in David McKitterick (ed.), *The Cambridge history of the book in Britain*. VI. *1830–1914* (Cambridge, 2009), pp. 416–42

Elkin, Judith 'Trends in publishing and supply of children's books', in Judith Elkin and Ray Lonsdale (eds.), *Focus on the child: libraries, literacy and learning* (1996), pp. 98–132

Ellis, Alec *A history of children's reading and literature* (Oxford, 1968)

Ellis, Peter Berresford and Jennifer Schofield *Biggles! The life story of Capt. W. E. Johns, creator of Biggles, Worrals, Gimlet and Steeley* (Godmanstone, 1993)

Engel, Matthew *Tickle the public: one hundred years of the popular press* (1996)

English, James F. *The economy of prestige: prizes, awards and the circulation of cultural value* (Cambridge, MA, 2005)

'Winning the culture game: prizes, awards, and the rules of art', *New Literary History* 33:1 (2002), pp. 109–35

Escarpit, Roger *The book revolution* (London and Paris, 1966)

Eve, Martin Paul *Open access and the humanities: contexts, controversies and the future* (Cambridge, 2014)

Expanding the book market: a study of reading and buying habits in GB (2005)

Faber, Geoffrey *A publisher speaking* (1934)

Farthing, Rys *The cost of going to school, from young people's perspective* (2014)

Feather, John *A history of British publishing* (1988)

A history of British publishing, second edition (2006)

Feather, John and Hazel Woodbridge, 'Bestsellers in the British book industry 1998–2005', *Publishing Research Quarterly* 23 (2007), pp. 210–23

Feaver, William *When we were young: two centuries of children's book illustration* (1977)

Fellowes, E. H. *Memoirs of an amateur musician* (1946)

Field, Michele *The publishing industry* (1986)

Findlater, Richard *Author! Author! A selection from* The Author, *the* Journal of the Society of Authors *since 1890* (1984)

Banned! A review of theatrical censorship in Britain (1967)

(ed.) *Public Lending Right: a matter of justice* (1971)

What are writers worth? (1963)

Finkelstein, David 'Literature, propaganda and the First World War: the case of *Blackwood's Magazine*', in Jeremy Treglown and Bridget Bennett (eds.), *Grub Street and the ivory tower: literary journalism and literary scholarship from Fielding to the internet* (Oxford, 1998), pp. 91–111

'The globalization of the book 1800–1970', in Simon Eliot and Jonathan Rose (eds.), *A companion to the history of the book* (Oxford, 2007), pp. 329–40

Finkelstein, David and Alistair McCleery *The Edinburgh history of the book in Scotland. 4. Professionalism and diversity 1880–2000* (Edinburgh, 2007)

Fisher, Allan 'Evangelical-Christian publishing: where it's been and where it's going', *Publishing Research Quarterly* 14 (1998), pp. 3–11

Fitzgibbon, Constantine *The life of Dylan Thomas* (1965)

Flanagan, Richard 'Colonies of the mind; republics of dreams: Australian publishing past and future', in David Carter and Anne Galligan (eds.), *Making books: contemporary Australian publishing* (Brisbane, 2007), pp. 132–48

Flanders, Amy 'The Press in London', in Wm Roger Louis (ed.), *The history of Oxford University Press. 3. 1896–1970* (Oxford, 2013), pp. 137–88

Folio Society *Folio 21: a bibliography of the Folio Society* (1968)

Follett, Brian *Joint Funding Council's libraries review group report* (Bristol, 1993)

Forman, Denis *Persona Granada: memories of Sidney Bernstein and the early years of Independent Television* (1997)

Foster, Malcom *Joyce Cary* (1968)

Fountain, Nigel *Underground: the London alternative press, 1966–74* (1988)

Fox, Geoff 'Movable books', in Kimberley Reynolds and Nicholas Tucker (eds.), *Children's book publishing in Britain since 1945* (Aldershot, 1998), pp. 86–109

Francis, Hywel 'Survey of Miners' Institute and Welfare Hall libraries in South Wales', *Library History* 3:1 (1973), pp. 28–32

Francis, Rob *Publishing market profile: India* (2008)

Fraser, Robert *Book history through postcolonial eyes: rewriting the script* (2008)

  'School readers in the empire and the creation of postcolonial taste', in Robert Fraser and Mary Hammond (eds.), *Books without borders. 1. The cross-national dimensions in print culture* (Basingstoke, 2008), pp. 89–106

  'War and the colonial book trade: the case of OUP India', in Robert Fraser and Mary Hammond (eds.), *Books without borders. 2. Perspectives from South Asia* (Basingstoke, 2008), pp. 137–50

Fredriksson, Einar H. (ed.) *A century of science publishing: a collection of essays* (Amsterdam, 2001)

Freedman, Jenna 'Grrrl Zines in the library', *Signs: Journal of Women in Culture and Society* 35:1 (2009), pp. 52–9

Friedman, Alan J. and Carol C. Donley *Einstein as myth and muse* (Cambridge, 1986)

Friend, Tad 'The parachute artist: have Tony Wheeler's guidebooks travelled too far?', *New Yorker* 18 April 2005, pp. 78–91

Fuller, Danielle, and DeNel Rehberg Sedo *Reading beyond the book: the social practices of contemporary literary culture* (New York, 2013)

Fuller, Danielle, DeNel Rehberg Sedo and Claire Squires 'Marionettes and puppeteers? The relationship between book club readers and publishers', in DeNel Rehberg Sedo (ed.), *Reading communities: from salons to cyberspace* (Basingstoke, 2011), pp. 181–99

Fyfe, Aileen 'The information revolution', in David McKitterick (ed.), *The Cambridge history of the book in Britain. 6. 1830–1914* (Cambridge, 2009), pp. 567–94

Gale, Maggie B. 'The London stage', in Baz Kershaw (ed.), *The Cambridge history of British theatre. 3. Since 1895* (Cambridge, 2004), pp. 143–66

Galey, Alan 'The enkindling reciter: e-books in the bibliographical imagination', *Book History* 15 (2012), pp. 210–47

Gallagher, Patrick and Paul Donovan *A hundred years of Allen & Unwin* (Sydney, 2014)

Galligan, Anne 'The culture of the publishing house: structure and strategies in the Australian publishing industry', in David Carter and Anne Galligan (eds.), *Making books: contemporary Australian publishing* (St Lucia, Queensland, 2007), pp. 34–50

Gammons, Helen *The art of music publishing* (Oxford, 2011)

Gardiner, Leslie *Bartholomew: 150 years* (Edinburgh, 1976)

Garland, Ken *Mr Beck's Underground map* (Harrow Weald, 1994)

Garnett, Kevin, Gillian Davies and Gwilym Harbottle *Copinger and Skone James on copyright*, fourteenth edition (1999)

Gassert, Imogen 'C. W. Daniel: maverick pacifist publisher in the First World War', *Publishing History* 48 (2000), pp. 5–40

Gennard John *A history of the National Graphic Association* (1990)
  Mechanical to digital: the Print Employers' Organisation (Edinburgh, 2010)

Gennard John, with Peter Bain *A history of the Society of Graphical and Allied Trades* (1995)

Gennard, John, with Geoffrey Hayward *A history of the Graphical Paper and Media Union* (2008)

Gerbaudo, Paolo *Tweets and the streets: social media and contemporary activism* (2012)

Gershuny, Jonathan *Changing times: work and leisure in postindustrial society* (Oxford, 2000)
  'Mass media, leisure and home IT: a panel time-diary approach', *IT & Society* 1:1 (2002), pp. 53–66

Gershuny, Jonathan I. and Kimberly Fisher 'Leisure in the UK across the 20th century', in A. H. Halsey and Josephine Webb (eds.), *Twentieth-century British social trends* (Basingstoke, 2000), pp. 620–49

Gibby, Richard and Andrew Green 'Electronic legal deposit in the United Kingdom', *New Review of Academic Librarianship* 14 (2008), pp. 55–70

Gibson, Mel *Remembered reading: memory, comics and post-war constructions of British girlhood* (Leuven, 2015)

Giles, Jim 'Internet encyclopaedias go head to head', *Nature* 438 (2005), pp. 900–1

Gill, Eric *Art* (1934)

Glaister, Geoffrey Ashall *Encyclopaedia of the book*, second edition (1996)

Glasgow, Eric 'The origins of the Home University Library', *Library Review* 50 (2001), pp. 95–8

Goaman, Karen and Mo Dodson 'A subversive current? Contemporary anarchism considered', in Jon Purkis and James Bowen (eds.), *Twenty-first century anarchism: unorthodox ideas for a new millennium* (1997), pp. 83–98

Goldthwaite, John 'Notes on the children's book trade: all is not well in Tinsel Town', in Sheila Egoff, G. T. Stubbs, and L. F. Ashley (eds.), *Only connect*, third edition (Toronto, 1980)

Gombrich, E. H. *The story of art* (pocket edition) (2006)

Gomez, Jeff *Print is dead: books in our digital age* (New York, 2008)

Goodell, Rae *The visible scientists* (Boston MA, 1977)

Goody, Alex *Technology, literature and culture* (Cambridge, 2011)

Gordon, Giles *Aren't we due a royalty statement? A stern account of literary, publishing, and theatrical folk* (1993)

Gough-Yates, Anna *Understanding women's magazines* (2002)

Gould, Thomas H. P. 'Protocols and challenges to the creation of a cross-disciplinary journal', *Journal of Scholarly Publishing* 42.2 (2011), pp. 105–41

Graham, Eleanor 'The Puffin years', *Signal* 12 (1973), pp. 115–22

Graham, Jacqueline 'Publicity', in Peter Owen (ed.), *Publishing now* (1993), pp. 147–54

Graham, Judith 'Picture books', in Kimberley Reynolds and Nicholas Tucker (eds.), *Children's book publishing in Britain since 1945* (Aldershot, 1998), pp. 60–85

Graves, Norman and Brendan Murphy 'Research into geography textbooks', in Ashley Kent (ed.), *Reflective practice in geography teaching* (2000), pp. 228–37

Gray, Alasdair *A life in pictures* (Edinburgh, 2010)

Green, E. H. H. *Ideologies of conservatism: conservative political ideas in the twentieth century* (Oxford, 2002)

Green, Jonathon *Days in the life: voices from the English underground, 1961–1971* (1998)

Green, S. J. D. 'A people beyond the book? Seebohm Rowntree, the decline of popular biblicism and the fate of Protestant England, c.1900–1950', in Michael Ledger-Lomas and Scott Mandelbrote (eds.), *Dissent and the Bible in Britain, c.1650–1950* (Oxford, 2013), pp. 256–76

   The passing of Protestant England: secularisation and social change c.1920–1960 (Cambridge, 2011)

Greenfield, George *Scribblers for bread: aspects of the English novel since 1945* (1989)

Gregory, Jane and Steve Miller *Science in public: communication, culture and credibility* (Cambridge, MA, 2000)

Griest, Guinevere *Mudie's Circulating Library and the Victorian novel* (Bloomington, IA, 1970)

Grieves, Keith 'Nelson's history of the war: John Buchan as a contemporary military historian 1915–22' *Journal of Contemporary History* 28:3 (1993), pp. 533–51

Grimley, Matthew 'The religion of Englishness: puritanism, providentialism, and "national character", 1918–1945', *Journal of British Studies* 46 (2007), pp. 884–906

Groombridge, Brian *The Londoner and his library* (1964)

Gross, Alan G., Joseph E. Harmon and Michael Reidy *Communicating science: the scientific article from the 17th century to the present* (Oxford, 2007)

Gross, Paul R. and Norman Levitt *Higher superstition: the academic left and its quarrels with science* (Baltimore, 1994)

Grove, Laurence and Peter Black 'The invention of comics', in *Comic invention* [exhibition catalogue] (Glasgow, 2016)

Grove, Valerie *So much to tell* (2010)

Gunelius, Susan *Harry Potter: the story of a global business phenomenon* (Basingstoke, 2008)

Gupta, Shyam Lal 'Educational publishing in India', in D. N. Malhotra and Narendra Kumar (eds.), *Indian publishing since independence* (Delhi, 1980), pp. 71–84

Gupta, Suman, *Globalization and literature* (Cambridge, 2009)

Gutjahr, Paul 'The Bible-zine *Revolve* and the evolution of the culturally relevant Bible in America', in Charles L. Cohen and Paul S. Boyer (eds.), *Religion and the culture of print in modern America* (Madison, WI, 2008), pp. 326–48

Gutteridge, L. E. S. 'A history of Wisden', *Wisden Cricketers' Almanack centenary edition* (1963), pp. 74–88

Hack, Jefferson and Jo-Ann Furniss *Dazed and confused: making it up as we go along* (New York, 2011)

Hadow, W. H. *Report of the consultative committee on books in public elementary schools* (1928)

Haines, Joe *Maxwell* (1988)

Hale, Charles 'The integration of photo and type', *Typographica* 1 (1949), pp. 15–18

Halsey, A. H. *Decline of donnish dominion* (Oxford, 1995)

Hamill, Lynne 'Changing times: home life and domestic', in Richard Harper (ed.), *The connected home: the future of domestic life* (2011), pp. 29–56

Hammerton, Sir John *Child of wonder: an intimate biography of Arthur Mee* (1946)

Hammond, Andrew *Cold War literature: writing the global conflict* (2006)

Hammond, Mary 'Book history in the reading experience', in Leslie Howsam (ed.), *The Cambridge companion to book history* (Cambridge, 2015), pp. 237–52

    'The multimedia afterlives of Victorian novels: the Readers Library Photoplay editions in the 1920s', *Nineteenth Century Theatre and Film* 37 (December 2010), pp. 28–44

Hammond, Paul 'The New Jerusalem Bible', *Theology* 89 (1986), pp. 309–10

Hampden, John *The book world today: a new survey of the making and distribution of books in Britain* (1957)

Hancock, Susan (ed.) *A guide to children's reference books and multimedia material* (Aldershot, 1998)

Hanson, Dian *The history of girly magazines: 1900–1969* (Cologne, 2006)

Harcup, Tony *A Northern Star: Leeds other paper and the alternative press 1974–1994* (Pontefract, [1994])

Hare, Steve *Penguin portrait: Allen Lane and the Penguin editors, 1935–1970* (1995)

Harley, Jane 'The King Penguin series: an historical survey', *Matrix* 5 (1985), pp. 143–50

Harris, Harriet *Fundamentalism and evangelicals* (Oxford, 1998)

Harris, José 'Society and the state in twentieth-century Britain', in F. M. L. Thompson (ed.), *The Cambridge social history of Britain 1750–1950. 3. Social agencies and institutions* (Cambridge, 1990), pp. 63–118

Harrison, John R. *The reactionaries* (1966)

Hart-Davis, Rupert *Hugh Walpole: a biography* (1952)

Harvey, Barbara *Visiting the National Portrait Gallery: a report of a survey of visitors to the National Portrait Gallery* (1987)

Hartley, Jenny *The reading groups book, 2002–3 edition* (Oxford, 2002)

Harvie, David, Geoff Lightfoot, Simon Lilley and Kenneth Weir 'What are we to do with feral publishers?', *Organisation* 19:6 (2012), pp. 905–14

Haskell, Francis *The ephemeral museum: old master paintings and the rise of the art exhibition* (2000)

Hastings, Adrian 'Some reflexions on the English Catholicism of the late 1930s', in Garrett Sweeney and Adrian Hastings (eds.), *Bishops and writers: aspects of the evolution of modern English Catholicism* (Wheathampsted, 1977), pp. 107–25

Hastings, Selina *Rosamond Lehmann* (2002)

Hayden, Terry 'Subject discipline dimensions of ICT and learning: history, a case study', *International Journal of Historical Learning, Teaching and Research* 2:1 (2001), pp. 17–36

Haynes, Jim *Thanks for coming! An autobiography* (1984)

Hazelgrove, Jenny *Spiritualism and British society between the wars* (Manchester, 2000)

Healy, Maura and Michael Marland *Language across the curriculum: a selection of books for secondary school teachers* (1979)

Heasman, Esther, *Publishing market profile: Canada* (2004)

Hedstrom, Matthew *The rise of liberal religion: book culture and American spirituality in the twentieth century* (Oxford, 2012)

Heelas, Paul *Spiritualities of life: romantic themes and consumptive capitalism* (Oxford, 2008)

Heelas, Paul and Benjamin Seel 'An ageing New Age?', in Grace Davie, Paul Heelas and Linda Woodhead (eds.), *Predicting religion: Christianity and alternatives in the West* (Aldershot, 2003), pp. 229–47

Heinsheimer, H. W. *Menagerie in F sharp* (New York, 1947)

Heinze, Andrew *Jews and the American soul: human nature in the twentieth century* (Princeton, NJ, 2004)

Held, David, Anthony G. McGrew, David Goldblatt and Jonathan Perraton *Global transformations: politics, economics and culture* (1999)

Hench, John B. *Books as weapons: propaganda, publishing and the battle for global markets in the era of World War II* (New York, 2010)

Hentea, Marius 'Late modernist debuts: publishing and professionalizing young novelists in 1920s Britain', *Book History* 14 (2011), pp. 167–86

Hibberd, Dominic 'A publisher of First World War poetry: Galloway Kyle', *Notes & Queries* 33:2 (1986), pp. 185–6

    Harold Monro: poet of the new age (Basingstoke, 2000)

Hibberd, Dominic and John Onions (eds.) *The winter of the world: poems of the First World War* (2007)

Hick, John *An autobiography* (Oxford, 2002)

Hicks, Dave *Bias in geography textbooks: images of the Third World and multi-ethnic Britain.* Working paper, Institute of Education (1982)

Hilgartner, Stephen 'The dominant view of popularization: conceptual problems, political uses', *Social Studies of Science* 20 (1990), pp. 519–39

Hill, Alan *In pursuit of publishing* (1988)

Hill, Doug *Not so fast: thinking twice about technology* (Philadelphia, 2013)

Hill, Jeffrey *Sport, leisure and culture in twentieth-century Britain* (Basingstoke, 2002)

Hilliard, Christopher *English as a vocation: the* Scrutiny *movement* (Oxford, 2012)

    'The two-penny library: the book trade, working-class readers, and "middlebrow" novels in Britain, 1930–42', *Twentieth-Century British History* 25:2 (2014), pp. 199–220

    To exercise our talents: the democratization of writing in Britain (Cambridge, MA, 2006)

Hillier, Bevis *John Betjeman: new fame, new love* (2002)

    John Betjeman: the bonus of laughter (2004)

Hillman, David, Harri Peccinotti and David Gibbs *Nova: the style bible on the 60s and 70s* (1993)

Hinnells, Duncan *An extraordinary performance: Hubert Foss, music publishing and the Oxford University Press* (Oxford, 1998)

Hitchcock, Steve, Leslie Carr and Wendy Hall 'Web journals publishing: a UK perspective', *Serials* 10 (1997), pp. 285–9

Hobson, Harold, Phillip Knightley and Leonard Russell *The pearl of days: an intimate memoir of the* Sunday Times, *1822–1972* (1972)

Hodges, Sheila *Gollancz: the story of a publishing house 1928–1978* (1978)

Hogarth, Grace 'Children's publishing in the 1930s: memoirs of an American in London', *Signal* 61 (1990), pp. 51–63

Hoggart, Richard *An imagined life: life and times, 1959–91* (1992)

The uses of literacy: aspects of working-class life with special reference to publications and entertainments (1957; repr. 1971)

Holgate, Andrew and Honor Wilson-Fletcher (eds.) *The cost of letters: a survey of literary living standards* (Brentford, 1998)

Holland, Stephen *The mushroom jungle: a history of post-war paperback publishing* (1993)
  The trials of Hank Janson (Tolworth, 2004)

Hollinger, David *After cloven tongues of fire: Protestant liberalism in modern American history* (Princeton, 2013)

Hollis, Richard *Graphic design: a concise history* (2001)
  Swiss graphic design: origins and growth of an international style 1920–1965 (2006)

Holman, Valerie *Print for victory: book publishing in England 1939–1945* (2008)
  'The art book', in Simon Ford (ed.), *Information sources in art, art history and design* (Munich, 2001)

Holmes, Sir Charles *National Gallery Trafalgar Square: illustrated guide* (1926)

Holmes, Su *British television and film culture in the 1950s* (Bristol, 2005)

Hooper, Walter (ed.), *C.S. Lewis: collected letters. 2. Books, broadcast and war, 1931–1949* (2004)

Hooper-Greenhill, Eilean *Museums and the interpretation of visual culture* (2000)

Hopkins, Gerard *The battle of the books* (1947)

Hopkinson, Tom *Picture Post 1938–50* (Harmondsworth, 1970)

Houlden, Leslie 'A wilderness voice', *Theology* 89 (1986), pp. 339–41

Housmans Diary Group '50 years at Caledonian Road', in *Housmans Peace Diary 2009* (2008)
  'Peace News – 75 and counting', in *Housmans Peace Diary 2011* (2010)

Howard, Michael S. *Jonathan Cape, publisher* (1971)

Howe, Ellic *The British Federation of Master Printers, 1900–1950* (1950)

Howsam, Leslie *Past into print: the history of publishing in Britain* (2009)

Hoyles, Martin *Bread and roses: gardening books from 1560 to 1960* (1995)

Humble, Nicola *Culinary pleasures: cookbooks and the transformation of British food* (2005)
  The feminine middlebrow novel, 1920s to 1950s (Oxford, 2001)

Hunt, Stephen *Anyone for Alpha?* (2001)

Hurd, Michael *Vincent Novello – and company* (1981)

Hutton, Ronald *The triumph of the moon: a history of modern pagan witchcraft* (Oxford, 1999)

Ireland, Phillipa 'Laying the foundations: New Beacon Books, Bogle L'Ouverture Press and the politics of Black British publishing', *E-rea: Revue Électronique d'Études sur le Monde Anglophone* 11:1 (2013). http://erea.revues.org/3524

Jackson, Kate *George Newnes and the new journalism in Britain, 1880–1910: culture and profit* (Aldershot, 2001)

Jackson, Sheila 'A Puffin illustrator of the forties', *Signal* 70 (1993), pp. 37–45

Jacobson, Timothy Curtis *et al. Knowledge for generations: Wiley and the global publishing industry 1807–2007* (New York, 2007)

Jaillant, Lise *Cheap modernism: expanding markets, publishers' series and the avant-garde* (Edinburgh, 2017)

James, Elizabeth (ed.) *Macmillan: a publishing tradition* (Basingstoke, 2002)
  (ed.) *The Victoria and Albert Museum: a bibliography and exhibition chronology, 1852–1996* (1998)

Jeanneret, Marsh 'Universities as publishers', *Scholarly Publishing* 1 (1969), pp. 3–4

Jeffries, John 'European documentation centres in the UK', *Government Publications Review* 4:2 (1977), pp. 127–9

Jenkins, Edgar W. 'E. J. Holmyard (1891–1959) and the historical approach to science teaching', in Michael R. Matthews (ed.), *International handbook of research in history, philosophy and science teaching* (Dordrecht, 2014), pp. 2,383–2,408

Jennings, Elizabeth *Poetry to-day, 1957–60* (1961)

Johanson, Graeme *Colonial editions in Australia, 1842–1972* (Wellington, 2000)

Johansson, Eve 'The reference work of the British Library Official Publications Library', *Government Publications Review* 3 (1976), pp. 271–6

John, Juliet *Dickens and mass culture* (Oxford, 2010)

Johnson, Buzz *'I think of my mother': notes on the life and times of Claudia Jones* (1985)

Johnston, W. & A. K. Johnston *An Edinburgh centenary: 100 years of map making* (Edinburgh, 1925)

Jones, H. Kay *Butterworths: history of a publishing house* (1980)

Jones, Peter (ed.) *Imagist poetry* (Harmondsworth, 1972, 2001)

Jones, Philip Henry and Eiluned Rees (eds.) *A nation and its books: a history of the book in Wales* (Aberystwyth, 1998)

Jones, Terry and Edward Enninful (eds.) *i-D covers 1980–2010* (Cologne, 2010)

Jonsson, Joanna *Writing for broadcasting* (1949)

Joseph, Michael *The adventure of publishing* (1949)

   This writing business (1931)

Joshi, Priya *In another country: colonialism, culture and the English novel in India* (New York, 2002)

Kaye, Elaine *C. J. Cadoux: theologian, scholar and pacifist* (Edinburgh, 1988)

Keates, J. S. *Understanding maps* (1992)

Keay, Douglas 'Aids, education and the year 2000!' *Woman's Own* 31 October 1987, pp. 8–10

Kee, Robert *The Picture Post album* (1989)

Keen, Andrew *The cult of the amateur: how blogs, MySpace, YouTube and the rest of today's user-generated media are destroying our economy, our culture, and our values* (2008)

Keir, David *The house of Collins: the story of a Scottish family of publishers from 1789 to the present day* (1952)

Keller, Michael A. 'Science, scholarship and internet publishing: the HighWire story', *Content* 6:2 (1998)

Kelly, Thomas *A history of public libraries in Great Britain: 1845–1975* (1977)

Kemsley, Walter *Martin Eve remembered* (Woodbridge, 1999)

Kenna, Carol, Lyn Medcalf and Rick Walker *Printing is easy . . .?* (1986)

Keppel, Gilles *Allah in the West* (1997)

Kiberd, Declan *Ulysses and us: the art of everyday living in Joyce's masterpiece* (2010)

King, Edmund G. C., 'A captive audience? The reading lives of Australian prisoners of war, 1914–1918', in Shafquat Towheed and Edmund G. C. King (eds.), *Reading and the First World War: readers, texts, archives* (Basingstoke 2015), pp. 153–67

   '"Books are more to me than food": British prisoners of war as readers, 1914–1918', *Book History* 16 (2013), pp. 247–71

   'E. W. Hornung's unpublished "diary", the YMCA, and the reading soldier in the First World War', *English Literature in Transition, 1880–1920* 57:3 (2014), pp. 361–87

   'Reading and World War I', in *History of reading: an introduction to reading in the past.* OpenLearn, Open University (2016)

King, Emily 'Time Out cover design, 1970–81', in Jeremy Aynsley and Kate Forde (eds.), Design and the modern magazine (Manchester, 2007), pp. 56–82

King, John A Christian view of the mushroom myth (1970)

Kingsford, R. J. L. The Publishers Association, 1896–1946 (Cambridge, 1970)

Kirschenbaum, Matthew Track changes: a literary history of word processing (Cambridge, MA, 2016)

Kirschenbaum, Matthew and Sarah Werner 'Digital scholarship and digital studies: the state of the discipline', Book History 17 (2017), pp. 406–58

Kloester, Jennifer Georgette Heyer (2001)

Knapp, John C. and Azalea M. Hulbert Ghostwriting and the ethics of authenticity (New York, 2017)

Knight, David 'Getting science across', British Journal for the History of Science 29 (1996), pp. 129–38

Public understanding of science: a history of communicating scientific ideas (2006)

Knight, Kobold A guide to fiction writing (1945)

Kohnstamm, Thomas Do travel writers go to hell? (New York, 2008)

Kovecci, Eugene 'Solution to information problems or obsolescence?', in Proceedings of the 1965 international federation for documentation (1966)

Krishnamurthy, Ramesh 'The corpus revolution in EFL dictionaries', Kernerman Dictionary News 10 (2002), pp. 1–6

Kugelmann, Robert Psychology and Catholicism: contested boundaries (Cambridge, 2009)

Kuzyk, Raya 'Reference into the future', Library Journal 132:19 (2007), p. 8

Lafaye, Vanessa Blackwell Publishing 1990–2007: a brief history (Oxford, 2009)

LaFollette, Marcel Making science our own: public images of science, 1910–1955 (Chicago, 1990)

Laity, Paul (ed.) Left Book Club anthology (2001)

Lambert, J. W. and Michael Ratcliffe The Bodley Head: 1887–1987 (1987)

Lambert, Yves 'A turning point in religious evolution in Europe', Journal of Contemporary Religion 19 (2004), pp. 29–45

Lane, Allen 'Penguins and Pelicans', Penrose Annual 40 (1938), p. 42

Lanier, Jaron You are not a gadget: a manifesto (2010)

Larken, H. W. Compositor's work in printing (1961)

Larrea, Carlota and Alexis Weedon 'Celebrating book culture: the aims and outcomes of UNESCO's World Book and Copyright Day in Europe', Publishing Research Quarterly 23 (2007), pp. 224–34

Law, Graham and Robert L. Patten 'The serial revolution', in David McKitterick (ed.), The Cambridge history of the book in Britain. 6. 1830–1914 (Cambridge, 2009), pp. 144–71

Lawrence, Margot 'Prayer and Mammon', in David Martin and Peter Mullen (eds.), No alternative: the Prayer Book controversy (Oxford, 1981), pp. 179–82

Lea, F. A. The life of John Middleton Murry (Oxford, 1959)

Leasor, James Author by profession (1952)

Leavis, F. R. Mass civilisation and minority culture (Cambridge, 1930)

Leavis, Q. D. Fiction and the reading public (1932)

Lee, Hermione '"Crimes of criticism": Virginia Woolf and literary journalism', in Jeremy Treglown and Bridgett Bennett (eds.), Grub Street and the ivory tower: literary journalism and literary scholarship from Fielding to the internet (1998), pp. 112–34

Lee, Jenny 'Exploiting the imprint', in David Carter and Anne Galligan (eds.), *Making books: contemporary Australian publishing* (St Lucia, Queensland, 2007), pp. 17–33

Legat, Michael *An author's guide to literary agents* (1995)

Lehmann, John *I am my brother: autobiography II* (1960)
  The ample proposition: autobiography III (1966)

Leslie, Jeremy *Issues: new magazine design* (2000)

Lessig, Lawrence *Free culture* (2005)

Levine, Charles 'The coming boom in English lexicography', *Kernerman Dictionary News* 9 (2001)

Lewis, Jeremy *Penguin special: the life and times of Allen Lane* (2005)

Lewis, John *The Left Book Club: an historical record* (1970)

Lewis, John *Typography: basic principles. Influences and trends since the 19th century* (1963)

Lindsay, Jack 'Publishing', in *Arena, a magazine of modern literature: the USA threat to British culture*, special edition of *Arena*, new series 8 (June/July 1951)

Literature in the 21st century: understanding models of support for literary fiction Canelo/Arts Council England report (2017). www.artscouncil.org.uk/sites/default/files/down load-file/Literature%20in%20the%2021st%20Century%20report.pdf

Liveing, Edward *Adventure in publishing: the house of Ward Lock 1854–1954* (1954)

Lloyd Jones, Linda and Jeremy Ainsley *Fifty Penguin years* (Harmondsworth, 1985)

Long, Patricia M. 'The commercial circulating library in the 1970s', *Library and Information History* 5:6 (1981), pp. 185–93

Lonsdale, Ray and Sheila Ray 'Librarianship', in Peter Hunt (ed.), *International companion encyclopaedia of children's literature* (1996), pp. 615–33

Lorant, Stefan *101 best picture comparisons from Lilliput: or Chamberlain and the beautiful llama* (1940)

Losowsky, Andrew (ed.) *We love magazines* (Luxembourg, 2007)

Louis, Wm Roger 'The Waldock Inquiry, 1967–1970', in Wm Roger Louis (ed.), *The history of Oxford University Press. 3. 1896–1970* (Oxford, 2013), pp. 757–89

Low, Gail *Publishing the postcolonial: Anglophone West African and Caribbean writing in the UK, 1950–1967* (2010)

Luckham, Brian *The library in society: a study of the public library in an urban setting* (1971)

Luckmann, Thomas *The invisible religion: the problem of religion in modern society* (1967)

Luhrmann, Tanya *When God talks back: understanding the American Evangelical relationship with God* (New York, 2012)

Luna, Paul 'Books and bits: text and technology 1970–2000', in Simon Eliot and Jonathan Rose (eds.), *A companion to the history of the book* (Oxford, 2007), pp. 383–94

Lunn, Arnold *Now I see* (1932)

Mabe, Michael 'Scholarly publishing', *European Review* 17 (2009), pp. 3–22

Mabe, Michael and Mayur Amin 'Growth dynamics of scholarly and scientific journals', *Scientometrics* 51 (2001), pp. 147–62

Macdonald, Alastair *Mapping the world: history of the directorate of overseas survey, 1946–1985* (1996)

Macdonald, Kate 'The symbiotic relationship of Thomas Nelson & Sons with John Buchan within the publisher's series', in John Spiers (ed.), *The culture of the publisher's series. 1. Authors, publishers and the shaping of taste* (Basingstoke, 2011), pp. 156–70

'Translating propaganda: John Buchan's writing during the First World War', in Mary Hammond and Shafquat Towheed (eds.), *Publishing in the First World War: essays in book history* (Basingstoke, 2007), pp. 181–201

Mackenzie, Norman and Jean Mackenzie *The time traveller: the life of H. G. Wells* (1973)

Mackian, Sara *Everyday spirituality: social and spiritual worlds of enchantment* (Basingstoke, 2012)

Macmillan, Frederick *The Net Book Agreement 1899 and the book war 1906–1908* (Glasgow, 1924)

MacQueen, Adam *Private Eye: the first 50 years* (2011)

Maher, Terry *Against my better judgement* (1994)

Maiden, John *National religion and the prayer book controversy* (Woodbridge, 2009)

Mair, Carlene *The Chappell story, 1811–1961* (1961)

Malhoutra, D. N. and Narendra Kumar *Indian publishing since Independence* (Delhi, 1980)

Mandelbrote, Giles (ed.) *Out of print and into profit: a history of the rare and secondhand book trade in Britain in the 20th century* (2006)

Mann, Peter H. *A new survey: the facts about romantic fiction* (1974)
    Books: buyers and borrowers (1969)
    Books and reading (1971)

Marcus, Laura 'Virginia Woolf and the Hogarth Press', in Ian Willison, Warwick Gould and Warren Chernaik (eds.), *Modernist writers and the marketplace* (Basingstoke, 1996), pp. 124–50

Marsden, William Edward *The school textbook: geography, history and social studies* (2001)

Marshall, Alan *Changing the word: the printing industry in transition* (1983)

Marston, Maurice *National Book Council: a survey of fourteen years' work* (1940)

Martin, Andy *Reacher said nothing: Lee Child and the making of* Make me (2015)

Maschler, Tom 'How it all began', in *Booker 30: a celebration of 30 years of the Booker Prize for Fiction 1969–1998* (1998), pp. 15–16
    Publisher (2005)

Mass-Observation *A report on Penguin world* (1947). Mass-Observation archive, MS 1332. University of Sussex. Digital edition, *Mass-observation online* www.amdigital.co.uk/m-collections/collection/mass-observation-online
    Books and the public (2 July 1942). Mass-Observation archive, MS 1332. University of Sussex. Digital edition, *Mass-observation online* www.amdigital.co.uk/m-collections/collection/mass-observation-online
    The press and its readers (1949)
    Wartime reading (1940). Mass-Observation archive, MS 1332. University of Sussex. Digital edition, *Mass-observation online* www.amdigital.co.uk/m-collections/collection/mass-observation-online

Maw, Martin 'Printing technology, binding, readers, and social life', in Wm Roger Louis (ed.), *The history of Oxford University Press*. 3. *1896–1970* (Oxford, 2013), pp. 277–307

Mayer, Jean-François 'Biens de salut et marché religieux dans le Cultic milieu', *Social Compass* 53 (2006), pp. 97–108

McAleer, Joseph *Passion's fortune: the story of Mills & Boon* (Oxford, 1999)
    Popular reading and publishing in Britain, 1914–1950 (Oxford, 1992)

McAllister, Gilbert et al. *The book crisis* (1940)

McChesney, Robert W. *Digital disconnect: how capitalism is turning the internet against democracy* (New York, 2013)

McCleery, Alistair 'Lady Chatterley's lover recovered', *Publishing History* 59 (2006), pp. 61–84

'The paperback evolution: Tauchnitz, Albatross and Penguin', in Nicole Matthews and Nickianne Moody (eds.), *Judging a book by its cover: fans, publishers, designers and the marketing of fiction* (Abingdon, 2007), pp. 3–18

'"Sophisticated smut": the Penguin edition of *Lady Chatterley's lover*', *Script & Print: Bulletin of the Bibliographical Society of Australia & New Zealand* 29 (2006), pp. 192–204

McCleery, Alistair, David Finkelstein and Jennie Renton *An honest trade: booksellers and bookselling in Scotland* (Edinburgh, 2009)

McColvin, Lionel *How to use books and enjoy them* (1933)

'Public, national and other libraries', in John Hampden (ed.), *The book world today: a new survey of the making and distribution of books in Britain* (1957), pp. 163–79

McDonald, Peter D. *The literature police: apartheid censorship and its cultural consequences* (Oxford, 2009)

McDonald, Ronan *The death of the critic* (2007)

McElroy, Mary 'Athletes displaying their lives: the emergence of the contemporary sports autobiography', in W. Umphlett (ed.), *The achievement of American sport literature* (Rutherford, NJ, 1991), pp. 165–83

McGonigal, James *Beyond the last dragon: a life of Edwin Morgan* (Dingwall, 2010)

McGurl, Mark *The program era: postwar fiction and the rise of creative writing* (Cambridge, MA, 2009)

McKay, George (ed.) *DIY culture: party and protest in nineties Britain* (1998)

McKay, Jenny *The magazines handbook* (2000)

McKenzie, D. F. 'History of the book', in Peter Davison (ed.), *The book encompassed: studies in twentieth-century bibliography* (Cambridge, 1992), pp. 290–301

McKitterick, David *A history of Cambridge University Press. 3. New worlds for learning, 1872–1972* (Cambridge, 2004)

'Changes in the look of the book', in David McKitterick (ed.), *The Cambridge history of the book in Britain. 6. 1830–1914* (Cambridge, 2009), pp. 75–116

'Introduction', in David McKitterick (ed.), *The Cambridge history of the book in Britain. 6. 1830–1914* (Cambridge, 2009), pp. 1–74

'Looking further', in Wm Roger Louis (ed.), *The history of Oxford University Press. 3. 1896–1970* (Oxford, 2013), pp. 807–13

'Second-hand and old books', in David McKitterick (ed.), *The Cambridge history of the book in Britain. 6. 1830–1914* (Cambridge, 2009), pp. 635–73

McKnight, David and Mitchell Hobbs '"You're all a bunch of pinkos": Rupert Murdoch and the politics of HarperCollins', *Media, Culture & Society* 33 (2011), pp. 835–51

McLean Rathgeber, Eva-Maria 'Nigerian university presses: problems and prospects', *African Book Publishing Record* 5 (1979), pp. 13–18

McLean, Ruari *Jan Tschichold: typographer* (1975)

Magazine design (Oxford, 1969)

Modern book design (1958)

McMenemy, David *The public library* (2009)

McRobbie, Angela *Feminism and youth culture: from 'Jackie' to 'Just Seventeen'* (Basingstoke, 1991)

Meadows, A. J. *Communicating research* (San Diego, CA, 1998)

Mears, Daniel and Christopher Ellison, 'Who buys New Age materials?', *Sociology of Religion* 61 (2000), pp. 289–313

Melman, Billie *The culture of history: English uses of the past, 1800–1953* (Oxford, 2006)

Mennell, Stephen *All manners of food: eating and taste in England and France from the middle ages to the present* (Oxford, 1985)

Meynell, Francis *My lives* (1971)

Michel, Marilouise 'Samuel French Ltd.', in Jonathan Rose and Patricia J. Anderson (eds.), *Dictionary of literary biography*. 106. *British literary publishing houses, 1820–1880* (1991), pp. 138–42

Miles, Barry *London calling: a countercultural history of London since 1945* (2010)

Miller, David and Richard Price *British poetry magazines 1914–2000: a history and bibliography of British magazines* (2006)

Miller, Harvey 'Phaidon and the business of art book publishing: 1923–1967', *Visual Resources: An International Journal of Documentation* 15:3 (1999), pp. 343–53

Miller, Karl *Authors* (Oxford, 1989)

Miller, Laura J. *Reluctant capitalists* (Chicago, 2006)

Milner, Andrew *Literature, culture and society* (1996)

Mintz, Adam 'The Talmud in translation', in Sharon Liberman Mintz and Gabriel M. Goldstein (eds.), *Printing the Talmud: from Bomberg to Schottenstein* (New York, 2005), pp. 121–41

Mitchell, Bertoli *Book publishing in Britain* (1999)

Moggridge, D. E. 'A risk-bearing author: Maynard Keynes and his publishers', in Elizabeth James (ed.), *Macmillan: a publishing tradition* (Basingstoke, 2001), pp. 218–29

Monk, Ray *Bertrand Russell, 1921–1970: the ghost of madness* (2000)

Montefiore, Hugh *Oh God, what next?* (1995)

Montgomery, Robert and Robert Threlfall *Music and copyright: the case of Delius and his publishers* (Aldershot, 2007)

Moore, Geoffrey *Poetry to-day* (1958)

Moore, Harry T. *The intelligent heart* (1955)

Moore, Jerrold Northrop *Elgar and his publishers: letters of a creative life* (Oxford, 1987)

Moore, Reginald 'The development of sports publishing: some marginal notes', *British Book News* (March 1976), pp. 157–61

Moran, James *Printing presses: history and development from the fifteenth century to modern times* (1973)

Moran, Joe *Star authors: literary celebrity in America* (London, 2000)

Morgan, Charles *The house of Macmillan, 1843–1943* (1943)

Morgan, Jamie and Mitzi Lorenz *Buffalo: the style and fashion of Ray Petri* (New York, 2000)

Morgan, Ted *Somerset Maugham* (1980)

Morison, Stanley *First principles of typography* (Cambridge, 1936)

Morpurgo, J. E. *Allen Lane, king penguin: a biography* (1979)

Morris, Colin *God-in-a-box: Christian strategy in the television age* (1984)
    Include me out! Confessions of an ecclesiastical coward (1968)

Morris, Sally, Ed Barnas, Douglas LaFrenier and Margaret Reich *The handbook of journal publishing* (Cambridge, 2013)

Morrison, Blake 'Poetry and the poetry business', *Granta 4: beyond the crisis* (Spring 1981)

Morus, Iwan R. *Frankenstein's children: electricity, exhibition and experiment in early nineteenth-century London* (Princeton, NJ, 1998)

Mosch, Ulrich, 'Musikverlage, Komponisten-Institute und das zeitgenössische Schaffen', in Otto Kolleritsch (ed.), *Der musikverlag und seine komponisten im 21. Jahrhundert: zum 100-jährigen Jubiläum der Universal Edition* (Vienna, 2002), pp. 30–43

Moss, Elaine 'Kathleen Hale and Orlando the Marmalade Cat', *Signal* 9 (1972), pp. 123–7

Moss, Elaine *Part of the pattern: a personal journey through the world of children's books, 1960–1985* (1986)

Mottram, Eric 'The British poetry revival, 1960–1975', in Peter Barry and Robert Hampson (eds.), *New British poetries: the scope of the possible* (Manchester, 1993), pp. 15–50

Moyle, Donald, and Jean Ainslie *Teaching reading: an annotated bibliography*, second edition (1981)

Muggeridge, Malcolm *Christ and the media* (1977)

Muir, P. H. (ed.), *Talks on book-collecting* (1952)

Mumby, Frank *Publishing and bookselling: a history from the earliest times to the present day* (1930)

Munford, W. A. *Penny rate: aspects of British public library history, 1850–1950* (1951)

Murphy, Andrew *Shakespeare in print: a history and chronology of Shakespeare publishing* (Cambridge, 2007)

Murray, Simone *Mixed media: feminist presses and publishing politics* (2004)

   The adaptation industry: the cultural economy of contemporary literary adaptation (New York, 2011)

Musson, A. E. *The Typographical Association: origins and history up to 1949* (Oxford, 1954)

Nadal, Ira Bruce *Double act: a life of Tom Stoppard* (2004)

Nash, Andrew 'Literary culture and literary publishing in inter-war Britain: a view from Chatto & Windus', in Simon Eliot, Andrew Nash and Ian Willison (eds.), *Literary cultures and the material book* (2007), pp. 323–42

   'Publishers' archives, authors' papers and literary scholarship', in David Sutton and Ann Livingstone (eds.), *The future of literary archives: diasporic and dispersed collections at risk* (Leeds, 2018), p. 115–25

   'Sifting out "rubbish" in the literature of the twenties and thirties: Chatto & Windus and the Phoenix Library', in John Spiers (ed.), *The culture of the publishers' series. 1. Authors, publishers and the shaping of taste* (Basingstoke, 2011), pp. 188–201

   'The changing face of the publishing house: 1880–1980', in David Finkelstein and Alistair McCleery (eds.), *The Edinburgh history of the book in Scotland. 4. Professionalism and diversity 1880–2000* (Edinburgh, 2007), pp. 185–202

   'The material history of the novel I: 1940–1973', in Peter Boxall and Bryan Cheyette (eds.), *The Oxford history of the novel in English. 7. British and Irish fiction since 1940* (2016), pp. 21–36

   'The material history of the novel II: 1973–present', in Peter Boxall and Bryan Cheyette (eds.), *The Oxford history of the novel in English. 7. British and Irish fiction since 1940* (2016), pp. 401–16

   'The production of the novel, 1880–1940', in Patrick Parrinder and Andrzej Gąsiorek (eds.), *The Oxford history of the novel in English. 4. The reinvention of the British and Irish novel 1880–1940* (Oxford, 2010), pp. 3–19

Nash, David *Christian ideals in British culture: stories of belief in the twentieth century* (Basingstoke, 2013)

National Book Council *Report of a special committee of the National Book Council appointed to consider a plan for increasing the national interest in books* (1934)

National Book League *Books for schools* (1979)

    Education a touring exhibition (1965)

    Enquiry into expenditure by local education authorities on class books for schools (1951)

    Exhibition of books 1951 Festival of Britain (Cambridge, 1951)

Negroponte, Nicholas *Being digital* (1995)

Nelson, Elizabeth *The British counter-culture, 1966–73: a study of the underground press* (Basingstoke, 1989)

Nelson, Theodore Holm *Literary machines* (Sausalito, CA, 1980, 1987)

Newbolt, Henry *The Newbolt Report: the teaching of English in England* (1921)

Newdigate, Bernard *The art of the book* (1938)

Newsinger, John *The Dredd phenomenon: comics and contemporary society* (Bristol, 1999)

Nicholas, David et al. 'Peer review: still king in the digital age', *Learned Publishing* 28 (2015), pp. 15–21

Nineham, Dennis (ed.) *The New English Bible reviewed* (1965)

    The use and abuse of the bible (1976)

Noda, Nathaniel T. 'Copyrights retold: how interpretive rights foster creativity and justify fan-based activities', *Seton Hall Journal of Sports and Entertainment Law* 20 (2010), pp. 131–64

Norrie, Ian *Mumby's publishing and bookselling in the twentieth century*, sixth edition (1982)

    Sixty precarious years: a short history of the National Book League, 1925–1985 (1985)

Norrington, A. L. P. *Blackwell's 1879–1979: the history of a family firm* (Oxford, 1983)

Nott, James J. *Music for the people: popular music and dance in interwar Britain* (Oxford, 2002)

Nott, Kathleen *The emperor's clothes* (1953)

[Novello], *A century and a half in Soho: a short history of the firm of Novello, publishers and printers of music, 1811–1961* (1961)

Nuttall, Barry 'Local government information: a "grey" area', *Aslib Proceedings* 34:11 (1982), pp. 473–9

Nyburg, Anna *Émigré: the transformation of art publishing in Britain* (2014)

O'Conner, Joseph *Inishowen* (2000)

O'Connor, Sands *Black British children's literature* (Basingstoke, 2017)

O'Connor, Sara, Neal Hoskins and Kate Wilson 'Digital developments: panel on book apps and digital publishing', in Bridget Carrington and Jennifer Harding (eds.), *Beyond the book: transforming children's literature* (Newcastle upon Tyne, 2014), pp. 44–53

O'Hagan, Andrew *The secret life* (2017)

Ohmann, Richard *Selling culture: magazines, markets, and class at the turn of the century* (1998)

Ollard, Richard *A man of contradictions: a life of A. L. Rowse* (1999)

    (ed.) *The diaries of A. L. Rowse* (2003)

Oluwasanmi, Edwina, Eva McLean and Hans Zell (eds.) *Publishing in Africa in the seventies* (Ife-Ife, Nigeria, 1975)

Onibonoje, G. O. 'Wanted! A cultural revolution, not a dialogue', in Edwina Oluwasanmi, Eva McLean and Hans Zell (eds.), *Publishing in Africa in the seventies* (Ife-Ife, Nigeria, 1975), pp. 262–76

Ormond, Richard *National Portrait Gallery in colour* (1979)

Ortolano, Guy *The two cultures controversy: science, literature and cultural politics in postwar Britain* (Cambridge, 2009)

Orwell, George 'Bookshop memories', in Sonia Orwell and Ian Angus (eds.), *The collected essays, journalism and letters of George Orwell*. 1. *1920–1940* (1970), pp. 273–7

    'Boys' Weeklies', *Horizon* 3 (1940), pp. 174–200

    I belong to the left: 1945 (1999)

    The road to Wigan Pier (1937)

Owen, William *Magazine design* (1991)

The Oxford history of the Irish book, 5 vols. (Oxford, 2006–)

Oxford music: the first fifty years, '23 –'73 (Oxford, 1973)

Packer, James *Fundamentalism and the word of God* (1958)

Panofsky, Ruth 'One series after the other: the Macmillan company of Canada', in John Spiers (ed.), *The culture of the publisher's series*. 2. *Nationalisms and the national canon* (Basingstoke, 2011), pp. 184–98

Paret, Peter 'John Keegan's *The price of admiralty* and popular history', *Journal of Military History* 54:2 (1990), pp. 227–31

Parker, Martin 'Becoming editor: or, Pinocchio finally notices the strings', *tripleC* 11:2 (2013), pp. 461–74

Parker, Peter *Isherwood: a life* (2004)

Parker, Philip *2009 report on gardening magazines* (San Diego, CA, 2009)

    The 2009 import and export market for dictionaries, encyclopedias, and serial installments thereof excluding single sheets in the UK (San Diego, CA, 2009)

Parry, Roger *The ascent of media: from Gilgamesh to Google via Gutenberg* (2011)

Parsons, Gerald 'There and back again? Religion and the 1944 and 1988 Education Acts', in Gerald Parsons (ed.), *The growth of religious diversity: Britain from 1945*, vol. 2 (1994), pp. 161–98

Partridge, Christopher *The re-enchantment of the West*. 1. *Alternative spiritualities, sacralization, popular culture and occulture* (2005)

Patterson, Diana (ed.) *Harry Potter's world wide influence* (Newcastle upon Tyne, 2009)

    'J. K. Rowling and Harry Potter: publishing, but not as we know it,' *Journal of the Edinburgh Bibliographical Society* 1 (2006), pp. 11–19

Pearsall, Phyllis *A–Z maps: the personal story, from bedsitter to household name* (1990)

Pearson, Lucy (ed.) *Jacqueline Wilson* (Basingstoke, 2015)

    The making of modern children's literature in Britain: publishing and criticism in the 1960s and 1970s (Farnham, 2013)

Peterson, Olga M. 'So you're celebrating British book week!', *ALA Bulletin* 37:9 (1943), pp. 283–6

Petersen, William S. *John Betjeman: a bibliography* (Oxford, 2006)

Pett Ridge, W. 'Guide to Fleet Street', *Bookman* 22 (1902), pp. 53–4

Phillips, Angus 'Does the book have a future?', in Simon Eliot and Jonathan Rose (eds.), *A companion to the history of the book* (Oxford, 2007), pp. 547–59

    'Trade publishing', in Keith Robbins (ed.), *The history of Oxford University Press*. 4. *1970 to 2004* (Oxford, 2017), pp. 333–52

Phillips, J. B. *The price of success: an autobiography* (Wheaton, IL, 1985)

Phillips, Justin C. *S. Lewis at the BBC: messages of hope in the darkness of war* (2002)

Picton, Hugh 'Electronic official publishing', in V. J. Nurcombe (ed.), *Official publishing past, present and future: SCOOP 30 years on anniversary seminar* (2002), pp. 35–42

Pierson, Christopher *The modern state*, second edition (2004)

Piette, Adam 'Pointing to east and west: British Cold War poetry', in Tim Kendall (ed.), *The Oxford handbook of British and Irish war poetry* (Oxford, 2007), pp. 632–52

Pimlott, Herbert '"Eternal ephemera" or the durability of "disposable literature": the power and persistence of print in an electronic world', *Media, Culture & Society* 33:4 (2011), pp. 515–30

Pipes, Alan *Production for graphic designers* (2009)

Pittock, Murray (ed.) *Robert Burns in global culture* (Lanham, MD, 2011)

Potter, Jane *Boys in khaki, girls in print: women's literary responses to the Great War 1914–1918* (Oxford, 2005)

'For country, conscience and commerce: publishers and publishing, 1914–1918', in Mary Hammond and Shafquat Towheed (eds.), *Publishing in the First World War: essays in book history* (Basingstoke, 2007), pp. 11–26

Powers, Alan *Front cover: great book jacket and cover design* (2001)

Poyner, Daniel (ed.) *Autonomy: the cover designs of 'Anarchy' 1961–1970* (2012)

[Printing Industries Sector Working Party] *The future of the printing industries: report to the National Economic Development Council* (1983)

Public libraries and their use: a research report on the use of public library buildings with implications for their distribution, location and design (1973)

Publishers Association, *Publishing and the economy* (2013)

Pullinger, David 'Journals published on the net', *Serials* 7 (1994), pp. 243–8

Pullinger, David and Christine Baldwin *Electronic journals and user behaviour: learning for the future from the SuperJournal project* (Cambridge, 2002)

Puttick, Elizabeth 'The rise of mind-body-spirit publishing: reflecting or creating spiritual trends?', *Journal of Alternative Spiritualities and New Age Studies* 1:1 (2005), pp. 129–49

Pyne, Lydia *Bookshelf* (2016)

Quail, John *The slow burning fuse: the lost history of the British anarchists* (1978)

Quinn, Anthony *A history of British magazine design* (2016)

Radway, Janice *A feeling for books: the Book-of-the-Month Club, literary taste, and middle-class desire* (Chapel Hill, NC, 1997)

Rainbird, George *The Rainbird archive: an autobiographical bibliography* (1985)

Ramdarshan Bold, Melanie 'The return of the social author: negotiating authority and influence on Wattpad', *Convergence: The International Journal of Research into New Media Technologies* (2016). http://journals.sagepub.com/doi/abs/10.1177/1354856516654459

Ramone, Jenni and Helen Cousins (eds.) *The Richard and Judy Book Club reader: popular texts and the practices of reading* (2011)

Rampley, Matthew *Exploring visual culture: definitions, concepts, contexts* (Edinburgh, 2005)

Raven, Charles *Teilhard de Chardin: scientist and seer* (1962)

Rawlinson, Andrew *The book of enlightened masters: western teachers in eastern traditions* (Chicago, 2007)

Ray, Sheila G. *The Blyton phenomenon* (1982)

Ray Murray, Padmini and Claire Squires 'The digital publishing communications circuit', *Book 2.0* 3:1 (2013), pp. 3–24

Raymond, Harold *Publishing and bookselling: a survey of post-war developments and present-day problems* (1938)

Rayner, Samantha '"A new spirit of hope": educating the book trade, 1920–1930', *Publishing Research Quarterly* 29:2 (2013), pp. 134–50

Read, Herbert 'The crisis in bookcraft', *The Penrose Annual* 43 (1949), pp. 13–18

Rebellato, Dan *1956 and all that: the making of modern British drama* (1999)

Reed, David *The popular magazine in Britain and the United States (1880–1960)* (Toronto, 1997)

Reid, Gavin *The gagging of God* (1969)

Report on the British press: a survey of its current operations and problems with special reference to national newspapers and their part in public affairs (1938)

Reynolds, Barbara (ed.) *The letters of Dorothy L. Sayers. 3. 1944–1950: a noble daring* (Cambridge, 1998)

(ed.) *The letters of Dorothy L. Sayers. 4. 1951–1957: in the midst of life* (Cambridge, 2000)

Reynolds, David *In command of history: Churchill fighting and writing the Second World War*, second edition (2004)

Reynolds, Kimberley *Left out: the forgotten radical tradition in children's publishing in Britain, 1910–1949* (Oxford, 2016)

'Publishing practices and the practicalities of publishing', in Kimberley Reynolds and Nicholas Tucker (eds.), *Children's book publishing in Britain since 1945* (Aldershot, 1998), pp. 20–41

Reynolds, Kimberley and Nicholas Tucker (eds.) *Oral archives: a collection of informal conversations with individuals involved in creating or producing children's literature since 1945* (1998)

Reynolds, Siân *Britannica's typesetters: women compositors in Edinburgh* (Edinburgh, 1989)

Richards, Graham 'Psychology and the churches in Britain 1919–39: symptoms of conversion', *History of the Human Sciences* 13 (2000), pp. 57–84

Richardson, F. R. 'The circulating library', in John Hampden (ed.), *The book world* (1935), pp. 195–202

Richardson, Paul and Graham Taylor *PA guide to The UK publishing industry*, second edition (2010)

Ricketson, Sam and Jane C. Ginsburg *International copyright and neighbouring rights* (Oxford, 2006)

Roberts, A. D. *Introduction to reference books* (1948)

Roberts, John Michael 'How are George Orwell's writings a precursor to studies of popular culture?', *Journal for Cultural Research* 18:3 (2014), pp. 216–33

Roberts, R. Ellis *H. R. L. Sheppard* (1942)

Roberts, Robert *The classic slum: Salford life in the first quarter of the century*, new edition (1990)

Roberts, Ryan *John Fuller and the Sycamore Press: a bibliographic history* (Oxford, 2010)

Rolph, C. H. (ed.), *The trial of Lady Chatterley*, second edition (Harmondsworth, 1990)

Rose, Jonathan 'J.M. Dent and Sons,' in Jonathan Rose and Patricia J. Anderson (eds.), *Dictionary of literary biography. 112. British literary publishing houses, 1881–1965* (1991), pp. 81–94

'Lady Chatterley's broker: banking on modernism', in Pamela L. Caughie (ed.), *Disciplining modernism* (Basingstoke, 2010), pp. 182–96

'Modernity and print I: Britain 1890–1970', in Simon Eliot and Jonathan Rose (eds.), *A companion to the history of the book* (Oxford, 2007), pp. 341–53

'Rereading the English common reader: a preface to a history of audiences', *Journal of the History of Ideas* 53 (1992), pp. 47–70

The intellectual life of the British working-classes (New Haven, CT, 2001)

The literary Churchill: author, reader, actor (New Haven, CT, 2014)

Rose, Stuart 'An examination of the New Age movement: who is involved and what constitutes its spirituality', *Journal of Contemporary Religion* 13 (1998), pp. 5–22

Rosenthal, Tom 'Walter and Eva Neurath: their books married words with pictures', *Logos* 15:1 (2004), pp. 12–19

Rota, Anthony *Apart from the text* (1998)

Roth, Ernst *The business of music: reflections of a publisher* (1969)

Rowberry, Simon Peter 'Ebookishness', *Convergence: The International Journal of Research into New Media Technologies* 23:3 (2017), pp. 289–305

Rowbotham, Sheila *Edward Carpenter: a life of liberty and love* (2008)

Rubery, Matthew *The untold story of the talking book* (Cambridge, MA, 2016)

Rudd, David *Enid Blyton and the mystery of children's literature* (Basingstoke, 2000)

Sabin, Roger *Adult comics: an introduction* (1993)

Sackville-West, Vita *Some flowers* (1937)

Said, Edward W. *Culture and imperialism* (1994)

Orientalism (1979)

Samuels, Stuart 'The Left Book Club', *Journal of Contemporary History* 1:2 (1966), pp. 65–86

Sanders, Andrew 'Hatching classics', in William Wootten and George Donaldson (eds.), *Reading Penguin: a critical anthology* (Newcastle upon Tyne, 2013), pp. 111–16

Sanders, F. D. *British book trade organisation: a report on the work of the joint committee* (1939)

Sanders, Mark, Phil Poynter and Robin Derrick (eds.) *The impossible image: fashion photography in the digital age* (2000)

Sands-O'Connor, Karen *Children's publishing and Black Britain, 1965–2015* (2017)

Saunders, Frances Stoner, *Who paid the piper? The CIA and the cultural Cold War* (1999)

Sayle, A[my] *Village libraries: a guide to their formation and upkeep* (1919)

Schäfer, Jürgen *Documentation in the O.E.D.: Shakespeare and Nashe as test cases* (Oxford, 1980)

Schiffrin, André *The business of books: how international conglomerates took over publishing and changed the way we read* (2000)

Schiller, Kurt 'A happy medium: ebooks, licensing, and DRM. (cover story)', *Information Today* 27:2 (2010), pp. 1–44

Schmidt, Leigh 'The making of modern "mysticism"', *Journal of the American Academy of Religion* 71 (2003), pp. 273–302

Scotland, James *The history of Scottish education* (1969)

Scourfield, Jonathan, Sophie Gilliat-Ray, Asma Khan and Sameh Otri *Muslim childhood: religious nurture in a European context* (Oxford, 2013)

Seaton, A. V. 'Book towns as tourism developments in peripheral areas', *International Journal of Tourism Research* 1:5 (1999), pp. 389–99

'Hay on Wye, the mouse that roared: book towns and rural tourism', *Tourism Management* 17:5 (1996), pp. 379–85

Secord, James 'Science, technology and mathematics', in David McKitterick (ed.), *The Cambridge history of the book in Britain. 6. 1830–1914* (Cambridge, 2009), pp. 443–74

Seville, Catherine 'Copyright', in David McKitterick (ed.), *The Cambridge history of the book in Britain. 6. 1830–1914* (Cambridge, 2009), pp. 214–37

'Peter Pan's rights: "To die will be an awfully big adventure"', *Journal of the Copyright Society of the USA* 51 (2003), pp. 1–77

The internationalisation of copyright law: books, buccaneers and the black flag in the nineteenth century (Cambridge, 2009)

Seymour, W. A. (ed.) *A history of the Ordnance Survey* (Folkestone, 1980)

Shackel, Brian and David Pullinger *Blend-1: background and developments* (1984)

Sharratt, Bernard 'Roman Catholicism in the 1960s', in Garrett Sweeney and Adrian Hastings (eds.), *Bishops and writers: aspects of the evolution of modern English Catholicism* (Wheathampsted, 1977), pp. 127–58

Sheed, F. J. *Ground plan for Catholic reading: with a note on reading and education* (1937)

Sidelights on the Catholic revival (1941)

The Church and I (1974)

Sheed, Wilfrid *Frank and Maisie: a memoir with parents* (1985)

Sheldon, Leslie E. 'Evaluating ELT textbooks and materials', *ELT Journal* 42:4 (1988), pp. 237–46

Shepherd, Geoffrey 'Swallowing the ASB 1980', in David Martin and Peter Mullen (eds.), *No alternative: the prayer book controversy* (Oxford, 1981), pp. 80–95

Sheppard, Robert *The poetry of saying: British poetry and its discontents, 1950–2000* (2005)

Sherry, Norman *The life of Graham Greene, 1955–1991* (2004)

Shipcott, Grant *Typographical periodicals between the wars* (Oxford, 1980)

Shone, Richard and John-Paul Stonard (eds.), *The books that shaped art history: from Gombrich and Greenberg to Alpers and Krauss* (2013)

Silver, Larry 'The crisis in publishing and the problem of art history tenure', *The Art Book* 12:2 (2005), pp. 23–4

Simonis, H. *Street of ink: an intimate history of journalism* (1917)

Skelton, Matthew 'The paratext of everything: constructing and marketing H. G. Wells's *The outline of history*', *Book History* 4 (2000), pp. 237–75

Skelton, Robin (ed.) *Poetry of the forties* (1968)

Slienger, Carl *Radical footnotes: periodical for the narrative of working class publishing* 1:1 (Summer 2008)

Slinn, Judith, Sebastian Carter and Richard Southall *History of the Monotype Corporation* (2014)

Smith, Barbara 'British official publications' parts I–III, *Government Publications Review* 4:3 (1977), pp. 201–7; 5:1 (1978), pp. 1–12; and 6:1 (1979), pp. 11–18

Smith, James B. 'The British information research department and Cold War propaganda publishing', in Greg Barnhisel and Catherine Turner (eds.), *Pressing the fight: print, propaganda and the Cold War* (Amherst, MA, 2010), pp. 112–25

Smith, Kelvin *The publishing business: from p-books to e-books* (Lausanne, 2012)

Smith, Nicola 'Book learning', *New Media Age* (2011), pp. 20–2

Smith, Philip N. *et al.* 'Journal publishing with Acrobat: the CAJUN Project', *Electronic Publishing* 6 (1993), pp. 481–93

Snape, Robert 'Libraries for leisure time', in Alistair Black and Peter Hoare (eds.), *The Cambridge history of libraries in Britain and Ireland. 3. 1850–2000* (Cambridge, 2006), pp. 40–55

Snowman, Daniel *Past masters: the best of 'History Today'* (2001)

Sobel, Dava *Longitude: the true story of a lone genius who solved the greatest scientific problem of his time* (1996)

Southall, Brian *Northern songs: the true story of the Beatles' song publishing empire* (2006)

Southwell, Tim *Getting away with it: the inside story of 'Loaded'* (1998)

Spain, Nancy *Mrs Beeton and her husband* (1948)

Sperling, Matthew 'Books and the market', in Peter Robinson (ed.), *The Oxford handbook of contemporary British and Irish poetry* (Oxford, 2013), pp. 191–212

Spivey, Nigel *Phaidon 1923–1998* (1999)

Spread the Word, *Writing the future: Black and Asian writers and publishers in the UK marketplace* (2015). www.spreadtheword.org.uk/wp-content/uploads/2016/11/Writing-the-Future-Black-and-Asian-Authors-and-Publishers-in-the-UK-Marketplace-May-2015.pdf

Spurling, Hilary *Paul Scott: a life* (1990)

Squires, Claire 'Book marketing and the Booker Prize', in Nicole Matthews and Nickianne Moody (eds.), *Judging a book by its cover: fans, publishers, designers, and the marketing of fiction* (Aldershot, 2007), pp. 70–82

'Literary prizes and awards', in Graeme Harper (ed.), *A companion to creative writing* (Chichester, 2013), pp. 291–303

Marketing literature: the making of contemporary writing in Britain (Basingstoke, 2007)

'Publishing's diversity deficit', *CAMEo Cuts* 2 (Leicester, 2017). www2.le.ac.uk/institutes/cameo/cameo-cuts-1/cuts-2

'The history of the book in Britain from 1914,' in Michael F. Suarez and H. R. Woudhuysen (eds.), *The Oxford companion to the book*, vol. 1 (Oxford, 2010), pp. 188–93

'Too much Rushdie, not enough romance?', in Bethan Benwell, James Procter and Gemma Robinson (eds.), *Postcolonial audiences: readers, viewers and reception* (2012), pp. 99–111

St Clair, William *The reading nation in the romantic period* (Cambridge, 2004)

St John, John *William Heinemann: a century of publishing, 1890–1990* (1990)

Stanislawksi, Michael 'The "Vilna Shas" and Eastern European Jewry', in Sharon Liberman Mintz and Gabriel M. Goldstein (eds.), *Printing the Talmud: from Bomberg to Schottenstein* (New York, 2005), pp. 97–102

Stannard, Martin *Evelyn Waugh* (1984)

Stapleton, Julia *Sir Arthur Bryant and national history in twentieth century Britain* (Oxford, 2005)

Steer, Roger '"Without note or comment": yesterday, today and tomorrow', in Stephen Batalden, Kathleen Cann and John Dean (eds.), *Sowing the word: the cultural impact of the British and Foreign Bible Society 1804–2004* (Sheffield, 2004), pp. 63–80

Steinberg, S. H. and John Trevitt *Five hundred years of printing* (1996)

Stevenson, Iain *Book makers: British publishing in the twentieth century* (2010)

'Cartographic publishing', in David Finkelstein and Alistair McCleery (eds.), *The Edinburgh history of the book in Scotland. 4. Professionalism and diversity, 1880–2000* (Edinburgh, 2007), pp. 337–41

'The book trade', in J. H. Bowman (ed.), *British librarianship and information work 2001–2005* (Aldershot, 2007), pp. 312–27

Stevenson, Randall *The Oxford English literary history. 12. 1960–2000: the last of England?* (Oxford, 2004)

Stockham, K. A. (ed.), *British county libraries, 1919–1969* (1969)

Stocks, Mary *Unread best-seller: reflections on the Old Testament* (1967)

Stockwood, Mervyn *Chanctonbury Ring: an autobiography* (1982)

Stoinova, Ivanka 'Der Untergang der Casa Ricordi: Kurze Geschichte und einige Gedanken über eine erzwungene Erschöpfung', in Otto Kolleritsch (ed.), *Der Musikverlag und seine Komponisten im 21. Jahrhundert: zum 100-jährigen Jubiläum der Universal Edition* (Vienna, 2002), pp. 86–99

Stolow, Jeremy *Orthodox by design: Judaism, print politics, and the ArtScroll revolution* (Berkeley, CA, 2010)

Stoney, Barbara *Enid Blyton, a biography* (1974)

Straus, Peter 'Format', in Peter Owen (ed.), *Publishing now* (1993), pp. 68–74

  'The use and effect of literary prizes in the twentieth century', in Robin Myers, Michael Harris and Giles Mandelbrote (eds.), *Books for sale: the advertising and promotion of print since the fifteenth century* (New Castle, DE, 2009), pp. 145–68

Stray Christopher and Gillian Sutherland, 'Mass markets: education', in David McKitterick (ed.), *The Cambridge history of the book in Britain. 6. 1830–1914* (Cambridge, 2009), pp. 359–81

Street, Seán *The A to Z of British radio* (Lanham, MD, 2009)

Striphas, Ted *The late age of print* (New York, 2009)

Strong, L. A. G. *The writer's trade* (1953)

[Strong, L. A. G.] (ed.) *Beginnings* (1935)

Stuart, A. 'Reading habits in three London boroughs', *Journal of Documentation* 8:1 (1952), pp. 33–49

Suarez, Michael, F. S.J., and H. R. Woudhuysen (eds.) *The Oxford companion to the book* (Oxford, 2010)

Suber, Peter *Open access* (Cambridge, MA, 2012)

Sutcliffe, Peter *The Oxford University Press: an informal history* (Oxford, 1978)

Sutcliffe, Steven *Children of the New Age: a history of alternative spirituality* (2004)

  '"Wandering stars": seekers and gurus in the modern world', in Steven Sutcliffe and Marion Bowman (eds.), *Beyond the New Age: exploring alternative spirituality* (Edinburgh, 2000), pp. 17–36

Sutherland, John *Bestsellers: popular fiction of the 1970s* (1981)

  Fiction and the fiction industry (1978)

  Offensive literature: decensorship in Britain, 1960–1982 (1982)

  Reading the decades: fifty years of the nation's bestselling books (2002)

Swinnerton, Frank *Figures in the foreground: literary reminiscences, 1917–1940* (1970)

Tabbi, Joseph and Michael Wutz *Reading matters: narrative in the new media ecology* (1997)

Tanselle, G. Thomas *Book-jackets, their history, forms, and use* (Charlottesville, NC, 2011)

Taraporevala, R. J. *Competition and its control in the British book trade, 1850–1939* (1973)

Taylor, A. J. P. *English history 1914–1945* (Oxford, 1965)

Taylor, D. J. *The prose factory: literary life in England since 1918* (2016)

Taylor, John *From Ovaltiney to angry old man* (2007)

Taylor, John Seaby 'Sexist bias in physics textbooks', *Physics Education* 14 (1979), pp. 277–80

Taylor, Steve and Neville Brody *100 Years of magazine covers* (2006)

Thatcher, Martyn and Anthony Quinn *Kitchener: the man, the poster and the legacy* (2016)

Theophano, Janet *Eat my words: reading women's lives through the cookbooks they wrote* (Basingstoke, 2002)

Thomas, Tig (ed.) *True to the trefoil: a celebration of fictional girl guides* (Bath, 2010)

Thompson, John B. *Books in the digital age: the transformation of academic and higher education publishing in Britain and the United States* (Cambridge, 2005)

   Merchants of culture: the publishing business in the twenty-first century (2010)

Thompson, Judith and Paul Heelas *The way of the heart: the Rajneesh Movement* (1986)

Thompson, Phyllis *Minka and Margaret* (1976)

Thorp, Roger 'Publishing on art: a crisis?', *The Art Book* 13:1 (February 2006), pp. 27–8

Thorsheim, Peter 'Salvage and destruction: the recycling of books and manuscripts in Great Britain during the Second World War', *Contemporary European History* 22:3 (2013), pp. 431–52

Thring, G. Herbert *The management of literary property: book and serial rights, with a letter to the author from Bernard Shaw* (1933)

Thwaite, Ann *A. A. Milne: his life* (2013)

Tobey, Ronald C. *The American ideology of national science, 1919–1930* (Pittsburgh, PA, 1971)

Tobin, Carol M. 'The book that built Gale Research: The *Encyclopedia of Associations*', in James Rettig (ed.), *Distinguished classics of reference publishing* (Phoenix, AZ, 1992), pp. 89–97

Todd, Richard *Consuming fictions: the Booker Prize and fiction in Britain today* (1996)

Towheed, Shafquat 'Two paradigms of literary production: the production, circulation and legal status of Rudyard Kipling's Departmental Ditties and Indian Railway Library texts', in Robert Fraser and Mary Hammond (eds.), *Books without borders. 2. Perspectives from South Asia* (Basingstoke, 2008), pp. 125–36

Towheed, Shafquat and Edmund King *Reading and the First World War: readers, texts, archives* (Basingstoke, 2015)

Towler, Robert *The need for certainty: a sociological study of conventional religion* (1985)

Townsend, John Rowe *Written for children: an outline of English children's literature* (1965)

Travell, John *Doctor of souls: a biography of Dr Leslie Dixon Weatherhead, 1893–1976* (Cambridge, 1999)

Trease, Geoffrey *A whiff of burnt boats* (1971)

   Tales out of school, second edition (1964)

Trenaman, Joseph 'Books, radio and television', in John Hampden (ed.), *The book world: a new survey of the making and distribution of books in Britain* (1957), pp. 198–206

Trevelyan, G. M. *English social history* (1948)

Trewin, John and Evelyn Mansfield King *Printer to the House: the story of Hansard* (1952)

Triggs, Teal *Fanzines* (2010)

Trivedi, Harish 'The "book" in India: orality, manu-script, print (post)colonialism', in Robert Fraser and Mary Hammond (eds.), *Books without borders. 2. Perspectives from South Asia* (Basingstoke, 2008), pp. 12–33

   Truly yours: one hundred and fifty years of play publishing (1980)

Tungate, Mark *Branded male: marketing to men* (2008)

Tunstall, Jeremy *The media in Britain* (1983)

Turner, Jane (ed.), *The dictionary of art* (1996)

Twyman, Michael *Printing 1770–1970: an illustrated history of its development and uses in England* (1970)

Tymn, Marshall B. and Mike Ashley (eds.) *Science fiction, fantasy and weird fiction magazines* (Westport, CT, 1985)

Tynan, Katherine 'War books and others', *The Bookman* (October 1916), p. 21

Unwin, Philip 'A new reading public?', *Bookseller* (5 April 1934)

Unwin, Stanley *How governments treat books* (1950)

   'Introduction', in John Hampden (ed.), *The book world* (1935)

   The truth about a publisher (1960)

   The truth about publishing (1926)

   'The advertising of books', in George Stevens and Stanley Unwin (eds.), *Best-sellers: are they born or made?* (1939), pp. 11–37

Van Hove, Hildegard 'L'émergence d'un marché spirituel', *Social Compass* 46 (1999), pp. 161–72

Velterop, J. J. M. 'Keeping the minutes of science', in Mel Collier and Kathryn Arnold (eds.), *Electronic library and visual information research* (1995), pp. 11–17

Vincent, Nigel and Chris Wickham *Debating open access* (2013)

Viswanathan, Gauri *Masks of conquest: literary study and British rule in India* (Delhi, 1998)

wa Thiong'o, Ngũgĩ *Decolonising the mind: the politics of language in African literatures* (Oxford, 1986)

Wace, Michael 'From Carroll to Crompton: the work of a children's publisher', in Elizabeth James (ed.), *Macmillan: a publishing tradition* (Basingstoke, 2002), pp. 242–55

Walasek, Helen *Best of Punch cartoons* (2008)

Walford, A. J. *Guide to reference material*, vol. 3 (1970)

Wallace, Helen *Boosey & Hawkes: the publishing story* (2007)

Waller, Jane and Michael Vaughan-Rees *Women in wartime* (1987)

Waller, Philip *Writers, readers, and reputations: literary life in Britain 1870–1918* (Oxford, 2008)

Wallis, L. W. *A concise chronology of typesetting developments, 1886–1986* (1988)

   'Seven wonders of modern typesetting technology (1844–1994)', *Printing Historical Society Bulletin* 41 (Summer 1996), pp. 1–7

Waltz, Mitzi *Alternative and activist media* (Edinburgh, 2005)

Wand, William *Changeful page: the autobiography of William Wand* (1965)

Warburg, Frederic *All authors are equal* (1973)

   An occupation for gentlemen (1959)

Warburton, Eileen *John Fowles: a life in two worlds* (2004)

Ward, A. C. *Twentieth-century English literature* (1964)

Ward, Maisie *Unfinished business* (1964)

Ward, Martin L. *Readers and library users* (1977)

Ward, Simon 'The development of the book shop', in David Finkelstein and Alistair McCleery (eds.), *The Edinburgh history of the book in Scotland. 4. Professionalism and diversity, 1880–2000* (Edinburgh, 2007), pp. 83–91

Ware, Mark 'Online submission and peer review systems', *Learned Publishing* 18 (2005), pp. 245–50

Ware, Mark and Michael Mabe *The STM report: an overview of scientific and scholarly journal publishing*, fourth edition (2015)

Watson, Nicola J. *The literary tourist: readers and places in Romantic and Victorian Britain* (Basingstoke, 2006)

Watson, Rowan *Western illuminated manuscripts* (2011)

Waugh, Evelyn *Put out more flags* (1943)

Webb, Kaye *Lilliput goes to war* (1985)

Weedon, Alexis '"Behind the Screen" and "The Scoop": a cross-media experiment in publishing and broadcasting crime fiction in the early 1930s', *Media History* 13:1 (2007), pp. 43–60

'Elinor Glyn's system of writing', *Publishing History* 60 (2006), pp. 31–50

'Textual production and dissemination in book history: a case study of cross-media production between the wars', in Marianne Thornablen (ed.), *English now: selected papers from the 20th IAUPE conference in Lund, 2007* (Lund, 2008), pp. 318–31

'The book trade and internet publishing: a British perspective', *Convergence: The Journal of Research into New Media Technologies* 2:1 (1996), pp. 76–102

Werskey, Gary *The visible college: a collective biography of British scientists and socialists of the 1930s*, second edition (1988)

West, James L. W. III 'The Chace Act and Anglo-American literary relations', *Studies in Bibliography* 45 (1992), pp. 303–11

Wexler, Joyce Piell *Who paid for modernism? Art, money, and the fiction of Conrad, Joyce and Lawrence* (Fayetteville, AR, 1997)

Whalley, Joyce Irene and Tessa Rose Chester *A history of children's book illustration* (1988)

White, Eric W. *Poetry Book Society, 1954–1978: the first 25 years* (1979)

White, Gabriel *Edward Ardizzone: artist and illustrator* (1979)

White, Martin 'From PSLO to NESLI: site licensing for electronic journals in UK academic institutions', *New Review of Academic Librarianship* 3 (1997), pp. 139–50

Whited, Lana A. (ed.) *The ivory tower and Harry Potter: perspectives on a literary phenomenon* (2002)

Whiteley, Peter 'The gender balance of physics textbooks: Caribbean and British books, 1985–91', *Physics Education* 31 (1996), pp. 169–74

Whitley, Richard 'Knowledge producers and knowledge acquirers: popularization as a relation between scientific fields and their publics', in Terry Shinn and Richard Whitley (eds.), *Expository science: forms and functions of popularization* (Dordrecht, 1985), pp. 3–28

Whittington, Christine 'Unbeatable: the *Guinness Book of Records*', in James Rettig (ed.), *Distinguished classics of reference publishing* (Phoenix, AZ, 1992), pp. 138–46

Whitworth, Michael 'The clothbound universe: popular physics books, 1919–1939', *Publishing History* 40 (1996), pp. 52–82

Whyte, William 'Oxford University Press, 1896–1945', in Wm Roger Louis (ed.), *The history of Oxford University Press. 3. 1896–1970* (Oxford, 2013), pp. 59–95

Williams, Edward Everitt and Ruth Verrill Noble *Conference on international cultural, educational and scientific exchanges, Princeton University, November 25–26, 1946* (Princeton, NJ, 1946)

Williams, H. A. *Some day I'll find you* (1982)

Williams, Raymond *Culture and society* (1958)

The long revolution (1961, repr. 1965)

[Williams, William Emrys] *The Penguin story* (Harmondsworth, 1956)

Williamson, Hugh *Book design: the practice of an industrial craft* (1956)

Willison, Ian, Warwick Gould and Warren Chernaik (eds.) *Modernist writers and the marketplace* (Basingstoke, 1996)

Wilson, Nicola 'Boots Book-Lovers' Library and the novel: the impact of a circulating library market on twentieth-century fiction', *Information and Culture: A Journal of History* 49:4 (2014), pp. 427–49

   'Libraries, reading patterns, and censorship', in Patrick Parrinder and Andrzej Gąsiorek (eds.), *The Oxford history of the novel in English. 4. The reinvention of the British and Irish novel 1880–1940* (Oxford, 2010), pp. 36–54

Winder, Robert *The little wonder: the remarkable history of Wisden* (2013)

Wiseman, Leanne 'Copyright and the regulations of the Australian publishing industry', in David Carter and Anne Galligan (eds.), *Making books: contemporary Australian publishing* (St Lucia, Queensland, 2007), pp. 177–97

Within a mile of Edinburgh town: the history of Bertrams Limited (Edinburgh, [1955])

Wolfe, Kenneth *Churches and the British Broadcasting Corporation, 1922–56: the politics of broadcast religion* (1984)

[Worpole, Ken] *Local publishing and local culture: an account of the work of the Centerprise publishing project, 1972–77* (1977)

Worthen, John *D. H. Lawrence: a literary life* (1989)

   'D. H. Lawrence and the "expensive edition" business', in Ian Willison, Warwick Gould and Warren Chernaik (eds.), *Modernist writers and the marketplace* (Basingstoke, 1996), pp. 105–23

Wozencroft, Jon *The graphic language of Neville Brody* (1988)

Wright, David *Faber music: the first 25 years: 1965–1990* (1990)

Wright, Simon, 'Music hire libraries: printing music or printing money?' *Brio* 44:2 (2007), pp. 2–18

Yates, Martin *William Shakespeare in Penguin Books* (2010)

Yglesias, Roy 'Education and publishing in transition', in Asa Briggs (ed.), *Essays in the history of publishing* (1974), pp. 357–88

York, Michael 'New Age commodification and appropriation of spirituality', *Journal of Contemporary Religion* 16 (2010), pp. 361–72

Young, Edward 'The early days of Penguins', *The Book Collector* 1.4 (1952)

Zaid, Gabriel *So many books* (2004)

Zell, Hans 'Publishing in Africa', in Philip G. Altbach and Edith S. Hoshino (eds.), *International publishing: an encyclopedia* (New York, 1995), pp. 366–72

Zobl, Elke 'Cultural production, transnational networking, and critical reflection in feminist zines', *Signs: Journal of Women in Culture and Society* 35:1 (2009), pp. 1–12

Index

Lightning Source UK Ltd.
Milton Keynes UK
UKHW011245220621
385834UK00009B/371